PSYCHOTHERAPY: CLINICAL, RESEARCH, AND THEORETICAL ISSUES

PSYCHOTHERAPY: CLINICAL, RESEARCH, AND THEORETICAL ISSUES

HANS H. STRUPP

Vanderbilt University

JASON ARONSON, INC.

NEW YORK

Library of Congress Catalog Card Number : 72–94846
Standard Book Number : 87668–059–7

Designed by Jennifer Mellen

Manufactured in the United States of America

To
Lottie
Karen, Barbie,
and John

Acknowledgments

Grateful acknowledgment is made to Joan T. Reese and Anne L. Bloxom for valuable assistance in preparing the manuscript and indices.

Thanks are due the following journals and publishers for granting permission to reprint material appearing in this book:

Archives of General Psychiatry
Psychiatry
American Psychological Association
Behavioral Science
Journal of Clinical Psychology
Appleton-Century-Crofts
Psychotherapy: Theory, Research, and Practice
International Journal of Psychiatry
Basic Books
Macmillan
Journal of Contemporary Psychotherapy
Voices

Table of Contents

Preface

An author who decides to publish a collection of his papers usually feels called upon to supply a rationale. My reasons are twofold. First, Dr. Jason Aronson, editor of Science House, kindly invited me to undertake this task on the supposition that both clinicians and researchers concerned with the study of psychotherapy might be interested in such a collection; second, pondering Dr. Aronson's invitation, I was immodest enough to think that my publications over the past 15 years added up to something more than the sum of their parts. The reader must judge this for himself.

I feel that my investigative efforts have made some inroads on the vexing problems in the area of psychotherapy; perhaps as a result of this work I am more keenly aware that there is much unfinished business. If the future of psychotherapy is that of a scientific discipline, then it cannot be otherwise. But I believe we have learned to ask better questions than was possible even two decades ago, and we have evolved research techniques that, while admittedly crude, permit us to extend the frontiers of knowledge. I take satisfaction in having played a part in this movement.

In an area that is deeply concerned with personal matters, one's own experience necessarily shapes one's thinking and writing. I merely wish to note that my personal experience has been the longest and the most arduous part of my apprenticeship. Without this personal experience, I doubt very much that research in psychotherapy would have held, or continued to hold, a lasting fascination for me. Clearly, no sustained scientific, or for that matter human, endeavor is possible without a deep personal interest and commitment. I feel I have had both.

Personal factors aside, I have come to see the nature of the therapist's influence and the patient's susceptibility to that influence as one of the core problems in psychology. When I entered the field, there were only a few people who seriously devoted themselves to research in this area. Within two decades this picture has drastically changed. Today there is a burgeoning literature supported by an avid interest in the problems of personality and behavior change. However, it is not only a question of how we can change personality or modify behavior that undergirds this effort. As I see it, it is a problem of learning more about the principles that make it possible for one person to have a pervasive interest in another. In this light, research in psychotherapy is central to problems in child-rearing, education, crime and delinquency, propaganda, religion, and social influence in general. Research in psychotherapy is no longer the esoteric pursuit of people concerned with evaluating a particular treatment method, in the medical sense. Instead it is concerned with what it means to be human, how we grow up to become self-directing, self-controlling, and relatively independent adults who participate in realizing themselves and shaping their destiny.

12

A word about my theoretical orientation and the settings in which I did my work may be appropriate. In the late Forties I became heavily influenced by my teachers at the Washington School of Psychiatry, who included, among others, Drs. Frieda Fromm-Reichmann, Otto Will, Clara Thompson, Alfred Stanton, Ernest Schachtel, Cora Dubois, Mabel Cohen, and Leon Salzman. Apart from my training in research techniques and methodology, academic psychology in those days provided little stimulation. From 1955 to 1966 I profited greatly from my association with psychiatrists and psychoanalysts, mainly in the Department of Psychiatry at the University of North Carolina. Dr. D. Wilfred Abse provided a particularly fine model of the clinician. I came to espouse a more orthodox Freudian position although the work of Franz Alexander and his followers always appealed to me. Only after I left the medical setting in 1966 and became affiliated with an academic department of psychology (at Vanderbilt University) did I perceive more clearly the stultifying influence that organized psychoanalysis and psychiatry have exerted on developments in psychotherapy.

In 1967 I had the good fortune to be asked to work on a major project designed to explore the feasibility of large-scale studies in psychotherapy and to assess the promise of coordinated research. This exploration, initiated by the National Institute of Mental Health, involved close collaboration with Professor Allen E. Bergin of Columbia University that extended over several years. As a result of our joint endeavor and our intensive discussions with a group of the most outstanding researchers in the country, I gained a broader and, I believe, more balanced outlook on the scientific and clinical enterprise. I remain deeply grateful to Drs. Joseph D. Matarazzo and A. Hussain Tuma for creating this unique opportunity.

My current position is one of greater eclecticism and open-mindedness. I continue to admire Freud's seminal insights but have become increasing critical of many psycho-

13

analytic formulations that I now view as shackles to be thrown off by future developments. Reliance on empirical data and conceptual clarification of basic issues impress me as our best hope. In this quest, we must strive to overcome the constrictions imposed by professional guilds and to create a spirit of open inquiry wherever it may lead us. I believe we are well on our way toward this goal. Orthodoxies of any kind have no place in science, and, to reiterate, the future of psychotherapy should be that of a scientific discipline.

The organization of this volume is self-explanatory. To guide the reader I have prefaced each part by a short synopsis drawing attention to the highlights.

If the volume succeeds in stimulating further critical inquiry into some of the many unresolved issues in psychotherapy, I shall consider that its purpose has been well served.

Hans H. Strupp

PSYCHOTHERAPY:
CLINICAL,
RESEARCH, AND
THEORETICAL
ISSUES

Part I
Introduction

Since I entered the field of psychotherapy and made the understanding of the complex phenomena in this intriguing area my aim in life, no issue has held greater fascination for me than the nature of the psychotherapeutic influence: how does it come about that one person, by virtue of what he is or what he does, can exert such a lasting influence on another person that the changes that result from this encounter may be termed therapeutic? The problem, clearly, is not unique to psychotherapy; it is a basic issue in education, religious conversion, medicine, faith healing, and propaganda. What is the difference between psychotherapy and other areas of psychological influence? I believe that the difference lies in the fact that as psychotherapists and researchers we have set ourselves the task of arriving at a better scientific understanding of the forces operating within the dyadic framework of the therapeutic relationship. Our aim is (or should be) not merely the achievement of therapeutic results—important as this goal unquestionably is—but a conceptualization of *how* these results are achieved as well as the parameters of our efforts. To be sure, shamans, faith healers, and medicine men through the ages also had their rationales, but it was Freud who set the course of searching for answers based on the tenets of Western science. Assuredly, this is our article of faith, which I for one am quite willing to accept. Furthermore, if our goal is to develop psychotherapy as a *scientific discipline*, together with an improved technology for effecting therapeutic change, I believe that this course of action represents our best hope. Implicit here is the assertion that other approaches, advocated by some contemporaries who are embracing mysticism and "experiencing" of various sorts, may well lead to greater serenity, peace of mind, and happiness, but they are intrinsically antithetical to the view that psychotherapeutic phenomena should be studied and understood as phenomena of nature, capable of description, analysis, and control.

Throughout his life Freud was keenly interested in the nature of therapeutic action in psychoanalysis, and while in his later years other topics preoccupied him a great deal more, he periodically returned to the problem. There is reason to believe that he was always profoundly ambivalent about the therapeutic effectiveness of the techniques he developed: on the one hand he looked upon psychoanalysis as a therapeutic instrument of great penetration, precision, and promise although, especially in his early years, he was quite conservative in delimiting its range of applicability (to the so-called transference neuroses); on the other hand, he gradually shifted ground and, toward the end of his life, foresaw that the classical technique might have a brighter future as an investigative than as a therapeutic tool.

Like all therapeutic innovators, Freud stressed the unique features of psychoanalytic psychotherapy, and he

20

played down those elements it might have in common with other therapeutic approaches. He was particularly concerned about setting psychoanalysis apart from "suggestion" and hypnosis, both of which he depreciated. The unique technical feature of psychoanalysis, as Freud saw it, was *interpretation* of transference resistances and other unconscious material, to which everything else was subordinate. He deemphasized especially the personal contribution of the therapist, whom he regarded as a more or less impersonal manipulator of unconscious forces. To be sure, he occasionally conceded that the therapist provides the patient with a model of mature and nonanxious behavior, and he recognized that at certain times the therapist must act as a teacher and mentor to the analysand. In this vein, he described psychoanalysis as a procedure of re-education or after-education. However, to the extent that the therapist was able to remain aloof from emotional entanglements with the patient—personal analysis was designed to achieve this aim—to that extent psychoanalytic psychotherapy was conceptualized as an essentially impersonal set of technical operations. Thus, Freud was intent upon developing a therapeutic *technology*, very much akin to a refined surgical procedure. By the same token, the future of psychoanalysis as a therapeutic procedure was seen as a continued attempt to increase its precision and technical elegance. Toward the end of his life Freud had satisfied himself that the nature of the therapeutic action was well understood. In the light of more recent developments, this claim must be considered highly questionable. Moreover, Freud was inimical to "statistical" studies of therapeutic outcomes, which to him were a waste of time and effort.

Following Freud's death there occurred a resurgence of interest in the person of the therapist. A salient example of this trend was Franz Alexander's insistence on the importance of the "corrective emotional experience," which brought with it a renewed emphasis on the therapist's personal contribution. Also, as research in psychotherapy got under way in the 1940s, attention focused on the therapist's attitudes toward the patient and the emotional atmosphere within which the therapeutic work proceeds. Glover's survey of British analysts in the late Thirties had already shown quite convincingly—if proof was needed—that there were considerable idiosyncratic differences among therapists, and that the notion of the "calibrated" practitioner was obviously a myth. At any rate, that there were marked *individual differences* among therapists was an inescapable conclusion, as well as the thought that these differences in themselves might play an important role in therapeutic success or failure.

My own work, beginning with the exploration of differences in technique, suggested the formulation that the therapist's contribution was both *personal* and *technical*. This position, which I adopted primarily on the basis of the findings reported in Chapter Nine, remained my basic conviction for about a decade. This particular study, incidentally, provided me with greater insights into the operations of psychotherapists than any other empirical research I had done before or did after. The first two chapters presented in Part I set forth and expatiate this conception.

The therapist's personal contribution largely coincides with what Jerome Frank has termed the "nonspecific factors" in psychotherapy. The incisive analysis that Frank advanced in *Persuasion and Healing* (1961) stressed the ubiquitousness of nonspecific factors in all forms of psychotherapy—from faith healing to psychoanalysis. While fully acknowledging the cogency of his position, I used to believe that the skilled psychotherapist could potentiate the therapeutic influence by specific factors lying primarily along the *technical* dimension that had received such forceful attention in Freud's writings. In more recent years, too, the behavior therapists have added weight to the view that specific technical procedures employed by the trained psychotherapist are a major factor—and perhaps the overriding factor—in therapeutic change.

I believe the issue is far from settled, but I must concede that I have become increasingly skeptical about the therapeutic efficacy of technical maneuvers. For one thing, I have become more strongly impressed with the therapeutic effects of such nonspecific factors as faith, trust, hope, and favorable expectations of therapeutic change that any good psychotherapist inevitably engenders in his patients. For another, the research on placebo effects and placebo responsivity (Shapiro, 1971) has had a trenchant effect on my position. Altogether, the previously denigrated and rejected role of suggestion and suggestibility—in hypnosis, but also in other healing relationships—has fueled my doubts. We really know very little about the psychological phenomena loosely grouped under the headings of "suggestion" and "suggestibility." We can no longer afford the luxury of calling a process "suggestion" and let it go at that; the psychological forces at work in this process are very much in need of further explanation. Again, we are brought face to face with the basic question: What makes an individual influenceable by psychological techniques, what is the nature of these techniques, and what are the circumstances in which they become effective? We are merely begging the question if we assign the labels of "suggestion" and "suggestibility" to these phenomena. A host of writers, including Freud, have unfortunately brought these forces into ill repute, and it is only in recent years that the powerful force of suggestion in work on hypnosis and placebos has again engaged the serious attention of researchers. I am inclined to think that the answers to our question may be found as we are able to bring concerted investigative effort to bear on this problem.

As far as the technical operations of the psychotherapist are concerned, they are heavily suffused by the practitioner's faith in their efficacy, and it is difficult to disentangle the two. This is not to say that such procedures as desensitization and interpretations do not produce a given result. But other procedures applied within the framework

23

of a trusting relationship where the patient's expectancy of relief and cure is raised may accomplish the same result. In the end we may find that the specific technical operations may account for a very small part in the totality of the therapeutic effect. Needless to say, the hypothesis remains to be tested.

The therapeutic relationship consists of transactions between two persons; it is not, as Macalpine (1950) asserted, the relationship of an analysand to a therapist. For conceptual or research purposes one may focus on the therapist or on the patient, but one must never lose sight of the overriding importance of their interaction. Regardless of the therapist's stance, he influences and directs the patient. Different forms of therapy may leave the patient greater or lesser initiative; they may encourage him to take particular courses of action, either in the therapeutic relationship or outside, or they may strenuously insist that only intrapsychic forces are being dealt with. The fact remains that the therapist directs the patient, and the term "nondirective" therapy appears decidedly to be a misnomer. The therapist, as Haley (1963) has clearly shown, controls the patient—his associations, his feelings, as well as his actions. Within the framework of the therapeutic relationship the patient learns new or different ways of dealing with the therapist (as a representative of the adult world); he learns to feel differently about the people in his life and about himself; he learns to reconstruct his cognitions; and hopefully he learns to lead his life more autonomously, more constructively, and more satisfyingly.

In the following chapters in this part I attempt to shed light on these problems by showing that learning in psychotherapy proceeds on a broad front and that, unless the therapist focuses on the amelioration of a single symptom, he facilitates learnings of diverse and often very different kinds. But even in psychotherapy that deals with a specific symptom, the implications are broader. As the patient learns to cope more effectively with a segment of his behavior, in-

24

crements occur in his adaptive capacity that will radiate to other areas of his life, change his self-concept, and enhance his self-control.

In short, we are dealing with an educational process of considerable complexity, and it is quite likely that very similar kinds of learning occur in all forms of psychotherapy. The labels that seemingly separate the various therapeutic approaches dotting the contemporary scene probably disguise very marked similarities and commonalities, which should be of primary interest in the long run. Moreover, the fact that therapeutic changes are multidimensional has a far-reaching bearing on their measurement. If change occurs on many fronts, we ought to become more specific about the kinds of changes we are talking about when we rate a patient "improved" or otherwise. Outcomes, too, are heavily intertwined with cultural values—changes we consider healthy, desirable, moral, or whatever.

Finally, if it is true that psychotherapists carry out teaching tasks of various kinds, it would follow that they might achieve particular goals more effectively if they brought specific techniques to bear on them. If one wishes to learn ice-skating it is more effective to concentrate on skills related to this sport than to focus on physical fitness in general. Similarly, it is one thing to help a shy patient to become less inhibited and more trusting in his interpersonal relationships, but in and of itself this may not help him a great deal in asking a girl for a date. There may be important transfers of learning from therapy to the external world, and significant therapeutic benefits may accrue once a central problem in the patient's life has been dealt with; however, if we set more specific goals in psychotherapy and worked consistently toward their realization, we would become more efficient and effective therapists. "Traditional" forms of therapy have typically not proceeded in this fashion; behavior therapists have done so to a far greater extent. In any event, greater specificity must be our goal, which we can hope to approximate but never achieve.

References

Frank, J. D. 1961. *Persuasion and Healing: A Comparative Study of Psychotherapy.* Baltimore: Johns Hopkins Press.

Haley, J. 1963. *Strategies of Psychotherapy.* New York: Grune & Stratton.

Macalpine, I. 1950. "The Development of the Transference," *Psychoanal. Quar.,* 19: 501-539.

Shapiro, A. K. 1971. "Placebo Effects in Medicine, Psychotherapy, and Psychoanalysis," in *Handbook of Psychotherapy and Behavior Change: An Empirical Analysis,* ed. A. E. Bergin and S. L. Garfield, pp. 439-473. New York: Wiley.

1

THE THERAPIST: PERSONAL AND TECHNICAL FACTORS

The therapist's contribution to the therapeutic process is an important determinant of its course and outcome. His personality has long been recognized as a potent factor in therapeutic action, but the mainstream of psychoanalytic thinking has tended to characterize this influence as non-analytic, preliminary, subordinate, or even antagonistic to interpretive operations, which traditionally have been considered the hallmark of psychoanalytic psychotherapy. In more recent years, partly as a result of the work of Harry Stack Sullivan, Karen Horney, and other exponents of the "cultural" school, some of whose ideas were anticipated by Otto Rank and Sandor Ferenczi, the totality of the therapist's personality and the reality aspects of the therapeutic situation have received increasing attention. In keeping with these newer formulations I shall elaborate on the notion that the therapist's personality, attitudes, and values are very much in the picture at all times, and that they color and influence the direction and quality of his therapeutic operations.*

I have asserted (see Chapter Nine) that the therapist's contribution is both a personal and a technical one: the personal contribution was seen as uppermost, although technical procedures might materially further the therapeutic endeavor; on the other hand, in the absence of a favorable emotional matrix, no amount of expert technique could shift the psychodynamic balance in the direction of therapeutic growth. My purpose at this time is not to add another argument or opinion to an area already abounding in these commodities, but hopefully to stimulate systematic and controlled research that might cast further light on the issues. Such investigations may help to sort out the various influences impinging on the interpersonal process called psychotherapy and eventually permit the assignment of relative weights— statistical or practical—to the relevant variables. At present there is no precise knowledge of what makes psychotherapy effective or ineffective with certain therapists or patients; experimental designs that would produce such incontrovertible evidence probably lie far in the future (Frank, 1958).

In addition to theoretical considerations, certain practical implications are perhaps of greater and more immediate relevance. I am referring to the ubiquitous but insufficiently recognized effects of the therapist's attitudes as they permeate and color his clinical observations and judgments as well as the structure and feeling tone of his com-

*The research project of which this chapter forms a part was supported by research grants (M-965 and M-2171) from the National Institute of Mental Health, of the National Institutes of Health, U.S. Public Health Service. I am greatly indebted to the following persons for critical comments: Drs. D. Wilfred Abse, Lucie Jessner, Joseph J. Geller, Benjamin Wolstein, Jerome D. Frank, Merton M. Gill, and H. A. Meyersburg. The responsibility, needless to say, remains mine.

munications to the patient. As a sensitive human being the therapist is a highly complex scientific instrument, whose operational characteristics are still in great need of exploration and specification. It is a truism by now that the objectivity of information gathered about a patient in the social interaction of psychotherapy is at best relative, because it is filtered through and affected by the social interaction that itself is partly a function of the therapist's underlying personality structure. There is preliminary experimental evidence to show that the quality of the therapist's perceptions, evaluations, judgments, predictions, and interventions is subtly affected by his own unwitting emotional reactions.

Stone (1954) addresses himself to this point as follows:

> In no other field, save surgery, to which Freud frequently compared analysis, is the personal equation so important. It is up to us to know our capacities, intellectual and emotional, if we cannot always know one another so clearly in this respect. Again, special predilections, interests, emotional textures may profoundly influence prognosis, and thus—in a tangible way—the indications [p. 592].

This, coupled with an accumulating body of observations, leads to an increased realization that in psychotherapy, perhaps more than in most areas of scientific investigation, the participant observer becomes subject to the principle of indeterminacy, since it is impossible to make observations in the interpersonal field without altering that field in potentially important ways. To the extent that the therapist is clearly aware of the alterations he introduces, he may adjust and correct for his biases. To the extent that he is unaware of the ways in which he influences the interpersonal process, he is at the mercy of unknown forces and may merely observe and record events that his very operations have brought about. The adverse effects of gross distortions resulting from "blind spots" in the therapist were recognized early by Freud (1953), and the requirement for a didactic or training analysis was an ingenious step toward reducing therapist biases from this source. Considerably less attention has been accorded the more subtle variables influencing the therapist's mental processes, techniques, and theoretical predilections, such as temperamental, attitudinal, and cultural factors underlying his perceptions of the outside world.

THE THERAPIST-PATIENT RELATIONSHIP— CHANGING CONCEPTS

The dynamics of the therapist-patient relationship are the *sine qua non* of psychoanalytic psychotherapy, and all major contributions have taken as their point of departure Freud's revolutionary conceptions of transference and countertransference. I shall not go into the historical evolution of these concepts here. Major trends have been reviewed with admirable clarity by Orr (1954) and Thompson (1950); Wolstein's (1954) trenchant analysis represents another attempt to view current thinking in historical perspective. It is clear that under the impact of operationalism in science certain modifications have occurred since the time of Freud. In general, there is an increasing tendency to deal with the dynamics of the therapeutic situation in process terms, to think of transference and countertransference as phenomena along continua instead of regarding them as either "positive" or "negative." Furthermore, greater emphasis is being placed on the here-and-now experience in the therapeutic relationship. The formulation by Janet Rioch (1943) may serve as an example of this trend:

The therapeutic aim in this process is not to uncover childhood memories which will then lend themselves to analytic interpretation. . . . Psychoanalytic cure is not the amassing of data, either from childhood, or from the study of the present situation. Nor does cure result from the repetition of the original injurious experience in the analytic relationship. What is curative in the process is that in tending to reconstruct with the analyst that atmosphere which obtained in childhood, the patient actually achieves something new. He discovers that part of himself which had to be repressed at the time of the original experience. He can only do this in an interpersonal relationship with the analyst, which is suitable to such rediscovery. . . . Thus, the transference phenomenon is used so that the patient will completely re-experience the original frames of reference, and himself within those frames, in a *truly different relationship with the analyst*, to the end that he can discover the invalidity of his conclusions about himself and others [p. 151]. [The italics are mine.]

According to this viewpoint, the therapist is *more* than a sympathetic listener who interprets the patient's transference distortions, and his interpretations are not regarded as the only or the most effective factor in therapeutic success. He makes a significant emotional contribution that is positive if it succeeds in creating the kind of emotional atmosphere in which the patient's re-experiencing can take place. By the same token, "countertransference" reactions are interferences with this positive emotional contribution— that is, instances in which the therapist's own personality and unresolved emotional problems impede the full realization of the therapeutic goal.

When Freud introduced the term "countertransference" in 1910, he revised his earlier view of the analyst as an impersonal mirror by recognizing that "blind spots" in the analyst's personality structure might interfere with his usefulness as a therapist. The emphasis of Freud's original formulation and that of subsequent elaborations has been on *interferences* with the analytic process introduced by deficiencies, shortcomings, and characterological distortions of

31

the analyst. This led to recommendations about dangers to be avoided, attitudes to be discouraged, and so on. The objective was to keep the analytic field clean and uncontaminated by minimizing unwarranted intrusions and involvements of the analyst in the patient's transference maneuvers. There is no doubt that this did much to augment the objectivity of observations in the analytic situation and to decrease the possibility of influencing the phenomena under scrutiny. It furthermore approximated a definition of the analytic situation as a laboratory situation for studying and modifying interpersonal processes—an achievement of the first magnitude.

It is instructive to note that in the earlier formulations, countertransference was defined in relation to transferences of the patient, with little regard for the healthy or realistic aspects of the therapist's personality and his attitudes. Even today, as Orr (1954) points out, there is widespread disagreement as to what the term comprises. For example, distinctions have been made between positive and negative countertransference; some writers insist that all feelings of the therapist should be included; others differentiate between whole and partial responses to the patient; still others restrict the term to the therapist's unconscious reactions. Berman (1949) suggests a distinction between countertransference in the classic sense and the therapist's reasonable and appropriate emotional responses, which he calls "attitudes." He also addresses himself to certain contradictions in Freud's writings, and reasons, "The answer could simply be that the analyst is always both the cool detached surgeon-like operator on the patient's psychic tissues, and the warm, human, friendly, helpful physician [p. 160]." The rest of his paper is devoted to an enlightening discussion of the therapist as a human being whose attitudes are characterized by the term "dedication."

According to orthodox analytic principles, the therapist must not influence the transference situation by any means other than interpretations, which thus become the primary therapeutic agent. Furthermore, Freud and Fenichel imply that differences in the analytic atmosphere created by the analyst's personality do not exert an influence upon the transference situation and the therapeutic results. According to this view, the transference neurosis evolves more or less automatically, provided the therapist does nothing to interfere with its development.

In his last formulation Freud (1949) viewed the analyst as a new superego, who corrects errors in the patient's early upbringing: "The new superego now has an opportunity for a sort of *after-education* of the neurotic; it can correct blunders for which his parental education was to blame."

But then Freud immediately proceeds to sound a warning against the therapist's educational influence, disavowing that this is a legitimate part of his activity:

> However much the analyst may be tempted to act as a teacher, model and ideal to other people and to make men in his own image, he should not forget that this is not his task in the analytic relationship, and indeed that he will be disloyal to his task if he allows himself to be led on by his inclinations. He will only be repeating one of the mistakes of the parents, when they crushed their child's independence and he will only be replacing one kind of dependence by another. In all his attempts at improving and educating the patient the analyst must respect his individuality. The amount of influence which he may legitimately employ will be determined by the degree of inhibition in development present in the patient. Many neurotics have remained so infantile that in analysis too they can only be treated as children [p. 67].*

*There seem to be several contradictions in this passage that apparently flow from these assumptions: (1) Analysis and "after-education" are separate and distinct processes: analysis is the essence of therapy, after-education is at best a tolerable by-product. (2) The analyst is not or should not be a model or a teacher because such people make men in their own image, crush the child's independence

Strachey (1934), writing in the same vein, observes:

> ... the principal effective alteration consists in a profound qualitative modification of the patient's super-ego, from which the other alterations follow in the main automatically. . . . This modification of the patient's super-ego is brought about in a series of innumerable small steps by the agency of mutative interpretations, which are effected by the analyst in virtue of his position as object of the patient's id impulses and as auxiliary super-ego. The dosed introjection of good objects is regarded as one of the most important factors in the therapeutic process [p. 159].

Bibring (1937) recognizes that the therapist makes a positive contribution through his own personality, but considers this to be essentially nonanalytical:

> ... the therapeutic changes which take place in the super-ego are effected by purely analytical means, i.e., by

---

and fail to respect his individuality. None of these things is ipso facto true of educaton in the best or in the literal sense of the word. Rather the analyst and educator appear to have much in common, a fact that Freud (1935) recognizes when in a different context he says: ". . . psycho-analytic treatment is a kind of *re-education* [p. 372]."

Wolstein (1954), too, draws a sharp line between "analysis" and "reeducation." The danger of the latter is said to be that the therapist by making suggestions may exploit his position of authority "as a magical source of truth." "The aim of constructive analysis is definitely not reeducation. The goal is to find, by inquiring into transference distortions, what has blocked the patient's way to whatever reeducational sources he wishes in order to pursue his goals [p. 78]."

The point of view I am developing is that reeducation and analysis are not antithetical and that both are integral aspects of the therapist's function. As I shall attempt to show, the therapist really has no choice in the matter: either he will be a good model of reality or he will be a poor one, but in either event he will be more than the analytic operator. This appears to be true even though the patient's transference reactions may emerge relatively independently of the therapist's personality.

34

demonstrating contradictions in structure and development and by making an elucidation of them possible. . . . In my opinion the analyst's attitude, and the analytical atmosphere which he creates, are fundamentally a reality-correction which adjusts the patient's anxieties about loss of love and punishment, the origin of which lies in childhood. Even if these anxieties later undergo analytical resolution I still believe that the patient's relationship to the analyst from which a sense of security emanates is not only a pre-condition of the procedure but also effects an immediate (apart from an analytical) consolidation of his sense of security which he has not successfully acquired or consolidated in childhood. Such an immediate consolidation—which, in itself, lies outside the field of analytic therapy—is of course, only of permanent value if it goes along with the coordinated operation of analytic treatment [pp. 182-183].*

Why is the atmosphere created by the therapist in which a "reality-correction" takes place separate and distinct from the interpretive essence of analytic treatment? It may be that both are integral parts of analytic psychotherapy and that they operate conjointly as therapeutic factors. To tease out their relative contributions is an important research task that may approach a solution of the question of what is effective in psychotherapy.

---

*In a more recent article Bibring (1954) delineates five groups of basic therapeutic techniques : (1) suggestive, (2) abreactive, (3) manipulative, (4) clarifying, and (5) interpretive, and makes an important distinction—difficult though it may be to define it operationally—between "technical" and "curative" applications of these principles. He asserts that in psychoanalysis proper all therapeutic principles are employed; however, "insight through interpretation is the principal agent and all others are—theoretically and practically—subordinate to it [p. 762]." He also notes a contemporary shift in emphasis from insight through interpretation to "experiential manipulation" exemplified in the approach of Alexander and French. The formulations I advance here would appear to correspond to Bibring's conception of "influence through experience."

THE EMOTIONAL CONTEXT OF THE THERAPY SITUATION AND THE THERAPIST AS REALITY MODEL

In order to be effective, psychotherapy must be an emotional experience; intellectual understanding per se does not produce therapeutic change, although it frequently is a by-product or an accompaniment of emotional insight. This emotional experience, to use Franz Alexander's term, must be a corrective one. The therapist's foremost task is to create an appropriate context for this emotional experience, and the success of therapy may largely depend on the achievement of this aim. Consequently, his activity—including his attitudes and communications—must be placed in its service. This appears to be one of the cardinal reasons for strict adherence to the tenet that no communication between therapist and patient is inconsequential, because extraneous communications or interventions that are unrelated to the therapeutic objective potentially complicate and distort the field of interaction and becloud the therapeutic context.

What makes the therapist's task so enormously difficult is the patient's tenacious unconscious opposition to unlearning inappropriate patterns and learning new, less conflictual ones. The fundamental problem for therapeutic technique is the search for optimal procedures to effect lasting modifications of the patient's personality structure. The patient must be shown, clearly and unequivocally, *what* he has to change and *how* he can change it. Opinions differ as to whether he also has to be presented with substitute solutions, or whether the spontaneous growth or reparative processes, aided by the patient's conscious strivings, can take over.

In interpersonal relationships all of us operate on more-or-less unconscious assumptions or hypotheses about the other person, particularly with regard to the question of whether he represents a threat to our security. Realistically, the other person may be a threat to our security or he may not; however, a serious problem arises when, as a result of

36

unfortunate life experience, we are unable to make this discrimination. We are then treating the other person as though he were a representation of our past, and our reactions to him will be determined by the kinds of assumptions or hypotheses we were forced to adopt at that time rather than by the reality of the present situation. It seems to make little difference whether such distortions are called transference or parataxis; the process remains the same.

It is the therapist's job to demonstrate to the patient how he distorts current situations in terms of his past, and how such distortions tend to complicate his interpersonal relations with his adult contemporaries. The stereotypy and rigidity of the patient's emotional reactions and behavior patterns must be analyzed and understood. This may come about most effectively if the patient's current experience with the therapist contrasts with the inappropriateness and the futility of his past performances. The patient must be enabled to make meaningful comparisons between the present and the past, so that he will begin to question his own assumptions or hypotheses about other people and their reactions to him. In this framework the totality of the patient's defenses emerges and becomes subject to analysis. The point is that the patient's emotional experience—interaction—with the therapist must be sufficiently different from all previous interpersonal experience to highlight the patient's own contribution; yet, paradoxically, the emotional context must have common elements with the past to form a bridge. The emotional context created by the therapist *is* contemporary reality, and it provides the backdrop against which the patient's distortions eventually stand out in bold relief. Thus, the sharper the experiential contrast, the greater the likelihood of constructive personality change.

How does the therapeutic situation provide a new emotional context? The essential ingredients have often been described; they are summed up in Fromm-Reichmann's (1950) key phrase: the therapist listens. The therapist bends all his energies to the task of understanding the patient's communications, particularly their emotional implications and undercurrents. His attitude is respectful, accepting, nonvaluative, noncondemning, noncriticizing, and thus invariably in contrast to the patient's experiences with significant adults in his early life. The therapist, unlike significant people in the patient's past and present life, minimizes *his* emotions, feelings, and needs, and maximizes the patient's. Usually for the first time in his life, the patient has the unique experience of hearing himself, of experiencing himself. The importance of the therapist's attitude, as communicated nonverbally or by minimal verbal cue, can hardly be overestimated. The message to the patient is that of simple acceptance and worthwhileness as a human being, regardless of the symptoms and personality characteristics about which the patient and others (including the therapist) may have misgivings or regrets. In this way the therapist helps the patient toward greater self-acceptance and self-esteem ("If the therapist is tolerant and noncondemning, perhaps I can accept myself better, too").

The therapist's basic acceptance provides a powerful impetus for therapeutic movement because of its security-giving aspects. In a profound sense, the patient becomes attached to and forms a meaningful interpersonal relationship with the therapist, not only on the basis of his irrational and unreasonable expectations but also on the basis of the *reality of the situation.** It is an experience with a human being who is "different," who can be trusted, irrespective of the content of the patient's disturbing feelings or impulses.

---

*When Freud (1949) spoke of transference as "the best instrument" of cure, he addressed himself exclusively to the *irrational* elements in the patient-therapist relationship. He did not recognize that apart from transference feelings the patient may have reality-based feelings about the therapist, and that these may play a part in the curative effort. To the last, Freud viewed the patient's positive transference— that is, his infantile, irrational, and distorted investments in the therapist—as the true motive force for the patient's collaboration and the

The character of this basic relationship must be maintained throughout therapy, throughout each session, throughout each minute; it must never be shaken. In consequence, the only serious danger to the therapeutic relationship could come from an actual breach of this unspoken contract, or from misunderstandings of the therapist's veracity, honesty, or respect. If the patient can feel assured, deep within himself, of the reality of the relationship, errors in technique, including premature or erroneous interpretations, should be less of a threat to the therapeutic enterprise.

The security-giving aspects of the therapist's attitude must be experienced and felt by the patient; they cannot be communicated effectively by superficial verbal means, such as reassurances, effusiveness of warmth, joviality, and so on. This does not mean that the therapist's verbal statements, questions, and comments are unsuited to reflect his basic attitude of respect; the opposite is true, but essentially the patient must work through to the realization that his attitude exists, and that it is genuine, sincere, and reliable.

The therapist thus comes to serve as a *new model of reality* by the time-proven method of setting an example, which enables the patient to compare his approach to his feelings and attitudes with that of the therapist and note the differences. Gradually the patient perceives that feelings and actions are not identical, that he condemns himself equally for both, and that the critical and punitive attitudes that he had attributed to others are really his own. At the same time, the therapist does not take sides with the patient against people in the latter's environment; he implies that

strongest factor operating in the therapist's favor.

In contrast, Anna Freud (1954) states: " . . . so far as the patient has a healthy personality, his real relationship to the analyst is never wholly submerged. With due respect to the necessary strictest handling and interpretation of the transference, I feel still that we should leave room somewhere for the realization that analyst and patient are also two real people, of equal adult status, in a real personal relationship to each other [p. 618]."

understanding is more important than blame; that the past is no longer subject to change; that the patient has within himself the capacity to grow, to place a more positive evaluation on himself, to exercise a choice, and so on. The therapist attempts to be an objective and dispassionate observer and encourages the development of similar attitudes in the patient, who thus gains greater distance from himself —the "splitting of the ego," in analytic terminology.

As a new model of reality, the therapist represents reality in its constructive aspects. This means, among other things, that the therapist treats the patient as an adult capable of making his own decisions, who must assume and discharge adult responsibilities. Although the therapist respects the patient, he does not pamper him. Nor is acceptance of the patient's feelings tantamount to approval or approbation; feelings are neither "good" nor "bad"—they are simply data whose significance in the patient's living is to be studied and understood. Similarly, recognizing and accepting the patient's dependency needs does not mean that the therapist aids and abets them or that he participates in their perpetuation. This applies with equal force to the patient's need to please, to manipulate, or to gain attention. Thus the therapist sets realistic limits. As the therapist accepts the patient's unreasonable demands but does not satisfy them—the reaction, unconsciously expected by the patient, that prompted the emergence of these demands— the patient reacts with profound disappointment, resentment, and rage. But, as he gains a more realistic appreciation of the therapist's unwavering position as a reality model, he is gradually able to relinquish some of his intense demands and to channel others in more productive and, in the long run, more satisfying ways.

While the patient must experience the therapist's trust, maturity, and integrity, the therapist must be *sparing* in verbally communicating his interest, understanding, and respect, in accordance with the rationale that the patient must work out his own solutions. He gains strength through his own efforts, and his achievements will be more thorough and lasting if they are his own. A parent who promptly rushes to the aid of the child whenever he is trying to master a problem, is not doing the child a service because the child comes to feel that solutions to life's problems will always be presented on a silver platter. By analogy, the patient must be permitted to work on his problems at his own speed, without interference or pushing from the therapist. This speed may at times appear excruciatingly slow to the participant observer, and his temptation to accelerate it may be strong. If he succumbs to the temptation, he may seemingly speed up the therapeutic process, but in actuality he may be instrumental in fostering the patient's dependent needs instead of analyzing them. On the other hand, if he has sufficient patience and maturity, he helps the patient work through to a sense of unsuspected strength and to a realization that he can endure, survive, and integrate painful feelings. In this way, too, the therapist teaches by example that achievements are commensurate with the expended effort, and fosters self-confidence, self-reliance, and independence.

The therapist's attitude conveys his unfaltering willingness to help the patient in constructive efforts to master his problems, yet he does not solve them for him, nor does he do the work of therapy. While the therapist is giving, he is not all-giving. Rather, in contrast to the patient's early life experience, he teaches the patient that he too can give, that his gifts can be worthwhile, and that others do not necessarily or invariably reject the giver. The patient's giving is fostered through the injunction to communicate all of his thoughts, fantasies, feelings, and wishes. By withholding them he tends to repeat infantile patterns that, as Freud has so clearly elaborated, may have originated in interpersonal experiences—for example, attitudes surrounding bowel functions. The pleasure of withholding is frequently a conflictual one, reflecting the patient's attitude toward his mother: "I am punishing or fighting you by holding on to my thoughts, feelings, and feces. In this way, I gain power over you. I give you nothing." It is evident that a therapist who showers the patient with the gifts of interest, attention, and human kindness does not succeed in evoking the patient's retentive and negativistic attitudes, thus depriving himself and his patient of the opportunity of understanding them in all their ramifications.

It is clear that therapy, like any educational process, requires long periods of time. The extent to which the growth process may be accelerated by interpretations and other techniques is a major question for research in this area. The attitudes which have been mentioned may rank among the most important catalysts available.

While here-and-now experiences with the therapist have been stressed, no attempt has been made to deal systematically with etiological factors, or the technical operations of psychotherapy, including the analysis of transference distortions; *nor should anything I have said in the course of this chapter be construed as minimizing the importance or the potential effects of analytic interpretations.*

COUNTERTRANSFERENCES

The phenomena usually classed under the heading of countertransference appear to be relatively gross deviations of the therapist from his role as an objective participant observer and creator of a new reality model. Perhaps these deviations are viewed more fruitfully not as a class of phenomena by themselves, but as extremes of continua underlying the emotional context of therapy. When the therapist responds to the patient's transference behavior in terms of the patient's distorted expectations rather than in terms of a new reality model, he has abdicated his therapeutic role and minimized his usefulness to the patient. The therapist's distortions may be instigated by and represent a response to the patient's transference behavior; frequently, perhaps, this is the case. On the other hand, they may be distortions that the therapist would exhibit relatively independently of the patient's distortions. Furthermore, it appears that most deficiencies in the therapeutic emotional context created by the therapist are not the gross phenomena that have traditionally been grouped under the heading of countertransference, but rather more subtle shortcomings in the therapist's contribution.

Experimental evidence obtained under reasonably controlled conditions (see Chapters Nine, Ten, and Eleven) supports the contention that the therapist's unconscious attitudes may subtly color his "technical" thinking about a case, his diagnostic formulations, prognostic estimates, therapeutic plans, and goals, and ultimately the character of his communications or the patient's neurotic process itself; it is difficult to see how the therapist's conscious or unconscious rejecting attitudes, however subtle, that find their way into his therapeutic interventions, can fail to have a detrimental effect on the therapeutic enterprise. Fromm-Reichmann (1950) gives the following example:

> The emanation of the psychiatrist's general system of ethical values is not the only example of the possibility of inadvertent communication of his viewpoints and its influence on the course of treatment. The emanation of the psychiatrist's evaluation of and judgment about the symptomatology of his patients may turn out to be of equally great importance. One of the most impressive examples illustrating this fact presents itself in the history of the psychiatric evaluation of the symptom of stool-smearing. In the old days, stool-smearing was considered to be a symptom of grave prognostic significance in any psychiatric patient. Since psychiatrists have learned to approach this symptom in the same spirit of investigating its psychopathology and its dynamics as they approach any other symptom or mode of expression, it has lost its threatening aspects. In other words, stool-smearing patients of previous periods in psychiatric development

were sometimes destined to deteriorate and become incurable. This was not because of the inherent gravity of the symptom but because of the atmosphere of awe, disgust, and gruesomeness which it evoked in their moralistic, pedagogically minded psychiatrists and which they unwittingly conveyed to the patients [p. 36].

These attitudinal distortions may be particularly insidious if the therapist is firmly convinced of the "objectivity" of his thinking when actually he is projecting feelings and attitudes on to the patient that have little relation to the clinical material under consideration. Such projections may be exemplified as follows:

The therapist may feel that he "ought" to be stricter with a patient who is likely to make great demands on him. Similarly, he may feel that he should be more active with such a patient, and discourage the free expression of feelings. He may feel that the prognosis is poor, which may provide a "justification" for a lack of interest on his part and be concomitant with his feeling that the patient is not worth helping, that the great expenditure of energy and interest required for creating a favorable emotional context for psychotherapy is a "waste of time," and so on. He may feel inclined to recommend brief psychotherapy instead of more intensive treatment, or rationalize that the patient is not really in need of psychotherapy. He may consider it "appropriate" to manipulate the transference relationship by making recommendations to the patient on how to lead his life. He may counsel the avoidance of certain topics in therapy, focus on others, and in general take a more active part in changing the patient than he normally would if his emotional reactions were less aroused. A consciously felt disinclination to treat such a patient, resulting in a referral elsewhere, would appear to reflect an honest solution of the impasse.

Again, the therapist's choice of words in diagnosing and describing the patient's emotional dynamics may reflect

44

a subtle moral value judgment about the patient. A diagnostic label assigned to a patient may carry with it a trace of disapproval that may have a pervasive influence on succeeding therapeutic interactions; such terms as "psychopathic," "paranoid," or "character disorder," may be more revealing of the therapist's attitude than of the patient to whom they are assigned.

How do the therapist's attitudes express themselves in his communications to a patient, even in an initial interview? Experimental evidence (see Chapters Nine, Ten, and Eleven) supports the following distinctions between therapists who seem to function in the role of a professional helper, and those who are deficient in creating a potentially constructive emotional context for psychotherapy.

In the experimental investigation, the first group of therapists tended to recognize the existence of an emotional problem and communicated such understanding to the patient at some point in the interview. They recognized with the patient that he had overcome his resistance to change by seeking help, that there was a relationship between his physical symptoms and his emotional conflicts that could be elucidated in psychotherapy, and that the resulting clarification might lead to constructive personality change. They attempted to alleviate the patient's discomfort in the interview by putting him at ease and allaying some of his anxiety, by instilling some hope for the future, and by refraining from threatening his self-esteem. They felt the need to communicate to the patient something about treatment plans, on the assumption that the patient had a right to expect such a statement from the interviewer as an expert. They gave evidence of listening to the patient, of being respectful, nonderogatory, noncritical, and nonjudgmental in a moral sense. Their questioning was designed to facilitate the patient's self-exploration rather than to expound their own views or hypotheses based on fragmentary data.

Therapists of the second group either failed to make a

positive contribution, or gave evidence of reacting to the patient's communications in ways that appeared antithetical to the therapist's role. Most common seemed to be reactions in which the therapist responded with anger to the patient's anger and demanding attitudes, which in turn led to accusations, criticisms, or direct interpretive attacks on the patient's defenses. Often the therapist's negative attitudes toward the patient expressed themselves in relatively indirect ways that were highlighted because of their contrast to the performance of other therapists. Therapists with negative attitudes, for example, seemed cold, distant, and extremely impersonal, and treated the patient like a "specimen." Needless to say, these distinctions are schematic and probably overdrawn; also, one cannot be sure of what may be desirable, "therapeutic," or appropriate in a given set of circumstances. However, it is doubtful whether a patient who comes to perceive the interviewer as a cross-examiner, whose sole purpose appears to consist of exposing the patient's "weaknesses," is likely, if he remains in therapy at all, to develop an attitude leading to the eventual relinquishment of defenses.

Deficiencies in empathic understanding not only may reflect blind spots in the therapist's personality, but also may be intertwined with attitudes fostered by the culture of which the therapist and the patient are a part. Whereas the culture of nineteenth-century Vienna dictated the suppression and repression of sexual matters, contemporary American culture is more intolerant of overtly expressed hostility, arrogance, antagonism, and signs that an adult male is dependent, "immature," passive, weak, and helpless. Certainly the therapeutic task is contravened if the therapist reacts to these manifestations in the patient with anger, suppression, and rejection, instead of with an understanding that allows them to be brought into the open, where they can be understood in terms of the patient's emotional dynamics.

Clearly, intensive research effort must be applied to the

scrutiny of the therapist's attitudes, whether determined by the culture or his own personality. What the therapist perceives as ongoing processes between himself and the patient, the manner in which he evaluates his perceptions, and the therapeutic actions he takes as a consequence—these are to an important degree a function of his own personality and his culture.

A question arises concerning the genuineness of the therapist's attitude, his spontaneity, and freedom of self-expression. The argument runs something like this. If the therapist is "himself," is spontaneous, relaxed, and unselfconscious—qualities stressed by numerous writers—he is not in a favorable position to be an objective and dispassionate observer. If he attempts to be a "scientist," controlling his verbal communications, and appraising and anticipating their possible effects, he interferes with his spontaneity as a therapist and thereby damages the free give-and-take of the interaction. It has also been asserted that the ideal therapeutic attitude of acceptance, permissiveness, noncriticalness, and imperturbable equanimity is unattainable, and that the therapist who purports to carry it out is dissimulating, insincere, and dishonest with himself.

I believe that the imposition of some procedural rules is necessary, but does not preclude a genuine interest on the therapist's part in helping and understanding. It is certainly true that society has erected specific limits for the therapist's behavior that most therapists agree cannot be transcended even if it is therapeutically desirable. Furthermore, the goal of scrutinizing the interpersonal relationship between therapist and patient demands that the field be kept as "clean" as possible in order to evaluate the respective contributions of patient and therapist. If the therapist fails to impose controls over himself and his communications, this goal is almost impossible to achieve. This is a basic scientific requirement. Finally, certain aspects of the therapist's role are by definition "artificial"; so is the essence of the therapeutic situation as a laboratory situation for study-

47

ing the patient's personality in interaction with another human being.

The value of the emotional experience is not lessened by the fact that the patient pays for the therapist's time and thus for his interest and effort. The limitations of reality notwithstanding, the therapist can be genuinely interested in his task of studying and understanding interpersonal processes; he can respect the patient as a person, without compulsion to love him, to side with him, or to spoil him. The patient must learn to get along with minimum essentials from other people, and this to a very important extent is part and parcel of the therapeutic experience. He may have had an excess of pampering in his childhood, or he may have suffered from sore neglect, but he has never had the experience of being accepted simply as a human being. I am not referring here to the superficial hail-fellow-well-met "acceptance," typically extended in this culture to most strangers. This experience the therapist can and must provide. The patient soon realizes that the therapist has a life of his own, that he has family and friends, and so on, but these facets enter as little as possible into the interaction. The therapist does not become artificial by keeping his private life out of the picture, any more than an executive at a conference is artificial if he devotes himself undividedly to the task at hand without talking about the weather or his hobbies. A flaw in this analogy is that the executive, unlike the therapist, arouses no expectations of an intimate personal relationship—that is, the ambiguity of the therapeutic situation is lacking (see Bordin, 1955). In time, the patient comes to appreciate the therapist's unwavering attention during the therapeutic hour to the understanding of the patient's interpersonal processes. Perhaps his parents have never taken him seriously, and so he has never taken himself seriously. The therapeutic session may be the first situation in which someone takes him seriously, and this in turn permits him to assume a similar attitude toward himself. The therapist who has mastered the therapeutic role does

48

not feel constricted by it, and in time the patient will accept the reality of the situation and use it to advantage.

THE FUNCTION OF INTERPRETATIONS

What function do verbal communications serve in the therapeutic interaction? If the essence of the psychotherapeutic process is the interaction within the emotional context created by the therapist, it follows that verbal communications must be placed in the service of this interaction and must parallel it. Verbal communications are therapeutic to the extent that they coincide with the interaction of emotional contexts. The patient is encouraged to put his feelings into words, an assignment that poses considerable difficulties for any person who has developed great skill in keeping words and feelings apart. The therapist, in turn, attempts to understand the patient's emotional context, which is typically at variance with his verbal communications. When the therapist, with the help of a variety of clues (nonverbal, gestural, and so on), succeeds in identifying an emotional, attitudinal, or behavioral sequence inapporpriate to or incongruous with the realities of the situation as the therapist sees it, he may attempt to put this discrepancy into words. An interpretation, then, is an attempt to describe by means of verbal symbols an emotional reaction or a behavior pattern exhibited by the patient in relation to the therapist, of whose interpersonal or dynamic significance the patient is unaware or insufficiently aware. The occurrence and significance of such patterns are recognized by the therapist because his training and experience have augmented his capacity to perceive and interpret incongruous responses to what he knows is going on in the therapeutic situation. The interpretation is properly timed and potentially successful if the patient is emotionally ready to recognize with the therapist the inappropriateness of his performance. Interpretations may relate to other interpersonal situations, but they are most dramatic and probably most effective if they refer to

49

the here-and-now of the therapeutic situation, for intellectual reconstructions of the past that are not accompanied by appropriate affect may remain sterile. Freud (1949) observed that "the patient never forgets again what he has experienced in the form of transference [p. 70]." This learning refers to the emotional experience and only secondarily to its verbal counterpart. Verbal symbols aid and promote the process of achieving emotional understanding and insight, but they cannot take the place of the emotional experience. On the other hand, verbal symbols play an important part in binding the emotional experience to the patient's cognitive structure: mastery over emotional experiences is aided if they can be put into words and adequately described.

AN OPERATIONAL ANALYSIS OF THE THERAPIST'S ATTITUDE

In conclusion, an analysis of the major determinants of the therapist's attitude at a given point in therapy would help to identify antecedent variables and their relative influences, and aid in providing more precise knowledge about therapeutic principles. A cardinal task for research is to break down the totality of the therapist's activities into variables that are therapeutically "active" and those that are relatively "inert," and to assay the relative importance of the "active" variables.

It appears that the therapist's attitude toward a patient results from at least the following components, which, to complicate matters, undoubtedly interact:

1. The therapist's customary or characterological attitudes—that is, organized and perduring personality patterns, ways in which he relates to people "in general." Thus, he may be outgoing, reserved, spontaneous, stilted, and so on. The most important feature of these attitudes is that they are largely beyond conscious manipulation. For example, a therapist may have a life history of early rejection

by significant adults; he may have come to understand the implications of these vicissitudes through his personal analysis and developed a considerable degree of self-consciousness. However, he will continue to meet strangers with a certain reserve even though he consciously knows that they are less "dangerous" than the significant adults of his past. These basic attitudes shade imperceptibly into temperament, from which they may at times be indistinguishable.

2. The personality structure of the patient with whom the therapist is interacting. The therapist may react warmly toward schizoid patients, coldly toward paranoid ones, and so forth. These patterns may reflect attitudes that he holds toward himself or significant people in his early life, or which significant people in his early life held toward him. Depending on the therapist's degree of self-knowledge and self-awareness, these attitudes may play an important part in coloring his clinical evaluations of and his willingness and ability to do therapy with certain patients.

3. The patient's station in life, his socioeconomic status, intellect, sex, age, color, and so forth. These may evoke attitudes in the therapist that are conditioned by the culture of which both are a part. The degree to which these attitudes influence or distort the therapist's perceptions is again a function of his self-knowledge. Cholden (1956), addressing himself to psychotherapy of schizophrenics, observes that: "The therapist is reacting to both the real and the imagined person seen before him. The patient's response, too, results from the real and the imagined person he perceives. The unreal aspect of the relationship, as determined by past attitudes on the part of both, co-determines the relationship [p. 240]." Cultural values may also partly determine the meaning and "clinical significance" that the therapist will attach to attitudes and behaviors of the patient, such as anger, hostility, dependency, weakness, "immaturity," and so on.

4. The therapist's conceptions of therapy, therapeutic goals, and techniques, composed of a set of conscious or

51

preconscious attitudes. They also comprise the therapist's understanding of his role in the therapeutic undertaking, which partly dictates the attitude he adopts toward a given patient. He may accept the notion of the therapist as an "objective mirror" and structure his behavior accordingly. He may feel that the therapist should be relatively spontaneous, "giving," warm, and so on, and pattern his behavior vis-à-vis the patient in accordance with this conception. Most of these "conscious" attitudes may be ego-syntonic and thus interact with the unconsciously determined attitudes mentioned before. To some extent, then, the therapist's idea of the "optimum" attitude represents a rationalization, in that he finds theoretical sanction for the way he *must* behave or in the manner in which he feels most comfortable. There is reason to believe that the therapist's choice of theory and technique is determined—to some extent, at least—by these factors, which have never been systematically explored.

5. The patient's current and long-range needs. With regard to the long-range needs, the therapist's attitude may reflect his consciously formulated therapeutic goals, which in turn may be based on his therapeutic philosophy and theory; with regard to the patient's momentary needs, theoretical considerations are perhaps usually present, but so are unconscious factors that may produce serious distortions in the therapist's perceptions, evaluations, and attitude, and determine the character of his intervention, not excluding silence. Thus, countertransference reactions are operations in which the therapist relinquishes his defined therapeutic role in order to pursue the covert gratification of his own needs instead of adhering to his avowed therapeutic objectives.

6. Chance—that is, additional fluctuations in the therapist's attitude that are a function of day-to-day variations and are difficult to bring under scientific control.

How can an operational analysis of the therapist's attitudes be carried out? Methodologically, one can rely on the therapist's conscious report, the patient's report, and observations by external observers. Or, one can approach the problem indirectly, by studying the therapist's perceptions, evaluations, and clinical judgments, and determining their relationships to his attitudes, however these may be measured. In its bare essentials, the therapist's attitude toward a patient is either positive or negative, approaching or withdrawing, adient or abient. This is not to minimize the enormous subtlety and complexity of interaction patterns that undergo many shifts during any therapeutic hour. But as research efforts succeed in analyzing this composite and mapping out meaningful relationships to other variables there should result increased understanding, improved control, and greater predictability of the therapeutic process.

References

Berman, L. 1949. "Countertransferences and Attitudes of the Analyst in the Therapeutic Process," *Psychiat.*, 12: 159-166.

Bibring, E. 1937. "Symposium on the Theory of the Therapeutic Results of Psychoanalysis," *Int. J. Psychoanal.*, 18: 170-189.

——— 1954. "Psychoanalysis and the Dynamic Psychotherapies," *J. Am. Psychoanal. Assn.*, 2: 745-770.

Bordin, E. S. 1955. "Ambiguity as a Therapeutic Variable," *J. Cons. Psychol.*, 19: 9-15.

Cholden, L. 1956. "Observations on Psychotherapy of Schizophrenia," in *Progress in Psychotherapy*, Vol. I, ed. F. Fromm-Reichmann and J. L. Moreno, pp. 239-247. New York: Grune & Stratton.

Frank, J. D. 1958. "Some Effects of Expectancy and Influence in Psychotherapy," in *Progress in Psycho-*

therapy, Vol III, ed. J. H. Masserman and J. L. Moreno, pp. 27-43. New York: Grune & Stratton.

Freud, A. 1954. "The Widening Scope of Indications for Psychoanalysis: Discussion," *J. Am. Psychoanal. Assn.*, 2: 607-620.

Freud, S. 1935. *A General Introduction to Psychoanalysis.* New York: Liveright.

———— 1949. *An Outline of Psychoanalysis.* New York: Norton.

———— 1953. "The Future Prospects of Psycho-Analytic Therapy," in *Collected Papers*, Vol. II, pp. 285-296. London: Hogarth.

Fromm-Reichmann, F. 1950. *Principles of Intensive Psychotherapy.* Chicago: University of Chicago Press.

Orr, D. W. 1954. "Transference and Countertransference: A Historical Survey," *J. Am. Psychoanal. Assn.*, 2: 621-670.

Rioch, J. M. 1943. "The Transference Phenomenon in Psychoanalytic Therapy," *Psychiat.*, 6: 147-156.

Stone, L. 1954. "The Widening Scope of Indications for Psychoanalysis," *J. Am. Psychoanal. Assn.*, 2: 567-594.

Strachey, J. 1934. "The Nature of Therapeutic Action of Psychoanalysis," *Int. J. Psychoanal.*, 15: 127-159.

Thompson, C. 1950. *Psychoanalysis: Evolution and Development.* New York: Hermitage House.

Wolstein, B. 1954. *Transference: Its Meaning and Function in Psychoanalytic Theory.* New York: Grune & Stratton.

2

THE DUALITY OF THE
THERAPIST'S CONTRIBUTION

Some years ago I became interested in the study of psychotherapeutic techniques and found that very little empirical
research had been done on the problem. Not only were there
few published investigations on the subject but there were
also few systematic expositions about psychotherapeutic
technique, not excluding the psychoanalytic literature.
Apart from Freud's well-known papers on technique, very
little attention had been given to the problem in print
(Fenichel, 1941), and even considering the fecundity of
Freud's writings it is puzzling that he never produced a
comprehensive work on therapeutic technique. One reason
for this dearth may be traced to the acrimonious attacks to
which psychoanalysis was exposed from its inception so that
Freud and his co-workers preferred to communicate and
teach technique by word of mouth rather than in writing.

This also prevented charlatans, of whom there were many, to go through a "home study" course of psychoanalysis. This, however, is probably not the full explanation.*

At any rate, my research interest turned to the objective study of therapeutic techniques, and in the course of this effort I developed a conceptual tool, a system of content analysis that made it possible to abstract several dimensions from therapeutic communications and to arrive at crude quantifications (See Chapter Twenty-one). This work was guided by the rationale that in order to compare one therapist with another, one technique with another, one theoretical orientation with another, it is necessary to develop methods for mediating such comparisons. Of course, studies aimed at assessing the outcomes of psychotherapy must eventually make more specific assertions than that the patient was treated by "psychoanalysis," "psychoanalytically oriented therapy," etc. I am well aware that the system developed in the course of our work is but a beginning, and that the sensitivity of such instruments must be substantially increased before the kinds of comparisons of which I spoke can be carried out. After some experimentation (see Chapters Thirteen and Fourteen) I came to feel that while our method provided fairly adequate measures of structural characteristics of communications it was insufficiently sensitive to other essential ingredients of the therapist's communications, those in the attitudinal-emotional sphere, to which I was led to attribute more and more importance.

One reason for the shifting interest from therapeutic technique per se to the person of the therapist derived from continuing efforts to relate variations in technique to factors in the therapist's training and experience. I became impressed with the not very original observation that the person of the therapist and his technique are inextricably interwoven. This led to more curiosity about characteristics

*The writing of this chapter and the research on which it is based were supported by Research Grant M-2171 from the National Institute of Mental Health, Public Health Service.

56

that might distinguish the "good" psychotherapist. Again, the lack of solid empirical data was rather striking.

It is interesting to speculate about the reasons for the rather amazing dearth of empirical data on the personal and technical qualifications of a good psychotherapist. To be sure, there are well-formulated stereotypes on which a high degree of agreement could be reached (Holt and Luborsky, 1958) but few conclusive findings. There is some anecdotal evidence (Glover, cited by Kubie, 1956) that sometimes beginners achieve successes that they are unable to equal once they have acquired more thorough formal training, but to my knowledge this has not been well documented. On the other hand, a highly experienced and seasoned psychoanalyst might be presumed to achieve results that a first-year resident in psychiatry could not hope to obtain, and perhaps he should be able to reach this goal by a more straightforward route than his inexperienced colleague. Again, no reliable data are available. Furthermore, some therapists may be highly successful with certain kinds of patients but less so with others. We know that experienced therapists typically are very circumspect in their selection of patients. They know their own strengths and weaknesses and they will not undertake tasks that they believe they cannot tackle. This increased selectivity in itself should be reflected in the quality of their therapeutic work. But is it?

Numerous writers have emphasized one grave obstacle —the absence of outcome criteria on which agreement can be reached. Another factor prominently mentioned is the intervention of unpredictable events, such as occurrences in the patient's life situation that may affect the outcome and over which the therapist—and sometimes also the patient —has no control. Once the cogency of these arguments is admitted, we are still left with the above questions, and I do not believe that an important part of the explanation is attributable to the lack of adequate criteria and the effect of other events.

One of the really disconcerting facts is that so far we have been virtually unable to study highly experienced, well-trained, and seasoned therapists and to learn the reasons for their unquestioned success. We have not even been able to get the opinions of these outstanding men as to what in their judgment accounts for their achievements. What are the personal qualities of these men? Do they have something in common? Do they differ in significant respects? Are the similarities and differences related in any systematic way to the kinds of patients they choose and the therapeutic results they achieve with them? Apart from personal characteristics, which are probably of outstanding importance, do their technical operations have important elements in common or are the therapeutic styles highly idiosyncratic, even if the theoretical principles to which these therapists subscribe may be for practical purposes indistinguishable? What sharpens the therapeutic weapon of the successful therapist? Is there a subtle fusion between technical skills and personal attributes, and if so, how does this fusion come about? Can skill compensate for personality characteristics and vice versa?

For various reasons those therapists from whom we could presumably learn the most are, paradoxically, the most inaccessible to the researcher, and the preponderance of the published investigations deals with beginners who, because of the organizational structure of institutions, are being supervised, which makes it feasible to obtain measures of their performance. The situation is somewhat analogous to one in which the investigation of violin virtuosi would have to be approached via students because performers like Heifetz, Szigeti, or Oistrakh were unavailable or had never played in public. Prominence in the field or reputation in professional circles is probably a criterion of considerable validity; but there is no assurance that therapists who are frequent contributors to the literature and whose names are in the limelight are in fact the outstanding therapists. The fact that such persons enjoy a reputation for competence is presumptive evidence that it is deserved, but by the same token there are probably large numbers of truly outstanding therapists who rarely publish—perhaps for the very reason that they devote most of their time to therapy.

What I am advocating, then, is that we turn to those therapists who can teach us the most—highly experienced practitioners of the art rather than novices. The next question is how to study them or how to learn from them. Undoubtedly we would find that each of these therapists—and I hope we shall not omit women, because their contributions to psychotherapy have been truly remarkable, a fact that by itself might give rise to a number of fruitful hypotheses—could provide an eloquent enumeration of the factors that he or she considers paramount in therapeutic work. How could we be certain, however, that these factors are the real factors? I am not casting aspersions upon the veracity of our respondents, but it is the avowed business of science to entertain skeptical doubts.

As a beginning, we could listen as intently, systematically, and open-mindedly as possible to what these people have to tell us and we could try to tease out common elements from their accounts. This might be a kind of intuitive factor analysis, which might be highly revealing. It is remarkable that it has never been done. A second step might be to observe these therapists at work and to study whether their operations have common elements or whether their procedures are so idiosyncratic that no common denominators can be extracted. I rather doubt that the latter would be the case. All these steps, I should like to emphasize, call for systematic naturalistic observation rather than "controlled" investigations. Implicit in this statement is my genuine belief that the straitjacket of methodology that is so appealing to modern behavioral scientists may so narrow our relatively unaided powers of observation, which it seems to me have been sold far short today, that we may be seriously hindered in discovering anything new. This is a major criticism of much of the controlled research that has been published in the area of psychotherapy; it has stressed scientific rigor at the expense of breadth of vision. Experimental "gimmicks," of which we find many, give "operational definitions" of this and that variable but often they are far less "elegant" than appears at first glance. There is a widespread fascination with numerical scores and correlation coefficients derived from a card sort simply because they are quantitative indices; but it is often forgotten that these coefficients may be based on simple-minded descriptions. I am not saying that such research is necessarily without value but it is doubtful that it will advance the frontiers of knowledge in significant ways.

At this point, I should like to digress for a moment and make a distinction between what might be called functional and nonfunctional experimental models, and to enter a strong plea for the first type. Clinicians—psychiatrists and psychoanalysts—often fail to observe this discrimination and voice their opposition to *all* research in the area of psychotherapy on the mistaken, I believe, ground that the situations that the experimenter designs are artificial and divorced from their usual modus operandi. It seems to me that some objections to research in this area are well founded whereas others are not, and to reject all research because some happens to be poorly designed appears to be an indefensible attitude whose ultimate effect cannot fail but hamper progress.

Let me try to be more concrete. In recent years, under the impact of operationalism, there has been an increasing trend among investigators, particularly among psychologists, to search for techniques yielding readily quantifiable measures that can then be subjected to statistical analysis. These measures often seem rather plausible and at times have a deceptive simplicity. To cite some examples: Patients may be asked to complete a paper-and-pencil personality test from which a profile of their "needs" may be derived. Concurrently, the therapist may be asked to complete the identical test as he thinks the patient filled it out.

60

The degree of agreement is then used as an index of the therapist's "understanding," "empathy," or even of his therapeutic competence. Or the therapist is asked to complete the test as he would like to see the patient fill it out upon completion of therapy, which is interpreted as a measure of his therapeutic goals. Or the last-mentioned description is correlated with the therapist's self-description on the test, to yield an index of how much the therapist would like the patient to become like himself. Similar procedures have been used to obtain measures of "conflict" between the patient's "real" and "ideal" self, "assumed similarity," and many others. Cronbach (1955) has critically analyzed such procedures on statistical grounds and called attention to a number of artifacts. He has also questioned the psychological meaning of "discrepancy scores" and correlations based on these measures. Apart from these considerations—which are cogent and valid in their own right—I wish to take issue with these approaches on the ground that they impose a task on the therapist that is *non-functional.* That is to say, he is called upon to perform an operation that in the ordinary course of events he does not perform and that in some instances is utterly alien to him. It seems reasonable to expect a therapist who has gained a thorough knowledge of a patient's personality structure and conflicts to predict how he would behave in a given situation. For example, on the basis of the therapist's observations on how the patient has related to, say, authority figures in the past, his knowledge of the patient's characteristic way of relating to the therapist in the transference situation, the stage of the therapeutic work, and related data, the therapist should be able to reasonably predict the patient's manner of relating to an authority figure in the present, provided something is known about that authority figure's characteristics and the nature of the situation in which the patient encounters that person. Similarly, he might be asked to predict the direction in which therapeutic movement might occur, probable shifts in the patient's defenses, etc., although here allowance must be made for the possible influence of external events in the patient's life over which the therapist ordinarily exercises no control. Nevertheless, within relatively broad limits, predictions should be possible. I might mention that to my knowledge this type of investigation has been attempted so far only by Bellak and Smith (1956)—with somewhat discouraging results. However, I believe that in Bellak's pioneering study the therapist's task was unnecessarily and somewhat unfairly complicated in other respects.

It seems to me that the therapist is not in a particularly favorable position to make assertions about the manner in which a patient resolves a forced-choice item on a personality questionnaire, whose validity is usually open to question in the first place. In other words, there is typically a great paucity of data concerning the statistical relationships between the measures derived from a test and the respondent's personality dynamics as determined by other empirical means. The therapist might have a fairly good notion of the patient's self-concept at a given point in therapy, but he does not know what the patient is willing to divulge to an outsider or the extent of his willingness to reveal himself in an experimental situation.

A *functional* experiment, on the other hand, is one that does not remove the therapist from his usual habitat and does not divorce the experimental task from the normal mental processes used by the therapist in his daily work. I recognize that in science it is often necessary to sacrifice something of the fullness and richness of the natural situation to rigor and precision, but the compromise must not be excessive. The art in designing experiments in this area is to know where to draw the line. In my judgment the rarity of good experiments and the artificiality of others is directly traceable to the fact that the expert clinician-therapist usually lacks the scientific know-how to design a good experiment. Conversely, those who are experts in experimental design and psychological measurement often lack a deep understanding of the complex dynamics with which the therapist deals in his work. This problem will not be remedied until the therapist becomes a better scientist and the scientist becomes a better clinician. It is gratifying to note that progress is being made in this direction (see Chapter Twenty-seven).

To return to the main theme, there are characteristics, elements, ingredients, etc., in the personality of the therapist that, other things being equal, contribute markedly to therapeutic success or failure. It must also be pointed out that these characteristics are not static attributes but rather something that enters into the living relationship between patient and therapist such that the therapeutic work is substantially furthered or hindered. It was Freud's tendency to lay major stress on such factors as the patient's ability to invest objects (including the therapist) with libido, the strength of the instincts, and the destructiveness of the superego forces. These, in his judgment, accounted for the course and outcome of the transference neurosis.

Recognizing, however, that the personality and attitudes of the therapist must play a part, he postulated as early as 1910 the concept of countertransference (Freud, 1953), which made room for the fact that unresolved neurotic problems on the part of the therapist would impede the full development and resolution of the transference neurosis. This formulation stresses interference, impediments, and obstacles in the therapist's personality and attitudes, but it does not provide for positive influences that might have a beneficial effect. These characteristics were lumped under the heading of the analytic incognito—the recognition that the analyst should be nonjudgmental, accepting, etc. In other words, a somewhat static conception prevented an elaboration of the manner in which these characteristics might affect and interact with the patient's expectations, wishes, and impulses. It was assumed that the analytic attitude, unless it was interfered with by problems in the therapist, was a constant that did not require further critical dissection. Freud never really deviated from this position although in one of his last papers (1952) he makes some obscure references to the analyst's personality that in some respects must be "superior" to enable the patient to model himself in the analyst's image. I think it was this conception that for many years hampered investigations into personality differences among analysts. It could not possibly have escaped Freud that his disciples behaved in very different ways with patients (and himself) and it is a bit hard to understand why he did not make more of this variable. My own speculation is that his own nineteenth-century scientific orientation, which laid major stress on the objects of observation rather than the observer, precluded further elaboration, but on the other hand, the very fact that he recognized countertransferences early and recommended personal analysis for the therapist was a brilliant insight and a unique attempt to decrease if not eliminate the observer bias that is a problem in the natural sciences but a hundredfold more so in the sciences concerned with interpersonal processes. It is noteworthy that it was many years before interest in the therapist's personality and his contribution to the therapeutic process was revived.

I should like to draw attention to the nature of the therapeutic influence that Freud (1935) postulates as the prime mover. He states: ". . . as soon as the treatment has taken a hold upon the patient it appears that the entire productivity of the illness henceforward becomes concentrated in one direction—namely, upon the relationship to the physician [p. 386]." He goes on to describe the dynamics of the transference neurosis, its all-important central significance for cure, and then addresses himself to the "powerful propelling force" that is instrumental in recovery:

The outcome in this struggle [between repressive and expressive forces] is not decided by his intellectual insight —it is neither strong enough nor free enough to accomplish such a thing—but solely by his relationship to the

64

physician. In so far as his transference bears the positive sign, it clothes the physician with authority, transforms itself into faith in his findings and in his views. Without this kind of transference or with a negative one, the physician and his arguments would never even be listened to. Faith repeats the history of its own origin; it is a derivative of love and at first needed no arguments. Not until later does it admit them so far as to take them into critical consideration if they have been offered by someone who is loved. Without this support arguments have no weight with the patient, never do have any with most people in life. A human being is therefore on the whole only accessible to influence, even on the intellectual side, in so far as he is capable of investing objects with libido [p. 387].

If we don't accept the libido theory, we might simply say that a human being is accesible to influence, even on the intellectual side, in so far as he is capable of becoming emotionally involved with another person.

Freud, in discussing the dynamics of the transference, is explicit on this point. He asks the rhetorical question: How can the resistance be gotten rid of? and then answers himself by saying that the resistance will be withdrawn when its recognition has been made possible by the work of interpretation. He then proceeds to ask: What are the instinctive propelling forces at our disposal to bring this about? and replies: "First, the patient's desire for recovery, which impelled him to submit himself to the work in cooperation with us, and secondly, the aid of his intelligence which we reinforce by our interpretation [p. 379]."

As the battle of the repression is revived, the therapist acts as a helper to the patient's struggling ego. In all this—and this is the reason for holding up for examination material that is abundantly familiar—it is apparent that the therapeutic work is sustained by the patient's trust, confidence, belief, faith in the therapist's unwavering commitment and dedication to the therapeutic task and, ultimately, to the patient as a person in his struggle for growth, maturity, and independence. In the final analysis, the patient relinquishes his resistance out of love for the therapist; he goes through the painful struggle because there is the hope that things will come out differently; he gives up his repressions because he is deeply convinced that there is a new safety and security in the relationship. He borrows strength from his identification with the superior strength of the therapist. But the touchstone for these changes is the experience that, in a profound sense, the therapist has the patient's best interest at heart. His gradually growing trust in the therapist's integrity is often enough disturbed by his ambivalence and his destructive tendencies, so that if the therapist betrays any uncertainty of his own or, because of his own unresolved conflicts, has to fight or control the patient, the outcome is doomed to failure. True, the transference is made up of a good measure of infantile trust and mistrust, but if there is any play-acting in the objectivity, task-orientedness, and attitude of the therapist, if there is any punitiveness or sadism, it will not go undetected by the patient, who by his very illness has become acutely sensitized to duplicity and exploitation.

But very much more is needed on the therapist's side than objectivity, immunity from getting involved in neurotic interactions, etc. It seems to me that the therapist has to *care*; he must have a deep and genuine commitment to the patient and a pervasive dedication to help. Without these, the patient could never carry through the arduous and painful work of therapy. He must have a profound respect for the humanity of man, the intrinsic worth of human beings, and he must, first and foremost, respect himself. To the extent that he fulfills these conditions he can also respect, cherish, and love the healthy ego in the patient and support and sustain it in its struggle against the engulfing forces of repression. I firmly believe that only to the extent that the patient can identify with these attitudes can he make therapeutic progress, and the strength and pureness

66

of these attitudes must be inversely proportional to the internal obstacles to be overcome. In the light of these observations I do not consider it possible to treat the therapeutic process as a *purely technical* one; unless these technical operations are undergirded by something else—call it love for one's work, or whatever—therapy must remain a sterile, lifeless ritual.

What evidence about the influence of the therapist's personality and attitude upon the patient and the therapeutic interaction have we been able to glean from our own investigations? I should preface my brief summary by saying that all the evidence is indirect, and its bearing on the actual therapeutic interaction at present only presumptive. At the same time the findings confirm informal observations easily made at diagnostic conferences. In other words, while the validity of the results needs to be checked further and the implications further explored, I have greater faith in the evidence than some critics who have taken us to task for the seeming artificiality of our experimental situations.

First, we were able to demonstrate that the therapist's level of experience and his theoretical orientation exert an influence upon the character of his communications addressed to the patient (see Chapters Six, Seven, and Eight). In a series of experiments it was shown that experienced therapists tend to ask fewer exploratory questions and that their communications are more inferential (interpretive) than those of less experienced practitioners. Client-centered therapists, as might be expected, differed from analytically oriented therapists in terms of the preponderance of reflections-of-feeling. A larger study, using a motion-picture technique, corroborated the above findings and contributed a number of additional ones (see Chapters Nine, Ten, and Eleven). The experimental procedure consisted of a sound film of an initial interview between a middle-aged, male patient and a young resident, to which therapists in the audience were invited to respond as vicarious interviewers. To lessen as much as possible the artificiality of the task, 28 interruptions were inserted in the film sequence, each lasting 30 seconds; whenever the title "What would you do?" appeared, therapists wrote down what they would have said to the patient had they been the interviewer. Subsequently, they completed a comprehensive questionnaire on diagnostic impressions, treatment plans, goals, etc. By means of this technique, data were collected from some 200 therapists in several cities. The sample included primarily psychiatrists and psychologists and ranged widely in terms of experience level and training. I will only draw attention to what I consider the most important yield of this investigation.

Apart from certain variations in clinical evaluations and communications that were associated with the therapist's level of experience—the more experienced therapists tended to rate the patient's disturbance as more severe and more deep-seated, the prognosis more unfavorable, and they expressed more negative attitudes toward the patient— there was a noteworthy correlation between the therapist's self-rated attitude toward the patient, the character of his clinical evaluations, his treatment plans and, perhaps most important, the degree of empathy and warmth expressed in his communications to the patient. To put the matter more concretely: therapists who focused on, say, the paranoid features in the patient's emotional make-up tended to see the prognosis as less auspicious, their attitude was more negative, they preferred to see the patient less frequently and for shorter periods of time, they advocated greater activity and strictness in therapy, they tended to discourage free association, they were more inclined to make recommendations to the patient concerning his life situation. In their communications to the patient they tended to be colder and less empathic. Therapists, on the other hand, who stressed the hysterical features in the patient's personality structure—and it is well to remember that all therapists viewed the same film and had the identical clinical data from which to draw inferences—felt more positively toward the patient, their evaluations were more favorable, the prognosis better, they tended to advocate greater permissiveness and passivity in therapy, and the warmth and empathy of their communications were significantly greater.

Thus we found an interaction between the clinical observations of a therapist, the nature of his treatment recommendations, and his attitude toward the patient; these in turn exerted an effect upon the manner of his communications.

Obviously identical clinical evidence was interpreted very differently by different therapists, although this result, too, has important practical implications. It highlights the sorry state of contemporary psychiatric nosology, the well-known fact that diagnostic labels are of very questionable value, and that in fact they may obscure more than they elucidate.

The important lesson to be learned from this research, I believe, lies in the demonstration that the data of clinical observation are influenced by, or interact with, the therapist's attitudes, and that these in turn influence the character of his communications to the patient. Since the process of drawing inferences from clinical data and acting upon these inferences by verbal and, perhaps more importantly, nonverbal communications repeats itself many times during each therapeutic hour, since "feedback," which the therapist obtains from the patient, is at least in part a response to the therapist's "input," the truism that from the very beginning the therapist is a partner in a subtle interplay of forces may acquire some added meaning. In the extreme case, he may merely elicit confirmation of evidence he himself has introduced. In the experiment under discussion it was rather surprising how many respondents—and by no means only inexperienced ones—reacted to the patient's anger, hostility, and demandingness with attitudes that contained similar elements; they tended to punish, moralize, and reject. These manifestations often took rather subtle forms, as I have suggested, but they were nonetheless measurable. We have been trying to explore to what extent these findings hold true with different patients whose symptom pictures are perhaps more socially acceptable.

In a subsequent study (see Chapter Nineteen) we obtained further evidence to show that clinical evaluations, prognostic estimates, and therapist's attitude are inter-related. Using the ratings of two psychiatrists who independently interviewed some 20 inpatients, a high degree of correlation emerged between ratings of the patient's motivation for therapy, capacity for insight and prognosis, and the therapist's liking for the patient. We confirmed what has also been demonstrated in other studies, that the patient's capacity for insight seems to be a key variable in determining ratings of motivation for therapy, and in turn the therapist's attitude toward the patient: therapists seem to like those patients who, in their judgment, are better therapeutic risks. This evaluation in turn rests on a global assessment of "capacity for insight," that is, a readiness or suitability for those forms of psychotherapy that make heavy demands on the patient's conscious, intellectual participation and collaboration.

Wallach (see Chapter Twenty) prepared two case histories in which the patient's motivation for therapy was systematically varied and elicited judgments from therapists. He found that evaluations tended to be more favorable when the patient was perceived as more highly motivated for therapy. Wallach is currently exploring further the cues entering into ratings of "motivation for therapy."

The manner in which basic personality attributes determine modes of perceiving and reactions to a patient is suggested dramatically in a pilot study recently completed and currently being expanded into a larger investigation. Jones (1960) presented the sound film used in the earlier investigation to college students who had been selected on the basis of their scores on the F scale of authoritarianism originally proposed by Adorno et al. (1949). The rather extensive literature that has sprung up during the past decade depicts the authoritarian personality as dogmatic, unable to establish warm, effective, interpersonal relations, unable to tolerate weakness in either himself or others, and hostile toward those perceived as being of inferior status or power. These qualities are usually assumed to be incompatible with the image of a "good" psychotherapist. Jones found that the responses of high authoritarians indicated rejection of the patient, whereas low authoritarians in general were more accepting. The attitudes of the former group were strikingly more negative, they tended to moralize about the patient's behavior, expatiated on the wrongfulness of his actions, etc. In terms of their communications to the patient—it should be pointed out that none of the subjects had any training or direct experience with psychotherapy—high authoritarians were significantly more directive. While these findings are tentative, they corroborate the characterizations derived from two groups of therapists distinguishable in the earlier study: one group appeared to be more humane, permissive, democratic, and accepting, whereas the second emerged as more directive, disciplinarian, moralistic, and harsh. I should also point out in this connection that the influence of personal analysis on the experimental findings seemed to be that of a neutralizing agent on the therapist's self-rated attitude. That is to say, even if the therapist whose training had included personal analysis admitted a negative attitude toward the patient, there was a lesser likelihood that this attitude was communicated in his comments to the patient than in the case of unanalyzed respondents.

The skeptic has every right to question any hasty translation of these research results to the process and outcome of psychotherapy. What we have done is to demonstrate that in experimental, quasitherapeutic situations there is a tendency for attitudinal variables in the therapist to influence the character of his observations, the inferences he draws from them, as well as the "communications" to the patient. We are not even sure about the direction of causation. It may well be true that the therapist "feels better" when confronted with a patient who appears to fulfill the implicit criteria for his particular model of psychotherapy. However, the findings serve at least as a forceful reminder that in psychotherapy the therapist-scientist is exceedingly vulnerable to be influenced by and to influence in return the data of observation (the behavior of another human being), and that in extreme cases this reciprocal influence may be a highly adverse factor. Thus I find it difficult to see how it is possible for a therapist to integrate a useful collaborative relationship with a patient if *ab initio* he rejects the patient as a person and cannot see his neurotic symptoms and character deformations as reactions to and defenses against early traumatic experiences. Yet, this is precisely what seemed to happen in the experiment. By the same token, the personality of the therapist—and this is the usual working hypothesis in psychotherapy—may have a beneficial effect upon the patient, and it is the precise nature of this influence that must be studied in much greater depth and detail. As a matter of fact, the findings led to an attempt to formulate more clearly the characteristics of the therapist's contribution, particularly those aspects contributed by his personality and attitudes.

My attempt to delineate the character of the therapist's contribution to the treatment process (see Chapter One) proved to be a rewarding exercise from several points of view. For one thing, the existing literature shows that since Freud's introduction of the concept of countertransference most authors have stressed the deleterious results that "blind spots," unresolved transference problems, etc., may engender. However, very little mention has been made of the fact that in many respects the therapist represents a new model of reality to the patient that the latter uses in a variety of ways and, undeniably, for therapeutic purposes. Freud himself seemed to equivocate whether to recognize this influence as a legitimate therapeutic influence or, more accurately perhaps, as an essential ingredient in the analytic process. On the whole, I believe, he tended to view it as an adventitious byproduct. Subsequent writers have often followed this approach and distinguished between analysis proper (mediated primarily by interpretations) and extra-analytic influences that are in some way divorced from "the pure gold" of the former. In my view, the therapist's personality is almost inextricably interwoven with the technique, and it seems extremely difficult if not impossible to determine the particular antecedent of a given therapeutic result. I shall not repeat what I have said elsewhere about the positive contribution made by the therapist's personality to the treatment process, nor should that formulation be regarded as more than a very tentative and preliminary attempt in an area that needs much more exhaustive investigation. However, if this set of variables is properly taken into account, we may have at least a partial answer to the vexing problem that a technique in the hands of one therapist leads to gratifying therapeutic results whereas in the hands of another therapist, equally trained and experienced, it leads to a therapeutic impasse. Clara Thompson (1956) puts the problem thus: "In my early years as an analyst I was taught the idea that any well-trained analyst could do a good job on an analyzable patient. . . . I now believe that one analyst can sometimes take a particular patient further than another because his temperament and life experience fit him to understand this type of patient especially well [p. 534]."

I suppose few contemporary psychotherapists would take issue with this statement, which may be taken as commonplace until one tries to specify more stringently what is meant by "temperament" and "life experience." A decade earlier Fenichel (1945) commented in a similar vein: "Any honest analyst will admit that even though he is very thoroughly analyzed he does better work with certain types of patients than with others [p. 580]." More concrete data bearing on this problem were adduced in a study by White-horn and Betz (1954), which is also noteworthy in other respects. They reported that therapists who were found to be most successful with schizophrenics were not necessarily equally effective with neurotics or other types of psychotic patients. At this time I merely wish to suggest that this is an important area for research that, like so many others in psychotherapy, is largely unexplored. Too, research may lead to more precise statements about patient-therapist compatibility and may thus increase the likelihood of therapeutic success in a particular case. On a larger scale, greater precision in selecting a therapist for a particular patient may vastly strengthen the therapeutic efficacy of available techniques and add to the status of psychotherapy as a scientific discipline.

In addressing myself to the therapist's contribution to the treatment process I do not wish to create the impression that I consider it the crucial or the only factor in psychotherapy. As stated in Chapter Nine, I regard the therapist's contribution a dual one; it is both personal and technical. His personal attributes enable him to create the kind of interpersonal relationship in which constructive personality change can take place; his knowledge of psychodynamic principles and techniques permits him, in and through this relationship, to initiate the kinds of emotional unlearning and learning experiences that are considered necessary to the alleviation or resolution of neurotic conflict. The latter is impossible without the former; the former by itself, would never be sufficient. It seems that the pendulum has swung for some time between the therapist's personality and technique. In classical analytic thinking the contribution of the therapist's personality was deemphasized; in more recent formulations, for example those of Frank (1958, 1959), serious doubt is cast upon the uniqueness of technical ingredients claimed by psychoanalytic therapy. Also, the recent upsurge of existential analysis has cast aspersions upon Freud's technical-theoretical formulations.

It would be unfortunate if the hard-won insights of Freud were to become obscured by these tendencies of the *Zeitgeist*, nor does there appear to be a real danger.

However, it may be useful to indicate that research on the therapist's contribution is not antithetical to psychoanalytic formulations; rather it is an essential requirement in our never-ending struggle to advance the frontiers of knowledge and to gain insight into the nature of therapeutic factors in psychoanalytic and related forms of psychotherapy.

A major factor in the revival of interest in the therapist's personality was Alexander's conceptualization of the "corrective emotional experience," and it is fair to say that during the past decade this renewed interest in the person of the therapist has gained momentum. In his attempt to isolate the therapeutic factors in psychoanalysis, Alexander (1950) stated: "The crucial therapeutic factor is that the analyst's reactions are different from those of the parents [p. 486]." And elsewhere in the same paper:

No doubt, the most important therapeutic factor in psychoanalysis is the objective and yet helpful attitude of the therapist, something which does not exist in any other relationship [p. 487]. . . . To experience such a novel human relationship in itself has a tremendous therapeutic significance which cannot be overrated. . . . This attitude, combined with correct interpretation of material which is about to emerge from repression, together with the analysis of the ego's defenses, is primarily responsible for the therapeutic effectiveness of psychoanalysis.

And further: "The emotional content of the patient-physician relationship, the fact that the therapist's attitude is different from the original parental attitude, is the major dynamic factor which allows repressed material to become conscious [p. 496]." More recently, Alexander (1958) restates this emphasis in forceful terms:

The theory of corrective emotional experience leads to still another technical conclusion. This concerns the most

75

opaque (in my opinion) area of psychoanalysis, the question of the therapist's influence on the treatment process by the virtue of being what he is: an individual personality, distinct from all other therapists. The evaluation of this most elusive element in the therapeutic equation is at present quite beyond our ken. We know only that the blank screen model is an abstraction, which is too far removed from the actual events during treatment [p. 311].

In an important paper Frank (1959) explores the hypothesis that the patient's attitude of trust or faith may play a significant part in his response to all forms of psychotherapy. He hypothesizes that this favorable expectation is fostered by the therapist's own confidence in his ability to help, his ability to inspire confidence in the patient, to care deeply about him, to communicate the message that help will be forthcoming; and furthermore, that "the patient's favorable expectation, which is the major determinant of the therapist's influence over him, may have direct therapeutic effects that are not necessarily transient or superficial." Frank views these ingredients as a common factor in the effectiveness of all forms of psychotherapy. It is my impression that despite his cautions and disclaimers he is inclined to regard this common factor as the *major* factor.

The foregoing hypothesis, if substantiated, would be particularly damaging to the orthodox Freudian position, which draws a sharp line between the therapeutic objectives of psychoanalysis and those of other methods, including hypnosis, faith healing, brainwashing, etc., that Frank draws upon as analogues.

Macalpine (1950), in a lucid and incisive paper arrives at the following distinction between the nature of psychological influence in psychoanalysis and suggestion in hypnosis or similar situations:

. . . both hypnosis and psychoanalysis exploit infantile situations which they both create. But in hypnosis the

76

transference is really and truly a mutual relationship existing between the hypnotist and the hypnotized. . . . One is tempted to say that countertransference is obligatory in and an essential part of hypnosis (and for that matter of all psychotherapies in which the patient is helped, encouraged, advised or criticized). . . . In psychoanalytic therapy alone the analysand is not transferred to. The analyst . . . is never a coactor. The analytic transference relationship ought, strictly speaking, not to be referred to as a relationship between analysand and analyst, but more precisely as the analysand's relation to his analyst. . . . It is thereby not denied that analysis is a "team work"; in so far as it is, an "objective" relation exists between the analyst and the analysand. Because the analyst remains outside the regressive movement . . . suggestion can inherently play no part in the classical procedure of psychoanalytic technique. . . .

To make transference and its development the essential difference between psychoanalysis and all other psychotherapies, psychoanalytic technique may be defined as the only psychotherapeutic method in which a one-sided, infantile regression—analytic transference—is induced in a patient (analysand), analyzed, worked through, and finally resolved [pp. 535-536].

Frank concedes that his position and the analytic viewpoint need not be mutually exclusive, although I would strongly agree with Macalpine that psychoanalysis offers and demands considerably more than the "favorable expectancy" envisioned by Frank. It requires enormously hard work from the patient and makes similar demands on the therapist. In this connection Freud's (1935) distinction between "hypnotic" and "psychoanalytic" suggestion is of momentous significance. He states:

Hypnotic therapy allows the patient to remain inactive and unchanged, consequently also helpless in the face of every new incitement to illness. Analytic treatment makes as great demands for efforts on the part of the patient as on the physician, efforts to abolish the inner resistances. The patient's mental life is permanently changed by overcoming these resistances, is lifted to a higher level of development, and remains proof against fresh possibilities of illness. The labor of overcoming the resistances is the essential achievement of the analytic treatment; the patient has to accomplish it and the physician makes it possible for him to do this by suggestions which are in the nature of an *education*. It has been truly said therefore, that psycho-analytic treatment is a kind of *re-education* [p. 392]. In psycho-analysis we work upon the transference itself, dissipate whatever stands in the way of it, and manipulate the instrument which is to do the work. Thus it becomes possible for us to derive entirely new benefits from the power of suggestion; we are able to control it; the patient alone no longer manages his suggestibility according to his own liking, but in so far as he is amenable to its influence at all, we guide his suggestibility [p. 393].

This staggering task, however, cannot be accomplished unless the patient is deeply convinced that the analyst is a reliable partner in the enterprise, that his attitude encompasses uncompromising personal integrity, dedication, honesty, and faith in the fruitfulness of the task in whose name the sacrifices are demanded. It is this element that I think central to psychoanalysis as a therapeutic technique but that is not yet adequately conceptualized. In this sense, there is an "objective relationship" between patient and therapist, and it is no blot on the purity of analysis that it exists. It is this attitude, too, that seems to offer rich opportunities for new and better identifications.

Finally, I wish to reiterate my earlier hypothesis that it is the duality of the therapist's contribution—its technical and personal aspects—that goes to make up therapeutic success. We need to know very much more about each. But the greatest technical skill can offer no substitute for, nor will it obviate, the preeminent need for integrity, honesty, and dedication on the part of the therapist. Unless these are at the core of the therapist's personality, he will not be successful in helping the patient to develop them within himself.

References

Adorno, T. W., Frenkel-Brunswik, E., Levinson, D. J., and Sanford, R. N. 1949. *The Authoritarian Personality.* New York: Harper & Brothers.

Alexander, F. 1950. "Analysis of the Therapeutic Factors in Psychoanalytic Treatment," *Psychoanal. Quar.,* 19: 482-500.

———— (1958). "Unexplored Areas in Psychoanalytic Theory and Treatment," *Behav. Sci.,* 3: 293-316.

Bellak, L., and Smith, M. B. 1956. "An Experimental Exploration of the Psychoanalytic Process," *Psychoanal. Quar.,* 25: 385-414.

Cronbach, L. J. 1955. "Processes Affecting Scores on 'Understanding of Others' and 'Assumed Similarity,'" *Psychol. Bul.,* 52: 177-194.

Fenichel, O. 1941. *Problems of Psychoanalytic Technique.* New York: The Psychoanalytic Quarterly.

———— 1945. *The Psychoanalytic Theory of Neurosis.* New York: Norton.

Frank, J. D. 1958. "Some Effects of Expectancy and Influence in Psychotherapy," in *Progress in Psychotherapy,* Vol. III, ed. J. H. Masserman and J. L. Moreno, pp. 27-43. New York: Grune & Stratton.

———— 1959. "The Dynamics of the Psychotherapeutic Relationship: Determinants and Effects of the Therapist's Influence," *Psychiat.,* 22: 17-39.

Freud, S. 1935. *A General Introduction to Psychoanalysis.* New York: Liveright.

———— 1952. "Analysis Terminable and Interminable," in

Collected Papers, Vol. V, pp. 313-357. London: Hogarth.

———— 1953. "The Future Prospects of Psychoanalytic Therapy," in *Collected Papers,* Vol. II, pp. 285-296. London: Hogarth.

Holt, R. R., and Luborsky, L. 1958. *Personality Patterns of Psychiatrists.* New York: Basic Books.

Jones, W. S. 1960. Ph.D. dissertation, University of North Carolina.

Kubie, L. S. 1956. "Some Unsolved Problems of Psychoanalytic Psychotherapy," in *Progress in Psychotherapy,* Vol. I, ed. F. Fromm-Reichmann and J. L. Moreno, pp. 87-102. New York: Grune & Stratton.

Macalpine, I. 1950. "The Development of the Transference," *Psychoanal. Quar.,* 19: 501-539.

Thompson, C. 1956. "The Role of the Analyst's Personality in Therapy," *Am. J. Psychother.,* 10: 347-359.

Whitehorn, J. C., and Betz, B. J. 1954. "A Study of Psychotherapeutic Relationships Between Physicians and Schizophrenic Patients," *Am. J. Psychiat.,* 3: 321-331.

3

TEACHING AND LEARNING IN PSYCHOTHERAPY

Although different theories of psychotherapy emphasize divergent "mechanisms" for psychotherapeutic change, it is becoming increasingly clear that single principles are inadequate to account for the complex learning that occurs in psychotherapy. Instead, learning in psychotherapy appears to proceed on a very broad front. I would like to examine this problem in some detail, in keeping with my conviction that progress in this area will be furthered by greater specificity concerning the kinds of interventions the therapist employs and their effect on the patient.

In one of his last papers, Alexander (1963) commented on the remarkable fact that very few changes in the intricate procedure of psychoanalytic therapy have occurred since its guiding principles were formulated by Freud between 1912 and 1915. He asked: "Is it due to the perfection of the standard procedure which because of its excellence does not require reevaluation and improvement, or does it have some other cultural rather than scientific reason?" Alexander's career as a psychotherapist and his contributions to the problem of therapeutic technique bear eloquent testimony that any formulations cannot possibly be the final word in science; to act as if they were can only result in stultification of progress. While admitting that "Almost all statements concerning technique could be legitimately only highly tentative," Alexander (1963) noted that the essential psychodynamic principles of analytic therapy rest on solid observational foundations, which he summarized as follows (condensed quotation):

1. During therapy, unconscious (repressed) material becomes conscious. This increases the action radius of the conscious ego and permits greater ego control of previously repressed impulses and tendencies.

2. The mobilization of unconscious material is achieved mainly by two basic therapeutic factors: (a) interpretation of material emerging from free association; and (b) the patient's emotional interpersonal experiences in the therapeutic situation (transference). The therapist's relatively objective, nonevaluative, impersonal attitude is the principal factor in mobilizing unconscious material.

3. The patient shows resistance against recognizing unconscious content. Overcoming this resistance is one of the primary technical problems in therapy.

4. The patient will sooner or later direct his typical neurotic attitudes toward the therapist. He develops a transference that is the repetition of interpersonal attitudes, mostly the feelings of the child to his parents. The resolution of the "transference neurosis" becomes the aim of therapy [pp. 440-448].

Most analytic therapists will agree with Alexander's succinct summary of the process, but few have followed his

quest to explore what therapists actually do in the therapeutic situation. It became clear to Alexander, as it did to
Glover in the 1930s, and to a host of researchers since about
1940, that general formulations can serve only as the barest
scaffolding for the transactions between therapist and
patient. There must be a continuing search to identify and
refine the principles underlying the therapist's actual operations. Glover's pioneering survey of British psychoanalysts
was the first step in exploding the myth, since then articu-
lately elaborated by Kiesler (1966), that there is a standard
therapeutic technique and that the therapist's behavior in
therapy is uniform even if he shares with his colleagues a set
of common theoretical assumptions. Psychotherapy is an
immensely complicated process, and any system that
attempts to reduce it to a single or a few general statements
cannot escape the charge of oversimplification. Realizing
this, Alexander was firmly convinced that psychotherapy
must be studied "from the ground up," that is, through
painstaking observation of the process. Acting on this conviction, he initiated the program at Mount Sinai Hospital
to study the therapeutic process as objectively as possible.
Unfortunately, he did not live to see the completion of this
project, but even on the basis of the preliminary results he
arrived at two important conclusions (Alexander, 1963):

First, that the traditional descriptions of the therapeutic process do not adequately reflect the immensely complex interaction between therapist and patient. The patient's
reactions cannot be described fully as transference reactions.
The patient reacts to the therapist as a concrete person and
not only as a representative of parental figures. The therapist's reactions also far exceed what is usually called countertransference. They include, in addition to this, interventions
based on conscious deliberations and also his spontaneous
idiosyncratic attitudes. Moreover, his own values are conveyed to the patient even if he consistently tries to protect
his incognito. The patient reacts to the therapist's overt but
also to his nonverbal hidden intentions and the therapist

reacts to the patient's reaction to him. It is truly a transactional process.

Second, that the therapeutic process can best be understood in terms of learning theory. In particular, the principle of reward and punishment and also the influence of repetitive experience can be clearly recognized. In psychotherapy the reward consists in less conflicting, more harmonious interpersonal relations, which the patient achieves first by adequately relating to his therapist, then to his environment, and eventually to his own ego ideal.

Alexander's statement concerning the transactional character of the therapeutic relationship and his prophecy of a fruitful integration between the theory of psychoanalytic therapy and learning theory are of the utmost importance for the future of psychotherapy. Both assertions of course have been made before, but none of the earlier authors has been so thoroughly immersed in, and identified with, the evolution of analytic theory and practice. I believe it is evidence of the "cultural lag" and the encapsulation of psychoanalytic theory, to which Alexander alluded, that these reformulations are only now finding gradual acceptance within psychoanalysis. For the same reason, Alexander's conceptions of "learning theory" fail to reflect developments that have occurred during the last two or three decades in that area. It is also questionable whether the advancement of technique in psychotherapy is best assured, as Alexander believed, by closer naturalistic observation of the process. The latter approach assumes that it is possible to make observations in a complex field without theoretical presuppositions, a difficult problem whose implications are beyond the scope of our present discussion.

It is one thing to describe psychotherapy (including psychoanalysis) in terms of learning principles; it is quite another to take seriously the implications of this position. Apart from the fact that there is at present nothing resembling a unified learning theory, research findings obtained in laboratory settings cannot readily be applied to the psy-

84

chotherapy situation. Here I have set myself the task of compiling, in a very preliminary way, an inventory of some important things the patient learns in dynamic psychotherapy. In this way I propose to extend somewhat the statements made by Alexander and others on this subject. My purpose is to move closer to an understanding of the technical operations designed to reach these goals. It will become clear, I trust, that psychotherapy mediates different forms of learning and that these learnings follow different principles. To the dynamic therapist I wish to emphasize that psychotherapy is indeed a learning process and that "analysis of resistances" and "interpretations" are only two facets of the therapeutic influence albeit important milestones on the road to therapeutic learning. To the critics of dynamic psychotherapy I hope to present more concrete examples that may indicate that "reconstructing the past," "analyzing the transference," or providing "emotional insight" into the patient's motivations are not ends in themselves in dynamic psychotherapy, as is frequently alleged.

First, however, it seems apropos to advance some observations to show that (1) mere translation of one theory into the language of another does not seem to contribute substantively to the advancement of either; and (2) in psychotherapy, as an applied art or science, theoretical formulations follow, rather than precede, technical modifications. Hence, advances in psychotherapy are not likely to come from theoreticians or researchers but from therapists engaged in clinical pursuits.

Relative to the first point, it seems profitable to briefly revisit the first major systematic attempt to cast psychotherapy in terms of the principles of learning theory (Dollard and Miller, 1950). This work rests on the fundamental assumption that neurotic behavior is learned behavior; this being the case, it should be unlearned by the same principles by which it was taught. Dollard and Miller assert that the laws of learning promulgated by Pavlov, Thorndike, Hull, and their students should be of material help in this effort,

85

although they concede that principles and laws that are as yet unknown may play an important part. Of major significance in this book are the principle of reinforcement; repression viewed "as the inhibition of the cue-producing responses which mediate thinking and reasoning"; a reformulation of transference as a special case of the wider concept of generalization; and an elaboration of the dynamics of conflict from more basic principles. The bulk of their work is devoted to a recasting of Freudian theory in terms of these principles.

As Bandura (1961) correctly observed, Dollard and Miller's massive effort had remarkably little impact upon therapeutic practice, nor has it inspired a great deal of research along the lines implied by the authors. In part, the reason may be found in the general decline of all molar theories in contemporary psychology; to a larger extent, however, I am inclined to believe that Dollard and Miller provided merely a translation of psychoanalytic principles into learning theory terms. That is, they tended to accept as more or less established and immutable the technical procedures and formulations of the psychoanalytic theory of psychotherapy without raising questions about their range of applicability and a host of issues that recently have been brought to the fore (Goldstein, Heller, and Sechrest, 1966). Dollard and Miller (1950), for example, recognized and stressed that "the therapist (in traditional dyadic psychotherapy in an office setting) does not control the important primary rewards and punishments in the patient's life [p. 394]." However, they failed to raise such incisive questions as did Goldstein et al. (1966): Under what conditions does therapeutic learning become generalized to real life situations? Are there better techniques for insuring such generalizations than trusting to luck that somehow the patient will work out more adaptive solutions in the outside world? How can the therapist's influence be maximized, etc?

In addition—and perhaps more important—is the fact, already alluded to, that theories of psychotherapy are very

86

loosely articulated to technical procedures. Psychoanalytic theory provides a general, but vague, underpinning to therapeutic operations, and the same criticism applies to the theories developed by Rogers, Wolpe, and others. The evolution of the major theories of psychotherapy clearly shows that therapists first experimented with techniques, often in purely empirical fashion, and subsequently constructed a theory to fit their technical procedures. Ford and Urban (1963) observed that the major theories of psychotherapy are considerably more explicit about therapeutic goals than they are about the procedures by which these goals are to be reached. If this is true—and I believe it is—it follows that translations of one theory into the language of another remain a sterile exercise unless such translations become a prelude to innovations in practice whose viability can be corroborated in clinical work and perhaps documented by controlled research. Research per se, however, seems to have precious little effect on clinical practice.

This statement may sound odd coming as it does from an author who has invested a good many years in efforts to elucidate the process of psychotherapy through objective research. While objective research in psychotherapy has shown a stupendous growth during the past two decades, there is hardly a study that the average clinician (or researcher, for that matter) could cite as having significantly affected therapeutic techniques. One would expect that the substantive yield of this work, which is by no means inconsequential, would have exerted at least some influence on practice, but the evidence is hard to find. Is this merely a demonstration of cultural lag or does it go deeper? It is true, however, that the research contributions have produced a certain attitude change in therapists, who have become more mindful of the requirement to adduce empirical evidence for their assertions. Personally, I am convinced that the major function of research in an area like psychotherapy (and probably in others similarly complex) is to document in more or less precise fashion what therapists are doing, to compare their operations, and to raise questions concerning the adequacy of their theoretical formulations. In and of itself research does not result in new insights that, in my judgment, are the creation of practitioners who have become dissatisfied with the current status of the art. The same judgment must be entered about theoretical refinements or reformulations.

The assertion that theoretical advances stem from clinical innovations is well exemplified by the innovations introduced by Alexander and French. What created excitement in psychoanalytic circles in the 1940s and 1950s was the fact that these therapists began to experiment with changes in therapeutic procedures, such as planned interruptions, modifications of therapist behavior to provide a corrective emotional experience, and the like. The excitement and controversy were not primarily due to the theoretical reformulations but to the changes in technical operations that threatened time-honored practices. Consequently, the conclusion emerges that new departures in psychotherapy derive from changes in technical procedures, not from theoretical reformulations, however sophisticated the latter may appear. From the standpoint of the researcher, this conclusion suggests, from a different angle, that he needs to focus on the therapist's operations, that is, on empirical data of what he does rather than upon verbal descriptions of intentions, goals, and theories.

As a further example of this contention, Freud never wrote a systematic account of analytic technique, a point that has been noted repeatedly (Strachey, 1934; see also Chapter Twenty-three). From all accounts it is clear that as a therapist he never adhered closely to what later came to be termed the "classical model" technique; rather he experimented extensively with variations in technique and permitted himself considerable latitude in departing from what he espoused in writing. The formalization and the seeming imperviousness to change of the classical model technique are clearly a creation of his followers. The implications of this observation are that the institutionalization of a set of techniques from which no departures are permitted (except through such procedures as Eissler's "parameters," whose stipulations are probably unrealistic and unrealizable) can lead only to stagnation in the development of a science; and that, even if considered desirable by a professional organization, unwavering adherence to a technique is a virtual impossibility. Again, it may be noted that therapeutic practices change when perceptive practitioners begin to look at phenomena and accepted procedures in "unorthodox" ways and, to the chagrin of their mentors, tinker with sacrosanct practices. If the innovations work—and I believe the most creative therapists have been exceedingly pragmatic—the theory is modified to fit the changed practices.

PRODUCTS OF LEARNING IN PSYCHOTHERAPY

Following are a set of "lessons" the patient learns in analytically oriented therapy. The order in which they are presented is of no importance, nor is it contended that the items are independent; in fact, a good deal of overlap will be noted. Empirical support derives from a vast body of clinical experience as well as from retrospective accounts of former patients (Strupp, Wallach, and Wogan, 1964; Strupp, Fox, and Lessler, 1969). What the patient, in part, learns are new convictions or beliefs about himself and other people as well as new strategies for handling interpersonal experiences with the therapist, reinforced by subsequent reality testing. It is difficult to determine whether the new beliefs are the consequence of symptom relief or whether the acceptance of new beliefs results in the diminution of troublesome symptoms. With most therapists, I tend to believe the latter although I cannot prove it. It is interesting, however, that in the studies referred to patients after therapy typically talked much less about the symptoms that propelled them into therapy; that is, the place the symptoms played in their lives had changed or, stated otherwise, the experience of therapy had contributed to an emotional and cognitive restructuring of their view of themselves, others, and reality.

Typical "lessons" include:

1. The world is not such a bad place after all. People are more reliable and trustworthy than had been previously experienced. In some respects they are "bad" (that is, not satisfying to the patient) but in others they are much more valuable than he had believed.

2. One has to be less demanding of people; others resent and react negatively to exploitation. One has to scale down one's (infantile) demands and expectations if one wants to be "happier." This means he has to give up some things he always wanted (for example, praise, adulation, etc). One has to reduce one's narcissism, and accept limitations in oneself and others.

3. If one achieves something or gets pleasure out of some activity or experience, one's own satisfaction must be sufficient. One cannot expect others to praise and applaud nor can one bask in the glory of reflected feelings. Otherwise, one will be continually disappointed, and this disappointment tends to breed hostility and resentment, which in turn set in motion vicious cycles.

4. As a prime lesson, one learns to delay gratification. This learning is painful because often one cannot get what one wants in the form and at the time one wants it. He has to modify his wishes and desires, learn to accept "half a loaf," and in general get along with less (for instance, narcissistic supplies of all kinds). One also has to learn to endure tension, frustration, and privation—all of which are at first painful. (Compare Menninger's apt phrase that therapeutic gains are the products of the patient's frustrations and disappointments.)

5. Separation is painful but it need not last forever. At least, one can hope (sometimes against great odds) that gratification will eventually be forthcoming. Stated other-

90

wise, the gratification of interpersonal closeness need not be physical; it can be symbolic.

6. If one wants to reach a goal one has to institute realistic action. Sitting back and wishing is not likely to produce results. A large part of the satisfaction in any achievement is commensurate with the invested effort. By the same token, some things are realistically unattainable; therefore, the wish has to be abandoned or modified. (This, of course, is Freud's well-known distinction between passivity and activity, the former being a thoroughly infantile aim.)

7. Tension, suffering, anxiety, depression, etc., are not quite so bad as one had considered them to be. The patient realizes that he has greater strength than he has given himself credit for. Phobic fears have to be endured and inevitably one gains greater strength and self-confidence in the process. Ultimately, it does not help to avoid painful, difficult, and anxiety-provoking situations; avoidance may provide temporary relief but essentially it is a pseudo (neurotic) solution that intensifies rather than solves the problem. One has to learn to stand one's ground.

8. Certain interpersonal maneuvers do not work and are self-defeating. At the same time, they are not as dangerous as the patient had considered them to be, either when used by himself or others. Examples include: (a) Anger and hostile feelings in oneself and others are neither lethal nor dangerous. They will not destroy the other person or, via retaliation, oneself. Feelings, contrary to infantile beliefs, are not the same as acts and must not be confused with the latter. (b) Ingratiation typically does not work; for the most part it does not produce the approval one seeks, and when it does, it is at the cost of self-depreciation. (c) Negativism in adult interpersonal relations usually does not coerce the other person to do one's bidding. (d) Each person is an entity and ultimately has to stand on his own feet; therefore, attempts to "merge" with another person do not work. (e) The talion principle in interpersonal relations is self-defeat-

ing. For example, even if the other person has hurt one, nurturing a grudge against all people, or trying to "get even" with the aggressor results at least in wasteful effort and has other untoward consequences.

9. In contrast to the foregoing, cooperation as a technique for getting along with others generally brings the greatest returns. One cannot "buy" others but one can cooperate with those who are willing to cooperate. Other people, of course, are not obligated to cooperate, nor are efforts to subjugate them likely to "pay off." It is wise to avoid other persons whose exploitative tendencies have been identified. One is not beholden to others, nor are others likely to enjoy slavery (except for neurotic reasons of their own).

10. Honesty about one's feelings and motives, no matter how unpleasant or "immoral" they may seem to oneself, is a good policy. This does not mean that one needs to broadcast one's less desirable tendencies—although they are universal—or wallow in an orgy of guilt or self-pity because one is not perfect. These feelings have to be accepted as part of man's primitive strivings that are present throughout life. At the same time, recognition of their existence is no justification for acting on them. In the end, man is judged by his actions, not by his fantasies. By recognizing one's motivations, one can often take more appropriate action. On the other hand, one is responsible for one's actions; they cannot be blamed on others, nor can the therapist absolve the patient from guilt. The patient has to forgive himself.

Mowrer's (1961) assertion, that the analytic therapist "forgives." "absolves," and encourages "immoral behavior" is not in accord with Freud's teachings nor is it accepted technique. To accept feelings as "data" without value judgment is a very different process from approving them. Mowrer, in contrast, would prefer to see them condemned.

Analytic therapy, however, is in complete accord with Mowrer (1961), Glasser (1965), and other contemporary authors in insisting on the importance of accepting responsibility of one's feelings, motives, and actions (see point 14).

92

11. Every person has his rights, and one needs to learn to stand up for one's own. In this way one learns to respect others and oneself; often one can also gratify one's wishes more effectively in this manner.

12. One needs to respect, accept, and subordinate oneself to higher authority. It is futile to try to topple persons in higher positions, aggress, compete with, or rebel against them, or defeat them in other ways. Their power is never complete, and ordinarily one has the choice of leaving the domain of oppressors to search for a more congenial climate.

13. Accepting authority, however, does not entail abandoning one's freedom, a belief frequently held by patients. On the contrary, accepting authority frees the patient from struggles with others. As Fromm showed years ago, many people prefer an escape from freedom, which they see as threatening a symbiotic relationship.

14. It is crucial to accept full responsibility for one's psychological processes and for one's actions. With regard to the former, they must be recognized as part of man's biological heritage and of his past experience; the latter, insofar as they affect the lives of others, largely determine man's social worth. The past is irreversible, but man usually has considerable latitude in shaping the present. Blaming others for one's predicament is self-defeating and ineffectual. One of the most important findings from the accounts of former patients (Strupp, Fox, and Lessler, 1969) pertains to this "lesson" as the touchstone of successful therapy. With considerable regularity former patients expressed a heightened sense of responsibility that in turn permitted them to take active steps in shaping their fate or coming to terms with limitations in themselves and others. Stated otherwise, they gained an increased sense of strength and mastery.

15. Implicit in several preceding items is the process of achieving a clearer understanding of one's identity and role functions, whose central importance in personality development has long been recognized. The disastrous consequences of faulty identifications are most glaringly seen in homo-

sexuality and certain forms of schizophrenia but are equally important in neuroses and personality disorders. Also, the concept of sex-typing appears too narrow to account for the kinds of learning under this rubric in psychotherapy. Concretely, the patient learns not only to see himself more clearly as an adult man (or woman), but he acquires greater flexibility, depending upon the circumstances, to function as an authority or as a subordinate, a person who in some conditions is dependent and in others independent, who can assert himself and submit, who can compete when it is appropriate or abstain when it is inappropriate, who can be a parent as well as a son or daughter, etc.

The above inventory is illustrative of significant learnings that occur in psychotherapy but is in no way exhaustive; nor is there anything original about it. In fact, analytic therapists will regard the items as rather commonplace. My purpose in adducing these examples is to pave the way for a consideration of the techniques and procedures used by psychotherapists to mediate these cognitive and emotional reorientations.

To elaborate: learning in psychotherapy occurs on a *broad* front; the patient learns a variety of strategies and techniques for relating to himself and others; the "insights" he gains in the therapeutic situation necessarily must be tested and applied in real-life situations.

Learning in psychotherapy, almost by definition, occurs within the context of an interpersonal relationship, in the course of which the patient typically becomes dependent on the therapist as an authority, teacher, and mentor. Through the imposition of the "fundamental rule" and similar devices the therapist increases the patient's amenability to psychological influences and enhances the latter.

A variety of techniques is employed by the therapist in analytic therapy (as well as in other forms). The contention that analytic therapy solely employs interpretations is untenable (which, *mutatis mutandis,* is equally true of other schools). It is highly probable that different forms of psychotherapy employ techniques based on similar principles. However, the application is often haphazard and unsystematic, although the schools admittedly place different emphases on various techniques.

It is clear that analytic therapy employs such common techniques as those mentioned by Dollard and Miller (1950): (1) suggesting, urging, commanding, and forbidding; (2) reward and punishment, disapproval and approval; (3) permissiveness; (4) sympathetic interest and understanding; (5) reassurance; (6) questions designed to raise doubts about pat formulations entertained by the patient; and (7) interpretations that serve to label feelings, impulses, and patterns of behavior.

To a very significant extent learning in psychotherapy encompasses learning by imitation and identification. Throughout therapy the therapist serves as a model whose feelings, attitudes, values, and behavior (to the extent it can be observed in the therapeutic situation) the patient learns to accept, imitate, emulate, internalize, and respect. They become an integral part of his own view of the world and his system of values. While this process has long been recognized, beginning with Freud, it has generally been regarded as a "nonanalytic" influence. In contrast, learning by imitation and identification is probably the single most important aspect of the therapeutic influence and the fulcrum upon which the latter turns.

Whether one accepts Freud's (1921) original concept of defensive identification or any of the more recent formulations that variously stress developmental aspects, role practice (Sears, 1957), learning through reinforcement by punishment and reward, imitation (Bandura and Walters, 1963), an essential problem for psychotherapy with adult patients relates to the conditions, necessarily created by the therapist, which are instrumental in producing imitation, or identification, or both. To observe the occurrence of the process is but one step in specifying causal relationships. The recreation of a reasonable replica of the parent-child relationship in the transference situation is probably a highly important strategy in this regard. However, despite the sizable literature on the topic, it seems that we possess as yet little systematic knowledge concerning the precise manner in which therapeutic techniques instrument this form of learning.

To cite some specific examples of therapist behavior: throughout therapy he sets an example and portrays an ideal. When the patient is anxious, the therapist is calm; when the patient feels guilty about his feelings or past actions, the therapist, through his attitude more than by any other means, disagrees with the patient's a priori assumptions and evaluations of his behavior. When the patient attempts to provoke the therapist, the latter does not participate in the maneuver. When the patient is horrified by the enormity of his demands and expectations of others, the therapist accepts the feelings as "scientific data," although he places them continually in the context of infantile wishes and questions their adaptive value. When the patient feels overpowered or helpless in the face of manipulations by significant others, the therapist displays a sense of mastery and competence and at times may suggest alternative courses of action. When the patient attempts to "act out" passivity, erotic longings, etc., with the therapist, the latter thwarts these wishes by nonparticipation. And so on. Thus, the patient's learning is to a large extent experimental but it is also cognitive. However, cognitive learning is seen as maximally effective when feelings have become mobilized, most notably feelings about the therapist and the patient-therapist interaction.

Concomitant with the foregoing, the interpretation of unconscious fantasies is viewed as a part, but perhaps a less crucial part, of the therapeutic learning process. It would be foolhardy to follow the behaviorists in discarding the hard-won insights concerning these important internal determinants of attitudes and behavior. There can be no doubt that primitive fantasies influence the patient's feelings, attitudes toward others, and the quality of his interpersonal relations. Still it remains a moot question to what extent the process of making these fantasies conscious furthers in and of itself the therapeutic enterprise. Unquestionably, this process is part of the therapeutic process, but it may account for only a relatively minor portion of the therapeutic force and the change effected by it. On the other hand, I am convinced that interpretations of resistances, that is, those roadblocks that the patient erects to prevent a more open and closer relationship to the therapist, are of the greatest significance and tremendously important in facilitating the identificatory process.

For significant therapeutic learning to occur, the most important precondition is the patient's *openness* to the therapist's influence. Therefore, as I see it, the major effort in analytic therapy is devoted to creating a condition in the patient that permits the therapist to influence him through suggestions, interpretations, appeals to reason, and in general "imprinting" him. Thus, psychotherapy essentially consists first and foremost of social influence techniques or—if you will—behavior control. It is quite feasible to produce attitude and behavior change through the use of a variety of techniques, but, in my opinion, Freud will be conclusively upheld in his conviction that the analysis of transference phenomena is the single most effective technique for exerting a profound influence upon another person.

The transference paradigm, without question, is a highly ingenious design, unequaled by any other method yet created by psychologists (except perhaps through pharmacological agents and, more transiently, through hypnosis) for creating an almost incredibly intense state of openness, emotional arousal, or permeability in the patient. To be sure, this state is achieved only after a considerable amount of work has been accomplished, by means of interpretations of resistance and other techniques designed to break down the barriers impeding its development. Nor, as every therapist knows, does it typically last very long. However, the therapist works strenuously at creating and re-creating it. It is at those times when the therapist is sure of its existence that he injects the "corrective elements" considered most appropriate at that time. Similarly, it is this state of heightened influence or arousal that facilitates the patient's identification with the therapist: he has strong positive feelings toward the therapist, feels keenly dependent upon his love and approval, and "absorbs" his message in the deepest layers of his being.

In part the patient works consciously at following the basic rule—he becomes convinced that he does so in his own interest—but in an important sense he also complies to earn the therapist's approval that becomes an exceedingly crucial leverage. He goes through the agonizing process of subordinating himself to a powerful parent figure whom (following his past experiences) he never fully trusts, and he reexperiences a variety of painful feelings, ultimately out of love for the therapist and the rewards the latter dispenses. Likewise, he experiences consciously violent rage, disappointment, competitive strivings, envy, etc. Frequently, these wishes are thwarted once they are expressed, which again is painful.

Freud and his followers have amply described this process, familiar to all therapists and patients. What has long delayed research and further development are the excess baggage of the instinct theory and other esoteric concepts that have been invoked as explanatory principles. As time goes on, it will be necessary—and altogether possible—to conceptualize the process in terms of simpler psychological principles. This step, I am convinced, will revitalize the basic transference phenomena, whose importance for the understanding of the mechanisms operating in psychological influence is second to none.

Psychoanalysis hypothesizes that truly significant and basic therapeutic change is contingent upon the patient's undergoing the foregoing experience. While I am inclined to agree, the criterion of therapeutic effectiveness cannot be invoked to disprove the existence of the transference phenomena, as has often occurred, nor does it per se further our knowledge concerning them. It is conceivable that other technical procedures prove equally effective (which I consider unlikely) and it is quite possible that with many patients the "ideal" conditions for therapeutic change cannot be created. In other instances, the enormous expenditure of time and effort may not justify the utilization of the method. These questions are akin to engineering problems and essentially unrelated to the advancement of scientific knowledge.

The issue has been seriously confounded by analytic authors as well as proponents of other therapeutic approaches. Freud, perhaps unwittingly, started this unfortunate trend by asserting that in psychoanalysis research and therapy go hand in hand. Since Freud had come upon his important discoveries through his therapeutic efforts, his view is entirely understandable. Furthermore, to Freud research largely meant making observations and drawing inferences from data gathered within the framework of the analytic situation. As Alexander correctly observed, therapy is not research in any strict sense and the procedure of linking research with therapeutic effectiveness is indefensible and inevitably leads to an impasse. It goes almost without saying that a set of therapeutic operations may be effective for reasons quite apart from the theoretical assumptions; conversely, the effectiveness (or the lack) of particular therapeutic operations proves nothing about the adequacy of "correctness" of the theory. However, it is entirely legitimate to challenge the effectiveness of any set of therapeutic operations qua therapeutic operations and to insist on empirical demonstrations of their efficacy.

For example, it may turn out that behavior techniques are the most efficient ones, say, in simple phobias. There is no need for a big cannon to kill a mosquito; indeed, the procedure would be absurd. There may also be cases in which the elimination or alleviation of a disabling phobia or similar conditions may set in motion benign cycles that will produce far-reaching personality and behavior changes. Under other conditions it may be inexpedient, even in severe neuroses or behavior disorders, to use intensive and prolonged psychotherapy. But it seems highly unlikely, although it remains to be demonstrated, that behavioral techniques will prove very effective in producing significant improvements, however defined, in adults with severe neuroses or personality disorders of long standing. In fact, analytic exploration may provide important clues in such instances as to why this is so. The stumbling block is largely the criterion problem, that is, the difficulty of devising and agreeing on acceptable change measures. Unquestionably, changes resulting from all forms of psychotherapy are often not stupendous, which merely confirms the extraordinary difficulties in learning and unlearning. It is hard to believe that psychologists, who after all know a few things about learning, still expect miracles from psychotherapy. Such miracles are simply not to be expected. Realism, however, is not tantamount to nihilism nor should it induce a sense of complacency about existing knowledge or techniques.

To sum up, psychotherapy is a learning process of considerable complexity. The illustrations that have been used to call attention to various kinds of learnings often discussed in terms of global mechanisms (e.g., reinforcement, modeling, etc.) leave little doubt that single principles do not adequately describe the learning process. Therapeutic learning always proceeds on a broad front even though divergent theories may stress one form of learning at the expense of others.

The therapist's operations are typically not very well articulated to the kinds of changes of learning to be effected. Rather, it seems that the therapist sets in motion a complex process whose consequences are predictable only in a very broad sense. The task of the future is to achieve greater specificity concerning the effects of particular kinds of interventions.

100

Therapeutic learning appears to be most effective when there exists a strong emotional tie between patient and therapist, which the therapist controls and manipulates in the interest of effecting therapeutic change. Therapeutic learning appears to be predominantly experiential, although the therapist's explanations (interpretations) of the patient's experience may aid the process. As Fromm-Reichmann put it: the patient needs an experience, not an explanation.

The kinds of learning occurring in psychoanalytic therapy are not intrinsically different from those in other forms of therapy, although the objectives in long-term intensive therapy are obviously different from, say, those in a case of snake phobia. The former aims at effecting significant changes in the patient's identifications, role perceptions, self-control, etc. Even under the best circumstances such efforts require long periods of time.

While the goal of therapeutic efficiency (in terms of time, effort, etc.) is important, in the long run increased knowledge concerning the mechanisms involved in therapeutic learning is predictably more important. Greater knowledge may lead to greater efficiency, if only by defining the range of applicability. The transference paradigm is considered an exceedingly fruitful vehicle for illuminating the processes at issue, but little progress has been made in exploring its potential.

References

Alexander, F. 1963. "The Dynamics of Psychotherapy in the Light of Learning Theory," *Am. J. Psychiat.,* 120: 440-448.

Bandura, A. 1961. "Psychotherapy as a Learning Process," *Phychol. Bul.,* 58: 143-159.

—— and Walters, R. H. 1963. *Social Learning and Personality Development.* New York: Holt, Rinehart & Winston.

Dollard, J., and Miller, N. E. 1950. *Personality and Psychotherapy*. New York: McGraw-Hill.

Ford, D. H., and Urban, H. B. 1963. *Systems of Psychotherapy*. New York: Wiley.

Freud, S. 1921. "Group Psychology and the Analysis of the Ego," in *Sigmund Freud*, ed. J. Strachey, pp. 69-143. London: Hogarth, 1955.

Glasser, W. 1965. *Reality Therapy*. New York: Harper & Row.

Goldstein. A. P., Heller, K., and Sechrest, L. B. 1966. *Psychotherapy and the Psychology of Behavior Change*. New York: Wiley.

Kiesler, D. J. 1966. "Some Myths of Psychotherapy Research and the Search for a Paradigm," *Psychol. Bul.*, 65: 110-136.

Mowrer, O. H. 1961. *The Crisis in Psychiatry and Religion*. Princeton, N.J.: Van Nostrand.

Sears, R. R. 1957. "Identification as a Form of Behavioral Development," in *The Concept of Development: An Issue in the Study of Human Behavior*, ed. D. B. Harris, pp. 149-161. Minneapolis: University of Minnesota Press.

Strachey, J. 1935. "The Nature of the Therapeutic Action of Psychoanalysis," *Int. J. Psychoanal.*, 15: 127-159.

Strupp, H. H., Fox, R. E., and Lessler, K. J. 1969. *Patients View Their Psychotherapy*. Baltimore: Johns Hopkins Press.

———— Wallach, M. S., and Wogan, M. 1964. "Psychotherapy Experience in Retrospect: Questionnaire Survey of Former Patients and Their Therapists," *Psychol. Monog.*, 78 (Whole No. 588).

4

SPECIFIC VERSUS NONSPECIFIC FACTORS IN PSYCHOTHERAPY AND THE PROBLEM OF CONTROL

One of the chief purposes of psychotherapy, if not the primary purpose, is to promote the acquisition of self-control. Terms like "mastery," "ability to cope," "competence," "independence," and "autonomy" refer to the same phenomenon, Freud's capsule summary of psychoanalytic psychotherapy, "Where id was, there shall ego be," while anchored to assumptions and conceptualizations that are in need of thorough revamping, essentially describes the same process.

The course of therapy, in general terms, follows two usually intertwined courses of action: (1) to help the patient achieve greater control or mastery; (2) to help him abandon or modify unrealistic expectations of himself, others, and the environment. If the first is the goal, the therapist implicitly agrees with the patient's formulation of the problem; if the goal is the second, the therapist seeks to redefine the problem, promoting at the same time the patient's acceptance of the reformulation. "Acceptance" in this context means partly a conscious realization on the patient's part that his expectations of himself and others (self-concept) are in need of change but, more importantly, he must assimilate the redefinition on the deepest level. The ambiguous term "insight" refers to both processes, the second being the more consequential one. In any event, in some sense the patient must become aware of his assumptions, hypotheses, and beliefs about himself and others, the character of the interpersonal strategies he employs, the effect of his feelings and actions upon others, and the feelings and attitudes of others toward him. These assumptions, of course, are frequently implicit, complex, and highly symbolic.

MALADAPTIVE LEARNING AND THERAPEUTIC LEARNING

Leaving aside the issue of *how* beliefs, strategies for meeting problems in living, and emotional patterns have been learned, the pragmatic question becomes: *What* has been learned? Here traditional insight therapies diverge sharply from the behavioral therapies, both in terms of conceptualizations and in terms of therapeutic techniques. The behavior therapist, essentially, attempts to modify a patient's mode of response, which in turn may lead to changes in feelings and beliefs (however, these are not the focus of attention in therapy); the analytic therapist, on the other hand, ignores, at least for therapeutic purposes, specific responses and actions, and seeks to modify the patient's implicit (unconscious) beliefs, which are hypothesized to govern feelings as well as actions.

The above description is of course schematic, and, in practice it is difficult to differentiate between cognitive and emotional learning. Both probably occur to varying degrees in all forms of psychotherapy, and both appear to be necessary for significant therapeutic change. In this connection it is worth recalling that all major forms of psychotherapy (psychoanalysis, client-centered therapy, and behavior therapy) started out as relatively short-term endeavors, but over a course of time showed an unmistakable tendency to become longer and more drawn out. Thus it seems that all seasoned clinicians sooner or later have become impressed with the great difficulty of the therapeutic undertaking and the fact that troublesome patterns are usually deeply engrained. This realization is not mitigated by the observation that in a few instances patients do show rapid and dramatic change.

Furthermore, it is clear that no form of psychotherapy as it currently exists can possibly deal with the totality of the patient's emotional, cognitive, or behavioral repertoire. It is important to indicate which of its aspects are singled out by the therapist. Analytic therapy and behavior therapy focus on specific problems, whereas client-centered therapy and other humanistic forms of therapy attempt to deal with the total person. The former approaches may be likened to X-ray therapy, which is sharply localized, while the latter appear more akin to sun-lamp therapy in which the whole person is irradiated.

THERAPEUTIC TECHNIQUES AND CHANGES ARE BROAD-GAUGED

Considerable confusion persists regarding the definition of problems to which psychotherapy is applied, techniques employed to bring about personality and behavior change, and criteria for evaluating therapeutic outcomes. The difficulty revolves largely around the fact that (1) problems with which psychotherapy intends to deal fall into very different domains; (2) goals and techniques that are employed to reach these objectives are widely divergent; and that (3) diverse criteria are employed for assessing change. As pointed out elsewhere (Strupp and Bergin, 1969), psychotherapy cannot be described as a unitary process, and continued use of the term itself seems to perpetuate unclarities. Instead of speaking about "psychotherapy," it may be more fruitful to employ the admittedly more cumbersome *specific psychological techniques designed to accomplish specific personality and behavior change.*

Introducing new terminology, however, will not go very far in clarifying the issue although it appears to be one positive step. The problem lies deeper because it is not possible to apply specific techniques to specific problems without taking account of the interpersonal context within which the therapeutic transactions occur. To be sure, one may succeed in refining the therapeutic influence so that the kind of purity hinted at in the above formulation may be approximated, but even this will prove to be a difficult assignment. In this sense, therapists and investigators are correct in clinging to the term "psychotherapy" because the influence is, in fact, broad-gauged rather than specific.

Numerous studies (e.g. Strupp, Fox, and Lessler, 1969) suggest that changes occurring in psychotherapy are not necessarily a function of the interventions to which the therapist attributes them, and that it is virtually impossible to study techniques in pure culture. Any therapeutic technique is of course applied in a social context that prominently includes the patient's expectations of improvement. Followed to its logical conclusion, this line of argument leads to the formulation advanced by Frank (1961), that the patient's trust in the therapist's healing powers and a parallel belief on the therapist's part that his technical operations are effective encompass the substance of therapeutic outcomes. These are the nonspecific effects of psychotherapy that are receiving increased attention in the literature.

SPECIFIC VERSUS NONSPECIFIC EFFECTS OF PSYCHOTHERAPY

Can specific technical operations achieve goals that significantly exceed those of the nonspecific variety? Here we need to remind ourselves that both psychoanalysis and behavior therapy operate on the assumption that a therapeutic technology is superior to suggestion, persuasion, exhortation, and faith. I would assert categorically that it is quite unlikely that fundamental personality or behavior changes will occur as a function of minimal interventions. Nor do we need research to demonstrate the excruciatingly slow process encountered in the acquisition of complex skills and the unlearning of maladaptive habits, faulty strategies, or disturbed autonomic functions.

I suggest that the nonspecific effects are most conspicuous when psychotherapy is conducted over a short period, when the patient is in a state of acute distress that highly motivates him to seek change, and when certain other conditions are met. The studies on which Frank based his generalization (and many others that have appeared in the literature) are of this kind. These investigations (for a recent summary, see Shapiro, 1971) corroborate the well-known observation that any form of attention, encouragement, suggestion, etc., that rekindles the patient's hopes and raises his sagging morale will result in favorable changes that the patient (as well as clinical observers) will record as improvement. Accordingly, I present these alternative hypotheses:

1. The effects of all forms of psychotherapy are reducible to the nonspecific factors mentioned above.
2. While all forms of psychotherapy exert a nonspecific beneficial influence on the patient, the systematic application of specific techniques will result in changes that are quantitatively and/or qualitatively differentiable from the nonspecific ones.

If the first hypothesis is true, it will still be necessary to explore the nature of the nonspecific effects and to examine which aspects of the therapist's behavior are most conducive to changing the patient's general outlook on life and which

107

permit him to feel and act differently (as well as abandon certain symptoms). In other words, we cannot rest content with the assertion that certain undefined charismatic qualities of the therapist exert a psychological influence on the patient that augment his powers to cope with life's problems and in turn lead to diminution or disappearance of particular symptoms. Unlike religious conversion or faith healing, it is precisely the task of psychotherapy as a scientific discipline to make explicit the psychological mechanisms that are instrumental in producing change.

PAUCITY OF EVIDENCE FOR SPECIFIC EFFECTS

While the second hypothesis above is in principle testable, the preponderance of the available evidence does not support it. Nevertheless, I believe a good case can be made that the available evidence is inadequate and that the hypothesis has never been properly tested.

Eysenck (1965) and others following in his footsteps have castigated psychoanalysis and other forms of "traditional" psychotherapy on the ground of low improvement rates (compared to so-called untreated controls). Faulty as many of these comparisons have been, one would expect that if the second hypothesis were true, there would be, by now, reasonably convincing evidence that a set of specific therapeutic techniques, applied over a prolonged period of time, produces personality and behavior change that is quantitatively and/or qualitatively different from the kinds of changes regularly observed in accordance with the first hypothesis. To my knowledge, no such evidence exists. Furthermore, it is damaging to note that variations in technique appear to make little difference as far as outcome is concerned. Admittedly, the choice of criteria has been a foggy issue and related measurement problems have been formidable. But, as some critics have cogently argued, if specific effects were truly powerful, even crude assessment techniques would have demonstrated their existence. In

108

medicine no elaborate experimental designs are needed to demonstrate the effects of penicillin and other antibiotics in combating infections. Thus, in the absence of strong evidence to support the claim that the prolonged and systematic application of a set of psychotherapeutic techniques results in changes markedly exceeding those under the first hypothesis, it may be argued that none exist or, what may amount to the same thing, that they are so inconsequential as to elude existing measuring instruments regardless of their imperfections.

TOWARD SPECIFICITY OF TECHNIQUES

While the logic of these arguments appears compelling, and while the onus for demonstrating significant changes rests on the proponents of psychotherapy, not on the critics, I would, on the basis of clinical experience, counsel against a facile dismissal of the second hypothesis.

What would constitute a proper test? To answer this question we must look closer at the nature of the psychotherapeutic influence that, at least in some forms of therapy, includes prominently the application of relatively specific techniques. In practice, however, these techniques are often applied so diffusely and unsystematically as to defy reasonable articulation to any of the existing theories of psychotherapeutic technique. The task of the future is to *refine the application of relatively specific techniques in such a way as to markedly enhance the so-called nonspecific effects of psychotherapy.* This undertaking requires careful specification of the conditions under which focused interventions can achieve their maximum effect. In my judgment, this cannot be done unless the clinical context is taken into account, including such variables as the patient's expectations, the quality of the therapeutic relationship, and others. Such a context always exists, even in studies in which desensitization procedures are programed and presented by means of a computer (Lang, 1968) and where the experimenter

109

may negate or choose to ignore its effect. In the same way, such a context exists in Wolpean behavior therapy. For different reasons, but in a comparable manner, both Freud and the behavior therapists have minimized the therapist's faith, commitment, and therapeutic zeal. This position is quite understandable, if one considers the desire of these therapists to develop a therapeutic *technology* instead of promoting the view that "friendship heals." For these reasons, the technologically oriented therapists are highly task-oriented, and they do not try to achieve a close personal relationship with their patients. They construe the therapist's task as analogous to that of a surgeon or technician who is called in to correct a problem and leaves when the job is done.

The analogy, while crude, serves to underscore the point that (1) a technology in itself is neither good nor evil, but that it can be applied constructively or destructively depending on the technician's purposes or the purposes assigned to him by society; (2) Freud's ideal to help the patient find his own solutions, instead of imposing external ones, remains the best and most honest prescription for the therapist. This does not mean that psychotherapy should be dehumanized. In fact, I take it for granted that the psychotherapist, as well as the therapy researcher, is imbued by a profound respect for the patient as a person.

THE HYPOTHESIS OF THERAPIST CONTROL

There can be no doubt that the patient's relationship to the therapist (including transference reactions) embodies one of the most powerful forces in the therapeutic enterprise. This is an obvious point, but it is often grossly underestimated. Among the key working assumptions of analytic therapy are the following:

1. It is essential for the therapist to mobilize emotional forces in the patient that lead to total involvement and commitment.

110

2. By focusing the patient's total commitment upon himself, the therapist is placed in a position of virtually total control over the patient.

3. The therapist's position of total control is the most important single condition for the occurrence of maximum therapeutic effect.

Stated in the form of a (testable) hypothesis: The greater the therapist's control over the patient, the greater the likelihood of therapeutic change. There is no question that, among all forms of psychotherapy, analytic therapy strives for and often produces the greatest degree of total control over the patient. (The desirability of enhancing and prolongating this total control and the potential dangers of fostering excessive dependence on the therapist have been seriously called into question by Franz Alexander, whose recommendations to counteract these effects have given rise to considerable controversy among analysts.)

The total control hypothesis implies that other forms of therapy that do not explicitly foster it reach less deep, and that, therefore, the changes they produce must *ipso facto* be correspondingly less profound. Terms like "deep" and "profound" are of course precisely the ones in need of definition and measurement, and I have earlier noted a striking lack of evidence in this area. Again, one is tempted to conclude that either existing measurement techniques are grossly inadequate to record these changes or the total control hypothesis is false. If the latter alternative were true, it would follow that other techniques that are less time-consuming, less demanding, less expensive, and less painful to the patient are equally effective, and that the returns that may reasonably be expected from following the analytic course are incommensurate with the very considerable investment. At present, the question cannot be answered.

Actually, the concept of "total control" is of course an overstatement because during therapy the patient, in fact, leads his own life, holds a job, engages in a variety of interpersonal relationships, etc. Realistically, if not emotionally, he is always free to leave the therapeutic situation. Therefore, it seems more appropriate to speak about *relative* control, and it may be hypothesized that an *optimum* level of control may be necessary to effect particular therapeutic tasks. It is clear that *some* level of control is necessary for therapeutic change to occur, and the regulation of the level may be an important subject for empirical investigation. I realize this position is sharply at variance with views espoused by analytic and humanistic therapists. However, I contend that to the extent that the therapist works toward planful change, a measure of control in the foregoing sense is indispensable. In fact, I would reserve the term "psychotherapy" for such planful activity. In contrast, a meditative, contemplative encounter in which the patient finds his own solutions should be designated by some other name. This may turn out to be a rather important distinction.

It has been asserted, perhaps correctly, that analytic therapy is the only form of psychotherapy that does not exploit the patient's (infantile) trust in the therapist's omnipotence, whereas other forms use it, often without recognizing it, toward therapeutic ends. It is interesting to note a remarkable congruence between analytic therapy and behavior therapy in the treatment of phobias: both forms of therapy, following certain therapeutic interventions, urge the patient to test his reactions in the feared situation, and in both instances the therapist uses his influence to propel the patient in that direction. No doubt the patient has developed sufficient trust in the therapist to be willing to listen to his recommendations or exhortations, and somehow he has become deeply convinced that the feared consequences will not occur. But he must try and exert himself; he cannot remain passive. Mastery of a troublesome situation in which one had previously experienced defeat may generalize to mastery of other problems or at least efforts to face the challenge. These, let it be noted, are acts of will—voluntary achievements. While many problems with which the therapist must deal are not phobias, it may be quite useful to invoke (as the behavior therapists have done) the phobia situation as a model.

SPECIFIC PROBLEMS AND SPECIFIC THERAPEUTIC STRATEGIES

What is needed in psychotherapy as a technology for personality and behavior change is a *specific problem* that can be isolated, defined, and operated upon. The psychotherapist-technician has no techniques per se for dealing with problems formulated as *Weltschmerz,* existential despair, depression, etc. Such feeling states are hypothesized—by behavior therapists as well as by analysts—to be epiphenomenal. Behavior therapists accept the patient's view of the problem as the locus for attack (although they are beginning to see these problems in broader perspective); analysts attempt to subsume the problem under major headings (e.g., competition, rivalry, passivity), yet they strive to deal with specific problems as they emerge in therapy. That is, where specific problems do not exist or where they are obscured by defensive maneuvers, specificity must be created. The more specific the patient and the therapist can become about a problem, the greater the likelihood that the problem can be operated upon therapeutically. (This is often misunderstood by opponents.) Still, symptoms or problems cannot be dealt with in isolation, that is, without taking into account the situational context. It can be taken for granted, therefore, that all psychotherapy in the sense in which I use the term is reductionistic, and this realization may open the door to future technical developments. Moreover, therapists must become increasingly clear about what they can do and what they cannot do, and they must eschew tasks with which they are not equipped to deal.

Contemporary research on autonomic control (Miller, 1969) fits the specificity model, although there appears to be a tendency to attempt modification of autonomic responses,

113

including psychosomatic symptoms, without considering the broader social context or the possible symbolic functions the symptom may serve for the patient. It is quite likely, for example, that gastrointestinal symptoms, asthma attacks, and other psychosomatic conditions express strategies needed by the patient to control significant persons in his present (or past) life or to express resentment against them. Indeed, this is the standard psychoanalytic assumption. It is difficult to see how modification of the autonomic response in itself would abolish this problem, and in any case it seems essential to identify and study the broader interpersonal context and the *personal* meaning of a symptom. As this highly promising area of research is developed, we need to learn to what extent, if any, therapeutic changes are potentiated when the personal meaning of a symptom is taken into account. (This is the thrust of a research program employing computer-assisted informational feedback of bioelectric signals currently being implemented by the writer.)

FROM SUBORDINATION TO INDEPENDENCE

It is necessary for the therapist to gain ascendancy or control over the patient but to use the control for the purpose of stimulating independent and self-directive action. Fostering and perpetuating a profound dependency relationship to achieve this end may not be essential, and in fact it may often be contraindicated. At any rate, is this a necessary condition for therapeutic change to occur? Perhaps by focusing on a few specific but important problems and by helping the patient resolve them, it is possible to set in motion powerful reverberating circuits that enable him to become his own master and to solve problems more efficiently.

It is a paradox in modern psychotherapy that for the patient to achieve greater self-control, he must subordinate himself first to someone else's control. In order to become free, he must learn to become more disciplined—that is, he must learn obedience. This he can do only if he permits the therapist to influence him, and he will typically resist this effort. By clearing away the obstacles, the therapist gradually makes the patient amenable to his influence. He somehow persuades him to abandon the fight against submission and to relinquish his own self-willed and maladaptive controls (expressed, for example, through obsessional and compulsive symptoms). Paradoxically, once the patient feels "Thy will be done," he can begin to become his own master because he has started to accept a higher authority than himself. (I am aware of the religious and mystical parallels.) The neurotic patient, in many respects, subscribes to anarchy, and in order to improve he must learn to abide by "law and order." Needless to say, the lesson is often hard and rarely pleasant. It occurs within a framework of rather rigid therapeutic regulations that, however, provide great freedom for self-expression. True, in psychoanalytic therapy the patient finds his own solutions, but not before he has acquired a high level of self-discipline, mediated through obedience, delay of gratification, and "abstinence," that is, the opposite to pampering.

At this point it seems important to note that psychotherapy (and psychotherapists) seeks to accomplish a *variety of tasks,* and while all learning proceeds within the interpersonal framework of the therapeutic relationship, *we need to become increasingly explicit about the particular subgoals and the strategies needed to achieve them.* Furthermore, we need to know more about the *sequence* in which the tasks are to be tackled. Interpretations, or any other single communication, pale in significance compared to the forces that the therapist manipulates in the therapeutic relationship.

To illustrate, very different therapeutic strategies may be needed to abolish a phobia, change faulty beliefs and assumptions about oneself, become clear about one's aspirations and goals, develop different psychophysiological reactions to stress, become more self-assertive and more proficient in handling social situations, channel affect,

115

accept one's limitations, cope with separation and loss, deal with authority figures, and so on. In one instance, what may be needed is learning to make responses antagonistic to anxiety; in another, conditioning of autonomic responses may be called for; in a third, cognitive reorganization of implicit beliefs may be necessary; in a fourth, a sense of helplessness may need to be replaced by the acquisition of specific interpersonal skills not found previously in the patient's repertoire; in a fifth, the patient may need to learn to accept frustrations without developing a rage reaction. In my view, psychoanalytic therapists typically operate on these and other problems at different times in therapy, but they often proceed intuitively and unsystematically. Again, without negating the crucial import of the patient-therapist relationship, I suggest that specificity is both possible and necessary.

With respect to the problem of sequence, analytic therapists have operated on the assumption that problems and defenses are "layered," and that free association brings conflicts sequentially into view. It is certainly true that in the course of therapy a series of problems emerges and, when resolved or mitigated, tends to recede into the background. However, there is also evidence for recrudescence, and the notion of hierarchical structuring is at least open to question. Nor, as Paul Meehl (personal communication) has noted, does there seem to be a very convincing rationale why free association should be conducive to unraveling hierarchically organized conflicts, if such hierarchies indeed exist. The analytic view embraces the notion that when the "basic rule" is followed, important problems inevitably rise to the surface as repressions are dealt with. It is by no means certain that this process occurs regularly, nor may it be economical to let it run its course. In fact, there is clinical evidence to support the views that therapists, because of their own assumptions about the patient's central conflicts, guide him in particular directions. On the other hand, relying solely on the patient's productivity may be an invitation to interminable therapy.

On the basis of the preceding discussion I think that the second hypothesis (technical operations produce therapeutic effects over and beyond those that can be expected from nonspecific factors) may be true after all. Reasons for our failure to adduce strong confirmatory evidence appear to be in large part due to (1) inadequate and improper assessments of therapeutic outcomes (e.g., global measures of improvement); and (2) the fact that thus far psychotherapeutic techniques have been used without sufficient emphasis upon the therapeutic tasks to be accomplished, nor have techniques designed to reach specific ends been described and practiced with sufficient precision.

SUMMARY

This discussion may be summarized by a number of propositions:

1. A primary purpose of psychotherapy is the acquisition of self-control, mastery, competence, and autonomy.

2. The neurotic patient suffers from inadequate self-control, which may take the form of over- or under-control or misplaced controls. The nature of desirable controls is in part determined by the culture.

3. The existence and the nature of the inner controls can be inferred from behavior (e.g., "acting out," avoidance), emotional reactions, autonomic patterns of response (including psychosomatic symptoms), thought processes (obsessionalism, etc.), and so on. These are often, though perhaps not exclusively, guided by central processes, such as beliefs, assumptions about oneself and others, many of which are implicit and highly symbolic. One of the tasks of psychotherapy is to make these symbolic processes explicit. Feelings frequently are epiphenomena reflecting the existence of the foregoing underlying states.

4. Psychotherapy is a technology for personality and behavior change; concomitantly, the task of research is the

117

development of an increasingly refined technology and appropriate theories to account for these changes.

5. Since the majority of patterns with which the psychotherapist is called upon to deal are deeply engrained, it seems unlikely that significant therapeutic changes can be rapid or spectacular. In addition, limitations are imposed by biological factors, and maladaptive learning may have produced extensive modifications of the nervous system, some of which may be irreversible. The importance of these factors is only gradually being appreciated. In general, there is reason to believe that the kinds of changes that may be expected from psychotherapy, at least in part, are commensurate with the expended effort. One of the important future tasks for research is to elucidate the *limitations* of psychotherapy and to spell out what it can do effectively and what it cannot do. It is questionable whether such determinations can ever be highly precise.

6. Psychotherapy is not a unitary process. Instead, the problems to which therapeutic efforts are addressed vary widely, and so do the techniques that are employed toward their modification. This has led to considerable confusion, obscured the refinement of techniques, and clouded assessments of therapeutic outcome.

7. Nevertheless, psychotherapeutic changes always occur in the context of an interpersonal relationship, and are to some extent inextricable from it. While trite, this statement raises difficult, though potentially answerable, questions concerning the precise nature of the influence exerted by the therapist.

8. While all forms of psychotherapy exert a nonspecific influence, it may be hypothesized that the systematic application of specific and focused techniques, within this interpersonal framework, strengthen the therapeutic influence and lead to changes that are quantitatively and qualitatively differentiable from the nonspecific ones. The lack of convincing empirical evidence may be an indication that specific techniques have not been systematically applied, and that

their effects have been embedded in, and therefore over-shadowed by, the nonspecific effects. One important task for research, therefore, is the isolation of specific techniques that, however, cannot be studied outside the interpersonal context. The difficulty of this undertaking is obviously formidable.

9. The emotional involvement created within the psychotherapeutic situation can be augmented or minimized by specifiable technical maneuvers. Its most intense form is exemplified by the transference situation fostered in psychoanalysis, the pervasiveness of which is not always recognized by nonanalytic workers. It creates a situation of total emotional involvement unequaled in other forms of psychotherapy. Whether such total involvement is necessary or desirable for the occurrence of significant therapeutic change is an open question, but in any case it represents an important variable whose implications should be thoroughly explored. Minimally, it leads to a unique mobilization of powerful emotional forces. Furthermore, the total involvement into which the therapist, like a magnet, draws the patient's wishes, expectations, and emotions creates a most unusual laboratory situation, the potentialities of which are likewise in need of careful study.

10. While the total involvement mentioned above leads to total (or maximal) control on the part of the therapist, it remains to be explored whether it in fact potentiates the effect of specific therapeutic techniques. This kind of control is contingent upon the development of *trust* in the therapist, and in an important sense, psychotherapy may be viewed as a technology for eliminating the barriers against openness, honesty, and trust.

11. Psychotherapy as a therapeutic technology can operate only on specific problems, however the problem is defined. Where specific problems do not exist at the beginning of therapy—typically, the patient's definition of "the problem" is far from synonymous with the therapist's—*specificity must be created* as therapy proceeds.

12. In any form of psychotherapy the therapist must achieve some measure of ascendancy or control over the patient if his therapeutic interventions are to be effective, and such control exists even when the therapist chooses to ignore it.

13. In order for the patient to achieve self-control, mastery, and autonomy, he must learn to accept the therapist's authority and to subordinate himself to his control. This can occur only if the patient develops *trust* in the therapist's integrity and begins to see him as a person who is genuinely interested in his, the patient's, self-development and maturity.

14. With respect to the design of potentially fruitful research, the foregoing considerations have important implications. Of greatest significance, perhaps, is the necessity to *focus on both subjective and objective* aspects of the person's functioning. Concomitantly, it seems unlikely that the monitoring and recording of behavioral events, no matter how refined such measurements may become, can shed much light on the forces of which these outward manifestations are a function. Thus, one cannot eliminate, except at great risk, the clinical observer and his capacity for indwelling (Polanyi, 1966), that is, understanding, in the context of an interpersonal relationship free from sham, deception, and façade, the patient's inner world—his fantasies, beliefs, and working assumptions about himself and others. As an important goal, we must learn whether, and to what extent, *specific* learning experiences in psychotherapy can exceed *nonspecific* learning experiences mediated by the interpersonal aspects of the patient-therapist relationship.

References

Eysenck, H. J. 1965. "The Effects of Psychotherapy," *Int. J. Psychiat.*, 1 : 97-178.

Frank, J. D. 1961. *Persuasion and Healing*. Baltimore: Johns Hopkins Press.

Lang, P. J. 1968. "Fear Reduction and Fear Behavior: Problems in Treating a Construct," in *Psychotherapy Research*, Vol. III, ed. J. Shlien, pp. 90-102. Washington, D. C.: American Psychological Assn.

Miller, N. E. 1969. "Learning of Visceral and Glandular Responses," *Sci.*, 163: 434-445.

Polanyi, M. 1966. *The Tacit Dimension*. New York: Doubleday.

Shapiro, A. K. 1971. "Placebo Effects in Medicine, Psychotherapy, and Psychoanalysis," in *Handbook of Psychotherapy and Behavior Change: An Empirical Analysis*, ed. A. E. Bergin and S. L. Garfield, pp. 439-473. New York: Wiley.

Strupp, H. H., and Bergin, A. E. 1969. "Some Empirical and Conceptual Bases for Coordinated Research in Psychotherapy: A Critical Review of Issues, Trends, and Evidence," *Int. J. Psychiat.*, 7: 18-90.

——— Fox, R. E., and Lessler, K. 1969. *Patients View Their Psychotherapy*. Baltimore: Johns Hopkins Press.

5

THE TECHNOLOGY
OF PSYCHOTHERAPY

In psychotherapy (under which I continue to subsume psychoanalysis as a major subform) the resulting personality and behavior changes are ordinarily described as "therapeutic." However, the approach has broad implications for child rearing, education, rehabilitation, correction—in short, for any area that is concerned with the promotion of personality growth and the development of mature, self-directing, autonomous, and responsible adults who under ordinary circumstances can conduct their own affairs and are not in need of help, support, or guidance from others or society at large. I believe that the exploration of this psychological influence is the basic task facing the researcher in psychotherapy, to which the study of techniques per se is secondary. Conceptual clarification of these issues is an essential prerequisite for further meaningful research in this area.

122

FREUD'S DISSERVICE: A HISTORICAL NOTE

Certain terms in the area of psychotherapy have acquired the connotation of "dirty" words, with the result that the phenomena to which they refer have ceased to be respectable; more seriously, such value judgments have had the effect of delaying or even deterring exploration. Prominent among these terms are placebo effect (nonspecific, that is, broad interpersonal, factors) and suggestion. The blame for denigrating the concepts of suggestion and suggestibility must be placed at Freud's doorsteps.

Freud's early interest in hypnosis and the evolution of psychoanalysis as a set of therapeutic techniques hardly bears repetition. It is important to point out, however, that as Freud came to develop his basic concepts and the model of the psychoanalytic situation, he proceeded to draw a sharp distinction between psychoanalysis and other treatment approaches that in his judgment, were "merely" based on suggestion. The neurotic patient's tendency to transfer infantile patterns of behavior, expectations, and fantasies to the therapist was seen as part and parcel of his "suggestibility," and indeed the core of his "illness." (I shall return to this formulation later.) Psychoanalysis was designed, through dissection and neutralization of the patient's resistances, to deprive him of this weapon. In his later writings Freud admitted that the therapist does use suggestion but insisted that the thrust of the analytic technique was focused upon persuading the patient to relinquish his resistances by demonstrating to him that they were maladaptive, rooted in infantile experiences, fantasies, and misconceptions, hence anachronistic and unnecessary. Thus, the therapist supposedly did not "manipulate" * (another dirty

---

*Since the main thrust of this chapter will predictably be criticized on these grounds, it is important to stress the dictionary definition of the word "manipulate" : "to handle, manage or use, especially with skill, in some process of treatment or performance." I submit that this is precisely what psychotherapy is and what the patient has a right to expect.

word) the transference relationship, but he analyzed it. The model Freud was criticizing, I believe, was that of the domineering hypnotist who was bombarding the patient with authoritarian commands. He was very commendably advocating a permissive situation in which, ideally, the patient is encouraged to seek and find his own answers. Whatever the merits of Freud's distinction, the fact remains that the therapist exerts a powerful psychological influence on the patient, and it appears that the analytic situation was precisely designed to augment, intensify, and potentiate it. In fact, by creating a paradoxical situation in therapy that is ostensibly a relationship between two adults but that is also conducive to stimulating the reemergence of infantile patterns, Freud forged an exceedingly powerful tool for personality and behavior change.

Freud's distinction had, of course, the strategic advantage of extolling the uniqueness of psychoanalytic psychotherapy over all contenders, notably the crude practices that must have been extant at the time. In the long run, psychoanalysts could feel comfortably secure in the belief that they were practicing a superior brand of psychotherapy and that the psychological mechanisms they utilized in the patient or brought to bear on the interaction were qualitatively different from anyone else's. This belief is still widespread and neatly serves to undergird the analyst's professional grandiosity and presumption. The latter was scarcely Freud's intention, but his formulations had the effect of sequestering the psychotherapeutic influence as something "special" in human relations, thereby inhibiting investigations of what it might have *in common* with other techniques of psychological influence. Only in relatively recent years have attempts been made to bring about "translations" (Alexander, 1963; Dollard and Miller, 1950).

THE PATIENT'S SUSCEPTIBILITY TO PSYCHOLOGICAL INFLUENCE

What are the factors in the patient (pupil, delinquent,

124

medical patient, normal person) that render him open to psychological influence, or alternatively vitiate a therapist's efforts? I view this susceptibility as a universal continuum ranging from high susceptibility to virtual insusceptibilty.

CHILDHOOD ANTECEDENTS: It is quite likely that part of the susceptibility to social influence is biologically determined, that is, "wired" into the human organism, but in any case it is a basic tendency present soon after birth and of course heavily reinforced by mothering behavior in infancy and early childhood. As a result of early experiences the human infant under ordinary circumstances becomes highly susceptible and responsive to social cues, particularly if, we must surmise, the experience is perceived as intrinsically gratifying. Thus the child becomes dependent upon and seeks to perpetuate social interactions that are conducive to his receiving love, approval, and other rewards. He develops "basic trust," which also embodies blind faith in, and obedience to, a powerful external (parental) authority. Freud was undoubtedly correct in asserting that the adult's faith in God is a derivative of the child's sense of fear, awe, unquestioned submission, obedience and helplessness vis-à-vis an all-powerful parent figure. In turn, these feelings may be rooted in the child's own narcissistic fantasies of omnipotence. Throughout life the human being strives for independence and emancipation from these feelings while at the same time (because of his inherent weakness, finiteness, and fear of death) remaining forever vulnerable to reversion. Any influencer—therapist, physician, judge, educator, priest, leader, expert, or society at large—capitalizes on this by placing himself, often only temporarily, in the position of an all-powerful authority who exercises more or less complete control over the subject. More accurately, he encourages (manipulates) the subject to accept him in that powerful position from which he then proceeds to exert his influence. It is clear that whenever the subject is ill, weak, helpless, feels dependent or ignorant, the stage is set for

125

persons or organizations in authority to influence him. The psychoanalytic concept of regression refers to the same phenomenon. It is also clear, to cite but one example, that a patient in a state of crisis is highly amenable to the therapist's interventions (i.e., he is highly "motivated" to be influenced) and that such situations are typically coupled with the arousal of (primitive) affect.*

In short, under ordinary circumstances a child acquires a basic personality trait of suggestibility, persuadability, educability, psychological modifiability (treatibility, "analyzability") in later life. The ability to be hypnotized is probably part of this constellation. Once acquired, this tendency is exceedingly stable and persistent. Further, the strong human desire to belong to a group, to conform to its morals and mores, to be approved and loved by persons in authority (and one's peers) appears to be an integral part of the susceptibility to social influence. Highly pertinent to this discussion seems to be the finding reported by Josephine Hilgard (1970) that good hypnotic subjects appear to have a family background characterized in part by strict discipline in the context of a warm, loving parent-child relationship. It is clear that the psychotherapeutic enterprise, not to mention education, religion, propaganda, among others, is squarely built upon the supposition that most people are susceptible to, and influenceable by, psychological means, that they change attitudes, behavior, and beliefs as a response to such techniques, provided certain conditions are met. At the same time, however, people are more or less "resistant" to such influences.

Part of the reason for this resistance is the development of a "self-system," "ego," or whatever terminology may be employed to characterize the emergence of a person's self-directing, executive tendencies and his striving for

*It has recently been pointed out that the contemporary phenomenon of the "Jesus revolution" among alienated youth represents another version of the search for a benevolent paternal authority that many of the followers have never experienced.

126

autonomy and independence. It suffices to note that many impulses, wishes, and strivings are gradually brought under self-control, concomitant with the erosion or diminution of parental control. Nevertheless, the susceptibility to social cues remains present and perenially latent in everyone. Indeed, social living would be impossible without it.

DEFENSE MECHANISMS, RESISTANCE, AND TRANSFERENCE TENDENCIES

THE "NORMAL SOLUTION": There is reason to believe that when early experiences have been essentially satisfying, the growing child will partly assimilate ("introject") the control exerted by his parents and build his own control mechanisms; partly he will remain open and, under appropriate conditions, receptive to similar kinds of social influence; partly he will reject, and become resistant to attempts by others to control him. Thus, the "normal" child will become educable, teachable, adaptable, and, within limits, influenceable. At the same time, the acquisition of self-control must be seen as a major milestone in human development; it is largely a matter of how the growing human being responds to external constraints (discipline) and how he learns to discipline himself. Waelder (1960) epitomized the dilemma of child rearing in these terms: how to love without spoiling and how to discipline without traumatizing. The implications of the "normal solution" will emerge more clearly in the light of two broad classes of abortive attempts.

THE "NEUROTIC SOLUTION": The individual becomes "neurotic," that is, for complex reasons that have been amply discussed in the literature, he declares war on the mediators of social influence (usually his parents), and by means of various autonomic (unconscious) strategies and tactics seeks to ward off their influence by controlling them. He fights against submission, obedience, conformity, and compliance while at the same time craving these for the purpose of win-

127

ning the parents' love and approval. In short, he becomes "conflicted."

THE "PSYCHOPATHIC SOLUTION": The individual largely rejects the parental influence without first having assimilated the morals and values of the cultural group the parents represent. Such individuals do not grow out of the confines of the parental influence after having submitted to it in a deep sense; instead they reject it or pay only superficial allegiance to it. This group of individuals is exemplified by psychopaths and other "rebels." Traditionally, they have been considered very unpromising patients for psychotherapy, which makes good sense if the therapeutic relationship presupposes at least a rudimentary willingness on the patient's part to relive some parts—usually painful parts—of his childhood. These people are frequently described as having poor "impulse control," being given to antisocial "acting out," flouting accepted moral standards, preferring immediate gratification to what the adequately socialized person has come to accept as delays in gratification, and they are insensitive to the feelings of others.

To sum up, the normal individual has "come to terms" with the problem of social influence and has succeeded in modulating it; the neurotic continues to make an issue of it; and the psychopath has largely turned his back on it. With regard to later attempts at social influence, it would follow that the neurotic person is the most vulnerable of the three types precisely for the reason that he remains entangled in the issue of whether in interpersonal relationships he will fight for his independence (which often turns out to be a pseudo-independence) or whether he will abjectly submit to a feared authority figure (couched by Freud in terms of homosexual surrender and "passivity").

THE FEAT OF THERAPEUTIC PENETRANCE

The concept of "basic trust" refers to the child's pristine

and uncritical openness to social influence, his primitive yet pervasive faith in the goodness and beneficence of the nurturing adults, and his willingness to surrender to their unlimited power. This attitude is profoundly illustrated by Jesus' last words: "Father, into thy hands I commit my spirit" (Luke 23:46). The crucial context for significant therapeutic change lies precisely in a semblance of this attitude, which is concomitant with the complete (however temporary) abandonment of so-called defense mechanisms in relation to a healer experienced as possessing superior powers. However, such complete submission is extremely painful and occurs only under great duress. Furthermore, the pain is undergone only if it promises to liberate the individual from isolation by letting him become a full-fledged adult. The full implications of this observation need to be explored further.

Conversely, traditional defense mechanisms may be viewed as more or less adaptive techniques regulating the extent to which the person shall be susceptible to psychological influence from powerful authority figures. They may also be considered mechanisms for controlling oneself and others. In this light, the psychoanalytic emphasis on analyzing the patient's defenses makes good sense: by gradually eroding his habitual ("characterological") techniques for fighting off another person's influence, the therapist "opens up" the patient and, typically against the patient's will, paves the way for personality and behavior change. Time and again he forces the patient to experience the inutility and self-defeating character of his resistive maneuvers and, paradoxically, coerces him into renewed experiences of basic trust.

How does the therapist accomplish the feat of eroding the patient's defenses against influence by a powerful parent figure? The following appear to be basic components of the overall strategy:

1. The patient turns to the therapist for help. He is

129

driven by suffering and unhappiness to accept the advice, counsel, and ministrations of a healer-expert. If he is deeply distressed and propelled by inner forces (not by relatives, a court of law, etc.) to seek help from another person, he tends to be "motivated" to subordinate himself to a healer. On a deeper level, because of early childhood experiences, he seeks to reinstitute a parent-child situation in which he is taken care of, loved, forgiven, encouraged, coaxed, and so on. It may be postulated that the greater the reservoir of happy, rewarding experiences in early childhood—no matter how much they may be obscured or overlaid by subsequent disappointments and traumata—the greater the potential of the therapeutic situation for being similarly rewarding. Conversely, severe deprivations experienced early in life may render the patient chronically impervious to the potential benefits of a benign human relationship. This hypothesis is of course well documented by clinical experience, notably with certain schizophrenic or borderline patients. Ordinarily, these factors are termed "transference readiness," or, as I would prefer to call them, susceptibility to therapeutic influence. It is worth recalling that Freud considered patients suffering from what he called transference neuroses as the most promising candidates for psychoanalysis; in fact, he initially considered the technique contraindicated in all other instances.

2. Capitalizing on the patient's susceptibility to parental-type influences, the therapist initiates a benign, permissive relationship in which the patient is accepted, respected, encouraged to confide, and to communicate directly and uninhibitedly. Thus he is deprived of one set of "defensive" tactics that may be summarized by the question: How can I trust another person if he continually criticizes, nags, oppresses, corrects, pushes, blames, scolds, punishes, frightens, hurts, or rejects me? In other words, the patient is deprived of his customary "excuses" for fighting a powerful adversary.

In many forms of psychotherapy the creation of a relationship having the foregoing ingredients provides sufficient momentum for a corrective emotional experience. This experience embodies a reduction of guilt; it paves the way toward the abreaction of painful affect; it leads to the exploration and clarification of feelings, attitudes and values that for one reason or another had been troublesome. Thus, there results an improvement in morale, a rise in self-esteem and hope, and a diminution of anxiety and uncertainty. The key to these therapeutic changes seems to lie in the revival and deepening of a good parent-child relationship that places heavy reliance on the patient's susceptibility to a benign psychological influence. The vehicle for change is suggestibility and the patient's basic responsiveness to loved authority figures. In these forms of psychotherapy the therapist "does" nothing; however, he offers understanding, respect, encouragement, and—most important—a measure of love, all of which may mean a great deal to a person in distress. It is likely that a *very significant amount of psychotherapeutic change occurring in all forms of psychotherapy is attributable to these so-called nonspecific factors that derive their potency largely from their contact with loci of influenceability inherent in the "good" patient.* To the extent that the patient is capable of resonating to the ingredients of a good human relationship, and to the extent that the therapist is able to supply these in terms meaningful to the patient, to that extent therapeutic change may be predicted to occur.

This formulation fully allows for the disappearance or diminution of symptoms such as inhibitions and anxieties that often "melt" in the light of love. That the "dispensing" or provision of "therapeutic conditions" may be accomplished as readily—often more effectively—by a nonprofessional person is also congruent with this statement. In fact, professional training here has little to offer (except perhaps to mitigate the traditional "countertransference" tendencies in the therapist) and may indeed be detrimental, because it frequently fosters an intellectual distance-producing attitude in the trainee.

131

The foregoing essential aspects of psychotherapy, or for that matter of any healing relationship, are largely synonymous with the nonspecific factors delineated by Frank (1961, 1970), including prominently: (a) an intense, emotionally charged, confiding relationship; (b) a rationale or myth to account for the "causes" of the patient's distress; (c) new information concerning the "problem" and alternate solutions; (d) attempts to strengthen the patient's expectancy of help and arousal of hope (mediated by the therapist's personal qualities); (e) provision of success experiences that enhance the patient's mastery, competence, and self-esteem; and (f) the facilitation of emotional arousal. All of these play upon and utilize the patient's suggestibility, defined here as a primitive tendency to yield to social (parental) influence; and they lead to the so-called placebo effects (Shapiro, 1971), often confounded with "spontaneous remission" (Eysenck, 1952; 1960). Stated somewhat differently, the modern psychotherapist, at least on this level, relies to a large extent on the same psychological mechanisms used by the faith healer, shaman, physician, or priest, and the results, as reflected by the evidence of therapeutic outcomes, appear to be substantially similar.

As we have seen, the fulcrum on which the therapist's influence turns is delimited by the patient's motivation and his basic susceptibility to psychological influence. These are to some extent definable and measurable (compare the "therapeutic conditions" described by Rogers and researched by Truax and Carkhuff, 1967). However, the extent to which the patient responds is probably a fairly idiosyncratic matter, predictable only within broad limits. In the final analysis, the changes achieved in this context are contingent upon the degree to which the patient possesses and has retained the capacity to be a "good," obedient, pliable, conforming, and responsive child. Conversely, to the extent that the patient is lacking this capacity, and to the extent that the motivation to expose himself to a healer's influence is

132

absent, to that extent will the patient fail to take advantage of what the therapist at this level has to offer. He will experience the therapeutic setting as meaningless and empty, and he will reject the healer.

3. Assuming that the bedrock of psychotherapeutic change is largely coextensive with the patient's basic susceptibility to psychological influence, reconsider those individuals who are more or less impervious to it. It appears useful to distinguish two groups: (a) individuals who, because of seriously destructive relationships in early childhood or constitutional factors, are seriously deficient in suggestibility; and (b) a much larger group of individuals, ordinarily described as "neurotic," for whom the matter of parental influence has become an issue and who remain entangled in it. The first group, consisting of psychopaths, individuals suffering from so-called impulse-disorders, antisocial persons of various kinds to whom societal (parental) injunctions and approval are meaningless, is largely a lost cause for any form of psychotherapy; the second group overlaps with many "normals," but also comprises the more or less typical candidates for psychotherapy. The basic therapeutic problem here is to undermine or modify the techniques (defenses) by which the patient habitually wards off a healer's psychological influence, and thus to create a condition in which he can again experience "basic trust." When this goal has been reached, the operations described above can exert their "nonspecific" therapeutic effect.

THERAPEUTIC LEVERAGE THROUGH BASIC TRUST

Important aspects of this process have been incisively explored by Haley (1963). A salient example is the therapist's skill in creating a paradoxical situation (called by Haley a benign ordeal) where, on the one hand, the patient is encouraged to communicate with the therapist in "symp-

133

tomatic" ways. That is, he is enticed to fight off the therapist's influence in essentially the same way as he had learned to fight off the parents' socializing influence, and when he does so he is placed in a position that effectively makes it impossible to utilize these techniques. Consequently, he is faced with the dilemma of either assuming responsibility for the lack of progress and to quit therapy, which he ordinarily will not do because of the conditions described under (1), or he is forced to modify his usual strategies. which results in therapeutic change.

On a superficial level Haley's analysis creates the unfortunate impression that the therapist is a "manipulator" (in a pejorative sense) who continually engages in one-upmanship maneuvers. Haley also seems to disregard the patient's *motivation* for confronting the therapist. In agreement with dynamic teachings, I believe that the most important single factor supporting the patient's "resistance" is his anxiety, the dread of dire consequences (based on fantasy or actual experience) attendant upon the relinquishment of control to the therapist. It is difficult to determine the role of unconscious fantasies about "losing control" in the patient's struggle against the therapist, but I am reasonably convinced that "analyzing" them in and of itself produces relatively little change in the patient. What does produce change is *the patient's realization, on a deep level, that it is futile to fight the therapist with the weapons he has habitually used to control powerful, loved, but potentially dangerous authority figures,* and that these strategies, while "satisfying" in some sense, are basically self-defeating and unrewarding. That is, the patient must realize that the usual controlling techniques at his disposal do not get him what he wants, that what he wanted as a child may not be what he wants as an adult, and that most of his fears are groundless because they are based on erroneous beliefs of helplessness, weakness, and a need to be taken care of, as well as the notion that significant adults are extremely "dangerous."

134

A case in point is the child who has learned that the parents cannot be trusted to respect him as a person, to gratify his wishes (there is no need to discuss here the distinction between realistic and unrealistic ones), and to protect him, sometimes from his own impulses. As a consequence of such a profound disturbance of the child's security, he becomes devious. He keeps his feelings and wishes to himself, convinced that their exposure would lead only to further humiliation and frustration, and he develops techniques that serve the purpose of providing gratifications while preventing these from being detected. At the same time, the techniques developed in this context express a measure of *defiance* against the parental authority that has proven capricious, disappointing, and painful. The child also typically keeps from himself the intricacies of these maneuvers, of which masturbation, voyeurism, etc., but also other forms of "deviousness," are typical examples. What the child fails to appreciate is the enormous amount of *guilt* generated by what may now be termed a neurotic "symptom." The more guilty he feels, the more devious he becomes, but the secrecy of the pleasures also perpetuates the gratifications. Predictably, the process produces progressive estrangement from the parents and social influence. As sketched in this chapter, an important part of psychotherapy consists of *techniques* for restoring the condition of basic trust.

As Haley correctly points out, a fundamental problem in psychotherapy (and indeed in all human relationships) is the question of *who is in control*. While couching his operations in very different terms, Freud nevertheless evolved the ingenious technique of seemingly placing the patient in control of the therapist, while in actuality creating for the latter a position of immense power. *It is the judicious utilization of this power that uniquely defines the modern psychotherapist and that constitutes his expertise. The therapist's interpersonal power is deployed more or less deliberately in all forms of psychotherapy regardless of the specific techniques*

135

that may be utilized. In other words, if a symptom, belief, interpersonal strategy, or whatever, is to change, a measure of external force must be applied.

To elaborate on the term "judicious use of power," there appear to be essentially two ways of "changing" a person's learned behavior: either the contingencies of the situation force him to change his feelings, beliefs, attitudes, or symptoms, or he comes to realize that he *wants* to change some aspect of his personality or behavior. Without wishing to get embroiled in the hoary problem of free will versus determinism, a commonsense statement of the typical neurotic's position is that either he wants to do something but claims he cannot (e.g., a probic avoidance) or he does something and claims he cannot stop it (e.g., an obsession). In both situations the assertion is made that he has inadequate control over something that he, as well as others, feels he ought to have control over (see Chapter Four). At this point the orthodox analytic position diverges sharply from learning (behavioral) approaches. The former asserts that there are "reasons" (motives) that must be "understood" for the patient's symptomatic behavior and that this understanding on the part of the patient will in turn result in therapeutic change. The behavior therapists assert that it is sufficient to change the contingencies and consequences of the patient's behavior, with more expeditious and impressive results. I submit that the differences are more apparent than real. I fully agree with Haley that in analytic psychotherapy, too, the therapist manipulates the situation in such a way that it becomes impossible for the patient to behave in accustomed ways and that the structure of the relationship is such that he is forced to undergo change. By the same token, in desensitization therapy the patient is *forced* to experience graduated doses of anxiety under the guidance of the therapist.

The "insights" that the patient gains in analytic psychotherapy may be valuable in their own right; they may prove rewarding in demonstrating to the patient wishes, impulses, and fantasies whose existence he had only dimly suspected; they may be educational in a variety of other ways. However, they do not change behavior.* In order to change feelings, beliefs, attitudes, and behavior it is crucial to employ techniques that *force* such changes. If the "treatment" is successful, the patient will feel that he has acquired more adequate control, and indeed he has. Thus, it seems questionable that, as far as the abandonment of a "symptom" is concerned, the patient is achieving it by himself. (By implication, I assign to "insight" a rather secondary role.)

A simple example will illustrate the point: it is manifestly futile to tell a patient that he can be more trustful of the therapist or less anxious in a given situation. What does help is to *force* him to trust the therapist and sooner or later to expose himself to the anxiety-provoking circumstances. How can he be forced to trust the therapist? In psychoanalysis, he is forced to do so by the (seemingly) simple injunction to abide by the rule of free association; consequently, if he fails to follow the "basic rule," he ceases to be a "good patient" and it is pointed out that he does not "cooperate" with the therapist. It follows that the responsibility for progress has been thrust into the patient's hands, and he has to struggle with the problem of why he mistrusts the benevolent therapist. In this process he is shown that he manipulates the therapist, keeps secrets from him (see the earlier example), tries to undermine or ignore his authority, etc. He also comes to experience a good deal of anxiety (e.g., fear of censure, loss of love, annihilation, submission, "cas-

---

*It is interesting to note that some analysts nowadays refer analysands to behavior therapists for the treatment of particular symptoms but continue the "analysis" simultaneously or subsequently. Evidently, they are in accord with Freud's position toward the end of his career that the therapeutic value of psychoanalysis, in the sense of its original goal of behavior change, is severely limited. The aforementioned practice seems to indicate a further step away from Freud's original search for an effective psychotherapeutic technique.

tration"). These reactions are demonstrated as being ground-less and anchored in erroneous assumptions or beliefs about himself, the therapist's motives, and the world at large. This strategy also forces the patient to expose, at least in part, the techniques he unwittingly uses to control others, many of which are fraught with, and productive of, anxiety.

Trusting the therapist (and significant persons in general) has far-reaching implications. It is indeed a form of submission, a blind faith in the trustworthiness or basic goodness of the other person, and an abiding conviction that the other person will not use the power the patient has been forced to place in his hands against the patient except for "therapeutic" purposes. It means, among other things, that in the interest of the patient's maturation the therapist will at times inflict injuries to the patient's "narcissism" (his grandiosity, self-will, stubbornness, unbridled wishes), but that he will stringently abstain from embarrassing or humi-liating him, and that he will never misuse his power for selfish or ulterior purposes. Thus, *psychotherapy is a series of lessons in basic trust, together with the undermining of those interpersonal strategies the patient has acquired for controlling himself and others.* It places a high premium on open and direct communication, self-disclosure, and a basic willingness (and ability) to undergo deprivation, suffering, and self-examination, frequently subsumed under "ego strength."

In short, the interpersonal strategies (symptoms, de-fenses, characterological distortions), insofar as they are not fortuitous maladaptations (e.g., a snake phobia), are techni-ques for warding off trust in significant others; conversely, the anticipation of a trusting relationship often revives ex-tremely painful feelings of helplessness, loneliness, rejection, domination, or oppression, which presumably have led to anxiety and other defensive tactics in the first place. It follows that only in a very restricted sense is the patient re-living the past. Of crucial importance are the transactions with the therapist in the present. The concept of transference

138

highlights the patient's tendency to respond to powerful authority figures in accustomed ways. Accordingly, he tends to fight off the therapist's influence in ways similar to those he had used in fighting off his parents. Thus, *symptoms, at least in part, are techniques of social control* and can be modified if the therapist succeeds in forcing the patient to adopt different strategies or in giving up maladaptive ones.

PROBLEMS AND IMPLICATIONS

One of the basic unresolved problems in psychotherapy as well as in child development is the question of how external control is transformed into internal or self-control. How does the individual progress from a state of dependence to a relative state of independence? How does it come about that in some spheres and under some conditions he becomes resistant to external psychological influence, and in other respects remains influenceable, malleable, and open? By what mechanisms do some individuals acquire faulty control over certain physiological functions (e.g., breathing, gastric motility) resulting in the formation of psychosomatic symptoms? Contrary to the psychoanalysts who have proceeded on the assumption that in order to produce significant therapeutic change it is essential to search for "first causes" in the individual's life history, the behavior therapists have produced evidence that it is possible to effect personality and behavior change without recourse to such inquiries. Further, Miller's (1969) research has raised the possibility of directly modifying psychosomatic symptoms without delving into antecedent psychological factors. Thus far the evidence is far from conclusive and it would be premature to assert that psychodynamic considerations, including the provision of a therapeutic relationship along the lines sketched in this chapter, are expendable in this area.

To some extent control mechanisms are of course essential for social living, and there must be an optimum balance between openness to psychological influence and resistance

139

to it. The psychotherapist, through his interpersonal influence as well as through specific techniques he may employ for changing certain aspects of the patient's beliefs, feelings, and behaviors, attempts to modify and adjust these control mechanisms that govern the patient's suggestibility or influenceability.

The therapist thus injects himself into the socialization process, and he produces corrections of a "therapeutic" sort. He builds upon the parental authority, which in some respects has misfired, and paves the way for what Alexander has termed a "corrective emotional experience." However, he does more than take the place of a better parent, of a more rational authority, or of a better model who provides love, reasonableness, understanding of needs, wishes, and aspirations, thereby correcting the patient's experiential repertoire. He also uses the vantage point of the parental position as a power base from which to effect changes in the patient's interpersonal strategies, in accordance with the principle that *in the final analysis the patient changes out of love for the therapist.* The patient's experience may be formulated as follows: While it is painful to experience anxiety, give up a symptom, suffer disappointments, abandon stubbornness and grandiosity, have less "pleasure," get along with less approval from others, I will endure these privations because I realize that the higher authority wants me to do these things. More important, the therapist truly has my interest at heart, and by subordinating myself to him I will gain relief from my terrifying loneliness, alienation, and suffering. By subordinating myself to the therapist, whom I love and admire (but also fear and hate), I will become like him—share in his strength, fearlessness, maturity, independence, expertness in living, and so on. Once I do this, I will have gained the strength to strike out on my own and I can relinquish my struggle with authority figures. I will also have gained the acceptance of society.

It may be seen that therapeutic change thus involves a kind of *trade*—the exchange and modification of one set of (maladaptive) assumptions, behaviors, and strategies for another. This exchange is rooted in, and based upon, the reinstitution of a quasi-parent-child relationship, a readiness on the patient's part to endure the reliving (and consequent extinction) of painful experiences, together with the hope that another edition of the parent-child relationship will result in a happier outcome. It must also be assumed that unless there exists a residual memory of benign interpersonal experience, it is not likely that the patient can marshal much hope in therapeutic change. Moreover, unless the therapist somehow succeeds in becoming a loved figure for the patient, his efforts are likewise doomed to failure. Again, the major task of the therapist is to bring about an experience of *trust,* which alone permits him to apply the requisite *leverage* for therapeutically influencing the patient.

The forces sketched above are more readily discerned in intensive psychotherapy, but I propose that they are at work—perhaps in attenuated fashion—in any form of psychotherapy, behavior therapy, hypnotherapy, or any other healing relationship. In general terms, the patient trades a symptom or a maladaptive form of behavior for something else, that something else being the love or approval of an authority, even though the latter may be highly symbolic. He will not consummate the trade unless he becomes deeply convinced that the trade balance is favorable for him. The therapist's job is to create the proper conditions that may vary widely from patient to patient and from circumstance to circumstance. As Freud well recognized, the ever-present ambivalence, that is, the patient's mistrust, hostility, and rejection of a (parental) influencer constitutes a formidable obstacle to therapeutic change. The therapist's skill comes to fruition in his ability to ferret out the patient's deepest secrets, those obstacles he unwittingly places between himself and the therapist, and to maximize his opportunities for applying therapeutic leverage.

It is important to recognize that these opportunities

occur only intermittently and unpredictably. To be sure, as therapy progresses and as his emotional ties to the therapist deepen, the patient's general defensiveness may be expected to lessen. However, the therapeutic strategy must be aimed at making the patient aware of the frustrations inherent in his emotional isolation (the tendency to ward off the influence of another person and interpersonal relatedness in general), thereby arousing his affect and intensifying his conflict. When these experiences reach a certain strength, it is possible for the therapist to strike "while the iron is hot." Thus, he is in a position to exert a powerful influence and to have a strong impact on the patient's defenses.

In the above sense it is true that modern psychoanalysis is primarily concerned with the analysis of "ego defenses," *as they manifest themselves in the immediacy of the patient-therapist relationship,* not with the recall of "repressed" memories or other "unconscious content." To the extent that psychotherapy concerns itself with data in the here-and-now, it is, or has the potential of becoming, an empirical science. Reconstructions or the postulation of hypotheses about past experiences that *might* be the "causes" of what is happening in the present may be an interesting intellectual exercise, often quite gratifying to patient and therapist, but they are of little therapeutic value in their own right. The only possibility of effecting therapeutic change lies squarely in what can be forged out of the forces presently at work. This assertion seems so self-evident that it should hardly bear repeating were it not for the fact that it continues to be persistently misunderstood by the opponents of the dynamic therapies. Present events must be understood and explained in terms of the forces at work in the patient-therapist relationship, of which the major ones have been delineated above.

The analysis and understanding of current interpersonal dynamics must make allowance for "unconscious" beliefs and assumptions, fantasies, distortions, body armor, etc., that often govern aspects of the patient's behavior in

142

relation to the therapist (as well as other significant people in the patient's life). To deprecate or ignore them, as is done by many forms of today's nondynamic therapies, is to grossly underestimate the complexity of human behavior and its determinants. Presently it is important to distinguish whether one is studying these forces in their own right or whether one is primarily concerned with producing modifications of specific aspects of the patient's behavior. Freud's notion that the study of these forces and therapy go hand in hand is partly a convenient fiction that has opened the door to interminable therapy. On the other hand, the trouble is that we often do not know whether the dissection of a given belief system or fantasy will result in therapeutic gains, from which it follows that we need to achieve a better understanding of what will pay off and what won't. By focusing on one "problem" at a particular time as opposed to numerous others, the therapist is implicitly making such judgments anyway, although they do not seem to be very systematic. The standard injunction to analyze "from the surface" and "defenses first" vaguely calls attention to the overriding significance of present events or contemporary forces in the sense discussed in this chapter; however, the formulation is far too general to be of real value.

To put the matter bluntly, it is becoming increasingly clear that psychoanalytic writings about technique, while embodying important truths concerning the management of interpersonal forces in the therapeutic relationship are of very limited value to the practicing psychotherapist. What does the psychotherapist need to know, and what is excess baggage (that, moreover, has the unfortunate effect of obscuring what he should be concerned with)?

What the psychotherapist needs to know is how to operate within an interpersonal field of forces; he needs to understand the structure and the constraints he imposes upon the relationship and how the patient maneuvers under these pressures. He needs to have some hypotheses about *why* the patient maneuvers as he does, that is, why he maneuvers in a rigid, maladaptive ("transference") way as opposed to some other way. He needs to *understand* the patient as a struggling person; he needs to be clear about the nature of the influence he can exert on this field of forces in an attempt to modify a significant aspect of the patient's feelings and behavior. The therapist must have relatively specific goals as to what he can achieve at a particular juncture and what he may be able to achieve over a period of time; he must have some estimate of the probability of achieving a particular objective; he must understand the forces working against him, not only within the patient and in the therapeutic relationship, but also in the patient's total life, in order to cope with them adequately. In short, the therapist must be clear as to where the patient "lives," where he wants to go (which may need modification in terms of what, in the therapist's view, is possible and realistic); where he needs to go in order to suffer less (which inevitably engages the therapist's moral and cultural values); and what the therapist can do to help him get there.

What he does not need is constructs such as instincts, ego apparatuses, id, superego, a catalogue of defense mechanisms, narcissism, passivity, latent homosexuality, and many others. The utility and value of each concept or construct in current use need to be closely examined for their value in the context of therapeutic operations—a task that is long overdue. It may be surmised that as a result of this pruning a terser and much more concise vocabulary will result. Again, it is of the utmost importance to distinguish between the utility of concepts for therapeutic operations and for other purposes. Thus far, there has been an unfortunate intermingling of concepts and therapeutic techniques without much regard for the considerations mentioned above.

I have called attention in Chapters Three and Four to the fact that psychotherapy typically attempts *a variety of tasks,* that these tasks are often quite disparate, and that they may call for very different strategies. These tasks are grouped under the umbrella term "psychotherapy" because they all involve learning within the context of an interpersonal relationship that assigns to the therapist a position of great influence and power. It seems clear that the "modification" of a particular symptom or behavior is only one of the tasks—and often not a central one—undertaken by the therapist. Nevertheless, the evaluation of therapeutic outcomes—at least in American science—is largely based on *observable* changes of this kind. By the same token, the emphasis of this chapter rests on the understanding and management of interpersonal forces, hence on the development of psychotherapy as a technology. It is undeniably important to move in that direction.

As the contemporary pendulum has swung toward the perfection of a therapeutic technology, however, there has been a concomitant deemphasis on the *experiential* aspects of the psychotherapeutic enterprise. To be sure, these factors have been kept in the foreground by the existential and humanistic forms of psychotherapy, but it is important to underscore their presence in all psychotherapeutic forms. I wish to assert that they are present whether or not they are openly recognized or detected by our admittedly crude measuring instruments. While exceedingly elusive, the components appear just as real as symptom change. Alexander's concept of the "corrective emotional experience" appears to encompass the phenomena only partially.

Unlike the medical patient whose personality remains essentially unchanged when he is treated for an infection or a broken leg (although here, too, a prolonged or serious illness may have a profound personal significance), the psychotherapy patient, unless the symptom is trivial, undergoes a personally meaningful experience. He loses not only a symptom or modifies some aspect of his behavior, but he often changes his outlook on life, his values, his view of himself. Psychotherapy, especially when carried on for extended periods of time, *may* effect profound changes of this kind. Just as education, in the best sense of the term, consists of something other than the acquisition of facts or skills, so psychotherapy may affect the patient in a deep sense. If he is successful, the therapist launches the patient on a different course of life, inculcates some of his values, fosters self-examination, self-knowledge, and honesty, and he participates in the individual's personal development. There are no known "techniques" for effecting such an outcome nor can the outcome be "measured" on a scale or assigned a monetary value.

When Freud abandoned the search for techniques designed to "cure" hysteria and instead turned attention to the life style of the persons in whom hysterical symptoms frequently occurred, he began to forge a tool for the personal development of the individual. His ambivalence concerning psychoanalysis as a therapeutic technique is probably traceable to his inability or unwillingness to draw a clear distinction between psychoanalysis as a treatment technique and psychoanalysis as an educational enterprise. He wanted it both ways, which in retrospect proved impossible. That is, psychoanalysis as an educational enterprise. He wanted it symptoms has not proven to be very impressive. It is a vulnerable target for behavior therapists whose techniques, at least with certain disorders, are far more effective. Today psychoanalysts, to the extent that they have clarified their goals, tend to lean toward a conception of psychotherapy as an educational process designed to enhance the individual's personal development. Toward the end of his life, this was the position Freud began to embrace.

Even when these goals are raised to preeminence, the objective is still to investigate and mitigate the barriers against interpersonal trust, that is, the entanglements resulting from conflicts between individual strivings and the demands for obedience and acculturation. As these problems are dealt with and resolved, the individual becomes freer to examine his place in the world, to struggle with existential issues, and to evolve his own philosophy of life. In this endeavor he may greatly profit from whatever wisdom,

146

perspective, and insight the therapist has acquired through his own (and hopefully richer) life experience.

Psychotherapy in this sense far transcends conceptions of "behavior modification," and the question of "therapeutic outcomes" as usually formulated assumes a ring of superficiality. The quest for self-knowledge and individuation (in Jung's sense) is a quest for meaning, not for adaptation or adjustment to conditions as they are. In this sense, psychotherapy is revolutionary because it incisively questions prevailing values. Above all, it extols the individual, and, unlike any other human enterprise in contemporary society, persists in the most critical and personal examination of an individual's place in the world.

References

Alexander, F. 1963. "The Dynamics of Psychotherapy in the Light of Learning Theory," *Am. J. Psychia.,* 120: 440-448.

Dollard, J. and Miller, N. E. 1950. *Personality and Psychotherapy.* New York: McGraw-Hill.

Eysenck, H. J. 1952. "The Effects of Psychotherapy: An Evaluation," *J. Con. Psychol.,* 16: 319-324.

———— 1960. *Behavior Therapy and the Neuroses.* New York: Pergamon Press.

Frank, J. D. 1961. *Persuasion and Healing: A Comparative Study of Psychotherapy.* Baltimore: Johns Hopkins Press.

———— 1970. "Therapeutic Factors in Psychotherapy," paper presented at the meetings of the Association for the Advancement of Psychotherapy, New York City.

Haley, J. 1963. *Strategies of Psychotherapy.* New York: Grune & Stratton.

Hilgard, J. 1970. *Personality and Hypnosis.* Chicago: University of Chicago Press.

Miller, N. E. 1969. "Learning of Visceral and Glandular Responses," *Sci.*, 163: 434-445.

Shapiro, A. K. 1971. "Placebo Effects in Medicine, Psychotherapy, and Psychoanalysis," in *Handbook of Psychotherapy and Behavior Change: An Empirical Aanlysis,* ed. A. E. Bergin and S. L. Garfield, pp. 439-473. New York: John Wiley.

Truax, C. B., and Carkhuff, R. R. 1967. *Toward Effective Counseling and Psychotherapy: Training and Practice.* Chicago: Aldine.

Waelder, R. 1960. *Basic Theories of Psychoanalysis.* New York: International Universities Press.

Part II
The Therapist's Contribution:
Empirical Studies (1)

$\mathbb{H}$ow similar or different are the techniques of psychotherapists? Of what factors in their professional training and experience are observed differences a function? How important a contributor to differences in technique is the therapist's theoretical orientation?—whether his training had included personal therapy? Do psychiatrists, psychologists, and social workers differ from each other? To what extent do characteristics of the patient influence the therapist's technique? Are differences in technique systematically related to the therapist's clinical impressions, diagnostic judgments, prognostic ratings? How do these judgments affect the therapist's communications? What part do the therapist's attitudes toward the patient play? Do they affect the degree of empathy he communicates to the patient?

Little specific information on these and related issues

151

was available when the studies presented in this section were undertaken. Undoubtedly part of the reason was that few people believed that such data were needed. While clinical psychoanalysis tacitly acknowledged the existence of individual differences in therapists, it was assumed that these differences mattered little, so long as they did not interfere with the progress of therapy. The therapist's didactic (or training) analysis was designed to eliminate, or at least sharply reduce, so-called countertransference reactions. For the rest, thorough training in psychoanalytic technique was to carry the major weight in the therapist's total effort. Specifically it was denied that the therapist's personality, particularly its positive aspects, constituted a potent force in the therapeutic endeavor. It was argued that the course and outcome of psychotherapy were predominantly determined by: (1) Variables in the patient, such as degree of impairment, ego strength, motivation to seek change, "analyzability," chronicity of his problems, youth, education, and so forth; (2) the therapist's technical expertise in applying psychoanalytic principles; and, to a lesser extent, (3) situational variables, such as family pressures, economic constraints, etc., that might adversely affect the process of the intrapsychic changes that were the main focus of therapy.

To be sure, some questionnaire data obtained by Glover (1955) from British analysts in the late Thirties drew attention to marked individual differences among practitioners whose training had presumably been quite homogeneous. Some years later, Franz Alexander (1963) emphasized the importance of what he termed the patient's corrective emotional experience, which, in his view, was mediated by the analyst on the basis of what he "was" rather than what he "did." Furthermore, Alexander (1958) had become keenly aware of the therapist's personality as a potent force in therapy, describing it as "the most opaque area" in need of exploration.

The students of Carl Rogers, beginning in the early 1940s, undertook numerous studies centered on quanti-

152

fication of various aspects of the therapeutic interaction. The thrust of the early work was designed to enhance the therapist's nondirectiveness, operationally defined as the ratio of communications called "nondirective" in relation to all the therapist's communications. Later, Rogers (1957) deemphasized formal techniques, elevating such therapist qualities as genuineness, warmth, unconditional positive regard, and congruence to a position of preeminence. He went so far as to describe these as the necessary and sufficient conditions for constructive personality change.

When I began to undertake research in this area in the early 1950s, my work was guided by these considerations:

1. In order to achieve a better understanding of the therapeutic process it is essential to describe and quantify salient aspects.

2. In order to assess the relative effectiveness of different therapeutic techniques, ways and means must be found to compare the activities of the psychotherapist along meaningful dimensions.

3. Until we are able to carry out such comparisons, it is futile to discuss outcomes of different forms of psychotherapy on the basis of simple percentage figures.

4. Individual differences among therapists appear to be a potent variable determining a patient's acceptance or rejection for therapy, as well as the course and outcome of any psychotherapeutic endeavor.

5. While patient differences are undeniably important and perhaps the most significant factor in therapeutic change, the crux of psychotherapy research relates to the nature of the psychological influence the therapist brings to bear on the patient and the conditions enhancing or impeding it.

In retrospect, I was dimly aware that the therapist's personality and techniques are almost inextricably intertwined.

A major problem confronting the would-be researcher in this area was the absence of adequate methodological tools that would permit even the most elementary comparisons of psychotherapists. Consequently I proposed to execute comparisons between different psychotherapists and to relate observed differences to major variables in their professional training and experience, using the best available methods; I also began to devote concerted effort toward the development of more adequate tools for carrying out comparisons between therapists and their techniques. The first objective led to the studies described in this part of the volume; the second gave rise to the system of content-analysis explained in Part VII. As the system took form, it was employed in some of the later studies described in this part and applied to the analysis of interviews reported in the literature (see Part III).

It was also clear from the beginning that in order to carry out comparisons between therapists it was mandatory to hold constant as many patient and situational variables as possible. Only in this manner would it be appropriate to attribute observed differences among practitioners to variables within them. This requirement resulted in the choice of analogue procedures that unify the studies reported in the following pages. While this compromise obviously introduced a measure of artificiality, it assured a relatively high degree of experimental control and research economy.

Starting with a fairly primitive technique in which therapists were presented with cards on which selected patient statements had been printed, the work progressed to the use of sound films, the most recent of which were specifically constructed for the present research purpose. (The quality of the analogues I employed was directly a function of the degree to which the research was financially supported by granting agencies; in other words, if the researcher operates on a shoestring budget, he is forced to employ primitive techniques.) The first three chapters were culled from my doctoral dissertation, which I completed as

154

a part-time graduate student earning his living through other, less exciting pursuits. The next three chapters form another series: they are based on a large-scale study involving well over 200 psychotherapists spanning a wide range of experience and several theoretical orientations. The final study included in this part was essentially a replication of the earlier work. Employing a somewhat more refined methodology, it was particularly addressed to the question of whether patient differences accounted for appreciable variations in therapist activity.

Two sets of findings emerging from this research (which covered the period of about a decade) impress me as particularly noteworthy:

1. I was struck by the vast differences among individual psychotherapists. The qualitative differences, while more difficult to demonstrate, far outweighed any quantatative considerations. This realization gave rise to the distinction between Group I therapists, whom I described as more tolerant, more humane, more permissive, more "democratic," and more "therapeutic"; and Group II therapists, whom I characterized as more directive, disciplinarian, moralistic and harsh. The implications of these findings are spelled out in the discussion on pp. 365-373 . The hypothesis stated at the end of that section draws attention to the distinction between *specific* and *nonspecific* factors in psychotherapy, a problem that has continued to occupy me as a crucial issue in this field.

2. I was equally impressed by the remarkable degree to which the therapist's judgments about a patient were intertwined with his feelings and attitudes toward that person. The results pointed up the basic question of how much in clinical work is "out there" (that is, in "reality," in the patient) and how much is "within" (that is, the therapist's own reactions to the other person). The latter reactions, I came to appreciate, must have a pervasive influence on what occurs in the therapeutic relationship, and thus, from a

somewhat different angle, they inspired a skeptical view of technique ("specific") variables as a potent force in all forms of psychotherapy. I believe that these results document, in the clinical area, what Rosenthal (1966) and others have since identified as observer effects in behavioral science research. I also believe that the full implications of these suggestive results are yet to be explored.

References

Alexander, F. 1958. "Unexplored Areas in Psychoanalytic Theory and Treatment," *Behav. Sci.,* 3: 293-316.

—— 1963. "The Dynamics of Psychotherapy in the Light of Learning Theory." *Am. J. Psychiat.,* 120: 440-448.

Glover, E. 1955. *The Technique of Psychoanalysis.* New York: International Universities Press.

Rogers, C. R. 1959. "The Necessary and Sufficient Conditions of Therapeutic Personality Change," *J. Cons. Psychol.,* 21: 95-103.

Rosenthal, R. 1966. *Experimenter Effects in Behavioral Research.* New York: Appleton-Century-Crofts.

6

ROGERIAN AND
PSYCHOANALYTIC TECHNIQUES

The research effort by Carl Rogers and his students to
describe and elucidate the process of nondirective counseling
has provided objective evidence in an area in which such
evidence has been sorely lacking. Unfortunately, this impetus has not extended to other theories of psychotherapy, particularly those based more explicitly upon psychoanalytic
principles, which today claim a numerically much larger
following. The result of this development is a reasonably
well-documented body of knowledge concerning client-centered counseling but almost a total absence of empirical data
on psychoanalytically oriented therapy (cf. Saslow's recent
review, 1954).*

---

*Grateful acknowledgment is made to Professor Curtis E. Tuthill, Dr.
E. Lakin Phillips, and Leon Salzman, M.D., for valuable suggestions
and criticisms.

It is not surprising that much of the published research has focused upon the results of treatment and upon the development of methodologies for the description of the interpersonal process of therapy. It was also inevitable that the patient, for whose benefit the treatment is conducted, would receive a fair share of attention from investigators; it is less apparent why so little research effort has been expended upon the psychotherapist. Yet, it is almost axiomatic that the therapist's personality and attitudes are the prime determiners of the character of his therapeutic operations. On the nondirective side, several investigators have given attention to the therapist's verbal behavior (Porter, 1942; Seeman 1949; Snyder, 1945; among others), but with the exception of a few isolated studies, no systematic attempt has been made to study the techniques of psychotherapists not subscribing to the Rogerian frame of reference. The work reported by Fiedler (1953) in Mowrer's recent compendium represents an important beginning, but it must be broadened in scope and supplemented by a good deal of down-to-earth exploratory research to give us a better idea of what is meant by such dimensions as "expertness," "ideal therapeutic relationship," etc. In short, as research into the process of psychotherapy increases and as psychotherapy acquires the status of a scientific discipline, we may expect to see a concomitant rise in the number of investigations concerning the contributions of the psychotherapist to the treatment situation.

In keeping with this orientation, this chapter attempts an empirical comparison between the psychotherapeutic techniques used by Rogerian and psychoanalytically oriented psychologists. Techniques of psychotherapy are rational and systematic procedures designed to produce an amelioration of the patient's mental health. Every communication by the therapist is ideally placed in the service of the overall objectives of therapy, as conceived and elaborated in the prominent theories. Techniques may therefore be considered as theory translated into action. Without getting embroiled in

158

discussions about the extent to which Rogers' client-centered theory is basically different from psychoanalytic principles, or whether Rogers' theory is in fact nondirective, it is evident that differences in emphasis do exist among the major theories of psychotherapy. So much is certain. But what about theory in action? Do the operations of psychotherapists proceed in accordance with the theoretical precepts to which they claim allegiance? If so, we would know at least that different theories lead to specific therapeutic procedures predictable from the theory, although the therapeutic effectiveness of any procedure is thereby no further elucidated. If not, theory would have little practical import for therapy.

Investigations of the techniques of Rogerian counselors have shown (Porter, 1942; Seeman, 1949; Snyder, 1945) that they make considerable use of the techniques advocated by Rogers, such as reflections of feeling, nondirective leads, etc. With respect to psychoanalytically oriented therapy we have few objective data. It is well known, of course, that the ultimate emphasis of psychoanalytic technique rests upon interpretation, especially of the transference situation in the broadest sense. However, interpretations are not to be made frequently, indiscriminately, or at all in the initial phases of therapy (Fromm-Reichmann, 1950, ch. VIII). What techniques, then, does the psychoanalytically oriented therapist use at the beginning of therapy when the patient has as yet produced little information and the therapist is still unclear about the underlying dynamics? By singling out the Rogerian and psychoanalytic systems for the present comparison, we hope to provide objective evidence on the operational similarities and differences of two important theoretical orientations.

Specifically, followers of Rogers' system, in accordance with the principles enunciated in *Counseling and Psychotherapy* (1942) and *Client-centered Therapy* (1951), should be distinguishable from non-Rogerian therapists in regard to technique in (1) a larger number of "reflective" responses, (2) fewer interpretations, (3) fewer exploratory questions, (4)

159

less reassurance, (5) fewer instances of passive rejection and outright antagonism. Analytically oriented therapists, on the other hand, should differ from Rogerians in (1) offering a larger number of interpretations, (2) more explorations, and (3) fewer reflective responses.

Finally, it was hypothesized that the variable of personal analysis might disclose systematic differences in verbal techniques. Our concern here is exclusively with a limited aspect of the therapeutic process only—the therapist's verbal contribution, which is at no time considered coextensive with his total contribution to the treatment situation. But since techniques are described, advocated, taught, and manipulated, it is a legitimate undertaking to inquire into their application and to explore the extent to which they are a function of the practitioner's theoretical orientation.

METHOD

To study the therapist's verbal behavior under reasonably standardized conditions it was considered advisable to avoid the complexities of the actual therapeutic situation, but rather to have the therapist respond to a carefully preselected sample of patient communications. Thus, a series of 27 short paragraphs of patient statements was culled from published therapeutic interviews and typed on individual cards. A bare minimum of background information preceded each statement. It was stipulated that the materials pertained to early interviews to forestall the possible criticism that the interpersonal relationship between therapist and patient would make it difficult to formulate a response. The 27 statements were regarded to be a fairly representative cross section of verbalizations typically heard from neurotic patients in early interviews. Represented in the series were a variety of complaints, statements by a seriously disturbed near-psychotic patient, suicide threats, and other transference reactions, such as blocking, negativism, requests for direct advice, and open hostility.

Such "miniature therapeutic situations" obviously introduce a certain degree of artificiality and fall short of replicating the actual therapeutic session. While the degree of correspondence between the therapist's actual operations (the criterion) and his performance in a "test" situation should eventually be explored, we may, for the present, grant a certain conditional validity to our experimental procedure.

PROCEDURE AND SUBJECTS

Therapists who had indicated a willingness to participate were visited and interviewed individually. Cooperation was surprisingly good, and very few of the therapists who were approached refused. Each interview lasted about one and a half to two hours.

The respondent was presented with the experimental series of patient statements and requested to state what response, if any, he would make to the hypothetical patient. Information concerning the therapist's training, experience, theoretical orientation, etc., was collected at the end of the session.

The subjects were 15 psychologists engaged in the practice of psychotherapy; 8 were Rogerians and 7 were psychoanalytically oriented. Practically all respondents were attached to clinics in the Washington, D. C., area, and in addition to psychotherapy performed diagnostic and related functions. The data were supplemented by responses similarly collected from 25 psychiatrists and 9 psychiatric social workers, who constituted two psychoanalytically oriented reference groups.

Seven psychologists had more than five years of experience in therapy, and will be referred to as "experienced therapists." Table 1, which presents the respondents' experience level, also indicates that five Rogerians and six non-Rogerian psychologists had undergone personal analysis as part of their training. Rogerians and non-Rogerians appear

161

162

TABLE 1

THE SAMPLE BY EXPERIENCE LEVEL AND PERSONAL ANALYSIS

Group	Personal analysis			No personal analysis			Total
	Experi-enced	Inex-perienced	Sub-total	Experi-enced	Inex-perienced	Sub-total	
Rogerian psychologists	3	2	5	1	2	3	8
Psychoanalytically oriented psychologists	3	3	6	0	1	1	7
Total	6	5	11	1	3	4	15

to be well equated as regards experience level and personal analysis.*

RESULTS

Therapists' responses were categorized by Bales' system of interaction process analysis (1950), a well-known general purpose framework for describing social interactions. This system commended itself for present purposes because of its theoretical neutrality as to the conflicting schools of psychotherapy and because of the concentrated effort that has gone into the formulations.

The psychologists' responses yielded a total of 553 score units (mostly simple sentences or thought segments). The reliability of the categorizations was tested by several methods and found to be 78 per cent.†

Table 2 shows Bales' 12 categories, together with the responses of Rogerians and non-Rogerians assigned to each. Figure 1 presents the same results in profile form. The t values (computed by the formula for uncorrelated percentages) indicate highly statistically significant differences

---

*A certain degree of heterogeneity must be assumed among the respondents. There is no "pure" Rogerian just as there is no "pure" psychoanalytically oriented therapist. Most Rogerians must have come in contact with psychoanalytic concepts, particularly those who had undergone personal psychoanalysis. The converse is not necessarily true. Also, while there is considerable diversity in psychoanalytic thinking, most therapists surveyed here (including psychiatrists and social workers) had come under the influence of the Washington School of Psychiatry, and thus espoused neo-Freudian principles and concepts. The classificatory problem was resolved by including all psychoanalytically oriented therapists in one group and all therapists who acknowledged Rogerian influences in the other.

†Since data were collected from psychiatrists and social workers for related projects, the reliability was tested upon a stratified random sample of 20 per cent of the cases. The reliability percentage figure represents the average agreement among three judges who independently scored 370 response units.

TABLE 2

SCORING CATEGORIES AND RESPONSE FREQUENCIES

Category No.	Interaction process analysis definition	"Psychotherapeutic" definition*	Rogerians' responses		Non-Rogerians' responses		t
			N	%	N	%	
1	*Shows solidarity*, raises other's status, gives help, reward	Gives reassurance, encouragement, shows compassion, tenderness.	8	2.6	13	5.3	1.69
2	*Shows tension release*, jokes, laughs, shows satisfaction.	Not applicable†	0	0	0	0	
3	*Agrees*, shows passive acceptance, understands, concurs, complies.	Shows passive acceptance, understanding, is permissive (includes silences).	16	5.2	39	15.8	4.10‡
4	*Gives suggestion*, direction, implying autonomy for other.	Proposes course of action, defines ("structures") the therapeutic situation.	3	1.0	15	6.1	3.46‡
5	*Gives opinion*, evaluation, analysis, expresses feeling, wish.	Interprets, analyzes behavior patterns; thought in process, inferential reasoning.	11	3.6	25	10.0	3.10‡
6	*Gives orientation*, information, repeats, clarifies, confirms.	Restates, clarifies, "reflects" (Rogerian response).	231	75.5	35	14.2	14.26‡

No.	Category	Example*					
7	*Asks for orientation,* information, repetition, confirmation.	Asks factual questions, expresses lack of knowledge, uncertainty.	0	0	17	6.9	4.60‡
8	*Asks for opinion,* evaluation, analysis, expression of feeling.	Explores, asks for elaboration or expression of feeling (includes open-ended questions, "non-directive leads").	30	9.8	88	35.6	7.37‡
9	*Asks for suggestion,* direction, possible ways of action.	Not applicable.†	0	0	0	0	
10	*Disagrees,* shows passive rejection, formality, withholds help.	Shows passive rejection, disbelief; ignores requests or complaints; thwarts, frustrates.	3	1.0	13	5.3	3.14‡
11	*Shows tension,* asks for help, withdraws out of field.	Not applicable.†	0	0	0	0	
12	*Shows antagonism,* deflates other's status, defends or asserts self.	Shows antagonism, aggression, sarcasm, irony, cynicism.	4	1.3	2	.8	.56
	Total		306	100.0	247	100.0	

* This column gives examples of the kinds of responses by therapists included in the categories, which were in no way redefined.
† The absence of responses in these categories is probably a function of the experimental conditions under which responses were elicited.
‡ Significant at the .01 level of confidence.

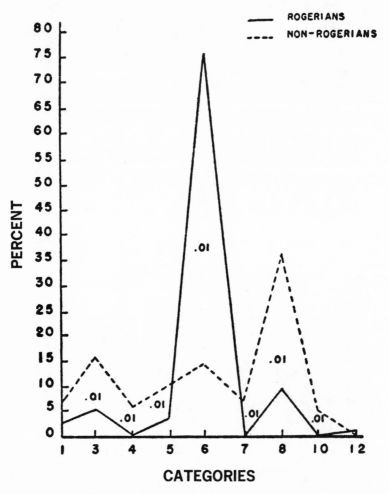

FIGURE 1. Response distributions of Rogerian and psychoanalytically oriented psychotherapists.

between Rogerian and analytically oriented therapists in almost all applicable categories. A chi-square test for the distributions is significant beyond the .001 level of confidence.

Figures 2 and 3 attempt a comparison between experienced and inexperienced therapists in each of the two groups. Rogerian therapists show a highly significant decline

166

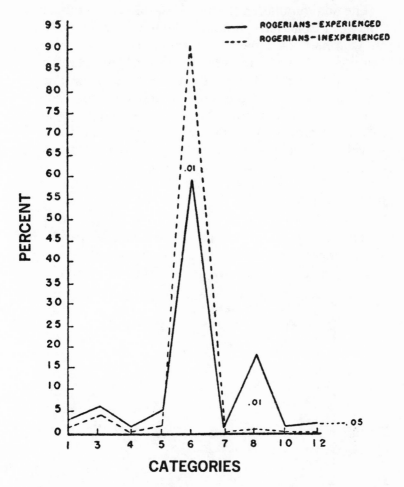

FIGURE 2. A comparison of the response distributions of experienced and inexperienced Rogerian psychotherapists.

in reflective responses (Category 6) with increasing experience, and a corresponding rise in exploratory responses (Category 8). The difference in Category 12 appears to be of little practical importance. Chi square is again highly statistically significant. Differences between experienced and inexperienced analytically oriented practitioners seem to be due to chance.

The final tabulation (Figure 4) shows considerable overlap between Rogerian therapists who had been analyzed and those who had not. Noteworthy differences are observed in Categories 3 and 8: analyzed therapists give significantly fewer responses classifiable as passive acceptance and explorations. Because of the small number of clinicians involved in this comparison, the results must be considered highly tentative. (Chi square was significant at about the .14 level.) A similar comparison for non-Rogerian therapists proved unfeasible for the same reason.

DISCUSSION

The sharp differences between Rogerian and psychoanalytically oriented psychologists constitute a striking finding, which in general confirms the predictions made from theor-

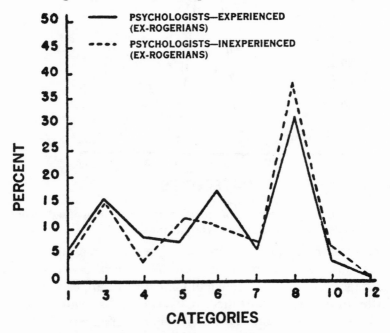

FIGURE 3. A comparison of the response distributions of experienced and inexperienced non-Rogerian psychotherapists.

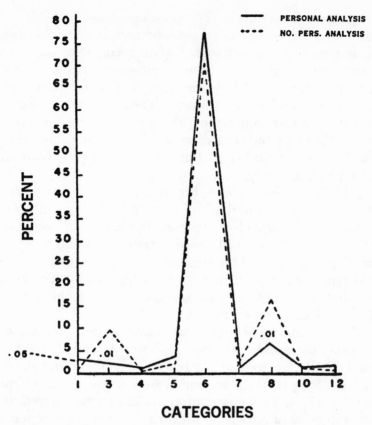

FIGURE 4. Response distributions of analyzed and unanalyzed Rogerian psychotherapists.

etical expositions. Thus, it is noted that Rogerians rely heavily on reflective techniques, with a corresponding neglect for other types of responses. The present frequency of reflective responses (75 per cent) falls about midway between two comparable figures reported for actual therapeutic interviews. Using a somewhat different classification scheme, Snyder (1945) categorized 62.6 per cent of counselor responses as "nondirective," whereas Seeman (1949) gave a figure of 85 per cent. Non-Rogerians, while showing a pronounced predilection for exploratory responses, reveal more that minimal frequencies in such categories as passive

169

acceptance, structuring, interpretation, and possibly re-assurance, direct factual questions, and passive rejection. Their responses are distributed more evenly over the range of techniques than those of the Rogerians and, as was shown in another context, closely resemble the response patterns of psychiatrists and social workers. These results, of course, indicate nothing concerning the relative effectiveness of these techniques, but regardless of other considerations there is at least the possibility that undue preoccupation with any one technique may lead to stereotypy.

The data presented in Figure 2 indicate a noteworthy decline of responses in the Rogerians' most favored category, which is not paralleled by non-Rogerians. An analogous difference was observed between experienced and inexperi-enced psychiatrists. This suggests that an increase in pro-fessional experience leads to a diversification of technique, and that, conversely, reliance on one specific technique is a characteristic of inexperience.

The differences between analyzed and unanalyzed Rogerian therapists, exhibited in Figure 4, while based on a small number of cases, are in general agreement with similar analyses for psychiatrists, non-Rogerian psychologists, and social workers. This observation applies particularly to the larger number of responses categorized as passive acceptance (no distinction was made between silent responses and other signs of passive acceptance, such as "Yes," "Mmmh," etc.). The statistically significant difference in exploratory re-sponses was not observed in any other analyses. While only inadequately explained at this time, this finding is of signifi-cance here because it clearly cuts across the Rogerian-non-Rogerian cleavage that these analyses have demonstrated.

The results of this investigation leave little doubt that adherence to the Rogerian frame of reference is an impor-tant determinant of a psychotherapist's techniques, trans-cending professional affiliation and experience level. Also, within the limits imposed by the experimental situation, psy-choanalytically oriented psychologists, psychiatrists, and social workers form a rather homogeneous group with respect to their therapeutic operations. Future investigations must refine these analyses and specify the conditions under which a given technique achieves a particular therapeutic effect.

SUMMARY

The major results of this study, one in a series of investigations to elucidate the psychotherapist's contribution to the treatment situation, may be summarized as follows.

1. Sharp differences exist between the response patterns of Rogerian and non-Rogerian therapists. As might be expected, Rogerians show a strong predilection for reflective responses, with a concomitant lack of responses in all other categories. Psychoanalytically oriented psychologists distribute their responses more evenly over a variety of techniques although they prefer explorations at this stage of therapy. The latter group agrees closely with psychiatrists and social workers whose techniques were investigated in related projects.

2. Rogerians disclose a significant decline in reflective responses as the level of their professional experience increases. While non-Rogerian psychologists fail to show a comparable trend, there is other evidence that an increase in experience leads to a diversification of therapeutic technique. Exclusive reliance on one technique appears to be a correlate of inexperience.

3. Analyzed Rogerians, like other therapists whose training has included personal analysis, show significantly fewer silent responses (passive acceptance).

This study thus provides preliminary objective evidence on the techniques of psychotherapists (psychologists) who are following respectively Rogerian and psychoanalytic principles, and documents pronounced differences in therapeutic technique specifically attributable to the clinician's theoretical viewpoint.

References

Bales, R. F. 1950. *Interaction Process Analysis.* Cambridge, Mass.: Addison-Wesley Press.

Fiedler, F. E. 1953. "Quantitative Studies on the Role of Therapists' Feelings toward Their Patients," in *Psychotherapy: Theory and Research,* ed. O. H. Mowrer, pp. 296-315. New York: Ronald.

Fromm-Reichmann, F. 1950. *Principles of Intensive Psychotherapy.* Chicago: University of Chicago Press.

Porter, E. H., Jr. 1942. "The Development and Evaluation of a Measure of Counseling Interview Procedures, *Educ. Psychol. Meas.,* 3: 105-125, 214-238.

Rogers, C. R. 1942. *Counseling and Psychotherapy.* Boston: Houghton Mifflin.

——— 1951. *Client-centered Therapy.* Boston: Houghton Mifflin.

Saslow, G. 1954. "Psychotherapy," *An. Rev. Psychol.,* 5: 311-336.

Seeman, J. A. 1949. "A Study of the Process of Nondirective Therapy." *J. Cons. Psychol.,* 13: 157-168.

Snyder, W. U. 1945. "An Investigation of the Nature of Nondirective Psychotherapy," *J. Gen. Psychol.,* 33: 193-223.

172

7

TECHNIQUE, PROFESSIONAL AFFILIATION, AND EXPERIENCE LEVEL

To the extent that psychotherapy aspires to scientific status, it must be based upon rational procedures that are capable of precise formulation and communication. Thus, psychotherapeutic operations are not teachable unless the requirement of communicability is met. To this end, psychotherapy must strive to make its working assumptions, hypotheses, and operations increasingly explicit and objective.*

Previous research in this field has dealt primarily with changes in the client as a result of therapy, diagnostic studies of the person seeking help, and the development of process measures. Few investigations have concerned themselves with the person of the therapist, and the character of his

---

*Grateful acknowledgment is made to Professor Curtis E. Tuthill, Dr. E. Lakin Phillips, and Leon Salzman, M.D., for valuable suggestions and criticisms.

173

contribution to the dyadic interpersonal situation known as psychotherapy. In Mowrer's (1953) recent compendium only one chapter (Fiedler's) specifically addresses itself to this problem. Yet it is almost axiomatic—and has been recognized in psychoanalytic writings since the time of Freud— that the therapist's personality, attitudes, past interpersonal experiences, and emotional blind spots are among the prime determiners of his therapeutic operations. It is believed that a program of research focusing on the therapist's contribution to the treatment situation is potentially productive for advancing our knowledge of psychotherapy.

As a first step, a series of exploratory studies directed at the therapist's verbal techniques has been conducted. This research attempts to answer the following questions: What techniques are used by psychotherapists of two theoretical orientations (Rogerian and psychoanalytic)? Are there systematic differences in technique attributable to professional affiliation and level of experience? Are there similar differences with respect to the therapeutic problem to which the therapist is addressing himself at the moment? What is the effect of the therapist's personal analysis upon his verbal operations? The first problem has been dealt with in the previous chapter. The second will occupy our attention in the next few pages. The remaining ones will be the subject of subsequent chapters.

METHOD

As described in the preceding chapter, it was considered advisable to avoid the complexities of the actual therapeutic situation, and to study therapists' verbal behavior through the use of a preselected sample of patient communications. The series of 27 short paragraphs of patient statements was used.

PROCEDURE AND SUBJECTS

Again, therapists who had agreed to participate were

visited and interviewed individually, each interview lasting about one and one-half to two hours.

The respondent was presented with the experimental series of patient statements and requested to state what response, if any, he would make to the hypothetical patient. The therapist was permitted to give as many or as few responses as he chose; "silent" responses were also considered acceptable, in contrast to the related study by Phillips and Agnew (1953), which restricted responses by a multiple-choice answer form. Therapists were asked to assume that the patient statements occurred early in treatment, that the problem came up for the first time, and that none of the patients were hospitalized. All responses and comments were recorded by the investigator.

Information concerning the therapist's training, experience, theoretical orientation, etc., was collected at the end of the interview.

The subjects were 25 psychiatrists, 7 psychologists, and 9 psychiatric social workers. All claimed allegiance to psychoanalytic or neo-Freudian principles, and most of them had received training from, or reported they had been influenced by, the Washington School of Psychiatry—a powerful agent molding the "therapeutic climate" in the Washington, D. C., area.

Fifteen psychiatrists, three psychologists, and seven social workers had five or more years of experience in psychotherapy and will be treated as "experienced therapists" in subsequent analyses. While such a dichotomy implies a certain arbitrariness, the distinction is quite clear cut in the case of psychiatrists: the experienced therapists were for the most part fully qualified analysts engaged in private practice of psychoanalysis, whereas the inexperienced group ($N = 10$) was made up largely of psychiatric residents with relatively little experience in therapy. The former group thus includes the greatest concentration of professional experience.

Psychologists and social workers were typically employed by local mental hygiene clinics, and in addition to

175

TABLE 1

SCORING CATEGORIES AND RESPONSE FREQUENCIES

Category No.	Interaction process analysis definition	"Psychotherapeutic" definition*	Psychiatrists		Psychologists		Social workers	
			n	%	n	%	n	%
1	Shows solidarity, raises other's status, gives help, reward.	Gives reassurance, encouragement, shows compassion, tenderness.	41	4.0	13	5.3	35	10.1
2	Shows tension release, jokes, laughs, shows satisfaction.	Not applicable.†						
3	Agrees, shows passive acceptance, understands, concurs, complies.	Shows passive acceptance, understanding, is permissive (includes silences).	184	18.1	39	15.8	70	20.3
4	Gives suggestion, direction, implying autonomy for other.	Proposes course of action, defines ("structures") the therapeutic situation.	65	6.4	15	6.1	16	4.6
5	Gives opinion, evaluation, analysis, expresses feeling, wish.	Interprets, analyzes behavior patterns; thought in process, inferential reasoning.	164	16.1	25	10.0	23	6.7
6	Gives orientation, information, repeats, clarifies, confirms.	Restates, clarifies, "reflects" (Rogerian response).	108	10.6	35	14.2	59	17.1

7	*Asks for orientation*, information, repetition, confirmation.	Asks factual questions, expresses lack of knowledge, uncertainty.	31	3.0	17	6.9	18	5.2
8	*Asks for opinion*, evaluation, analysis, expression of feeling.	Explores, asks for elaboration or expression of feeling (includes open-ended questions, "non-directive leads").	367	36.2	88	35.6	118	34.3
9	*Asks for suggestion*, direction, possible ways of action.	Not applicable.†						
10	*Disagrees*, shows passive rejection, formality, withholds help.	Shows passive rejection, disbelief; ignores requests or complaints; thwarts, frustrates.	44	4.3	13	5.3	5	1.4
11	*Shows tension*, asks for help, withdraws out of field.	Not applicable.†						
12	*Shows antagonism*, deflates other's status, defends or asserts self.	Shows antagonism, aggression, sarcasm, irony, cynicism.	13	1.3	2	.8	1	.3
	Total		1,017		247		345	

* This column gives examples of the kinds of responses by therapists included in the categories, which were in no way redefined.
† The absence of responses in these categories is probably a function of the experimental conditions under which responses were elicited.

psychotherapy performed diagnostic and related functions.*

RESULTS

Quantification of therapists' responses was accomplished by means of Bales' (1950) system of interaction process analysis, a well-known general purpose framework for describing social interactions. The system commended itself for present purposes because of the painstaking labor that went into its development, and its theoretical neutrality with respect to the teachings of conflicting "schools" of psychotherapy.

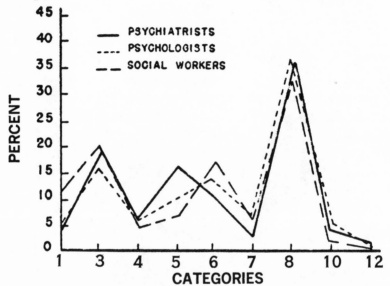

FIGURE 1. Response distributions of psychotherapists by professional affiliation.

Table 1 presents Bales' 12 categories, together with the response frequencies of psychiatrists, psychologists, and social workers.

*For a systematic comparison between the techniques of these psychoanalytically oriented psychologists and a comparable group of Rogerians see the previous chapter.

178

The reliability of the writer's categorizations was tested upon a stratified random sample of 10 cases comprising a total of 370 score units. Two judges who had been trained in the Bales method independently scored the ten "test" cases. Average rater agreement was 78 per cent.

Figure 1 presents the frequencies shown in Table 1 in profile form. Table 2 attempts a systematic comparison between the professional groups with respect to the percentages in any one response category. The t values (computed

TABLE 2

COMPARISONS (t VALUES) BETWEEN PROFESSIONAL GROUPS

Category	Psychiatrists versus psychologists		Psychiatrists versus social workers		Psychologists versus social workers	
1	.93		4.36†		2.09*	
3	.85	P	.92		1.41	
4	.18	P	1.20	P	.83	Ps
5	2.40*	P	4.48†	P	1.48	Ps
6	1.64		3.25†		.97	
7	2.79†		1.83		.85	Ps
8	.15	P	.63	P	.35	Ps
10	.67		2.42*	P	2.79†	Ps
12	.63	P	1.50	P	.83	Ps

P—The response frequency of psychiatrists exceeds that of the other group.
Ps—The response frequency of psychologists exceeds that of the other group.
* Significant at the .05 level using a two-tailed test.
† Significant at the .01 level using a two-tailed test.

by the formula for uncorrelated percentages) disclose the following statistically significant differences:

1. Psychiatrists tend to give a larger number of interpretive responses (Category 5) than either psychologists or social workers.
2. Psychiatrists and psychologists exceed psychiatric social workers in passive rejections (Category 10).
3. Psychiatric social workers make greater use of reassurance (Category 1) than either psychiatrists or psychologists.

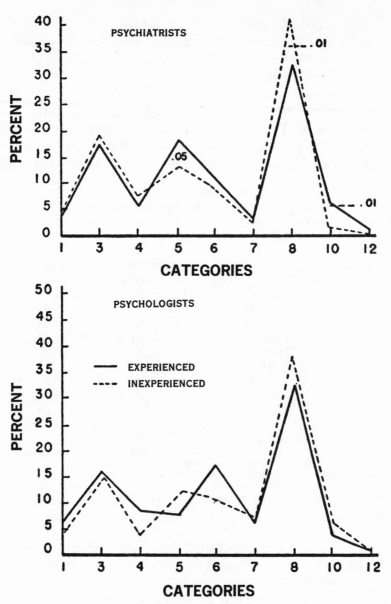

FIGURE 2. Response distributions of experienced and inexperienced psychotherapists. (Experienced psychiatrists $N = 15$, $n = 595$; inexperienced psychiatrists $N = 10$, $n = 422$; experienced psychologists $N = 3$, $n = 117$; inexperienced psychologists $N = 4$, $n = 130$.)

180

Inconsistent differences in Categories 6 and 7, while possibly quite real, have been disregarded for the present.

The next analysis addresses itself to the question of are there significant differences between the response distributions of experienced and inexperienced therapists within a professional group? In other words, what is the effect of length of professional experience upon technique?

Figure 2 shows the results in profile form, significant differences being indicated in the graph by the appropriate significance level. Social workers, while showing a response pattern similar to psychologists, have been omitted because of the very small N for inexperienced practitioners.

The distributions are again rather similar; however:

1. Experienced psychiatrists use more interpretations and a larger number of passive rejections.

2. Inexperienced psychiatrists reveal a predilection for exploratory responses (Category 8).

With respect to psychologists, none of the differences are statistically significant, but the shift in Category 8 seems to be in the same direction.

DISCUSSION

The most striking finding emerging from the comparison between psychotherapists of different professional affiliations but comparable theoretical orientation is the large degree of similarity of their response profiles.

Of the three statistically significant differences between professional groups, only one (reassurance) appears to be attributable to professional affiliation. The second (interpretation) is more adequately accounted for on the basis of experience level, and the third (passive rejection) is somewhat in doubt.

The preponderance of reassuring responses by social workers is a move away from insight-producing "uncovering" therapy, in that this technique assuages but actually changes little. This is not to say that a certain amount of reassurance may not be desirable, beneficial, or useful in the early stages of therapy, particularly with a seriously disturbed or very anxious patient.

The finding that psychiatrists exceed psychologists and social workers in the number of passive rejection responses is a provocative one, but because of the relatively small frequencies it is merely reported as suggestive of a possibly important difference (see below).

With regard to experience level, it is interesting to note that psychiatrists show somewhat greater divergence than psychologists. This may be a function of the greater differential in experience between experienced analysts and psychiatric residents than between psychologists of varying degrees of professional experience. While the sample of psychologists was small, the group appears to be fairly homogeneous as long as we disregard Rogerian therapists whose techniques, as we have shown in the previous chapter, are radically different.

The principal technique differences between experienced and inexperienced psychiatrists concern interpretations, explorations, and passive rejections.

As a psychiatrist becomes more experienced, he appears to place greater emphasis upon interpretations. It was also demonstrated (Strupp, 1954) that this characteristic not only differentiates reliably experienced psychiatrists from inexperienced ones but also from psychologists and social workers.

The significance of this result is twofold: (1) It attests to the emphasis given to interpretations by experienced psychiatrists in that this professional group follows, perhaps more closely than any other, psychoanalytic doctrine, which extols interpretation as the hallmark of intensive psychotherapy; (2) it contravenes to some extent the recommendations of such authorities as Fromm-Reichmann (1950) who caution against interpretations before sufficient information

182

to document this therapeutic maneuver has been obtained. Thus, psychiatrists, as the most thoroughly trained group of therapists, might be expected to be more wary of interpretations, but if such cautiousness does exist, it is not revealed by the present data.

Concerning the statistically highly significant difference between experienced and inexperienced psychiatrists in Category 8, the following observations appear warranted. Inexperienced therapists display a tendency to ask more exploratory questions, which by and large are made at the expense of interpretations and passive rejections. It appears altogether reasonable for a therapist, when confronted with a patient about whom he knows little, to ask for further information; but here we have objective evidence that inexperienced psychiatrists reveal a more pronounced tendency to develop a patient's theme along exploratory lines whereas experienced psychiatrists proceed more readily to interpretations. While we cannot answer the question as to which is more effective therapeutically, there is at least the suggestion that to the extent that explorations are a sign of inexperience, less experienced therapists with medical training subscribe to the precept: If in doubt, ask for more information.

This result gains further meaning in the light of the comparison between experienced and inexperienced Rogerian therapists presented in the previous chapter. It was shown there that inexperienced Rogerians give a significantly larger number of reflective responses than their more experienced colleagues, the reflective response being the most favored variety. In the present study, Category 8, the preferred response of psychiatrists, reveals the same relationship. The implication is clear: regardless of whether we deal with the Rogerian or the psychoanalytic frame of reference, the most popular (stereotyped?) technique derives a good deal of its popularity from inexperienced therapists, and undergoes a pronounced decline as the therapist becomes more experienced. It is true that this trend is more

183

pronounced for Rogerian psychologists than for analytically oriented psychiatrists, but the same conclusion seems justified: an increase in experience leads to a diversification of therapeutic technique, and, conversely, reliance on one specific technique is a characteristic of inexperience.

Because of the small frequencies, it is difficult to say whether passive rejection is a technique preferred by experienced psychiatrists or by psychiatrists in general, although we are inclined to tentatively accept the former interpretation.

SUMMARY AND CONCLUSIONS

The salient results of this, the second in a series of investigations to elucidate the psychotherapist's contribution to the treatment situation, may be summarized as follows:

1. The response profiles of the three professional groups manifest a considerable degree of similarity. Of the statistically significant differences, only one appears to be a function of professional affiliation, namely the psychiatric social workers' predilection for reassurance.

2. Comparisons between experienced and inexperienced practitioners among psychiatrists and psychologists (with social workers omitted because of a small N for inexperienced workers) disclose the following reliable differences: (a) experienced psychiatrists give a larger number of interpretive responses; (b) inexperienced psychiatrists show a preference for exploratory responses; (c) experienced psychiatrists use more passive rejections.

Thus, professional affiliation exerts a relatively minor influence upon the kinds of techniques used by psychiatrists, psychologists, and psychiatric social workers. As long as the variable of theoretical orientation is held constant, all therapists adhering to psychoanalytic principles employ very similar techniques. When experience level is taken into

184

account, psychologists emerge as a somewhat more homogeneous group compared to psychiatrists, for whom more conspicuous differences between experienced and inexperienced therapists are in evidence. Intensive training in psychotherapy seems to stress interpretations at the expense of exploratory (probing) responses and leads to a general diversification of technique. Previous evidence from Rogerian therapists provides added support for this latter conclusion.

References

Bales, R. F. 1950. *Interaction Process Analysis.* Cambridge, Mass.: Addison-Wesley Press.

Fromm-Reichmann, F. 1950. *Principles of Intensive Psychotherapy.* Chicago: University of Chicago Press.

Mowrer, O. H., ed. 1953. *Psychotherapy: Theory and Research.* New York: Ronald.

Phillips, E. L., and Agnew, J. W. 1953. "A Study of Rogers' 'Reflection' Hypothesis," *J. Clin. Psychol.,* 9: 281-284.

Strupp, H. H. 1954. "An Empirical Study of Certain Psychotherapeutic Operations: An Exploration of the Verbal Response Techniques of Psychiatrists, Psychologists, and Psychiatric Social Workers." Ph.D. dissertation, George Washington University.

8

EFFECT OF
PERSONAL ANALYSIS

Chapters Six and Seven have presented objective evidence on the techniques of Rogerian and psychoanalytically oriented psychotherapists and the verbal behavior of psychiatrists, psychologists, and psychiatric social workers of varying levels of experience. Those chapters also set forth the rationale for focusing attention upon the psychotherapist and for studying systematically the concomitants of his techniques. This chapter is an extension of the previous inquiry, and attempts to answer the question, what is the effect of the therapist's personal analysis upon his therapeutic techniques?*

Since the time of Freud no training requirement for

---

*The writer wishes to express his appreciation to Dr. Dorothy E. Green for valuable statistical advice.

the psychotherapist has been considered more important than his personal analysis, and the curricula of psychoanalytic training institutes have traditionally been built around this aspect of the candidate's training. In view of the voluminous literature on the subject, little need be said about the arguments commonly advanced in favor of this training requirement. Fromm-Reichmann's summary (1950), while perhaps unduly restrictive, is representative of current thinking:

> And so it is that, because of the interrelatedness between the psychiatrist's and the patient's interpersonal processes and because of the interpersonal character of the psychotherapeutic process itself, any attempt at intensive psychotherapy is fraught with danger, hence unacceptable, where not preceded by the future psychiatrist's personal analysis [p. 42].

If this position is correct, the experience of personal analysis should have a demonstrable effect upon the character of the therapist's operations. Even if present-day methods for objectively examining such an elusive variable are crude, there must be systematic differences between the techniques of therapists whose training has included personal analysis and those whose training has not.

THREE KINDS OF PATIENT MANEUVERS

SUICIDE THREATS : A suicide threat is one kind of power operation by which the patient attempts to bring a significant person under his control. The reaction is, of course, the culmination of a long series of frustrations, rebuffs, and injuries that have been inflicted in reality or fantasy upon the victim, and constitutes a grandiose attempt at revenge by turning the tables upon the perceived aggressor. Without attempting to give the dynamics more than cursory treatment, it may be recognized that a suicide threat contains as its essential ingredients: (1) profound disappointment, frustration, and suffering; and (2) pervasive reactions of rage, aggression, and hostility.

Operationally, self-destructive threats expressed by a patient may serve to evoke the therapist's pity and commiseration, they may be designed to perpetuate a dependent relationship, or they may represent a maneuver to dominate and to make the therapist responsible for the patient's actions.

With regard to recommended therapeutic approaches, Fromm-Reichmann (1950) states: "A thorough investigation of the validity of the causes for the patient's discouragement, unhappiness, or despair must be the starting point of every therapeutic approach to suicide, or suicidal attempts and fantasies [p. 198]." By the same token, reassurance or pity appears to be ill-advised: "If the therapist offers encouragement to patients' parataxic expectations by actually falling into the role of practical adviser, he retards the process of insight into the immature character of such expectations; hence he retards the process of resolving them [pp. 208-209]."

The first hypothesis tests whether therapists do what they preach: Hypothesis 1—When confronted with suicide threats, psychotherapists include in their responses (1) a relatively large number of explorations; (2) a relatively small number of responses that convey reassurance; and (3) a relatively small number of interpretations.

If the therapist who has undergone personal analysis is more clearly aware of the dynamics of the situation, Hypothesis 1 may be extended by stating that the predicted trend is more pronounced for therapists whose training has included personal therapy.

TRANSFERENCE REACTIONS: In its special psychotherapeutic meaning, transference refers to all processes whereby the patient reenacts in the therapeutic situation unresolved interpersonal conflicts, and casts the therapist into the role of the significant adult who figured prominently in the earlier experience. Transference constitutes the cornerstone of all modern conceptions of psychoanalytic therapy and is increasingly utilized by other forms of therapy as well. This emphasis also implies that a significant segment of the therapeutic work consists in clarifying the doctor-patient relationship and concomitantly the distortions that complicate the patient's living.

The giving of interpretations has to be carefully planned and timing is all-important. Interpretations that are offered prematurely, that is, before the establishment of a relatively durable doctor-patient relationship and relaxation of the patient's emotional defenses, are useless if not positively harmful. Still, transference reactions manifested by the patient at almost any stage of the treatment are likely to be dealt with by means of interpretations, particularly by analyzed therapists who themselves have been exposed to the psychoanalytic maxim of giving primary attention to transference phenomena. Thus, the second hypothesis is: Hypothesis 2—When confronted with transference reactions, psychotherapists employ a relatively large number of interpretations. Analyzed therapists exhibit this tendency to a greater extent.

SCHIZOID PRODUCTIONS: The third hypothesis deals with the productions of a single patient who appears seriously disturbed, and who gives the impression of being on the verge of a schizophrenic break. It appears plausible that such a patient would be treated differently early in therapy than one who is less disturbed, anxious, and confused. For one thing, the therapeutic effort obviously must be directed at bringing about a diminution rather than an increase in anxiety; for another, the therapist must attempt to obtain a fuller picture of the underlying dynamics. Since the technique of silence is often used to create "a sort of vacuum [which] pushes the patient into taking the initiative in the relationship" (Whitaker and Malone, 1953, p. 221), it necessarily increases the patient's anxiety, for which reason it would be contraindicated with a very anxious patient. As for the second objective, a fair number of exploratory questions may be anticipated. On the assumption that the analyzed therapist will be more sensitive to the requirements of the situation, the third hypothesis may be stated: Hypothesis 3—When confronted with the productions of a seriously disturbed, near-psychotic patient, psychotherapists employ (1) a relatively small number of silent responses, and (2) a relatively large number of explorations. Analyzed therapists follow this trend in more clear-cut fashion.

METHOD, PROCEDURE, AND SUBJECTS

A fuller description has been given in the previous chapter. Samples of psychotherapists' verbal behavior were elicited by presenting a series of 27 cards containing short paragraphs of patient statements selected from published therapeutic interviews. Included in the series, which was considered a fair cross section of verbalizations heard from neurotic patients in early interviews, were four suicide threats, six transference reactions (including an insistent request for direct advice, denials of the need for therapy,

TABLE 1

THE SAMPLE BY PROFESSIONAL AFFILIATION, EXPERIENCE LEVEL, AND PERSONAL ANALYSIS

Group	Personal analysis			No personal analysis			Total
	Exp.	In-exp.	Sub-total	Exp.	In-exp.	Sub-total	
Psychiatrists	14	3	17	1	7	8	25
Psychologists	3	3	6	0	1	1	7
Psychiatric social workers	6	1	7	1	1	2	9
Total	23	7	30	2	9	11	41

190

and examples of competitiveness and open hostility), and six complaint statements of a seriously disturbed near-psychotic patient.*

Subjects were the same 25 psychiatrists, 7 psychologists, and 9 psychiatric social workers who participated in the previous research (see Chapters Six and Seven). All were psychoanalytically oriented. Length of experience in psychotherapy ranged from 1 to 12 years, with a median of 5 years. Practically all of the experienced therapists (five years and above), and about half of the inexperienced therapists (less than five years) had undergone personal analysis as part of their training. These data are shown in Table 1. While no systematic information was obtained concerning the length of a respondent's personal analysis, it is safe to assume that for the most part it had been fairly extensive—

TABLE 2

BRIEF DESCRIPTION OF SCORING CATEGORIES

Category number	Core meaning
1	Reassurance
2	Not applicable*
3	Silence (passive acceptance)
4	Structuring
5	Interpretation
6	Reflection of feeling
7	Factual questions
8	Exploration
9	Not applicable*
10	Passive rejection
11	Not applicable*
12	Antagonism

* Probably a function of the experimental conditions under which responses were elicited.

certainly beyond one year. A few therapists who had only recently started their analysis were included in the unanalyzed group.

*Adapted from Rogers' case "Miss Tilden," reported in Snyder (1947); by permission of Professor Snyder.

RESULTS

Quantification of the therapists' responses was accomplished by means of Bales' (1950) system of interaction process analysis. A total of 1,609 score units was categorized by this method. Rater agreement was tested on a stratified random sample of 370 score units (10 cases) and found to be 78 per cent. A brief description of the scoring categories is given in Table 2.†

Figure 1 presents the response profiles of analyzed and unanalyzed therapists, regardless of professional affiliation.

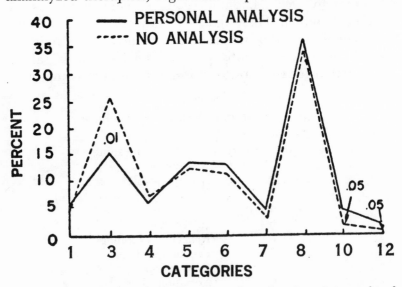

FIGURE 1. Response distributions of analyzed and unanalyzed therapists (personal analysis, $n = 1,173$; no personal analysis, $n = 436$).

The statistical analyses test the significance of percentage differences in a particular response category; t values significant at the .01 or .05 level are indicated in the figure. The findings may be summarized as follows:

1. The two response profiles show considerable overlap

---

†For a fuller description of the scoring categories, see Chapters Six and Seven.

192

in several of the major categories; nevertheless, a chi square computed on an over-all basis is significant beyond the .001 level of confidence.

2. A pronounced discrepancy occurs in Category 3, denoting that analyzed therapists give significantly fewer silent (passive acceptance) responses, and conversely that unanalyzed therapists are more passive.*

3. Small, but statistically significant differences in Categories 10 and 12 (passive rejection and antagonism), while possibly quite real, are based upon small frequencies and should be regarded as tentative.

Since the mean length of experience of analyzed therapists was significantly greater than that of unanalyzed therapists ($F = 6.33$, p $< .05$), there was reason to question whether the significant difference between analyzed and unanalyzed therapists with respect to the number of silent responses was attributable to personal analysis, or whether it was rather a function of length of experience. The analysis of covariance technique was employed to determine whether the difference between the number of silent responses by analyzed and unanalyzed therapists was significant when the effect of experience was controlled. The obtained F value of 9.39 ($p < .01$) indicates that, as far as the present data are concerned, the difference in silent responses between analyzed and unanalyzed therapists is attributable to the variable of personal analysis. This result was to be expected since the correlation between length of experience and number of silent responses is .12, which is not significantly different from zero.

To test the three specific hypotheses, therapists' responses to each subseries (suicide threats, transference reactions, and schizoid productions) were compared with responses to all other statements. These operations were per-

---

*The findings reported for Rogerian therapists (see Chapter Six) corroborate this result.

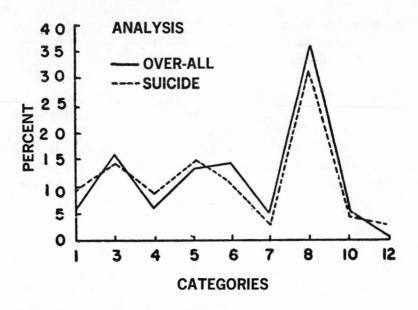

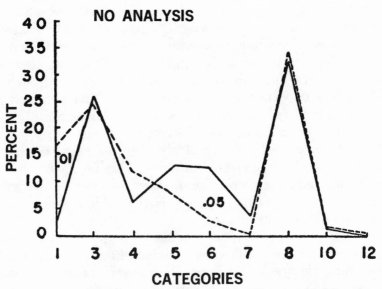

FIGURE 2. Response distributions of analyzed and unanalyzed therapists to suicide threats and to all other statements (personal analysis : suicide, $n = 182$; over-all, $n = 991$; no personal analysis : suicide, $n = 64$; over-all, $n = 372$).

194

formed separately for analyzed and for unanalyzed therapists. Subseries responses were, of course, always excluded from the over-all frequencies.

SUICIDE THREATS: Figure 2 shows the response profiles of analyzed and unanalyzed therapists to suicide threats and to all other statements. The following differences may be observed:

1. Unanalyzed therapists give a *larger* number of reassuring responses (Category 1) to suicide threats; for analyzed practitioners the trend is in the same direction $(t = 1.95, p < .06)$.
2. Unanalyzed therapists disclose a significant decrease in reflective responses (Category 6).
3. Both groups show a slight preference for structuring responses (Category 4) when dealing with suicide threats; however, neither difference is significant at the .05 level (analyzed group: $t = 1.63$, $p < .11$; unanalyzed group: $t = 1.94, p < .06$).

None of the above outcomes is in accordance with Hypothesis 1; in fact, the increment in reassuring responses is in opposition to the prediction, except that unanalyzed therapists appear to give a relatively larger number of reassuring responses than do analyzed workers.

TRANSFERENCE REACTIONS: Figure 3 compares the response profiles of analyzed and unanalyzed therapists to transference reactions and to all other statements. The following observations may be made:

1. Both groups show an increase in interpretive responses (Category 5), but the difference is statistically reliable only in the case of the analyzed therapists.
2. Both analyzed and unanalyzed practitioners tend to give a larger proportion of silent responses (Category 3), but again the difference is significant only for the former group.

195

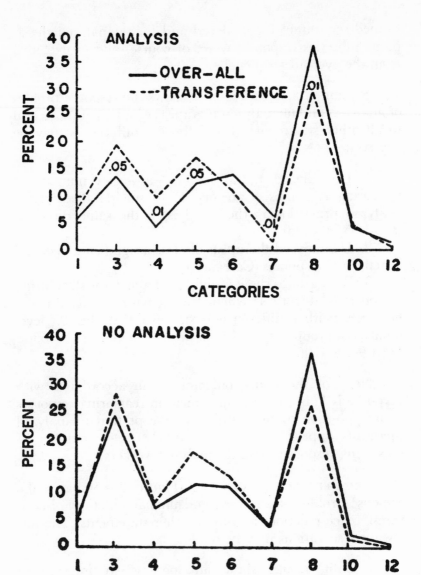

FIGURE 3. Response distributions of analyzed and unanalyzed therapists to transference reactions and to all other statements (personal analysis : transference, $n = 273$; over-all, $n = 900$; no personal analysis : transference, $n = 99$; over-all, $n = 337$).

196

It should be recalled here that this category revealed a significant discrepancy in the comparison of over-all distributions, unanalyzed workers exceeding the analyzed therapists.

3. Increments in structuring (Category 4) and decrements in exploratory responses (Category 8) are apparent for the analyzed group. These trends appear to be paralleled by the unanalyzed group, but here the differences are not significant, probably because the absolute numerical frequencies are considerably smaller. The difference in Category 7 is inconsistent and may be due to chance.

Hypothesis 2, which predicted an increase of interpretive responses, is thus partially confirmed; however, the verbal behavior of analyzed therapists seems to follow the same trend as that of their unanalyzed confreres. Collateral statistical treatments indicated that psychologists and social workers do *not* contribute to this shift.

Schizoid productions: Figure 4, which presents the by now familiar comparisons for schizoid productions, leads to the following interpretations:

1. Analyzed therapists' responses are characterized by a marked *decrease* in silent responses (significant at the .05 level), whereas unanalyzed therapists reveal an *increase* (not statistically significant).

2. Analyzed therapists use a proportionate number of explorations with this patient; unanalyzed workers, on the other hand, give significantly fewer exploratory responses.

3. The differences in Category 7 (direct questions) are traceable to an artifact in the items of the subseries. Another inconsistent difference in Category 6 may be due to chance.

Hypothesis 3 is partially confirmed by these results, particularly with respect to the decrease in silent responses for analyzed workers. If it is recalled that analyzed therapists were shown to be more active in the over-all com-

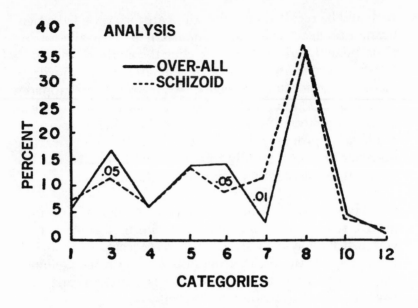

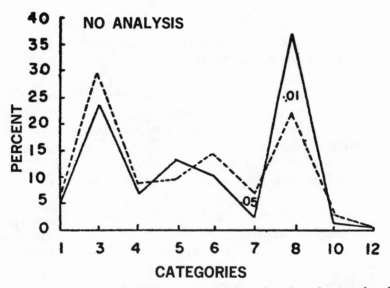

FIGURE 4. Response distributions of analyzed and unanalyzed therapists to schizoid productions and to all other statements (personal analysis : schizoid productions, $n = 274$; over-all, $n = 899$; no personal analysis : schizoid productions, $n = 94$; over-all, $n = 342$).

198

parisons, it follows that the gap between the analyzed and the unanalyzed groups is widened when responses to this patient occupy the focus of the statistical treatment. Exploratory responses, while undergoing no shift in the case of analyzed therapists, reveal a pronounced decrease in the unanalyzed group. This result is likewise in the predicted direction.

DISCUSSION

In interpreting the results of this study certain limitations must be kept in mind:

1. Therapists' responses were secured by means of an experimental model whose validity remains to be tested. It is thus not known to what extent the therapist's behavior in the experimental situation coincides with his behavior vis-à-vis a patient.
2. The experimental statements were brief and out of context; there was a minimum of background information on each patient; and, of course, the all-important therapist-patient relationship was lacking.
3. The three specific hypotheses were tested only in an approximate manner, and the tests are altogether relative since the reference distributions were composed of heterogeneous elements whose representativeness is not known. The number of suicide, transference, and schizoid items, moreover, was small so that reliable differences were difficult to demonstrate.

Within these limitations, the present investigation provides objective evidence on a problem about which much has been written but on which no quantitative data have yet been adduced.

The finding that analyzed therapists tend to be more active than their unanalyzed colleagues is a provocative one, but it runs counter to an intuitive hunch to the effect that the experience of personal analysis enables the therapist to maintain distance from the patient's maneuvers, and consequently that he feels less compelled to respond to any and all of the patient's communications. Rather, the present results may signify that the analyzed therapist is more skilled or more willing to formulate an immediate response. An alternative interpretation might be that the unanalyzed therapist is more passive when confronted with a series of patient statements in an experimental setting, but that this trend would be reversed in actual therapy. He might be more wary, more hesitant, and more unsure of himself and of his therapeutic procedures when called upon to give an account of himself, so to speak, to an outsider. It must be remembered here that length of experience per se *does not* account for the difference that, by this evidence, seems to be due to personal analysis or some related variable.

With respect to suicide threats, it is seen that contrary to recommendations made in the literature, *all* therapists tend to emphasize reassuring responses. At the same time, we may observe a consistent but statistically not significant increase in structuring responses that attempt a clarification of the patient's and the therapist's roles in the treatment situation. Such responses emphasize the reality aspects in opposition to the parataxic character of the patient's perceptions. The latter finding, however, must be regarded as very tentative. Also, it should not be forgotten that exploratory responses, while evidently not subject to shift in this instance, account for about a third of all therapist responses.

In accordance with psychoanalytic theory, therapists appear to single out transference phenomena for interpretive attention, although the experience of personal analysis seems to have little effect on the therapist's verbal behavior in this case. As has been shown in the previous chapter, a predilection for interpretations is a distinguishing feature of all psychiatrists. The data would indicate that transference reactions act as a signal for the therapist to interpret, to be silent, or to define the therapeutic situation. Also, he seems to be less inclined to ask the patient for an elaboration of his feelings. However, since the findings for the smaller unanalyzed group lack conclusiveness, it would be less than cautious to attribute the observed differences to the variable of personal analysis.

The data presented for the productions of a very anxious and near-psychotic patient point to differential handling by analyzed and unanalyzed therapists, and tend to confirm the third hypothesis. Silent responses appear to be sensitive to this kind of stimulus material such that analyzed therapists become more active (the evidence is not conclusive for unanalyzed practitioners). The decline in exploratory responses by unanalyzed therapists may be the complement of this trend. In the context of the present results, this may perhaps be regarded as tentative evidence for the analyzed therapist's greater sensitivity to the demands of the therapeutic situation; and if one meaning underlying silent responses is the attitude of "playing it safe," there may be here an indication of the analyzed therapist's greater versatility and readiness for verbal participation. However, this extrapolation is clearly a speculation.

In conclusion, this study has presented incomplete but certainly provocative evidence concerning differences in the therapeutic behavior of analyzed and unanalyzed psychotherapists. Contrary to prediction, personal analysis seems to lead to greater rather than to diminished activity on the therapist's part. The implications as well as the generalizability of these findings remain to be explored further, but there can be no doubt that the problem is one of the first magnitude—for theory, for practice, and for training.

SUMMARY

The major results of this third and concluding chapter in a series of investigations to elucidate the psychotherapist's contribution to the treatment situation, may be summarized as follows:

1. Compared with unanalyzed therapists, analyzed practitioners tend to be more active, as evidenced by a significantly smaller number of silent responses.

2. *Suicide threats* evoke an increased number of reassuring responses from both therapist groups.

3. In dealing with *transference phenomena,* analyzed therapists tend to prefer interpretations, silence, and structuring responses. The results for the unanalyzed group are inconclusive.

4. *Schizoid productions* of a seriously disturbed patient appear to induce a smaller number of silent responses in analyzed therapists and a smaller number of exploratory responses in unanalyzed therapists. Since the foregoing results are significant only for one group, they must be considered tentative.

Within the limitations of this study, personal analysis has a demonstrable effect on the therapist's verbal behavior, independent of the therapist's level of experience.

This series of investigations has indicated the feasibility of studying objectively some aspects of the psychotherapist's techniques. There is reason to believe that this focus on the therapist's contribution to the treatment situation is of theoretical and practical value for advancing our knowledge of the process of psychotherapy.

References

Bales, R. F. 1950. *Interaction Process Analysis.* Cambridge, Mass.: Addison-Wesley Press.

Fromm-Reichmann, F. 1950. *Principles of Intensive Psychotherapy.* Chicago: University of Chicago Press.

Snyder, W. U., ed. 1947. *Casebook of Nondirective Counseling.* Boston: Houghton Mifflin.

Whitaker, C. A., and Malone, T. P. 1953. *The Roots of Psychotherapy.* Philadelphia: Blakiston.

9

THE THERAPIST'S PERFORMANCE: A. PSYCHIATRISTS

Research on psychotherapy may be focused on three elements: the therapist, the patient, and the therapist-patient interaction. This chapter is concerned with the therapist's contribution to the treatment process—what the therapist *does*, and how his procedures are related to and influenced by his background, training, experience, and personality. Research on the therapist's contribution is not, of course any more important than research on the personality processes that psychotherapy seeks to influence, but it is a necessary link in improving our understanding of what psychotherapy is about.*

---

*This investigation was supported by a research grant (M-965) from the National Institute of Mental Health, U.S. Public Health Service. Grateful acknowledgment is made to Winfred Overholser, M.D., Executive Officer of the Department of Psychiatry, under whose

The performance of any two therapists, even in clearly defined and highly specific situations, will reveal differences. It is the antecedents of such differences that constitute the focus of our inquiry. By the same token, there will be many similarities, which will be equally important.

Systematic differences in performance may be a function of the therapist's training, experience, and personality —to name a few of the more important variables. The effects may be relatively independent of the particular interpersonal situation (for example, an inexperienced therapist may not interpret at all or too much irrespective of the patient or the situation), or the effects may be highly specific (a therapist may respond to a patient's expression of hostility if it touches, say, his professional status but he may passively accept most other forms of overt hostility). In any case, it is clear that therapeutic techniques are not applied *in vacuo,* and that they are differentially affected by factors in the therapist's personality. His performance is determined—in part, at least—by the way in which he perceives the patient's behavior, interprets its meaning in the framework of his clinical experience *and* his own personality, and the way in which this meaning is reflected in his response. It is one of

general supervision this work was carried out. To Leon Yochelson, M.D., consultant to the project, I am indebted not only for many constructive criticisms, suggestions, and comments but also for his unwavering support and friendly encouragement. It is also a pleasure to acknowledge the contributions of my research associates, Mrs. Rebecca E. Rieger and Mrs. Louisa R. Bilon. I wish to thank my friends, Drs. Dorothy E. Green and J. B. Chassan, for valuable advice on statistical problems.

The wholehearted collaboration of the following organizations is sincerely appreciated : Saint Elizabeth's Hospital; Johns Hopkins Hospital; Maryland Psychiatric Society; Washington Psychiatric Society; Postgraduate Center for Psychotherapy; Veterans Administration Hospital, Perry Point, Md.; Michael Reese Hospital; and the Chicago Institute for Psychoanalysis. My debt to them is second only to that owed to the therapists who donated valuable professional time to this project. Without their interest, earnest participation, and patience, the work could not have been done.

the peculiarities of the therapeutic situation that the therapist's interpersonal perceptions are immediately translated into action deliberately designed to effect a change in the patient's perceptions and behavior.

This chapter explores how the therapist structures the therapeutic problems (perceptions and evaluations), how these conceptualizations are related to what he proposes to do (treatment plans, goals, proposed procedures), and what he actually does (technique). Our aim is to investigate these interrelationships as well as to explain possible differences among therapists in terms of systematic effects produced by their training, experience, and personalities.

METHODS AND PROCEDURE

If we are interested in comparing the therapeutic behavior of one therapist with that of another, and if we want to study similarities or differences between groups of therapists, we must be able to make specific statements about the conditions that evoke this behavior. This is a basic requirement of any scientific investigation, which it has been extraordinarily difficult to approximate in psychotherapy research. It is impossible to have more than one therapist conduct an interview with the same patient at the same time, nor are we likely to succeed in selecting "comparable" patients. It follows that we have to compromise. One compromise that has often proven fruitful in science is to sacrifice some of the "realism" of the situation in exchange for improved experimental control.

To study the performance of psychotherapists under comparable controlled conditions we decided to use a sound film of an initial interview, to which subjects responded as vicarious interviewers. The respondents (therapists in the audience) were instructed to behave as if they were interviewing the patient. The major difference between a "real" interview and the experimental situation is the fact that the interaction is not between the audience therapist and the

205

patient but between the film therapist and the patient. Consequently, the "interventions" of the audience therapist have no effect upon the patient or the course of the interview. Furthermore, the audience therapist's response is not exclusively to the patient, but rather to the totality of the patient-therapist situation as portrayed on the screen. This investigation, then, rests on the assumption that the audience therapist's simulated interviewer behavior bears a relationship to his performance as a therapist in similar real-life therapy situations, and that valid inferences can be drawn from this sample of his behavior. It is not maintained that the interview between the film patient and any audience therapist would have proceeded exactly as indicated by the therapist's hypothetical responses.

The film, part of a series produced by the Veterans Administration for training purposes, was originally entitled "A Clinical Picture of Claustrophobia." A 30-minute film, it has been described by its producers as an unrehearsed interview from which no significant parts were deleted.*

In the film the patient, a middle-aged man, complains of anxiety and gastrointestinal symptoms that appear to be of psychogenic origin. He relates an episode on a crowded street car in which he experienced an intense panic reaction; subsequently, he was unable to go out of the house unless he was accompanied by his wife, who was an invalid. He describes an intense conflict with his mother, who emerges as a domineering and overprotective woman, and speaks at length about his "bad luck" in all phases of his life—his father died at an early age, leaving him with family responsibilities that were not shared by his brother—concluding that "I had three strikes against me before I even came to the

─────────────
*The "Psychotherapeutic Interviewing Series" was directed by Dr. Jacob Finesinger and Dr. Florence Powdermaker. The film was Part V of the series and was filmed in 1952. Grateful acknowledgment is made to Dr. Harvey J. Tompkins, Director, Psychiatry and Neurology Service, of the Veterans Administration, for granting permission to adapt the film for experimental purposes.

206

plate." He speaks freely and his anger and resentment build up. His demanding attitudes come clearly to the fore, culminating in the statement—only half doubted—that the world owes him a living. While it is not clear that he has had psychotherapy before, he makes mention of previous interviews. He speaks of having obtained some "insight" but the fabric of his rationalizations and projections of blame belie this. The interview ends somewhat abruptly after the patient has made a passionate plea for help, couched in an intense demand for reassurance.

The therapist in the film is a young, inexperienced resident, who uses Finesinger's (1948) technique of minimal activity. Essentially, he lets the patient tell his own story, frequently repeating a word or phase, and otherwise focusing very little. At times, he asks an informational question that seems to have the effect of diverting the patient from an emotionally charged topic. The therapist's attitude may be described as benevolent but rather distant; he is quite passive and offers no reassurance. The abrupt ending leaves it unclear how the interview was terminated or whether any treatment plans were formulated.

Here are a few highly condensed excerpts from the sequence:

P.: I have always been afraid . . . (T.: Mm.) . . . because (*laughs*) my association with my mother just made me scared to death. I have always been anxious and my association with her the first 20 years of my life has caused my marked anxiety . . . (T.: Mmm.) . . . and from 20 years from then up to now economic conditions have also caused it.

T.: You say the street car swayed?

P.: I just never liked to . . . to . . . to be in a position where I could not throw my arms and get out if I wanted to, and this was one [being hemmed in by a big woman on a street car] that I could not get out fast enough . . .

207

and it caused this panic reaction. (T.: Mmm.) And when I finally got off . . . it took two blocks to regain my composure, and then I went on to work.

T.: You felt hemmed in by this woman there?

P.: And now the heart action has decreased, and now my trouble, doctor, is I am dizzy.

T.: Huh . . .

P.: [Being hemmed in] causes a very uncomfortable, smothering sensation in my chest to be hemmed in; it just feels like maybe somebody is sitting on it . . . and then it keeps my stomach turning, quivering all the time . . . and it just makes me so anxious . . . (T.: Uh.) . . . to the point where I become overwhelmed with the anxiety by thinking about it and then I bring on this sensation, and then the sensations bring on my fear . . . (T.: Mmm.) . . . and then I just keep myself in a circle.

T.: Like someone sitting and twisting . . .

P.: . . . so you see, all my anxieties stem from my economic worries . . . (T.: Mmm.) . . . and of course I developed a lot of antisocial attitudes along the way.

T.: You say your mother was with you in W—— for three years?

P.: . . . after all, regardless of how many things that I think she has done that I don't like, that caused me difficulty, after all, she is still my mother; we can't get away from that.

T.: How? How is that?

P.: I want to get well, so I get the hell out of this thing.

T.: You say, anxiety in association with your mother?

P.: . . . every association that I've had has wound up unpleasantly. Even my work. Either I'd get fired or else

208

I'd quit. So I have just come to the conclusion that I started out with three strikes against me before I came to the plate. It looks like it.

T.: What do you mean, "three strikes"?

P.: I said to myself, "Just why the hell was all this handed to me? Why did I, why was I . . . why couldn't it have been Bill Smith over there? . . . [it] makes me emotional . . . fill up even if I think about it . . . just feel like you want to bawl, cry . . . always had something to cause me to live some other way and it has been economic.

T.: Like you want to bawl, huh?

P.: But getting back to the sensations, that's the bugaboo . . . Now I have asked every doctor I have seen the same question . . . These sensations have been so horrible, and they're attacking me so viciously that . . . are they undermining my nervous system, are they going to cause me to have a heart disease . . .? That's all I want to ask you. Are they going to kill me? Will they cause me to have . . . will they cause my heart to flop out from under me some day or will they damage my nerve tissue or even my . . . my thinking? (End of film)

These quotations convey something of the patient's personality, his attitudes, and his approach to the therapist. The therapist's interventions, which are typical of his behavior throughout the interview, are minimal, noncommittal, and marked by uncertainty. It was thought that this factor tended to minimize possible competition on the part of the audience therapists.

To prepare the film for "audience participation," the interview sequence was interrupted at a number of predetermined points, giving the audience therapist an opportunity to indicate what he would have done had he been the interviewer. After numerous try-outs, 28 points of interruption were selected from an originally much larger number. They usually occurred immediately *before* an intervention by the film therapist (never after), at natural "breaks" in the patient's recital following the recounting of what might be potentially "significant" dynamic material, and at points immediately preceding a change of topic introduced by the film therapist. Certain points were selected on the basis of intuitive hunches. Finally, an attempt was made to obtain a fair sample of the respondent's therapeutic behavior without excessive interruption of the film sequence.*

Choice points were identified by a uniform title (WHAT WOULD YOU DO?) and a number from 1 to 28. An appropriate number of frames was inserted into the film sequence so that each title appeared on the screen for 30 seconds at the normal projection speed. The time limit was kept to a predetermined optimum to allow the respondent a reasonable amount of time, sufficient for most therapists, to consider and write down his comments. Nevertheless, the time limit set a pace that precluded lengthy deliberations. The experimental version of the film ran for approximately 50 minutes, including pauses. Once the operator had started the projector, the film ran continuously to insure complete uniformity for each presentation.

The film was shown to groups ranging in size from less than 10 to well over 100. Instructions were presented orally by the investigator. The purpose of the experiment was briefly described, with emphasis on the comparative study of therapeutic techniques. Therapists in the audience were then requested to assume the role of a therapist with the patient in the film and to record their comments—what the patient would hear or see—on an answer sheet. They were cautioned that a pause in the film sequence was not to be

*I wish to thank the following psychiatrists for their helpful comments on this phase : Drs. Jay L. Hoffman, Leon Salzman, Norman Taub, Otto A. Will, Jr., and Leon Yochelson. The responsibility, of course, remains mine.

210

construed as a requirement to respond, but that silences or other nonverbal communications were perfectly acceptable. The audience was also informed that this was a first interview, and that the film therapist knew no more about the patient than the respondent. (Some therapists criticized the investigator for not pointing out that the patient had had previous contact with psychiatrists, a fact that emerged as the interview unfolded.) The problem was simply presented as a situation in which a patient with an emotional problem approaches a professional person for help ("How would you help him?"). The instructions further stated that the therapist should assume that he had agreed to see the patient just once. It was the therapist's decision whether he wanted to treat him or make some other disposition. No guidence was given as to the kind of interview to be conducted (diagnostic, therapeutic, etc.).

Following the film showing, therapists were requested to complete a comprehensive questionnaire on diagnostic impressions, treatment plans and goals, formulations of the patient's dynamics, problems in treatment, estimates of the patient's anxiety, emotional maturity, social adjustment, prognosis with and without therapy, the respondent's attitude toward the patient and the therapist in the film, and an evaluation of the latter's performance. Appended to the questionnaire was a biographical information blank containing 24 questions about the therapist's training, theoretical orientation, and current therapeutic activities. The entire experimental procedure usually required approximately two hours.

The experimental procedure yielded two kinds of data: comments directed to the patient portrayed in the film (techniques) and responses to the questionnaire. The second group may be subdivided into diagnostic impressions and evaluations, treatment plans and goals, including technique problems, and biographical data that served as reference variables.

211

The sample

Complete data were collected from 237 therapists representing these professional groups:

Psychiatrists (including 32 analysts)	91
Residents in psychiatry	43
Total (medical training)	134
Psychologists	79
Psychiatric social workers	17
Others	7
Total sample	237

This chapter will include primarily the responses of therapists whose training had been in medicine ($N = 134$).

Statistics on age, experience, and personal analysis are presented in Table 1. Additional information may be gleaned from the following distributions:

Status of psychoanalytic training:

	N	%
Completed psychoanalytic training (Member of the American Psychoanalytic Association, $N=21$)	33	25
In training	18	13
Plans	25	19
No psychoanalytic training	47	35
No answer	11	8

Status of personal analysis:

	N	%
Completed personal analysis	49	37
Presently undergoing analysis	39	29
Plans	15	11
No personal analysis	25	19
No answer	6	5

Amount of training in psychoanalytic principles and techniques (self-estimate):

	N	%
None	13	10
Very little	27	20
A fair amount	54	40
A great deal	34	25
No answer	6	5

Amount of experience in psychotherapy, not counting personal analysis (self-estimate):

	N	%
None	11	8
Very little	22	17
A fair amount	55	41
A great deal	40	29
No answer	6	5

Present competence as a psychotherapist (self-estimate):

	N	%
Fully competent	31	23
Reasonably competent	67	50
Slightly competent	17	13
Not very competent	17	13
No answer	2	1

Theoretical orientation:

	N	%
Freud—Orthodox	13	10
Sullivan	27	20
Alexander	8	6
Psychoanalytically oriented—general	75	56
Eclectic	10	7
Meyer	9	7
Miscellaneous	13	10
No answer	15	11
	170*	

*Exceeds number of cases since there were some multiple responses.

Quantitative analysis and statistical treatment

QUANTITATIVE ANALYSIS OF THERAPISTS' COMMUNI-
CATIONS: The systematic analysis of several thousand comments given by over 200 therapists required some method
of quantification. A system of analysis was employed whose
development and operational characteristics are described
in greater detail in Chapter Twenty-four. The system yields
five measures for any therapist communication. There are
two sets of categories (Type of Therapeutic Activity and
Dynamic Focus) and three intensity scales (Depth-directedness, Initiative, and Therapeutic Climate). The components
are as follows:

Type of Therapeutic Activity specifies the outer form
or structure of a therapeutic intervention and provides a
gross analysis of the therapist's techniques. The major categories are:

Facilitating communication (minimal activity)
Exploratory operations
Clarification (minimal interpretation)
Interpretive operations
Structuring
Direct guidance
Activity not clearly relevant to the task of therapy
Unclassifiable

Certain subcategories serve to refine the primary ratings.

Depth directedness is based on the conception that
inference is an integral part of all therapeutic communications and that it is always present to some degree. Each communication is rated by means of an eight-point scale.*

---

*This scale is identical to the four-point scale described in Chapter
Twenty-four. The expansion of the scale merely represents the introduction of "half-steps" that have been found useful. The original
conception remains unchanged.

0	1	2	3	4	5	6	7	8
Non-inferential		Mildly inferential		Moderately inferential			Highly inferential	

Dynamic Focus refers to the frame of reference adopted by the therapist at a particular juncture and characterizes the manner in which he focuses the therapeutic spotlight. Two major sectors are used to differentiate whether the therapist "goes along" with the patient (*A*) or whether he introduces a different focus (*B*). Sector *A* includes silences, passive acceptance, simple reflections of feeling, and minimal questions. Sector *B* is analyzed in terms of five subcategories:

> Requests for additional information
> Focus on dynamic events in the *past*
> Focus on dynamic events in the *present*
> Focus on the dynamics of the therapist-patient relationship (analysis of the transference)
> Focus on the therapist-patient interaction in terms of the therapist's role as an expert, authority, etc.

Initiative measures the extent to which the therapist assumes responsibility for guiding the patient's communications in a given channel. Seven degrees are distinguished: †

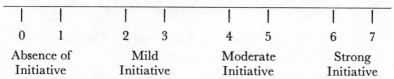

Therapeutic Climate or emotional overtones discernible in a communication are quantified by means of a bipolar scale:

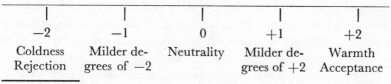

---

†In this case, the original scale consisted of four major scale steps.

215

RATER AGREEMENT: To estimate the reliability of the system a random sample of 20 answer sheets was selected

TABLE 1

SUMMARY STATISTICS OF AGE, EXPERIENCE, PERSONAL ANALYSIS

	N	Mean	SD
Age	131	38.25 years	10.67
Experience in therapy	131	6.78 years	7.22
Personal Analysis	74*	384.19 hours	245.22

* Includes respondents who responded affirmatively and indicated the number of hours.

TABLE 2

AGREEMENT BETWEEN TWO INDEPENDENT RATERS

System Component	Agreement on 20 cases (Number of judgments=1,673)
Type	86.9%
Depth-directedness	94.7%
Dynamic Focus	77.9%
Initiative	96.0%
Therapeutic Climate	17 nonzero judgments were made, of which 4 were disagreements.

Note.—All percentages are significant beyond the .01 level.

and scored independently by two raters.‡ The indices presented in Table 2 are based on a unit-by-unit analysis. Agreement on a unit (therapist communication) means that both raters assigned it to the same category, or that they gave it an intensity score no more than one-half step apart. It was difficult to test rater agreement on Therapeutic Climate because of the relative infrequency of nonzero scores. There is reason to believe that scores on this dimension are heavily influenced by voice inflections and other

‡Reliability data for typescripts of actual interviews have been reported in Chapter Fourteen.

nonverbal clues that are inevitably lost in written materials. Since the evidence in many instances was insufficient so that a "neutral" (zero) score had to be assigned, it may be assumed that the scores on this component almost certainly represent a gross underestimate.

The over-all disagreement was 11.2 per cent, which is considered acceptable. Since most ratings were made jointly by two raters, thus permitting discussions and resolutions of disagreements, the stability of the ratings used in the subsequent analyses is probably even higher.

STATISTICAL TREATMENT: The statistical analyses, for the most part, were concerned with the systematic comparison of therapists' response distributions grouped according to one or more independent variables. While all analyses imply at least a crude hypothesis, the fact remains that the work is to a large extent exploratory. For this reason, it appeared important to accept conservative standards; accordingly, the .05 level of probability (two-tailed test) has been used as a minimum level for rejecting the null hypothesis. Since the system components are correlated, the danger of compounding statistical significance when comparing the results of the various components has also been kept in mind. In view of the crudeness of the measurements it seemed prudent to avoid the assumptions underlying such statistical techniques as the t test and analysis of variance and to use instead their nonparametric counterparts (Siegel, 1956).

More specifically, comparisons were performed separately on each component of the system. In the case of categories, analyses were based on the distribution of frequencies within a category. For example, a therapist giving 10 "silent" responses was given a score of 10, etc. In the case of the continua, the hypothesis was tested that the more intense scores discriminated between groups of therapists. To maintain the ordinal character of the scale, we compared by the chi-square technique the proportion of therapists

217

who obtained *any* scores of 5 or above on these scales. A similar procedure was followed for scores on Therapeutic Climate, where greater importance was assigned to non-zero scores. Negative ("cold," rejecting) scores were judged particularly critical. Consequently, the comparisons involve the proportion of therapists in a given group who gave negative or positive scores respectively, the two kinds of scores being treated independently.

The major statistical techniques were the Mann-Whitney U test (when two independent samples were being compared) and the Kruskal-Wallis one-way analysis of variance (when more than two independent samples were being tested).

Finally, to quantify therapists' questionnaire responses, many of which were of the free-answer type, it was necessary to develop content codes after surveying the range of response for each item. All free-answer questions were then scored jointly by two trained raters.

RESULTS

Diagnostic and prognostic evaluations

DIAGNOSIS: This was the first item in the questionnaire, and required the respondent to indicate the patient's dominant personality type. As shown in Figure 1, eight pre-coded alternatives, taken from an article by Raines and Rohrer (1955), were listed. "Anxiety" was the preferred label, given by almost 40 per cent of the respondents. Actually, this is no more than a phenomenological description since the patient had mentioned the word on numerous occasions. Multiple diagnoses tended to include "Anxiety" in most instances. "Hysteria" and "Paranoid" were chosen with almost equal frequency, followed by "Obsessive," "Character Disorder," "Psychopathic," and some minor ones.

DEFENSE MECHANISMS: Most prominently mentioned were projective tendencies, including paranoid trends. Rationalization and intellectualization ranked next, followed by somatization, etc. On the average, two or more defense mechanisms were mentioned, the nomenclature itself showing wide variations.

FORMULATIONS OF DYNAMICS: In this free-response item, respondents were requested to formulate the dynamics of the patient's difficulties. Four major classes were defined, as illustrated by the following examples:

1. Nondynamic formulations

He is a dependent person who felt not adequate to cope with his problems.

Dynamics formulated around family interpersonal relationships.

The patient has never matured emotionally beyond the point of infancy or early childhood.

Hostile dependency. Symptoms probably a reaction to rejected need for dependency.

2. Genetic formulations

a. Descriptive

Seductive dominating mother, weak ineffectual father. Very dependent male with difficulty in identification with either parent.

Unresolved oedipal conflicts and guilt in death of father.

Patient lost capacity for healthy self-assertiveness or appears to have been incapable of changing direction. He was thoroughly castrated by mother. Dad?

b. Operational

An older indulged son feels displaced by a younger sibling, reacts with anger at being no longer the baby, but is forced to repress his anger.

The patient probably felt rejected by his mother and identified with his father, who left him "to hold the bag" so

219

to speak, and brother, identified with mother, was accepted.

His identity as a male is seriously disturbed, marked by fixation at an infantile level, marked castration anxiety, assumption of narcissistic feminine identification with a castrating mother.

3. Emphasis on Current Situation
a. Descriptive

Obsessive-compulsive character traits with self-defeating operations and self-burdening; strong guilt feelings over responsibility toward mother and wife.

Never freed himself from mother. His aggression is tremendous but can't find acceptable expression.

Chronic morbid resentment state based on unsatisfied dependency needs, "the world owes me a living."

b. Operational

Intense hostility toward a domineering mother, who expected a strong sense of responsibility that he must defeat in his neurotic actions.

The patient's anxiety attack started with his being thrown against a "fat woman," which caused a "warm feeling." The following phenomena represent his attempt to defend himself against awareness of longing for dependency on his mother, which he felt momentarily satisfied in contact with the fat woman.

Onset situation incomplete. Rage at mother and wife; impulse to hurt leads to rising titre; resentment at woman hemming him in on streetcar; streetcar almost hits truck equated with his almost out-of-control impulses leading to panic.

4. Formulations combining genetic and current emphases
a. Descriptive

Domineering, manipulative, phobic mother with passive father. Patient feels many unsatisfied dependency needs, which he tries to wring from the environment.

A closely bound-to-mother individual who has had difficulty in reaching any degree of maturity and is angry

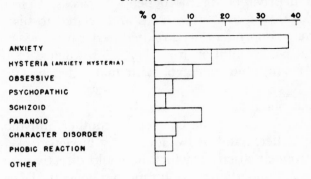

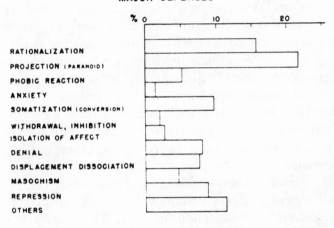

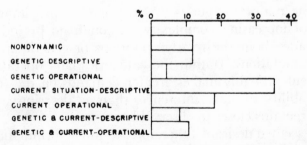

FIGURE 1. Diagnoses, defense mechanisms, and formulations of dynamics.

at the deprivation of his dependent needs. Considerable secondary gain, anger repressed and related to his cardiac symptoms; dependent need related to dizziness.

Passive orientation to father, ambivalence to mother. Easily corruptible superego, with many dependency strivings.

b. Operational

Intense rage at the enveloping mother and the abandoning father, handled by developing anxiety to keep him away from situations in which he could directly express his feelings . . . underlying love for mother beneath the rage.

Guilt and anxiety leading to incorporative attitudes. Regressive oral demanding attitudes toward mother repressed because of fear. Illness of his wife followed by mother's leaving home left patient without fulfillment of dependent needs. This resulted in insecurity and phobic mechanisms to get support. (Symbolic expression of fragmentary incorporative attitude toward mother in G. I. symptoms.)

Hostile identification with mother is basic issue; underlying depression in relation to father's death with suppressed rage and acting out as alternative defenses against passive (homosexual) trends. Suspect patient is hypertensive.

Most likely dynamics is rage at father (seen as a maternal but absent person), defended by phobic displacement, obsessive-compulsive mechanisms. etc. These are not sufficient to ban anxiety, and he feels anxiety directly.

The major categories are arranged approximately in order of increasing complexity, although no prejudgment was made about the relative positions of genetic and current formulations. Within the categories, an "operational" statement probably makes greater demands on the respondent's ability to make inferences than a "descriptive" one, which remains closer to observable events.

It seemed desirable, therefore, to judge formulations by an over-all criterion that came to be known as Dynamic Quality. This rating was made on a four-point scale, ranging from 1 (low) to 4 (high). In arriving at this global judgment, the following criteria were kept in mind:

1. Complexity. Does the formulation attempt to explain one or several facets of the patient's problem? Does it integrate a number of seemingly disparate manifestations? Is it a "rich" or a "meager" formulation?

2. Degree of inference. Is the formulation inferential or does it remain at a descriptive level? Does it state or imply a hypothesis that may have a bearing on therapy?

3. Precision. Is the language precise or is it "loose"? Are technical terms used in a strict sense or is technical language used as a jargon? Does a formulation seem to apply to the patient specifically or is it worded so generally that it might apply to anyone?

4. Operational aspects. Does the formulation indicate how the patient "handles" his conflict or does it describe a state? Is the conflict set forth in terms which are at least potentially verifiable or is the likelihood of verification virtually nonexistent?

Rater agreement on the over-all rating, between two independent raters, was 88 per cent (disregarding discrepancies of one scale step).

OTHER DIAGNOSTIC EVALUATIONS: Several diagnostic assessments were obtained through precoded items. Each item was followed by a four-point intensity scale, and the added alternative "Too little evidence to make a judgment at this time." Response distributions are presented in Figure 2. (In some cases, categories containing very small frequencies were combined with the adjoining one.) The alternative "Too little evidence" actually lies outside the scale continuum and signifies a respondent's refusal to make a judgment. It may also indicate the degree of inference involved in a rating, as perceived by the respondents. Thus, Ego Strength shows 16.5 per cent of the responses in that category, whereas Disturbance discloses less than 1 per cent. By

223

EGO STRENGTH

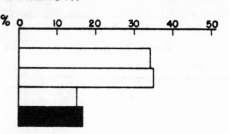

FAIR AMOUNT
RELATIVELY LITTLE
VERY LITTLE
TOO LITTLE EVIDENCE

ANXIETY

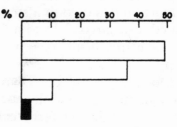

GREAT DEAL
FAIR AMOUNT
RELATIVELY LITTLE
TOO LITTLE EVIDENCE

INSIGHT

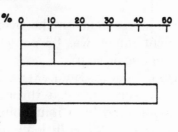

FAIR AMOUNT
RELATIVELY LITTLE
VERY LITTLE
TOO LITTLE EVIDENCE

DISTURBANCE

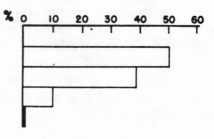

SERIOUSLY DISTURBED
MODERATELY DISTURBED
MILDLY DISTURBED
TOO LITTLE EVIDENCE

224

CAPABILITY OF SELF-OBSERVATION
vs. RATIONALIZATION

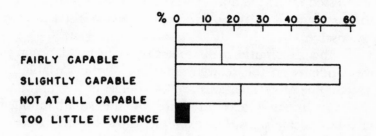

EMOTIONAL MATURITY

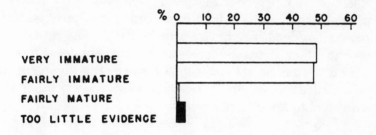

SOCIAL ADJUSTMENT

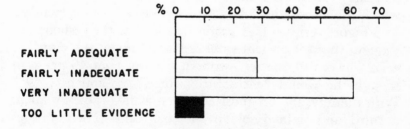

FIGURE 2. Ego strength, anxiety, insight, capability of self-observation versus tendency for rationalization, emotional maturity, social adjustment, and disturbance.

this standard, therapists by and large thought there was sufficient evidence on such items as Anxiety, Insight, Self-Observation, Emotional Maturity, and Disturbance but they expressed greater tentativeness on Ego Strength and Social Adjustment. Relatively few respondents refused to commit themselves.

The distributions disclose fair agreement among the respondents on the relative intensity of the variable being rated. The quantifications are, of course, crude, and part of the agreement is accounted for by the small number of available scale steps. For example, the subjective difference between "a great deal" of anxiety and "a fair amount" of anxiety may be slight, but the discrepancy between " a great deal" and "relatively little" anxiety seems considerable. In this case, 85 per cent of the respondents agreed that the patient experienced at least a fair amount of anxiety, but 11 per cent judged it to be "relatively little." The distributions on the other items are comparable, except for Emotional Maturity and Social Adjustment where the divergent minorities of about 10 to 15 per cent observed on other items dwindled to about 1 per cent.

PROGNOSIS: Diagnostic evaluations were followed by two questions relating to prognosis. Respondents were asked: "Assuming your recommendations for treatment were followed, how would you rate the prognosis for this patient?" Responses were made on five-point scales, to which the alternative "Too little evidence," was appended.

Figure 3 shows that more than half of the respondents thought that the patient would remain "about the same" or even "get a little better" without therapy, but 40 per cent thought he would "get a little worse" or "much worse." With therapy, the prognosis was seen as favorable by about a third and unfavorable by 45 per cent. These ratings involve relatively complex predictions so that the absence of a consensus is not startling. Also, favorableness of the prognosis partly depends on the respondent's frame of reference, treatment goals, etc. Even if the crudeness of the judg-

PROGNOSIS WITHOUT THERAPY

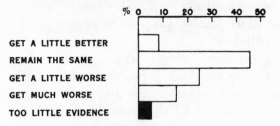

PROGNOSIS WITH THERAPY

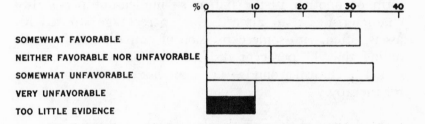

ATTITUDE TOWARD PATIENT

REASONS

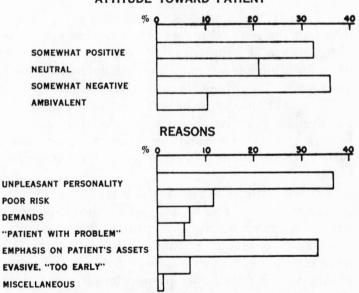

FIGURE 3. Prognosis without therapy, prognosis with therapy, attitude toward the patient, and reasons for the attitude.

227

ment is conceded, the fact remains that a notable percentage of the respondents took an optimistic view whereas a somewhat more sizable proportion regarded the outlook pessimistically.

ATTITUDE TOWARD THE PATIENT: Figure 3 indicates that the proportions of positive and negative attitudes were almost equal; about a fifth professed a neutral attitude, and the reaction of a tenth was ambivalent. When asked for the reasons for their reaction, 43 respondents left the question blank. Of those who replied, 36 per cent referred in one form or another to the patient's "unpleasant personality characteristics"; an almost equal percentage stressed his assets, often with some expression of empathy. It is worth noting that 11 per cent disliked him on what might be called "technical grounds," i.e., poor risk or poor motivation for therapy.

Formulations of therapeutic plans, goals, and techniques

THERAPEUTIC GOALS AND APPROACHES (Figure 4): More than half the respondents set rather modest goals consisting of some form of symptom relief. This was true particularly when a distinction was made between intermediate and ultimate goals. Even those therapists who described their goal as "a certain amount of insight" generally regarded this as the ultimate objective. Virtually no therapist indicated that he would strive for extensive personality reorganization. Only three therapists refused to accept the patient for treatment.

If we consider areas in which therapists expected the patient to "move" and areas in which they expected him to remain relatively unchanged, practically no one expected any basic personality change, whereas the possibility of more superficial changes was conceded by a fair proportion. However, a slightly larger proportion did not foresee even this as a likely occurrence. The greatest improvements, relatively speaking, were expected with regard to symptoms, work adjustment, and interpersonal relations, but minorities specified that little or no movement was to be anticipated in these areas. Many therapists took a rather pessimistic view of the patient's disturbance and of his capacity to profit from psychotherapy.

Asked to specify areas or problems which might be most amenable to therapy, therapists mentioned three major areas: (1) interpersonal relations (mostly with mother and wife, to a lesser extent with father, brother, and authority figures); (2) specific emotional dynamics (self-destructive tendencies, etc.); (3) external reality (work, jobs, living arrangements, etc.).

A similar question, designed to elicit information on areas in the patient's living that might receive primary focus, produced a shift in the response pattern; interpersonal relations and external reality were named more frequently and emotional dynamics less frequently. The differences may be a function of the wording of the two questions.

Closely related to the questions of focus were two items pertaining to attitudes or kinds of behavior that the therapist would encourage (or discourage) in therapy with this patient. Encouraged were: (1) a sense of responsibility, feelings of worthwhileness, self-esteem, independence, and the patient's masculine role; (2) increased socialization, gainful employment, "living in the present"; (3) the expression of feelings without guilt; (4) the development of insight. Discouraged were: (1) intellectualization, obsessive ruminations (resistances); (2) self-pity, self-depreciation, helplessness, demands; (3) acting out of anti-social impulses.

Among areas to be avoided (early) in therapy, the following were mentioned: sexual and homosexual impulses, oedipal material, and the patient's concept of his own masculinity. Next in frequency ranged interpersonal relations with his mother and wife. Small frequencies were accumulated under the headings of intellectual discussions, anger, hostility, death wishes, early life experiences, unconscious material, fantasies, dreams. Twenty-six respondents speci-

229

GOALS

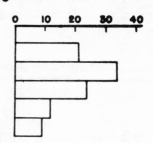

SYMPTOM RELIEF I
SYMPTOM RELIEF II (HIGHER LEVEL)
SOME INSIGHT I
SOME INSIGHT II (HIGHER LEVEL)
MISCELLANEOUS

AREAS AND DEGREE OF CHANGE

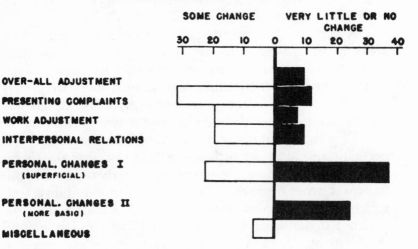

SOME CHANGE | VERY LITTLE OR NO CHANGE

OVER-ALL ADJUSTMENT
PRESENTING COMPLAINTS
WORK ADJUSTMENT
INTERPERSONAL RELATIONS
PERSONAL. CHANGES I (SUPERFICIAL)
PERSONAL. CHANGES II (MORE BASIC)
MISCELLANEOUS

SPECIFIC AREAS OF FOCUS

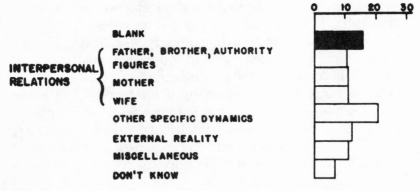

INTERPERSONAL RELATIONS
BLANK
FATHER, BROTHER, AUTHORITY FIGURES
MOTHER
WIFE
OTHER SPECIFIC DYNAMICS
EXTERNAL REALITY
MISCELLANEOUS
DON'T KNOW

230

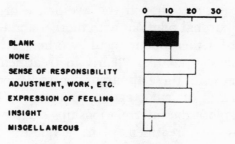

BEHAVIORS TO BE ENCOURAGED

```
                              0   10   20   30
BLANK
NONE
SENSE OF RESPONSIBILITY
ADJUSTMENT, WORK, ETC.
EXPRESSION OF FEELING
INSIGHT
MISCELLANEOUS
```

BEHAVIORS TO BE DISCOURAGED

```
                              0   10   20   30
BLANK
NONE
RESISTANCE
SELF—PITY
ACTING—OUT
MISCELLANEOUS
```

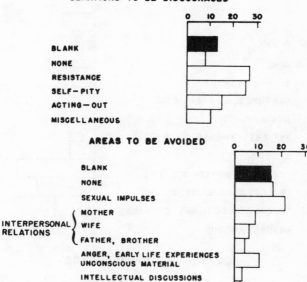

AREAS TO BE AVOIDED

```
                                      0   10   20   30
BLANK
NONE
SEXUAL IMPULSES
                    ⎧ MOTHER
INTERPERSONAL       ⎨ WIFE
RELATIONS           ⎩ FATHER, BROTHER
ANGER, EARLY LIFE EXPERIENCES
UNCONSCIOUS MATERIAL
INTELLECTUAL DISCUSSIONS
ACTING—OUT
MISCELLANEOUS
```

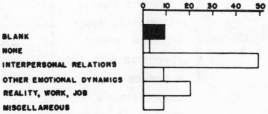

FOCUS

```
                              0   10   20   30   40   50
BLANK
NONE
INTERPERSONAL RELATIONS
OTHER EMOTIONAL DYNAMICS
REALITY, WORK, JOB
MISCELLANEOUS
```

FIGURE 4. Therapeutic goals and approaches.

231

fically indicated, however, that no areas should be avoided. Some therapists counseled the avoidance of certain areas (e.g., interpersonal relations with mother and wife) that were singled out for therapeutic focus by others. It is conceivable that the time stipulation ("early in treatment") may have been the cause for these apparent contradictions.

PROBLEMS OF THERAPEUTIC TECHNIQUE (Figure 5): In order to explore the interrelationships between perceptions, evaluations, and treatment plans, a question was included

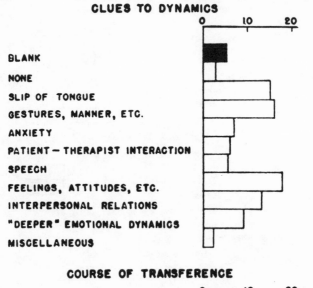

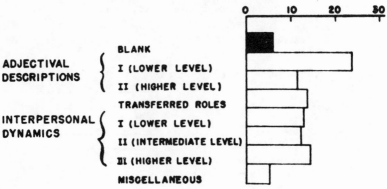

FIGURE 5. Problems of therapeutic technique.

232

HANDLING OF TRANSFERENCE

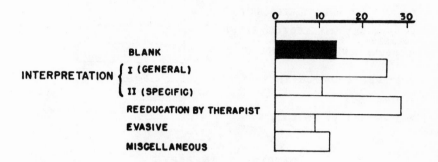

COUNTER TRANSFERENCE

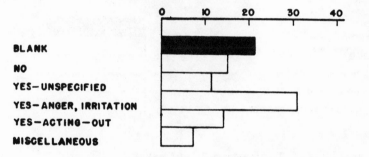

HANDLING OF COUNTER TRANSFERENCE

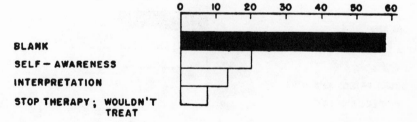

FIGURE 5. (Continued overleaf).

233

DIFFICULTIES IN THERAPY

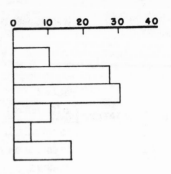

REFUSAL TO ACCEPT RESPONSIBILTY, DEPENDENCE

RESISTANCE : INTELLECTUALIZATION OBSESSIVE RAMBLING

MANIPULATION AND CONTROL OF THERAPIST

POOR MOTIVATION FOR THERAPY

ACTING—OUT

POSSIBILITY OF PSYCHOSIS

DANGERS IN THERAPY

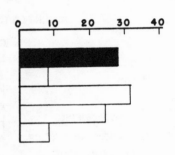

BLANK

NONE

TECHNIQUE ERRORS

" GOING TOO FAST "

COUNTERTRANSFERENCE

"ACTING—OUT" BEHAVIOR

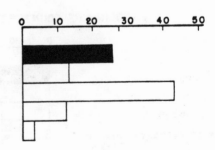

BLANK

NO

YES

QUALIFIED ANSWERS

MISCELLANEOUS

FIGURE 5. (cont.).

234

HANDLING OF "ACTING—OUT" BEHAVIOR

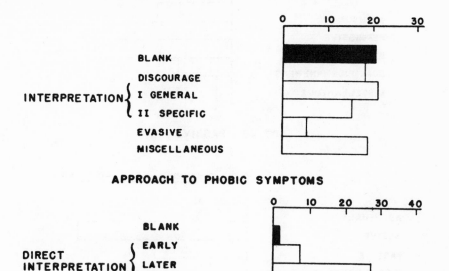

APPROACH TO PHOBIC SYMPTOMS

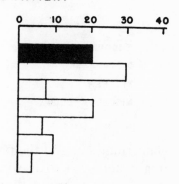

RECOMMENDATIONS TO PATIENT

FIGURE 5. (Continued overleaf).

235

STRICT — PERMISSIVE

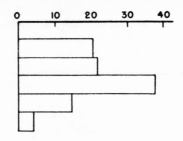

AS USUAL
PERMISSIVE
STRICT
QUALIFIED ANSWERS
MISCELLANEOUS

ACTIVE — PASSIVE

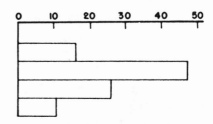

AS USUAL
ACTIVE
PASSIVE
MISCELLANEOUS

FREE ASSOCIATION

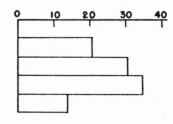

ENCOURAGE
DISCOURAGE
NEITHER
MISCELLANEOUS

FIGURE 5. (cont.).

concerning clues in the patient's behavior that the therapist might not wish to use in an initial interview but that he might keep in mind for later reference. Such clues might facilitate inferences concerning the nature of the patient's emotional conflict and generate hypotheses to be tested in subsequent therapeutic sessions.

236

The majority of the 200 clues referred to observations about the patient's feelings and attitudes (anger, hostility, "the world owes me a living") with frequent elaboration of their dynamic significance. Another cluster dealt with non-verbal clues (gestures, manner, bodily movements, etc.). A relatively large number referred to a slip of the tongue occurring in the interview (speaking about his father's death, the patient substituted the word "mother"). References to "deeper dynamics," i.e., highly inferential statements, were comparatively infrequent.

Responses relating to the course of the transference seemed to fall into three major categories: (1) adjectival descriptions; (2) statements in terms of transferred roles (often tautological); and (3) statements in terms of inter-personal dynamics. This sequence implies a hierarchy of increasing complexity and specificity, and it will be shown that the kind of formulation chosen was actually associated with the respondent's length of experience in therapy. The following examples illustrate responses assigned to the major scoring categories:

(1) Adjectival Descriptions
    Negative.
    Resentful, complaining.
    First positive, then negative.
(2) Transferred Roles
    [Course of the transference is that of] the relationship with his mother.
    With me, I would expect him to be a child with father—wanting help with wife and mother.
    [He would see me as] Mother, with expectations of being smothered by therapist, too.
(3) Interpersonal Dynamics
    [Transference] Probably would be fairly quickly established and therapist would probably first be the good father. Later, his [patient's] need for dependency gratification would make things stormy.

Possibly anxiety about possible illnesses in therapist. Hostile defensiveness if pressed.

I would expect him to develop hostile feelings that he would not be able to express but that would cause him to have symptoms and perhaps to stay away.

Two principal methods for handling transference problems were suggested: one is best described as interpretive, i.e., pointing out the distortive elements in the patient's maneuvers; the other refers to a skillful use of the therapist's role in changing the patient's attitudes and actions, by firmness, reassurance, or other re-educative techniques. In the latter method, interpretations are not necessarily excluded, but the major emphasis is upon the therapist as a person, authority figure, or reality model.

A patient who is very demanding, aggressive, and manipulative is likely to evoke emotional reactions from the therapist. More than half of the respondents expected to get involved in countertransference reactions with this patient. Most frequently mentioned were anger, annoyance, irritation, and impatience. Less often mentioned was the danger of acting out in response to the patient's manipulative and controlling tendencies, which might lead the therapist to abdicate his therapeutic role. More than 20 per cent of the therapists failed to answer this question. Almost three times as many therapists did not answer the second part of the question asking for specific statements about the "handling" of possible countertransference reactions. Those who replied stated they would try to be aware of the problem and act accordingly. A smaller number said they would discuss it with the patient or interpret it.

Related to questions about transference and countertransference were several items concerning difficulties and/or dangers that might arise in the therapy. With regard to difficulties, respondents mentioned prominently the patient's attempt to manipulate and control the therapist. Of equal magnitude were resistance, intellectualization, and

238

obsessive rambling. Akin to the foregoing were comments about the patient's refusal to accept responsibility, his dependence and parasitic trends, his projections of blame, and his poor motivation for therapy. The possibility of a psychotic episode was also anticipated by a fair number of therapists.

The question about dangers elicited responses that tended to be centered around techniques, with a variety of problems that could not easily be subsumed under common denominators. Frequent comments referred to an incorrect handling of the transference relationship, and an appreciable number cautioned against the therapist's "going too fast." They suggested the need for a sympathetic and understanding attitude to prevent the patient from becoming too anxious or developing a psychosis.

Three items dealt with more specific technique problems. The first asked whether the respondent expected the patient to engage in much acting out behavior, and, if so, how he would deal with it. The preferred methods for handling the problem were to be interpretation and control by firmness, strictness, or setting limits. Miscellaneous recommendations were made for supportive measures, including reassurance, focus on the patient's personality assets, and re-education.

Considerable divergence of opinion was expressed regarding the optimal method for dealing with the patient's phobic symptoms. The majority considered direct interpretation of these symptoms contraindicated at any time; a somewhat less sizable group thought interpretation should occur at a much later time; another group advocated more or less idiosyncratic approaches; and a small minority thought that the therapist should interpret them as early as possible.

A similarly divergent distribution was obtained on the question of recommendations to the patient to change his present mode of living or his environment. About one-third of the responses were in the negative, with most members of

FORM OF THERAPY

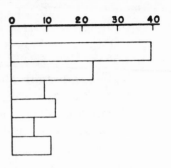

PSYCHOTHERAPY — GENERAL
PSYCHOTHERAPY — INTENSIVE, INSIGHT
PSYCHOANALYSIS
SUPPORTIVE, GROUP, ETC.
THERAPY PLUS ADJUNCTS
MISCELLANEOUS

FREQUENCY OF WEEKLY SESSIONS

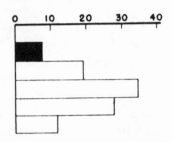

BLANK AND MISCELLANEOUS
I SESSION
1 — 2 SESSIONS
2 — 3 SESSIONS
3 OR MORE SESSIONS

LENGTH OF TREATMENT

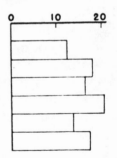

LESS THAN 6 MONTHS
6 MONTHS — I YEAR
1 — 2 YEARS
2 — 3 YEARS
MORE THAN 3 YEARS
EVASIVE

FIGURE 6. Form of therapy, frequency of sessions, and length of therapy.

240

SYMPTOM RELIEF

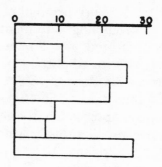

LESS THAN 3 MONTHS
3 - 6 MONTHS
6 MONTHS — 1 YEAR
1 - 2 YEARS
MORE THAN 2 YEARS
EVASIVE

COMPROMISES

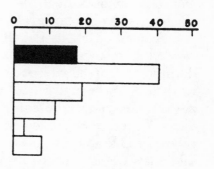

BLANK
CLINIC, FEWER SESSIONS, ETC.
DRUGS
ENVIRONMENTAL MANIPULATION
HOSPITALIZATION
MISCELLANEOUS

CHANGES ATTEMPTED

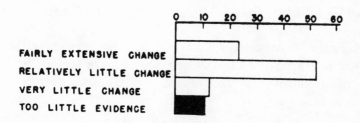

FAIRLY EXTENSIVE CHANGE
RELATIVELY LITTLE CHANGE
VERY LITTLE CHANGE
TOO LITTLE EVIDENCE

241

this group pointing out that recommendations were outside the therapist's province and unrelated to the therapeutic problem. Twenty per cent of the respondents qualified their replies, counseling deferment of a decision. Certain respondents indicated a willingness to make recommendations, primarily with respect to the patient's job, living arrangements for his mother, wife, etc.

Another set of questions sought to explore further the therapist's approach to therapy, and to determine the extent to which the therapist's "usual" techniques might be modified by or adapted to the particular set of problems presented by this patient. One out of five therapists indicated that he would be no more strict or permissive with this patient than with any other. A similar number preferred permissiveness. Forty per cent, however, voted for strictness, basing their judgment mostly on technical requirements. A minority qualified their responses by stating they would be strict in some areas, permissive in others, etc.

A question about the therapist's level of activity was worded as follows: "Assuming that the patient's behavior during the first hour is rather typical of him, would you tend to be more active (i.e., intervene frequently) or more passive (i.e., intervene infrequently) in subsequent interviews?" Here the division of opinion appeared even more pronounced than in the preceding item: Almost 50 per cent said they would tend to be rather active; a quarter said "rather passive"; others qualified their response or gave a noncommittal answer.

Free association was discouraged by a third; encouraged by a fifth; neither encouraged nor discouraged by another third.

FORM OF THERAPY, FREQUENCY OF SESSIONS, AND LENGTH (Figure 6): The preferred method of treatment was described simply as "psychotherapy." Thirty respondents qualified their responses by adding such terms as "intensive," "insight," "uncovering," or "analytically oriented." It is not certain, however, that those respondents who failed to define "psychotherapy" more closely did not in fact refer to more intensive therapy. Psychoanalysis, as the most extensive and intensive form of therapy, was recommended by less than 10 per cent. Other minorities recommended supportive therapy, group therapy, and various combinations.

Further information on the method of treatment—at least on its external aspects—is provided by the frequency of weekly sessions suggested by the respondents. The modal response was one to two times per week. Almost equally preferred, however, were interviews at the rate of two to three times per week. A sizable minority thought the patient should be seen only once a week. Therapists who voted for three or more sessions per week comprised only 10 per cent.

Considering the divergence of goals and modes of treatment, it is not surprising that the length of therapy was estimated quite differently. Therapists who distinguished between intermediate and ultimate goals expected to achieve the former in one year or less whereas the latter were estimated most prominently in the two-to-three-year range. As many therapists anticipated the treatment to last six months or less, as three years or more. An appreciable proportion gave evasive answers.

A more specific question dealt with the length of time required to relieve the patient's symptoms. The majority estimated that this could be done in one year, a fair percentage being even more optimistic. To the extent that the therapist views symptoms as rooted in the patient's personality structure whose modification is the more important task of psychotherapy, he might feel reluctant to take a stand on a question that might strike him as thoroughly nondynamic. The large percentage of abstentions or noncommittal answers on this item may be partly explained by this reasoning.

In view of the patient's poor economic condition, his wife's invalidism, etc., it appeared appropriate to consider the possibility of compromises in case the recommendations for treatment were unfeasible for practical reasons. The most

243

frequent response concerned changes in external arrangements of therapy, such as fewer sessions per week, referral to a clinic, or less intensive treatment. A moderate proportion suggested such adjuncts as tranquilizing drugs. It is noteworthy that negligible minorities recommended hospitalization or electric shock therapy.

As a global estimate of the kinds of changes in the patient's personality structure the respondents would attempt, the following responses appear instructive: a quarter of the responding therapists described their over-all goals as a fairly extensive change; more than half contented themselves with relatively little change; and 12 per cent said they would strive for very little change.

Analysis of systematic differences

VARIABILITY AS A FUNCTION OF EXPERIENCE: In view of the wide range of professional experience among the therapists, analyses were performed to determine the degree of association between length of experience and the various questionnaire items. The sample was divided into three groups: Group I included psychiatrists having 0 to $1\frac{3}{4}$ years of experience in therapy; Group II, two to five years of experience; and Group III, six years and above. Responses to each questionnaire item were then broken down in terms of this grouping, and the chi-square technique applied to test the significance of the differences in the three groups.

The results can be summarized by the statement that length of professional experience seemed to have a negligible bearing upon therapists' diagnostic and prognostic evaluations. In the case of continuous variables, product-moment coefficients of correlation were also computed. These are presented in Table 3.

The significant correlation between Ego Strength and experience as well as age indicates that with increasing experience therapists tended to judge the patient's ego strength to be *less*. Similarly, older therapists evaluated the

244

TABLE 3

PRODUCT-MOMENT COEFFICIENTS OF CORRELATION BETWEEN ATTITUDINAL AND BIOGRAPHICAL VARIABLES

(Average N=115)

Variable	Prognosis with Therapy	Attitude toward Patient	Experience (in years)	Experience (self-estimate)	Competence as Therapist (self-estimate)	Age
Ego Strength	.37†	.15	.20*	.07	.03	.23†
Anxiety	.08	.20*	−.09	−.03	.00	−.12
Insight	.38†	.33†	.12	.11	−.05	.03
Self-observation versus Rationalization	.36†	.35†	−.10	−.02	.04	−.09
Emotional Maturity	−.41†	−.20*	.05	.04	.03	.03
Social Adjustment	.28†	.21*	.15	.08	−.09	.10
Disturbance	−.17	−.04	−.07	−.10	.02	−.05
Prognosis without Therapy	.05	−.11	.14	−.01	.08	.21*
Prognosis with Therapy	—	.39†	.16	.07	−.08	.06
Attitude toward Patient	—	—	.02	.05	−.09	−.11
Experience (in years)	—	—	—	.72†	−.65†	.85†
Experience (self-estimate)	—	—	—	—	−.80†	.64†
Competence as Therapist (self-estimate)	—	—	—	—	—	−.56†

* Significant at the .05 level.   † Significant at the .01 level.

prognosis *without* therapy as less favorable than younger therapists. However, on both items the evidence was inconsistent and tentative. With respect to formulations of the patient's dynamics, experienced therapists contributed a larger number of "superior" formulations (the correlation, not shown in Table 3, was $r = .22$).

These results are plausible if it is recalled that many of the questionnaire items called for relatively simple judgments and predictions, so that an inexperienced therapist— or even a layman—might make a more or less informed guess. On the other hand, certain items, like formulation of the patient's emotional dynamics, made considerably greater demands on the therapist's technical knowledge; hence the experienced therapist was at an advantage. There was no conclusive evidence that experienced therapists preferred a particular kind of formulation, as measured by the classifications mentioned.

These tests also proved nonsignificant almost without exception on questions dealing with therapeutic plans, goals, and techniques. A parallel analysis comparing analysts (mean experience 13.7 years), psychiatrists (mean experience 7.3 years), and residents (mean experience .9 years) was likewise inconclusive except that analysts tended to judge the length of therapy to be longer than either psychiatrists or residents (who did not seem to differ significantly). Analysts preferred three or more weekly sessions, in contrast to psychiatrists, who preferred one or two weekly interviews.

In both analyses, the more experienced therapists, irrespective of whether they described themselves as analysts, tended to state the course of the transference in terms of interpersonal dynamics, whereas inexperienced respondents tended to prefer descriptions in terms of transferred roles.

VARIABILITY AS A FUNCTION OF ATTITUDE TOWARD THE PATIENT: The next analysis concerned a breakdown of responses to each questionnaire item in terms of the therapist's attitude toward the patient.

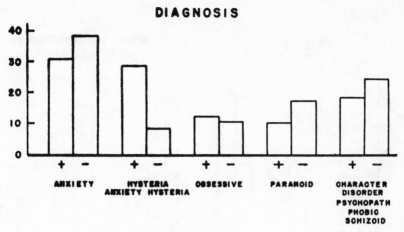

DIAGNOSIS

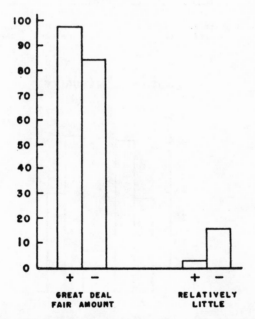

ANXIETY

FIGURE 7. Clinical evaluations in terms of therapist's attitude toward the patient, based upon statistically significant chi squares. Each bar indicates the percentage of therapists choosing a particular response alternative depending upon their attitude toward the patient. (+ = positive attitude, $N = 40$; − = negative or ambivalent attitude, $N = 65$; neutral attitude, $N = 28$, omitted.) (continued overleaf)

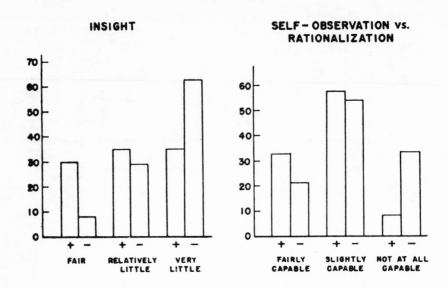

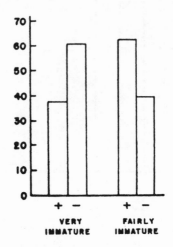

FIGURE 7. (cont'd.).

248

SOCIAL ADJUSTMENT

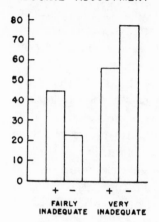

PROGNOSIS WITH THERAPY

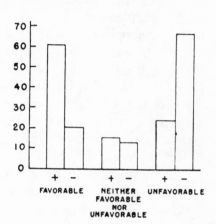

REASONS FOR ATTITUDE TOWARD PATIENT

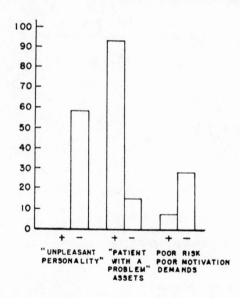

FIGURE 7. (cont'd.).

249

Table 3 shows a positive correlation between prognosis and attitude. It is not surprising that prognosis is correlated with diagnostic evaluations, but it is noteworthy that most of the relationships shown in Table 3 are paralleled by the therapist's attitude toward the patient. A slightly different method of analysis lends greater concreteness to these findings (see Figure 7). In each instance, chi squares were computed for the distributions of the positive and negative groups; the small ambivalent group was included in the negative group; the neutral group, because of its relative smallness, was omitted. The results were significant at least at the .05 level, and usually at the .01 level or beyond.

Therapists indicating a negative attitude toward the patient were more likely to choose such diagnostic labels as psychopath, character disorder, paranoid, and phobic; tended to see the patient as less anxious, having less insight,

TABLE 4

COMPARATIVE DATA ON PROBABILITY LEVELS OF CHI SQUARE FOR FULL SAMPLE AND PSYCHIA⁻RIST SAMPLE

Topical Area and Questionnaire Items	Full Sample ($N=168$)*	Psychiatrists only ($N=105$)†
Goals and Approaches		
Areas to be Avoided	.01	NS
Problems of Therapeutic Technique		
Dangers in Therapy	.02	NS
Handling of Countertransference	.05	NS
Recommendations to Patient	.001	.02
Strict-Permissive	.001	.05
Active-Passive	.05	.01
Free Association	.01	NS
Form of Therapy, Frequency, Length		
Form of Therapy	.05	.05
Frequency of Sessions	.05	.05
Symptom Relief (time estimate)	.001	.05
Changes Attempted	.05	NS

* "Neutral" group omitted; "ambivalent" group omitted.
† "Neutral" group omitted.
NS = Not significant.

250

being less capable of self-observation, more immature emotionally, and more poorly adjusted socially. A negative attitude toward the patient was associated with significantly poorer prognosis, and therapists responding in this manner were more likely to comment about the patient's "unpleasant personality characteristics."

Of the 27 chi squares relevant to therapeutic goals and techniques, 6 were significant at or beyond the 5 per cent level. It will be seen from Table 4 that the number of significant chi squares is almost doubled when the statistic is computed on the full sample of therapists (psychiatrists, psychologists, and social workers). Since the direction of change is quite consistent, it may be assumed that the trends are attenuated when the size of the sample is reduced. It appears less likely that the observed trends are more pronounced in the nonpsychiatrist groups.* While greater confidence, obviously, can be placed in those results that are significant in both samples, it seemed justifiable to present graphically the results for the full sample. This has been done in Figure 8.

Only one of the questions pertaining to therapeutic goals and approaches yielded a significant chi square, and this may be due to the particular grouping of responses. This result indicates (full sample only) that therapists whose attitude toward the patient was negative were more likely to suggest avoidance of certain areas in therapy, such as the patient's relationship with his wife, sexual impulses, hostility, anger, death wishes, unconscious material, fantasies, and dreams.

Under the heading "Problems of Therapeutic Tech-

---

*The experience levels of the various attitudinal groups, on the other hand, are more sharply differentiated for psychiatrists than for the full sample. In the former group, therapists professing a positive attitude had a mean experience of 4.72 years; neutral, 8.46 years; negative and ambivalent, 6.55 years. Analysis of variance yielded an F of 15.74, which is significant at the .001 level. For the full sample, the mean differences were statistically nonsignificant.

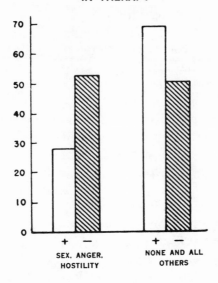

AREAS TO BE AVOIDED
IN THERAPY

70 —

60 —

50 —

40 —

30 —

20 —

10 —

0 —

+ —   + —

SEX. ANGER.   NONE AND ALL
HOSTILITY   OTHERS

DANGERS IN THERAPY

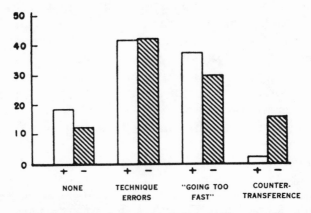

50 —

40 —

30 —

20 —

10 —

0 —

+ —   + —   + —   + —

NONE   TECHNIQUE   "GOING TOO   COUNTER-
      ERRORS   FAST"   TRANSFERENCE

FIGURE 8. Responses in terms of therapist's attitude toward the patient, based upon statistically significant chi squares. Each bar indicates the percentage of therapists (full sample) choosing a particular response alternative depending upon their attitude toward the patient. (+ = positive attitude, $N = 75$; − = negative attitude, $N = 93$; neutral attitude, $N = 45$, and ambivalent attitude, $N = 21$, omitted.)

RECOMMENDATIONS

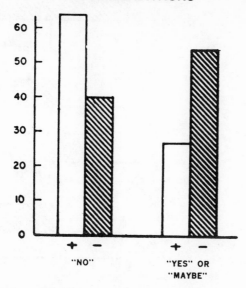

HANDLING OF COUNTERTRANSFERENCE

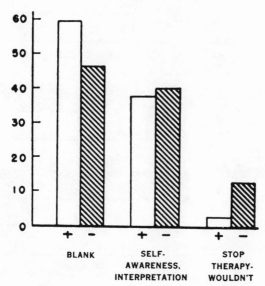

FIGURE 8. (cont'd.).

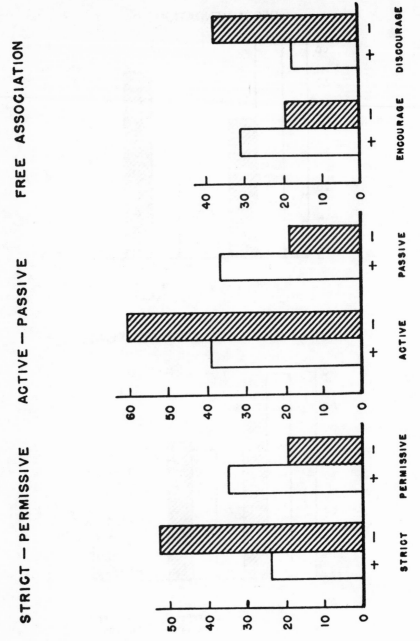

FIGURE 8. (cont'd.).

254

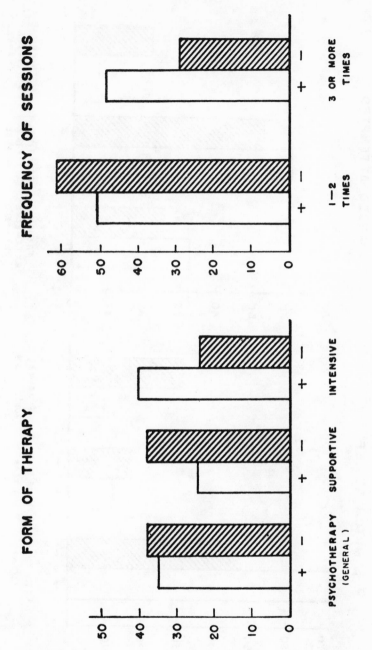

FIGURE 8. (cont'd.).

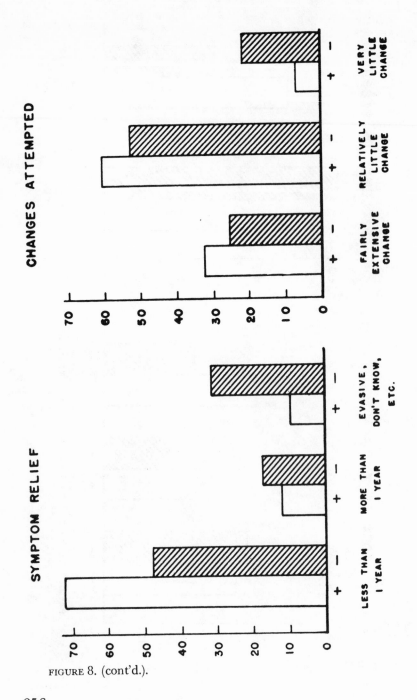

FIGURE 8. (cont'd.).

256

nique," the null hypothesis was rejected for several question-naire items. Descriptively, these results may be stated as follows:

Therapists expressing a negative attitude toward the patient were more likely to anticipate dangers to successful therapy from the therapist's anger, irritation, and other countertransference reactions (full sample only). On the other hand, therapists holding a positive attitude were more likely to mention the danger of pressing the patient too hard in therapy and recommended a sympathetic and under-standing attitude by the therapist. While there was a slight (but inconclusive) trend for the "dislike" group to expect more countertransference reactions, this group was more likely to discontinue therapy if the therapist became aware of countertransference, or not to accept the patient for treatment in the first place. Therapists admitting a negative attitude were more likely to make recommendations to the patient concerning changes in his mode of living—an approach often strongly disadvised by the "like" group.

The evidence was clear-cut that therapists whose atti-tude toward the patient was positive tended to characterize their proposed techniques as permissive, whereas a signi-ficantly larger proportion of the "dislike" group voted for strictness.

Similarly, with respect to the therapist's activity or passivity, a positive attitude toward the patient was asso-ciated with passivity, a negative attitude with activity.

Free association tended to be encouraged by therapists feeling positively about the patient, but was discouraged by those holding a negative attitude (full sample only).

With regard to the form of therapy, frequency of ses-sions, etc., a positive attitude was associated with the more intensive forms of treatment, including psychoanalysis, whereas therapists feeling negatively toward the patient were more likely to recommend supportive therapy or other adjuncts. A positive attitude was correlated with more fre-

257

quent weekly visits, fewer evasive answers about symptom relief, and plans for more extensive change in the patient's character structure (full sample only). Responses to the last item indicated that compared to therapists expressing a positive attitude, four times as many therapists holding a negative attitude planned for "very little change."

Attempts were also made to explore the possible influences of theoretical orientation and personal analysis upon therapists' response patterns. With respect to theoretical orientation, it proved difficult to isolate "pure" groups since respondents often acknowledged multiple influences. Several criteria were used to define "orthodox" and "neo-Freudian" groups, but these were so small as to preclude the application of rigorous statistical techniques. The results of this analysis must therefore be regarded as inconclusive. Similar difficulties were encountered with regard to personal analysis. Here an attempt was made to match a sample of psychiatrists whose training had included personal analysis with a comparable nonanalyzed group, experience, age, and sex being held constant. Even with an N of 28 in each group it proved impossible in most instances to test for the significance of differences on the various item responses. While the evidence must be judged indeterminate, it may be worth mentioning that the observed differences appeared, for the most part, small.

Analysis of therapists' communications to the patient

OVER-ALL RESPONSE DISTRIBUTIONS: Table 5 presents frequencies and percentages of therapists' responses, as distributed within each system component. As might be expected in a first interview, many communications were designed to obtain a fuller picture of the patient's person and problem. Highly inferential communications as well as comments revealing a high level of initiative were relatively rare.

EXPERIENCE IN PSYCHOTHERAPY: It seems reasonable

258

TABLE 5

SUMMARY DISTRIBUTIONS OF PSYCHIATRISTS' RESPONSES, QUANTIFIED BY A
MULTIDIMENSIONAL SYSTEM OF ANALYSIS
($N=126$ Psychiatrists)

System Component	Responses N	%
Type		
Silence	975	27.3
Passive Acceptance	169	4.7
Exploratory Operations	1,689	47.3
Clarification	128	3.6
Interpretive Operations	175	4.9
Direct Guidance	302	8.5
Miscellaneous and Unclassifiable	134	3.7
Total	3,572	100.0
Depth-directedness		
Level 1 Mildly inferential	202	8.2
2	459	18.6
3	1,125	45.4
4	495	20.0
5 Moderately inferential	104	4.2
6	60	2.4
7	20	.8
8 Highly inferential	9	.4
Total*	2,474	100.0
Dynamic Focus		
No Change in Focus	510	20.6
Reflections of Feeling	116	4.7
Requests for Additional Information	1,092	44.2
Dynamic Events—Past	151	6.1
Dynamic Events—Present	288	11.6
Therapist as Expert	284	11.5
Analysis of Transference	33	1.3
Total*	2,474	100.0

(Continued overleaf.)

Initiative

Level 1 Mild		170	6.9
2		387	15.6
3		1,086	43.9
4 Moderate		514	20.8
5		175	7.1
6		65	2.6
7 Strong		77	3.1
Total*		2,474	100.0

Therapeutic Climate

−2	5	.2
−1	31	1.2
0	2,326	94.0
+1	108	4.4
+2	4	.2
Total*	2,474	100.00

* Excludes silences and unclassifiable responses.

to hypothesize that a highly experienced therapist will conduct an initial interview differently from an inexperienced resident. Table 6 shows the results of the analysis of variance that may be summarized as follows: *

1. Inexperienced psychiatrists tended to ask more exploratory questions than experienced therapists.

2. Experienced psychiatrists tended to give a larger number of interpretive responses than inexperienced psychiatrists. These communications tended to be more inferential, and their dynamic focus concerned dynamic interpersonal events in the patient's past and present life.

3. Experienced therapists showed a higher degree of

---

*Unless otherwise indicated, the reference to statistical results in this section is Table 6. The descriptive statements are based on statistically significant group comparisons, as shown in that table. When more than two groups were involved, an attempt was made to "locate" the significant over-all difference by comparing subgroups with each other. Such references in the text describe subsidiary comparisons which were statistically significant at an acceptable level. Occasional exceptions to this procedure are specifically noted.

initiative in their communications than inexperienced practitioners.

4. Experienced therapists tended to change the dynamic focus of their communications more than the less experienced respondents.

5. Experienced therapists tended to be slightly "warmer."

The above changes appeared to be progressive with increasing experience.

ANALYSTS, PSYCHIATRISTS, RESIDENTS: A parallel analysis was performed on a somewhat different criterion—the respondent's self-description of his status within the profession. The analysis is analogous to the first one because the three groups were markedly divergent in terms of professional experience: Analysts' mean experience was 13.7 years; psychiatrists', 7.3 years; residents', .9 years. However, the variable of personal analysis and analytic training seems to enter more prominently into this grouping. The first group (with one exception) had both personal analysis and analytic training; the third group, for the most part, had neither; the middle group was divided. (On an over-all basis, the correlation between professional experience and personal analysis was .43.)

The following differences were statistically significant:

1. The number of interpretive communications given by analysts was proportionately larger than that of residents. As expected, such communications tended to be more inferential.

2. The relative degree of initiative shown by analysts was greater than that of residents.

3. Analysts tended to shift the dynamic focus from passive acceptance to past and current interpersonal events more than psychiatrists and residents.

4. While the over-all comparison was nonsignificant, the relative frequency of responses whose emotional tone

TABLE 6
SUMMARY OF STATISTICAL ANALYSES*

| Variable | System Components | | | | | | | | | | | | Subgroups | N |
| | Type | | | | Depth-directedness | Dynamic focus | | | | | Climate | | | |
	Silence	Explorations	Interpretations	Direct Guidance		Maintain focus	Addit. Info.	Dynamic Events	Therap. as Expert	Initiative	"Cold"	"Warm"		
Experience	—	.05	.01	—	.01	.05	.05	.02	—	.01	—	.09	0–1.75 yrs. 2–9 yrs. 10–30 yrs.	40 53 34
Grouping within Profession	—	.06	.01	—	.01	.001	—	.01	—	.02	—	—	Analysts Psychiatrists Residents	30 57 43
Personal Analysis†	.02	.02	—	—	—	—	—	—	—	—	—	—	Personal Analysis No Personal Analysis	28 28
Membership in Amer. Psy. Ass'n.	—	—	—	—	—	—	—	—	—	—	—	—	Members Non-members	18 14

Variable	Category	N										
Length of Analysis	More than 500 hours	22	—	—	—	—	—	—	—	—	—	.01
	Less than 500 hours	13	—	—	—	—	—	—	—	—	—	—
Theoretical Orientation†	Orthodox Freudians	16	—	—	—	—	—	—	—	—	—	—
	Neo-Freudians	16	—	—	—	—	—	—	—	—	—	—
Attitude toward Patient	Positive (+)	39	.05	.07	—	—	—	.03	—	—	—	—
	Neutral (0)	26	—	—	—	—	—	—	—	—	—	—
	Negative (−)	51	—	—	—	—	—	—	—	—	—	—
	Ambivalent (±)	13	—	—	—	—	—	—	—	—	—	—
Prognosis	Favorable (+)	41	.05	.05	.05	—	—	—	.05	—	—	—
	Noncommittal (0)	17	—	—	—	—	—	—	—	—	—	—
	Unfavorable (−)	58	—	—	—	—	—	—	—	—	—	—
Attitude-Prognosis (Jointly)	Att.: +; Prog.: +	22	—	.05	—	—	—	.05	—	—	—	—
	Att.: −; Prog.: −	33	—	—	—	—	—	—	—	—	—	—

* Significance levels (two-tailed tests) are based on the Mann-Whitney *U* test (comparisons of two groups) or the Kruskal-Wallis one-way analysis of variance (comparisons of more than two groups). Probabilities of .10 or less are given in the table; p values greater than .10 have been omitted (indicated by a dash). The statistic used for Depth-directedness, Initiative, and Climate (over-all comparisons) was chi square.

† Matched samples.

was judged "cold" was greater among analysts than among residents (ratio of $3:1$). Differences among "warm" responses were not statistically significant.

5. The decline of exploratory communications with experience, reported above, was significant at the .06 level for the present grouping. The direction of change was identical.

PERSONAL ANALYSIS: While the foregoing results suggest that the observed differences are primarily a function of experience, it is possible that personal analysis might make a contribution of its own. In order to explore this question, two samples were equated in terms of experience and at each experience level a therapist with a personal analysis was matched with a therapist without this training. The matched samples are described in Table 7. The results indicate that the only significant differences concern the relative frequency of silent responses and exploratory questions: analyzed therapists gave a significantly larger number of silent responses, this difference being achieved at the expense of exploratory questions.

To learn whether these differences might be more pronounced at the high or the low end of experience, the matched samples were equally divided into a high and low experience group. Comparisons showed that the difference in silent responses was particularly prominent among inexperienced therapists, suggesting that personal analysis might have a greater influence at the lower end of the experience continuum. These results are supported by another analysis in which 18 members of the American Psychoanalytic Association were compared with 14 nonmembers (both groups had a mean experience of approximately 14 years but most members of the second group had no personal analysis). No statistically significant differences were observed in these highly experienced groups. Nor did therapists whose analyses exceeded 500 hours differ in their responses from therapists whose personal therapy was relatively less extensive.

264

TABLE 7

SUMMARY OF BIOGRAPHICAL VARIABLES FOR TWO MATCHED SAMPLES OF
PSYCHIATRISTS
($N=28$)

Variable	Personal Analysis	No Personal Analysis
Age (mean)	38.4 years	38.2 years
Experience in therapy (mean)	6.4 years	6.4 years
Personal Analysis (mean)	458.8 hours	—
Analysts	10	1
Psychiatrists	10	17
Residents	8	10
Total Sample (M.D. degree)	28	28
Theoretical Orientation:		
Psychoanalytically oriented—general	19	15
Freud—orthodox	1	0
Sullivan	2	3
Meyer	0	3
Miscellaneous	6	7
Male/Female	24/4	25/3

THEORETICAL ORIENTATION: Despite the difficulties of isolating "pure" groups, an attempt was made to match two presumably divergent samples: those who subscribed to an "orthodox Freudian" orientation and those who might be called "neo-Freudians." Each group included 16 therapists, all of whom had undergone personal analysis. The orthodox Freudians' median experience level was 8.5 years, median length of personal analysis 650 hours; the neo-Freudians had a median experience of 7.0 years, and the median length of their analyses was 250 hours. Statistical comparisons failed to reveal any reliable differences between these groups.

ATTITUDE TOWARD THE PATIENT: It was shown in the preceding section that the therapist's conscious attitude toward the patient tended to be correlated with his clinical evaluations as well as his treatment plans, goals, and proposed techniques. This finding suggested the hypothesis that the therapist's self-rating of his conscious attitude might carry over to his communications; specifically, that therapists expressing a negative attitude would tend to be "colder," that is, more rejecting in their communications than therapists professing a positive attitude.

Comparisons between groups of therapists professing a positive, neutral, negative, or ambivalent attitude disclosed a statistically significant difference relative to exploratory questions; however, since this finding was not corroborated on related system components, it may be considered due to chance.

With regard to Therapeutic Climate, chi square for "cold" responses was significant at the .07 level of confidence, for "warm" responses it was significant at the .05 level. Therapists indicating a negative attitude gave three times the number of "cold" responses as therapists having a positive attitude. The "ambivalent" attitude group was differentiated reliably from each of the remaining groups by giving the largest proportion of "warm" responses. The positive attitude group did not differ significantly from the negative one in terms of "warm" responses.

PROGNOSIS: In view of the correlation between therapists' self-estimates of their attitude toward the patient and their prognostic ratings, a parallel analysis was conducted by grouping respondents according to their prognostic estimates. The results may be summarized as follows:

1. Statistically significant group differences were observed with regard to silent responses. Therapists expressing a noncommittal prognostic estimate tended to give the smallest number of silent responses.

2. Respondents giving a favorable prognosis were more likely to accept the patient's focus without attempting to shift it.

3. Therapists giving a noncommittal prognosis tended to show more initiative in their communications than the other two groups.

266

4.   Therapists whose prognosis was unfavorable gave more than four times as many "cold" responses than respondents who considered the prognosis favorable. (The noncommittal group appeared closer to the "favorable" one.)

5. The relative frequency of "warm" responses was greatest among therapists whose prognosis was noncommittal, and relatively low (one-half or less) in both the "favorable" and the "unfavorable" groups.

ATTITUDE AND PROGNOSIS CONSIDERED JOINTLY: To cast further light on the above findings, two extreme groups were isolated and compared. The first group included therapists whose attitude toward the patient was positive and whose prognosis was favorable (mean experience=5.6 years), the second those whose attitude was negative and whose prognosis was unfavorable (mean experience=6.6 years).* The group comparisons revealed few technique differences, except that the second group tended to change the focus by asking significantly more exploratory questions. In terms of Climate, however, the differences reported separately for Attitude and Prognosis were accentuated. Only 1 therapist in the first group obtained a "cold" response, in contrast to 10 in the second group—a ratio of almost 1 : 7. "Warm" responses revealed a small difference in the predicted direction, which was not statistically significant.

It may be appropriate to reiterate the earlier statement that the scores on Climate represent almost certainly a gross underestimate, so that many potentially "positive" or "negative" responses had to be treated as "neutral" for lack of sufficient evidence. Consequently, the frequencies involved in these comparisons are relatively small, but the relationships between film responses and therapist's attitude and prognosis nevertheless emerge as quite consistent. "Cold" responses, by this evidence, appear to be a more sensitive

---

*The mean difference was statistically nonsignificant.

indicator of the therapist's conscious attitude than "warm," empathic ones.

Further exploration of the empathy variable

The findings highlighting the interrelationships between the emotional tone of therapists' communications, conscious attitude, and clinical evaluations led to further explorations. In scoring the responses to the points of interruption in the film, our* attention was called early to marked qualitative differences in terms of responses to particular choice points (some of which appeared especially critical) as well as the over-all response patterns. As we developed a greater appreciation for the range of response, we became increasingly impressed by differences in therapists' underlying attitudes toward the patient, their willingness or unwillingness to engage in a therapeutic relationship, and their empathy. To be sure, some protocols did not lend themselves to this kind of analysis, mostly because the respondent had been unable or unwilling to make his stand sufficiently explicit, so that his written statements that at best conveyed only a pale impression of the sound of his voice left the question indeterminate. But a substantial number of protocols did provide sufficient evidence, and often very clear-cut evidence.

RESPONSES TO SELECTED CHOICE POINTS: Before dealing with certain global impressions gained from complete protocols, I should like to present some examples of responses to "critical" choice points. Often there seemed to be a noteworthy consistency between therapists' responses to several of these choice points.

One of the most controversial and seemingly most diagnostic passages occurred at the end of the interview. Somewhat unexpectedly perhaps, the patient makes an impassioned plea for reassurance by expressing concern about

*I wish to take this opportunity to repeat my sincere appreciation to Mrs. Rebecca E. Rieger, my research associate, who made a vital contribution to this phase of the work.

his anxiety symptoms, which, he fears, might lead to a heart attack. The question expresses both his obsessive ruminations and his intense anxiety. It may be a "loaded" question in the sense that his unconscious objective is to put the therapist "on the spot," to force him to commit himself. It also expresses the patient's dependency needs, his demands for a magical protector, and his passive-aggressive submission to an authority figure. The passage ends with the question: "That's all I want to ask you. Are they [these attacks] going to kill me? Will they cause me to have . . . will they cause my heart to flop out from under me some day or will they damage my nerve tissue or even my . . . my thinking?"

Here are some typical examples of therapists' responses:

> I feel that your emotional difficulty is really more important than any heart disease you might have. We can have you checked physically to determine your physical health.
>
> You prefer to talk of your symptoms—not your feelings. They are not the real problem.
>
> You must be convinced by now that they won't damage you after all these years. Tell me, how would your life be different if you didn't have them?
>
> No; but the attacks are causing you a lot of distress.
>
> No; these are only the effects of things you don't understand within yourself.
>
> What we can do here is see what we can find out about the attacks, what sets them off.
>
> No, your physical symptoms will not harm you. But it is important to understand what they do for you.
>
> No, this will not happen.
>
> I seem to feel that you know there is a connection between how you feel and the way you think life has treated you.
>
> Naturally, you are concerned about yourself.

In the following replies the therapist sidesteps the issue. He may feel that by doing so he is avoiding a trap, but in any event he is deliberately or unknowingly neglecting the patient's feelings. It is predictable that this evasion would be experienced by the patient as a rejection or at least as a "letting down." If it is kept in mind that the interview is drawing to a close, the possibility of increasing rather than allaying the patient's anxiety should be a matter of serious concern to the therapist. Operationally, such therapists either subtly changed the focus by asking a related question, or they threw the question back. The latter maneuver, used quite frequently by inexperienced therapists, appeared to be an evasion because the patient had talked about his feelings at some length.

You say you have these attacks at home now?
Even your thinking, huh?
Why should they damage you?
These are things you fear?
I'd like to discuss the types of work that you have done, for a while.
What did the other doctors tell you?
How do you feel when you feel "safe"?
What do you think?
Do you think they will?

There was a small group of therapists who decided either to make no reply at all or to launch a frontal attack upon the patient's neurotic defenses:

With your good luck, you're going to live and suffer.
Do you want to be a chronic invalid and be taken care of?
What difference would it make if I said yes or no? (Perhaps I might go on, not antagonistically, to explain that's not the problem.)
They might.
I don't know.

270

The following responses reflect the therapist's desire to avoid an authoritative answer and yet to give a forthright reply that may have the effect of allaying the patient's anxiety, at least temporarily:

As far as I know that will not cause a heart attack or damage your nerve tissue, but you surely want more than this. You want help for these symptoms, and I'll have to know more.

I know these feelings are very uncomfortable, I can't answer your question completely. I feel it's something that should be looked into.

That's a very important question, of course, but something we'll have to go into fully later. First we need a fuller understanding of you and your problem. I'd like to talk with you again and go into everything in more detail. Let's make another appointment if it's all right with you.

These examples may convey something of the wide range of responses and their individual flavor. They also show how different therapists attempted to meet the problem inherent in the patient's concluding question. Apart from the patient's needs at the moment, it was clear that certain therapists emerged as persons, as individuals, as human beings who were not averse to use the pronoun *I*, whereas others considered it important to remain anonymous. It was our impression that some of the most highly experienced therapists appeared most clearly as persons, both in an accepting and a rejecting sense; conversely, inexperience tended to go together with anonymity.

An interesting difference in responses was observed with regard to a passage in which the patient mentions a constructive striving toward health that, to the superficial viewer, might easily be considered subordinate to his recital of symptoms, etc. After detailing a number of symptoms, the patient says:

P.: You see what I mean? Pressure. Put your hand on your other hand; you got pressure. (T.: Mmm.) Well, that's just like it feels; that's the sensation of being hemmed in; you're cornered; you don't know which way to go. You are tired of the surroundings you are in and what you have been doing; you can't find anything that takes its place, that seems to be ... to ... fulfill the bill for you. (T.: Mmm.) But it's the sensations that worry me. (T.: Mmm.) This other stuff, huh, I can forget ... (T.: Mmm.) ... or have to if I want to regain my health.

The "obvious" thing to do at this point is to ask for further information: "Forget what?" "What other stuff?"

It seems to require greater alertness and self-awareness to focus on the patient's striving for health, which appears heavily overlaid by his emphasis on symptoms: "You feel as if you'd like to be healthier, too?" "You really want to get over these feelings?" "How do you feel you can regain your health?" "What kind of help might you expect from me?"

Among therapists whose conscious attitude toward the patient (expressed independently in the questionnaire) was positive and who gave a favorable prognosis ($N = 22$), 32 per cent focused on the "health" aspect, whereas among the negative attitude—unfavorable prognosis group ($N = 33$), only 1 therapist (3 per cent) took this approach. Among the latter group, 12 therapists included the phrase "other stuff" in their responses, whereas in the former group only 2 therapists did, one of whom combined the remark with a reference to the patient's health. This piece of evidence suggests that the second group tended to be more preoccupied with "pathology" than the first one.

An illuminating contrast in approach is provided by therapists' responses to an episode in which the patient relates an experience of being discharged from a job. Comments encompassed empathic remarks about the patient's misfortune, his underlying feelings, requests for further information, and moral judgment or condemnation.

. . . So, when I got fired from the First National Bank in H—— for writing a little old stinking $35 check on my personal account and didn't have the money to cover it, I got fired for that . . . see . . . And in my home town, a thing like that gets around pretty quick, in a small community. I couldn't find a damn job. I didn't have any place to sleep. I didn't have a damn thing to eat. Being an Episcopalian, I went to a person who I knew . . . she ran a boarding house, and I chopped wood at night for my supper, see, to get something to eat. And that was the beginning of all my antisocial attitudes. And if that isn't three strikes against you before you come to bat, I'd like to know what in the hell it is.

You seem to have had a hard time of it, especially after your father died.
    You feel badly about that time in your life.
    I can see things were pretty rough for you.
    You seem angry when you talk of this.
    Tell me about these antisocial attitudes.
    Despite the rough time, you seemed to know how to get work and take care of yourself.
    How do you think the bank manager should have handled the situation?
    How did the bank happen to fire you for what seemed just like an error?
    Fired for writing a bad check, huh?
    What would you have the bank do?
    You did write the check and expected to get away with it?
    You feel sorry for yourself; no one seemed interested.

Comparisons of responses to single items (stopping points) were often less revealing of the therapist's attitude

273

toward the patient, but the totality of the response pattern frequently provided important clues. On the basis of these observations it was decided to attempt an over-all evaluation of the protocols.

OVER-ALL EVALUATION OF PROTOCOLS: The objective of arriving at a global judgment of the degree of empathy shown by therapists was to determine whether such ratings could be made reliably, that is, whether independent raters could agree on the evaluation, and to explore the relationships between over-all ratings to other relevant therapist variables. Considering the exploratory character of this analysis, we restricted ourselves to a few gross categories. The major criteria are given below:

Score +. Therapist recognizes the existence of an emotional problem and communicates such understanding to the patient somewhere in the interview. Such communications may convey reassurance but this may not necessarily be the case.

Therapist recognizes that the patient is seeking help, that he is in need of help, that psychotherapy can help him, that there may be a relationship between patient's physical symptoms and his emotional conflicts, and that insight or understanding of the latter may alleviate the former.

Therapist communicates that he understands that the patient is suffering, that he is anxious and in a state of discomfort.

Therapist attempts to alleviate the patient's discomfort in the interview by putting him at ease, by trying to alleviate his anxiety, by instilling some hope for the future, by recognizing his past accomplishments despite difficulties, by raising his self-esteem.

Therapist feels the need to communicate to the patient something about treatment plans, referral, etc., that is, he recognizes that the patient has a right to expect a statement or recommendation from the interviewer as an expert, that the interview must serve a useful purpose to the patient, either by opening further possibilities or by making certain that the present experience is a constructive one.

Therapist gives evidence of listening to the patient's story, either by pertinent remarks or questions or by respectful silence. There should be no evidence that therapist changes a topic in order to impose his own frame of reference or trend of thought (especially in the beginning), nor should he respond with silence to urgent pleas from the patient.

The phrasing of comments should be respectful, non-derogatory, sympathetic, noncritical, nonjudgmental. There should be a complete absence of communications that by themselves would be assigned a score of −.

Score −. Therapist is cold, distant, unperceptive, unfeeling, and impersonal. Such attitudes would be inferred from a total absence of communications receiving a score of + or, more directly, from overt evidence: communications that seem to imply derogation, criticism, antagonism, hostility, disrespect, moral judgment, condemnation, accusation, impatience, punishment, nonacceptance of the patient as a person, or rejection. Included also would be communications by which the therapist implies or states openly that the patient is malingering, that he is anti-social, lazy, derelict in his duties to his family, exploiting, manipulating, sponging on others, psychopathic, unconventional, "crazy," ridiculous, silly, exaggerating, falsely accusing others, or imposing on the interviewer in any manner.

Therapist devotes large portions of the interview to gathering facts about the patient's life history. The interview resembles a cross-examination.

Therapist "gives" nothing to the patient such as recommendations for treatment, recognition that a problem exists, that psychotherapeutic help is available, that problems like his can and have been helped by psychotherapy; reassurance; acknowledgment that the patient is having a hard time, that his emotional and/or reality problems complicate his living.

Therapist responds with silence to patient's plea for reassurance, or uses rote devices to throw back the question. Therapist fails to respond to patient's underlying feelings throughout the interview.

Therapist gives interpretations that in the context of an initial interview and the patient's emotional state seem premature, inappropriate, etc. This judgment would apply with particular force to interpretations that are given very early in the interview, confront the patient directly with an important aspect of his problem, are not stated tentatively but rather authoritatively; that, because of their directness would be experienced by the patient as an attack on his self-esteem and consequently rejected; interpretations that seem "over the patient's head."

Score 0. The record provides insufficient evidence to warrant either a score of + or −, either because communications are minimal or because their emotional tone is "neutral." Therapist does not emerge sufficiently to be judged on the aforementioned criteria. (Records receiving a score of 0 tend to lean toward the − side, principally because there is an absence of positive indicators.)

Score ±. The record gives evidence of both + and − indicators, as previously defined, and it is difficult to determine which of these preponderate.

RATER AGREEMENT: Two successive ratings were made by two trained raters working independently. Rater agreement is reported in Table 8. Since there were indications of a certain affinity between + and ± ratings, and between 0 and − ratings, differences within these groupings were countered as "partial agreement." It is believed that sound recordings of the therapist's voice would have substantially increased the reliability of the judgments.

RELATIONSHIPS OF EMPATHY RATINGS TO OTHER VARIABLES: The four empathy ratings were combined into a single rating, and compared with therapists' self-ratings of their *attitude* toward the patient. Chi square was significant

276

TABLE 8

AGREEMENT WITHIN AND BETWEEN TWO INDEPENDENT RATERS
($N=131$)

	Full* Agreement	Partial† Agreement	Disagree- ment
Rater 1: Rating 1 versus Rating 2	69 (53%)	35 (27%)	27 (20%)
Rater 2: Rating 1 versus Rating 2	52 (40%)	38 (29%)	41 (31%)
Rater 1 versus Rater 2: Rating 1	51 (39%)	33 (25%)	47 (36%)
Rater 1 versus Rater 2: Rating 2	57 (44%)	28 (21%)	46 (35%)

* Using four categories: +, −, 0, and ±.
† Combining categories + and ±, and 0 and −.

at the .02 level of confidence. The distributions indicated that almost two-thirds of the therapists expressing a positive attitude received positive empathy ratings; negative attitude tended to be related to negative empathy ratings in approximately the same manner.

A similar analysis relating empathy ratings to therapists' *prognostic estimates* yielded a chi square that was significant at the .05 level, signifying an association between favorableness of the prognosis and greater empathy.

There was no statistically significant association between empathy ratings and *experience* in psychotherapy. A very slight trend (significant only at the .13 level of confidence) indicated that therapists having 10 or more years of experience tended to obtain a larger proportion of positive ratings.

When empathy ratings were related to the samples matched on *personal analysis,* the results were strongly in favor of the analyzed group, as shown in Table 9. Table 9 also indicates that the distribution of empathy ratings shows no differentiation in the less experienced groups, but the differences become greatly pronounced in the more experienced groups. Experienced nonanalyzed therapists had more than three times the number of negative empathy ratings as experienced analyzed therapists.

277

A further breakdown in terms of the therapist's self-rating of his attitude was undertaken in order to explore possible relationships between empathy and attitude. The results indicated that on an over-all basis the nonanalyzed group somewhat exceeded the analyzed group in terms of negative attitudes, but the difference was not statistically significant. In the less experienced group, analyzed therapists tended to have a more positive attitude; however, in the more highly experienced group the trend appeared to be almost reversed. Although these findings must be considered highly tentative because of the small size of the subsamples, in the experienced analyzed group a conscious *negative* attitude appeared to be associated more often with a *positive* empathy rating, whereas in the nonanalyzed group there appeared to be greater congruence between negative attitude and lack of empathy. Moreover, no experienced analyzed therapist having a positive attitude

TABLE 9

DISTRIBUTIONS OF EMPATHY RATINGS AND SELF-RATINGS OF ATTITUDE IN TWO GROUPS OF PSYCHIATRISTS, MATCHED IN TERMS OF PERSONAL ANALYSIS

Experience in Therapy	Attitude toward Patient	Personal Analysis			No Personal Analysis		
		Empathy Rating			Empathy Rating		
		+	−	Total	+	−	Total
0–3 years	+	3	6	9	2	2	4
	−	4	1	5	4	6	10
Total		7	7	14	6	8	14
3.5–30 years	+	4	0	4	2	4	6
	−	7	3	10	2	6	8
Total		11	3	14	4	10	14
Combined	+	7	6	13	4	6	10
	−	11	4	15	6	12	18
Total		18	10	28	10	18	28

obtained a negative empathy rating; in contrast, such a discrepancy was observed among four members of the nonanalyzed group.

The data suggest that at the higher levels of experience a therapist whose training had included personal analysis was better able to empathize with his patient regardless of his (the therapist's) conscious attitude, or perhaps in spite of a conscious (negative) attitude. On the other hand, a nonanalyzed therapist having a negative conscious attitude toward his patient was more likely to communicate this attitude to the patient. Furthermore, experienced nonanalyzed therapists were more prone to profess a positive attitude even though their communications to the patient revealed a lack of empathy, while no experienced analyzed therapist claimed a positive attitude that was not associated with empathy. In other words, personal analysis seemed to have little effect on the therapist's conscious attitude toward the patient—a majority in both groups admitted a negative reaction—but it had a differential effect upon the degree of empathy communicated to the patient.

DISCUSSION

The findings have numerous implications for psychotherapy. The importance one attaches to the implications is, of course, contingent upon the extent to which one can generalize from an experimental situation to the "naturally occurring" events in the interview process. It is not contended that the behavior of the psychiatrist in an initial interview with a "real" patient bears a one-to-one relationship to his performance in the experiment—an objection sometimes raised by respondents. What is asserted is that the evaluative processes, as they were studied under experimental conditions, are sufficiently similar to the "normal" behavior of the therapist to generate important hypotheses about his behavior in a first interview. Hypotheses thus derived are valuable if they raise further questions for research, and if they can be applied to practice and training in psychotherapy.

Two broadly defined groups of therapists appear to emerge from this investigation, whose attitudes and approach may be characterized schematically as in Table 10:

TABLE 10

Group I	Group II
Therapist's Attitude toward Patient:	
Somewhat Positive	Somewhat Negative
"Reason":	
"He is suffering and needs help."	"Unpleasant personality characteristics," poor risk, poor motivation for therapy
Diagnosis: (preferred)	
Hysteria (anxiety hysteria)	Paranoid, character disorder, psychopath, anxiety
Clinical Evaluation:	
A great deal of anxiety	Slightly less anxiety
Relatively more insight	Relatively less insight
Relatively more capable of self-observation versus rationalization	Relatively less capable of self-observation versus rationalization
More mature emotionally	Less mature emotionally
Fairly inadequate social adjustment	Very inadequate social adjustment
Prognosis with therapy:	
Favorable	Unfavorable
Treatment Plans:	
	Avoid dealing with sexual impulses, hostility, anger, death wishes, unconscious material.
Danger in "pushing" patient too fast. Therapist must be sympathetic, understanding.	Danger of therapist's irritation, anger, impatience, other countertransference reactions.
Handle countertransference by being aware of it or handle in therapy.	Handle countertransference by discontinuing therapy or not accepting patient at all.

280

Would not make recommendations to the patient about his mode of living. This is not the problem in therapy.	Might make recommendations to the patient to change his present mode of living or his environment.
Would tend to be permissive with patient.	Would tend to be strict with patient.
Would tend to be passive in therapy.	Would tend to be active in therapy.
Would encourage free association.	Would discourage free association.
Recommend intensive (insight) therapy.	Recommend supportive therapy, group therapy, drugs, other adjuncts.
3 or more weekly interviews.	1 or 2 weekly interviews.
Symptom relief expected in 1 year or less.	Evasive about length of time needed to accomplish symptom relief.
Would attempt relatively greater changes in patient's character structure.	Would attempt relatively little change in patient's character structure.

Therapist's experience:	
Relatively low	Relatively high

The above relationships are by no means invariant; we are dealing with *statistical trends,* and there were many subgroups of therapists who did not follow the pattern. However, the conclusion is suggested that clinical impressions and therapeutic planning are influenced by attitudinal variables within the therapist. Group I therapists appear to be more tolerant, more humane, more permissive, more "democratic," and more "therapeutic." Group II therapists emerge as more directive, disciplinarian, moralistic, and harsh. This contrast suggests the hypothesis that Group I therapists are "warmer" in their communications to the patient and that "cold," rejecting comments will be less frequent.

What is meant by this distinction? On the one hand, it is a basic attitude of understanding, respect, and compassion—what Albert Schweitzer calls "reverence for life."

281

It is the ability to listen to the patient's story without preconception, prejudgment, or condemnation. It is the ability to pierce the neurotic distortions, the socially unacceptable attitudes and acts, the more unsavory aspects of his personality, and to see behind it a confused, bewildered, and helpless individual trying to shape his destiny, hampered and hindered by his neurotic conflicts and maladaptations. On the other hand, it is an attitude of coldness, calculation, "clinical evaluation," distance, "objectivity," aloofness, moral judgment, and condemnation. It is a readiness to take the neurotic defenses and the patient's character structure at face value, and to react to them with irritation, impatience, annoyance, and anger. It also is an attitude of forming a judgment about the patient's illness almost from the beginning of the interview, often accompanied by a diagnostic label of "psychopathic," "paranoid," etc.

If further evidence can be adduced that motivational factors within the therapist are related to his perceptions, evaluations, and techniques with a given patient, we would be faced with many more problems than can be explained by the empirical data now at our disposal. For example, a therapist who finds himself responding negatively to a patient in an initial interview, whether or not he is aware of the underlying reasons, might have to be particularly circumspect about his emotional reactions lest they have a detrimental effect upon his evaluations and therapeutic interventions, and he may have to ask himself whether he can be therapeutically effective under these conditions. A therapist whose initial attitude is neutral or positive, needless to say, may not be free from countertransference distortions either, but to the extent that he feels free from an immediate avoidance reaction he will—at least initially—have fewer problems in treatment than one who from the start has to deal with a problem within himself. It remains to be explored whether the rather large-scale avoidance reactions are specific to this patient, whether they occur more frequently with certain kinds of patients, and if so, what patient attitudes are principally responsible for a negative or positive trigger effect. It is not inconceivable that culturally determined stereotypes have a more pervasive influence upon the alleged nontreatability of certain behavior disorders than has hitherto been realized; and that these stereotypes may exert a vitiating influence upon the treatment of other conditions to which the stigma of social reprehensibility may become more subtly attached.

Glover (cited by Kubie, 1956) has drawn attention to the observation that analysts sometimes seem to achieve their greatest successes when they are beginners, to which Kubie adds his disappointment in a youthful expectation that increasing analytic experience would yield a higher percentage of therapeutic successes and a more precise understanding of how successes are achieved. These comments appear pertinent to the finding that, in the psychiatrist group, therapists professing a negative attitude toward the patient were significantly more experienced in therapy than those holding a positive attitude. The last named group, as a matter of fact, ranked lowest in experience—lower than either the ambivalent or the "neutral" group (which had the highest level of experience). Length of experience, on the other hand, was not significantly correlated with prognosis (although the trend was in the direction suggested by attitude) or other clinical evaluations, nor with length or other aspects of treatment. It was shown, on the other hand, that the quality of the therapists' dynamic formulations or their formulations of the course of the transference (also in part a qualitative judgment) did correlate with experience. We may wonder, therefore, whether inexperienced therapists are more accepting of the patient because of their youthful enthusiasm, or whether the more experienced practitioners are more disillusioned, more discouraged—or simply more realistic. The present data, unfortunately, do not permit a definite answer; they do support, however, the relevance of Kubie's thoughtful question.

The analyses suggested that the empathic as well as the

unempathic approach was in part a reflection of the thera-pist's *conscious* attitude. That is, to some extent at least, therapists were aware of their positive or negative reaction to the patient and their willingness or unwillingness to enter into a therapeutic relationship with him. Undoubtedly they were less aware of the manner in which their attitude inter-acted with their clinical evaluations. In the light of this evidence, is it possible that the therapist's attitude, as con-veyed by his communications to the patient, tends to bring about a realization of the therapist's expectations? For psy-chotherapy, the crux of the matter is not the perceptions and clinical evaluations or even the therapist's conscious attitude toward the patient; it is the manner in which these variables influence and structure the therapeutic relation-ship. This is one of the important problems requiring further exploration.

Consider, in this connection, the essentials of psycho-therapy, as described in an essay by Masserman (1957):

> The warm, unashamedly personal acceptance of each patient not as another "interesting case" in support of some preconceived theory, or as an object of inexorable analysis, or even a grist for another therapeutic mill, but as a hurt, frightened, and troubled human being seeking relief and guidance. . . .
> . . . the first objective will be *to help the patient recognize that his previous patterns of behavior were neither as necessary nor as advantageous as he had im-plicitly assumed them to be.* . . . It is . . . equally necessary *to utilize optimal transference situations and other thera-peutic opportunities to impart the second essential portion of the dual dicta of insight: namely that new patterns of conduct are really preferable* . . . Such reorientations . . . may be rendered more effective by . . . Re-education of the patient by the therapist through reason, demonstration and, implicitly or explicitly, personal example. [Italics in the original.]

284

On this basis, the therapist's contribution to the treatment process is a dual one: it is personal and technical. His personal attributes (maturity, warmth, acceptance, etc.) enable him to create the kind of interpersonal relationship in which constructive personality change can take place; his knowledge of psychodynamic principles and techniques permits him, in and through this relationship, to initiate the kinds of emotional unlearning and learning experiences that are considered necessary to the alleviation or resolution of neurotic conflicts. The latter would be impossible without the former; the former, by itself, would never be sufficient. To recast this in the form of a hypothesis:

1. Psychotherapy is maximally effective when the therapist is able (a) to relate to the patient in a warm, empathic manner, so that the person of the therapist, as revealed in this relationship, will in time serve as a new, more mature, and more desirable model of reality than past interpersonal relationships which have distorted the patient's perceptions of himself and others; and (b) by appropriate technical devices (interpretations, etc.) to demonstrate, clearly and effectively, the self-defeating character of the patient's previous patterns of interpersonal behavior. (The formulation, timing, and communication of these insights requires consummate skill that is probably best acquired through a combination of intensive personal analysis and supervised experience.)

2. Psychotherapy is less effective when only the first condition is met.

3. Psychotherapy is least effective when the first condition is lacking, irrespective of the status of the second condition.

I sincerely believe that the cause of psychotherapy as a scientific procedure for helping people with their neurotic conflicts will be advanced as we succeed in refining and testing this hypothesis.

References

Finesinger, J. E. 1948. "Psychiatric Interviewing: I. Some Principles and Procedures in Insight Therapy," *Am. J. Psychiat.*, 105: 187-195.

Kubie, L. S. 1956. "Some Unsolved Problems of Psychoanalytic Psychotherapy," in *Progress in Psychotherapy*, ed. F. Fromm-Reichmann and J. L. Moreno, pp. 87-102. New York: Grune & Stratton.

Masserman, J. H. 1957. "Evolution vs. 'Revolution' in Psychotherapy: A Biodynamic Integration," *Behav. Sci.*, 2: 89-100.

Raines, G. N., and Rohrer, J. H. 1955. "The Operational Matrix of Psychiatric Practice. I. Consistency and Variability in Interview Impressions of Different Psychiatrists," *Am. J. Psychiat.*, 111: 721-733.

Siegel, S. 1956. *Nonparametric Statistics for the Behavioral Sciences*. New York. McGraw-Hill.

10

THE THERAPIST'S PERFORMANCE: B. A COMPARISON OF TWO PROFESSIONAL GROUPS

In the course of psychotherapy ordinarily it is not possible to make systematic observations about the effects of therapist variables upon the treatment process, yet there is little doubt that the totality of the therapist's personality—his age, sex, experience, maturity, attitudes, and a host of other factors—is subtly intertwined with his therapeutic techniques and the theoretical framework he brings to bear upon his therapeutic operations. It is also apparent that the scientific study of the therapeutic process requires precise information concerning the relative contributions of these variables to answer the central question of therapeutic change. We cannot make any definitive statements about the supposed effects of technique A or technique B as long as the person of the therapist is omitted from consideration. Wolberg's statement (Wolff, 1956) that therapists "seem to do well or poorly because of subtle personality factors rather than because of their particular orientation [p. 110]" may be correct or an overstatement, but the answer will not be forthcoming until we can assess the relative influences of the relevant variables. This goal, unfortunately, lies far in the future.*

On a less ambitious level, it appears reasonable to inquire how different therapists approach a patient during an initial interview, what impressions they form, how they conceptualize their observations, and how they respond to the patient facing them. By taking such data as a starting point, one might be able to investigate the extent to which variations in therapist performance are determined by variables in his background, experience, and personality. This focus on the therapist, rather than the more usual one on the patient, characterized the investigation discussed in this chapter.

A series of results based upon the performance of 134 psychiatrists has been reported in the previous chapter giving a more detailed description of the rationale, procedure, and results, and discussing their implications at greater length. This chapter presents a number of parallel analyses based on the performance of a group of therapists whose background training was in psychology rather than in medicine.

METHOD AND PROCEDURE

Using the method described in the previous chapter, complete data were collected from 235 therapists in several

*This research was supported by a research grant (M-965) from the National Institute of Mental Health, Public Health Service, and carried out at George Washington University, School of Medicine. I wish to acknowledge my appreciation to Winfred Overholser, M.D., and Leon Yochelson, M.D., for encouragement and advice.

cities.* Comparisons were made between 55 psychiatrists and 55 psychologists, matched on length of experience in psychotherapy and personal analysis (Table 1). In addition, reference will be made to certain parallel analyses performed separately for psychiatrists and psychologists.

RESULTS

To facilitate comparisons between the results obtained for psychiatrists and psychologists, the order of presentation follows that of Chapter Nine.

DIAGNOSIS: Like psychiatrists, analytically oriented psychologists chose a variety of diagnostic labels, "anxiety" being the preferred diagnosis. The response distributions of the matched samples did not differ significantly.

DEFENSE MECHANISMS: Psychologists mentioned almost the same number of defense mechanisms as psychiatrists (an average of about three). Chi square did not indicate statistically significant differences between the two samples.

FORMULATION OF DYNAMICS: The kinds and quality of dynamic formulations, as defined previously, did not differentiate the matched samples. In fact, the distributions disclosed a marked degree of similarity.

OTHER DIAGNOSTIC EVALUATIONS: A number of diagnostic assessments were obtained through precoded items. These included: Ego Strength, Anxiety, Insight, Capability of Self-observation and Self-appraisal as opposed to the Tendency for Rationalization, Emotional Maturity, Social Adjustment, Disturbance. The evaluations of psychiatrists and psychologists appeared to be very similar. No chi square value was significant at an acceptable level.

---

*For results dealing with the responses of 134 psychiatrists (analysts, psychiatrists, and residents in psychiatry) see Chapter Nine. For a comparison of the performance of 64 psychoanalytically oriented psychologists with that of 14 psychologists following the client-centered theory of Rogers, see Chapter Eleven.

TABLE 1

SUMMARY OF BIOGRAPHICAL VARIABLES FOR MATCHED SAMPLES OF PSYCHIATRISTS AND PSYCHOLOGISTS

	N	Length of Experience (years)		Personal Analysis (hours)		Age (years)	
		M	S.D.	M	S.D.	M	S.D.
Psychiatrists—Analyzed	32	4.5	3.5	322	228	34.4	6.2
Psychologists—Analyzed	32	4.6	3.5	319	210	38.4	8.6
Psychiatrists—Nonanalyzed	23	2.3	2.4	—		32.5	5.4
Psychologists—Nonanalyzed	23	2.3	2.1	—		30.8	6.2
All Psychiatrists	55	3.7	3.3	(322)	(228)	33.7	6.0
All Psychologists	55	3.7	3.2	(319)	(210)	35.2	8.5

PROGNOSIS: While respondents differed in their prognostic estimates, differences between psychiatrists and psychologists were statistically nonsignificant.

ATTITUDE TOWARD THE PATIENT: The matched samples were undifferentiated in terms of their attitudes toward the patient (self-ratings on a five-point item); nor did psychiatrists differ from psychologists regarding the reasons given for their professed conscious attitude.

Analysis of Systematic Differences

In order to investigate further the possible reasons for differences in therapists' evaluations the full psychiatrist sample ($N = 134$) was successively broken down according to a number of therapist variables. The results of these analyses may be summarized as follows:

1. Length of experience appeared to have a negligible bearing on therapists' evaluations. Significant but moderate correlations were observed between experience and estimates of Ego Strength and quality of the dynamic formulation, that is, the more experienced therapists estimated the patient's ego strength to be less, and they contributed a larger proportion of "superior" formulations.

2. Similarly, older therapists judged the prognosis without therapy to be more unfavorable.

3. Breakdowns in terms of theoretical orientation and personal analysis were inconclusive, chiefly because of difficulties in isolating "pure" groups.

4. A number of statistically significant correlations obtained between therapists' attitude toward the patient and clinical evaluations: therapists indicating a negative attitude were more likely to choose such diagnostic labels as psychopath, character disorder, paranoid, and phobic. They also tended to see the patient as less anxious, having less insight, being less capable of self-observation, more immature emotionally, and more poorly adjusted socially.

291

5. A statistically significant correlation was observed between prognosis and therapists' attitude ($r = .39$) that signified that therapists having a positive attitude toward the patient tended to give a more favorable prognosis. Prognostic estimates were also shown to be correlated with other clinical evaluations, and followed a pattern similar to that reported for therapists' attitude.

In order to determine the extent to which these relationships were paralleled in the sample of psychologists it would have been desirable to conduct the analyses on the matched samples. Unfortunately, the relatively small size of these samples rendered this unfeasible. As a compromise, the full sample of psychologists was used. In evaluating the results it must be kept in mind that the psychiatrist sample was notably larger (134 versus 64), more experienced (mean of 6.8 years versus 3.1 years), and somewhat older (38.2 years versus 35.6 years). In addition, the range of experience, as indicated by the standard deviation, was twice as great for psychiatrists as for psychologists. Despite these shortcomings it seemed appropriate to report the results for two reasonably large groups of therapists participating in this investigation. The layout of Table 2 is directly comparable to the one presented in Chapter Nine for the full psychiatrist sample. The results for the full psychologist sample may be summarized as follows:

1. As in the psychiatrist sample, length of experience was significantly correlated with Ego Strength, and quality of dynamic formulation (chi square significant at the .01 level). In addition, however, experience correlated significantly with Social Adjustment and Attitude toward the Patient. If self-estimates of experience rather than number of years were taken as the reference variable, Insight, Disturbance, and Prognosis without Therapy also disclosed significant correlations. Increasing experience tended to covary with the more unfavorable estimates.

TABLE 2

PRODUCT-MOMENT COEFFICIENTS OF CORRELATION BETWEEN ATTITUDINAL AND BIOGRAPHICAL VARIABLES—AVERAGE N
(PSYCHOLOGISTS) = 55

Variable	Prognosis with Therapy	Attitude toward Patient	Experience (in years)	Experience (Self-estimate)	Competence as Therapist	Age
Ego Strength	.26*	.08	.31*	.23	−.09	.19
Anxiety	.24	.23	.23	.16	−.06	.10
Insight	.27*	.18	.24	.29*	−.22	.12
Self-observation versus Rationalization	.29*	.28*	.15	.13	.07	−.02
Emotional Maturity	−.13	−.11	−.11	−.05	.00	−.19
Social Adjustment	.17	−.06	.30*	.26*	−.01	.27*
Disturbance	−.31*	.10	−.21	−.33†	.18	−.27*
Prognosis without Therapy	−.18	−.16	.23	.35†	−.20	.23
Prognosis with Therapy		.42†	.17	.19	−.08	.03
Attitude toward Patient			.25*	.17	−.11	.08
Experience (in years)				.73†	.57†	.66†
Experience (self-estimate)					.64†	.60†
Competence as Therapist (self-estimate)						−.41†

* Significant at the .05 level. † Significant at the .01 level.

293

2. Therapists' age correlated significantly with estimates of the patient's Social Adjustment and Disturbance, the direction of the correlation being similar to that reported in the preceding paragraph.

3. Breakdowns in terms of personal analysis and theoretical orientation were unfeasible for the psychologist sample as well.

4. Correlations between therapists' attitude and clinical evaluations appeared to be of a somewhat lower order than that reported for psychiatrists. Statistical significance was obtained in the case of Self-observation versus Rationalization and quality of the dynamic formulation.

5. As in the case of psychiatrists, prognosis correlated significantly with therapists' attitude $(r = .42)$. Prognostic estimates were also found to be significantly correlated with such clinical evaluations as Insight, Self-observation versus Rationalization, and Disturbance.

While the correlations for psychologists did not disclose a one-to-one relationship to those reported for psychiatrists, the pattern must be judged rather similar if allowance is made for inevitable sampling fluctuations and the sample differences already mentioned.

THERAPEUTIC GOALS AND APPROACHES: The distributions of responses given by the matched samples of psychiatrists and psychologists differed significantly in terms of therapeutic goals $(p < .01)$. Psychiatrists tended to specify more modest goals, such as symptom relief, whereas a larger proportion of psychologists stressed greater insight, greater self-acceptance, etc. Virtually no member in either group envisaged an extensive reorganization of the patient's personality.

Responses did not differ significantly on the following questionnaire items: areas in which therapists expected the patient to "move" and areas in which they expected him to remain relatively unchanged; areas or problems that might prove most amenable to therapy; areas in the patient's living that might receive primary focus in treatment; attitudes or kinds of behavior that the therapist would encourage (or discourage) in therapy with this patient; areas that should be avoided (early) in therapy.

PROBLEMS OF THERAPEUTIC TECHNIQUE: Psychiatrists appeared to differ very little from psychologists on a number of questions including clues derived from the patient's behavior during the interview; descriptions of the course of the transference and its technical handling; anticipation of countertransference reactions and methods of dealing with them; difficulties and/or dangers that might arise in the course of therapy; approach to the patient's phobic symptoms; the desirability of making recommendations to the patient to change his present mode of living or his environment; therapist's activity or passivity.

The matched samples diverged significantly with regard to their expectations of acting out behavior and its therapeutic handling. A larger proportion of psychiatrists expected the patient to engage in this form of transference reaction ($p < .02$); they were also more likely to state that they would actively discourage its development by firmness, strictness, setting limits, etc. ($p < .05$). Responses to a question dealing with the desirability of strictness or permissiveness very probably reflected the same line of thinking in that psychiatrists advocated strictness more than their psychologist colleagues ($p < .01$). Similarly, psychiatrists tended to be more outspoken about discouraging free association with this patient, in contrast to a larger proportion of psychologists who explicitly encouraged it ($p < .01$).

FORM OF THERAPY, FREQUENCY OF SESSIONS, AND LENGTH: Comparisons of the response distributions for the matched samples indicated that psychologists tended to advocate the more intensive forms of psychotherapy with this patient than psychiatrists ($p < .05$). There was no statistically significant difference regarding the frequency of weekly sessions, but the trend was for psychiatrists to prefer one weekly interview. There was a slight tendency for psy-

295

chiatrists to estimate the duration of psychotherapy to be shorter than psychologists ($p < .10$): more psychiatrists than psychologists estimated the length of treatment to be less than one year.

The distributions did not differ significantly regarding the time required to achieve symptom relief. A question relating to possible alternatives to the respondent's first choice of treatment elicited a somewhat larger proportion of recommendations for pharmacological therapy (presumably tranquilizing drugs) from psychiatrists, but differences in the over-all distributions were nonsignificant.

Analysis of Systematic Differences

The results for breakdowns of the full psychiatrist sample in terms of selected therapist variables may be summarized as follows:

1. The responses of psychiatrists, broken down by experience level, revealed almost no statistically significant differences, with these exceptions: analysts (the most highly experienced group) judged the length of therapy to be longer than either psychiatrists or residents. Analysts preferred three or more weekly sessions, in contrast to psychiatrists who showed a predilection for one or two weekly interviews. The more experienced therapists tended to characterize the course of the transference in terms of interpersonal dynamics rather than in descriptive terms, which were preferred by the less experienced psychiatrists.

2. The therapist's conscious attitude toward the patient was found to be significantly associated with his responses pertaining to possible recommendations to the patient regarding his mode of living; with strictness versus permissiveness; activity versus passivity; form of therapy; frequency of sessions; and the time required to achieve symptom relief.

Comparable analyses, for the full psychologist sample, disclosed the following results:

296

1. A breakdown in terms of experience produced very few statistically significant differences, with one notable exception: experienced therapists were *less* likely to recommend the more intensive forms of psychotherapy (p < .05).

2. Attitude toward the patient was significantly associated with strictness versus permissiveness; anticipations of acting out; and discouragement of certain attitudes and behaviors. Stated otherwise, therapists expressing a negative attitude toward the patient tended to advocate strictness on the therapist's part (p < .01); were more likely to expect acting out behavior (p < .09); and were more likely to discourage self-pity, self-depreciation, self-punishing behavior, refusal to accept responsibility, and projections of hostility (p < .06).

3. Therapists giving a negative prognosis were more likely to expect the patient to act out than therapists whose prognosis was favorable.

THERAPISTS' COMMUNICATIONS (FILM RESPONSES): Therapists' communications to the patient (film responses) were quantified by means of a system of analysis described in Chapter Twenty-one. The distributions obtained under the various components (Type of Therapeutic Activity, Depth-directedness, Dynamic Focus, Initiative, and Therapeutic Climate) were then compared by means of the nonparametric Mann-Whitney U test to determine the degree of divergence between the two matched samples. These results may be summarized as follows:

1. Psychiatrists differed from psychologists by asking a significantly larger number of exploratory questions (p < .01).

2. Psychologists in turn showed a relatively greater preference for the reflection-of-feeling technique usually associated with Rogers' client-centered theory (p < .001).

3. Psychologists tended to change the dynamic focus less than psychiatrists and were more likely to accept the patient's frame of reference (p < .002).

4. The two matched samples were not differentiated in terms of the relative frequency of "silent" responses, communications in which the therapist emerges as an expert or an authority, highly inferential communications, communications changing the dynamic focus to interpersonal events of the present or the past, communications showing a high level of initiative, and "warmth" or "coldness" of emotional tone.

ANALYSIS OF SYSTEMATIC DIFFERENCES

Level of Experience

As in the preceding sections, the results obtained from breakdowns of the full psychiatrist sample were compared with corresponding analyses based on the full psychologist sample. For the psychiatrist sample, the following findings appeared to be attributable to length of experience in psychotherapy:

1. Inexperienced psychiatrists tended to ask more exploratory questions than experienced therapists.
2. Experienced psychiatrists tended to give a larger number of interpretive responses than inexperienced practitioners. Related analyses disclosed that these communications were more inferential, and that their dynamic focus concerned dynamic interpersonal events in the patient's past and present life.
3. Experienced therapists showed a higher degree of initiative in their communications than inexperienced practitioners.
4. Concomitant with the above findings, experienced therapists tended to change the dynamic focus of their communications more than the less experienced respondents.
5. Experienced therapists tended to be slightly "warmer."

298

Most differences between inexperienced and experienced psychologists were statistically nonsignificant. However, communications in which the therapist emerged as an expert or as an authority tended to increase with experience ($p < .05$), and "warm" responses showed increments in the same direction ($p < .05$).

Personal Analysis

Psychiatrists whose training had included a personal analysis differed from nonanalyzed psychiatrists, with whom they were matched in terms of experience (N in each sample was 28), by giving a significantly larger number of silent responses at the expense of exploratory questions. This difference appeared to be more pronounced at the lower end of the experience continuum. Two similarly matched samples of psychologists (N in each sample was 33) were statistically undifferentiated in terms of their film response distributions on all components of the system of analysis.

However, comparable analyses between psychiatrists and psychologists (see Table 1) disclosed that analyzed psychiatrists tended to exceed analyzed psychologists in "silent" responses ($p < .11$) and exploratory questions ($p < .09$). Psychologists, on the other hand, showed a consistent preference for reflections of feeling. A comparison between nonanalyzed psychiatrists and nonanalyzed psychologists corroborated the differences regarding explorations and reflections of feeling, but not regarding silence. This suggests that analyzed psychiatrists tended to be the relatively most "silent" of the samples, and that the other variations between psychiatrists and psychologists do not seem to be a function of the personal analysis variable.

Theoretical Orientation

A comparison between two samples of psychiatrists whose respective theoretical orientations were orthodox

299

Freudian and neo-Freudian failed to disclose any statistically reliable differences in their film responses. A similar comparison for psychologists proved unfeasible because of small N's for "pure" subgroups.*

Attitude toward the Patient

A breakdown of the psychiatrist sample in terms of the therapist's expressed conscious attitude toward the patient revealed no notable differences in techniques per se, but disclosed that therapists indicating a negative attitude gave a significantly larger number of responses whose emotional tone was rated "cold"; "warm" responses did not differ significantly. Psychologists, in contrast, did not reveal statistically reliable differences in terms of therapeutic climate, but certain technique differences were observed:

1. Psychologists expressing a "neutral" attitude toward the patient asked a significantly larger number of exploratory questions ($p < .02$).
2. Concomitantly, those expressing a neutral attitude tended to accept the patient's focus least; on the other hand, psychologists professing a positive attitude were more likely to accept the patient's focus ($p < .02$).

Prognosis

The following statistically reliable differences were observed when the psychiatrist sample was broken down in terms of the respondents' prognostic estimates:

1. Psychiatrists expressing a noncommittal prognostic estimate tended to give the smallest number of silent responses.

---

*Certain differences between analytically oriented psychologists and those following the client-centered theory of Rogers will be reported in Chapter Eleven.

2. Respondents giving a favorable prognosis were more likely to accept the patient's focus.

3. Therapists giving a noncommittal prognosis tended to show more initiative in their communications than the favorable or unfavorable groups.

4. Therapists whose prognosis was unfavorable gave more than four times as many "cold" responses than respondents who considered the prognosis favorable.

5. The relative frequency of "warm" responses was greatest among therapists whose prognosis was noncommittal and relatively low in both the favorable and unfavorable groups.

The analysis for psychologists was not directly comparable because the number of respondents giving a noncommittal prognosis was too small. Results based on a comparison between respondents giving a favorable and an unfavorable prognosis showed that the latter group exceeded the former in the relative frequency of exploratory questions ($p < .05$).

EXPLORATION OF THE EMPATHY VARIABLE: As the analysis of the data progressed, it became apparent that therapists' responses to various choice points in the motion picture as well as the over-all response patterns differed rather markedly in feeling tone, understanding of the patient's plight, willingness to extend a helping hand, etc.—qualities that appeared to transcend the quantifications already discussed. This impression was strengthened by the observation that therapists admitting to a negative attitude toward the patient tended to be "colder" in their communications. For these reasons, an attempt was made to define criteria for judging the degree of empathy conveyed by the therapist.

Despite the crudeness of the measures, which are described at length in Chapter Nine, it was possible to demonstrate fair rater agreement. Successive ratings by each of two raters showed a consistency ranging from 69 per cent to 85 per cent; inter-rater agreement ranged from 64 per

301

TABLE 3

AGREEMENT WITHIN AND BETWEEN TWO INDEPENDENT RATERS ON OVER-ALL RATINGS OF EMPATHY ($N = 93$)

	Full Agreement*	Partial Agreement†	Disagreement
Rater 1: Rating 1 versus Rating 2	72 (77%)	7 (8%)	14 (15%)
Rater 2: Rating 1 versus Rating 2	60 (65%)	13 (14%)	20 (21%)
Rater 1 versus Rater 2: Rating 1	47 (51%)	14 (15%)	32 (34%)
Rater 1 versus Rater 2: Rating 2	40 (43%)	27 (29%)	26 (28%)

Note.—N comprises 64 psychoanalytically oriented psychologists, 14 Rogerians, and 15 psychiatric social workers.
* Using four categories: $+$, $-$, 0, and $\pm$.
† Combining categories $+$ and $\pm$, and 0 and $-$.

cent to 72 per cent. These indices were similar for the psychiatrist and nonmedical therapist samples, which were judged separately. The results for the latter sample (including 15 psychiatric social workers) are presented in Table 3.

In the psychiatrist sample, empathy ratings showed statistically significant associations with therapists' conscious attitude and prognosis, indicating that positive empathy tended to covary with positive attitude and favorable prognosis. For the nonmedical therapist sample, comparable analyses revealed a similar trend, but chi square was not significant at an acceptable level ($.20 < p > .15$). There was a slight tendency for experienced psychiatrists to have higher empathy ratings ($p = .13$); for nonmedical therapists, chi square was significant at the .09 level.

When the empathy ratings of psychiatrists whose training had included personal analysis were compared with nonanalyzed psychiatrists of comparable professional experience, the results were in favor of the analyzed group ($p < .07$). At the lower experience levels (less than three years), there appeared to be no difference between analyzed and nonanalyzed therapists in terms of empathy ratings; however, at the higher levels of experience, analyzed therapists obtained a larger proportion of positive empathy ratings. For a similarly matched sample of nonmedical therapists ($N = 33$ in each group, including 29 psychologists and 4 psychiatric social workers), the over-all results were statistically nonsignificant, but at the higher levels of experience the above mentioned trend appeared to be in evidence (Table 4).

A further breakdown in terms of the therapist's conscious attitude toward the patient showed that in the experienced analyzed group of psychiatrists, a negative attitude appeared to be associated more often with a positive empathy rating, whereas in the nonanalyzed experienced group there seemed to be greater congruence between negative attitude and lack of empathy. No corroboration for this finding was found in the nonmedical therapist sample. It is

TABLE 4

DISTRIBUTIONS OF EMPATHY RATINGS AND SELF-RATINGS OF ATTITUDE IN TWO GROUPS OF PSYCHOLOGISTS, MATCHED IN TERMS OF PERSONAL ANALYSIS

Experience in Therapy	Attitude toward Patient	Personal Analysis Empathy Rating			No Personal Analysis Empathy Rating		
		+	−	Total	+	−	Total
0–2 years	+	2	5	7	5	5	10
	−	2	7	9	3	3	6
Total		4	12	16	8	8	16
2.5–12 years	+	6	3	9	3	3	6
	−	4	4	8	3	8	11
Total		10	7	17	6	11	17
Combined	+	8	8	16	8	8	16
	−	6	11	17	6	11	17
Total		14	19	33	14	19	33

apparent that the results pertaining to the relationships between empathy ratings, personal analysis, and conscious attitude must be viewed with considerable caution, first, because of the very small size of the subsamples, and second, because the error of measurement in each variable is undoubtedly compounded when these variables are considered jointly.

SUMMARY

This investigation was undertaken for the purpose of obtaining empirical evidence on therapists' performance in an initial interview and to explore the effects of relevant therapist variables upon: (1) clinical judgments, including diagnostic and prognostic evaluations; (2) formulations of treatment plans and goals; (3) communications addressed to the patient. The clinical evaluations of psychiatrists were similar to those of psychologists of comparable experience despite marked intragroup differences. In some respects, psychologists as a group appeared to be more passively expectant in their therapeutic approach than psychiatrists. Psychiatrists' communications showed a preference for exploratory questions whereas psychologists disclosed a predilection for reflections of the patient's feelings. In both groups of therapists, clinical evaluations tended to become more unfavorable with increasing experience. In terms of therapeutic technique, experienced psychiatrists tended to give a larger number of interpretations and showed more initiative. Psychologists did not show this pattern in clearcut fashion. However, experienced therapists in both groups tended to be "warmer" in their communications to the patient.

Therapists' attitudes toward the patient, among psychiatrists as well as among psychologists, were shown to be correlated with certain clinical evaluations, treatment plans, and the emotional tone of their communications. In discussing the implications of these findings (see Chapter Nine), attention has been called to the potential effects of an inter-action between therapists' emotional reactions to a patient, assessments of the "objective" clinical evidence, and the character of the therapeutic interventions.

References

Wolff, W. 1956. *Contemporary Psychotherapists Examine Themselves.* Springfield, Ill.: Charles C. Thomas.

11

THE THERAPIST'S
PERFORMANCE:
C. A COMPARISON OF
TWO ORIENTATIONS

As a technique for producing changes in the personality structure of a patient, psychotherapy does not exist apart from the person of the therapist. While it is axiomatic that the therapeutic instrument comprises the therapist, his personality, theory, and techniques, little systematic attention has been paid by researchers to these variables.*

In a sense, the therapist is a reader of imaginary dials who acts "therapeutically" upon the information indicated by these measuring instruments within himself. When supplied with certain information, say, the behavior of a patient, he will register this information in certain ways, and he will

*This research was part of a larger project supported by a research grant (M-965) from the National Institute of Mental Health, Public Health Service. The author is indebted to Rebecca E. Rieger for her assistance and valuable comments.

react to it in certain other ways. The therapist's theory, experience, and personality determine the kinds of dials he uses as well as their calibration. His therapeutic actions are their reflection.

In order to obtain empirical data on the calibration of the therapist as a clinical instrument, we can supply a certain identical input (patient behavior) and note (1) how this input is perceived and evaluated; (2) what deductions and inferences are drawn from it; and (3) how these processes are translated into therapeutic action. Assuming that this testing procedure will disclose differences among therapists, one can investigate systematic influences that might produce the discrepancies. For example, therapists may use different sets of measuring instruments whose readings have no relation to each other. They may use similar instruments, but the calibration may differ. They may interpret differentially the meaning of the same pointer reading. Any one of these possibilities, plus many others, may result in divergent therapeutic communications.

This analogy is of course a gross oversimplification of the therapist's activity in the therapeutic situation, but it may help to make explicit the objectives of the larger investigation of which this chapter forms a part: the study of the therapist's performance in a first interview. We asked, if a group of therapists observes the same patient, how do they perceive the clinical problem? What kinds of evaluations result from their perceptions? How are their perceptions and evaluations related to their communications? And, can differences in their performance be accounted for in terms of common underlying variables? Specifically, this chapter is concerned with a comparison between psychotherapists (psychologists) following psychoanalytic principles and therapists following the client-centered theory of Rogers.

METHOD AND PROCEDURE

The method and the procedure used in this investigation are detailed at some length in Chapters Nine and Ten.

THE SAMPLES

Cooperation was obtained from psychiatric and psychological societies, hospitals, training centers, and therapeutic institutes. Data were collected in Washington, Baltimore, New York, Perry Point, and Chicago. The total sample comprised 235 psychotherapists, 134 of whom were members of the medical profession (analysts, psychiatrists, and residents in psychiatry); 17 were psychiatric social workers. This chapter is concerned with the responses of 14 psychologists who described their theoretical orientation as unqualifiedly Rogerian (8 were affiliated with the Counseling Center of the University of Chicago). This group is compared to 64 psychologists who professed to follow psychoanalytic principles broadly defined. Actually, they selected a total of 93 "labels," which were distributed over 14 categories; 72 per cent of the choices were accounted for by psychoanalytic orientation (general or orthodox), Sullivan, and eclectic.*

Summary statistics on age, experience, and personal analysis are presented in Table 1. The following data shed some further light on the composition of the samples:

Two-thirds of the psychoanalytically oriented psychologists (Sample A) held the Ph.D. degree, as compared with 36 per cent of the psychologists who followed Rogers' theory (Sample R).

Sixty per cent of the members in both groups said they had a fair amount or a great deal of experience in therapy and considered themselves competent therapists. All members of Sample R said they practiced client-centered therapy exclusively. Sample A showed a wider distribution, but

*Grateful acknowledgment is made to all psychologists who gave generously of their time to make this study possible. Thanks are also due the following organizations: VA Benefits Office, Washington, D. C.; VA Hospital, Perry Point, Md.; Maryland Psychological Association; Postgraduate Center for Psychotherapy, New York, N. Y.; Counseling Center, University of Chicago.

TABLE 1
SUMMARY STATISTICS OF AGE, EXPERIENCE, PERSONAL ANALYSIS

	Sample A*			Sample R†		
Statistic	$N\ddagger$	Mean	SD	$N\ddagger$	Mean	SD
Age	65	35.6 yrs.	8.7	13	33.4 yrs.	6.4
Experience in therapy	62	3.3 yrs.	3.1	12	3.0 yrs.	2.4
Personal analysis	33	291 hrs.	198	9	142 hrs.	101

* Psychoanalytically oriented psychologists.

† Rogerian psychologists.

‡ Fluctuations reflect absence of complete information and/or not having had personal analysis.

most replies fell within the broad category of psychoanalytically oriented psychotherapy. Most Rogerians indicated that they had received very little training in psychoanalytic principles and techniques; 69 per cent of Sample A claimed "a fair amount" or "a great deal."

Sixty-four per cent of Sample R had received their personal analysis within the client-centered framework. The responses of members of Sample A who indicated that they either had completed or were in the process of undergoing personal analysis (more than half the group) suggested that their analyses were based upon psychoanalytic theory.

Approximately one-half of the members in both groups stated that they devoted more than 25 per cent of their time to the practice of psychotherapy. Almost two-thirds of Sample R specified their therapy as being primarily with neurotic patients. Thirty-eight per cent of Sample A responded similarly, but another third said that their patients represented a wider range of personality disorders.

Sample A appeared to treat their "average patient" for longer periods than Sample R: 38 per cent of the former group described the length of therapy as exceeding one year, as contrasted with 14 per cent in the latter. On the other hand, Rogerians predominantly saw the "average patient" twice a week, whereas the modal frequency for Sample A was closer to one weekly session.

RESULTS

Therapists' responses to the film, that is, communications to the patient, were quantified by a multidimensional system of analysis that has been described in Chapter Twenty-four. Questionnaire responses to each item were coded and the frequencies tabulated. In view of the small size of Sample R, response categories within an item had to be combined. Typically, this resulted in 2 × 2 tables that were tested by means of chi square (corrected for continuity).*

CLINICAL EVALUATIONS AND THERAPIST ATTITUDES: Responses to the question of diagnosis revealed no significant differences. It seems noteworthy, however, that no member of Sample R chose such labels as psychopath, schizoid, paranoid, or character disorder, which were used by appreciable minorities of Sample A, as well as by psychiatrists whose response distributions have been presented in Chapter Nine. Asked to state the patient's major defense mechanisms, Sample R named a relatively smaller number than Sample A (ratio of 1 : 3), but the distributions did not appear to differ significantly. Nor did the samples differ in terms of qualitative descriptions of the patient's emotional dynamics.

Evaluations of the degree of ego strength, anxiety, insight, social adjustment, and disturbance disclosed no statistically significant differences.

The members of Sample R judged the prognosis with therapy to be more favorable than the members of Sample A ($p = < .05$): no Rogerian therapist considered it unfavorable. By contrast, an unfavorable prognosis was given by 40

---

*A table showing the response distributions of the two samples in percentages and giving probability values for $p = < .10$ has been deposited with the American Documentation Institute. Order Document No. 5887, remitting $1.25 for microfilm or $1.25 for photocopies.

per cent of the therapists in Sample A, who were in closer agreement with the predictions made by psychiatrists.

A large proportion of Rogerian therapists professed a positive attitude toward the patient than analytically oriented psychologists ($p = < .02$). Members of the University of Chicago Counseling Center unanimously described their attitude as positive. Those responding negatively often stated that their attitude was influenced by the patient's hostility, anger, and dependency; those responding positively stressed his personality assets or saw him as "a patient with a problem," a response often given with some empathy.

PLANS, GOALS, AND DIFFICULTIES IN THERAPY: Sample R showed greater reluctance to set up therapeutic goals than Sample A ($p = < .001$), but the two samples did not differ significantly as to estimated length of treatment or time needed to accomplish symptom relief. It seems pertinent to note that psychoanalysts were less optimistic than either of the psychologist groups.

Concerning difficulties expected in treatment, Sample R therapists were significantly less likely to mention the patient's parasitic attitudes, poor motivation for therapy, acting out, or the possibility of psychosis ($p = < .02$). Nor were countertransference or problems of technique mentioned with any degree of frequency by Sample R ($p = < .01$). One-half of Sample R anticipated countertransference problems with this patient, as compared with almost 80 per cent in Sample A; twice as many Rogerians answered the question in the negative ($p = < .07$). No Rogerian mentioned areas in the patient's living that should be avoided, at least early in therapy, whereas numerous areas were mentioned by Sample A therapists ($p = < .001$). Similarly, Rogerians were less likely to name areas in the patient's living that should be singled out for focus in therapy ($p = < .001$).

Rogerians either declined to specify attitudes or behaviors that the therapist should encourage in therapy with his patient or stressed the expression of feelings. Sample

A therapists were more likely to stress a sense of responsibility, increased socialization, relating feelings and symptoms to interpersonal situations, etc. ($p = < .02$).

Conversely, Sample A therapists were more likely to discourage attitudes and behaviors, such as intellectualization, obsessive ruminations, self-pity, self-depreciation, helplessness, refusal to accept responsibility, demanding attitudes, and acting out; Rogerians, by comparison, tended to say they would discourage nothing or leave it to the patient ($p = < .001$).

No member of the Rogerian group advocated strictness by the therapist, as contrasted with more than a third of the members of Sample A who considered strictness therapeutically desirable ($p = .02$). A question about therapists' activity or passivity did not differentiate the two groups, possibly because the terms of reference were not clearly defined. Free association was discouraged by an appreciable proportion of Sample A therapists, but not by Sample R ($p = < .06$).

A question was asked about clues in the patient's verbal or nonverbal behavior that might not be used immediately but kept in mind for possible later reference. All members of Sample A who answered the question (85 per cent) mentioned one or more clues. Four Rogerians specifically stated "none" ($p = < .001$). Rogerians commented about the patient's feelings and attitudes but, in contrast to Sample A, paid less attention to such clues as gestures, bodily movements, manner of speaking, the patient's past or present interpersonal relations with his mother, wife, brother, or father—with or without inference about their dynamic significance.

Descriptions of the course of the transference did not diverge significantly, but members of the two samples disagreed about approaches to the problem ($p = < .001$). Rogerians predominantly encouraged or fostered a "corrective emotional experience" by conveying respect or clarifying feelings. Members of Sample A, on the other hand, tended to advocate interpretation and other procedures, such as reassurance and firmness, in which the therapist uses his role to induce changes in attitudes and actions.

Responses to a question dealing with "acting out," an aspect of the transference problem, revealed a similar pattern: no statistically significant differences with respect to its occurrence, but divergence in terms of "handling." Here, too, Rogerians recommended understanding, clarification, and reflections; analytically oriented therapists preferred an interpretive approach ($p = < .001$).

EVALUATION OF AND ATTITUDE TOWARD THE FILM THERAPIST: A number of questions were included to study similarities or differences between the film therapist's and the respondent's approaches to interviewing. It was hoped that in this way it might be possible to obtain a clearer picture of the respondent's own procedure.

Sample R therapists were more definite in their assertion that they would have conducted the interview "in a very different manner" ($p = < .02$). They dissociated themselves from his approach and tended to evaluate his performance as "a very inadequate job"; the majority of therapists in Sample A considered his performance reasonably adequate ($p = < .01$).

Within each sample, there was notable disagreement as to whether the therapist had been too passive or given insufficient support, but the intersample comparisons were nonsignificant.

Rogerians and psychoanalytically oriented therapists disagreed very markedly about the amount of time they would have devoted to obtaining data on the patient's life history: 75 per cent of Sample R stated that they would have spent somewhat less or considerably less time than the film therapist; almost one-half of Sample A said they would have devoted somewhat more or considerably more time ($p = < .001$). The transcript shows that about 10 per cent of the therapist's interventions can be construed as case history questions in the usual sense. These questions were usually asked in the context of the patient's story, and attempted to clarify a time, place, or interpersonal event. On the other hand, the therapist frequently repeated a word or phrase in a questioning tone of voice, apparently to obtain further data on a feeling or attitude.

The two samples revealed a statistically highly significant difference in terms of their attitude toward the therapist. The majority of Rogerian therapists described their attitude as negative, whereas most analytically oriented therapists professed a positive or neutral attitude ($p = <$ .001).

A supplemental question disclosed that the respondents' criticisms were directed at the film therapist's technique as well as at his person. Prominently mentioned by both samples were the following objections: therapist was not in control of the situation, engaged in too much activity but not of the "right" kind or not at the "right" time, too much interference with patient's talk, too much "accenting" (repeating last word), wrong emphasis, no plan. Rogerians criticized him especially for failing to focus on the patient's feelings and attitudes, and for a lack of empathy.

INTERVIEWING TECHNIQUES: Analyses of therapists' communications to the patient disclosed that Rogerians strongly favored the reflection-of-feeling technique, which comprised 67 per cent of their responses. The comparable percentage for analytically oriented psychologists was 17. The technique preferred by Sample A consisted of exploratory questions (40 per cent). The number of "silent" responses given by Sample R was significantly smaller than that of Sample A. Communications showing a high degree of inference or initiative were rare in Sample R; Sample A had three to eight times as many responses in these ranges.

As might be expected, Sample R therapists adhered quite consistently to the reflection-of-feeling technique, even when the patient pleaded for a direct answer from the therapist. Many analytically oriented therapists responded to this plea with a direct answer.

DISCUSSION

In interpreting these findings it must be kept in mind that the sample of Rogerian therapists was small. This deficiency was partly mitigated, however, by the fact that this group was compared with a considerably larger sample of analytically oriented therapists to whom they were roughly comparable in terms of training and level of experience. Furthermore, on a number of questionnaire items, Sample R revealed almost complete unanimity that undoubtedly reflected homogeneous training in a single setting (The University of Chicago Counseling Center); Sample A, on the other hand, was made up of therapists from a variety of backgrounds. It may be noted that psychoanalysts (members of the American Psychoanalytic Association), whose training might be considered reasonably homogeneous, varied more widely in their responses.

The results showed a number of pronounced differences in approach that highlighted discrepancies between therapists subscribing to psychoanalytic principles and the client-centered framework. Both positions are too well known to require exposition in this context. It seems appropriate, however, to quote what Rogers (1956) considers to be the distinctive emphases of client-centered therapy:

> A second distinctive aspect [the first is the emphasis on research] is the deep confidence in the capacity of the individual, which client-centered therapists have found to be justified by their experience. Rather than seeing man as essentially a destructive animal [the reference is evidently to the death instinct postulated by Freud late in his career, one of the most disputed and least accepted tenets in contemporary analytic thinking], with the primary problem of the control of his impulses, we have found man to be essentially constructive, if he can be released from his defensiveness. Our experience is that, to the extent that he can fully accept his experience and him-

self, he becomes satisfactorily self-controlled. Our view of the basic nature of man differs sharply from those of most therapeutic orientations, which believe that guidance and control must be arranged by the expert.

A third point of difference relates to a difference in theory. The theory of therapy which is developing in client-centered therapy stresses the importance of the immediate moment of experience in the relationship, not the genetic causation of behavior in the client, nor the formulation of some theoretic picture in the mind of the therapist [p. 207].*

---

*It is difficult to see how the terms "guidance and control," in the sense that Rogers seems to use them, do in fairness characterize the mainstream of contemporary psychoanalytic thinking. A semantic confusion seems to arise from the conception that the psychotherapist who functions in the role of a professional expert *ipso facto* manipulates the patient or controls him, and that guidance in the educational sense is synonymous with authoritarianism. Compare, in this connection, the formulations of a prominent psychoanalyst regarding therapeutic goals and the part played by the therapist (Fromm-Reichmann, 1950) :

Treatment, of course, is aimed at the solution of the patient's difficulties in living and the cure of his symptomatology. Ideally these therapeutic goals will be reached by the growth, maturation, and inner independence of the patient. . . . This goal will also be actualized by the development of his capacity for self-realization, his ability to form durable relationships of intimacy with others, and to give and accept mature love [p. 34].

. . . security and inner independence of the authoritarian values attributed to the conventional requirements of our culture are indispensable for the therapist who wants to guide his patients successfully toward finding out about the degree of cultural adjustment which is adequate to their personal needs [p. 33].

The psychiatrist's respect for his patients will also help him to safeguard against the previously mentioned mistake of assuming an attitude of personal "irrational authority" instead of listening and conducting therapy in the spirit of collaborative guidance. This irrational authoritarian behavior will be harmful not only because it interferes per se with the patient's tendency toward growth and maturation but also, and more important, because it constitutes a

317

Rogers' conception of the "ideal" therapist is that of a participant in an interpersonal situation whose primary function is to empathize with and understand the patient within his (the patient's) frame of reference. From this vantage point, the therapist is imposing an external frame of reference if he attempts to diagnose, assess, or prognosticate. The same dictum would apply to hypotheses or hunches the therapist may have about the etiology of the patient's conflict or how best to help him through psychotherapy. By this definition, the therapist who explicitly or implicitly goes beyond the patient's phenomenological self-descriptions is not client-centered.

---

traumatic repetition of the authoritarian aspects of the cultural pattern of behavior in general and of the parental pattern in particular, to which most mental patients have been harmfully subjected in their past [p. 17].

In his third point of difference, Rogers asserts that the experiential element in the psychotherapeutic situation is more important than the formulation of some theoretic picture in the mind of the therapist. This statement carries with it the implication that the therapist cannot adequately empathize with the patient, thereby helping to actualize the immediate moment of experience, if he attempts to understand rationally what is going on. Rogers has elaborated on this alleged dilemma in another paper (1955). I, for one, know of no evidence that the therapist's private thoughts about the nature of the patient's emotional problem, its severity, etiology, etc., in and of themselves preclude or interefere with empathy, nor that the exclusion of the therapist's rational processes assures it. I feel that any psychotherapist does more than empathize with his patient : whether he interprets a feeling or attitude in terms of current or past interpersonal relationships, or whether he selects a particular feeling or attitude for reflection, he seems to follow a design for action dictated by his theory.

Psychotherapy based on psychoanalytic principles does differ from other forms of psychotherapy in its emphasis on giving the patient a rational understanding of his interpersonal processes as they emerge in the therapeutic relationship. The emotional experience remains uppermost, but, in addition, the patient gains a conscious appreciation of his own contribution to his difficulties in interpersonal relations.

318

Certain objections voiced by Rogerian therapists regarding the experimental procedure are understandable from this point of view. While they cooperated willingly, they made it clear that ordinarily they do not work this way.

On this basis, too, the following results are consistent with the client-centered viewpoint: a reluctance to make a diagnosis beyond the general label "anxiety," to formulate therapeutic goals, to mention dangers that might be encountered in therapy or cautions that would have to be observed, to encourage or discourage specific attitudes or behaviors in the patient, to treat him with strictness, to discourage the free expression of feelings (free association), or generally to consider problems of technique or "handling." Rogerians were also disinclined to make inferences about the patient's behavior in the interview situation, the etiology of his disturbance, or the dynamic import of his behavior. Finally, they deemphasized case history questions.

One of the sharpest discrepancies between client-centered and analytically oriented therapists related to the question of prognosis: *no* Rogerian gave an unfavorable estimate, whereas 40 per cent of Sample A took a pessimistic view. How can this finding be explained?

First, it must be considered that our knowledge of neurotic disorders and psychotherapy is not sufficiently developed to permit specific predictions about the outcome of treatment even when a great deal is known about the patient. Such predictions undoubtedly become increasingly accurate as therapy progresses, and the therapist comes to learn more about the nature of the conflict, its ramifications, its history, and the patient's current level of functioning. Thus, a prognostic estimate based on a single interview may be little more than a guess, which may reveal more about the therapist than about the patient.

Second, the key issue in this comparison seems to be the high degree of uniformity among Rogerians, which was not paralleled by the analytically oriented therapists whose responses appeared to be more "normally" distributed. If therapists were talking about a specific event, the predictions of some obviously must be right and the predictions of others must be wrong. Unquestionably, therapists were not talking about a specific event but about a therapeutic outcome concerning which a wide range of ideas and opinions was entertained.

In an attempt to shed some light on this result, I will examine the following alternatives: (1) Rogerians gave a more favorable prognosis because they perceived the patient as less disturbed; (2) Rogerians planned for more modest therapeutic goals and therefore gave a more optimistic prognostic estimate; (3) prognostic estimates may be relatively unrelated to the presenting problem or the therapist's past successes with similar patients, but reflect more directly the therapist's attitude, his theoretical orientation, or combinations of these.

1. The available evidence indicates that therapists in both samples tended to regard the patient as seriously disturbed. They were also reasonably agreed that he suffered a great deal of anxiety, that he was emotionally immature, socially maladjusted, and that he had relatively little insight. There is no reason to believe, therefore, that Rogerians judged the patient's difficulties as less severe.

2. It is difficult to judge similarities or differences in therapeutic goals because of the vagueness of the terms of reference. Rogerians tended to advocate greater self-acceptance; analytically oriented therapists tended to strive for some insight. However, the latter group generally did not recommend the more intensive forms of psychotherapy usually associated with psychoanalysis. On this basis, it seems fair to say that the Rogerians' more favorable prognostic estimates were not a function of more limited therapeutic goals.

3. It has been reported in Chapter Nine that there was a highly significant statistical relationship between psychia-

320

trists' prognostic estimates and their self-ratings of their conscious attitude toward the patient ($r = .39$). For psychoanalytically oriented psychologists, the correlation was $r = .42$. Among Rogerians, the invariance between attitude and prognosis was almost complete. Eight therapists at the University of Chicago Counseling Center expressed a positive attitude and rated the prognosis favorable.

In the case of psychiatrists, it was found that both attitude and prognosis were significantly associated with other clinical evaluations and treatment plans. In addition, therapists' attitudes tended to be reflected in the emotional tone and the degree of empathy of their communications. These findings suggested the interpretation that clinical assessments tended to reflect, in part at least, the therapist's emotional reaction to the patient. It seems reasonable to assume that clinical evaluations, treatment plans, and goals are a function of the diagnosis. Comparisons of therapists (based on the total sample) giving a "pure" diagnosis of Hysteria, Obsessive-compulsive, Paranoid, and Anxiety showed a number of statistically significant differences in terms of clinical evaluations, etc. (see Chapter Nine). It was pointed out in the same connection that the choice of certain diagnostic labels (paranoid, psychopath) may signify a subtle value judgment that in turn may be determined by the therapist's attitude toward the patient. The data seemed to favor this conclusion.

On the other hand, if the therapist had undergone personal analysis, his empathy tended to be greater irrespective of his conscious attitude. In other words, personal analysis seemed to introduce some distance between a negative reaction to the patient and the therapist's ability to empathize with him. It is possible, then, that the therapist's conscious attitude toward the patient is less important than what he does about it. It should be recalled that the operational definition of therapist's conscious attitude toward the patient, as used in this investigation, was a self-rating on a

321

five-point scale. Apart from considerations of reliability, this rating was undoubtedly influenced by therapists' willingness to express their genuine conscious attitude, unconscious distortions, etc. It is difficult to say to what extent such ratings represent countertransference reactions even if there were greater agreement about the term (Orr, 1954). It seems that Gitelson's (1952) description of reactions to the patient as a whole, which he terms transferences of the analyst as distinguished from reactions to partial aspects of the patient (countertransference), fits the present ratings reasonably well:

> It is my impression that total reactions to a patient are *transferences* of the analyst to his patients and are revivals of ancient transference potentials. These may be manifested in the over-all attitude toward patients as a class or may exacerbate in the "whole response" to particular patients. These attitudes may be positively or negatively toned. They are likely to manifest themselves early in the contact with a patient and determine the tendency of the analyst towards the whole case [p. 4].

To integrate a workable therapeutic relationship, the therapist, according to psychoanalytic theory, must convey an attitude of acceptance, patience, respect, etc. He must also be able to empathize (Fenichel, 1945, p. 580). This does not mean that he must have or should have a positive attitude toward *all* aspects of the patient's behavior. Rather, it is recognized that the therapist, like other people, may experience emotional reactions. However, he is enjoined to be vigilant to make sure that they do not interfere with the therapeutic process and if they do, to seek clarification through self-analysis or other means.

The emphasis on diagnosis and etiology, according to analytic theory, determines at least partially the therapist's approach to therapy. Reich (1949) says:

322

It should be clear that one approaches an aggressive patient unlike a masochistic one, a hyperactive hysteric unlike a depressive one, that one changes one's attitude to one and the same patient according to the situation, that, in brief, one does not behave neurotically oneself, even though one may have to deal with some neurotic difficulties in oneself.

One cannot give up one's own individuality, a fact which one will consider in the choice of patients. But one should be able to expect that this individuality is not a disturbing factor and that the training analysis should establish the necessary minimum in plasticity of character [p. 139].

From these considerations it would follow that, ideally, the prognosis for any one patient represents a realistic assessment of the severity of the disturbance reflecting clinical experience regarding the response of similar patients to psychotherapy.

While evidence has been presented in Chapter Nine that a prognostic estimate *may* be based on the therapist's emotional reaction to the patient rather than on the clinical evidence, it does not follow that an unfavorable prognosis is *ipso facto* proof of a rejecting attitude on the therapist's part. It may well be a realistic assessment of the clinical picture.

It appears that the results obtained from client-centered therapists must be explained on different grounds. First, one of the most important conditions for constructive personality change postulated by Rogers (1957) is the therapist's "unconditional positive regard" for the patient. This means a "prizing" of the person, the absence of *conditions* of acceptance and of a selective evaluating attitude. Unconditional positive regard appears closely related to empathy, another of Rogers' (1957) key postulates, which is defined as the therapist's "experiencing an accurate, empathic understanding of the client's awareness of his own experience [p. 99]."

Second, in explicitly rejecting the usefulness of diagnosis for psychotherapy, Rogers (1957) denies that the therapist's approach or operations should be influenced or modified by the type of patient or disturbance [p. 101]. This would also imply that prognostic estimates, to the extent that they attempt to take into account the severity or chronicity of the patient's disturbance, are pointless.

Thus, it appears logical that the client-centered therapist who fully accepts the theory must describe his attitude toward the patient as positive and give a favorable prognosis. The ratings under discussion seem to reflect very clearly the respondents' theoretical orientation and are perhaps best explained on this basis.

Whether a conscious attitude toward the patient is a more or less individual expression of the therapist's emotional reaction or whether the attitude is an intrinsic part of the therapist's theoretical framework, or both, the more important question relates to the manner in which this attitude is expressed in the therapeutic situation. Some evidence (see Chapter Nine) has been adduced that there is in fact a carry-over. It remains to be demonstrated to what extent the therapist's initial attitude toward the patient influences the course and outcome of therapy, but there seems to be a very real possibility that the therapist making a negative evaluation and/or reacting negatively to the patient may unwittingly contribute to the realization of the events he diagnoses or predicts. On the other hand the therapist who brings a genuinely positive approach to bear upon the relationship may thereby promote a more favorable outcome.* Both psychoanalytic and client-centered theory emphasize that the person of the therapist, as revealed in this relationship, will in time serve as a new, more mature, and more desirable model of reality than past interpersonal relation-

*If it turns out that the therapist's personality—his dedication, faith, belief—is indeed a primary force in modern psychotherapy, painstaking research may still give a clearer picture of the components. See in this connection (Frank, 1958).

ships that have distorted the patient's perceptions of himself and others (see Chapter One):

> What is curative in the [therapeutic] process is that in tending to reconstruct with the analyst that atmosphere which obtained in childhood, the patient actually achieves something new. He discovers that part of himself which had to be repressed at the time of the original experience. He can only do this in an interpersonal relationship with the analyst, which is suitable to such a rediscovery. . . . Thus, the transference phenomenon is used so that the patient will completely reexperience the original frames of reference, and himself within those frames, in a truly different relationship with the analyst, to the end that he can discover the invalidity of his conclusions about himself and others (Rioch, 1943, p. 151).

Rogers (1956) puts it this way:

> In a minimal way, the client may perceive from the first the unconditional positive regard of the therapist for him. The perception is continually strengthened as he discovers that each facet of himself which is exposed—contradictions, weaknesses, strengths, abnormal feelings, tender feelings, vicious attitudes, antisocial behaviors, fears and despairs—are all met with equal positive regard, because each of these elements is a part of him, and he is prized unconditionally. The client then gradually takes in the experience of being loved—a love which is nonpossessive and nondemanding, warm but not oversolicitous. As he lives for a sequence of hours in this atmosphere, the experience has two primary results. It permits him to relax the tight defensive structure of his concept of himself and to admit into awareness and fully experience attitudes which previously he had found too threatening. . . . In the second place, the attitude of the therapist toward him is gradually internalized so that he can take the

same attitude toward himself. He comes to prize himself, to feel that he *is* of value [p. 204].

Much remains to be learned about the therapist's personality and its contribution to the treatment process, but, as I have suggested in Chapter Twenty-one, this focus on the person of the therapist may be one of the most fruitful avenues for research in this area.

SUMMARY

In this investigation, designed to obtain empirical evidence on psychotherapists' performance in an initial interview for the purpose of studying the influence of relevant therapist variables, Rogerians were generally disinclined to make plans for treatment or to set up therapeutic goals. Their prognostic estimates were more favorable, and they rated their attitude toward the patient as more positive than analytically oriented therapists.

In discussing the implications of these findings, attention has been drawn to the interrelationships between therapist's attitude toward the patient and clinical evaluations, including diagnosis and prognosis. In view of the self-realizing character of one's expectations, the therapist's attitude toward the patient may have important effects upon the course and outcome of psychotherapy.

This investigation has stressed the great need for research on the therapist's contribution to the treatment process.

References

Fenichel, O. 1945. *The Psychoanalytic Theory of Neurosis.* New York: Norton.

Frank, J. D. 1958. "Some Effects of Expectancy and Influence in Psychotherapy," in *Progress in Psychotherapy,* Vol. III, ed. J. H. Masserman and J. L. Moreno, pp. 27-43. New York: Grune & Stratton.

Fromm-Reichmann, F. 1950. *Principles of Intensive Psychotherapy.* Chicago: University of Chicago Press.

Gitelson, M. 1952. "The Emotional Position of the Analyst in the Psychoanalytic Situation," *Int. J. Psychoanal.,* 33: 1-10.

Orr, D. W. 1954. "Transference and Countertransference: A Historical Survey," *J. Am. Psychoanal. Assn.,* 2: 621-670.

Reich, W. 1949. *Character-analysis.* New York: Orgone Institute Press. Third edition.

Rioch, Janet. 1943. "The Transference Phenomenon in Psychoanalytic Therapy," *Psychiat.,* 6: 147-156.

Rogers, C. R. 1955. "Persons or Science: A Philosophical Question," *Am. Psychol.,* 10: 267-278.

——— 1956. "Client-centered Therapy: A Current View," in *Progress in Psychotherapy* 1956, ed. F. Fromm-Reichmann and J. L. Moreno, pp. 199-209. New York: Grune & Stratton.

——— 1957. "The Necessary and Sufficient Conditions of Therapeutic Personality Change," *J. Cons. Psychol.,* 21: 95-103.

THE THERAPIST'S PERFORMANCE: D. A FURTHER STUDY OF PSYCHIATRISTS (WITH M. S. WALLACH)

The investigation discussed in this chapter is part of an ongoing research program reported in Chapter Nine as well as in Chapters Nineteen and Twenty. See also Strupp (1960). In past work, we have been concerned with the psychotherapist's perceptions of patients, the manner in which interview impressions influence clinical judgments, treatment plans, etc., as well as the character of the communications the therapist addresses to the patient. Guided by the data of our earlier work, we have become increasingly interested in *attitudinal* factors within the therapist that seem to be closely associated with his initial impressions of a patient. We have also attempted to relate differences in a therapist's clinical evaluations as well as his communications to patients to his theoretical orientation, experience, and other biographical variables.*

A detailed description of the experimental method and procedure is given in earlier chapters. Despite numerous shortcomings, which we have attempted to make explicit (Strupp, 1962), we believe that the technique is a potentially fruitful device for studying interviewer differences, with a view toward elucidating variables in their background, training, experience, and personality that might account for observed variations.

Salient findings of the earlier work may be briefly summarized as follows.

1. Therapists differed markedly in their perceptions of the patient, in their diagnostic and prognostic formulations, clinical judgments, treatment plans, and attitudes toward the patient depicted in the film.

2. Similar variations were observed with respect to the character of their communications, as measured by a system of content analysis developed as part of the investigative effort (see Chapter Twenty-one).

3. Certain systematic differences in therapists' responses were traced to factors in their theoretical orientation, level

*This research was supported by Research Grant MH 02171 from the National Institute of Mental Health, Public Health Service. A great debt of gratitude is owed to the psychiatrists and residents of the Deparment of Psychiatry at the University of North Carolina School of Medicine for their participation in this study. Each person donated several hours of valuable time. The fact that virtually the entire psychiatric staff agreed to participate is particularly gratifying, since it provided us with a sample spanning the whole gamut of professional experience.

George C. Ham, M.D., former chairman of the Department, encouraged and facilitated our work. Dr. Joan W. Jenkins actively participated in various stages of the work. Dr. Lyle V. Jones, Director of the Psychometrics Laboratory at the University of North Carolina, provided valuable advice on statistical problems. Mrs. Sophie Martin handled the experimental procedure with great diligence and skill.

of experience, whether they had undergone personal analysis, and the like.

4. Most important, for theoretical as well as practical purposes, were rather striking interrelationships between therapists' attitudes toward the film patient (as rated by themselves and inferred from the emotional tone of their characterizations) and clinical judgments, treatment plans, and the emotional quality of their communications. For example, therapists indicating a negative attitude toward the patient were more likely to choose such diagnostic labels as psychopath, character disorder, paranoid, and phobic; they tended to see the patient as less anxious, having less insight, being less capable of self-observation, more immature emotionally, and more poorly adjusted socially. Similarly, a negative attitude toward the patient was associated with significantly poorer prognosis, greater anticipation of countertransference reactions, greater readiness to make recommendations to the patient concerning changes in his mode of living, a tendency to be strict and active in therapy, to discourage free association, to see the patient less frequently in therapy, etc.

With regard to therapists' communications, there was a significant relationship between the degree of empathy shown the patient (rated by independent judges) and the therapist's self-rated attitude. Judgments of prognosis related to empathy in a similar manner.

The implications of these findings raise the possibility that the therapist's attitude toward the patient, as conveyed by his communications, may bring about a realization of the therapist's conscious as well as unconscious expectations. The latter may act as a self-fulfilling prophecy having far-reaching consequences for the course of psychotherapy. We reasoned that the crux of the matter is not the therapist's perceptions of the patient or even the therapist's conscious attitude; rather, it is the manner in which these variables influence and structure the developing therapeutic relation-

330

ship through verbal as well as nonverbal communications.

While the findings of the previous investigation were based on sizable samples (134 psychiatrists and 55 psychoanalytically oriented psychologists), they nevertheless represented responses to a *single* patient in idiosyncratic fashion. The patient was a middle-aged man of lower-middle-class background who was interviewed by an inexperienced psychiatric resident *after* having had a period of psychotherapy with another therapist. Moreover, the patient was a rather hostile, demanding, and provocative individual, who might have elicited undue counter-anger, rejection, and negative attitudes in many therapists. Hence, it appeared logical to strive for greater diversification of the stimulus situation, and to request respondents to react to at least two films.

1. By presenting respondents (psychotherapists) with two sound motion pictures depicting initial interviews with patients differing in terms of sex, motivation for therapy, nature of the neurotic problem, etc., we proposed to investigate differences (or similarities) in the viewers' perceptions, clinical judgments, attitudes toward the patient, their eagerness to work with these patients in psychotherapy, and the like.

2. Also, we desired to shed light on differences (or similarities) in the respondents' manner of communicating with different patients presenting themselves to a psychotherapist. The problem of central concern in both of these questions is whether therapists react and relate to different patients in a relatively invariant manner or whether patient characteristics exert a marked effect upon the therapists' evaluations and response style.

3. We anticipated that the data obtained in the present investigation would permit replication and extension of the findings previously reported, particularly those bearing on the interrelationships among clinical evaluations, treatment plans, attitude toward the patient, and the tenor of the communications addressed to the patient.

METHOD AND PROCEDURE

The sound films

The sound films used in this investigation were part of a series that had been produced for experimental purposes in collaboration with the Communications Center of the University of North Carolina. (A detailed description of the rationale and development of these films is presented by Strupp and Jenkins, 1963.) Since it was not considered feasible to show more than two films to any one respondent, the first two films (in the series of six) were selected.

Each film (running time, including titles, approximately 15-20 minutes each) presents an interview with a different neurotic patient. The interviews were chosen to portray diverse neurotic and character problems, but not grossly unusual or atypical ones. The therapist's contribution was intentionally kept to a minimum. That is, we deliberately presented him as a facilitator of communication, "playing down" efforts at interpretation. Both the patient's and the therapist's parts are played by actors (advanced drama students).

No information about the patients was given apart from the transactions in the interview. Admittedly, this puts the viewer who may be used to detailed diagnostic work-ups, case history material, etc., at a disadvantage, but the procedure achieves the greatest economy and maximally standardizes the information available to each viewer.

Each film contained eight stopping points (30 seconds each), at which time the film sequence is interrupted and the uniform title "WHAT WOULD YOU DO?" appears on the screen.

FILM 1: This interview was originally presented (Wolberg, 1954, pp. 277-280) as an example of negative feelings expressed toward the therapist in an initial interview, and the therapist's dealing with them by acceptance. Since the original sound recording or supplementary data were not

332

available, the interview was reconstructed entirely from information given in the above source and slightly edited. To quote the therapist's description of the patient:

The patient stomps into the office with a swagger. She is a young woman with a short haircut and a severely tailored suit. She radiates an air of masculinity, and is obviously disturbed and hostile. She opens the interview by announcing, "The first thing I'm going to tell you is that because of a past experience I am against psychiatry completely. I'm coming here against my will—definitely against my will." She goes on to say that she was asked to leave college because of homosexuality and masculine mannerisms, her way of dressing, and so on. Ostensibly she would like to retain her preference for homosexuality but become less "obvious" about it and conform more to social conventions. While rather hostile and defensive at the beginning of the interview, she softens as she goes on and finally confesses " . . . there is this tremendous fear that I am not myself."

A few excerpts from the film follow:

P1: Several years ago I had two psychiatrists working with me. One was a society doctor who got me in and gave me 10-minute sessions talking about nothing and charged me fifteen bucks; the other was a complete ass, who just sat on a chair and did nothing. . . .

P4: . . . In fact, it's not the homosexualism that bothers her (a college counselor), it's the way I dress and walk and things. I was a little out of hand at school. They don't say that but that's what I say. (*Stopping Point 2*)

T4: What sort of trouble did you have?

T8: Well, when you are with them, how do you act with the girls?

P9: I am aggressive, naturally.

T9: Do you ever take the passive role with them?

333

P10: No.

T10: And what about your relations with men?

P11: I am very much in love with a man now, and he is also a homosexual. My only associations which are very satisfying are with gay boys. (Laughs.) If I talk to you much longer, you'll get my lingo. Isn't it awful? (*Stopping Point 5*)

T11: You seem to be ashamed of it.

P12: I'm not ashamed of the fact that I'm a homosexual, but I am ashamed of the fact that I'm obvious. That's what I'd like to change. . . . Right now, if I were to choose, I think I would be homosexual—because my whole environment as a child and ever since I can remember has been one which was conducive to homosexuality. But I'm unhappy, you see. (*Stopping Point 6*)

T12: Maybe you feel that if you were to start therapy, I am likely to change your preference for homosexuality.

P13: (aggressively): Well, are you? (*Stopping Point 7*)

FILM 2: Interview 2 was originally published as an illustration of some of the processes occurring in an initial session (Wolberg, 1954, pp. 293-302). The therapist states:

The patient telephoned for an appointment stating that he had been referred by a psychiatrist in San Francisco. When he appeared, he presented the appearance of a pleasant, poised young man, somewhat timid in manner.

As the interview opens, the patient formulates his problem by saying, "I'm not as complete a person as I might be." He spends the better part of the interview explaining rather circumstantially his relationships with two girl friends. Both affairs ended by the patient's being rejected. He speaks easily and garrulously throughout, and at one point warns the interviewer that his previous therapist felt his "glibness" was a problem. It emerges that his parents were divorced when he was a young boy,

334

and that he was brought up by his father and stepmother. The latter is described as "a person who deprecated me and my accomplishments constantly; a person who, of course, took me to the dentist twice a year and performed all the routine functions of a mother without really letting herself—uh—be a mother." He has difficulties forming friendships and attributes this problem to "the fact that I had been deprecated, I had been deprecated by my stepmother throughout life. . . ." In the original interview the therapist proceeds to ask a series of detailed case history questions (not included in the film), giving this rationale: "Since the patient is garrulous, to allow him to explore several other things that occurred to the patient would divert us from important tasks." As the film interview terminates, the patient states: ". . . Dad was always the most stabilizing influence in this whole set-up. He was wonderful."

A few excerpts from the interview follow:

T2: . . . Now the best way I can preface what I want to say is that I went to see Dr. Brown in San Francisco. I did have a problem, sort of an immediate problem, which in turn led to other problems. There was a girl with whom I had been going for the past year, and we had just broken off, and I was very upset about that. And, I had, we had been having an affair which seemed to complicate the matter considerable, since I wanted to be married and she in turn had had a previous engagement which had been broken. And my first really severe emotional, what I consider a bust-up was when she broke off the affair, and I, I lost control of myself pretty well.

   P6: . . . As I look back on it now it seems to be almost a shadow. Oh, it comes back—every so often. I think that my conduct today would be entirely different. I mean I can't visualize myself doing some of the incredibly insane things I did at the time. I mean I, I persisted, I was jealous, I-I-I didn't know whether to phone her or not. I put her on the spot. I made things rough and miserable for her. I made them miserable for myself. (*Stopping Point 2*)

P14: . . . My mother got involved, and she became just like every other mother, very possessive and jealous of her son. . . . She said, "She's no better than a whore." I took great offense to that. I got sore as hell. . . .

Now why I'm here today . . . I know you want to get to that. Well right now I have actually never felt in a way so confident except maybe when I was in high school or in the Army. But it may be because I think introspectively. I guess introspection isn't too good either. (*Stopping Point 7*)

Procedure

The two sound films were administered to each respondent in individual sessions. The order of presentation was varied systematically, so that half the group viewed Film 1 first and half the group Film 2. Both films typically were shown at one sitting. The respondent was seated in a comfortable chair, and spoke his comments at the stopping points into a microphone that was connected to a tape recorder.*

Respondents were told that they were to be shown two films of initial interviews, that the presentation of each film

---

*Since this procedure represented a departure from the earlier one, in which respondents recorded their responses in writing, we investigated systematically possible differences between the two methods of response (Jenkins, Wallach, and Strupp, 1962). In general, interviewers preferred the verbal to the written means of responding to film patients, and there was a tendency for greater verbal output to occur with the former method. While the evidence was not entirely conclusive, the verbal response method, despite the much greater expenditure of time and energy, was considered preferable because it reduced the amount of artificiality in the experimental analogue, thus yielding a better sample of typical interviewer behavior.

336

would be interrupted at certain points, and that each stopping point would last approximately 30 seconds. They were asked to assume the role of a therapist with the film patient and to address their comments and questions directly to the patient. If they preferred to remain silent or to communicate nonverbally at any point of interruption, they were free to do so. In that event, they were requested to say "No comment," and/or to describe their gestures. No information concerning the patients portrayed in the films was provided, nor did the experimenter (a woman) answer questions concerning the original filming procedure, the authenticity of the patients, and the like. Such data were provided upon termination of the experiment, if requested by the respondent.

Following the presentation of each film, the respondent was requested to complete a comprehensive questionnaire relating to diagnostic impressions, clinical judgments, treatment plans, the interviewer's attitude toward the patient, etc. In addition, the respondent was asked to furnish basic biographical data (such as age, sex, length of experience, personal analysis, etc.).* Finally, there was a 17-item questionnaire in which information was elicited concerning the subject's usual mode of conducting psychotherapy. (The results of this questionnaire are reported in Chapter Twenty-two.)

The experimental procedure, which typically occupied two hours, yielded two major kinds of data: (1) comments to the patients portrayed in the films; and (2) responses to the questionnaire items.

The sample

Complete data were collected from 59 psychotherapists (all physicians), representing various degrees of training and

---

*This questionnaire was patterned after the one described in Chapter Nine, although it incorporated some modifications in item type and content, suggested by our cumulative research experience.

experience, ranging from first year residents in psychiatry to highly experienced psychoanalysts. All respondents were affiliated with the Department of Psychiatry at North Carolina Memorial Hospital, the teaching hospital of the University of North Carolina. Table 1 summarizes pertinent biographical data obtained from the respondents.

QUANTITATIVE ANALYSIS AND STATISTICAL TREATMENT

Quantitative analysis of therapists' communications

Therapists' responses were quantified according to a revised version of the system of content analysis described in Chapter Twenty-one. Although the original version has been applied in a number of investigations (see Chapters Nine, Ten, Eleven, Thirteen, Fourteen; also see Auerbach, 1963), it appeared desirable to introduce a modified version. There were two major reasons for this step. First, simplification of the scoring procedure seemed indicated (the original version called for simultaneous assessments on five separate components, entitled respectively Type of Therapeutic Activity, Depth-directedness, Dynamic Focus, Initiative, and Therapeutic Climate). Secondly, it appeared that there was considerable overlap among the five components. The revised scoring system was intended to retain a maximum of information yielded by the earlier version by combining the various components into a single system. As will be noted from Table 2, the revised system attempts both a categorization of responses and provides for an intensity measure (under Interpretive Operations). The component Therapeutic Climate was not retained in the revised version of the system. This decision principally derived from the consideration that a very large proportion of all responses was not differentiable on this component in previous work, and that a measure of the therapist's "warmth," which, in terms of the rating process, seemed largely synonymous with

338

TABLE 1

BIOGRAPHICAL DATA OF RESPONDENTS
$N=59$*

Category	Number
Age 25–29	13
30–34	15
35–39	21
40+	10
Mean	36
Range	26–64
Level of Training	
Analyst	4
Psychiatrist	22
3 or 4 Year Resident	12
2 Year Resident	12
1 Year Resident	9
Hours of Personal Therapy	
None	28
Less than 100	4
100–299	9
300–499	7
500+	10
No answer	1
Range	10–900
Hours per Week Devoted to Therapy	
0–4	2
5–9	12
10–14	18
15–19	17
20+	10
Mean	14
Range	3–30
Years of Experience in Therapy	
Less than 3	26
3–5	15
6–9	7
10–14	8
15–19	1
20+	2
Range	1 month–33 years

* The 3 female and 56 male respondents all possessed the M.D. degree and 35 listed psychotherapy as their major interest.

TABLE 2

REVISED SYSTEM OF CONTENT ANALYSIS

Code	Description
00	Facilitating Communication (Minimal Activity)
01	Silence
02	Passive acceptance, acknowledgment.
10	Exploratory Operations Simple questioning: asking for further information, clarification, elaboration, examples; simple probes, case history questions; accenting by repeating one or more words.
20	Clarification Reflection of feeling, restatements for purposes of clarification, essentially noninterpretive summaries.
30	Interpretive Operations
31	Mildly interpretive. Questioning to stimulate the patient's curiosity, encourage self-exploration, direction to explore feelings rather than facts.
32	Moderately interpretive. Implicit or explicit challenge of what the patient has said, pointing out inconsistencies without overtly interpreting their meaning.
33	Frankly interpretive. Analysis of defenses, establishing connections, definitions of the patient's problem; interpretations.
50	Direct Guidance Suggestions for activity either within or outside of the therapeutic framework; giving information, stating an opinion, answering direct questions, speaking as an authority.
60	Activity Not Clearly Relevant to the Task of Therapy. Greetings, small talk, endings, etc.
70	Unclassifiable.

"empathy," was being obtained separately. Thus, the revised system provides essentially for exclusive scoring in that a single score is typically assigned to a therapist communication.*

In addition to the foregoing quantification, two additional types of measures were obtained: (1) the total number of words the respondent spoke at each stopping point, as well as the total number of words spoken by each subject in response to each film; and (2) the latency of response at each stopping point, as well as the average latency of response for each subject for each film. (Silent responses received no latency score since it was assumed that practically all silences are a product of a rather rapid decision to offer no verbal response.)

Over-all ratings of empathy

Following the procedure and scoring criteria outlined in Chapter Nine, protocols were rated on the dimension of empathy. This judgment was a global assessment based on the complete set of responses to each film. The following distinctions were made. Score + : The set of responses gives evidence of empathy on the part of the respondent. Score − : The set of responses is essentially nonempathic. Score 0: This judgment was made when the judge felt that in a given set of responses (1) empathy was not present or (2) there appeared to be an equal number of empathic and nonempathic responses in the set.

---

*The unit of response categorized was the entire communication at a stopping point. Under certain conditions, according to scoring rules established in advance, it was possible for a communication to receive a multiple score. For example, in a few cases in which more than one category appeared appropriate for a single response, two (but no more than two) scores were allowed. Coders had been previously trained to a high level of reliability, and agreement among two of three raters was considered necessary to classify a response. In a few instances where agreement among two of three raters did not exist initially, differences were discussed and a consensus reached.

By assigning weights of 2 to a "plus" rating, 1 to a "zero" rating, and 0 to a "minus" rating, each respondent's score for each film was the sum of all ratings assigned independently by seven judges.* Thus, the higher the score, the more confidence one would have in asserting that the respondent was being empathic.

Quantitative treatment of questionnaire items†

Separate statistical treatment was indicated for the portion of the questionnaire that dealt with the respondent's diagnostic impressions and evaluations, proposed treatment plans, and attitudes toward the patient (completed for each of the two patients shown in Films 1 and 2) and the second segment (completed only once for each respondent) dealing with his usual therapeutic practices.

DIAGNOSTIC IMPRESSIONS: The 47 items comprising this section of the questionnaire were intercorrelated separately for each patient. All 47 items showed one or more statistically significant ($p < .05$) intercorrelations, but factor analysis of this large an item composite did not seem feasible (considering the relatively small sample of respondents). Twenty-one of the items, for one or both films, clearly were most often intercorrelated, whereas the remaining 26 items demonstrated many fewer statistically significant intercorrelations. We thus utilized the 21 most highly intercorrelated items and performed two factor analyses.

The next step consisted of computing factor scores for each respondent. These scores were based upon those items that had the highest loadings on a given factor and thus

---

*In addition to the authors, the following persons served as judges: Ronald E. Fox, Joan W. Jenkins, Peter N. Mayfield, Gary M. Olson, and Michael Wogan.

†In this section we shall outline only the more complex analyses. Omitted are simple comparisons (e.g., differences in ratings for Films 1 and 2 on particular questionnaire items), which will be discussed in the Results section.

342

served to define the dimension. Separate factor scores were computed for Films 1 and 2. The respondent's score on a given factor thus served as a means of indicating his relative standing on a particular dimension represented by the factor. Finally, the respondents' factor scores were used as variates in the major analysis of this investigation, whose objective it was to explore the relationships among the factors in this portion of the questionnaire to the respondents' usual therapeutic practices (see below), biographical variables, and therapeutic communications.

USUAL THERAPEUTIC PRACTICES: The analysis of this segment of the questionnaire (comprising 17 items) forms the subject of Chapter Twenty. Briefly, these items were subjected to factor analysis, which yielded six factors, four of which were sufficiently clear to lend themselves to interpretation. It should be pointed out that the results of the first factor analysis were replicated upon a larger sample of 248 psychotherapists. These factors were identified as follows: Factor I: Maintenance of personal distance; Factor II: Preference for intensive (psychoanalytic, uncovering) psychotherapy; Factor III: Preference for keeping verbal interventions to a minimum; and Factor IV: Psychotherapy as an artistic activity, with emphasis on flexibility. Chapter Twenty should be consulted for a fuller description of these dimensions and their relationships to other therapist variables.

Content coding

Therapist responses to the two films were transcribed, and the typescripts were scored independently by four (in some cases, only three) raters who had been given extensive training previously in the use of the modified system of content analysis. Table 3 indicates the number of responses coded in each category.

Nearly perfect agreement (99 + per cent) among raters was obtained for the 01 category. In the 02 category there

TABLE 3
FREQUENCY DISTRIBUTION OF CODED RESPONSES

Code Number and Description		Film 1		Film 2		Total	
		n	%	n	%	n	%
01	Silence	48	11.6	83	19.2	131	15.5
02	Acknowledgment	14	3.4	36	8.3	50	5.9
10	Exploratory	220	53.1	229	53.0	449	53.0
20	Clarification	11	2.7	14	3.3	25	3.0
30	Interpretive	85	20.5	68	15.8	153	18.1
50	Guidance	34	8.2	1	0.2	35	4.1
70	Unclassifiable	2	0.5	1	0.2	3	0.4
	Subtotal	414		432		846	
	Double Codings	54		37		91	
	Total	468		469		937	

was 70 per cent perfect agreement in every instance at least two of the judges coded the response as 02. For the most often used coding category, 10, perfect agreement was observed 71 per cent of the time (at least two of three or three of four raters agreeing raises agreement level to 95 per cent). The coding categories of 20 and 50, which accounted for but 60 of the responses, showed respectively 50 per cent and 100 per cent agreement by all, or all but one, rater. For the category of "interpretation," 80 per cent agreement by all, or all but one, rater was obtained, but this figure was reduced to 50 per cent when the criterion for agreement was tightened by asking judges to specify the exact level of interpretation (31, 32, or 33). Double coded responses (91) led to a lower level of reliability, but 70 per cent of the time all (or all but one) of the raters agreed that double coding was called for.

EMPATHY RATINGS: Empathy was rated as previously described. For Film 1 there were 13 cases in which 4 of the 7 raters were in agreement, and 30 cases in which 5 or more raters were in agreement. For Film 2 there were 23 instances of agreement by four raters and another 23 times where

344

agreement was for five or more raters. The ratings were weighted $(+ = 2; 0 = 1; - = 0)$ and summed across raters. In this way, each respondent obtained a score which was employed in subsequent analyses. This score represents the pooled judgment of all raters.

RESULTS

Comparisons between film patients 1 and 2

To compare the respondents' evaluations made of the patients presented respectively in Film 1 and Film 2, *t* tests were performed on all questionnaire items. Of the 47 comparisons, 15 (approximately 31 per cent) were statistically significant at or beyond the .05 level (two-tailed test). Items

TABLE 4

SIGNIFICANT MEAN DIFFERENCES IN THERAPISTS' EVALUATION OF PATIENTS
1 AND 2

Item No.	Variable	Patient 1	Patient 2	$p<$
3	Degree of defensiveness	+		.02
6	Degree of disturbance	+		.001
9	Adequacy of social adjustment		+	.001
10	Motivation for therapy		+	.05
14	Prognosis without therapy		+	.01
16	Ease of empathizing	+		.01
17	Willingness to treat	+		.01
18	Personal reaction to patient	+		.01
20	Amount of emotional investment	+		.001
30	Likely to become impatient		+	.05
37	Likely to lose interest		+	.01
40	Feel warmly toward patient	+		.01
42	Psychotic break a possibility	+		.05
46	Patient has reality problems	+		.01
49	Type of patient a poor candidate	+		.02

+ indicates greater mean.

345

showing statistically significant mean differences are presented in Table 4, together with the directions of the differences.

These differences seem to be explicable on the basis of two sets of factors: (1) the "built-in" characteristics of the film patients, which were responsible for their being perceived differently, and (2) the therapists' attitudes toward the patients, particularly with reference to their liking for and willingness to treat them.

To elaborate on these points, Patient 1 was portrayed as a young woman who expressed herself as being violently opposed to psychiatry at the outset and whose attitude toward professionals in this field was one of bristling hostility. True, this façade belied an underlying feeling of helplessness (inferred by many viewers), but the fact remained that her Defensiveness (Item 3) was great and her motivation for Therapy (Item 10), at least viewed superficially, was poor. Therapists tended to agree that such patients are usually poor candidates for psychotherapy. These reasons seem to be the basis for the significant differences on these items between this patient and Patient 2.

The second set of differences appear to refer to an attitudinal component, which may be termed Liking-Willingness to Treat-Warmth-Empathy. It will be noted that these items (16, 17, 18, 20, 40) showed differences in favor of Patient 1. Thus, there is no doubt that Patient 1 was "preferred" to Patient 2 by our respondents.

The latter attitudinal component, too, seems to account for certain additional differences in the evaluations of the two patients, which corroborate findings reported in Chapter Nine pertaining to statistically significant relationships between therapists' attitudes (in the earlier case toward *one* patient) and the character of clinical evaluations, treatment plans, and the like. Specifically, it appears that a generally more positive attitude toward Patient 1 on the part of the respondents coincided with higher ratings on Disturbance (Item 6), poorer prognosis without therapy (Item 14), and

346

greater likelihood of becoming psychotic (Item 42). Although one cannot be certain, the greater severity of reality problems attributed to her (Item 46) may have a similar basis. (Seen "objectively," both patients clearly had serious reality problems, although Patient 1's homosexuality seems to have been regarded as more "serious" than Patient 2's promiscuity.)

Finally, the respondents' more positive attitudes toward Patient 1 undoubtedly led them to assert that they were less likely to become impatient with the patient in therapy (Item 30) or to lose interest soon (Item 37).

Patient 2, it will be recalled, was presented as a glib young man, who seemed to have a pronounced problem with heterosexual relationships. However, he seemed eager to obtain professional help, a fact that evidently earned him higher ratings on Motivation for Therapy (Item 10) and lower ratings on Defensiveness (Item 3). It should be added that he tended to be seen as less seriously disturbed and as having a better social adjustment than Patient 1.

Nevertheless, the consensus indicated that Patient 2 was less easy to empathize with ("average"), and respondents tended to be "neutral" in wanting to see this patient in psychotherapy. Their personal reaction, too, tended to be "neutral" and "warmth" seemed to be lacking (Item 40). Emotional Investment (Item 20) was somewhat less than "moderate." In brief, a decided absence of enthusiasm for accepting this patient in therapy seemed to prevail. One important clue for this attitude may be obtained from responses to Item 30, which gave indications that therapists were concerned lest they become impatient and lose interest in the patient's therapy (Item 37).

It is possible that the respondents' lack of interest in treating this patient was rationalized by more favorable ratings on Prognosis-without-Therapy (Item 14), although they seemed to be agreed that both patients had much to gain from psychotherapy (Item 15).

Attention should be called to a number of items that

347

failed to differentiate between the two patients. According to the respondents' mean judgments, both patients were appraised as approximately equal in anxiety, emotional maturity, capacity for insight, and past success in coping with their problems. The optimal intensity of therapy was rated fairly high for both patients, and the prognosis with therapy was regarded as quite promising. It is noteworthy that none of the items that dealt with departures from the therapist's "usual" technique as a function of particular patient characteristics or countertransference reactions (Items 21-28) differentiated the two patients. Similarly, a number of the Likert-type items (29-49) showed no statistically significant differences.

In Chapter Nine extensive discussion was devoted to the distribution of individual items dealing with diagnosis, prognosis, treatment plans, etc., with emphasis on the variability of the respondents' evaluations. We have omitted such discussion from this chapter. However, inspection of the relative magnitudes of the standard deviations pointed to considerable divergence in the therapists' appraisals for both patients. For example, the standard deviations on the recommended duration of therapy (Item 13b) was particularly large (true for both patients), which is not surprising since, obviously, the item called for a rather ambitious prediction. Variability was considerable on numerous items, including such clinical indicators as Defensiveness, Anxiety, Capacity for Insight, and the like, on which greater unanimity might have been expected. Items in which the respondent is asked to rate personal reactions of course invite idiosyncratic responses, so that variability in those instances may be expected. It was precisely the observation of marked individual differences in clinical evaluations that provided the point of departure for our earlier effort to account for such differences in terms of the respondents' biographical variables (age, experience, personal analysis, theoretical orientation, etc.) and liking for the patient. The latter variable, in particular, disclosed marked congruency

348

with numerous clinical judgments, treatment plans, as well as communications addressed to the patient.

A major purpose of the present replication was to identify *dimensions* in therapists' clinical evaluations, treatment plans, as well as attitudes toward patients, and to relate such dimensions to the communications addressed by the respondents to the film patients. We attempted to achieve this objective by starting with a relatively large item pool, whose intercorrelations were subjected to factor analytic procedures. The hope was to arrive in this way at a more stable measure than was provided by single items. In the following section, therefore, we shall address ourselves to the process of developing factor scores that were used in subsequent analyses. This approach did not account fully for the variance contributed by a number of single items; thus, it will be necessary in later sections to have recourse to individual items and their relationships to other measures.

Factor analyses of questionnaire items

In carrying out the factor analyses for the data of Film 1, the principal axes solution was employed, followed by varimax rotation to orthogonal simple structure, as programed by Johnson (1961) for the UNIVAC 1105. The pattern of decrements in successive characteristic roots from the principal axes solution suggested that no fewer than five and no more than eight factors should be retained for rotation. Rotated solutions were obtained based upon the largest four, five, six, seven, and eight principal axes. The eight-factor solution was judged most suitable, since the smallest rotated factor still displayed sizable projections of two variables. By a comparable procedure seven factors were extracted and rotated for the data of Film 2. In each analysis the smallest rotated factor did not lend itself to clear interpretation; thus, the results presented for Film 1 and Film 2 are for seven and six factors respectively. While there were some slight variations (in terms on highest loadings) in the item composite of the five factors that were common to both films, the discrepancies were sufficiently slight to justify single descriptions of these factors. Based on items having the highest loadings on each factor, the following brief characterizations are offered.

FACTOR A (4 items): The highest loadings occurred on items dealing with the respondent's feeling that he finds it easy to empathize with the patient, his willingness to treat him, his liking for him, and his feeling warmly toward him. In Film 2, the amount of improvement expected (prognosis) also entered prominently into this composite. This factor, which emerged as the strongest one for both films, appeared quite clear in its meaning and was labeled "Empathy-Liking-Willingness to Treat." Clearly, it refers to the therapist's interest, investment, and positive attitude toward the patient.

FACTOR B (3 items): This factor was defined by items asserting that psychotherapy with the patient would be a rewarding experience for the therapist, or alternatively, that the patient might be a poor candidate for psychotherapy. Also part of the cluster was a rating of the patient's capacity for insight (Film 1) and an assessment of the likelihood that the patient would continue in psychotherapy until some of his major problems were resolved. We designated the factor "Patient's Suitability for Psychotherapy," but recognized that the therapist's assessments included an appraisal of his own as well as the patient's *motivation* for collaborative work.

FACTOR C (3 items): The items that were identical for both films comprised estimates of the likelihood that the therapist might become impatient, angry, and rejecting toward the patient. The term "Countertransference Potential" appears to be an adequate description of this composite.

FACTOR D (2 items for Film 1; 3 items for Film 2): In the two items that were common to both films the therapist asserted his expectation of being able to work steadily with

350

the patient in psychotherapy and the suitability of his own personality to treat the patient. Film 2 included an additional item stating that psychotherapy with the patient would be a rewarding experience for the therapist. This factor appears to combine elements of the three preceding factors but deals more specifically with the "Therapist's Own Suitability to Treat the Patient." This designation was therefore chosen.

FACTOR E (2 items): This doublet of items, identical for both films, comprised estimates of the patient's emotional maturity and his capacity for insight. By implication, these items seem to refer to the patient's suitability for psychotherapy, but the assessments evidently are couched to a greater extent in "clinical" terms. The label "Clinical Assessments of Emotional Maturity" did not impress us as very felicitous, but no better term occurred to us; nor does the factor appear to be well defined by the small number of items.

FACTOR F (2 items, Film 1 only): The items defining this factor referred to the possibility that the therapist may reject and lose interest in the patient. The provisional label "Disinterest-Rejection" was accordingly assigned.

FACTOR G (2 items, Film 1 only): The items deal with the patient's motivation for therapy, as assessed by the therapist, as well as the likelihood of her continuing in treatment until some of her major problems are resolved. We selected the designation "Patient Motivation" for this factor.

FACTOR H (2 items, Film 2 only): The meaning of this factor is certainly unclear and must await clarification through further work. The two items presently included deal with the patient's degree of ego strength and the therapist's denial that the patient has few attractive qualities. We named the factor provisionally "Patient's Attractive Qualities."

It may be noted that the first four factors are reasonably distinct, clear-cut, and well defined. This assertion is

351

further substantiated by the fact that it was possible to isolate identical factors for both films through independent statistical analyses. Factors E, F, G, and H, on the other hand, must be considered quite tentative and provisional.

As previously noted, the items included in each factor formed the bases of factor scores that were computed for each respondent, separately for each film. We shall next examine the statistical relationships among these factor scores, as well as their relationships to other variables included in this investigation.

Interrelationships among factors

Table 5 presents the statistical relationships among factor scores for each of the films. In general, the relationships for Film 1 parallel fairly closely the relationships for Film 2, although some of the discrepancies seem to exceed fluctuations ordinarily to be expected. These divergences may be a function of personality differences between the two patients; however, it seems hazardous to attempt interpretations. Nevertheless, there are consistent indications that Patient 2 posed a greater threat to the respondents in terms of the countertransference reactions he might evoke, and his suitability for therapy seemed more closely intertwined with the therapist's own suitability than was true of Patient 1 (note the correlates of Factors C and D for the two films).

It will be noted that on the whole the correlation coefficients between clinical and attitudinal variables are quite consistent. For both patients, favorable clinical assessments tend to coincide with favorable attitudes on the part of the therapist and vice versa. Patients who are considered well motivated for therapy, whose prognosis is considered good, who are said to have reasonably great ego strength, emotional maturity, capacity for insight, and whose social adjustment is rated favorably are individuals toward whom therapists tend to feel positively disposed. Therapists like to treat such persons, find them easy to empathize with, are confident in their ability to help, anticipate therapy to be a

352

TABLE 5

INTERCORRELATIONS AMONG PATIENT FACTORS FOR FILMS 1 AND 2

N varies from 52 to 59

Factors	B-1	B-2	C-1	C-2	D-1	D-2	E-1	E-2	F-1	G-1	H-2
A. Empathy-Liking and Willingness to Treat	.47†	.57†	−.52†	−.66†	.35†	.62†	.51†	.26*	−.45†	.50†	.46†
B. Suitability for Therapy			−.32*	−.56†	.30*	.76†	.75†	.43†	−.39†	.59†	.58†
C. Countertransference Potential					−.17	−.51†	−.31*	.00	.74†	−.33*	.36†
D. Therapist's Own Suitability to Treat							.29*	.25	−.22	.32*	.44†
E. Clinical Assessment									−.30*	.44†	.43†
F. Therapist Disinterest-Rejection (Film 1 only)										−.36†	—
G. Patient Motivation (Film 1 only)											—
H. Patient Attractive Qualities (Film 2 only)											

* $p < .05.$ † $p < .01.$

353

rewarding experience, feel warmly toward the patient, and regard their own personality as well suited. The converse, of course, holds true as well. Several items that asserted unfavorable reactions on the part of the therapist (Factor C) predictably disclosed consistently negative relationships with clinical assessments. At the risk of stressing the obvious, it must be reiterated that the direction of causation is indeterminate, so that the therapist's attitude toward the patient cannot be considered the antecedent of his clinical evaluations, nor can it be said that therapists feel more positively about certain patients *because* they appear to be better prospects for psychotherapy. Both sets of variables are undoubtedly closely intertwined and simultaneously affect the respondent's ratings. It is noteworthy, however, that these relationships have also been demonstrated in several other studies that elicited ratings under different conditions and circumstances. In each instance the foregoing relationships were found. The conclusion can be accepted with considerable confidence that the findings are not unique to a given set of patient characteristics, but hold true for a wide range. To be sure, some patients, because of their character structure, motivation, and attitudes, elicited stronger emotional reactions from the clinician-viewers—either pro or con— than others, but the virtually inextricable interrelationship and mutual influence of personal-attitudinal variables and clinical appraisals must by now be accepted as a valid generalization. Of particular importance, because of their relevance to subsequent psychotherapy, are clinical assessments included in Factors B, E, and G (for example, Motivation for Therapy and Capacity for Insight).

Some qualifications, however, must be noted. In Chapter Nine it was shown that Diagnosis, Problems of Therapeutic Technique, and Form, Frequency, and Length of Therapy were similarly related to the respondent's self-rated attitude toward the patient. In the present investigation, it was not possible to demonstrate comparable relationships in all of these areas. In the case of frequency of sessions and recommended duration of therapy, the statistical relationships were inconclusive, so that these items were not included in the factor analyses. With respect to problems of therapeutic technique, the wording of the items in the present study was perhaps less likely to elicit responses resulting in statistical relationships pointing in the indicated direction. In the earlier study, for example, the therapist was asked whether he would tend to be "active" or "passive" with the patient (an item that resulted in clear-cut differences between respondents who expressed respectively a positive or negative attitude). In the present investigation, we attempted to place the respondent's answers in relation to his technique with other patients. The comparable items (24 and 25) read, respectively: (Rate, from very little to very great) "The chances that you will be more active (passive) than usual in therapy with this patient." The implication of a possible countertransference reaction in the present study is thus suggested much more strongly and may be the reason for the low relationships between these technique-oriented items and attitudinal ones. Again, this fact accounted for technique-oriented items to be omitted from the factor analyses. Nevertheless, some of the *item* inter-relationships appear worthy of further discussion.*

---

*In the earlier investigation major emphasis was placed on the statistical associations between individual *items*, particularly between the respondent's conscious attitude toward the patient (positive or negative) and other variables. For the most part, these associations were tested by chi square. In contrast, the present study placed major emphasis on product-moment coefficients of correlation, which were then used selectively in the factor analyses that have been described. This procedure made fuller use of the available information than did the chi-square analyses and capitalizes less on peculiarities of the sample. The recourse to individual items in the following paragraphs, while seemingly a departure from this principle, was dictated by a desire to explore more speculatively certain relationships suggested by the earlier work, which, for the reasons indicated above, were not further clarified by the factor analyses. There was the further desire to pursue as far as possible comparisons with the previous research.

Table 6 is designed to show statistical relationships between items dealing with attitudinal (emotional) reactions and technical operations. It must be borne in mind that while the respondents' emotional reactions are more or less directly based on their impressions from the sound films, supposed effects of these impressions on technique are an extrapolation that, however, may be based on their experiences with similar patients. Since the respondents were reporting *conscious* emotional reactions to the two patients, the term "countertransference reactions" should, strictly speaking, not be invoked, because the concept is generally accepted to refer to *unrecognized* effects of the therapist's personality upon the therapeutic interaction. However, as Orr (1954) has pointed out in his review, the concept is used to encompass a wide variety of phenomena and its usage is far from precise.

It is seen that a number of the statistically significant relationships, while manifestly meaningful, are scattered, which may be due to the relatively limited size of the sample and corresponding fluctuations. Furthermore, some of the relationships which obtain for Patient 1 do not hold true for Patient 2, and vice versa. This, in itself, is not surprising and almost to be expected, because we are in fact dealing with the responses to very different individuals who, as has already been pointed out, elicited different reactions from the viewers. (The correlations of Factor C, Countertransference Potential, illustrate the same point, although in somewhat more gross fashion.)

Essentially, there appear to be three major ways (as the respondents view it) in which the therapist's emotional response to the patient affects his technique: (1) he might become too firm; (2) he might become too active; (3) he might become too passive. Excessive firmness (strictness, as it was called in the earlier study) appears to be the most common, or the most readily admitted, effect on technique. Impatience, anger, and rejecting attitudes on the part of the therapist are likely to give rise to excessive firmness. On the other hand, the more the therapist considers his personality well-suited, the more he is convinced that the patient will stay in therapy (as opposed to leaving precipitously); the easier he finds it to empathize with the patient; the more warmly he feels toward him; and the less he believes he will react with excessive firmness. These sets of relationships are quite consistent and hold true for both patients.

Statistically related to the danger of the therapist's becoming too active were impatience, anger, and rejecting attitudes, but these reactions are envisaged by the respondents only for Patient 2. In addition, the wish not to get involved with this patient in therapy was found to be correlated with potentially greater activity on the therapist's part. On the other hand, therapists tended to feel that they might become too passive in therapy with this patient if they felt discouraged about the progress and if the patient became too demanding. Doubts concerning the therapist's ability to work well with the patient also showed a significant correlation with the danger of excess passivity. Impatience and excessive permissiveness were similarly correlated for this patient.

Furthermore, the encouragement of free association was a concomitant of the therapist's conviction that therapy would be rewarding, that his personality was well suited to treating the patient, and of a generally positive attitude toward the patient. These findings seemed to hold true for both Patients 1 and 2. As has been shown in one of our related investigations (Strupp, Wallach, and Wogan, 1964) therapists prefer to treat patients by means of intensive therapy, in which free association of course plays an important part, and they feel more positively disposed toward patients whom they consider suitable for this method of treatment. Excessive firmness and excessive activity, in terms of the present results, appear to be reactions that the therapist fears he might resort to if the patient falls short of being an "ideal" patient for the psychoanalytic model technique. However, in the context of the present investigation, this

357

TABLE 6

COEFFICIENTS OF CORRELATION BETWEEN SELECTED THERAPISTS' RATINGS FOR FILMS 1 AND 2*

N varies from 52 to 59

Item	Description	Item 30 Likely to be more active		Item 31 Likely to be more passive		Item 32 Likely to be more firm		Item 33 Likely to be more permissive		Item 34 Encourage free association	
		Film 1	2	1	2	1	2	1	2	1	2
35	Likely to evoke anxiety	−.30†									−.32†
36	Likely to be impatient		.34‡			.40‡	.50‡		−.32†		
37	May make me angry		.28†			.41‡	.45‡				
38	Apt to become rejecting		.39‡			.36‡	.50‡				
39	Danger of being manipulated					.37‡					
41	May feel discouraged				.31†						
43	Likely to lose interest					.34‡					
44	Well able to work with patient				−.32†	−.36‡				.30†	
45	Therapy rewarding									.36‡	.37‡
46	Feel warmly toward patient						−.48‡				
50	Own personality well-suited					−.44‡					.29†
51	Patient might become demanding				.29†						
53	Wish not to get involved		.44‡			.28†	.37‡				

358

	Item							
28	Own feelings might interfere						.27†	
22	Ease of empathy	−.27†					−.27†	
29	Patient likely to stay in therapy				−.32†	−.46†		
54	Patient has few attractive qualities				−.28†	.33‡		−.33‡
24	Personal reaction to patient				.43‡	−.40‡		
12	Degree of emotional maturity		−.34‡	.29†	−.51‡	.35‡		
15	Motivation for therapy		−.28†		−.44‡			

* Nonsignificant correlations omitted. † $p < .05$. ‡ $p < .01$.

statement may be expanded to refer more specifically to patients who, the therapist anticipates, are likely to evoke countertransference reactions because of their manipulative tendencies. Patient 2, on the basis of the evidence, clearly was seen as a "manipulator," of whom the respondents became wary.

Correlations between factor scores and experience level, personal analysis, and rated empathy

Findings obtained under this heading further substantiate the respondents' preference for Patient 1 as a more promising candidate for psychotherapy. Therapists whose training had included more personal analysis (in terms of number of hours) considered their own suitability for treating Patient 1 (Factor D) greater than therapists with less personal analysis ($r = .31$). Length of experience in psychotherapy failed to correlate significantly with any of the factor scores, which suggests that length of experience in psychotherapy per se was a negligible factor entering into the various assessments of either patient. On the other hand, therapists who expressed greater empathy, liking, and willingness to treat Patient 1 (Factor A), who considered the patient more suitable for psychotherapy (Factor B), and who assigned her higher ratings in terms of emotional maturity (Factor E), also achieved higher ratings (from independent judges) on the degree of empathy expressed in their communications (r's ranging from .29 to .36; see Table 7).

Correlates of factors with usual therapeutic practices (UTP) factors

Most of the correlations between the factor scores and the UTP factors failed to reach statistical significance, the only noteworthy exceptions referring to several factors derived from Film 1, which were significantly correlated with Factor II (Preference for Intensive Psychotherapy). It

360

emerged that therapists who expressed a greater preference for the more intensive forms of psychotherapy, which in terms of our sample means primarily psychoanalysis, tended to experience greater empathy, liking, and interest in treating Film Patient 1 ($r = .39$). Similarly, therapists who expressed a preference for intensive therapy tended to see the patient as more mature (that is, more suitable for intensive psychotherapy, $r = .32$), regarded her as more highly motivated for therapy ($r = .35$), and denied the likelihood of losing interest and rejecting her ($r = -.32$). These results suggest that Patient 1 was seen as a better candidate for intensive therapy than Patient 2—at least by therapists who preferred doing intensive psychotherapy.

Interrelationships among content analysis measures and rated empathy

Before discussing the statistical relationships between the factor scores and the therapists' communications addressed to the film patients, which were quantified by means of the content analysis system previously described, it will be necessary to consider the interrelationships among the content categories themselves. In quantifying the therapists' communications, several additional measures were used. One of these, the degree of empathy, rated by independent judges, has already been described. Several additional measures were used, which will now be briefly defined.

The *number of words* used by the respondent is self-explanatory. This measure is, of course, inversely related to the number of silences and passive acceptances.

Complex responses are responses at a given point of interruption that were assigned a double content code, e.g., a question (10) and an interpretation (30). A rating of + was given to respondents who had two or more "complex" responses in their comments to Film Patients 1 *and* 2. All others were given a rating of 0.

Non-giving responses were defined by the total number

361

of responses coded 01, 02, and 10. Such comments (silence, passive acceptance, and questions) were viewed as maneuvers in which the respondent elicits ("takes in") data and information from the patient, as contrasted with clarifications, interpretations, and "direct guidance," by means of which the therapist is "going out" or "giving" to the patient. For purposes of this index, responses to Films 1 and 2 were combined.

Latency of response is defined by the number of seconds elapsed before the therapist started to respond after the film sequence was interrupted by the title "WHAT WOULD YOU DO?" This index was computed separately for Films 1 and 2 and represents the means for each respondent. Silences at a given stopping point were omitted from this index. It can be readily seen that the longer the respondent's latency at a given stopping point, the less are his chances that he can emit a large number of words because the stopping point was limited to a standard 30 seconds.

The scores for the various content categories were separately intercorrelated for Film 1, Film 2, and for both films combined. Ratings of empathy were included in this composite in an effort to determine the extent to which they might be related to the content measures. The latter findings, indeed, appear to be of greatest interest for the purposes of this investigation.

1. Therapists who use a greater number of words in their responses are more likely to receive high ratings on empathy (Film 1, $r = .30$; Film 2, $r = .47$). This may not be a direct function of the number of words used, but clearly the degree of empathy was more difficult to judge from short responses than from longer ones; therefore, the judges were more likely to assign positive empathy ratings to longer responses, simply because there was more "evidence" on which to base such ratings. By the same token, frequent silences and passive acceptance in a respondent's record, which in a larger context than that provided by the films

362

might well be indicative of empathic listening, proved a deterrent to his receiving a positive empathy rating (Film 1, $r = -.41$; Film 2, $r = -.31$).

2. Positive empathy ratings were more likely to be assigned to therapists who offered interpretations (Film 1, $r = .35$; Film 2, $r = .29$) and who gave "direct guidance" (Film 1, $r = .39$; Film 2, r not significant) than to therapists who tended to be silent, passively acceptant, and who asked clarifying questions.

These statistical relationships between quantity of "verbal output" and empathy may to some degree reflect certain artifacts in the ratings of empathy, but the associations are sufficiently low so as to allow for the operation of many other factors, apart from the relatively low reliability of the empathy scores.

Relationships between factor scores and therapists' communications

Table 7 summarizes the statistical relationships between factor scores, communication measures, rated empathy, and selected biographical variables. (The relationships of empathy to the factor scores have already been discussed.) The following trends may be discerned:

FILM 1:

1. Therapists who in their questionnaire responses express greater empathy, liking, and willingness to treat the patient tend to use a greater number of words in their comments, give more "complex" responses, and advance a significantly smaller number of "non-giving" comments.

2. Therapists whose responses are *rated* as "empathic" on an overall basis are more likely to include in their comments a larger number of "direct guidance" responses; they employ a greater number of words; they give a larger num-

363

TABLE 7

CORRELATIONS BETWEEN FACTOR SCORES, COMMUNICATION, EMPATHY, EXPERIENCE, AND PERSONAL ANALYSIS*

N varies between 52 and 59

Factors	Content Categories				Number of Words	Complex Responses	Non-giving Responses	Rated Empathy
	01 and 02	10	30	50				
Film 1								
A. Empathy-Liking and Willingness to Treat	−.21				.31†	.30†	−.29†	.36‡
B. Suitability for Therapy	−.23		.22			.21	−.21	.30†
E. Clinical Assessments	−.41‡		.35‡	.39‡	.30‡	.36‡	−.60‡	.29†
Rated Empathy				.36‡				
Experience		−.25						
Personal Analysis								.27†
Film 2								
B. Suitability for Therapy	.30†	−.27†		−.24				
D. Therapist's Own Suitability		−.21		−.37†				
E. Clinical Assessments	.29†	−.36‡						
H. Patient Attractive Qualities				−.24	−.33†	−.27†		
Rated Empathy	−.31†		.29†		.47‡	.22	−.49‡	

* Nonsignificant correlations below .20 not included.   † p < .05.   ‡ p < .01.

ber of "complex" responses; and there is a marked negative relationship between empathy and non-giving responses.

FILM 2:

1. Therapists who rate the patient as more suitable for psychotherapy tend to give a larger number of silent and passively acceptant responses, and they ask significantly fewer simple questions (presumably of an information-seeking nature).

2. The more the therapist considers himself "suitable" to work with the patient in psychotherapy, the fewer "direct guidance" responses he is likely to advance. This finding coincides with a similar one reported in Chapter Nine, and suggests that " direct guidance" responses tend to be offered with greater frequency when the therapist is disinclined to enter into a therapeutic relationship with the patient. It may be a way of "giving him some advice and sending him on his way." On the contrary, as shown in the preceding paragraph, silence and passive acceptance appear to be more indicative of the therapist's willingness to work with the patient in therapy, as is a smaller number of information-seeking questions. In other words, both frequent questioning and "direct guidance" emerge as distance-producing techniques, at least in an initial interview.

3. The more attractive qualities the patient is seen to possess, the smaller is the number of words the therapist addresses to him and the fewer "complex" responses he gives.

4. Higher empathy ratings are seen as correlating negatively with silence and passive responses. Both in Films 1 and 2—and these are the only congruent findings for the two films—the number of words used by the respondent correlates with positive ratings of empathy, and correlates negatively with the number of "non-giving" responses. As already noted, these findings are to some extent contaminated in that positive empathy ratings are partly a function of lengthier statements and also of more "giving" responses.

365

DISCUSSION AND CONCLUSIONS

In general, the results and conclusions of the earlier investigation were replicated, although—and this is hardly surprising—this was not true of each and every finding. On the basis of these results, we feel confident in quoting the statement by which we characterized (see Strupp, Wallach, and Wogan, 1964) the therapists' attitudes in the study of former therapy patients:

> Therapists derive greater enjoyment from treating patients with whom they established (or expect to establish) a productive working relationship: they prefer to work with patients whom they consider suitable for intensive psychotherapy, that is, those who have greater personality assets and potential resources, and in whose therapy they can invest themselves emotionally. This is not to be considered synonymous with the assertion that therapists prefer to work with patients who are not seriously disturbed, but understandably they tend to select those who in their judgment possess appreciable potential for reconstructive therapy.

To this may be added the observation derived from the present investigation, as well as its predecessor, that therapists tend to communicate differently with patients whom they consider "suitable" candidates for psychotherapy (i.e., in therapy with *the respondent*) than with those with whom they do not wish to enter in a therapeutic relationship. In the former instance, the communications tend to be more empathic; in the latter, a disproportionate frequency of certain distance-producing techniques, such as silences, questioning, and giving advice, was observed.

While the measurement of the respondent's empathy is considered a problem of signal importance, in our judgment far overshadowing the assessment of communications in terms of their structural characteristics (e.g., silence, ques-

366

tioning, interpretations, etc.), we do not feel that we have made significant progress in assessing this variable. Its definition, characterization, and quantitative assessment remain surrounded by grave difficulties, whether one works with sound recordings or typescripts. The demarcation of units and the possibility of achieving satisfactory rater agreement remain seemingly insurmountable obstacles. The addition of a larger context would probably be of help, but only if the preceding problems can be tackled. (Fox and Goldin [1964] have presented a careful review of the literature, together with an insightful discussion of the basic problems.)

What are the practical implications of this research? How do they affect the work of the psychotherapist? The search for answers to these questions, after all, is the ultimate justification for undertaking investigations in this area, and for requesting the busy clinician to participate in experimental tasks that are basically alien to him and that require, however we may rationalize it, self-disclosures and intrusions into his privacy. The sacrifice demanded by research of this kind should not be dismissed lightly. Throughout the presentation of results we have been at pains to point out that we are dealing only with trends. Yet at this point we wish to present our conclusions with a certain measure of assertiveness and conviction—more than is perhaps justified by the data. However, the fact that a fair amount of congruent evidence has been amassed in a variety of studies lends veridicality to our statements.

The most important, and potentially the most far-reaching, implications of our investigations relate to the personal involvement of the psychotherapist in his diagnostic evaluations, his prognostic judgments, the formulation of his treatment plans, and the manner in which he communicates with the patient. All of these are closely intertwined and unquestionably play an important part, not only in terms of a particular therapist's decision to accept a particular patient for psychotherapy, but—and this is of greater consequence—in terms of the course and outcome of the

367

interaction between the two participants. Our findings underscore the crucial significance of the therapist's initial attitude and the character of his emotional reactions to a patient. It has long been recognized that the diagnostician, the clinician, and the therapist can learn much about the interviewee's personality structure and functioning by consulting his own feelings, his personal attitudes, and his spontaneous emotional responses. We believe that an even greater emphasis should be placed on these reactions, preferably *before* they are transmuted into seemingly objective assessments of the nature of the patient's emotional disturbance, the degree of his illness, the chances for his improvement through psychotherapy, and before a therapeutic regimen is decided upon. We cannot assess with certainty the extent to which in a particular instance the therapist vis-à-vis a patient is acting as an "objective" clinician and the extent to which he is responding as a person. It is undeniably true that he is always doing both: he is appraising, judging, and responding in the total context of his clinical experience, which has included many patients with similar problems and similar personality structures; however, he is also responding as a human being to another human being. He brings to bear upon the interaction his own past, his prejudices, his likes, his dislikes, and the totality of his character structure, which is attuned in a particular way to similar or different characteristics in another person. It is almost axiomatic—and the statistical findings confirm it— that the therapist's personal responses and his clinical judgments are confounded.

This formulation brings to the fore both the inherent strength and weakness of the clinical method. In its positive aspects, the therapist's own feelings and emotional responses equip him to function as a superbly sensitive clinical instrument that far surpasses any "objective" techniques for assessing the personality "state" of another person, his mood, feelings, attitudes, etc. On the negative side, this sensitivity renders him subject to distortions, faulty assessments, and personal-idiosyncratic judgments that he might project onto the patient.

The recognition and description of this state of affairs are hardly a new discovery; indeed, they are the foundation upon which the clinical method rests. What we have done in the course of our investigations is to document the existence of these facts and to elucidate in a modest way their pervasive influence upon the transactions between patient and therapist.

As a function of his training, which stresses objectivity, detachment, and accuracy, the clinician is often impelled to minimize his native sensitivity as well as his personal response to the patient. Perhaps too frequently he is enjoined to turn a deaf ear to his inner promptings and personal reactions, to disregard them, and to highlight the "objectivity" of his findings and appraisals. Moreover, it is frequently more expedient, less emotionally disturbing, and professionally more "acceptable" to spread the mantle of objectivity on one's observations in interpersonal settings. As long as the clinician can separate and clearly keep apart the subjective and the objective elements in his operations, he is able to function appropriately and (assuming he has had the necessary training and experience) adequately in the clinical role. It is when the two segments interact in unknown and unconscious ways that the interest of the patient may be served less well. The perpetual problem with which the clinician is faced at every juncture in his work is (to adapt another saying) to be able to distinguish what is within himself and what is within the patient, and to know the difference.

The concept of countertransference, while accounting for these variables to some extent, actually covers the vicissitudes we have described only very inadequately. The concept is too restrictive and seems to cover only the gross and relatively enduring reactions of the therapist. His personal response to the patient, we submit, is rather a more ubiquitous, continuous, and infinitely more subtle phenomenon than is generally acknowledged.

Obviously, we cannot claim to have investigated the phenomenon in many of its ramifications. Existing measuring instruments are too crude, static, and inflexible to accomplish such a feat. At best we can say that we have focused attention upon it and to have shown some of its effects.

We must also reiterate a point that has been intimated in our earlier publications: the fact that widely and popularly held attitudes concerning the desirability or undesirability of particular social behaviors and personality characteristics influence the clinician's assessments and his therapeutic operations in as yet poorly understood ways. For example, most clinicians exhibit as little tolerance for the irresponsible, ingratiating, and deceitful behavior of the psychopath as the proverbial "man in the street." In the present study, as it turned out, we were pitting a seemingly hostile, homosexual, yet attractive girl against a manipulative, glib, young man, who apparently was suffering from a character disorder of considerable proportions and with whom promiscuity was one focal symptom. The girl was overtly hostile to psychiatrists and opposed to help via psychotherapy; the young man was seemingly more seriously interested in enlisting the help of a professional person.

Interestingly enough, the results clearly showed that most respondents, while recognizing the difference in the two patients' motivation to enter therapy, felt more positively disposed to the girl than to the young man, even though both patients appeared to be intelligent and had many positive personality characteristics that might be characterized as substantial ego "resources." We believe the differences in the evaluations of these two patients, resulting in the respondents' preference for the girl, were derived essentially from their preference for a person who, while hostile, was open, honest, and straightforward in expressing her feelings. The young man, on the other hand, was perceived as an indivi-

370

dual who in a glib way tended to gloss over his exploitative tendencies.

No one can cite pertinent statistics of treatment outcome for persons with such divergent emotional difficulties, nor would anyone be presumptuous enough to claim with certainty that treatment with the one person would be more successful than with the other. True, the respondents differed little in such broad prognostications. But, they showed important differences in terms of their attitudes toward the two patients, finding the girl easier to empathize with, more rewarding as a potential patient. Also, they felt less threatened by her hostility than by the young man's subtle manipulative trends, which, superficially, were not outstanding but which were frequently detected by the viewers. We can only speculate about the effect of such differing attitudes in the therapeutic situation. Conceivably, one person is "easier" to treat than another. But, we must entertain the possibility that the therapists' *initial* attitude may have far-reaching consequences upon the character and the outcome of the therapeutic relationship with the two patients.

In all of these respects the present study confirms the findings of the earlier investigation in which only one patient was presented to the viewers, but substantially similar findings and tentative conclusions were obtained. Future work might be designed to pinpoint the differences in therapists' perceptions; in fact, we have ourselves produced four additional films depicting different patients, which might serve this function. However, it is doubtful that the findings can go much beyond the ones that have already been presented. It may turn out to be more fruitful to investigate the therapist's reaction to a patient in an individual case, rather than to study group trends that, while more reliable and trustworthy on statistical grounds, tend to obscure what might be demonstrated much more convincingly in a single instance. It may suffice to have demonstrated the presence of such trends. The next task might be to study more intensively and at closer range the "fit" between a particular patient and a particular therapist. Such intensive scrutiny, if undertaken in a clinical setting, possibly with the assistance of senior supervisors, might go a long way toward reducing a subsequent therapeutic impasse or failure. The initial selection and assignment procedure is an extraordinarily important step in psychotherapy and psychoanalysis, and is undoubtedly deserving of greater attention than it ordinarily has been accorded. (We are aware, of course, of such procedures as a "trial analysis" that have traditionally been advocated to handle the problem.) Another suggestion for further work is to map out, much more systematically than has hitherto been done, the immediate emotional reactions of trained as well as untrained persons to attitudes, personality traits, and interpersonal techniques manifested by a variety of individuals. This research lies in the area of interpersonal perception, which we consider a most promising field of inquiry. It is our impression that judgments about another person, whether positive or negative, whether ultimately valid or invalid, are arrived at with considerable rapidity, perhaps in a few seconds or minutes. It remains to be investigated whether and to what extent such initial impressions are modifiable or, alternatively, persistent.

In conclusion, we do not wish to convey the impression that the therapist's liking for the patient is the beginning and end-all of psychotherapy or psychoanalysis. Goethe's dictum, *Gefühl is alles!*, does not encompass the enterprise of psychotherapy, existentialists and Daseins-analysts notwithstanding. Technical training and skill, we wish to reiterate, are as much a part of the psychotherapist's tools as is his empathic understanding of the patient. Psychotherapy is—and will undoubtedly remain for a long time to come—a highly refined clinical art. Some of its aspects, although they may turn out to be the not really important ones, are subject to scientific study and scrutiny. But, the scientific method, in our view, is the clinician's servant, not his master. And, we may reach a point at which the very real

372

limitations of this approach to the understanding of the psychotherapeutic process and its essence—the factors that are fundamentally instrumental in the permanent modification of neurotic patterns—may have to be honestly faced and acknowledged.

References

Auerbach, A. H. 1963. "An Application of Strupp's Method of Content Analysis to Psychotherapy," *Psychiat.,* 26: 137-148.

Fox, R. E., and Goldin, P. C. 1964. "The Empathic Process in Psychotherapy: A Survey of Theory and Research," *J. Ner. Men. Dis.,* 138: 323-331.

Jenkins, J. W., Wallach, M. S., and Strupp, H. H. 1962. "Effects of Two Methods of Response in a Quasi-therapeutic Situation," *J. Clin. Psychol.,* 28: 220-223.

Johnson, E. S. 1961. "Varimax Rotation," NCGFOL, Feb. 7, Programing Note No. 58, Computation Center, The University of North Carolina, Chapel Hill, N.C.

Orr, D. W. 1954. "Transference and Countertransference: A Historical Survey," *J. Am. Psychoanal. Assn.,* 2: 621-670.

Strupp, H. H. 1960. *Psychotherapists in Action: Explorations of the Therapist's Contribution to the Treatment Process.* New York: Grune & Stratton.

——— 1962. "The Therapist's Contribution to the Treatment Process: Beginnings and Vagaries of a Research Program," in *Research in Psychotherapy,* Vol. II, ed. H. H. Strupp and L. Luborsky, pp. 25-40. Washington, D. C.: American Psychological Assn.

——— and Jenkins, J. W. 1963. "The Development of Six Sound Motion Pictures Simulating Psychotherapeutic Situations," *J. Ner. Men. Dis.,* 136: 317-328.

———— Wallach, M. S., and Wogan, M. 1964. "Psychotherapy Experience in Retrospect: Questionnaire Survey of Former Patients and Their Therapists," *Psychol. Monog.*, 78 (whole No. 588).
Wolberg, L. R. 1954. *The Technique of Psychotherapy.* New York: Grune & Stratton.

Part III
The Therapist's Contribution: Empirical Studies (2)

T he chapters included in this part represent quantitative analyses and comparisons of therapist activity in actual psychotherapy interviews. The first study was designed to explore consistencies and variations in the communications of one therapist (Dr. Lewis R. Wolberg) over the course of short-term therapy (nine treatment sessions).

The second chapter attempts a comparison of therapist activity in analytic (Dr. Lewis R. Wolberg) and client-centered therapy (Dr. Carl Rogers). While the patients are very different, the analyses highlight technique differences that for the most part are consonant with the theoretical positions of the therapists under study.

The system of content-analysis described in Part VII was utilized in all instances.

While the quantifications are obviously crude, they

may be seen as steps in providing empirical data on therapist activity, a goal considered essential to the progress of research in psychotherapy.

13

ANALYSIS OF TECHNIQUE
IN BRIEF PSYCHOTHERAPY

I have called attention (see Chapter Twenty-one) to the need for comparative studies of psychotherapeutic techniques and proposed a system of analysis for abstracting and measuring certain relevant aspects of therapeutic communications. Here I wish to apply this method to a case treated by short-term psychotherapy based on psychoanalytic principles in an attempt to illustrate this approach and to indicate some of its potentialities.*

*This research was supported by a research grant (M-965) from the National Institute of Mental Health, of the National Institutes of Health, U. S. Public Health Service, to the George Washington University School of Medicine, Department of Psychiatry. Grateful acknowledgment is made to Winfred Overholser, M.D., under whose general direction the work was carried out, and to Leon Yochelson, M.D., consultant to the project. I also wish to express my appreciation to Mrs. Rebecca E. Rieger, whose assistance has been invaluable.

The proposed system yields five measures relative to any therapist communication. There are two sets of categories—Type of Therapeutic Activity and Dynamic Focus—and three intensity scales—Depth-directedness, Initiative, and Therapeutic Climate.

THE CASE HISTORY

The case history to be analyzed in this chapter was published by Wolberg (1954, pp. 688-780) and comprises nine treatment sessions, which were transcribed and fully reported, minor changes having been made only for the purpose of concealing the patient's identity. In addition to the therapist-patient communications, the transcript includes comments by the therapist.

By way of introduction Wolberg states:

The type of treatment employed was insight therapy with re-educative goals. The problem for which therapy was sought was a "run-of-the-mill" type of situation often encountered in practice. I was happy that the psychopathologic material elicited in this case was not so startling as to excite concentration on psychodynamics. In teaching therapy there is so often a temptation to focus on the spectacular, to wallow so in symbolic representations of conflict and in the manifold defenses that the human mind employs in seeking surcease from turmoil, that one may fail to emphasize what is really important in treatment: the study of the relationship that develops between the patient and the therapist. I felt that the case I chose would permit us to explore such aspects as the conduct of an initial interview, the establishment of a working relationship with the patient, the techniques for arriving at the dynamcs of a neurosis, the promotion of activity toward therapeutic change, and the termination of therapy [pp. 688-689].

380

And further,

> The case was chosen not for its dramatic interest—since there was nothing spectacular about the involved dynamics—but because it delineates within the nine sessions that comprised the total treatment period, important processes observed in the opening, middle and terminal phases of therapy [p. 688].

According to this rationale, the case should be equally well suited for present purposes because it might yield a useful profile of the therapist's activity at various stages of treatment. By the same token, it should disclose clear-cut differences in therapist activity correlated with the dynamic events of each therapeutic hour. To be sure, the profile mirrors Wolberg's technique, which may or may not be representative of other therapists' procedures. This question will remain unanswered until analyses of comparable therapeutic sessions conducted by other therapists provide additional data.

PROCEDURE

While no summary can adequately convey the richness of the actual therapist-patient interaction, it is impossible to reproduce here the case history in its entirety. It will therefore be necessary to condense radically the happenings during each therapeutic hour, and to refer interested readers to the original source.

Seven of the nine interviews were scored jointly by two raters from the transcript; two interviews were rated independently by the same raters to obtain a measure of rater agreement. Editorial remarks were disregarded as far as possible in an effort to base the analysis upon the interaction itself. Since the original sound recording was not available, it is conceivable that some nuances were lost.

381

Before presenting the case history, I will discuss the quantitative measures used, in order to highlight the kinds of information yielded by the multidimensional analysis. Subsequently, the reader can judge for himself to what extent these results gain in meaning when the totality of the interaction is considered.

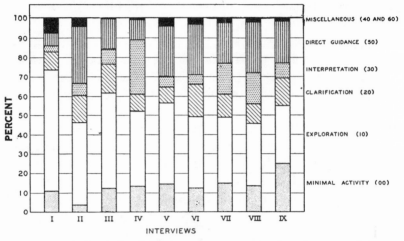

FIGURE 1. Analysis of therapeutic communications in terms of type.

DISCUSSION OF RESULTS

TYPE OF THERAPEUTIC ACTIVITY: Figure 1 presents a profile of the therapist's verbal communications for the nine interviews in regard to *type*.* The breakdown is by major categories, the frequencies for each interview having been converted to percentages. The total number of interventions over the nine interviews was 1,075. Within interviews, the frequencies ranged from 79 to 174, with a median of 114. Actually, the longest interview ran overtime, so that the upper limit was 154 (the last one). The smallest number of interventions occurred in the second session $(N = 79)$.

---

*See the Appendix for data on the statistical analyses and significance levels (Pp. 399-401).

Minimal activity (Category 00, including such verbalizations as "Mm-hm," "I see," and so on) ranged from about 2.5 per cent in the second interview to 24.7 per cent in the ninth, with a median of about 13 per cent. The frequencies of all other activities ranged, in absolute numbers, from 75 to 151, with a median of 97. Assuming the typical session to last about 50 minutes, this would mean approximately 2 interventions per minute—a fairly high level of verbal activity.

Exploratory operations (Category 10) ranged from 31.5 per cent in Interview VIII to 64.8 per cent in the initial interview. With the exception of the first interview, in which the therapist asked a great many exploratory questions, the "exploratory level" remained fairly constant throughout treatment, comprising somewhat better than a third of all communications.

Clarification (Category 20), which includes reflections of the patient's feelings, restatements of content, and non-interpretive summaries, was used rather sparingly. It comprised approximately 10 per cent of all interventions.

With respect to interpretive operations (Category 30), there were sharp fluctuations: interpretations ranged from less than 2 per cent in the initial interview to 28.1 per cent in Interview IV. There was a gradual rise from Interview I to Interview IV, a sharp drop for the two succeeding interviews, and another increase (beginning with Interview VII), which was maintained, with minor changes, until termination. The data for Depth-directedness will further elucidate this finding.

Structuring (Category 40) made up 5.6 per cent of the communications in Interview I but occurred so infrequently thereafter that it was lumped with other miscellaneous communications (greetings, small talk, and so on) in Category 60.

Category 50, which for lack of a better term was labeled "direct guidance," includes communications in which the therapist emerges as an expert or authority, states opinions, gives approval, provides reassurance, and so on (see also Category B-4, under Dynamic Focus). This type of activity was used minimally in Interview I (6.5 per cent) and reached its peak in Interview II (27.8 per cent), with Interviews V, VI, and VIII following closely. It is the frequency of this form of activity that typifies this therapist's approach as re-educative. It is also interesting, in this connection, that Interview IV, which showed a spurt in interpretive communications, had a concomitant decline in Category 50. In other words, interpretive and re-educative techniques alternated, to some extent at least.

DEPTH-DIRECTEDNESS: In order to give a graphic presentation of the relative depth of the therapist's communications, three levels were distinguished. Level I includes communications scored $1+$ or less on the five-point scale; Level 2 comprises the range of $2-$ to $2+$; and Level 3 is made up of interventions rated $3-$ or higher. Figure 2 shows the relative frequency of each level within an interview.

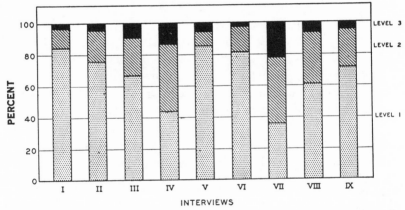

FIGURE 2. Analysis of therapeutic communications in terms of Depth-directedness.

It is readily apparent that Level 1 exceeded 80 per cent in Interviews I, V, and VI, with Interviews II and IX not far removed; in other words, most therapist communications in these interviews were rather close to the "surface" and relatively noninferential. By contrast, Interview VII showed

384

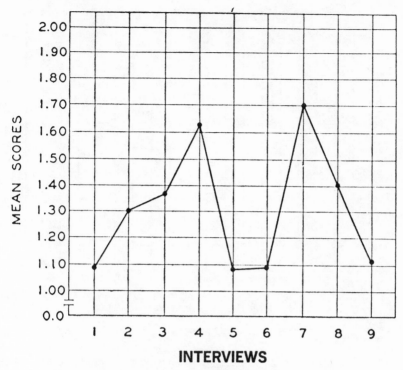

FIGURE 3. Distribution of mean Depth-directedness scores.

the highest proportion of inferential communications, followed by Interview IV. Intermediate depth occurred in relatively higher proportions in these two interviews as well. The bar diagrams also point to an increase in inferential activity from Interview I through Interview IV, a sharp decline for Interviews V and VI, another spurt in Interview VII, and again a decline to the end of treatment.

The *mean depth* for each interview has been plotted in Figure 3. This analysis follows closely the trend of Figure 2, although the means are heavily depressed by the preponderance of low scores; nevertheless, the gradual increase, the two peaks at Interviews IV and VII, the sharp drop in the middle phase, and the gradual decline at the end clearly emerge.

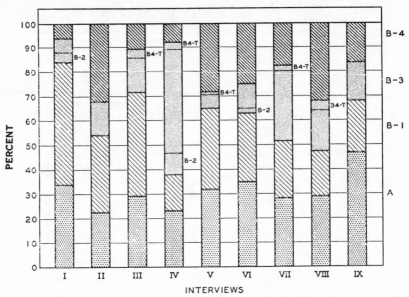

FIGURE 4. Analysis of therapeutic communications in terms of Dynamic Focus.

DYNAMIC FOCUS: Figure 4 presents a breakdown of therapist communications in terms of Dynamic Focus. Sector A (no shift in dynamic focus) accounted for some 22 percent in Interviews II and IV, at its lowest, and for 46.7 per cent in Interview IX, at its highest; for the remaining interviews, the rate was fairly constant—in the neighborhood of 30 per cent.

Requests for additional information (B-1) ranged from 14.9 per cent in Interview IV to 50 per cent in Interview I, and a sizeable proportion of the activity in most interviews was taken up by this particular focus, with a median of 28.2 per cent.

Greater interest attaches to the focus of communications commonly called interpretations. Here, the therapist's interpretive efforts were concerned primarily with dynamic events in the *present;* focus on dynamic events in the patient's past occurred only in Interview IV (8.6 per cent),

386

Interview I (3.7 per cent) and Interview VI (1.2 per cent); transference dynamics were minimally dealt with in Interviews III, VIII, IV, VII, and V (in descending order, percentages ranging from 3.7 to .8). Dynamic interpretations of the patient's contemporary interpersonal relations accounted for 42.5 per cent of all therapist interventions in Interview IV and 28.1 per cent in Interview VII—the most "interpretive" interviews.

In all interviews, with the possible exception of the two highly interpretive ones, the therapist introduced a fair measure of guidance into the situation. Category B-4, which is closely related to category 50 under *type,* accounted minimally for 6.5 per cent of all interventions in Interview I, and maximally for about a third in Interviews II and VIII.

INITIATIVE: The data presented so far suggest that the therapist was quite active in his participation, that his interpretations were phased, and that he favored the current-interpersonal focus. However, regardless of technique, to what extent did he assume the initiative in guiding the patient's communications into a goal-directed channel? Figure 5 presents a tabulation of initiative scores, which have been grouped into three levels: Level 1, scores of 1 +

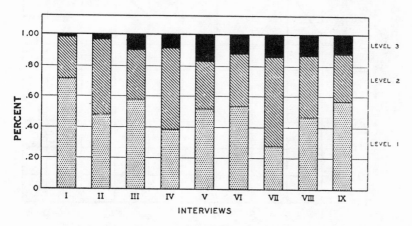

FIGURE 5. Analysis of therapeutic communications in terms of Initiative.

and below; Level 2, scores of 2− through 2+; and Level 3, scores of 3− or above.

Mild initiative was displayed to a rather variable degree, ranging from 28.9 per cent in Interview VII to 72.2 per cent in the initial interview. It was outweighed, however, by moderate and high scores in Interviews II, IV, and VII. Extreme scores showed a steady increase to Interview V, a level that was maintained, with minor fluctuations, throughout the remainder of treatment.

A somewhat dissimilar picture is conveyed by the mean scores (Figure 6). Here, the plateau is worthy of note, as are the valleys in Interviews I, III, and IX, indicating that the therapist's initiative was relatively low in these sessions. Again, the mean scores are greatly influenced by the high proportion of low scores. For this reason, it may be instructive to consider the *absolute* number of extreme (Level 3)

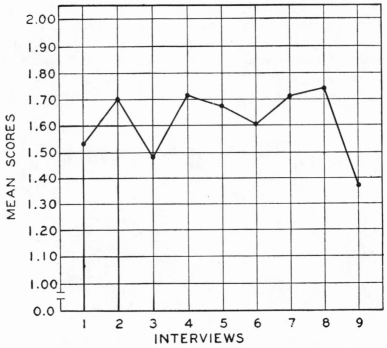

FIGURE 6. Distribution of mean Initiative scores.

388

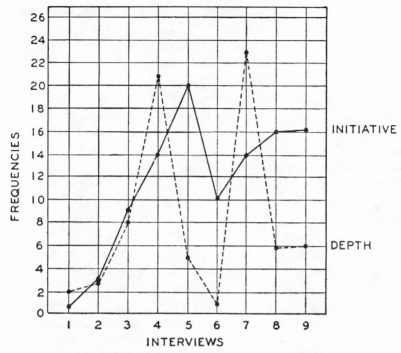

FIGURE 7. Distribution of extreme (level 3) scores on Depth-directedness and Initiative.

scores and to relate them to comparable scores on Depth-directedness. This has been done in Figure 7.

It is seen that both Depth and Initiative rose concomitantly to the middle of treatment, but that the former reached its peak in Interview IV—already identified as the first highly interpretive one—whereas Initiative did so in the following hour, in which depth sharply dropped. Interview VI was characterized by relatively low Depth and Initiative. From then on, the plots diverge: *depth* showed another peak in the second higher interpretive interview (Interview VII), whereas the plateau of Initiative was maintained. To pursue his goals, the therapist used *both* interpretation and initiative—exemplified by re-educative techniques—which seemed to implement each other. The

389

observed differences in phasing may be of more than passing interest.

THERAPEUTIC CLIMATE: The relative absence of non-zero scores, augmented perhaps by the procedure of scoring from the printed page, presented difficulties and contributed to a certain tenuousness of results on this component. There was never any question concerning minus scores, which were clearly not present; but with respect to positive scores, differentiations between scores of +1 and +2 were not feasible. In absolute numbers, Interview V ranked lowest, with 3 positive scores, and Interviews II and IV highest, with 8 positive scores. Even so, there is little question but that the therapist was accepting, sympathetic, warm, and benevolent.

SUMMARY OF THE ANALYSIS: The quantitative analyses make it abundantly clear that the therapist's techniques showed systematic variations over the course of this short-term therapy. The initial interview was largely devoted to an exploration of the patient's problem; the next two interviews revealed an intensification of therapeutic activity, both in terms of inferential operations and initiative; Interviews IV and VII emerged as deeply interpretive ones, the intervening ones appearing as less "dramatic"; data for the remaining sessions pointed to a phasing out of interpretive activity, but initiative was maintained at a relatively high level. The therapist's interpretive operations were geared to the dynamics of the patient's current interpersonal relations, and transference analysis and focus on genetic antecedents were generally deemphasized. Throughout the course of treatment, but especially in the second half, the therapist stood out as a person who, in the role of an expert, gave guidance, stated opinions, and engaged in procedures which are best characterized as re-educative. He was clearly more active than passive, both in terms of frequency of interventions and in directing the course of therapy. The aptness of Wolberg's descriptive label—"insight therapy with re-educative goals"—is certainly corroborated by the quantitative analysis. The most noteworthy single result is perhaps the *phasing* of therapeutic activity, which is reflected so clearly in the tabulations. It seems that the therapist gradually prepared the patient for deeper interpretations, which he advanced in the fourth session. Then he waited for the consolidation of insights before renewing his interpretive endeavors in Interview VII. Thereafter, he diminished his interpretive activity, while maintaining a degree of therapeutic pressure until the end.

SYNOPSIS OF THE CASE HISTORY

It is now appropriate to take a look at the interactive events in this case history, with emphasis upon those facets that might illuminate the quantitative analysis. In order to minimize possible biases of my own, I shall rely mostly on the therapist's comments and summaries. Wolberg (1954) relates the background in these words:

I received a telephone call from a former patient who asked if I could see a friend of hers in consultation. Her friend, a retired business woman, had, during the past two years, become progressively more depressed, and in the past six months had retreated from her customary social contacts. An attractive widow, and comfortably situated financially, there was no objective reason why she should act in this manner. She had tried to convince her friend to seek therapy six months previously, but the reaction to this suggestion was a bad one. However, her friend had telephoned her this morning and had asked to be referred. My comment was that I would want to see her friend in consultation before I could decide whether I was the best person to treat her particular problem. If she would ask her friend to call me, I would be pleased to give her an appointment. That afternoon the patient telephoned me and I set up an appointment for an initial interview [p. 690].

INTERVIEW I: The initial interview was designed to establish rapport, to make a tentative diagnosis, to get an idea of the psychodynamics involved, to evaluate the feasibility of treatment, and to make arrangements for therapy. The therapist decided to accept the patient for treatment, asked a fairly large number of diagnostic questions, and made the tentative diagnosis of a "psychoneurotic depression engrafted on a personality disorder [p. 699]." He felt that "the involved psychodynamics were unclear, but a number of elements were suggested, namely, the possibility of having experienced shattered security and self-esteem due to maternal neglect, the need to submit herself to exploitation as evidenced in her relationship with her husband, the low estimation of herself along with self-neglect, and the blocking of her ability to relate to people [p. 699]."

INTERVIEW II: The therapist structured the therapeutic situation by explaining the procedures and goals of therapy. The patient provided further data on her history and touched upon her need to help people who in turn seemed to exploit her.

INTERVIEW III: Toward the end of the interview, in which the patient had shown resistance, as evidenced by her demands on the therapist to supply her with "answers" and by self-recriminations, the therapist summed up the events in these words:

> Th [89].* So, as a child you were unhappy, and you married to get away from it; but you were still unhappy. Then you met the middle man, and you put everything into that relationship, but it ended. You took care of an orphan and that ended tragically for you, too. You married John and felt exploited and used. And with the last man, too, things ended by your feeling that you got little out of it. That's quite a series of depriving incidents. [90]

*The numberings 89, 90, and so on that appear in this section were given the therapist's communications for the purposes of the present study.

392

No matter what you did and gave, it ended as if you had nothing to give [pp. 718-719].

In his comments about the interview, the therapist wrote:

As tension accumulates in the interview, she comes out with suppressed and partially repressed material, with some catharsis. She attempts to act-out an impulse to be exploited in the transference, which I circumvent. She continues to try to force me into a directive role, and finally she becomes aware of her intent. At the end she seems to accept my structuring of the therapeutic situation. We seem to be entering into the middle phase of treatment [p. 720].

INTERVIEW IV: In his comments on this interview, the therapist noted:

In this session the patient has arrived at several insights. She sees a pattern weaving through her life and connects it with what happened to her in her childhood. She realizes the values of her neurotic patterns, but also appreciates their destructive effects. At the end of the session she challenges her need to pursue the pattern of her giving presents to be loved [pp. 723-733].

The tenor of the therapist's interpretive activity is epitomized by the following quotation:

Th [57]. Maybe you feel people wouldn't like you unless you did.
    Pt. Unless I would do something.
    Th [58]. If this is so, how do you think this would make you feel?
    Pt. Terrible, feeling always they won't like me.
    Th [59]. That they'd reject you. And, if this is so, isn't it possible that if you have to keep doing things to

393

keep people liking you, you would either want to run away from the relationship or else continue to have to do things for the person over and over [p. 724]?

The following samples illustrate the therapist's re-educative techniques:

> *Th* [76]. It is possible for you to find many things in your life that you don't like. All people do things about which they may have shame. You can catalogue all the bad things you have done and make testimony that sounds overwhelming, but when you compare your life to any other person's life, your sins will probably compare to theirs. So far, you haven't told me a thing that would justify your feeling the way you do [p. 725].
> *Th* [168]. The important thing is to understand your patterns of living thoroughly, see how they cross you up, why they occurred and are still occurring, and then challenge them [p. 732].

> INTERVIEW V: The therapist noted:

> In this session the patient begins to make positive plans for the future. An attempt to deal with deeper unconscious material is revealed in a dream; however, the patient resists this effort and seeks to keep the interview on her immediate environmental situation. I act more directive in suggesting a positive course of action [pp. 741-742].

(These encouragements concern a course in antiques, in which the patient has expressed an interest.) It seemed that the patient had assimilated the therapist's previous interpretations to some extent.

INTERVIEW VI: The therapist commented, "This session is illustrative of sessions in which not much seems to be happening. The working-through process may be going on

394

nevertheless [p. 742]." To the patient, the therapist put the matter in this way:

Th [*53*]. There is one thing you may have to watch for when you meet a worthwhile person. In the face of this man's apparent good qualities, you may say to yourself, "Well, gosh, he'll never see anything in *me*. Why should I get myself messed up over him? If he sees something in me, it's because he just wants sex, or because he wants to take advantage of me, or something like that; it isn't likely that he respects me for myself." And after that, you won't give him a chance; you'll just run like a deer. Now you've got to build up this estimate of yourself, if things are to be different. We have a fairly good idea of the origin of this bad estimate of yourself in your early upbringing. But this has produced in you an extremely insidious situation, in which you keep on despising yourself, in which you feel you have no inherent qualities, in which you feel that you can only be loved for what you can do for people, and not for yourself. Now these patterns keep messing you all up [p. 747].*

---

*The direct quotations given in this section were chosen to provide convenient summaries of a particular session or to illustrate certain aspects of Wolberg's technique; they are not necessarily representative of his technique throughout treatment. It may be of interest, in this connection, to quote Wolberg (Wolff, 1956) on what he considers to be the essentials of his therapeutic approach in general:

The particular kind of therapy that I utilize is psychoanalytic therapy. This varies from formal psychoanalysis on a four- or five-times-a-week basis, with an establishment of a transference neurosis, to an approach on a once-a-week basis in which there is face-to-face interviewing. While in the latter approach a transference neurosis is avoided as much as possible, therapy, even on a once-a-week basis, depends on an adequate dealing with transference and resistance. Dreams are employed constantly and, in my opinion, are the most effective medium of approach to the unconscious. I find that from time to time I modify my methods, employing, on the one hand, supportive devices when the individual is extremely

In his remarks about this hour, the therapist called attention to the presence of deeper unconscious conflicts that he suspected that the patient was unwilling to explore. He decided to strive for limited therapeutic goals, because of her age.

INTERVIEW VII : This interview was characterized by a further exploration of the patient's neurotic patterns and the therapist's suggestion that she participated in their per-

---

sick and manifests symptoms of adaptational collapse or impending psychosis and, on the other hand, devices to expedite awareness of unconscious material through hypnoanalysis. . . .

I would say that my therapeutic system breaks down into four essential parts. The first deals with the development of a working relationship with a patient. In this phase, we work through characterologic resistances that prevent the individual from relating to me. Essentially, analytic techniques are employed here, and I am more or less active until I am certain that I have a good relationship with the patient. Once this relationship is assured, the second phase of therapy begins, which involves investigation of the sources of the individual's problems. Here I employ dream analysis, the investigation of the current life situation, the verbal associations of the patient, and any transference manifestations that he exhibits in his relationship with me. The third phase of therapy consists of translating insight and understanding into action. The final phase involves terminating the treatment process and handling dependencies that may exist. This framework might rightfully be called eclectic since it utilizes concepts derived from various disciplines, including psychoanalysis, psychobiology, casework and psychological counseling. The objective of this framework is reconstruction of the personality, although there is recognition of, and allowance for, the fact that this goal may have to be scaled down in instances where motivation is lacking or there is diminutive ego strength.

Both directive and nondirective approaches are utilized, depending on the needs of the patient and the specific phases during therapy. For instance, I am more inclined to be directive at the start of therapy, at the time when the working relationship is being set up. During the explorative phases of therapy, passivity is the keynote. In handling resistances of the patient, particularly toward activity and change, much greater activity may be required. Finally, in the terminal phases of therapy, a more nondirective approach is mandatory [pp. 114-115].

petuation more than she had realized. The therapist felt that the patient was more hopeful and less self-defeating, but that she evinced reluctance to "go deeper." The patient seemed exceptionally cooperative and task-oriented.

INTERVIEW VIII: The therapist considered this session typical of the middle phase of treatment [p. 760] and called attention to the patient's growing insight in the direction of change [p. 769]. Her insight was tested and challenged repeatedly, but she asserted herself by making constructive plans for her life.

INTERVIEW IX: In this, the final interview, the patient announced her decision to terminate treatment in what appeared to be a confident tone. The therapist accepted her plans, but warned of recurrences of her difficulties, which might necessitate further therapy. He appeared to encourage her newly won self-confidence, and helped her to consolidate her gains.

In his final comment, Wolberg emphasizes that good results were achieved in an unusually short time, and he attributes this to the patient's motivation for therapy, the relative lack of resistance, and the fact that there was no strong secondary gain. Concerning his technique, he mentions that the work proceeded almost entirely on a characterologic level, and that the effect of treatment was mostly of a re-educative nature despite his dealing with resistance, and, in a few instances, with transference [pp. 779-780].

This very brief summary of the treatment history may give some glimpse of the interactive events upon which the quantitative analysis was based. It lies outside the scope of this comparison to relate specific incidents of the case history to the quantitative indices, although such a task would be quite feasible. My main purpose has been to show that the profiles bear a meaningful relationship to dynamic events in psychotherapy and that they help to characterize both the kinds of technique that are used throughout as well as their ebb and flow from hour to hour.

At this point the critical reader may well ask, "What

does this quantitative analysis add to my knowledge? After all, if I want to learn something about this patient, her problem, and the therapist's techniques, all I have to do is to read the transcript and come up with the same answers. I will be able to tell that interpretive techniques are used in conjunction with re-educative measures, that the therapist is quite active in his approach, that he seems benevolent and supportive, and so on. And I might even tell you that Interviews IV and VII are more interpretive than the initial or the terminal interview. Aren't you just demonstrating the obvious? Besides, you haven't said a word about the effectiveness of this particular therapeutic technique. Isn't it conceivable that identical or more beneficial results would have been achieved had the therapist employed different methods?"

I would reply that these criticisms are quite cogent as far as this particular case history is concerned. But suppose the investigative task is to compare the therapeutic techniques of two, three, or more therapists with comparable patients. How could one make such comparisons without being able to say that Therapist A is using more of this and less of that at various stages of therapy than Therapist B? And how could one place any confidence in the accuracy and objectivity of one's observations unless one used some kind of a calibrated measuring instrument? I would concede that the present tool is a far cry from a precision instrument, as precision is thought of in the physical sciences. But at least it permits the investigator to conduct a systematic inquiry and to make observations that can be closely approximated by independent observers. The fact that the results seem to corroborate information obtained by less rigorous means, instead of detracting from the quantitative measures, attests to their potential validity.

As for the second stricture, concerning the absence of qualitative judgments, my answer would be that this avoidance is deliberate. I believe that a concerted effort must be made to separate descriptions from value judgments; once it is possible to specify, with increasing accuracy, the relevant aspects of therapeutic interactions, one can turn to external criteria of effectiveness—such as "cures," improved adjustment, or better functioning—and relate them to internal measures, as obtained by the present system of analysis. If it becomes further possible to achieve better control over such elusive variables as the initial degree of disturbance, the personality of the therapist, the intervention of influences outside the therapeutic framework, and the like, questions as to the relative effectiveness of different techniques may come nearer solution. The strife among the warring factions represented by the different schools of psychotherapy is fueled by the continuing lack of adequate quantitative criteria, and it may not be expected to subside unless and until a measure of scientific rigor can be brought to bear upon the exceedingly complex phenomena within their domain.

APPENDIX

RATER AGREEMENT: In order to estimate the reliability of the scoring system, two of the nine interviews were analyzed independently by two raters. The indices presented in Table 1 are based upon a unit-by-unit analysis; agreement on a unit (therapist communication) means that both raters assigned it to the same category (on Type or Focus, respectively), or that they gave it an intensity score (on Depth-directedness or initiative, respectively) no more than one-half step apart. For the last mentioned scales, product-moment coefficients of correlation were computed, in addition.

CORRELATION BETWEEN DEPTH-DIRECTEDNESS AND INITIATIVE: Since the two scales appear to be interrelated, it seemed desirable to investigate whether they may be regarded as independent measures. Accordingly, product-moment correlation coefficients were computed for three selected interviews, V, VII, and IX. The respective r's were

TABLE 1

AGREEMENT BETWEEN TWO INDEPENDENT RATERS

System Component	Interview VII (N=114) %	Interview IX (N=154) %
Type	80.7	80.5
Depth-directedness	86.0 (r=.86)	94.0 (r=.885)
Dynamic Focus	80.7	85.7
Initiative	87.7 (r=.87)	93.5 (r=.93)
Therapeutic Climate	Agreement on 7 out of 9 nonzero scores	Agreement on 3 out of 5 nonzero scores

All percentages are significant beyond the .01 level.
All correlation coefficients are significant beyond the .01 level.

TABLE 2

LEVELS OF SIGNIFICANCE

Figure	Type of Analysis	Result	Degrees of Freedom	p Level
1	Chi-square	χ^2 = 142.08	32	<.001
2	Chi-square	χ^2 = 171.73	16	<.001
3	Analysis of variance	F = 20.45	26	<.001
4	Chi-square	χ^2 = 231.83	24	<.001
5	Chi-square	χ^2 = 79.20	16	<.001
6	Analysis of variance	F = 8.17	26	<.001

.13, .61, and .63. While the reliability of the two scales is high, it appears that in certain interviews the two scales yield rather similar information; nevertheless, even with an r of .63, only slightly more than a third of the variance is accounted for. In other interviews, the two scales do not covary to any appreciable degree. It must be concluded that Depth-directedness and Initiative, as measured by the two scales, are often fairly highly correlated, but that this is not always the case. Experience indicates that deeply interpretive communications usually are rated high on Initiative also, but that the converse is not necessarily true.

SIGNIFICANCE LEVELS: Table 2 presents the levels of significance for the analyses that have been presented in the body of this paper.

References

Wolberg, L. R. 1954. *The Technique of Psychotherapy.* New York: Grune & Stratton.

Wolff, W. 1956. *Contemporary Psychotherapists Examine Themselves.* Springfield, Ill.: Charles C. Thomas.

14

THERAPIST ACTIVITY IN ANALYTIC AND CLIENT-CENTERED THERAPY

"In science we need flexible minds and rigid concepts, but in psychoanalysis we have rigid minds and flexible concepts" (Wolff, 1956, p. 233). This statement by a leading analyst, which is equally applicable to other forms of psychotherapy, epitomizes a growing awareness among research-minded psychotherapists that the fluidity of concepts, the ambiguities of language, and the idiosyncratic frames of reference espoused by competing schools represent serious barriers against furthering our knowledge of the psychotherapeutic process. From numerous quarters in recent years has come the cry for simpler concepts, for operational definitions, and for identifying the common denominators underlying all psychotherapeutic procedures. This trend implies, among other things, that differences in theory are meaningless if they fail to carry over into practice, and that focus upon the actual operations may be more fruitful for testing theoretical differences than prolonged controversy about the uniqueness of a given system.*

The analysis of therapeutic protocols has occupied the time of researchers for some years, but rarely has an attempt been made to go outside a school of thought and to compare the techniques of, say, a nondirectivist with those of an analyst. Yet, such comparisons will inevitably play a part in future attempts to evaluate the relative effectiveness of competing approaches to psychotherapy.

This chapter presents a preliminary descriptive analysis of two varieties of psychotherapeutic techniques: insight therapy with re-educative goals based on psychoanalytic principles, and client-centered therapy. The analysis is mediated by a multidimensional system, designed to quantify the common denominators in the verbal operations of therapists irrespective of their theoretical orientation. The data obviously do not permit an evaluation of the respective merits of short-term analytic and client-centered therapy.

THE TWO CASE HISTORIES

The first case history, published by Wolberg (1954, pp. 688-780), was discussed in detail in Chapter Thirteen. It comprises nine treatment sessions with a retired business woman, a widow in the middle years of life, who had become progressively depressed, and retreated from her customary social contacts. Concerning his technique, the therapist (Wolberg) mentions that the work proceeded almost

*This research is part of a larger project that is supported by a research grant (M-965) from the National Institute of Mental Health, of the National Institutes of Health, U. S. Public Health Service. Grateful acknowledgment is made to Winfred Overholser, M.D., under whose general direction this work was carried out, and to Leon Yochelson, M.D., project consultant. In addition, I am greatly indebted to my former research associate, Rebecca E. Rieger, A.M., who contributed materially to the execution of this study.

entirely on a characterologic level, and that the effect of treatment was mostly of a re-educative nature, despite the fact that he interpreted some of the patient's defenses. A follow-up indicated that the results of treatment had been durable.

The second case history is that of Mary Jane Tilden, counseled by Rogers in a series of eleven interviews (Snyder, 1947, pp. 128-203). Unfortunately, the author was not aware that this case is available in its entirety, which necessitated the selection of reasonably complete interviews from the beginning, middle, and terminal phases of treatment from the published portions.

Miss Tilden was described as a 20-year-old, attractive young woman brought to the clinic by her mother, who complained that the patient was sleeping all the time, brooding, and ruminating. Miss Tilden seemed to be with-drawing progressively—she had given up her job and lost interest in her social life. Miss Tilden was treated by non-directive therapy. Rogers felt that 11 counseling hours were followed by a period of improved adjustment; nevertheless, the evaluation of final outcome remained somewhat in doubt since, shortly after a year had elapsed, there seemed to be a recurrence of the earliest symptomatology.*

THE SYSTEM OF ANALYSIS

The system of analysis whose development and operational characteristics are delineated in Chapter Twenty-one yields five measures relative to any therapist communication. There are two sets of categories (Type of Therapeutic Activity and Dynamic Focus), and three intensity scales (Degree of Inference, Initiative, and Therapeutic Climate). These components may be briefly characterized as follows:

---

*Although one cannot be sure, this case may pertain to that period in the evolution of client-centered therapy in which Rogers (1946) detects "vestiges of subtle directiveness."

404

TYPE OF THERAPEUTIC ACTIVITY: The categories specified the outer form or structure of a therapeutic intervention
and provide a gross analysis of the therapist's techniques.
The major categories were:

00   Facilitating Communication (Minimal activity).
10   Exploratory Operations.
20   Clarification (Minimal interpretation).
30   Interpretive Operations.
40   Structuring.
50   Direct Guidance.
60   Activity not clearly relevant to the task of therapy.
70   Unclassifiable.

Sixteen subcategories served to refine the primary rating.

DEGREE OF INFERENCE: This intensity scale was based
on the conception that inference is an integral part of all
therapeutic communications and that it is always present to
some degree. Each communication was rated by means of
a five-point scale ranging from low to high inference. Scale
points were defined a priori rather than via empirical judgments, but examples of typical communications were used
to define each scale point.

DYNAMIC FOCUS: Dynamic Focus referred to the frame
of reference adopted by the therapist at a particular juncture, and characterizes the manner in which he focuses the
therapeutic spotlight. Two major sectors were used to differentiate whether the therapist "goes along" with the
patient (A) or whether he introduces a different focus (B).
Communications assigned to Sector B were further analyzed
in terms of five subcategories:

B-1   Requests for additional information.
B-2   Focus on dynamic events in the *past*.
B-3   Focus on dynamic events in the *present*.
B-4T   Focus on dynamics of the therapist-patient rela-
       tionship (analysis of the transference).

405

B-4   Focus on the therapist-patient interaction in terms of the therapist's role as an expert, authority, etc.

INITIATIVE: The second intensity scale measured the extent to which the therapist assumes responsibility for guiding the patient's communications in a given channel. Initiative was conceived as ranging from low to high, and ratings were made on a four-point continuum. As in the case of Degree of Inference, scale points were defined by reference to appropriate examples.

THERAPEUTIC CLIMATE: Emotional overtones discernible in a communication were quantified by means of a bipolar scale: 0 = neutral; $+ 1$ = mild degree of warmth; $+ 2$ strong degree of warmth; $- 1$ mild degree of coldness; $- 2$ strong degree of coldness. A "warm" communication is one in which the therapist empathizes, shows understanding, or supports; a "cold" communication is one in which the therapist rejects, withdraws support, or punishes.

PROCEDURE

Seven of the nine Wolberg interviews and three representative interviews from the Miss Tilden case were scored jointly by two raters from the printed scripts. Two of the Wolberg interviews were rated independently by the same raters to obtain a measure of rater agreement.

RESULTS

RATER AGREEMENT: Table 1 presents results based on a unit-by-unit analysis of two interviews scored independently by two raters. Agreement on a unit (therapist communication) means that both raters assigned it to the same category (on Type and Focus, respectively), or that they gave it an intensity score (on Degree of Inference or Initiative, respectively) no more than one-half step apart. For the last two

406

scales, product-moment coefficients were computed in addition.

TABLE 1

AGREEMENT BETWEEN TWO INDEPENDENT RATERS*

System Component	Wolberg Interview VII (N=114) %	Wolberg Interview IX (N=154) %
Type	80.7	80.5
Degree of Inference	86.0 (r=.86)	94.0 (r=.885)
Dynamic Focus	80.7	85.7
Initiative	87.7 (r=.87)	93.5 (r=.93)
Therapeutic Climate†	—	—

* All percentages and correlation coefficients are significant beyond the .01 level.
† Nonzero scores too infrequent.

THE WOLBERG CASE: The therapist's activity, as mirrored by the multidimensional system of analysis, is presented in Figures 1, 2, 3, and 4. Within each interview, frequencies have been converted into percentages. In the

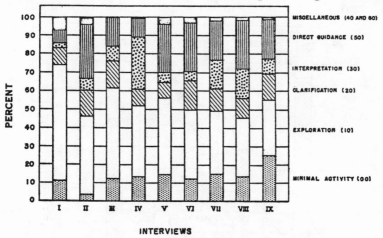

FIGURE 1. Therapist activity in the Wolberg case in terms of Type of Therapeutic Activity. (Interviews: I, $N = 108$; II, $N = 79$; III, $N = 108$; IV, $N = 174$; V, $N = 123$; VI, $N = 85$; VII, $N = 114$; VIII, $N = 130$; IX, $N = 154$. Total number of therapist interventions: $N = 1,075$.)

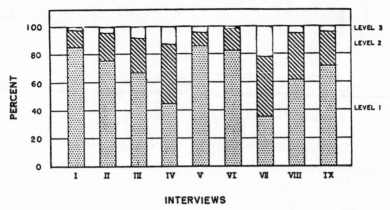

FIGURE 2. Therapist activity in the Wolberg case in terms of Degree of Inference.

case of Degree of Inference and Initiative, the designation Level 1, 2, and 3 signifies that scores have been grouped; Level 3 refers to the most intense scores. Chi squares computed for each component of the system were significant beyond the .01 level, indicating that the fluctuations in

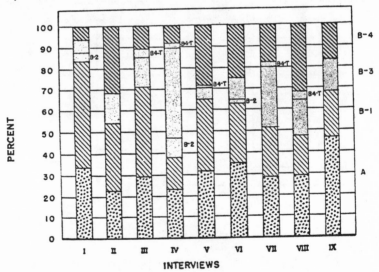

FIGURE 3. Therapist activity in the Wolberg case in terms of Dynamic Focus.

408

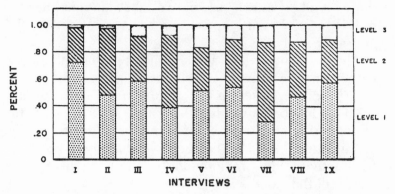

FIGURE 4. Therapist activity in the Wolberg case in terms of Initiative.

therapist activity for the interview series are not attributable to chance.

The therapist's techniques show systematic variations on all components over the course of therapy.* The initial interview is devoted largely to an exploration of the patient's problem; the next two interviews reveal an intensification of therapeutic activity, both in terms of inferential operations and Initiative; Interviews IV and VII emerge as interpretive ones, the intervening sessions as less "dramatic"; data for the remaining sessions point to a phasing out of interpretive activity, but Initiative remains at a relatively high level.

The therapist's interpretations are geared to the patient's current interpersonal relations, with relatively little emphasis on the therapist-patient relationship or on genetic antecedents. Throughout treatment, but especially in the second half, the therapist stands out as a person who, in the role of an expert, gives guidance, states opinions, and engages in procedures that may be labeled re-educative. He is clearly more active than passive, both in terms of frequency of intervention and in directing the course of

---

*Therapeutic Climate had to be omitted because there were very few nonzero scores.

therapy. Wolberg's own descriptive label "insight therapy with re-educative goals" appears to be corroborated by the quantitative analyses.

The most noteworthy single result is perhaps the *phasing* of therapeutic activity. It seems as if the therapist gradually prepares the patient for more inferential formulations, which he advances in the fourth session. Then he waits for a consolidation of insight before renewing his interpretive efforts in Interview VII. Thereafter, he diminishes his interpretive activity while maintaining a degree of therapeutic pressure till the end.

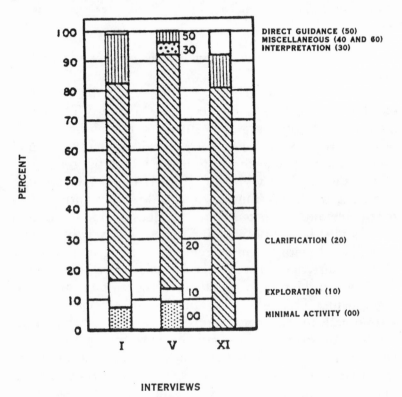

FIGURE 5. Therapist activity in the Miss Tilden case in terms of Type of Therapeutic Activity. (Interviews: I, $N = 57$; V, $N = 23$; XI, $N = 53$. Total number of therapist interventions: $N = 133$.)

410

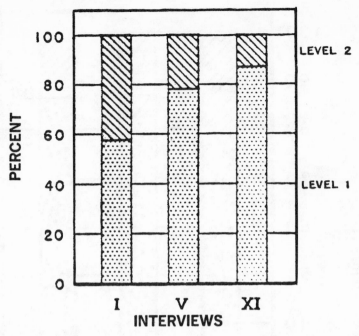

FIGURE 6. Therapist activity in the Miss Tilden case in terms of Degree of Inference.

THE CASE OF MISS TILDEN: The analysis comprises three selected interviews; they are, however, separated in time and they presumably represent different stages of therapy.

Reference to Figures 5, 6, 7, and 8 indicates that the profiles of therapist activity are quite similar from interview to interview. As might be expected, reflections of feeling account for a large percentage of all interventions (75 per cent); interpretations are virtually absent; explorations are used minimally in the initial session and are almost non-existent later on; direct guidance is equally rare. The data on Degree of Inference and Initiative corroborate these findings: neither maximal Degree of Inference nor maximal Initiative is used to any appreciable degree, but the initial interview is relatively more inferential than the final one. (In

411

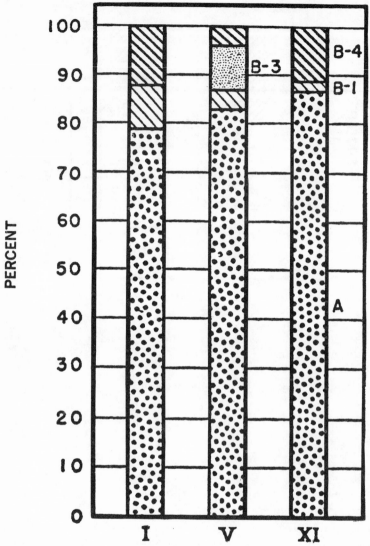

FIGURE 7. Therapist activity in the Miss Tilden case in terms of Dynamic Focus.

this instance, chi square exceeded the .01 level of probability; all others failed to reach the .05 level). In most of his interventions, the therapist accepts the patient's focus; only very

412

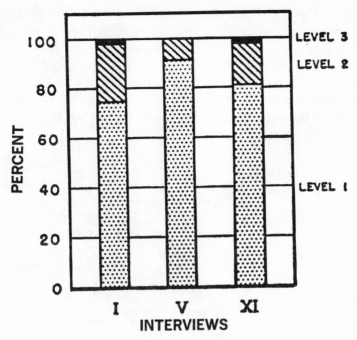

FIGURE 8. Therapist activity in the Miss Tilden case in terms of Initiative.

rarely does he assume the role of an expert or an authority.

INTERTHERAPIST COMPARISONS: While the preceding analyses have shown that Wolberg's technique varies systematically over the course of treatment whereas Rogers' does not, the question may still be asked, how do the two therapists compare at different stages of therapy? To explore this problem, three interviews from the beginning, middle, and terminal phases of the Wolberg series were selected and compared with the Miss Tilden case. Since the distributions of the categories within Type and Dynamic Focus vary so greatly for the two therapists, the only meaningful comparisons concern the continua of Degree of Inference and Initiative. The results of this analysis are presented in Table 2.

In the case of Degree of Inference, a significant chi square indicates that Wolberg's technique is significantly more inferential than Rogers'; with respect to Initiative, Wolberg exerts stronger guidance in the middle and terminal interviews, but not in the initial one. The latter finding is accounted for by the fact that Wolberg employs a great many exploratory questions of a diagnostic character in his first session, which in terms of Initiative receive scores similar to the reflection-of-feeling technique, which Rogers employs throughout.

TABLE 2

CHI-SQUARE COMPARISONS OF THERAPIST ACTIVITY IN INITIAL, MIDDLE, AND TERMINAL INTERVIEWS

	Wolberg I ($N=108$) versus Rogers I ($N=57$)	Wolberg IV ($N=174$) versus Rogers V ($N=23$)	Wolberg IX ($N=154$) versus Rogers XI ($N=53$)
Degree of Inference	19.32†	9.39†	4.66*
Initiative	.19	22.79‡	9.85†

* Significant between the .02 and .05 level.
† Significant at the .01 level.
‡ Significant at the .001 level.

DISCUSSION

A multidimensional system of analysis has been applied to the therapist's communications in two forms of therapy in an effort to measure aspects that may be common to both. With respect to the Miss Tilden case, the system of analysis yields data that are substantially in agreement with other analyses that have been performed on interviews conducted by nondirective counselors. By and large, these results also agree with Rogers' recommendations on therapeutic technique. Wolberg's technique, too, is in agreement with his descriptive account but, to my knowledge, no comparable quantitative studies have been published. While not crucial, such evidence attests indirectly to the validity of this system

414

of analysis. Of at least equal importance, however, is the tentative demonstration that the method facilitates the comparative treatment of therapeutic techniques—a treatment that is quantitative and highly objective, and that does not prejudge a particular communication as desirable or undesirable on a priori grounds.

To be sure, the present two case histories are comparable only in superficial respects and they do not lend themselves to a rigorous evaluative comparison. However, they suggest a number of questions that appear to be basic to all psychotherapy research. Consider the following two points.

We know that both patients entered psychotherapy seeking alleviation of their emotional problems. Did their difficulties have any common basis? What was the relative degree of their disturbance? Even if both had been diagnosed as "depressed," or by any other label, we would know but little about the common denominators of the underlying dynamics. As Kubie (1956) has pointed out, the time is ripe for fresh attempts to identify the common principles of the "neurotic process." It is clear that studies in which patients are matched with experimental "controls" remain largely meaningless unless this Herculean research task can be accomplished.

Secondly, what happened in the therapeutic sessions that led both therapists to evaluate the outcome as "successful"? Both therapists are highly experienced men in their field; both had a rationale for their respective procedures that on the evidence of this study differed quantitatively (Degree of Inference and Initiative) and perhaps qualitatively (Type and Dynamic Focus). Rogers, in keeping with his theory, consistently reflected the patient's feelings, whereas Wolberg, combining analytic principles with reeducative techniques, attempted to effect therapeutic changes in his patient mainly by means of interpretation and guidance. But even if the patients could be equated it would not be possible to attribute differences in therapeutic outcome (whose measurement is another staggering problem)

415

to variations in technique as long as relevant factors in the therapist's personality are left out of account. Certainly, Wolberg was more "directive" (by Rogerian standards). But both therapists conveyed an attitude of respect for their patients and implied their right to self-direction; both appeared to be warm, accepting, and noncritical; both encouraged the patient's expression of feelings; and both, by their therapeutic performance, seemed to engender a feeling of greater self-acceptance in their patients. These attitudes on the part of the therapist—he may have them in common with the mature person who can also be a good parent*— are as yet largely unexplored by objective research, but they may be the touchstone of *all* therapeutic success, regardless of the theory.† Given the "basic therapist personality" it may still be possible that some therapeutic techniques or combinations of techniques catalyze the therapeutic process whereas others are relatively inert; on the other hand, no amount of training in technique may compensate for deficiencies in the therapist's "basic attitudes." To approach these problems by research is difficult, but by no means impossible.

It seems that altogether too little attention has been paid by researchers to the therapist and his contribution to the therapeutic process. In keeping with this conviction, I

*I have in mind Fromm's "productive character" (1947).

†There is increasing evidence that the therapist's attitude may "cut across" theoretical orientations. For a comprehensive statement of the client-centered position, see Rogers' discussion (1951, pp. 19-64). On the other hand, Wolberg's transcript offers evidence that respect for the patient, his capacities, his right to self-direction, and his worth as a human being can be conveyed even when the therapist makes interpretations. Fiedler's studies (1950a, 1950b, 1951) suggest that "experts," irrespective of whether they subscribe to the analytic, Adlerian, or client-centered viewpoint, create highly similar "ideal therapeutic relationships" but, as Bordin (1955, pp. 115-116) has pointed out, Fiedler's findings cannot be regarded as evidence for or against the question of the importance to be attached to differences among theories.

have focused upon one facet—the therapist's techniques—and attempted to abstract common denominators from the therapist's verbal operations. The isolation and measurement of common denominators in varying therapeutic techniques appear to be a needed research task that must be expanded by research on the therapist's personality, from which technique seems to be inseparable.*

SUMMARY

Intertherapist comparisons showed that the analytically oriented therapist used techniques that were generally more inferential and that showed greater Initiative than those of his client-centered counterpart. While the initial interviews did not differ significantly in terms of Initiative, the approach of the two therapists was nevertheless divergent on other dimensions.

The primary implications of this preliminary comparison relate to the comparative study of therapeutic techniques, which is considered one of the most important frontiers of research in psychotherapy. The isolation and measurement of common denominators in the techniques of therapists adhering to different schools should lead to more definitive studies of the therapist's personality, particularly of those attitudes that, wittingly or unwittingly, he brings to bear upon the therapeutic interaction.

---

*A three-year investigation, completed in the 1950's, deals with the techniques, therapeutic formulations, and attitudes of more than 200 therapists who responded as vicarious interviewers to a sound film of an initial interview.

References

Bordin, E. S. 1955. *Psychological Counseling.* New York: Appleton-Century-Crofts.

Fiedler, F. E. 1950a. "The Concept of an Ideal Therapeutic Relationship," *J. Cons. Psychol.,* 14: 239-245.

——— 1950b. "A Comparison of Therapeutic Relationships in Psychoanalytic, Nondirective, and Adlerian Therapy," *J. Cons. Psychol.,* 14: 436-445.

——— 1951. "Factor Analyses of Psychoanalytic, Nondirective, and Adlerian Therapeutic Relationships," *J. Cons. Psychol.,* 15: 32-38.

Fromm, E. 1947. *Man for Himself.* New York: Rinehart.

Kubie, L. S. 1956. "Some Unsolved Problems of Psychoanalytic Psychotherapy," in *Progress in Psychotherapy 1956,* ed. F. Fromm-Reichmann and J. L. Moreno, pp. 87-102. New York: Grune & Stratton.

Rogers, C. R. 1946. "Significant Aspects of Client-centered Therapy," *Am. Psychol.,* 1: 415-422.

——— 1951. *Client-centered Therapy.* Boston: Houghton Mifflin.

Snyder, W. U. (Ed.) *Casebook of Non-directive Counseling.* Boston: Houghton Mifflin.

Wolberg, L. R. 1954. *The Technique of Psychotherapy.* New York: Grune & Stratton.

Wolff, W. 1956. *Contemporary Psychotherapists Examine Themselves.* Springfield, Ill.: Charles C. Thomas.

Part IV
Studying the
Psychotherapeutic
Process *in vivo*

In approaching the study of the psychotherapeutic process the investigator faces two choices: (1) He can attempt to study the naturally occurring phenomena and devise ways of quantifying them; or, (2) he can turn to experimental approaches, in the course of which he studies part-processes in the laboratory or in quasi-therapeutic situations (analogues). The latter course implies a recognition that the naturally occurring events are intrinsically too complex and not amenable to experimental control or manipulation, at least with our current techniques. The chapters included in Part II describe studies of the analogue variety, or they are concerned with analyses of therapist activity in recorded interviews, quantified *after the fact*. In contrast, the chapter included in this part deals with the ongoing process of therapy.

421

Apart from its concern with methodological issues, the study presents a number of findings that may be expected to interest the practicing clinician. The following appear to be particularly noteworthy:

1. Therapists tend to report positive attitudes when they have a high degree of motivation and investment in the patient during a given hour, when their empathy is high, when the hour is considered productive, and when they are satisfied with the progress.

2. Therapists tend to value manifestations in which the patient is moving in the direction of greater maturity, shows a cooperative attitude with the therapist, seems to be working on his problem, and seemingly is achieving insight. The emergence of affect and the absence of submissiveness belong to this pattern.

3. Therapists tend to feel positively toward a patient when he is nondefensive and showing signs of "maturity." At such times they are more likely to be "giving." Conversely, therapists tend to be displeased when the patient is resisting.

All of this may mean no more than that therapists are human: they feel pleased when the work is progressing, and they feel frustrated when the patient is thwarting their efforts. However, it is quite clear that the therapist's interventions are distinctly a function of his emotional and attitudinal response to the patient—they are not the communications of an impersonal operator or of a technician. The research reported here thus corroborates a major theme, perhaps the *Leitmotif* of my investigational efforts in this area, to which repeated attention has been called in Part II. I am referring to the demonstration that the therapist's attitudes toward a patient permeate his diagnostic formulations, clinical judgments, prognostic estimates, as well as the quality of his communications. For these reasons, the therapist's cognitions and emotions may have an exceedingly important effect on the course and outcome of therapy with a particular patient. The implications of these findings are bound to be far-reaching; they clearly deserve further exploration.

15

LONGITUDINAL STUDY OF
PSYCHOTHERAPY
(WITH J. B. CHASSAN
AND J. A. EWING)

PROBLEMS OF METHODOLOGY AND
QUANTIFICATION

Accurate description is the first requirement in any science:
without it, measurement and prediction are an impossibility.
One of the often-repeated criticisms of psychoanalysis and
psychotherapy has been aimed at this alleged deficiency,
and, one must admit, with considerable justification. Aside
from quantitative measurement and prediction that may be
viewed as later and more refined developments, it should be
possible, minimally, to agree on observable phenomena in
the psychotherapeutic situation. Yet, when serious attempts
have been made to study this problem, the results have
usually been disappointing. The extent of this disillusionment is difficult to gauge because many efforts in this direc-

424

tion that were considered abortive by the investigators have never been published. In the absence of such reports it it difficult to assess whether the difficulties are indeed insuperable. However, if the direction of developments in psychotherapy is toward greater precision, and if psychotherapy aspires to the status of a science, the difficulties must be faced and resolved. The failures that have been experienced are perhaps largely due to faulty methodologies rather than to an inherent impossibility of describing adequately the phenomena of psychotherapy.

The requirement for a consensus among observers is elementary and needs little further elaboration. If Therapist A asserts that Event X is happening at a particular time, but an independent observer, B, describes the occurrence as Event Y, and independent observer, C, describes the occurrence as Event Z, the trustworthiness (reliability) of their observations is seriously in question.

The principal sources of their disagreement appear to be:

1. Observers are poorly *calibrated*; that is, they may have different theoretical preconceptions (*orientations*), their level of expertness in observing therapeutic phenomena may differ, etc.

2. The phenomena under observation themselves may be so unclear, fluid, and hazy that observer agreement is in principle impossible and that the observations are little more than the *projections* or fantasies of the observers (this is the usual criticism of the opponents of psychotherapy).

3. The methods by which observations are recorded are faulty, so that it is difficult or impossible to ascertain whether observers in fact agree or disagree.

For the moment we shall disregard sources of disagreement (1) and (2). It will be assumed that observers are equally well trained and that they have a relatively uniform approach to their observations, although it is conceded that unreliability will be introduced in this way. We reject the

425

notion that the phenomena of psychotherapy are *instrinsically* unreliable, and, in contrast, accept as a working assumption that the difficulties lie primarily in the methods used for describing and recording the data.

When one takes a closer look at these difficulties, he finds that they are twofold: (1) the problem of demarcating meaningful units of observation, and (2) the technical problem of specifying dimensions or categories. Solution of these problems is absolutely essential and prerequisite to significant research advances in this area. If one could achieve a level of agreement (reliability) of say, 80 to 85 per cent, one would have built a foundation from which a variety of research operations, such as comparisons between the techniques of different therapists and patients' intrapsychic reactions and responses to particular kinds of therapists' communications could be fruitfully undertaken.

With regard to problem (1) the investigator has available essentially two approaches: he can decide on arbitrary units, such as time units, sentences, paragraphs, etc., that are easy to demarcate but that often lack psychological significance; or he can select psychological units, such as *themes*, which emerge in a single hour or over a course of hours (Cohen and Cohen, 1961). These are maximally meaningful but almost impossible to demarcate. In most research studies undertaken so far, the first course has usually been chosen.

Problem (2) is by far the more difficult one, although since about 1940 many attempts have been made to devise conceptual schemes as well as categories, dimensions, and rating devices to capture "relevant" aspects of the content of psychotherapy. Such schemes are typically attempts at content-analysis, but they vary greatly in their focus, level of abstraction, and the content they include as well as exclude. I will not undertake a review of pertinent content-analysis systems; several summaries of the literature have previously been published (Auld and Murray, 1955; Dittes, 1959; Strupp, 1962; Marsden, 1965). A number of schemes described in these sources has been reported as possessing

426

adequate reliability; however, it is noteworthy that no single system has received sustained interest from many investigators other than the originator; instead, investigators have typically preferred to develop systems of their own. It is also important that most systems thus far reported in the literature have been anchored to a particular theory of psychotherapy (the client-centered viewpoint is perhaps best represented), thus effectively precluding comparisons between therapeutic interviews of therapists subscribing to different theoretical orientations. Some systems (like the Bales system of interaction process analysis, Bales, 1950) that are not subject to this stricture have been considered too general to be of incisive value for research in psychotherapy.

An important advantage of the psychoanalytic situation is that it is unique as a method of observation. This has been stressed by a number of authors including Janis (1958) and Greenacre (1954). If the value of psychoanalysis as a method of observation is granted, a significant question arises: Why has it been so sorely neglected by researchers in the area of psychotherapy as well as by personality psychologists in general? The answer may be found in the sharp (and often unjustified) criticisms made against the data generated in this way. Among these, the following may be discerned:

1. In order to make the kinds of observations that analysts claim to be regular, repeatable, and recurrent, one must be indoctrinated in the theory of psychoanalysis. Persons not so indoctrinated do not make the same observations.

2. The data generated in the psychoanalytic situation are purely artifactual, that is, they are a function of the frustrations imposed upon the patient. Consequently they have relatively little bearing upon the patient's attitudes and performance in extra-analytic situations.

3. Whenever one attempts to test the reliability of one analyst's observations (through the use of external observers), the agreement tends to be so low and the contradictions in

427

the inferences drawn from the observations so pervasive that serious doubt must be entertained about the utility of such data.

Criticisms (1) and (3) are related. Criticism (2) touches upon the question of therapeutic effectiveness and the relevance of studying interpersonal and intrapsychic data in the transference situation for the purpose of effecting changes in the patient's *adjustment*. While this criticism can potentially be refuted by empirical data (although this remains a task for the future), we shall not concern ourselves with it at this time as it lies outside the scope of the present discussion.

Insofar as criticism (1) advocates the abandonment of the psychoanalytic theoretical framework in favor of a completely atheoretical scheme, it can be safely rejected. As Tolman (1953) has shown, the fact that an observer who is trained to make observations along particular lines that another observer not possessing such training would fail to make does not per se disqualify the former as long as the observations are not *automatically* determined by the theoretical frame of reference.

If it were true that inter-rater agreement is of a very low order, the argument against the utility of the psychoanalytic situation as a method of observation (not necessarily as a treatment technique) would indeed be a formidable one. Here we return to our previous contention that the techniques that have thus far been employed for establishing rater consensus have been inadequate or faulty, and that improvement in the techniques would markedly raise the consensus. A distinction must be made here again between the data of observation and the metapsychological (or theoretical) implications. A theory as such cannot be validated by observational means; however, it must be conceded that in the domain of observations with which the psychoanalytic observer deals, almost any observation implies an inference. It is necessary, therefore, to keep the level of inference sufficiently low, but not so low as to become meaningless. For example, observers might agree very well that on a particular day the patient is wearing a green tie (a very low inference but presumably not a very relevant observation); however, they might agree far less on whether the patient is anxious (a relatively high-order inference, but presumably a highly relevant judgment).

One attempt to devise a system for quantifying the therapist's communications has been made by one of the authors (see Chapter Twenty-one). It consisted of three dimensions (Depth-directedness, Initiative, Warmth-Coldness) and two sets of categories (Type of Communication and Dynamic Focus) that served to quantify each communication by the therapist. In Chapters Nine, Thirteen, and Fourteen, it was shown that the system possesses adequate reliability, it discriminates the therapist's activity within single hours and over a series of hours with reasonable sensitivity, and it permits meaningful comparisons between the communications of therapists subscribing to different theoretical orientations, differing in terms of experience and similar variables.

Despite this demonstrated utility, we feel that the system has some significant deficiencies. First, it overemphasizes the structural aspects of the therapist's communication and it is insufficiently sensitive to the attitudinal-emotional facets of his communications. While the system does a reasonably adequate job in specifying whether a communication by the therapist is a question, an interpretation, and the like, and while similarly it assesses reasonably well the degree of initiative, the depth of inference, and the dynamic focus of a communication, it performs poorly in the attitudinal-emotional area.

From the standpoint of the investigator, techniques are needed to assess both the quality of the emotional relationship including subjective, experiential factors in therapist and patient, and the technical operations of the therapist (technique). In addition, of course, there must be developed parallel techniques for quantifying the patient's *state* at a given time, as it is subjectively experienced by the patient as well as it is evaluated by external observers.

The requirements for quantitative assessments are similar whether one is dealing with the communications of the therapist or the patient. It may be stated categorically that existing techniques for measuring essential aspects of the therapeutic encounter are exceedingly primitive and inadequate. New approaches are needed; of this we are convinced, even though we are not prepared to offer radical solutions. The latter seem to lie far in the future. At this time we should like to pursue somewhat further the problem of the deficiency of existing measures.

Bellak and Smith's Contribution

Bellak and Smith (1956) published a paper that represented an original approach to the problems to which this chapter addresses itself.* It is regrettable that their study has never been replicated, nor has anyone, to our knowledge, pursued their lead.

In brief, they recorded psychoanalytic sessions and asked two psychoanalysts to make certain ratings of the events in these sessions. Two other analysts were asked to predict, independently, the nature of subsequent analytical sessions, using the same rating instrument. According to Bellak and Smith:

> The kind of study we have undertaken forces the participants to attempt to describe more accurately what they see, to agree on definitions of phenomena, and to make more explicit the hypotheses under which they operate. The participants were surprised to find that an implicit prediction was part of their every interpretive statement [p. 386].

---

*One of the authors (JBC) has independently pursued research designed to develop adequate systems for quantifying clinical process data. (Chassan, 1962).

430

The variables selected by these investigators included transference (positive, negative), acting out, insight, working through, resistance, anxiety, aggression (extra- and intra-), passivity, guilt, depression, elation, oral strivings, anal strivings, phallic strivings, oedipal strivings, genital strivings, homosexuality, scoptophilia. In addition, their list included the following defenses: projection, rationalization, isolation, denial, intellectualization, displacement, reaction formation, regression, reversal, identification with aggressor. The process ratings and predictions were made on an all-or-none basis, and raters were asked to distinguish between *conscious* and *unconscious* phenomena. In addition, there were some features in this investigation that need not concern us in the present context. Without reporting the results in detail, it may be stated that Bellak and Smith found relatively good rater agreement, correlation coefficients ranging from .11 to .78, for variables on which both raters made a rating in a given week. They state:

> If ratings had been required on all variables, lower figures would have resulted, (but) such required ratings would be logically and clinically entirely meaningless (since) any scientist addresses himself to a limited area of functioning; to variables which, at the moment, seem important to him. The statistical picture would be rather more distorted than truthful if he were forced to rate variables he considered irrelevant at the time [p. 406].

They concluded that analysts were able, quantitatively, to agree on the *structure* of the case; that is, they agreed generally on the variables each member of a pair rated relatively high or relatively low. However, they were unsuccessful in predicting the variables in which positive or negative change would occur over a (relatively short) period of time. We agree with the authors' conclusion that despite their failure to demonstrate accuracy of prediction "the results of the study show a gratifying measure of agreement in the des-

431

cription by four or five analysts in psychoanalytic language of the psychodynamics of a patient. This alone is more than has ever been established experimentally and statistically before [p. 411]."

Basing their judgment on the results of their investigation, Bellak and Smith believe that psychoanalytic concepts are poorly defined, and that analysts proceed therapeutically in idiosyncratic ways in accordance with their own personality characteristics, although their subjective preferences may eventually be corrected to produce considerable agreement in the long run. They suggest that a team of psychoanalysts and social scientists be formed to attempt better definitions of the basic vocabulary. In addition, they feel that longer training of participants in the rating procedure as well as better acquaintance with the problems of quantitative rating on the part of the participants would be helpful.

The foregoing recommendations are certainly desirable; however, it may be questioned whether they would in and of themselves produce marked increments in rater agreement. The major obstacle, as we see it, is that even with better definitions of the variables, one still does not know the meaning of a particular rating. Is it an average based upon the fluctuations of a given variable during the hour? Does it represent a single observation at a given point in time during the hour? If so, at what time? It appears that the ratings used by Bellak and Smith are ratings based upon global impressions averaged by the observer for a given hour. On the basis of their findings one does not know the weighting procedures these observers have used and the manner in which they arrived at their ratings.

We disagree with Bellak and Smith in their emphasis upon *predictive* ratings. The task they imposed upon their predictors appears difficult and essentially unrealistic. First, there is the general problem of clinical predictions, which has been well described by Holt (1958). In essence, he argues that often the clinician is asked to generate information in the absence of empirically established relationships between the predictor variables and a given criterion. Bellak and Smith's criterion is so inadequately defined (it is merely a time interval) that the cards are stacked against the clinicians making predictions. If one considers the multitude of intervening events that may influence a patient's feeling state it becomes apparent that his status at an unspecified future date is virtually impossible to predict. The raters were asked to make predictions about impulses and defenses, which by their very nature are unstable. The problem is compounded by the impossibility of controlling the patient's life situation. Obviously, the patient is always in interaction with a complex environment, which somehow must be taken into account in predictive judgments. In the circumstances, the reported failure to demonstrate stable relationships is hardly surprising.

Prospectus

Despite these strictures Bellak and Smith's effort provides an excellent starting point for a system by means of which observations can be made systematically and that yields quantifications of significant aspects of the therapeutic process. Before it can reach maximum usefulness, however, a number of problems will have to be resolved.

1. As Bellak and Smith recognized, it will be necessary to develop better operational definitions of the variables to be rated. The observer-rater must be given specific and unambiguous criteria concerning the observational referents of, say, an anal impulse. The danger is that theoretical preconceptions may automatically determine such ratings. For instance, a patient displaying anger, hostility, and spite may be rated as exhibiting *anal trends* because the theory presupposes a relationship between anality and hostility. Ratings should largely be based on *observable* behavior, without reference to inferred unconscious processes. Ratings also

433

should make minimal theoretical assumptions. These requirements, while difficult to meet, are not impossible.

2. Appropriate units of observation have to be defined. There are indications that smaller units can be more reliably rated than larger units. Because a variable is likely to fluctuate markedly during a therapeutic session, the hour unit is probably much too large. Smaller time units (five minutes, or even less), may prove to be much more satisfactory. (See Pilot Experiments below.)

3. The reliability of ratings will have to be studied extensively, particularly the problem of inter-rater agreement. How well do raters agree on an observation? Are there differences between highly experienced therapists as raters and inexperienced judges? How much training is necessary to achieve a satisfactory level of agreement? What kinds of training are designed to achieve this objective? These are some of the questions to be answered.

4. Variables should be selected in such a way that for the particular unit to be rated a reasonably complete picture of the patient-therapist interaction results. Thus, in addition to ratings aimed at a description of the patient state, there should be parallel ratings of the nature of the therapist's interventions (technique), his attitudes toward the patient, and the prevailing attitudinal climate of the relationship.

5. Given a rating instrument meeting the above criteria, systematic assessments can be made. It must be decided whether ratings are to be made by the therapist, the patient, independent observers, or in some combination. Once such assessments are made for a number of patient-therapist pairs over an extended period of time, such questions as the following may be approached: (A) What kinds of variables remain relatively stable over time, and which ones change? How does stability or change relate to progress or lack of progress in therapy, as assessed by the more commonly used process notes or clinical observations? (B) How do changes in one clinical variable relate to changes in other variables?

What are the relationships to technique, therapist's attitudes, and the emotional climate of the relationship?

It should be noted that the preceding questions may be answered by relying on the empirical data, obviating predictions such as were used by Bellak and Smith.

6. The exploration of these problems requires the solution of a number of statistical issues relative to time-series and the independence of repeated measurements.

The foregoing listing encompasses a program of research in which only the barest beginnings have been made. Obviously, it will not solve *all* the problems with which research in psychotherapy and psychoanalysis is beset. But it could provide an important starting point for more adequate descriptions of the therapeutic process, which at the present stage of development of this amorphous field would indeed constitute a tangible advance.

PILOT EXPERIMENTS

In the following pages we shall present the results of some preliminary attempts to develop an instrument that might meet the criteria that have been outlined and to begin experimentation along the lines indicated. The study by Bellak and Smith has been reported in some detail because in important respects the following experiments represent a continuation of their effort. However, on the basis of our results and experience gained in conducting these experiments, we have come to the conclusion that significant modifications of their system are indicated. The nature of the proposed modifications that should be undertaken prior to further experimentation on a larger scale will be made explicit.

A Modification of Bellak and Smith's Instrument

It was our objective to carry further Bellak and Smith's

attempt to provide adequate descriptions of the dynamic process of psychotherapy by requiring the therapist to make systematic ratings of the interaction, such ratings to be made following each therapeutic hour. Following these workers, we proposed to use the single hour as a convenient unit of observation, although it now appears that this unit is too large and too global.

For the reasons previously stated, the idea of obtaining predictions from the therapist (or from independent judges) was abandoned. Instead, ratings were to be based on the events occuring during the hour to be rated. The extent to which such ratings might be predictive of subsequent events in therapy would thus become an empirical question that might be answered by studying changes in the ratings over time.

Second, it was considered inadvisable to require raters to make evaluations of *unconscious* processes, for the reason that such ratings require a very high level of inference. They would be more highly dependent upon the theoretical predilections of the raters than more directly observable events; consequently, it seemed unlikely that a satisfactory level of agreement could be obtained. (Experiment 3 confirmed this assumption.) It was clear that even ratings of so-called observable events required varying degrees of inference that, we anticipated, would dilute rater agreement (as it evidently had in Bellak and Smith's study).

Third, we attempted to distinguish several degrees of intensity (or relative frequency), a possibility that has been considered by Bellak and Smith, but that they abandoned in favor of all-or-none ratings. In order to retain simplicity of the rating process, we devised a uniform five-point scale that therapists were asked to use in rating each variable (see Figure 1).

Finally, several variables from Bellak and Smith's list were eliminated * and several new ones added.† In addition, we attempted to obtain ratings in two areas not included in the original list. These were: therapeutic technique

436

Patient Code: _____ Therapist: _____ Therapy Hour No: _____ Date: _____ 196 _

Please rate *all* items using the following code:

0	No evidence, absent	None	Absent, very seldom	Absent
1	Slight evidence	Slight	Occasional	Mild
2	Fairly strong evidence	Moderate	Fairly frequent	Moderate
3	Strong evidence	Great	Frequent	Intense
4	Extremely strong evidence	Extremely great	Extremely frequent	Extremely intense

Note: As far as possible, make ratings on the basis of behavior observed or evidence
obtained during the hour rather than on the basis of inferences or theoretical constructs.

No.	Patient Variable	0	1	2	3	4	No.	Therapist Variable	0	1	2	3	4
1	Dominance						22	Interventions					
2	Dependence						23	Interpretations					
3	Resistance						24	Depth of interpretation					
4	Anxiety						25	Initiative					
5	Affect						26	Warmth					
6	Sadism						27	Coldness					
7	Masochism						28	Support					
8	Hostility, anger												
9	Defensiveness						29	Motivation, dedication, "investment"					
10	Transference-positive						30	Positive attitudes					
11	Transference-negative						31	Negative attitudes					
12	Competitiveness, rivalry						32	Countertransference problems					
13	Depression						33	Empathy					
14	Elation						34	Productivity of hour					
15	Insight						35	Satisfaction with progress					
16	Working through							Comments:					
17	Oral strivings												
18	Anal strivings												
19	Phallic strivings												
20	Oedipal strivings												
21	Genital strivings												

FIGURE 1.

---

*Omitted were : Acting out, Aggression (Extra- Intra-), Passivity, Guilt, Homosexuality, Scoptophilia, as well as the 11 "classic" defenses. These variables seemed on an a priori basis too difficult to rate because of (seven variables) and the therapist's feelings toward the patient and about the therapeutic process (seven items). The rationale for including these variables derived from previous research in this area in which the potential influence of the therapist's attitudes toward the patient with respect to technique and clinical evaluations had been demonstrated (see Chapters Nine, Nineteen, and Twenty-one).

Thus, the modified instrument was designed to provide information in each of the following areas: (1) the patient's feelings, attitudes, emotional reactions in the transference situation; (2) the frequency and kind of interventions by the therapist (technique); and (3) the therapist's feelings and attitudes toward the patient, about himself, and about the therapeutic process.

EXPERIMENT 1—DEGREE OF INFERENCE: In this experiment we set ourselves the task of determining empirically the degree of inference entering the rating process. In studying the variables included in the rating instrument it becomes apparent that some are much closer to observable events than others. For example, when the patient expresses hostility (anger) toward the therapist, there are presumably much more direct and specific behavioral manifestations than when he evinces phallic strivings. The latter must be inferred from trends in the patient's free associations and the total context of impulse and defense constellations. Thus, in order to make a rating of the intensity of such a variable, the therapist (or independent observer) must go through a

---

their being too general, not sufficiently process-oriented, too inferential, and the like. Bellak and Smith gave no rationale for their list except that the variables had been "agreed upon." Our own list, too, was intuitively derived. It is clear that in subsequent work greater attention must be given to the selection of variables to be rated. The number of empirically distinguishable dimensions is probably limited, and factor analytic techniques might prove useful in isolating such underlying dimensions.

†Added were: Dominance, Dependence, Affect, Sadism, Masochism, Hostility (anger), Defensiveness, Competitiveness (rivalry). This left 13 variables common to the two lists.

highly complex process of clinical inference, invoke his clinical experience and theoretical knowledge, finally arriving at a quantitative rating that represents a rather high-order abstraction. The farther a variable is removed from directly observable events, the higher is the degree of inference required. Furthermore, it may be hypothesized (and this hypothesis will be tested in Experiment 2) that the greater the degree of clinical inference required in making a rating the lower will be the level of agreement among independent observers (including the therapist). Conversely, observers may be expected to agree best on variables that refer to directly observable events.

This problem of inference has been one of the great stumbling blocks in describing the events in psychoanalysis and psychotherapy. Because many events with which the psychotherapist deals are highly complex and far from being directly observable, and because a high level of clinical inference is often required in describing the nature of the events, it is likely that an independent observer will not traverse the same road of clinical inference traveled by the therapist. The result is that their respective descriptions may fail to agree, or, because the two observers may focus on different levels of abstractions or different facets of the matrix of events, it is difficult to determine from their respective descriptions whether they agree or disagree, or to assess the extent of their agreement.

Another way of stating the problem is to say that, in psychoanalytic terms, there is no one-to-one relationship between behavioral indicators and their psychological antecedents. Long ago Freud differentiated between different viewpoints (such as the dynamic, structural, economic, genetic, and the like). Furthermore, he recognized that any psychic event is complexly determined (*overdetermined*). Accordingly, it is possible (and often highly useful) to give different descriptions of a single event. These descriptions may be given from different *viewpoints* that, however, are (from the observer's position) very difficult to keep apart.

439

Typically, a description of an event in psychotherapy or psychoanalysis represents a mixture, which further complicates the problem of achieving a consensus among independent observers.

For example, a patient at a given point in therapy may become silent. This is a behavioral indicator on which observers presumably can agree with a high degree of precision. The length of the silence can be measured objectively, but not so the determinants. It is readily apparent that a large number of *explanations* can be given of this occurrence. He may be showing resistance to an interpretation given by the therapist earlier, he may be struggling against the expression of erotically tinged feelings toward the therapist, he may mourn a childhood object, he may try to defeat the therapist, there may be a struggle between superego and id resulting in an impasse, and so on. It may be seen that a host of possible formulations may be advanced (many of them considerably more complex than the brief examples given). How is one to decide whether they are in agreement or in disagreement? Which one describes what is *really* going on?

From these considerations it becomes apparent that ideally one should construct rating scales that take account of the multidimensionality of events. Such scales should specify not only the particular *viewpoint* one wishes the rater to adopt, but they should be capable of mirroring the total constellation of vectors. It seems unlikely that such scales can be constructed at the present state of knowledge. It must also be recognized that the scales that were posited by Bellak and Smith, as well as our proposed modification, represent a mixture of levels of abstraction and *viewpoints*.

There are essentially two approaches to developing and refining such scales, recognizing that even with highly refined scales accurate measurement of the complex events in psychotherapy may only be approximated. The first approach, followed by Bellak and Smith, is to draw on theoretical and clinical knowledge and to define variables corresponding to what one considers to be important (relevant) concepts. The second is to proceed empirically by selecting variables that stay close to observables, make a minimum of theoretical assumptions, and avoid inference as far as possible. Variables like anger, friendliness, sadness, etc., might exemplify this approach. The possibility exists (and it has much to commend it) to combine the two approaches. Thus, one might posit a number of variables suggested on the basis of theoretical and clinical observations, determine how reliably they can be rated (rater agreement), and study their relative statistical independence. It may turn out, for instance, that hostility and anger are largely synonymous, in which case it would not be necessary to obtain ratings on each as a separate variable. The desideratum would be to develop scales of variables that are highly relevant clinically and theoretically (for purposes of describing ongoing events and making predictions), and highly independent of each other. The latter consideration is dictated by a desire for research economy, since for practical purposes the demands one can make on therapists (or raters) are necessarily limited. Besides, any rating scheme in order to be useful must provide for reduction of the phenomenal complexity and must abstract from the latter a small number of dimensions that are maximally heuristic.

In the present experiment, proceeding from the variables that had already been included in the rating instrument, we addressed ourselves to the problem of assessing empirically the degree of inference required in arriving at a given rating. Our objective was to arrive at a rank ordering of the variables in terms of the degree of inference required for judging each. We did not attempt to treat the three components of the rating instrument (clinical variables, technique variables, and attitudes) as separate entities but proposed to include all variables in the final rank ordering.

PROCEDURE: Eleven judges (trained clinical psychologists having the Ph.D. degree) were given the following instructions:

441

As part of an ongoing investigation, we should like to request your cooperation in rating the *degree of inference required* in assessing each of the variables listed below. Using the following scale, please indicate alongside each variable how much inference would be required in rating it:

1. virtually no inference required; almost directly observable
2. slight
3. some
4. a fair amount of inference required; a fairly typical clinical judgment
5. moderately high ·
6. high
7. extremely high degree of inference required; almost impossible to observe directly

The framework for making the above evaluations is the *typical* neurotic patient and the *typical* therapy hour. In other words, we are asking you to put yourself in the position of the therapist (or a direct observer of the therapeutic interaction) and to rate the degree of inference that would be required in making an evaluation of each variable. The unit of observation is the therapeutic hour.

(There followed a list of the 35 variables included in the rating instrument.)

RESULTS: The ratings obtained from the 11 judges were averaged (arithmetic mean) and for each variable a standard deviation was computed. The resulting rank ordering in terms of mean values is presented in Table 1. The results are almost self-explanatory. As might be expected, the more theoretically *neutral* variables grouped themselves at the lower end of the continuum, whereas those referring to impulses and concepts deeply anchored in psychoanalytic theory tended to be given higher (more inference required) ratings. Variables higher on the scale, too, tended to have greater dispersions; however, it is noteworthy that a vari-

TABLE 1

DEGREE OF INFERENCE ENTERING INTO RATINGS BY EXTERNAL OBSERVERS

$N=11$ Judges

Rank	Var. No.	Variable	Mean*	S.D.
1	22	Frequency of therapist's interventions	1.364	.674
2	23	Frequency of therapist's interpretations	1.818	1.789
3	14	Elation	2.182	.874
4	8	Hostility, anger	2.273	.786
5	5	Affect	2.363	1.026
6	13	Depression	2.545	.820
7	4	Anxiety	2.727	1.191
8	25	Therapist's initiative	2.818	1.251
9	1	Dominance	2.909	1.221
10	28	Therapist's support	3.091	1.514
12	2	Dependence	3.182	1.789
12	9	Defensiveness	3.182	1.168
12	27	Therapist's coldness	3.182	1.251
14.5	12	Competitiveness, rivalry	3.273	1.618
14.5	26	Therapist's warmth	3.273	1.272
16	30	Therapist's positive attitudes	3.545	1.440
17.5	31	Therapist's negative attitudes	3.636	1.501
17.5	3	Resistance	3.636	1.120
19	10	Transference—positive	4.000	1.612
20.5	15	Insight	4.182	1.662
20.5	35	Therapist's satisfaction with progress	4.182	1.601
22	11	Transference—negative	4.364	1.501
23	34	Therapist's estimate of productivity of hour	4.545	1.635
25	24	Depth of interpretations	4.636	1.361
25	29	Therapist's motivation	4.636	1.963
25	33	Therapist's empathy	4.636	1.026
27	7	Masochism	4.727	1.555
28	6	Sadism	4.818	1.538
29	16	Working through	4.909	1.700
30	21	Genital strivings	5.000	1.949
31	20	Oedipal strivings	5.182	1.662
32	32	Countertransference problems	5.273	1.555
33.5	17	Oral strivings	5.545	1.573
33.5	18	Anal strivings	5.545	1.635
35	19	Phallic strivings	6.000	1.549

* Based on ratings on a seven-point scale where
  1 = virtually no inference required
  7 = extremely high degree of inference required (see text).

443

able like frequency of the therapist's interpretations, which ranked low in terms of inference, had a rather marked standard deviation.

EXPERIMENT 2—A STUDY OF RATER AGREEMENT: This study is an attempt to provide preliminary information on the extent to which independent observers agree when judging the therapeutic interaction by means of the modified rating instrument. Achievement of a high level of consensus among independent observers has repeatedly been mentioned as one of the fundamental objectives of research in this area. Unless therapist and independent observers agree in judging the phenomena occurring during the therapeutic hour, little reliance can be placed on results that take such ratings as their point of departure.

Bellak and Smith obtained "considerable agreement" among their judges. As has already been mentioned, their tetrachoric coefficients of correlation ranged from .11 to .78. These results represented the degree of agreement in judgment in those instances in which both raters felt that a judgment was possible. If one of the raters did not rate a given variable, that variable presumably was omitted. Contrary to the results to be presented in this study, their coefficients were based on agreements for *all* variables rated (rather than on *single* variables), called by them the "dynamic structure of the case." There were other important differences in their procedure, which make it difficult to assess the comparability of our results with theirs. The chief difference perhaps is that in the present study the *over-all* agreement among judges and therapist was assessed (rather than among pairs), which represents a more stringent criterion.

PROCEDURE: Four advanced graduate students in clinical psychology (interns) observed therapeutic interviews through a one-way screen and listened to the verbal interchange between patient and therapist by means of a microphone-loudspeaker setup. The patient, a 21-year-old college student, was seen in psychoanalytically oriented psycho-

444

therapy by an experienced clinical psychologist. Interviews were conducted on a twice-a-week basis, although only one interview per week was observed by the raters. The patient's difficulties were essentially characterological and related to a conflict between extreme passivity and rebelliousness toward his father. Observations were made during the first few months of treatment. Following each therapy interview, the therapist met with the student group and discussed problems of psychodynamics and technique. He also informed the group (although not systematically) about events that had occurred during unobserved interviews that had been held in the interim. Ratings were made typically before the discussions, but in some instances contamination may have taken place. If so, this should have led to an artificial inflation of the inter-rater agreement.

The raters had relatively little training and experience in psychotherapy, although they were familiar to some extent with most of the pertinent concepts. No systematic training in applying the rating instrument was given.

Ratings were obtained for 11 therapy hours spaced over a period of three to four months.

RESULTS: Since we were interested in studying the degree of agreement for each variable included in the rating instrument (rather than the over-all agreement on all variables during a given hour), we proceeded to analyze each variable separately. The intraclass coefficient of correlation, R, as described by Haggard (1958), was used to determine the amount of agreement among therapist and judges. This measure, a variant of the analysis of variance technique, is a rather rigorous index of the amount of correlation between the ratings of all judges. For example, the R for Variable 1 (Dominance) indicates the degree of agreement among the judges (therapist and raters) on this variable for the 11 hours of therapy under consideration. Table 2 presents the R's for all variables included in the modified rating instrument.

Inspection of this table indicates that the agreement among the judges tended to be rather low: the highest

445

TABLE 2

INTRACLASS COEFFICIENTS OF CORRELATION (R)
BASED ON OBSERVATIONS DURING 11 THERAPY HOURS BY 5 RATERS

Variable	R
1. Dominance	.345
2. Dependence	.583
3. Resistance	.099
4. Anxiety	.380
5. Affect	.648
6. Sadism	.014
7. Masochism	.138
8. Hostility, anger	.358
9. Defensiveness	.085
10. Transference, positive	*
11. Transference, negative	.178
12. Competitiveness, rivalry	.216
13. Depression	.504
14. Elation	*
15. Insight	.369
16. Working through	.291
17. Oral strivings	.034
18. Anal strivings	*
19. Phallic strivings	*
20. Oedipal strivings	*
21. Genital strivings	.083
22. Interventions	*
23. Interpretations	.046
24. Depth of interpretation	*
25. Initiative	.053
26. Warmth	.204
27. Coldness	.031
28. Support	.060
29. Motivation, dedication, "investment"	*
30. Positive attitudes	.081
31. Negative attitudes	*
32. Countertransference problems	*
33. Empathy	.322
34. Productivity of the hour	.245
35. Satisfaction with progress	*

* Negative value (see text).

agreement was obtained for Affect (.648), Dependence (.583), and Depression (.504), with most values being considerably lower. In 11 instances the obtained R was a negative value, which for practical purposes signifies no agreement among the raters. There was no evidence that the judges agreed better among themselves than they did with the therapist, which might have been expected on the basis that they represented a more homogeneous (if relatively untrained) group and occupied a similar vantage point as far as their observations and ratings were concerned.

On the basis of these findings, which are considered highly tentative, the reliability of the rating instrument appears deficient. Possible reasons for the lack of reliability are:

1. The variables and scale points were not sufficiently well defined. Bellak and Smith had earlier stressed the importance of arriving at better definitions of the variables to be rated, which, if accomplished, might result in higher rater agreement. Furthermore, providing anchoring definitions for each scale point might give the judges a more uniform frame of reference for making ratings.

2. The judges were inexperienced therapists who undoubtedly had widely different conceptions of the variables they were asked to assess. Greater training and experience in psychotherapy as well as in applying the rating instrument might appreciably augment the rater agreement.

3. The time unit in which observations were made was too large (a full therapeutic hour). The large time unit is considered a major source of unreliability, since under the conditions of this experiment it was not clarified whether a rating was to represent an average rating for the total hour, a measure of the maximum intensity reached during the hour, or whatever. It is considered essential to use much smaller units of observation (perhaps five minutes or even shorter) in future experimentation. (Dr. Henry L. Lennard,

447

in personal communication, has made similar observations.)*

EXPERIMENT 3—RELATIONSHIP BETWEEN DEGREE OF IN-
FERENCE AND RATER AGREEMENT: By means of further statistical analysis of the data obtained in Experiments 1 and 2 we tested the hypothesis that an important determinant of rater agreement is the degree of inference required in making a clinical judgment. In other words, the higher the degree of inference entering into a clinical judgment, the lower will be the agreement among independent judges; and, conversely, the closer to observable events the clinical judgment, the higher will be the rater agreement.

PROCEDURE: For purposes of this analysis we rank ordered the first 21 variables in the modified rating instrument (omitting technique and attitudinal variables) in terms of the degree of inference obtained in Experiment 1. We then proceeded to obtain a rank order coefficient of correlation (rho) between these rankings and ranks assigned to the coefficients (R) obtained in Experiment 2, representing the level of agreement among independent judges. The pertinent data are presented in Table 3.

The resulting rho was .712, which is significant beyond the .01 level (one-tailed test), thus strongly supporting the hypothesis. It is concluded that ratings of clinical variables calling for a high degree of inference give rise to deficient rater consensus (at least in the absence of extensive training of judges in observing psychotherapeutic phenomena and/ or in the use of the rating instrument). The result also underscores the need for better definitions of the clinical variables

*In a more recent pilot experiment, each of three experienced psychiatrists conducted 20 psychoanalytic interviews with three college students who had been selected for their "normality" on the basis of psychological tests. The conditions and procedures were highly similar to the ones described in the foregoing experiment, except that the two observers in each instance were more highly experienced. The level of rater agreement did not appear to be superior to that reported here.

TABLE 3

RELATIONSHIP BETWEEN DEGREE OF INFERENCE AND RATER AGREEMENT

Variable	Degree of Inference Mean	Rank	Rater Agreement R	Rank
14. Elation	2.182	1	neg.	18.5
8. Hostility, anger	2.273	2	.358	6
5. Affect	2.363	3	.648	1
13. Depression	2.545	4	.504	3
4. Anxiety	2.727	5	.380	4
1. Dominance	2.909	6	.345	7
2. Dependence	3.182	7.5	.583	2
9. Defensiveness	3.182	7.5	.085	13
12. Competitiveness	3.273	9	.216	9
3. Resistance	3.636	10	.099	12
10. Transference—positive	4.000	11	neg.	18.5
15. Insight	4.182	12	.369	5
11. Transference—negative	4.364	13	.178	10
7. Masochism	4.727	14	.138	11
6. Sadism	4.818	15	.014	16
16. Working through	4.909	16	.291	8
21. Genital strivings	5.000	17	.083	14
20. Oedipal strivings	5.182	18	neg.	18.5
17. Oral strivings	5.545	19.5	.034	15
18. Anal strivings	5.545	19.5	neg.	18.5
19. Phallic strivings	6.000	21	neg.	18.5

to be rated, particularly in the sense of clarifying the behavioral indicators of variables calling for a high degree of inference.

EXPERIMENT 4—THREE PRELIMINARY APPLICATIONS OF THE MODIFIED RATING INSTRUMENT: This pilot study is an attempt to apply the modified rating instrument in long-term psychotherapy. The data were provided by two therapists: JAE, an experienced psychiatrist whose psychoanalytic training was nearing formal completion, rated two of his analytic patients (T and R) and HHS, a clinical psychologist, rated one patient (WA). This patient was seen in psychoanalytically oriented psychotherapy.

Patient T, a married woman, was rated for 327 hours. She suffered from a serious character disorder with much impulsive behavior, periodic episodes of overwhelming anxiety, and at times a clinical picture of a borderline psychotic state. Her therapy was characterized by marked fluctuations of mood and a major degree of conscious uncooperativeness for over a year. The gradual elucidation of negative transference led to some marked improvements in the treatment relationship. Following this, it became possible to work on various complex aspects of her development and her current life situation. The latter remained very bad and resulted in her receiving much psychic trauma. Although she grew more able to tolerate many of these blows, they did present a major "outside" interference, which led to considerable fluctuation in the psychoanalytic situation. Eventually she decided that such difficulties were ones that she did not have to accept and she took some realistic steps to deal with this toward the end of this period of therapy. Therapist JAE was well aware of the tenuous nature of the therapeutic relationship for most of the first year. This, and the patient's "borderline" state, led to a very special type of handling which JAE believes is reflected in the ratings.

Patient R, a young professional man, was rated for 157 hours. His problem was that of a moderate obsessive-compulsive character neurosis with some recent anxiety attacks connected with increasing awareness of aggressive impulses. Treatment of this case involved dealing with a fairly rapidly developing transference neurosis. There were major defenses against awareness of affects, using typical isolation mechanisms. Considerable satisfactory progress was made during the hours rated, so that throughout this time there was gradual increasing therapeutic interaction. After the period that was rated, the analysis was continued to termination with relief of symptoms and much improvement in interpersonal relations.

Patient WA, a 20-year-old girl, in therapy for about three years, was seen typically on a twice-a-week basis.

450

Ratings were made for 173 hours. She was the daughter of a professional man who was unusually active and devoted to his work although he was advanced in years and on the verge of retirement. The mother was a rather overprotective authoritarian woman. There were two younger sisters.

The patient was originally referred because of difficulties in her schoolwork, both academic and interpersonal. Following verbal disagreements with schoolmates and teachers, she was asked to withdraw from college. She returned home, where she regressed to a passive, helpless state. Her parents alternatively tended to encourage and to condemn her regressive behavior.

Clinically, Miss WA was an extremely dependent and immature young woman. Her passive-aggressiveness was pervasive. She had a severe character problem, complicated by a very impoverished ego development. Her primary defense was to dominate people through her dependency and demandingness.

Therapy was aimed at fostering insight into her unconscious mechanism to maintain the status quo of dependency, and at providing, through the therapeutic relationship, a more suitable reality model than she had experienced in the past. This proved to be an exceedingly difficult task, and progress was slow and halting. Nevertheless, the patient eventually gained enough ego strength to resume her academic work and to become somewhat more outgoing and self-reliant.

All ratings were made for *consecutive* hours. Therapist JAE's patients were rated from the beginning of therapy, but Patient R's therapy continued beyond the 157 hours included here. Patient WA had been in therapy for about two years at the time the ratings were initiated. Her therapy (and that of Patient T) were rated to termination. In other words, Patient T's therapy was rated in its entirety; Patient R was rated from the beginning but continued beyond the cut-off point; and Patient WA was rated from the middle period to termination.

451

It is apparent that these rating data lack comparability. Not only are there marked differences in type of patient, form of therapy, and background training of the two therapists, but there was also relatively little congruency in terms of the period of therapy being rated. The assumption here is that any course of psychoanalysis or psychotherapy has a relatively regular pattern—a somewhat distinct introductory period, a long middle period (characterized by "working through"), and a termination period.

Eventually, of course, one would hope to obtain ratings covering the complete therapy of different patients who might be matched on a variety of characteristics. In the same manner one might match therapists, different forms of therapy, and other variables. Once such controls are imposed, one would be able to provide empirical answers to the question of whether there is a "typical" course of therapy under specified conditions. One would also be able to investigate deviations from such a typical course once it was established.

This objective far exceeds that of the present pilot study. Our limited goal was to apply the modified rating instrument in a few cases, to study the resulting distributions of ratings, to explore the statistical interrelationships among the variables being rated, and to gather some preliminary data on the rating characteristics of two therapists working with different patients. Whatever tentative comparisons we might make between therapists and between patients must be considered highly speculative. A final objective of this pilot work was to investigate statistical problems relating to repeated ratings of the same patient on identical variables over an extended period of time. The problem of the reliability of ratings, which has previously been discussed, is ignored here, simply because it was not possible to gather pertinent data in the privacy of individual therapy. The findings that have already been presented strongly suggest, however, that this problem must be dealt with systematically before ratings of this kind are collected in the future.

452

Results—statistical treatment: The statistical analysis of the data of this study falls under the heading of *time-series analysis*. Tests of statistical significance applied to time-series data, particularly tests for a true or significant correlation between two series, must take into account the extent of redundancy introduced by a succession of observations on the same subject as measured by sets of appropriately defined autocorrelations. The papers by Bartlett (1935, 1946) contain theoretical discussions, and Quenouille (1952) provides a nonmathematical discussion of the methodology.

All ratings were punched on IBM cards, and distributions for all variables were prepared. We then intercorrelated the ratings for each patient-therapist pair. This procedure resulted in three tables of intercorrelation in which N represents the number of therapy hours rated by each therapist.

In addition, statistical analyses were performed to explore the extent to which a rating on a given variable made during one hour was correlated with comparable ratings in preceding hours.

Distribution of Ratings

Table 4 shows the distributions of each therapist's ratings in percentages. Examination discloses marked divergences in these distributions which appear to be attributable primarily to the following sources:

1. Differences between the patients who were being seen in therapy resulting in differences in the clinical phenomena that emerged over the course of treatment.

2. Differences in the form of therapy conducted by Therapist HHS and Therapist JAE, as these therapists saw it.

3. Differences in the way the two therapists understood the rating scales and the manner in which they used them.

4. Combination of the foregoing.

453

TABLE 4

DISTRIBUTIONS OF THERAPISTS' RATINGS FOR THREE PATIENTS
(IN PERCENTS)

Variable	Patient	None Absent 0	Slight Mild 1	Fairly Strong Moderate 2	Great Frequent 3	Extremely Great or Frequent 4
1. Dominance	WA	49.7	7.5	28.3	12.1	2.3
	T	21.4	19.0	53.2	6.4	
	R	10.8	5.7	70.7	12.7	
2. Dependence	WA	23.7	2.9	26.0	28.9	18.5
	T	46.5	35.5	17.7	.3	
	R	48.4	31.8	19.1	.6	
3. Resistance	WA	2.3	5.2	27.7	42.8	22.0
	T	31.2	22.3	32.1	12.8	1.5
	R	11.5	22.3	54.1	12.1	
4. Anxiety	WA	10.4	20.2	52.0	16.8	.6
	T	43.7	27.8	22.6	5.5	.3
	R	34.4	42.7	18.5	4.5	
5. Affect	WA	16.8	32.9	30.1	14.4	5.8
	T	10.7	26.0	47.7	13.8	1.8
	R	12.1	46.5	35.0	6.4	
6. Sadism	WA	16.2	9.2	29.5	23.7	21.4
	T	99.4	.3	.3		
	R	99.4	.6			
7. Masochism	WA	38.7	11.6	22.5	22.0	5.2
	T	90.2	5.8	3.4	.6	
	R	98.7	1.3			
8. Hostility, anger	WA	8.1	19.1	35.8	16.8	20.2
	T	59.3	19.0	14.4	6.4	.9
	R	61.1	21.0	14.6	2.5	.6
9. Defensiveness	WA	4.0	9.2	28.3	31.8	26.6
	T	41.0	16.2	32.4	10.1	.3
	R	25.5	17.2	48.4	8.3	.6
10. Transference- positive	WA	7.5	6.9	35.8	47.4	2.3
	T	37.0	31.8	26.9	4.3	
	R	51.0	35.0	14.0		
11. Transference- negative	WA	7.5	26.6	31.8	20.2	13.9
	T	71.9	14.4	11.9	1.8	
	R	61.1	28.7	10.2		
12. Competitiveness	WA	72.2	6.4	13.3	6.9	1.2
	T	93.6	3.4	2.4	.3	.3
	R	49.0	23.6	18.5	8.3	.6

TABLE 4 (CONT'D.)

Variable	Patient	None Absent 0	Slight Mild 1	Fairly Strong Moderate 2	Great Frequent 3	Extremely Great or Frequent 4
13. Depression	WA	43.4	45.1	9.2	1.2	1.2
	T	61.8	21.4	11.6	4.0	1.2
	R	96.2	3.2	.6		
14. Elation	WA	93.1	5.2	1.7		
	T	93.9	3.7	1.8	.6	
	R	99.4	.6			
15. Insight	WA	11.0	35.8	45.1	8.1	
	T	59.3	18.3	19.0	2.8	.6
	R	65.0	19.7	14.6		.6
16. Working	WA	4.0	20.8	47.4	27.2	.6
through	T	29.7	24.5	39.8	5.5	.6
	R	43.3	20.4	34.4	1.9	
17. Oral strivings	WA	86.7	1.7	3.5	4.6	3.5
	T	57.8	19.6	18.3	4.0	.3
	R	46.5	24.8	21.7	7.0	
18. Anal strivings	WA	45.1	1.7	13.3	20.8	19.1
	T	92.4	5.8	1.2	.3	.3
	R	86.0	7.6	5.1	1.3	
19. Phallic strivings	WA	95.4	.6	1.7	2.3	
	T	92.7	2.4	4.0	.9	
	R	79.6	9.6	10.2	.6	
20. Oedipal	WA	65.9	2.3	9.8	18.5	3.5
strivings	T	72.8	15.6	9.2	2.1	.3
	R	78.3	9.6	9.6	1.9	.6
21. Genital strivings	WA	100.0				
	T	95.1	2.1	1.8	.6	.3
	R	98.8	.6	.6		
22. Interventions	WA	1.7	9.8	57.2	30.1	1.2
	T	13.1	43.7	40.1	3.1	
	R	9.6	38.2	52.2		
23. Interpretations	WA	.6	8.1	52.0	38.7	.6
	T	49.5	34.2	15.9	.3	
	R	26.1	56.0	17.2	.6	
24. Depth of inter-	WA		9.2	27.7	47.4	15.6
pretations	T	50.5	8.9	27.5	11.0	2.1
	R	26.7	15.9	31.2	24.2	1.9
25. Initiative	WA	1.2	11.6	38.1	45.1	4.0
	T	88.1	8.6	2.4	.6	.3
	R•	91.7	7.6	.6		

TABLE 4 (CONT'D.)

Variable	Patient	None Absent 0	Slight Mild 1	Fairly Strong Moderate 2	Great Frequent 3	Extremely Great or Frequent 4
26. Warmth	WA	1.2	15.6	52.6	30.1	.6
	T	70.6	24.8	4.6		
	R	90.4	9.6			
27. Coldness	WA	87.3	10.4	2.3		
	T	99.1	.9			
	R	98.1	1.9			
28. Support	WA	2.9	12.7	45.1	38.1	1.2
	T	38.5	46.8	14.4	.3	
	R	71.3	28.0	.6		
29. Motivation	WA	1.2	11.0	40.5	43.9	3.5
	T	76.8	11.3	11.9		
	R	75.8	15.3	8.9		
30. Positive	WA	.6	11.0	43.9	42.2	2.3
Attitudes	T	38.2	38.2	22.9	.6	
	R	35.7	40.1	24.2		
31. Negative	WA	75.7	18.5	4.0	1.7	
Attitudes	T	85.3	9.2	4.0	1.5	
	R	96.8	2.5	.6		
32. Counter-	WA	79.8	17.3	2.3	.6	
transference	T	72.5	16.8	10.1	.6	
problems	R	84.1	12.7	3.2		
33. Empathy	WA	1.2	11.0	46.2	38.7	2.9
	T	83.8	7.6	8.6		
	R	71.3	14.6	13.4	.6	
34. Productivity	WA	1.7	15.0	39.3	39.3	4.6
of hour	T	22.6	31.2	36.4	9.5	.3
	R	8.9	30.6	48.4	11.5	.6
35. Satisfaction with	WA	.6	16.8	48.6	31.2	2.9
progress	T	26.0	27.2	37.0	9.2	.6
	R	14.0	26.7	48.4	10.2	.6

While the respective influences cannot be isolated apart, there are indications that the two distributions for Therapist JAE are more alike than either is to the ratings of Therapist HHS. Furthermore it will be seen that Therapist JAE sees his therapeutic operations differently from Therapist HHS.

456

We thus infer very tentatively that the observed differences may reflect more strongly different uses of the scales by the two therapists as well as differences in therapeutic technique rather than true patient differences. (Therapist JAE conducted a form of therapy that followed more closely the "classic" psychoanalytic model, whereas Therapist HHS employed a modified form of psychoanalytically oriented psychotherapy.) These divergencies seem to overshadow true differences among the three patients.

To document these inferences we shall comment upon the empirical findings in somewhat greater detail.

Therapist HHS saw Patient WA as exceedingly passive (showing an absence of *dominance*), which apparently was not true for Patients R and T; similarly, Patient WA was rated high on *dependence* much more frequently than either of the other patients. Passivity and dependence were indeed outstanding features of this patient's psychopathology. Her *resistance,* too, was rated as extremely great. Patient R emerges as more dominant than Patient T, but the degree of their dependence appears about equal, and the distribution of their ratings on resistance does not appear to vary markedly. Anxiety ratings seem to follow a similar pattern.

With respect to ratings of *affect*, Patient T receives the preponderance of high ratings; however, in this instance, all three dyads are reasonably comparable and well distributed over the range of the scale.

Therapist JAE gives virtually nothing but zero ratings on *sadism*, where Therapist HHS's ratings are distributed over the entire range. In the case of *masochism*, a very similar situation obtains. It is difficult to believe that one patient was so completely different in these respects and it seems very probably that the two therapists had markedly divergent definitions of these variables and made their ratings in very different ways.

There is little question but that Therapist HHS tended to give more extreme ratings on *hostility* than his colleague, whose two patients appeared very similar in this respect.

457

The same is largely true for ratings on *defensiveness, positive transference*, and *negative transference*. In each instance, Therapist JAE gives sizeable proportions of zero ratings whereas these are very small for Therapist HHS.

Patient T shows very little *competitiveness*, as reflected by the ratings, whereas the remaining two patients, for once, appear more similar.

Patient R emerges as the least *depressed* one of the three; again Therapist HHS tends to give more non-zero ratings.

Elation is one of the few clinical variables that shows very similar distributions for the three dyads, but a very large percentage of all ratings are still zero. Still, non-zero ratings, where they occur, may be important.

Therapist HHS's patient is credited more frequently with achieving *insight* than Therapist JAE's patients. The evidence suggests that we are dealing with a definitional problem rather than a clinical one. *Working through* discloses a similar situation.

The pattern of ratings for the two patients treated by Therapist JAE on *oral strivings* are highly similar; in this instance, Therapist HHS gives a preponderance of zero ratings.

The ratings of *oral, anal, phallic, oedipal*, and *genital* strivings must be suspected of extreme unreliability. (See Experiments 1, 2, and 3.) This is suggested not only by divergent use of the scales by the two therapists, the results of the preceding experiments, but also by comments from various clinicians (including the two therapists) expressing considerable uncertainty about the empirical referents.

The distributions of ratings dealing with aspects of therapeutic technique disclose marked inter-therapist differences. Therapist HHS intervenes and interprets much more frequently (as he sees it), and he regards his interpretations as markedly "deeper" than does Therapist JAE. Therapist JAE seems reasonably consistent with himself, except that he made "deep" interpretations much more frequently with

458

Patient R than with Patient T. Therapist HHS obviously is pursuing a much more active technique, as evidenced by his ratings on *initiative*.

Extremely large differences between the two therapists are disclosed when their self-ratings of attitudes and motivations are examined. For the most part, these discrepancies seem to reflect true differences in the two therapists' approach to psychotherapy, but it is also apparent that their understanding of the various scales must have differed very considerably. For example, in three out of four sessions Therapist JAE rated his motivation as "absent." This simply cannot be true if the ratings are interpreted literally. The rating sheet listed this item as "motivation, dedication, 'investment'," and in fact Therapist JAE scored this as present only when it clearly exceeded the "baseline" motivation that initiated his acceptance of the patients in the first place. At the risk of repetitiveness, let it be said again that the calibration of raters must be achieved through advance training.

It is noteworthy that, making allowance for patient fluctuations, Therapist JAE was reasonably consistent with himself. Therapist HHS, perhaps because he was the originator of the scales and, as a psychologist, more aware of the necessity to achieve "good" distributions, may have attempted to make greater use of the entire range of the scales and, where possible, avoided zero ratings.

The two therapists observed countertransference reactions in 16 to 20 per cent of their interviews; here, too, we find reasonable agreement between the two therapists as far as their respective distributions is concerned. Therapist JAE seemed to have the most intense and/or frequent reactions to Patient T. Ratings on negative attitudes showed similar agreement and in general parallel the distributions on countertransference.

Patterns of Intercorrelations

In the following we shall discuss similarities and differ-

459

ences in the correlational patterns obtained for the three patient-therapist pairs. Since one of the two therapists (JAE) contributed two sets of ratings, it will be possible to learn something about his mode of interaction as well as his rating tendencies with *two* patients.

As already indicated, we cannot be sure whether a given finding is idiosyncratic with respect to the therapist, the patient, and their mode of interaction, or whether it represents an invariant relationship that would obtain were we to study *any* therapist-patient pair. Between these two extremes of complete idiosyncrasy and a high generalizability there may be intermediate positions. For instance, a statistical relationship may apply to therapy with a hysterical patient, but not to others; it may apply to a therapist following a particular theoretical orientation (in this case the psychoanalytic), but not to therapists following different persuasions; it may apply to therapists of a given level of experience, but not to others, etc. In brief, how much any finding here reported can be generalized is open to question; however, considerable clarification can be obtained empirically simply by studying additional patient-therapist pairs. Therefore, the problem is not insoluble in principle.

Some measure of ability to be generalized is possible by virtue of our having collected data on three patient-therapist dyads. It is for this reason that we shall examine in some detail the patterns of relationships among the variables for each dyad. Where similar patterns of relationships obtain in the three patient-therapist pairs, we may consider ourselves on safer ground than in instances where a relationship is found only for one dyad. However, in any event, the number of dyads is too small for trustworthy conclusions. We shall only discuss those relationships that were stable across the three dyads. For purposes of exposition, we shall subdivide our discussion among clinical, technique, and attitudinal variables (of the therapist).

1. Patient States—Since we are dealing with three different patients who were being seen in psychotherapy for very different clinical problems, a high degree of non-overlap is to be expected. In fact, this is what we found. The relationships, even where they reached statistical significance for the three dyads, were for the most part low, and in a number of instances the patterns for the three patients were highly idiosyncratic.* Table 5 summarizes the relationships pertaining to patient states.

TABLE 5

STATISTICALLY SIGNIFICANT COEFFICIENTS OF CORRELATION (PRODUCT-MOMENT R'S) CONSISTENT FOR THREE THERAPEUTIC DYADS

CLINICAL VARIABLES: PATIENT STATES

Variable	Correlate	Pt. WA $N=173$	Pt. R $N=157$	Pt. T $N=327$
1. Dominance	5. Affect	19†	28	20
	8. Hostility	31	16	14
2. Dependence	7. Masochism	51	18	15
	17. Oral strivings	16	40	26
4. Anxiety	5. Affect	19	32	36
5. Affect	1. Dominance	19	28	20
	4. Anxiety	19	32	36
	8. Hostility	36	24	33
	12. Competitiveness			
7. Masochism	2. Dependence	51	18	15
8. Hostility, anger	1. Dominance	31	16	14
	5. Affect	36	24	33
	18. Anal strivings	50	18	16
12. Competitiveness, rivalry	5. Affect	27	16	16
	20. Oedipal strivings	22	32	23
17. Oral strivings	2.Dependence	16	40	26
18. Anal strivings	8. Hostility	50	18	16
20. Oedipal strivings	12. Competitiveness	22	32	23

† Decimal points omitted.

*While it would be tempting to discuss "unique" patterns of interrelationships for a particular dyad, this procedure seemed too speculative, for the reasons already indicated.

It is somewhat surprising that therapists' ratings of the degree of *anxiety* experienced by the patients were not related systematically to other variables for the three dyads. In fact, only *affect* tends to be systematically related to anxiety for all three patient-therapist pairs. As will be seen in the following, similar observations hold true for a number of clinical variables.

Oral strivings, as might be expected, show systematic relationships to ratings of *dependence,* which in turn is related to *masochism.*

All three patients, when seen to exhibit *oedipal strivings* are also rated as being *competitive,* which in turn is associated with ratings of *affect.*

Patients are considered to show signs of *affect* when they are *dominant, anxious, hostile,* and *competitive.* It is noteworthy that a number of other variables usually considered to have an affective component (e.g., depression, elation, etc.) fail to follow this pattern.

Hostility and *anger* show systematic relationships to *dominance* and *affect,* and, not unexpectedly, they vary concomitantly with ratings of *anal strivings.*

2. Transference—The foregoing variables are of course a function of the transference relationship, but for purposes of exposition we have segregated them from variables that are more specifically and explicitly related to transference phenomena in a technical sense. (See Table 6.)

Resistance and *defensiveness* were found to be appreciably correlated, at least in two of the three dyads. Similarly, there is a fair amount of overlap between ratings of *resistance* and *negative transference.* Patients, too, are rated as *resisting* when they exhibit *hostility* and *anal strivings.* Significant statistical relationships between *resistance* and *affect* were demonstrated, but in one case the relationship was a negative one. A patient who is *defensive* also tended to be seen as *anxious,* but like many of the relationships we have commented upon, this one was at a rather low level.

Positive transference, according to the therapists' rat-

462

TABLE 6

STATISTICALLY SIGNIFICANT COEFFICIENTS OF CORRELATION (PRODUCT-
MOMENT R'S) CONSISTENT FOR THREE THERAPEUTIC DYADS
CLINICAL VARIABLES: TRANSFERENCE

Variable	Correlate	Pt. WA $N=173$	Pt. R $N=157$	Pt. T $N=327$
3. Resistance	5. Affect	−18*	21	18
	8. Hostility	35	21	32
	9. Defensiveness	68	17	47
	11. Negative transference	59	19	30
	18. Anal strivings	33	18	20
9. Defensiveness	3. Resistance	68	17	47
	4. Anxiety	19	18	26
10. Positive transference	1. Dominance	29	28	26
	5. Affect	33	33	25
	15. Insight	48	27	35
	20. Oedipal strivings	38	24	42
11. Negative transference	3. Resistance	59	19	30
	8. Hostility	53	30	56
15. Insight	1. Dominance	26	24	38
	5. Affect	17	30	38
	10. Positive transference	48	27	35
	16. Working through	69	43	64
	20. Oedipal strivings	43	28	32
16. Working through	1. Dominance	35	36	43
	5. Affect	33	31	38
	10. Positive transference	61	47	32
	15. Insight	69	43	64
	20. Oedipal strivings	39	17	28

* Decimal points omitted.

ings, is characterized by *dominance, affect, oedipal strivings*,
and the emergence of *insight*.

Negative transference, on the other hand, is accompanied by *hostility*, and, as has already been pointed out, by
resistance.

The achievement of *insight* and the process of *working
through* appear to be markedly similar, at least in terms of
the ratings under discussion, and they show highly com-

parable statistical relationships to other variables such as: *dominance, affect, positive transference,* and *oedipal strivings.* It may deserve comment that in each instance *insight* discloses the higher relationships; possibly this means that ratings on this variable are statistically more reliable.

STATISTICAL RELATIONSHIPS INVOLVING TECHNIQUE VARIABLES (Table 7): There was some evidence that *frequency of interventions* tended to be correlated with *depth*

TABLE 7

STATISTICALLY SIGNIFICANT COEFFICIENTS OF CORRELATION (PRODUCT-MOMENT R'S) CONSISTENT FOR THREE THERAPEUTIC DYADS
TECHNIQUE VARIABLES

Variable	Correlate*	Pt. WA $N=173$	Pt. R $N=157$	Pt. T $N=327$
22. Frequency of interventions	24. Depth of interpretations	41†	19	18
	28. Support	55	19	25
	1. Dominance	24	47	32
	10. Positive transference	31	32	18
	15. Insight	37	29	28
	16. Working through	36	43	31
23. Frequency of interpretations	24. Depth of interpretations	61	65	78
	10. Positive transference	43	19	15
	15. Insight	43	24	22
	16. Working through	47	26	17
24. Depth of interpretations	5. Affect	23	32	33
	7. Masochism	22	18	25
	10. Positive transference	48	29	23
	15. Insight	58	24	23
	16. Working through	62	21	16
	20. Oedipal strivings	33	28	35
25. Initiative	26. Warmth	60	40	23
	29. Motivation	59	27	18
28. Support	15. Insight	52	18	18

* In each instance, the correlations between one technique variable and other technique variables are presented first. These entries are followed by the correlations between technique and clinical variables.
† Decimal points omitted.

464

of interpretation but not with *frequency of interpretation* (only in two instances). On the other hand, *frequency of interpretation*, within the limits of the present study, must be considered virtually synonymous with *depth of interpretation*.

It is difficult to say whether *support* should be considered a technique variable per se, but irrespective of this issue *frequent interventions* tended to be seen as supportive, which was not consistently true for interpretations.

Turning to the relationships between technique and clinical variables, we found the following associations:

Therapists tended to *intervene frequently* when the patient was *dominant*, evincing *positive transference*, achieving *insight*, and *working through*. They tended to *interpret frequently* and *deeply* under similar conditions. In addition, *deep interpretations* were made in the context of *affect*, *masochistic strivings*, and *oedipal strivings*.

Therapists tended to be more *supportive* when the patient was achieving *insight*.

Statistical relationships involving attitudinal variables (Table 8): Parallel to the preceding section, let us first examine statistical relationships among attitudinal variables. Here the most pronounced associations were found, suggesting a high degree of overlap among these variables.

In each instance, the therapists felt they were experiencing *positive attitudes* when they had a high degree of *motivation and investment* in the patient, when their *empathy* was high, when the *hour* was *productive*, and when they were *satisfied with the progress*. Under these conditions they also felt they were being *supportive*.

The converse was true for only two variables. Therapists experienced *negative attitudes* when they were *dissatisfied with the progress* and when they considered the *hour unproductive*.

Warmth was appreciably correlated with the therapists' feelings of *motivation, dedication, and investment*, but

465

to no other attitudinal variables. *Coldness* disclosed highly inconsistent relationships, as was true for *countertransference problems.* The latter, in particular, one would expect to be highly idiosyncratic and situationally determined, hence hardly replicable across dyads.

Empathy, productivity of the hour, and *satisfaction with progress* seemed to tap highly similar attitudes, as shown by their high interrelationships, and they appeared to be a function of *positive attitudes.*

How do therapists react attitudinally to different kinds of clinical constellations? If, as we have done throughout this section, we restrict ourselves to statistically significant relationships replicated across the three patient-therapist pairs, the following regularities emerged:

TABLE 8

STATISTICALLY SIGNIFICANT COEFFICIENTS OF CORRELATION (PRODUCT-MOMENT R'S) CONSISTENT FOR THREE THERAPEUTIC DYADS
ATTITUDINAL VARIABLES

Variable	Correlate*	Pt. WA $N=173$	Pt. R $N=157$	Pt. T $N=327$
26. Warmth	29. Motivation	69†	27	53
	10. Positive transference	56	29	19
	15. Insight	59	31	20
	16. Working through	59	25	13
	25. Initiative	60	40	23
	28. Support	77	17	31
29. Motivation, dedica-tion, "investment"	26. Warmth	69	28	53
	30. Positive attitudes	84	26	49
	10. Positive transference	49	23	26
	15. Insight	54	26	33
	16. Working through	58	28	31
	23. Frequency of interpretations	54	39	18
	25. Initiative	59	27	18
30. Positive attitudes	29. Motivation	84	26	49

* In each instance, the correlations between one attitudinal variable and other attitudinal variables are presented first. These entries are followed, in turn, by the correlations between attitudinal variables and clinical variables and between attitudinal variables and technique variables.
† Decimal points omitted.

466

TABLE 8 (CONT'D.)

Variable	Correlate*	Pt. WA $N=173$	Pt. R $N=157$	Pt. T $N=327$
30. Positive attitudes	33. Empathy	86	39	39
(*cont'd.*)	34. Productivity of hour	77	58	57
	35. Satisfaction with progress	77	54	65
	1. Dominance	16	25	41
	5. Affect	18	39	32
	10. Positive transference	51	47	46
	15. Insight	56	30	54
	16. Working through	57	49	54
	22. Frequency of interventions	48	37	31
	23. Frequency of interpretations	53	32	21
	24. Depth of interpretations	54	44	21
	28. Support	74	27	12
31. Negative attitudes	34. Productivity of hour	−44	−21	−16
	35. Satisfaction with progress	−46	−25	−27
33. Empathy	30. Positive attitudes	86	39	39
	34. Productivity of hour	74	44	42
	35. Satisfaction with progress	76	46	43
	1. Dominance	21	17	21
	5. Affect	19	35	25
	10. Positive transference	54	24	13
	16. Working through	53	18	32
	20. Oedipal strivings	40	27	20
	22. Frequency of interventions	45	25	24
	24. Depth of interpretations	51	29	21
34. Productivity of hour	30. Positive attitudes	77	58	57
	31. Negative attitudes	−44	−21	−16
	33. Empathy	74	44	42
	35. Satisfaction with progress	84	84	79
	1. Dominance	18	41	45
	5. Affect	27	47	39
	10. Positive transference	56	45	44

467

TABLE 8 (CONT'D.)

Variable	Correlate*	Pt. WA $N=173$	Pt. R $N=157$	Pt. T $N=327$
34. Productivity of hour (*cont'd.*)	15. Insight	59	22	54
	16. Working through	59	36	55
	20. Oedipal strivings	42	31	40
	22. Frequency of interventions	43	37	40
	23. Frequency of interpretations	47	30	28
	24. Depth of interpretations	62	60	44
35. Satisfaction with progress	30. Positive attitudes	77	54	65
	31. Negative attitudes	–46	–25	–27
	33. Empathy	76	46	43
	34. Productivity of hour	84	84	79
	5. Affect	24	48	35
	10. Positive transference	50	41	45
	15. Insight	59	28	53
	16. Working through	59	39	58
	17. Oral strivings	–17	47	32
	20. Oedipal strivings	42	33	36
	22. Frequency of interventions	42	47	37
	23. Frequency of interpretations	47	30	23
	24. Depth of interpretations	52	58	34

It seems to make little difference which attitudinal variable is selected for discussion because almost identical patterns of relationships can be demonstrated between them and certain clinical variables. *Warmth, motivation (dedication, "investment"), positive attitudes, empathy, productivity of the hour,* and *satisfaction with progress* each show marked associations with: *positive transference, insight,* and *working through. Dominance* and *affect* seem to follow this pattern, but there are some exceptions, and the coefficients

468

appear to be somewhat lower. Finally, *oedipal strivings* are consistently correlated with *empathy, productivity of the hour,* and *satisfaction with progress.*

It is quite apparent that therapists value manifestations in which the patient is moving in the direction of greater maturity, in which he shows a cooperative attitude with the therapist, in which he seems to be working on his problem, and achieving insight. The emergence of affect and the absence of submissiveness belong to this pattern. Oedipal strivings, at least in part, may be viewed as strivings toward greater maturity. Conspicuous by their absence are comparable negative relationships, such as might exist between resistance and negative attitudes in the therapist. One among many possibilities is that therapists may be more reluctant to acknowledge negative attitudes when they experience them.

Finally, we shall comment upon consistent relationships between attitudinal variables in the therapist and therapeutic technique variables.

Therapist *warmth* was found to be appreciably associated with *initiative* and *support.* Warmth, however, followed a somewhat unique pattern which was not replicated for the remaining attitudinal variables, which in their patterns of correlation appeared to "hang together." With minor exceptions, *motivation* (dedication, "investment"), *positive attitudes, empathy, productivity of the hour,* and *satisfaction with progress* each was markedly correlated with *frequency of interventions, frequency of interpretations,* and *depth of interpretations.* In addition, *positive attitudes* correlated with *support.*

The direction of causation is of course indeterminate, but in general—and this appears to be the most conservative interpretation of the relationships—we may say that therapists feel positively toward a patient when the latter is cooperative, working through, nondefensive, and showing signs of "maturity." At such times, too, they are more likely

469

to be "giving," as evidenced by more frequent and deeper interpretations. It is also this constellation which engenders in them feelings of warmth and empathy, satisfaction with the hour, and progress in general.

This may mean no more than that therapists evince typically "human" reactions: they feel pleased when the work is progressing and they feel frustrated when (presumably for unconscious reasons) the patient is thwarting their efforts. On the other hand, we may have here another demonstration of previously established relationships among therapists' clinical judgments, communications, and attitudes. These relationships were found in an experimental situation in which therapists responded as vicarious interviewers to a patient portrayed in a sound film, as well as in initial diagnostic interviews (Chapters Nine, Twelve, and Nineteen). In the present study we now have evidence that these relationships obtain equally in long-term, intensive psychotherapy. In our earlier publications we called attention to the possibility of a self-fulfilling prophecy that through conscious and unconscious attitudes may influence the therapist's clinical judgments, prognostications, as well as the nature of his interventions. Such attitudinal reactions in the therapist, if communicated to the patient, may reinforce the patient's initial negative attitudes and ultimately result in an impasse.

For example, the patient may be in a state of negative transference and he may be highly resistive during a particular hour. What our findings suggest is that the therapist reacts negatively (rejectingly?) to such maneuvers; he may become silent, withdrawn, etc., in turn and decide to "wait it out." We also glean from our results that under these conditions he becomes dissatisfied with the progress, tends to feel unempathic, and shows less warmth. We are not arguing that under conditions of intense resistance the best clinical and therapeutic procedure may not be for the therapist to remain benevolent, neutral, silent, noninterpretive, etc. It is quite likely, however, on the basis of the present results,

470

that the therapists' maneuvers because of their underlying attitudinal component may reinforce the patient's resistance rather than diminish it. The phenomenon of counter-resistance in the therapist has long been recognized as a countertransference problem. We do not wish to suggest that the therapist invariably falls victim to it; however, the strong likelihood of a relatively frequent occurrence of this phenomenon must be entertained.

In part, therapy consists in *rewarding*, hence reinforcing, those attitudes, moves, feelings, etc., in the patient that are in the direction of what the therapist conceives to be mental health (in terms of our findings, this includes positive transference, dominance, affect, oedipal strivings, and the achievement of emotional insight), and *punishing* (i.e., disregarding, neglecting, treating with silence) those moves that maintain the patient's defensive structure. As far as the evidence from the present investigation can be trusted, it is clear that therapists become *active* (i.e., interpretive) when they see the patient as collaborating, and they tend to become *passive* (at least in terms of frequency of verbal communications) when the patient is "opposing" them. The foregoing has long been known. What this investigation has contributed is certain evidence that both sets of operations by the therapist are not carried out in an attitudinal climate of detachment and neutrality, but rather that the therapist responds rather strongly on an emotional level. It is likely that he may be able to react therapeutically irrespective of these attitudes; the findings do not instruct us about the extent to which he is successful in this endeavor. Ideally, his therapeutic interventions should be largely immune from his personal feelings. We doubt that this is always, or even very often, the case, and suggest that irrespective of the therapist's professional training (including his personal analysis), his therapeutic operations are a function of his emotional and attitudinal response to the patient to a larger extent than is acknowledged by psychoanalytic theory (and most other therapeutic theories extant).

471

Recommendations

The preliminary nature of the foregoing experiment obviously precludes any conclusions. However, there are a number of lessons to be learned from our experience, and it is in the spirit of facilitating future work that the following recommendations are set forth (see also the section entitled "Prospectus"):

1. The greatest need appears to be for better definitions of the variables to be rated. Factor analysis or similar techniques might be used to isolate major dimensions that might have heuristic value.

2. The number of variables employed in this experiment is too large. Items that are too inferential, too difficult to define, too difficult to rate for other reasons, that are overlapping to an appreciable extent with items that are less beset with the foregoing shortcomings, and items that are judged inadequate on other grounds need to be eliminated or redefined. Also, a number of items that have shown promise should receive increasing focus.

3. Therapists or other judges using the instrument must be given careful training in its application, and a clear-cut consensus must be reached among judges before further experimentation is undertaken.

4. The units of observation must be clearly demarcated, although it may prove difficult to break the therapeutic hour down into small yet *meaningful* units. Arbitrary time periods do not seem to be the answer to this problem.

5. Once the necessary spadework has been completed, there is need to repeat similar longitudinal observations with the same therapist, but also with similar types of patients and different therapists. When the technical prerequisites have been met, a higher degree of comparability of patient-therapist pairs may be anticipated.

6. Related to the preceding point, there is need to compare different parts of the same therapeutic experience, for

472

example, before and after significant personality modification is believed to have occurred.

7. In all comparative studies (such as might be undertaken under Points 5 and 6) it will prove useful to discuss the quantitative findings in relation to the clinical phenomena as they are observed by the therapist during each hour. The value of such comparisons has been shown in Chapter Thirteen and by Auerbach (1963).

8. Despite the inadequacy of the pilot experiments reported in these pages, it seems highly justified to persist in efforts to improve the agreement among judges or between the therapist and a panel of observers. The achievement of a solid consensus among observers of the psychotherapeutic process concerning the phenomena under scrutiny is obviously a task of the highest priority, upon whose satisfactory solution the comparative study of psychotherapeutic interviews—whether we are dealing with individual hours or an entire course of therapy—ultimately depends.

Concluding Comments

The reader who has patiently followed the tortuous exposition of the difficulties surrounding the quantification of process phenomena in psychotherapy and the preliminary experiments we have carried out may well wonder concerning the substantive yield of these labors. It is amply apparent that the work here presented allows no definitive conclusions. What we intended to convey in this presentation, which may be likened to a visit of the researcher's laboratory, was a close-up of the tremendous obstacles facing the researcher in this area. Our efforts as yet are halting, our methodology is imperfect, and we are not even certain that the direction we have taken will turn out to be promising in the long run. Indeed, there are indications that other "mining techniques" may be more fruitful.

Essentially, there are two courses of action open to the researcher in this area: he can attempt to study the naturally occurring phenomena in psychotherapy and devise ways and means of quantifying them. To do so, he must conceptualize dimensions or categories that, according to his lights, promise the greatest returns. (This course has been followed in the present investigation.) Or, he can turn to experimental approaches, in the course of which he studies part-processes in the laboratory or in quasi-therapeutic situations. This course implies a recognition that the naturally occurring events are intrinsically too complex and not amenable to experimental control or manipulation, at least with our current research technique. (This approach has been followed in other investigations performed by our group, to which reference has been made in this chapter.)

Each of these approaches has its advantages and its shortcomings. Our efforts along both of these dimensions bespeak our uncertainty and our doubts as to which is most deserving of future effort. Perhaps this question cannot be answered at the current state of our knowledge, and considerable work must be undertaken in both of these areas before more definitive answers can be forthcoming. We have made a number of suggestions along the way concerning possible improvements of the methodology we have employed here. We hope they will stimulate others to carry forward the work which is needed.

We have no illusions about the immediate future. We do not believe that "break-throughs" are in the offing, although new techniques and advances in seemingly unrelated areas may bring unexpected progress. The field is very young, and research in it is exceedingly difficult. Patience and persistence are perhaps the qualities most sorely needed at this stage. We should be wary of gimmicks and easy solutions that promise great returns for small investments of time and energy. On the other hand, there is no reason to believe that efforts to study the phenomena of psychotherapy by the tools of science are foredoomed to failure. The gold (or, as Freud foresaw, the amalgam) is there: the techniques for assaying it are as yet woefully inadequate. Some may feel that they are not worth developing; others (among whom we should like to be counted) remain convinced of the lasting value of the "substance." In the final analysis, it is a question of values—whether a given researcher considers a particular goal worthy of pursuit.

References

Auerbach, A. H. 1963. "An Application of Strupp's Method of Content Analysis to Psychotherapy," *Psychiat.*, 26: 137-148.

Auld, F., Jr., and Murray, E. J. 1955. "Content-analysis Studies of Psychotherapy," *Psychol. Bul.*, 52: 377-395.

Bales, R. F. 1950. *Interaction Process Analysis.* Reading, Mass.: Addison-Wesley.

Bartlett, M. S. 1935. "Some Aspects of the Time-Correlation Problem in Regard to Tests of Significance," *J. Royal Stat. Soc.*, 98: 536-543.

——— 1946. "On the Theoretical Specification and Sampling Properties of Autocorrelated Time-Series," *Supp. J. Royal Stat. Soc.*, 8: 27-41.

Bellak, L., and Smith, M. B. 1956. "An Experimental Exploration of the Psychoanalytic Process," *Psychoanal. Quar.*, 25: 385-414.

Chassan, J. B. 1962. "Probability Processes in Psychoanalytic Psychiatry," in *Theories of the Mind,* ed. J. Scher, pp. 598-618. New York: Free Press.

Cohen, R. A., and Cohen, M. B. 1961. "Research in Psychotherapy: A Preliminary Report," *Psychiat.*, 24: 46-61.

Dittes, J. E. 1959. "Previous Studies Bearing on Content Analysis of Psychotherapy," in *Scoring Human Motives,* ed. J. Dollard and F. Auld, Jr., pp. 325-351. New Haven, Conn.: Yale University Press.

Greenacre, P. 1954. "The Role of Transference: Practical Considerations in Relation to Psychoanalytic Therapy," *J. Am. Psychoanal. Assn.*, 2: 671-684.

Haggard, E. A. 1958. *Intraclass Correlation and the Analysis of Variance.* New York: Holt, Rinehart & Winston.

Holt, R. R. 1958. "Clinical and Statistical Prediction: A Reformulation and Some New Data," *J. Abnorm. Soc. Psychol.*, 56: 1-12.

Janis, I. L. 1958. "The Psychoanalytic Interview as an Observational Method," in *Assessment of Human Motives,* ed. G. Lindzey, pp. 149-182. New York: Holt, Rinehart & Winston.

Marsden, G. 1965. "Content-analysis Studies of Therapeutic Interviews: 1954 to 1964," *Psychol. Bul.*, 63: 298-321.

Quenouille, M. H. 1952. *Associated Measurements.* London: Butterworth Scientific Publications.

Strupp, H. H. 1962. "Patient-doctor Relationships: Psychotherapist in the Therapeutic Process," in *Experimental Foundations of Clinical Psychology*, ed. A. J. Bachrach, pp. 576-615. New York: Basic Books.

Tolman, R. S. 1953. "Virtue Rewarded and Vice Punished," *Am. Psychol.*, 8: 721-733.

Part V
The Outcome
Problem

Every psychotherapist is firmly convinced that a substantial proportion of his patients is helped by his ministrations and that they "improve" as a result of his efforts. Conversely, a sizable proportion of patients (typically in the vicinity of 66 per cent to 75 per cent) is willing to agree. Unfortunately, these statistics do not answer such questions as what is the character of the improvement? Are the changes lasting? Can they be attributed to particular therapeutic techniques, or are they a function of so-called non-specific factors (e.g., faith, hope, expectancies, etc.) that play such an important role in all healing relationships? To what extent do the changes exceed a base rate of spontaneous recoveries?

While the issues are real, the literature has not been particularly helpful in clarifying them. My own position,

479

based on empirical work cited below, is embodied in the following quotation:

> . . . the term psychotherapy as used today is a multi-faceted conglomerate with fuzzy meanings; that as long as there is no reasonable consensus about methods, objectives, and outcomes, comparisons between different forms of therapy will remain largely meaningless; and that the effectiveness of psychotherapy is largely a problem of definition—of the investigator's (or the public's) value judgments about worthwhile outcomes. Because psychotherapy has traditionally been regarded as a kind of medical treatment, the concept of cure has often been employed as a seemingly reasonable criterion. We have shown the inappropriateness of this notion. Patients change, but no one is "cured" in the sense of being restored to a *status quo ante*, nor does there seem to be such a thing as "spontaneous remission"—certainly not among the patients we studied. It is safe to predict that when the changes that may be expected from particular psychotherapeutic procedures are specified, medical analogizing will be abandoned.
>
> It would help greatly to view psychotherapy as a form of education or as Freud called it, "after-education." What the patient in psychotherapy acquires are new perceptions of himself and others; he learns new patterns of interpersonal behavior and unlearns maladaptive ones. . . .
>
> At its best, individual psychotherapy creates a learning situation unequaled by anything else that human ingenuity has been able to devise. While costly in terms of money, time, manpower, and dedication of the participants to the common task, it remains one of the few monuments to the individual's worth, self-direction and independence in a collectivist society which fosters conformity and erodes individual values and autonomy in a host of ways. . . . In essence, it is an unrealizable ideal of self-discovery through learning and teaching in the con-

480

text of a human relationship uninfluenced by ulterior motives of any kind. What the patient, if he is fortunate, may receive is a glimpse, or perhaps even a reasonable approximation, of this ideal.

Contrary to my earlier views, I have become increasingly skeptical that psychotherapy has anything "special" to offer, in the sense that its techniques exceed or transcend the gains that may accrue to a patient (or should we say learner?) from a highly constructive human relationship. This is a testable hypothesis—perhaps one of the most basic that can be posited in the area—and I continue to be vitally interested in its exploration. If evidence sustains the view that common factors in all constructive human relationships are supreme, we would still face the formidable task of analyzing them, but we might become far less impressed by the ambitious theoretical formulations bequeathed to us by earlier writers.

It is still possible that a set of specialized techniques may potentiate the effects derivable from a good human relationship. If this is the case—the two hypotheses need not be mutually exclusive—we must spell out with greater precision the particular techniques that help particular patients under particular circumstances. In other words, is psychotherapy a form of behavioral engineering (technology) or is it a growth experience? There is a chance that under particular circumstances it may be both.

The articles included in this part deal with a conceptual analysis of the outcome problem. The views expressed in the foregoing are partly based on retrospective reports of former patients (Strupp, H. H., Fox, R. E., and Lessler, K. 1969. *Patients View Their Psychotherapy*. Baltimore: Johns Hopkins Press.).

16

THE OUTCOME PROBLEM
REVISITED

For reasons that will become more apparent later, the outcome problem in psychotherapy has been receiving relatively scant attention in recent years—not because the problem has lost its importance but rather because of a realization on the part of researchers that a new approach to the issue must be found, and that more pressing matters must be dealt with first before we can address ourselves meaningfully to the question of the effectiveness of psychotherapy. This rationale partly accounts for the great interest in so-called process studies that have swept the scene during the last decade. It appears that in the furor for "easy" quantifications we have largely lost sight of the rich potentialities for research in the transference situation, which unquestionably represents the greatest single methodological discovery

482

for interpersonal research in the twentieth century.*

One of the major difficulties in psychotherapy research is that of adequately specifying the independent variable—the psychotherapeutic methods—to which therapeutic changes are being attributed. Knight (1941), for example, cites the following characterizations (among others):

1. With regard to the preponderant attitude taken or influence attempted by the therapist; e.g., suggestion, persuasion, exhortation, intimidation, counseling, interpretation, re-education, re-training, etc.

2. With regard to the general aim of the therapy; e.g., supportive, suppressive, expressive, cathartic, ventilative, etc.

3. With regard to the supposed "depth" of the therapy—superficial psychotherapy and deep psychotherapy.

4. With regard to the duration—brief psychotherapy and prolonged psychotherapy.

5. With regard to its supposed relationship to Freudian psychoanalysis as, for example, orthodox, standard, classical, or regular psychoanalysis, modified psychoanalysis, "wild" analysis, direct psychoanalysis, psychoanalytic psychotherapy, psychoanalytically oriented psychotherapy, psychodynamic psychotherapy, psychotherapy using the dynamic approach, and psychotherapy based on psychoanalytic principles.

6. With regard to the ex-Freudian dissident who started a new school of psychotherapy. Thus we have Adler's individual psychology with its Adlerian "analysis," Jung's analytical psychology with its Jungian "analysis," the Rankian "analysis," the Stekelian "analysis," and the Horney modifications [pp. 52-53].

*The writing of this paper was aided by Research Grant No. M.3171 (C3), of the National Institute of Mental Health, Public Health Service.

I am greatly indebted to Dr. Martin Wallach for a critical reading of the manuscript and for a number of valuable suggestions for improvement.

What do these techniques have in common? What are their unique differences? What variance is introduced by the person of the therapist practicing them—his degree of expertness, his personality, and attitudes? These are staggering research problems, and the available research evidence by and large is insufficient. It seems to me that we shall not be satisfied with studies of therapeutic outcomes until we succeed in becoming more explicit about the independent variable. Thus the very extensive research efforts that are beginning to get under way in the area of the therapist's contribution, including his personality and techniques, are crucial as a prerequisite. I shall merely mention in passing that variables in the patient's life situation, social class and other environmental factors, are also increasingly being studied. This work is bound to have a cumulative effect.

Let us stay, however, with the method of treatment and consider further its relation to outcomes, disregarding (what in reality cannot be disregarded) therapist variables and socioenvironmental factors. Some methods of psychotherapy are more intensive than others—in terms of effort, aim, duration, and the like. If we asked clinicians to rank order different methods of psychotherapy on this continuum, we would undoubtedly find that psychoanalysis, four times a week, for two or more years, would rank at the top and once-a-week supportive therapy in which the patient is seen for a total of 5-10 sessions would be rated somewhere near the bottom. Let us go a step further and predict that therapeutic outcome is (partly at least) commensurate with the effort expended—not an unreasonable assumption in education, training, and child-rearing. It would then follow that, other things being equal, the results achieved by psychoanalysis should be substantially greater than those resulting from minimal treatment methods. We shall for the moment set aside a specification of "greater" but merely suggest that even with crude measuring instruments (which is all we have at present) the demonstration of differences in outcome between the two methods should be a fairly simple matter.

The literature, unfortunately, is replete with quasi-documentation that has hopelessly fogged the issue.

A brief review of Eysenck's (1952) widely quoted survey, which capitalized upon and added considerably to the existing confusion, may be instructive. In order to make any meaningful statements about the effects of psychotherapy, Eysenck reasoned, it is necessary to compare psychotherapy patients with "untreated controls." The effects of psychotherapy, if any, would thus be demonstrated in terms of differences between the two major groups. The "base line" was provided by two studies, one dealing with the percentage of neurotic patients discharged annually as recovered or improved from New York State hospitals, the other a survey of 500 patients who presented disability claims due to psychoneurosis and who were treated by general practitioners with sedatives and the like. The assumption was made in these two studies that the patients did not receive psychotherapy, or at least not anything resembling "formal" psychotherapy. The amelioration rate in both studies was in the neighborhood of 72 per cent. Typical criteria of recovery were: (1) return to work and ability to carry on well in economic adjustments for at least a five-year period; (2) complaint of no further or very slight difficulties; (3) making of successful social adjustments.

The results of these studies were compared by Eysenck with 19 reports in the literature dealing with the outcomes of both psychoanalytic and eclectic types of psychotherapy. Pooling the results, he found that patients treated by means of psychoanalysis improved 44 per cent; patients treated eclectically improved 64 per cent; patients treated only custodially or by general practitioners improved 72 per cent. Thus, paradoxically, it appears that there is an inverse relationship between intensity of psychotherapeutic treatment and rate of recovery.

A situation in which clinical experience is completely at variance with statistical data usually calls for a searching analysis to discover possible sources of error. However,

Eysenck answered—to his satisfaction—the question that the "control" patients were as seriously ill as the treated patients, and that the standards of recovery were equally stringent for both groups. His paper also shows that contrary to the subsequent popularizations of his findings (by himself) he was well aware of the limitations of the comparison. However, he takes seriously his conclusion that "roughly two-thirds of a group of neurotic patients will recover or improve to a marked extent within about two years of the onset of their illness, whether they are treated by means of psychotherapy or not [p. 322]."

Several writers have taken Eysenck to task for his conclusions, pointing out numerous fallacies in his design. For example, his so-called untreated control groups are almost certainly deficient for the purpose; the criteria for discharge from a state hospital are undoubtedly very different from those of a psychoanalytic treatment center; and the "spontaneous recoveries" may, for all we know, be spurious. If this is true, or even if the "spontaneous recovery" rate is grossly overstated, Eysenck's uncritical acceptance of these figures and his unfortunate conclusion to abandon the training and practice of psychotherapy forthwith would be rash. Furthermore, if two-thirds of all people who suffer from a "neurosis" "recovered" within two years "after onset," emotional disorder would scarcely be the serious problem it manifestly is. Finally, one may take issue with Eysenck's assertion that psychotherapists must do significantly better than 72 per cent before they can make any legitimate claim for the efficacy of their procedures.

Even if Eysenck's arguments are ill-founded, we should take a close look at the results reported by the psychoanalytic treatment centers, because it may be presumed that the most intensive, the most ambitious, and the most thoroughgoing form of psychotherapy is practiced there. Eysenck's data abstracted from published reports are given in Table 1.*

Eysenck points out that in this tabulation he classed those who stopped treatment together with those who were

486

rated as not improved. This seemed reasonable to him on the ground that a patient who failed to finish treatment should be considered a therapeutic failure. However, if only those patients are considered who completed therapy— about one-third broke off treatment—the percentage of successful treatments rises to about 66 per cent (Eysenck). Although it may be true that errors in technique may have been responsible for some of the premature terminations, it seems quite unjustified to regard such cases as "therapeutic failures"; by the same token, the efficacy of insulin therapy is hardly adequately represented by including those diabetics for whom it was prescribed but who failed to adhere to the regimen.

Eysenck presented his tabulation of results from therapy under four headings: (1) cured, or much improved; (2) improved; (3) slightly improved; (4) not improved, died, discontinued treatment, etc. This criterion is undoubtedly crude; it may be unreliable; it may reflect an impossibly high standard of perfection; it may be entirely incomparable to the judgments made for the "control" cases or for the studies of "eclectic psychotherapy." But, over-all assessments are often the best we have, and in many areas of psychological measurement they have been shown to have a

---

*I have reexamined the original sources quoted in Part A of Eysenck's Table 1 in an attempt to reconcile the two sets of data. I have been utterly unable to do so. To be sure the various reports are not uniform, and it is difficult to bring the figures under common denominators. Nevertheless, on the basis of the published reports the therapeutic results are regularly more favorable to psychoanalysis than is suggested by Eysenck's tabulation—in some instances markedly so. There can be no doubt that Eysenck's zeal has led him to place the worst possible interpretation upon the results. It is also abundantly clear from the reports that exceedingly stringent criteria were employed in classifying outcomes. Thus, the standards employed in these sources were very different from the ones used elsewhere by Eysenck.

It is regrettable that in more recent years psychoanalytic institutes seem to have increasingly desisted from publishing such data, perhaps partly on the grounds that they are easily misinterpreted.

487

TABLE 1 (*From Eysenck, 1952*)

SUMMARY OF REPORTS OF THE RESULTS OF PSYCHOTHERAPY

	N	Cured; much improved	Improved	Slightly improved	Not improved; died: left treatment	% Cured; much improved; improved
(A) *Psychoanalytic**						
1. Fenichel (1930; pp. 28–40)	484	104	84	99	197	39
2. Kessel and Hyman (1933)	34	16	5	4	9	62
3. Jones (1936; pp. 12–14)	59	20	8	28	3	47
4. Alexander (1937; pp. 30–43)	141	28	42	23	48	50
5. Knight (1941)	42	8	20	7	7	67
All cases	760	335		425		44%

* Part B (Eclectic) omitted.

highly valid core. This would hold true on even stronger grounds where the raters have had ample opportunity to make observations and have intimate knowledge of the person being rated. Where would such conditions be met more perfectly than in psychoanalytic treatment? Irrespective of the validity or meaningfulness of Eysenck's comparisons, the statistics reported by the four* psychoanalytic treatment centers may be accepted as reasonable assessments. Still, there is the somewhat disconcerting fact that some 21 per cent of the patients treated were only "slightly improved" and 35 per cent fall into the limbo category "not improved, died, discontinued treatment, etc." However the data are analyzed, we are left with the conclusion that psychoanalysis was only slightly successful or unsuccessful for about 30 per cent of the patients who at one point were accepted for therapy. Since they were accepted for therapy we may presume that at that time, at least, they were considered suitable candidates for this form of psychotherapy. Apart from the fallibility of the criterion measure (which has been considered to be relatively slight), the lack of success may be attributed to the following factors, or a combination of these:

1. Errors in judgment about the analysand's suitability;
2. factors in the patient's psychopathology or character structure that emerged as insurmountable obstacles after therapy began;
3. deficiencies in the method of treatment;
4. inadequacies of the therapist's technical skills or shortcomings of his personality;

*The study of Kessel and Hyman (1933) is out of place in Part A of Eysenck's Table 1, which focuses on psychoanalytic institutes and treatment centers. In contrast, the source of Kessel and Hyman's data is obscure, and no information is given about the characteristics of their sample. Most damaging is the fact that the evaluations of treatment outcome were made by unqualified judges (internists), who themselves disavow any competence in psychoanalysis.

5. vicissitudes of the particular patient-therapist interaction that resulted in a therapeutic impasse; and

6. variables in the patient's (and/or the therapist's) life
situation that produced adverse effects.

Some of these factors may have been predictable at the
beginning of therapy provided more complete information
had been available; others may have been completely fortuitous and beyond human control. For example, if we had
precise information that patients with a certain character
structure fail to benefit markedly from psychoanalysis 80 to
90 per cent of the time, and if we could be sure that Patient X
is a member of that class, it would be unwise to recommend
psychoanalysis for him. Or, if we had precise information
that patients with a certain personality structure in 80 to 90
per cent of the cases come to grief when entering therapy
with a therapist having a particular personality structure,
one would advise them accordingly and help them select a
more suitable therapist. Fortuitous circumstances (e.g., a
fatal illness) need no further illustration. The point to be
made is this: Considering the extremely important implications of the decision in advising a patient to enter or not to
enter psychoanalysis (or, for that matter, any form of psychotherapy), it would be highly advantageous from the
therapist's as well as the patient's point of view to have
precise information about the outcome that might reasonably be expected. An increase in the power to predict the
outcome of psychotherapy would indeed represent a tremendous advance: not only would it conserve money, energy,
and professional manpower, it would enhance the scientific
status of psychotherapy to an unprecedented degree. In
order to compete with other forms of treatment, psychotherapy and psychoanalysis need not establish that they are
superior to anything else that is available; their claim to
existence, survival, and development rests on the establishment of a large number of empirical, highly predictable
relationships among key variables that are based on a coher-

490

ent theory of demonstrable utility. What is necessary is a theory that accounts for highly predictable *and* measurable therapeutic gains.

What is meant by "outcome"? In Eysenck's review and in many of the studies on which it is based, the term is used in extremely loose fashion. Eysenck himself treats neurosis in analogy to a form of physical illness, which allegedly one may contract at one time or another during one's lifetime, which seems to run an almost self-limiting course, and from which the patient somehow recovers through therapy or spontaneously. Anyone having the slightest familiarity with psychopathology and psychodynamics knows how erroneous and misleading such a conception is. I shall not pursue this point at the moment but plan to return to it in a somewhat different context. For the moment, it must be conceded that irrespective of our conception of neurosis or mental disorder there is such a thing as outcome from therapy. But, what kind of criterion is it?

Holt (1958), in an insightful and lucid article, tells us that there is a hidden trick in global predictions because they are not themselves a form of behavior but a judgment made by someone on a great deal of concrete behavior. This is true of grades in college, success in any type of treatment, and the like. "Because it is hidden by the label," Holt says, "there is a temptation to forget that the behavior you should be trying to predict exists and must be studied if it is to be rationally forecast." As long as one relies on global clinical judgments, like outcome, no matter how remarkable clinical judgments may sometimes be, one substitutes something for real information, and where there is no genuine information to begin with, none can be generated.

What needs to be done is
to decide what intervening variables need to be considered if the behavior is to be predicted (and) to deal with the inner constructs that mediate behavior and the determining situational variables as well. . . . The best

491

practice seems to be to give explicit consideration to this step (the formation of clinical judgments), and to supply judgment with as many relevant facts as possible. This means studying known instances, comparing people who showed the behavior in question with others who in the same situation failed to [p. 2].

To translate Holt's lesson to the therapy situation, it is futile to make judgments and predictions about outcome as long as we have paid insufficient attention to variables in the patient, the therapist, the method of therapy, the patient-therapist interaction, and the surrounding life situation. It is this realization, I believe, that in recent years has caused investigators in the area of psychotherapy to lose interest in "simplistic" (Luborsky's term) outcome studies of the kind we have been discussing and turned them to sustained research upon the psychotherapeutic process itself. Nevertheless, it seems to me, we shall again and again return, armed with more specific data, to the problem of outcome, no matter how arbitrary an end point it may represent.

The following sections deal with two areas having a bearing on the problem of outcome; both represent important frontiers of research, although clearly they are by no means the only, or even the most important ones. But in both researchers have had more than a modicum of success in mapping, in charting, and in establishing the kinds of empirical connections of which Holt speaks. To be sure, the progress cannot be termed spectacular or a "breakthrough," but it represents the constructive, painstaking, gradual effort that is needed. I am referring to the area of the patient's motivation for therapy, including patient-therapist compatibility; and, secondly, to analyses dealing with the criterion problem. Progress in the former area is more impressive than in the latter, but both unquestionably represent cornerstones on which the scientific edifice of psychotherapy must ultimately rest.

From a fairly large body of converging empirical evi-

492

dence, which I shall not review here, it is becoming increasingly clear that therapists have fairly specific—and presumably valid—notions about the kinds of attributes that a "good" patient should possess, as well as about those attributes that make a patient unsuitable for the more usual forms of investigative, insight-producing psychotherapy. Patients considered good prognostic risks tend to be young, physically attractive, well-educated, members of the upper-middle class, possessing a high degree of ego-strength, some anxiety impelling them to seek help, no seriously disabling neurotic symptoms, relative absence of deep characterological distortions or strong secondary gains, a willingness to talk about their difficulties, an ability to communicate well, some skill in the social-vocational area, a value system relatively congruent with that of the therapist, and a certain psychological-mindedness that makes them see their problems as emotional rather than physical. A number of these attributes appear to be statistically linked to social class. This linkage extends to the patient, the therapist, and the principles of psychotherapy to which he subscribes.*

Hence, therapists tend to select those patients whose attributes meet the above criteria. It is hard to say whether therapy is effective because therapists invest their best efforts when these conditions prevail or whether the existence of these conditions in itself presages favorable results. Both

---

*This formulation readily lends itself to the misinterpretation that promising candidates for psychotherapy are not really "sick." This inference would be quite unwarranted, and it is in part a reflection upon the primitive status of currently available assessment techniques. By superficial behavioristic standards a person may be described as "mentally healthy" if he meets gross behavioristic criteria of performance, such as functioning in a particular social role, earning a living, absence of gross disturbances in interpersonal situations, absence of gross psychopathology, and the like. Yet, such conformity or seeming adaptation may be achieved at tremendous psychic cost; the individual may feel intensely unhappy, inhibited, conflicted, etc. It appears that, broadly speaking, psychoanalysis pays the closest attention to, and evinces the greatest respect for, the individual's intrapsychic

statements are probably true to some extent, although variables within the patient and situational variables may play a more important part than the therapist's attitudes and expectations.

Every neurotic patient is unconsciously committed to maintain the status quo, and psychotherapy, particularly if aimed at confronting the patient with his inner conflicts, proceeds against the obstacle of powerful unconscious resistances. Therefore, unless there is a strong conscious desire to be helped and to collaborate with the therapist, the odds against a favorable outcome may be insuperable. Motivation for therapy is a global and a highly complex variable; research has shown that it is made up of combinations of the variables in the patient that have already been mentioned. But, it represents a clinical judgment made by the therapist, which in turn is colored to a significant extent by his own personality and attitudes. Because psychotherapy demands great investments of time and emotional energy from the therapist, it is hardly surprising that his willingness to enter into a therapeutic relationship with a particular patient becomes highly selective. We know that different therapists, depending on their own personality, have highly individual preferences, which it would be important to elucidate. It seems reasonable to hypothesize that therapeutic relationships in which the patient is highly motivated to seek thera-

---

organization and its function in the person's *fine* adjustment to himself and others. The latter is completely lost sight of in the statistical tabulations dealing with treatment outcomes. Unfortunately, there are no adequate measures of self-respect, a sense of worthwhileness as a person, emotional well-being arising from an ability to be at peace with oneself and others, a sense of relatedness, and identity—values that in this age of materialism largely seem to have lost their meaning. Unless we acknowledge that the integration and full unfolding of the human personality are worth striving for, no matter what the expenditure of therapeutic time and effort may be, and unless it becomes possible to reflect such achievements in tabulations of statistical results, we may be forced to concede that the future lies with tranquilizing drugs rather than with psychological techniques.

494

peutic help and in which the therapist in turn is highly motivated to put his skills at the patient's disposal have, other things being equal, the greatest chance of success.

For example, Kirtner and Cartwright (1958), studying 42 cases at the University of Chicago Counseling Center, found a significant association between treatment outcome and the manner in which the client conceptualized and presented his problem in the initial interview. Failure cases tended to intellectualize and discussed external manifestations of internal difficulties. Successfully treated cases, on the other hand, tended to deal with feelings in the therapeutic relationship and were eager to discover how they were contributing to their inner difficulties. No doubt, the second group was considered more suitable by the client-centered therapists. While it cannot be proven, it is entirely possible that those patients who felt they could be helped by client-centered therapy (and by client-centered therapists) continued to work on their problems, whereas those who did not, dropped out. One may also speculate that the therapist's motivation to help the latter group of patients, for a variety of reasons, was less. Thus, the therapist's attitude toward the patient may reinforce corresponding attitudes in the patient, leading to premature termination of therapy. There is no implication that this phenomenon is restricted to one form of therapy or to any one stage of therapy; however, the judgment of therapeutic failure, premature termination, therapeutic impasse, poor motivation for therapy, and the like, wherever it occurs, may signal an unwillingness or inability on the part of the therapist to work with a particular patient as much as it reflects limiting factors within the patient.

Empirical evidence bearing upon this problem has been adduced by our research group in a series of studies dealing with therapists' perceptions of patients, clinical judgments, treatment plans, and therapeutic communications. In some of these studies therapists were presented with a sound film of a therapeutic interview (see Chapter Nine); in others,

495

they based their evaluations on patients seen in diagnostic interviews (see Chapter Nineteen); in still others, we presented therapists with written case histories (see Chapter Twenty). The findings have been remarkably congruent, and are corroborated by similar studies in the literature. Certain systematic differences in therapist responses were traceable to such variables as level of experience, theoretical orientation, and personal analysis. However, in all investigations the therapist's attitude toward the patient as rated by himself showed a highly significant statistical relationship to his clinical judgments and treatment plans, and, where we obtained such data, to the emotional tone of his communications. In recent studies, an item that inquired whether the therapist felt warmly toward the patient proved particularly predictive. For example, negative attitudes toward the patient were found to be correlated with a more unfavorable diagnosis and prognosis, with recommendations for greater strictness and activity on the part of the therapist, with recommendations for less frequent interviews, with greater unwillingness to treat him, etc. The reverse was also true.

With regard to the therapists' communications, there was a significant relationship between the degree of empathy shown toward the patient and the therapist's self-rated attitude; therapists who felt more positively toward the patient also communicated with him more empathically. The variable of personal analysis entered into this statistical relationship in a very interesting way: if the therapist had undergone a personal analysis he was more likely to reveal a high degree of empathy in his communications irrespective of whether he described his attitude toward the patient as positive or negative. This finding was particularly pronounced for the more experienced therapists. Thus it seemed that in the case of experienced therapists their personal attitude toward the patient was less likely to influence the emotional tone of their communications to the patient provided their training had included a personal analysis; if it

496

had not, a negative attitude tended to be associated with lack of empathy.

These findings relate to the possibility that the therapist's attitude toward the patient, as conveyed by his communications, may bring about a realization of the therapist's conscious as well as unconscious expectations concerning the course and outcome of therapy. For psychotherapy the crux of the matter is not the perceptions and clinical evaluations or even the therapist's conscious attitude toward the patient; rather it is the manner in which these variables influence and structure the therapeutic relationship. This is one of the important problems requiring further exploration.*

It is as yet unknown to what extent the patient may fulfill the therapist's unverbalized prophecy. This much, however, is clear: in the absence of a keen and abiding interest and dedication on the part of the therapist, the patient cannot marshal the necessary strength and energy to fight his way to a healthier adaptation, or, to use Dr. Alexander's felicitous term, he cannot undergo a corrective emotional experience. This is particularly true in those situations in which the therapist aims at a thorough reorganization of the patient's personality by inducing him to relive his childhood traumas. Too, the infinite patience that dedicated therapists like Frieda Fromm-Reichmann, Otto Will, Harold Searles, and others have invested in therapy with schizophrenic patients bears eloquent tribute to the proposition that often therapeutic gains are commensurate with the efforts expended by the therapist, provided the patient possesses good basic personality resources.

On the experimental side, numerous studies attest that patients who appear to be motivated for psychotherapy (however the therapist understands this term) tend to be liked by therapists and the prognosis is seen as more favor-

---

*This discussion and the following paragraphs underscore the interdependence of "process" and "outcome" research and the importance of predictions at the beginning and throughout therapy.

able (see Chapter Twenty). Heine and Trosman (1960) have shown that mutuality of expectation is an important factor in the continuation of the therapeutic relationship. In this study, patients who continued in psychotherapy conceptualized their expectations of therapy in a manner more congruent with the therapist's role image, and may therefore have been more gratifying to the therapist. Similarly patients who were judged nondefensive, insightful, likable, and well motivated for therapy were seen by therapists as most likely to improve (see Chapter Nineteen). In the same vein, Sullivan, Miller, and Smelser (1958) summed up their findings by saying: "Those persons who are least equipped to meet life challenges are the ones who stand to gain least from psychotherapy [p. 7]."

Now it may be conceded that a high level of motivation on the part of the patient as well as on the part of the therapist is auspicious for successful psychotherapy, but what about that large group of patients who fail to meet the above high criteria? What shall be done with them? Secondly, nothing has been said about the chronicity and severity of the personality disorder the therapist is attempting to treat. Surely, no matter how highly a patient may be motivated to seek professional help and how eager he may consciously seek to do something about his difficulties, this desire may count for little if his personality structure poses insuperable difficulties to therapy.

To be sure, apart from the patient's motivation for therapy, there are clinical indicators that set limits to the therapist's best efforts. Freud dealt with these most eloquently and exhaustively in his paper "Analysis Terminable or Interminable" and elsewhere. The therapist cannot perform miracles, and he cannot exceed the limits set by constitutional and hereditary factors; nor can he always undo the crippling conditions brought about by extremely adverse childhood experiences. In this dilemma the therapist has essentially two choices: he can attempt to select patients whom he considers promising candidates for psychotherapy,

498

and with whom he feels he can work productively, rejecting all other applicants; he can recognize the limitations imposed by reality and do his best even if he realizes that in such instances his success may be less than spectacular. What he must not do—and here we return to the experimental findings cited earlier—is to let *irrational* personal attitudes about the treatability or nontreatability of certain patients and clinical conditions influence the best technical efforts he might otherwise put forth. At the present state of knowledge, the dividing lines between clinical indicators and limitations on the one hand, and personal attitudes of the therapist on the other, are unfortunately not as clear as one would like them to be. If they could be disentangled and assessed more objectively, the prediction of therapeutic outcomes would be markedly enhanced, and the percentage of patients who emerge from therapy as "slightly improved" or "unimproved" might dwindle further to approach that ultimate, irremediable hard core contributed by "chance."

Undoubtedly there is no simple relationship between diagnostic indicators and therapeutic outcomes, and much remains to be learned about the problem; in principle there seems to be no reason why it should not be susceptible to conceptual analysis and empirical research—the kind of "job analysis" approach Holt proposes. Traditionally, the "classical" neurotic conditions, like hysteria, have been considered ideally suited for psychotherapy and psychoanalysis, whereas severe character disorders and the psychoses have been relegated to the opposite end of the treatability continuum of psychotherapy. Such judgments are partly based upon clinical experience; but in part they also reflect subtle value judgments about the kinds of persons with whom psychotherapists prefer to work, as well as an appraisal in sociocultural terms of the patient's character structure and symptoms. Consequently, a patient meeting the psychotherapist's explicit as well as implicit criteria of a "good" or "promising" patient not only has a better chance of finding a competent therapist, but he may from the beginning elicit greater interest from the therapist, who in turn may become more willing to make an emotional investment in the treatment program and to devote greater energy to the treatment. How much the patient may fulfill the therapist's unverbalized prophecy is at yet unknown. However, it may turn out that a great deal more can be done for certain patients psychotherapeutically once it is possible to approach them and their difficulties in living more objectively.

After many of the variables that need investigation and specification have been sorted out, we may find that only a relatively restricted band of the population meets the criteria for a "good" patient. The available evidence points to a convergent trend, which was aptly summarized by Luborsky (1959): "Those who stay in treatment improve; those who improve are better off to begin with than those who do not; and one can predict response to treatment by how well they are to begin with [p. 324]." It may be noted that the criteria of suitability that have been identified by research coincide remarkably well with those outlined much earlier by Freud. What about the much larger group of people who by these standards are unsuitable for the more common forms of psychotherapy practiced today?

From a practical point of view, the answer seems to lie not in making them more amenable to available methods of psychotherapy—sometimes this can be done, although it is a difficult and time-consuming effort—but in becoming more selective about making the limited facilities and the limited professional manpower available to those who can benefit from it the most. Rather than being "undemocratic," this appears to be a counsel of reality. Research might make an important contribution by refining the selection of particular patients for particular therapists and for particular therapeutic methods. The challenge for the development of alternative techniques and treatment methods for those who cannot readily benefit from customary psychotherapy of course continues and will have to be met. To return once again to the statistical results previously cited, there is a strong possibility that a segment of the failure or near-failure cases can be accounted for in terms of poor selection methods of candidates. In some cases it may be better to acknowledge limitations imposed by reality, no matter how painful the consequences may be, rather than to attempt the impossible.

I shall turn next to another major stumbling block in psychotherapy research—the problem of criteria for evaluating results. Before the advent of the "modern era" in psychotherapy research, that is, before sophisticated methodologists and researchers versed in matters of objective investigation and experimental design concerned themselves with these matters, a group of prominent psychoanalysts, including such men as Glover, Fenichel, Strachey, Bergler, Nunberg, and Bibring (1937), addressed themselves to the issue. This occurred at the International Congress of Psychoanalysis at Marienbad, in 1936. While this group did not make any formal recommendation for judging outcomes, it dealt with the aims of psychoanalytic therapy and its modus operandi. Knight (1941), in a valuable paper, returned to the problem, listing three major groups of criteria, with several subheadings. Since this compilation has not been substantially improved upon, let me quote it in its entirety:

1. *Disappearance of presenting symptoms*
2. *Real improvement in mental functioning*
   a. The acquisition of insight, intellectual and emotional, into the childhood sources of conflict, the part played by precipitating and other reality factors, and the methods of defense against anxiety which have produced the type of personality and the specific character of the morbid process;
   b. Development of tolerance, without anxiety, of the instinctual drives;
   c. Development of ability to accept one's self objec-

501

tively, with a good appraisal of elements of strength and weakness;

    d. Attainment of relative freedom from enervating tensions and talent-crippling inhibitions;

    e. Release of the aggressive energies needed for self-preservation, achievement, competition and protection of one's rights.

3. *Improved reality adjustment*

    a. More consistent and loyal interpersonal relationships with well-chosen objects;

    b. Free functioning of abilities in productive work;

    c. Improved sublimation in recreation and avocations;

    d. Full heterosexual functioning with potency and pleasure.

Knight, too, called attention to certain limitations, that may detract from the full effectiveness of the therapeutic method. These will be recognized as the counterparts of the "good patient" variables previously mentioned. Limitations may be due to:

1. the patient's intelligence;

2. native ability and talents;

3. physical factors, such as muscle development, size, personal attractiveness, physical anomalies, sequelae of previous injury or illness, etc.;

4. permanent crippling of the ego in infancy and childhood;

5. life and reality factors that might impose frustrations, privations, etc., against which the patient must do battle, and that might produce relapses;

6. the patient's economic status, whether there is too little or too much money.

It is apparent that Knight's enumeration of criteria goes far beyond a definition of disabling illness and in fact it attempts a definition of positive mental health. It is also clear that the objectives of psychoanalytic therapy have always aspired to this ideal, and the outcome statistics reported by the various psychoanalytic treatment centers leave no doubt on this point. As early as 1930, Fenichel stated in this connection:

> We have defined the concept "cured" as rigorously as possible. We have included in this category only cases whose success involves not only symptom removal but which underwent character changes that are rationally and analytically completely understandable and which, where possible, were confirmed through follow-up. In view of this rigor, most of the cases designated as "much improved" are for practical purposes completely coordinate with the "cured" ones. "Improved" cases are those which have remained refractory in one form or another; in this category also belong those cases which for external reasons had to remain partial successes, as well as those which were discharged already in the phase of "transference cure," hence, psychoanalytically speaking they must be considered questionable [p.19].

By contrast, Eysenck's survey implicitly adopted a much less rigorous standard, oriented around symptom removal. His compilation is a telling example of the confusion that arises when one uncritically mixes studies in which a variety of criteria, frequently unspecified, are adopted. This dilemma, however, cannot be resolved until we succeed in developing more specific empirical indicators of treatment outcomes. Among other things, this requirement entails operational definitions that can be agreed upon by independent observers. For example, there may be reasonable agreement on the meaning of "symptomatic recovery," but a moment's reflection will reveal the difficulties inherent in such judgments as "increased productiveness" or "achievement of sufficient insight to handle ordinary psychological conflicts and reasonable reality stresses."

Knight seems to take it for granted that the evaluations

are to be made by the therapist. While it may be conceded that the therapist's knowledge of the patient's psyche is second to none, and that therefore he is in a unique position to perform the evaluative task, it must be remembered that his judgment is vulnerable on a number of grounds, including his personal involvement as well as the necessarily segmental view he obtains of the patient's life.

In an effort to objectify the therapist's observations many attempts have been made during the last two decades to develop measures of the patient's intratherapy behavior. These have usually taken the form of quantifying aspects of his verbal behavior in therapy. Another large group of studies has followed the phenomenological approach, by asking the patient to evaluate his own status. A third approach has dealt with assessments by means of psychological tests. Zax and Klein (1960), following a review of several hundred investigations, conclude that the most serious failing of these approaches is that the criterion measures have not been systematically related to externally observable behavior in the life space of the patients. Their own proposed solution is to develop "criteria of sufficient breadth that they are meaningful and representative of a wide range of functioning and yet, at the same time, circumscribed enough to be measured with reliability [p. 445]." They go on to say that the development of such criteria is in its infancy, largely because there is no unifying set of principles (a theory of "normal" behavior) to guide observations. Finally, they express the hope that it might be possible to develop "a relatively limited number of norms reflecting basic interpersonal environments which can be useful." The basic problem here seems to be one of bridging the gap between the person's inner psychic experience and his adaptation to an interpersonal environment.

Clearly, there can be no single criterion of mental health or illness. As Jahoda's (1958) excellent review of current concepts points out, mental health is an individual and personal matter; it varies with the time, place, culture

504

and expectations of the social group; it is one of many human values; and it should differentiate between the person's enduring attributes and particular actions. One value prominent in American culture is that the individual should be able to stand on his own two feet without making undue demands or impositions on others.

From the research point of view, Jahoda discerns six major approaches to the subject:

1. Attitudes of the individual toward himself.

2. Degree to which a person realizes his potentialities through action (growth, development, self-actualization).

3. Unification of function in the individual's personality (integration).

4. Individual's degree of independence of social influences (autonomy).

5. How the individual sees the world around him (perception of reality).

6. Ability to take life as it comes and master it (environmental mastery).

In her searching and incisive discussion of the directions for further research Jahoda clearly indicates that we must develop better empirical indicators of positive mental health in all of the above areas; beyond this it is necessary to specify the conditions under which it is acquired and maintained. The development of outcome criteria in psychotherapy largely overlaps these requirements and must follow a similar course. The patient's behavior in therapy will scarcely suffice as an ultimate criterion, but it will occupy a central position in the cluster of criteria that will undoubtedly emerge. The therapy situation is a unique "test situation" in this respect, whose rich potentialities we have barely begun to exploit. I should like to outline briefly some of the unique advantages as well as some of the limitations.

1. By virtue of its particular structure, the therapeutic situation, and particularly the psychoanalytic situation, re-

moves the conventional restraints in interpersonal communication and makes it possible to observe the patient's "real" feelings and emotional reactions with a minimum of distortions.

2. By inducing regression it uncovers invaluable data about the patient's most enduring patterns of interpersonal relatedness and facilitates the tracing of their genetic development.

3. It provides a penetrating view of the patient's motivational patterns, the manner in which basic strivings are bound intrapsychically, adapted to, and translated into action. Such microscopic observations are carried out over extensive periods of time. Thus it is possible to trace the relationship between an action and its underlying motivation, and to gain considerable information about the mediating processes. Hence the therapeutic situation avoids a frequent error in psychological research, namely the assumption of an invariant relationship between a behavioral act and the person's underlying motivation.

4. The therapeutic situation simulates an appropriately complex situation and thus meets the objections of oversimplification and artificiality frequently leveled against experimental analogues. (It has been said that the therapeutic situation represents a highly personal situation within a highly impersonal framework.)

5. In the therapeutic situation, the therapist gains important insights into the patient's inner experience, the manner in which he perceives himself, and his self-concept; but he also can assess the patient's social stimulus value—at least in relation to the therapist as a representative of the social environment, and observe discrepancies between inner experience and outward actions. Usually we are restricted in our knowledge of the other person and we can only make inferences from his actions, his verbal communications, and clues we get from his unwitting behavior. In individual therapy, by contrast, the patient himself, through the agency of his observing ego, adds important data about his inner

experience to the aforementioned ones. Thus a unique, panoramic view is obtained.*

6. The therapeutic situation yields unique data on the manner in which a particular input (clarification, interpretation, etc.) is perceived, experienced, and reacted to on verbal as well as nonverbal levels. Thus, we may gain considerable information about the manner in which an external stimulus is perceived and experienced, and we may note discrepancies between the "objective" aspects of the stimulus (at least as seen by the therapist) and the way in which it is experienced by the patient.

These are some examples to indicate the variety of ways in which the psychotherapeutic situation provides criteria—which in part have their own validity—about human mental functioning. But we demand that intratherapeutic criteria have a counterpart in the external world, that is, a validity beyond the therapeutic situation. It is noteworthy that in the various mental health criteria enumerated by Jahoda the therapeutic situation plays an important part in gathering more precise empirical indicators. The therapeutic situation itself should be used to a much greater extent than has been heretofore the case to generate and develop criteria of outcome. Nowhere else do we have an opportunity to make as penetrating, intensive, systematic, and undistorted observations as in the therapeutic setting.† Furthermore, it is in keeping with one of the

---

*Although it adds other complexities, group psychotherapy provides more than one representative of the social environment; and it permits the patient to test his motives, actions, inner processes, etc., against the background of the feelings of others.

†This recommendation is far from original. More than a quarter of a century ago, in the first five-year report of the Chicago Psychoanalytic Institute, Dr. Alexander (1937) concluded that the analyst and the patient are in the best position to judge the actual progress made and the weights to be assigned to analytic insight and the altered life situation in evaluating the therapeutic result. Unfortunately, very little has been done in the interim to design objective research investigations embodying this insight.

major working hypotheses of psychoanalysis, that the patient's relationship to the therapist (the transference) is the most faithful replica of the patient's capacity for intimate interpersonal relatedness; as a corollary it states that the patient's adaptation to his human environment outside the therapeutic situation "improves," that is, becomes less conflictual, and more satisfying to the extent that he is able to relate more effectively (in less conflictual ways) to the therapist. The skilled therapist is keenly aware of the shifts in the patient's patterns of relatedness (to him), and he regards them as sensitive indicators of therapeutic change and improvement. What I am advocating, then, is that as researchers we attempt to systematize and objectify these intratherapeutic observations and, wherever possible, relate them to the patient's interpersonal performances outside therapy.

In making this recommendation I am placing major emphasis upon the therapy situation as a miniature life situation, and I am stressing the alignment of psychic forces rather than specific behavioral acts in the outside world. This view is predicated on the (testable) assumption that there is a close association between the quality of the patient's relationship to the therapist and the quality of his relationships with others, including his adaptation to reality. I am also suggesting that the therapist, because he is in possession of incomparably fuller data about the patient's personality, is potentially in a superior position to assess the patient's "mental health." No therapist would maintain that the patient's behavior with close associates or his mastery of life's problems is unimportant, but he is probably correct in insisting that he (in collaboration with the patient) is better equipped to assess the patient's success in living than outsiders irrespective of the degree of their sophistication.

Among the difficulties of using the therapeutic situation as a criterion-generating situation we must note:

1. The problem of conceptualizing, specifying, and

508

quantifying the multidimensional observations made in therapy;

2. the therapist's reliability as an observer (by which is meant more than countertransference); and

3. limitations inherent in the two-person setting, which provide representative, but incomplete, data about the patient's interactions with others. Because of the transference relationship, the therapist tends to get a more or less distorted perspective of the patient's current reality functioning and to some extent he is forced to accept the patient's view of reality, although he will generally be able to make appropriate corrections.

These recommendations, which need to be spelled out in much greater detail before they can be translated into research operations, are in keeping with my conviction that the transference situation, as defined by Freud, is the richest source for observing and studying interpersonal data, and that it has a unique validity of its own. Nowhere else is it possible to study interpersonal processes as systematically, intensively, deeply, and with as much control over extraneous influences. The task for the future is to find ways and means for ordering and quantifying the observations, and to aid the human observer in dealing more systematically and more objectively with the complex data in his auditory-visual field. "Validation" cannot come from experimental analogues and similar devices, and a naive faith in their seeming objectivity may merely serve to deprive us of the potentialities inherent in the transference relationship.

References

Alexander, F. 1937. *Five Year Report of the Chicago Institute for Psychoanalysis, 1932-1937.* Chicago.

Eysenck, H. J. 1952. "The Effects of Psychotherapy: An Evaluation," *J. Cons. Psychol.,* 16: 319-324.

Fenichel, O. 1930. "Statistischer, Bericht über die therapeutische Tätigkeit 1920-1930," *Zehn Jahre Berliner Psychoanalytisches Institut,* pp. 13-19. Vienna: Int. Psychoanalytischer Verlag.

Glover, E., Fenichel, O., Strachey, J., Bergler, E., Nunberg, N., and Bibring, E. 1937. "Symposium on the Theory of the Therapeutic Results of Psychoanalysis," *Int. J. Psychoanal.,* 18: 125-189.

Heine, R. W., and Trosman, H. 1960. "Initial Expectations of the Doctor-Patient Interaction as a Factor in Continuance in Psychotherapy," *Psychiat.,* 23: 275-278.

Holt, R. R. 1958. "Clinical *and* Statistical Prediction: A Reformulation and Some New Data," *J. Abnorm. Soc. Psychol.,* 56: 1-12.

Jahoda, M. 1958. *Current Concepts of Positive Mental Health.* New York: Basic Books.

Jones, E. 1936. *Decennial Report of the London Clinic of Psychoanalysis, 1926-1936.* London.

Kessel, L., and Hyman, H. T. 1933. "The Value of Psychoanalysis as a Therapeutic Procedure," *J. Am. Med. Assn.,* 101: 1612-1615.

Kirtner, W. L., and Cartwright, D. S. 1958. "Success and Failure in Client-centered Therapy as a Function of Initial In-therapy Behavior," *J. Cons. Psychol.,* 22: 329-333.

Knight, R. P. 1941. "Evaluation of the Results of Psychoanalytic Therapy," *Am. J. Psychiat.,* 98: 434-446.

Luborsky, L. 1959. "Psychotherapy," in *Annual Review of Psychology,* Vol. X, ed. P. R. Farnsworth and D. McNemar, pp. 317-344. Palo Alto, Calif.: Annual Reviews.

Sullivan, P. L., Miller, C., and Smelser, W. 1958. "Factors in Length of Stay and Progress in Psychotherapy," *J. Cons. Psychol.,* 22: 1-9.

Zax, M., and Klein, A. 1960. "Measurement of Personality and Behavior Changes Following Psychotherapy," *Psychol. Bul.,* 57: 435-448.

17

THE OUTCOME PROBLEM:
A REJOINDER

The controversy about the value of psychotherapy has been
with us for some time, and it is not likely to be resolved by
argument or counterargument. The question in its crudest
form, "Does psychotherapy do any good?," is largely a
specious one, and most researchers and clinicians have lost
enthusiasm in attempting to answer it in these terms. Clinical observations amply document that many patients benefit
from an interpersonal relationship with a professional person
when they are troubled by difficulties in living and are seeking help. To argue otherwise is simply to close one's eyes to
the facts. Researchers have increasingly recognized during
the last decade that there are more important questions to
be answered by research, such as: What is the relative
effectiveness of different methods of psychotherapy? What
kinds of personality changes occur as a result of particular

kinds of therapeutic interventions? How do patient and therapist variables influence the therapeutic interaction?, etc. Researchers have also realized that many questions cannot be answered conclusively until we learn to measure with greater precision kinds and qualities of outcome, the nature of the patient's disturbance before therapy, changes in personality structure, and the important characteristics of the therapeutic influence as mediated by the therapist. Dr. Eysenck's 1952 article certainly did much to awaken investigators to "the many difficulties attending . . . actuarial comparisons" and the shortcomings of previous studies.

My own work (see the preceding chapter), which Dr. Eysenck attacks, took issue with his *conclusions*. There is little point in making comparisons until we know what we are comparing. Ratings of "improvement" are for the most part inadequate and insufficiently sensitive; and terms like "eclectic psychotherapy" are too vague when pitted against the "control groups" that are the fulcrum of Eysenck's argument. As others have pointed out before me, these "control groups" cannot be considered a legitimate base line.

Eysenck never showed that patients in psychoanalysis and psychotherapy derived no benefits—in fact, the reported figures, such as they are, point to very respectable success rates. Eysenck's conclusion, as I tried to show in my work, hinges upon the adequacy of the control groups, which, in my judgment, are highly suspect. His point is essentially that unless patients treated by psychotherapy or psychoanalysis improve significantly more than the so-called untreated controls, the former treatment methods are useless.

True, he admits that "The figures quoted do not necessarily disprove the possibility of therapeutic usefulness," but the whole tenor of his arguments over the years strongly suggests that he does not take this possibility very seriously. As Dr. Eysenck admits, each individual will have to decide what conclusions, if any, he is willing to draw. To this, I fully agree.

Whether behavior therapy, psychoanalysis, or some

512

other form of therapy is more efficient under specified conditions is certainly a legitimate question for future research. But this takes us back to the measurement problems I mentioned earlier. To be sure, it is important to free a patient from—say—a troublesome phobia, and everyone would agree that symptom relief is a *sine qua non* in psychotherapy. But, we must not lose sight of the patient's *intrapsychic* state—his sense of identity, feeling of worthwhileness as a person, and happiness. From an actuarial point of view, these factors may seem unimportant; to some therapists they may seem fuzzy and "soft"; but, to some psychologists, they are as real and essential as any behavioral criterion. Unfortunately, we have made little progress so far in measuring them and in including them in our criteria of "outcome."

18

THE LIMITATIONS
OF PSYCHOTHERAPY

Drs. Grinspoon, Ewalt, and Shader (1967) build a rather convincing case for the general ineffectiveness of long-term psychotherapy with chronic schizophrenic patients. At the same time, the use of drugs was not exactly impressive either, to wit: " . . . it should be emphasized that the observed changes did not suggest that the patient was any less schizophrenic. For the most part, it merely meant that the group exhibited less florid symptomatology." Nevertheless, considering the severity of the patients' disturbance, symptomatic improvement is not to be depreciated. If one accepts the authors' pessimistic conclusion, perhaps this is the best that can be done for such patients, given the present-day knowledge of our science and technology. Where does this leave us?

Before considering some of the implications, I wish to

record my impression that Grinspoon, Ewalt, and Shader's study is more impressive as a clinical report than as a carefully controlled experiment, but I am quite willing to accept the accuracy of their observations and the validity of their findings. Lest this comment be considered gratuitous, it may be pointed out that, contrary to arguments frequently seen these days, much can be learned from studies even if they do not fully meet the most rigorous canons of science. Undoubtedly, though, this report will be chalked up as another score by those embarked on a crusade to demonstrate the general inefficacy of psychotherapy, particularly that following the psychoanalytic model. Especially damaging in this instance is the fact that the psychotherapy was in the hands of experienced and skilled practitioners, rather than novices, which is more commonly the case. One wonders, however, about the conditions that induced these therapists to undertake the treatment.

Rather than demonstrating the ineffectiveness of psychotherapy *in general,* this paper underscores its limitation— a conclusion toward which I am inclining with increasing conviction. Psychotherapy, including psychoanalysis, is not a panacea. It never was, and I do not believe it ever will be. The question is how this myth ever got started and how it came to gain currency. Psychotherapy comprises a specialized set of techniques, applicable to specific circumstances and conditions, and no more. But also no less. Once clinical and laboratory research succeeds in spelling out with greater precision the particular techniques that help particular patients under particular circumstances, the field will gradually be freed from the confusion with which it is still beset. On the other hand, as long as the myth persists that psychotherapy (understood as a global entity) is a panacea for all of man's emotional and adaptational ills, therapists will come to grief, patients will be disillusioned, and the critics will continue to gloat.

Freud's basic conservatism in restricting the applicability of psychoanalysis essentially to the transference

515

neurosis is well known; likewise, he reiterated his emphasis on the prerequisite of a basically reliable ego. More recently, Anna Freud (1954) commented:

> If all the skill, knowledge and pioneering effort which was spent on widening the scope of application of psycho-analysis had been employed instead on intensifying and improving our technique in the original field (hysteric, phobic, and compulsive disorders), I cannot help but feel that, by now, we would find the treatment of the common neuroses child's play, instead of struggling with their technical problems as we have continued to do [p. 610].

One must agree with Grinspoon, Ewalt, and Shader that prolonged psychotherapy under the stated conditions is largely of academic interest. The fact that dedicated therapists like Frieda Fromm-Reichmann, Harold Searles, and Otto Will have achieved remarkable results with schizophrenic patients after many years of heroic effort does not mitigate this judgment. In this connection it may be noted that the outlook for their patients was probably more promising than was true of the patients under discussion. The latter appear to belong to the group of process schizophrenics, who, as we know, have the poorest prognosis.

If psychotherapy is more akin to a learning process than to medical treatment—a belief to which this writer subscribes—then learning can take place only if certain preconditions are met. To use a crude analogy, it is predictable that a person with an I.Q. of 80 will not benefit from a college education, which proves nothing about the value of educational techniques for those to whom they are suited. The future of psychotherapy, as I see it, lies in delineating patient, therapist, and technique characteristics that in proper combination have a reasonable chance of producing or enhancing a specified outcome. In this effort, concerted research efforts may be counted upon to reap rich results.

If this means, as I think it does, that psychotherapy in

its various forms has relatively little to offer to a rather large segment of the patient population, this is regrettable and perhaps even tragic; but such a realization may also spur efforts to seek solutions along different lines. Drugs may not be able to produce cures, but as the paper by Grinspoon, Ewalt, and Shader (together with research from other centers) shows, they help. Amelioration, perhaps for a longer time, may be the best that can be done for a large number of patients.

However, I do not believe that psychotherapy has fully realized its potential. In a revealing passage, the late David Rapaport (1960) stated:

> Therapies or therapists . . . end up by establishing their own McCarran Act: sooner or later they announce that this or that kind of patient is not the right kind for their kind of therapy. Not rarely they go further and announce that this or that kind of patient is "not treatable." In the long run, psychological theories of therapy must come to a point where they will make it possible to select the therapy which is good for a patient and not the patient who is good for a therapy [p. 115].

In a sense, Rapaport was unduly harsh in his judgment. I see nothing wrong with systematic explorations that may reach the conclusion that a given technique, or combination of techniques, is not suitable for a certain patient or patient groups. Why should a technique be applicable to all persons under all circumstances? A psychotherapist who undertakes the treatment of a patient against great odds deserves our admiration; but the total enterprise of psychotherapy should not be faulted if his "batting average" is low. By the same token, therapists as a group should not be induced to undertake the impossible or the improbable. I believe we are entering an era in which the claims and aspirations of psychotherapy will become more circumscribed and more focused. It may also spell a return to greater modesty, from which we should never have departed.

References

Freud, A. 1954. "The Widening Scope of Indications of Psychoanalysis," *J. Am. Psychoanal. Assn.,* 2: 607-620.

Grinspoon, L., Ewalt, J. R., and Shader, R. 1967. "A Preliminary Report on Long-Term Treatment of Chronic Schizophrenia," *International Journal of Psychiatry,* 4: 116-128.

Rapaport, D. 1960. *The Structure of Psychoanalytic Theory.* New York: International Universities Press. *Psychol. Is.,* Vol. II, No. 2 (Monograph 6).

518

Part VI
Who Are the "Good" Patients in Psychotherapy?

Beginning with Freud, much has been written about the "suitability" of patients for psychotherapy. In accordance with the disease model, Freud laid great stress on clinical considerations—severity of the patient's disturbance, degree of incapacitation, chronicity, "type" of neurosis, and so on. However, he also recognized that youth, level of education and sophistication, "strength of character" (later termed "ego strength"), ability and willingness to tolerate frustration, and—perhaps most important—motivation to undertake and persist in the hard work that, he felt, therapy inevitably entailed. On the subject of the therapist's personal attitude toward the patient, Freud vacillated: on the one hand he maintained that it was immaterial whether the therapist "liked" the patient, adding that he had been able to help many patients with whom he had little in common and whom, by implication, he did not care for as persons; on the other, he asserted that the therapist cannot possibly do good work with individuals whom he does not respect. In his later writings Freud did not concern himself greatly with the therapist's "liking," evidently believing that the concept of the countertransference was adequate to take care of most contingencies.

Since the decision to accept a patient for psychotherapy—particularly long-term psychotherapy—requires a rather major commitment on the part of the therapist, clinical and personal impressions are of critical importance in early interviews. In fact, numerous therapists (e.g., Gill, Newman, and Redlich, 1954) regard the initial interview as perhaps the single most important encounter between the participants. One reason for this position is the realization that, at least within limits, the therapists' initial impressions may act as a self-fulfilling prophecy, so that patients judged to have a good prognosis will in fact improve, and vice versa. It is also likely that therapists will invest greater effort in patients toward whom they are more positively disposed.

The two chapters in this part, while attacking the problem from somewhat different angles, present converging findings: *motivation for therapy* emerges as the key variable determining the therapist's liking for the patient as a person, as well as the quality of his clinical evaluations, particularly when the patient's disturbance is judged to be relatively mild. On the basis of other evidence, Luborsky (1959) noted: "Those who stay in treatment improve; those who improve are better off to begin with than those who do not; and one can predict response to treatment by how well they are to begin with [p. 324]."

Motivation for therapy undoubtedly embodies many components that are in need of greater specification. For one thing, it implies the patient's desire to get "well," to change in the direction of greater "mental health," to do what the therapist thinks is required to launch him on that

521

road. However, it probably means more. It includes a willingness to strive for the goals and values espoused by the therapist (as an agent of society or as a representative of American middle-class standards); a potential compliance with socially accepted and approved values; a striving to realize oneself "within" the social system, i.e., a readiness to become more socialized by submitting to the therapist's influence; a greater acceptance of parental and social authority; a commitment to the ethos of work, responsibility, independence, and achievement along socially valued lines; an implicit acknowledgment of wanting to be a "good child" vis-à-vis the therapist. In contrast, therapists tend to be rejecting of patients whom they view as "anti-social," "acting out," etc. (see Part II). These findings underscore the fact that therapists are not treating a "disease" (except in a highly metaphoric sense); instead, they see themselves (implicitly, but correctly, I believe) as functioning *in loco parentis*. Consequently, their clinical judgments are not medical assessments of a disease process but rather a mixture of moral approval (or disapproval) coupled with a prognostication of whether the client, as a function of the therapist's influence, is likely to change, grow up—become a mature adult, as defined by our culture.

References

Gill, M. M., Newman, R., and Redlich, F. C. 1954. *The Initial Interview in Psychiatric Practice*. New York: International Universities Press.

Luborsky, L. 1959. "Psychotherapy." In *Annual Review of Psychology*, Vol. X, ed. P. R. Farnsworth and Q. McNemar, pp. 317-344. Palo Alto, Calif.: Annual Reviews.

19

SOME DETERMINANTS OF CLINICAL EVALUATIONS (WITH J. V. WILLIAMS)

The use of the interview as a diagnostic technique continues in spite of the many questions raised about its reliability and validity. There is a subjective feeling of comfort and security to be had from seeing and talking with a person that persists even when the information gained, translated, and sorted into ratings, predictions, and the like, fails to correlate with other variables (Kelly and Fiske, 1951). Those who feel that the interview has little value state that in an unstructured situation there is too great a danger that the interviewer will be biased by his own needs and attitudes. Robinson and Cohen (1954) found reliable differences in the case reports of interns in clinical psychology that were related to the personality characteristics of the interns, and somewhat similar results were reported by Raines and Rohrer (1955) in a study of psychiatrists' ratings of naval officer candidates.

523

Although probable officer success could be predicted at a better than chance level, the psychiatrists did not agree with one another on their ratings, and they showed significant differences among themselves in the frequency with which they "observed" different personality types. The study discussed in Chapter Nine demonstrated that therapists reacted very differently to the patient in a film of an initial interview and that variations in their clinical evaluation of his personality and his suitability for psychotherapy were associated both with length of experience as a therapist and with attitude toward the patient. The more experienced therapists tended to like the patient less, and a negative attitude toward the patient was associated with a less favorable evaluation and with ratings of a poorer prognosis.*

This chapter attempts to clarify the interrelations of diagnostic and prognostic evaluations and attitudes toward the patient, as well as to assess the reliability of judgments based on a single interview. Although, for the most part, the determinants of these judgments will be the same for both of the psychiatrists involved, there will be other, more idiosyncratic factors that reflect the personality and values of the interviewer rather than the objective situation.

PROCEDURE

Briefly, two interviewers independently assessed 22 psychiatric patients and, after the interview, recorded their impressions on a simple rating form.

INTERVIEWERS: Interviewer 1 was a British psychoanalyst who visited the department for a period of three months. He is internationally known for his work in analytic group psychotherapy and has had extensive experience (over 30 years) with patients in individual psychoanalysis as

---

*This study was made possible through the support of a research grant (M-2171) from the National Institute of Mental Health, U.S. Public Health Service.

524

well. In terms of his theoretical orientation, he may be considered orthodox Freudian. This was his first experience with American patients.

Interviewer 2 was a young psychiatrist, a regular member of the departmental staff. He has had several years of experience in psychiatry and is currently pursuing psychoanalytic training. The two interviewers first became acquainted at the time of this investigation.

SUBJECTS: All subjects were psychiatric inpatients at North Carolina Memorial Hospital, the teaching hospital of the North Carolina School of Medicine. The criteria for the selection of subjects were (1) relatively recent admission to the hospital, so as to minimize the effects of psychotherapy they had received, and (2) reasonably good contact with reality and the ability to participate, to some extent at least, in the interview. For the purpose of the group situation the further constraint was added that either two men and two women or all members of the same sex be seen each week. Parenthetically, it might be stated that for the most part the inpatient service does not treat very severely disturbed or chronic patients, the average length of stay in the hospital being about one month. In all, 22 patients were included in this study (16 women and 6 men).

INTERVIEW SITUATION: In the course of a 2-month period all 22 patients were seen for a brief initial interview by both of the psychiatrists, who worked completely independently of each other. Therapist 1 saw the patients for an hour in groups of four. Therapist 2 conducted individual 15-minute interviews with each of the patients. Four patients were seen each week for six weeks,* the order of the interviews being alternated so that one week the group interview occurred first, the next week the individual interviews, etc. Neither therapist had any previous information about the

---

*One patient refused to participate, and another left the hospital before the second interview could take place, thus reducing the number from 24 to 22.

patients he was to see beyond the knowledge that they were all inpatients at the hospital where the experiment took place. There was no communication between the therapists until the ratings had been completed.

The two psychiatrist-interviewers were free to structure the interviews in any way they chose. All interviews were conducted in a room with a one-way vision screen and were observed by from 1 to 25 persons. These included staff psychiatrists, residents in psychiatry, groups of medical students on rotational assignment to psychiatry, and the investigators. There was a microphone in full view of the patients, and a tape recorder in the observation room recorded all the interviews. While the patients were aware that they were being observed, they were largely unaware of the purpose of the investigation. Most accepted it as part of the hospital routine; some were resentful, and a few were hostile. Certainly the presence of observers and the ambiguity of the situation contributed to their anxiety, particularly in the group situation.

Although no instructions were given to the therapists as to how they should conduct the interviews, the knowledge that they would not see the patients again, that they would be asked to fill out questionnaires, and that they had a very limited amount of time at their disposal probably led both therapists to structure the interview so as to gather as much information as possible. Both the group and the individual interviews tended toward the kind of question-and-answer interchange between therapist and patient that would lead to a diagnostic evaluation.

RATINGS

After each session the psychiatrist filled out a questionnaire giving his diagnostic impressions and recommendations for treatment and, for the purposes of this study, rated patients on the following 14 variables, using a 5-point scale: Dominance, Anxiety Shown, Emotional Maturity,

Hostility, Complainingness, Independence, Defensiveness, Capacity for Insight, Degree of Disturbance, Motivation for Therapy, Degree of Improvement Expected in Therapy, Therapist's Interest in Treating Patient, Amount of Support Therapist Would Give Patient, Therapist's Liking for Patient as a Person. The open-ended Recommendations for Treatment were similarly scaled, the more intensive forms of psychotherapy receiving higher scores.

A correlational analysis of these ratings was done, yielding an index of agreement on each variable for the two therapists, as well as the intercorrelation of the items for each therapist separately. In addition, partial correlations were run on what appeared to be the five key variables in this study. The differences between means of the two raters were analyzed using the t test.

RESULTS

The initial question to be asked of the data was whether the two therapists who interviewed the patients in different situations would agree in their impressions. Table 1 presents the product-moment coefficients of correlation between the ratings on each variable. Table 2 is an analysis of the difference between means. Table 1 indicates that 9 of the 15 coefficients exceeded the 5 per cent level of significance, indicating that the two raters agreed fairly well in their assessment of these patients. On the other hand, Table 2 demonstrates that there were often absolute differences in the use of the scale, even though relative placement of the patients might be the same. On some occasions these differences do contribute to a lack of correlation. Therapist 1, for example, saw all patients as very disturbed and did not believe in extending support, and he had an extremely restricted range on these variables. Perhaps lack of a common frame of reference was also manifested in low agreement on the more personal variables, such as interest in treating a particular patient. In this connection, it subse-

527

TABLE 1

AGREEMENT BETWEEN TWO INTERVIEWERS
$N=22$

Variable	r
Dominance	0.35
Anxiety	0.22
Emotional maturity	0.58*
Hostility	0.46†
Complainingness	0.51†
Independence	0.11
Defensiveness	0.46†
Capacity for insight	0.47†
Disturbance	0.01
Motivation for therapy	0.56*
Degree of improvement expected (prognosis)	0.53†
Interest in treating patient	−0.05
Support to be given	0.12
Liking for patient	0.69*
Treatment recommendations	0.53†

* Significant at 0.01 level.
† Significant at 0.05 level.

quently became known that one of the interviewers was considering his own overcrowded schedule and desire for variety, while the other was reacting in a less subjective fashion. The substantial agreement on a number of variables is noteworthy, however, particularly in view of differences in the raters' age, training, experience, and cultural background.

The second question to be asked was whether the same variables would be seen as interrelated for both therapists and, specifically, whether the same ones would be seen as important prognosticative signs. Table 3 reports the intercorrelations of all the variables computed separately for each rater. It may be noted that the five scales measuring Defensiveness, Capacity for Insight, Motivation for Therapy, Prognosis, and Liking for the Patient as a Person were highly intercorrelated for both therapists. This might be called the "good-patient" cluster. In addition, there was

TABLE 2

DIFFERENCES BETWEEN MEANS FOR THE TWO INTERVIEWERS
$N=22$

Variable	Mean*	S.D.*	t
Dominance	2.77	1.07	
	2.68	1.32	0.03
Anxiety	3.55	1.01	
	3.14	1.17	1.28
Emotional maturity	2.91	0.87	
	2.05	0.58	3.28†
Hostility	3.27	1.03	
	3.73	0.77	1.58
Complainingness	2.64	0.90	
	3.41	1.05	2.31‡
Independence	2.73	0.83	
	1.91	0.75	3.00†
Defensiveness	3.41	1.10	
	2.64	1.26	2.30‡
Capacity for insight	3.00	1.07	
	2.82	1.22	0.54
Degree of disturbance	4.59	0.59	
	3.45	0.74	4.56†
Motivation for therapy	3.18	1.10	
	2.86	1.28	0.95
Degree of improvement expected	3.59	1.26	
	3.00	1.07	1.23
Interest in treating patient	2.64	1.05	
	2.45	1.14	0.59
Support	2.05	0.84	
	3.59	0.67	5.78†
Liking for patient	3.05	0.72	
	2.41	1.01	2.23‡
Recommendations for treatment	3.18	1.53	
	3.27	1.28	0.02

* The ratings for Therapist 1 precede those for Therapist 2.
† Significant at 0.01 level.
‡ Significant at 0.05 level.

agreement that high Dominance was related to poor Motivation for Therapy and that Hostility was an indicator of defensiveness. On the other hand, there appeared to be

TABLE 3

INTERCORRELATIONS OF RATINGS ON THE VARIABLES FOR THE TWO THERAPISTS

Therapist 1 (first value) / Therapist 2 (second value)

Variable	Th	B	C	D	E	F	G	H	I	J	K	L	M	N	O*
A. Dominance	1	−0.41	0.44†	0.41	0.01	0.63	0.45†	−0.38	0.00	−0.49†	−0.21	−0.42	−0.25	−0.42	
	2	−0.43†	−0.36	0.05	−0.24	0.31	0.41	−0.27	0.15	−0.45†	−0.40	0.01	−0.10	−0.40	
B. Anxiety	1		0.06	0.03	0.18	−0.44†	−0.30	0.40	0.55‡	0.34	0.18	0.56‡	−0.03	0.09	
	2		0.42	0.15	0.65‡	−0.09	−0.29	0.32	0.04	0.52†	0.34	0.06	−0.23	−0.13	
C. Emotional maturity	1			0.15	−0.11	−0.43†	0.09	0.15	0.11	0.02	0.27	0.07	−0.45†	0.08	
	2			−0.02	0.05	0.23	−0.44†	0.49†	−0.39	0.46†	0.54†	0.26	−0.07	0.46†	
D. Hostility	1				0.37	0.04	−0.44†	−0.43†	0.19	−0.51†	−0.50†	−0.34	−0.01	−0.53†	
	2				0.38	−0.13	0.53†	−0.21	0.40	−0.09	0.06	0.47†	−0.04	−0.16	
E. Complainingness	1					−0.08	0.16	−0.10	−0.02	−0.12	−0.14	0.26	0.27	−0.41	
	2					−0.01	0.19	0.16	0.24	0.04	0.08	0.04	−0.09	−0.39	
F. Independence	1						−0.03	0.09	−0.34	0.00	0.16	−0.01	0.02	−0.14	
	2						0.01		−0.09	−0.06	0.12	−0.01	−0.08	0.11	
G. Defensiveness	1							−0.81‡	−0.17	−0.78‡	−0.67‡	−0.69‡	0.07	−0.63‡	−0.64‡
	2							−0.76‡	0.65‡	−0.77‡	−0.64‡	0.09	0.44‡	−0.55†	−0.68‡
H. Capacity for insight	1								0.00	0.73‡	0.71‡	0.72‡	−0.11	0.56‡	0.81‡
	2								−0.64‡	0.90‡	0.84‡	0.20	−0.21	0.64‡	0.67‡
I. Degree of disturbance	1									0.27	0.15	0.29	−0.15	0.27	
	2									−0.43†	−0.42	0.03	0.01	−0.58‡	
J. Motivation for therapy	1										0.78‡	0.81‡	−0.06	0.65‡	0.74‡
	2										0.87‡	0.24	−0.40	0.52†	0.72‡
K. Improvement expected in therapy	1											0.64‡	−0.16	0.55‡	0.63‡
	2											0.35	−0.20	0.66‡	0.63‡
L. Interest in treating patient	1												−0.09	0.40	
	2												−0.06	0.29	
M. Support	1													0.16	
	2													−0.02	
N. Liking for patient	1														0.51‡
	2														0.39
O. Recommendations	1														
	2														

*Computed only for selected variables. †Significant at 0.05 level. ‡Significant at 0.01 level.

idiosyncratic factors influencing the correlations for each therapist. For example, Hostility and Interest in Treating the Patient were highly related to the five key variables for Interviewer 1, as were Emotional Maturity and Degree of Disturbance for Interviewer 2.

As a next step in the statistical analysis, partial correlation coefficients involving the five "key variables" were computed separately for each interviewer. The relationship between Motivation for Therapy and Degree of Improvement Expected remained high ($r = 0.61$ and 0.48, respectively), even when the effect of the other three variables was held constant. This was the only third-order partial correlation that was significantly greater than zero for both therapists. When the effect of the variable Liking for the Patient as a Person was removed, little change in the magnitude of the partial correlation coefficients could be observed. This analysis suggests that Motivation for Therapy is the single most important variable affecting the clinical evaluations of the two interviewers and that liking for the patient may be a result of perceiving him as a "good patient" rather than a determinant of this perception.

Comparisons of the ratings made by the two interviewers with those made by the external observers proved inconclusive, although there was some evidence (significant at the 0.01 level in an analysis of variance design) that the interviewers tended to see the patients as less defensive and having a better prognosis.

COMMENT

Throughout this report little emphasis has been given to the fact that one of the psychiatrists interviewed the patients in a group situation, whereas the other conducted individual interviews. Since there were only two psychiatrists involved, there was an unfortunate confounding of the difference in situations with the difference in therapists. This could not be overcome, for practical reasons. Each

531

patient had already been interviewed by the resident and psychiatrist in charge of his case, as well as by the two therapists in this study, and could not be expected to go through the procedure several more times in the interest of a well-balanced design. Nor was it deemed advisable to alternate techniques for the therapists, as one was skilled in group interviewing and the other was not. Each used the method of his choice.

Certainly, it seemed that there were differences in the two situations. The observers' impression was that there was more verbal information communicated in the individual interviews, where the possibly inhibiting influence of the presence of other patients was not a factor. On the other hand, the interaction of the patients with each other, as well as with the therapist, in competition with other patients provided a valuable source of nonverbal information in the group situation.

The difference between the therapists has been mentioned and was very pronounced. The first therapist was considerably older, more experienced, and well established in the field. On the other hand, this was his first experience with American, and more particularly southern American, patients. While the second therapist was younger and less experienced, he was from the South, and almost all of his training was in the hospital, so that he was very familiar with the culture and the type of patient seen.

Inasmuch as the two agreed on their ratings, it may be said that neither experiential nor situational factors played a prominent role in the evaluation of these patients and that reliable ratings can be made in spite of all these differences, a finding that is very encouraging. On the other hand, inasmuch as the two disagreed, it cannot be definitely ascertained whether this was occasioned by the patients' reacting differently in the two situations or toward the two men or by the personalities of the therapist determining the way in which they perceived the patients. It is certainly possible that some patients reacted differently in the two situations.

The lack of significant interrater agreement on the two variables of Dominance and Anxiety, for example, might be a reflection of this difference. From another aspect, however, the difference between means and, more particularly, between intercorrelation patterns may reveal something about the therapist—his needs, values, and method of perceiving his environment.

Comparatively, the first therapist saw the patients as possessing more emotional maturity and independence and as complaining less. To him, they showed greater defensiveness and disturbance. In spite of liking them more, this therapist would extend less support. He seemed to manifest a clinical, impersonal view of the patients, seeing them as sick and in need of psychological help or analysis, rather than of warmth, understanding, or supportive care. He was primarily interested in treating the "good patient," and for him lack of hostility was correlated with this cluster.

The second therapist saw the patients as more immature, dependent, and complaining and as less defensive or disturbed. He would extend greater support, liked them less, and considered emotional maturity and a lesser degree of disturbance as important prognostic indicators. He seemed to regard the patients more personally than did the first therapist, both concerning the manifestation of their illness (a sort of childishness) and the prescribed cure (more of a supportive strengthening than giving of insight.)

These findings do call attention to idiosyncratic factors in therapists, which in this case resulted in their assigning differential weights to such variables as Dominance, Anxiety, Hostility, and Emotional Maturity. These tendencies, some of which are undoubtedly unconscious, may affect the therapist's evaluations, as well as his willingness to treat a particular patient. In addition, this technique enables the investigator to make indirect determinations of the therapist's attitudes, values, etc.—an approach that in our judgment is superior to more conventional self-reports.

From another vantage point, the results demonstrate

agreement of therapists' clinical judgments, with special reference to the patient's suitability for psychotherapy. Lack of defensiveness, capacity for insight, likability, and motivation for therapy appear to be ingredients of primary importance. Youthfulness, too, seems to be an asset, although the evidence on this point was merely suggestive. The work described in Chapter Nine showed attitude toward the patient to be related to clinical evaluation. Certain evidence from this study, particularly the partial correlations, indicates that therapists entertain more favorable attitudes toward patients whom they feel they can help, rather than that they feel they can help those whom they like. Undoubtedly, they view the patient not as a person in the abstract but, rather, in terms of his potentiality as a patient for psychotherapy. Holt and Luborsky (1958) reported rather similar results in their study of the personality patterns of psychiatrists. Psychologists' ratings of the "likability" of psychiatric residents proved to be the best single predictor of success as a psychiatrist, a finding they explained by the concept of the "valid halo." Specifically, they feel that the successful or good psychiatrist embodies the same qualities, and in much the same combination, as does the sort of person the psychologist-raters would like, and that the correlation is a reflection of this overlap. Since both ratings are global, and not mathematical combinations of discrete variables, the effect of this "valid halo" is maximized.

The same effect may be operative in rating patients' suitability for psychotherapy. Therapists prefer patients who appear to have an introspective curiosity about themselves, who show what Szasz (1958) has called "rudiments of the scientific attitude." Thus, they are evaluated in terms of their potential for the kind of psychotherapy that views emotional and intellectual insight as its principal achievement and curative agent. There is, then, a realization that a good many patients simply do not have the potentiality for such a development, and their prognosis accordingly is

534

considered poor. Rather than social class per se, as Hollings-head and Redlich (1958) have suggested, it appears that a certain kind of cognitive-emotional development, which admittedly may be correlated with social status, determines the judgment of a patient's suitability for insight-producing psychotherapy. Such a judgment, of course, reflects a congruency between the therapist's and the patient's social values. This investigation has presented an additional piece of evidence for this congruency.

SUMMARY

In the correlational analyses done to determine both the degree of agreement on each variable between therapists and the intercorrelation of the variables for each therapist, results indicate that agreement on 9 of the 15 variables surpassed the 0.05 level of confidence. Five of these, Defensiveness, Capacity for Insight, Motivation for Therapy, the Degree of Improvement Expected in Therapy, and the rater's Liking for the Patient as a Person, were highly interrelated for both therapists. In addition, the patient's Emotional Maturity and Degree of Disturbance were highly related to this group for one therapist; ratings of the patient's Hostility and the therapist's Interest in Treating the Patient were key variables for the other.

Partial correlations were computed for the five variables that were significantly intercorrelated for both therapists. The relationship between Motivation for Therapy and Degree of Improvement Expected remained high, even when the effect of the other variables had been removed. The removal of the variable Liking for the Patient as a Person seemed to have little effect on the relationship between the other variables.

In conclusion, it would seem that these therapists could agree quite well in their independent assessment of patient characteristics, and, furthermore, that both tended to see the same set of variables as interrelated. Nondefensive, insightful, likable, and well-motivated patients were seen as most likely to improve in psychotherapy, with motivation being the most independent predictor. In addition, there were idiosyncratic factors in the therapists that led to their assigning different weights to other variables and that affected both their evaluations of and their willingness to treat a patient.

References

Hollingshead, A. B., and Redlich, F. C. 1958. *Social Class and Mental Illness.* New York: Wiley.

Holt, R. R., and Luborsky, L. 1958. *Personality Patterns of Psychiatrists: A Study of Methods of Selecting Residents.* New York: Basic Books.

Kelly, E. L., and Fiske, D. W. 1951. *The Prediction of Performance in Clinical Psychology.* Ann Arbor, Mich., University of Michigan Press.

Raines, G. N., and Rohrer, J. H. 1955. "The Operational Matrix of Psychiatric Practice: Consistency and Variability in Interview Impressions of Different Psychiatrists," *Am. J. Psychiat.,* 111: 721-733.

Robinson, J. T., and Cohen, L. D. 1954. "Individual Bias in Psychological Reports," *J. Clin. Psychol.,* 10: 333-336.

Szasz, T. S. 1957. "On the Theory of Psychoanalytic Treatment," *Int. J. Psychoanal.,* 38: 166-182.

20

PSYCHOTHERAPISTS' CLINICAL JUDGMENTS AND ATTITUDES TOWARD PATIENTS (WITH M. S. WALLACH)

Theoretically, and from the standpoint of research, the therapist appears to be finding his way back into therapy. This trend is in keeping with a renewed interest in counter-transference or, more broadly, the therapist's contribution to the treatment process. Mensh (1956) states, ". . . study of the therapist is now more explicitly indicated, an emphasis which has appeared with trends toward introducing experimental design qualities into research in psychotherapeutic process [p. 342]." Butler (1952) asserts that ". . . exact observation of the therapist is a necessary precondition to understanding the behavior of the client [p. 378]"; similarly, Gitelson (1952), Jackson (1956), and Wolberg (1954) stress the importance of therapist variables. Perhaps the primary impetus for focusing upon the therapist stems from a belief that orthodoxy is waning and "Viewing therapy as a very intimate relationship and recognizing a trend toward less restrictive therapist roles, the expectation arises that differential therapist characteristics would have systematic effects on process and outcome" (Winder, 1957, p. 316).*

Previous attempts to explore the relationships between therapist variables and therapist performance in treatment have considered mainly those factors that most readily lend themselves to objective quantification: i.e., the therapist's professional affiliation, theoretical allegiance, length of experience, number of hours of personal analysis, etc. The potential importance of less tangible personality variables, long recognized in Freud's conception of countertransference, is beginning to attract the attention of investigators seeking objective documentation. For instance, Parloff (1956) found that the therapist relates most satisfactorily to those patients who most clearly approximate his "Ideal Patient." In Chapter Nine it was shown that the therapist's attitude toward the patient was significantly correlated with the form of therapy, frequency and length of treatment, the kinds of technical problems expected in therapy, and certain qualitative aspects of the techniques the therapist expected to employ. These observations strongly support the notion that emotional and attitudinal factors in the therapist may have an important bearing upon his clinical evaluations.

The therapist, as a function of his life experiences, approaches each initial interview with needs, expectations, and wishes of his own. If his expectations are sufficiently realized, he will consider the situation as "rewarding," and a "warm" attitude toward the patient is likely to develop. More specifically, if in an initial interview the prospective patient approximates the therapist's conception of an "ideal patient," he may develop a warm attitude toward the patient. While the conception of "ideal patient" may differ

*This research is part of a larger project supported by a research grant (M-2171) from the National Institute of Mental Health, Public Health Service.

538

from therapist to therapist, in a general sense, it may be assumed to imply a certain congruence between the kind of help the patient is seeking and the kind of help the therapist is able to provide, as well as an explicit or implicit belief on the patient's part that the treatment will be effective. Patients exhibiting such hopes and beliefs may be said to be "motivated for therapy" or "ready for a psychotherapeutic experience." Thus, patients whose beliefs, desires, and expectations are similar—in some respects at least—to corresponding expectations held by the therapist may be said to arouse a warmer attitude in the therapist. This attitude will be sufficiently strong to give rise to a kind of "halo effect" overshadowing certain "reality factors." Operationally, this may be evidenced by the character of the therapist's perception of the patient, treatment planning, and the like.

The initial halo effect will be self-realizing. This is to say, having achieved a "comfortable" or "warm" feeling toward the patient, the therapist will continue to focus on perceptions that are likely to engender further this effect, and he will propose a therapeuetic regime that will reflect this attitude. Moreover, he may be more inclined to view the patient as a "good patient" and work toward a closer therapeutic contact with the patient. The present investigation aims to explore the relationships between the therapist's attitude toward the patient on the one hand and his perceptions of the patient and treatment plans on the other. The causal direction, of course, remains an open question.

HYPOTHESES

1. A patient's verbal or nonverbal expectations concerning his "motivation for therapy" or "readiness for therapy" are an important determinant of the therapist's attitude toward the patient. In particular, the more highly motivated patient will engender in the therapist a warmer attitude.

2. The therapist's attitude toward the patient, whether

a function of the patient's motivation for therapy or other factors, is correlated with the therapist's perception of, and treatment plans for, the patient. More specifically, a warmer therapist attitude toward the patient is associated with more favorable perceptions of the patient, including clinical judgments, prognostic estimates, and treatment plans implying closer therapeutic contact.

PROCEDURE

To test these hypotheses it was planned to present a group of therapists with a patient manifesting relatively high motivation for therapy, and a comparable group of therapists with the same patient showing relatively low motivation for therapy. Furthermore, to lend greater generalizability to the findings, therapists were presented with two patients.

Two written case histories of neurotic patients were adapted for experimental purposes. Each case history consisted of alternate forms identical in all respects, except that one form presented the patient as highly motivated and the second form as poorly motivated for therapy. "Motivation" was communicated primarily in terms of the patient's eagerness to seek and accept psychotherapeutic help. Each case history was followed by an identical questionnaire of 27 items eliciting the respondents' clinical impressions, treatment plans, and attitudes toward the patient. Subjects were presented with the case histories of both patients, the degree of motivation being varied systematically. In addition, several biological questions were appended to the second questionnaire.

SAMPLE: Data were collected from medical psychotherapists actively engaged in the practice of psychotherapy. Three sources were utilized: (1) physicians known to the investigators personally, (2) colleagues of psychologists at selected installations, and (3) psychiatrists selected at random from the Directory of the American Psychiatric Asso-

540

ciation. Of 300 sets of material distributed personally or by mail, 82 were included in the analysis. One hundred and eighty-four sets were never returned, 26 respondents asked to be excused, and 8 respondents completed and returned the questionnaires after the analysis of the data was well in progress. Analysis of the biographical data (age, sex, professional level, years of experience, number of hours of personal analysis) supplied by respondents indicated that the sample was drawn from a relatively homogeneous universe of experienced medical psychotherapists (see Table 1), and that in terms of these variables the various subsamples showed no significant variations.

RESULTS

POSITION EFFECTS: As a first step in the statistical analysis it seemed important to investigate the possible influence of order of presentation (patient and degree of motivation) upon questionnaire responses. Since 24 multiple-choice items were answered under 4 experimental conditions, 96 comparisons were called for. Chi squares and t tests of these comparisons yielded 15 results significant at beyond the .1 level. These significant position effects appeared to be largely due to the fact that one of the patients seemed objectively more disturbed, so that respondents studying the male (more disturbed) patient first tended to attribute greater personality strengths and assets to the female (less disturbed) patient when her case was presented second.

EFFECTS OF COMMUNICATED PATIENT MOTIVATION: Chi square or t tests were employed to ascertain effects of the patient's motivation, as communicated in the case histories, upon responses to the 24 multiple-choice items. Five figures significant at or beyond the .05 level were obtained for the male case, and nine figures significant at this level were obtained for the female case.

When Mr. J. was presented as possessing high motiva-

541

TABLE 1

BIOGRAPHICAL DATA OF RESPONDENTS

	N	Male	Female	Mean Age	Mean Hours of Personal Analysis		Mean Years of Experience
Psychiatric Residents	11	10	1	33.91	140	(2)*	3.05
Psychiatrists	37	34	3	35.86	487	(26)	7.27
Psychoanalysts	34	30	4	44.47	625	(34)	14.31
Totals	82	74	8	39.17	549	(62)	9.62

* Figures in parentheses indicate number of respondents who had personal analysis.

tion for therapy, respondents tended to attribute to him greater ego strength, more anxiety, more insight into his problems, greater motivation for therapy (check item), and they expressed greater willingness to accept the patient for treatment. Contrary to the hypothesis, therapists' attitudes toward the patient did not vary significantly. However, there was a (statistically nonsignificant) trend in the predicted direction—a slight tendency for therapists to claim a warmer attitude toward the patient when he was presented as being more highly motivated for therapy.

When Mrs. D. was presented as possessing high motivation for therapy, respondents estimated ego strength, insight into her problems, and motivation (check item) as being greater. They likewise judged her social adjustment as more adequate, more often recommended psychotherapy or psychoanalysis without adjunctive forms of treatment (drugs, shock), and indicated that they would strive to accomplish a more extensive change in the patient's character structure. Presenting Mrs. D. with high motivation also accounted for a more favorable prognosis with treatment and a greater willingness on the part of the therapist to take her into treatment. Finally, as hypothesized, therapists claimed a warmer attitude toward the patient when high motivation was communicated.

EFFECTS OF PERCEIVED PATIENT MOTIVATION: The preceding comparisons were made in terms of the level of motivation communicated in the case material that did not necessarily coincide with the patient's motivation as actually perceived by the respondents. For the male case, there was high agreement between the kind of motivation communicated and the kind of motivation perceived by respondents. For the female case, however, the disparity between communicated and perceived motivation was greater, as evidenced by 13 shifts (16 per cent). Ten of these respondents "misread" the case history intended to convey low motivation by estimating the patient's motivation to be relatively high. Consequently, it was thought advisable to determine the relationship between perceived motivation and other variables, and chi-square tests were performed between the respondent's estimate of the patient's motivation and each of the other 23 multiple-choice items.

For the male case, questionnaire items already cited as being significantly related to communicated motivation were again significantly related to perceived motivation. In addition, five other items were significantly related to perceived motivation at or beyond the .05 level. Respondents who perceived Mr. J. to be highly motivated also tended to estimate social adjustment to be more adequate, suggested more frequent therapeutic sessions, stated that they would be less willing to alter the kind of therapy they usually conduct, estimated the prognosis to be more favorable with treatment, and found it easier to empathize with the patient.

For the female case, estimates of greater ego strength, more insight, better social adjustment, more favorable prognosis with treatment, greater willingness to accept the patient in treatment, and warmer therapist attitudes accompanied perceived motivation, as they did communicated motivation. On the other hand, perceived high motivation (unlike communicated high motivation) was not significantly related to form of treatment or to the extensiveness of attempted change in the patient's character structure. However, respondents who perceived Mrs. D. as highly motivated for therapy also tended to judge her as being more emotionally mature and less seriously disturbed.

EFFECTS OF THERAPISTS' ATTITUDES: In order to test the second hypothesis, the respondents' stated attitudes toward the patient were compared, by chi square, with the 23 remaining multiple-choice items.

For the male case, eight items varied significantly with the therapist's attitude toward the patient, and only one of these (willingness of the therapist to alter his usual way of conducting therapy) was in the opposite of the predicted direction. Briefly, a positive therapist attitude was found to be associated with: a diagnosis of psychoneurosis rather

544

than one of psychosis or personality disorder, estimates of greater ego strength and insight, *less* willingness to alter his usual therapeutic procedure, more favorable prognostic estimates with or without treatment, greater willingness to accept the patient for treatment, and greater ease of empathizing with the patient.

For the female case, six items showed a significant relationship with attitude at the .05 level, and all differences were in the predicted direction. Therapists who claimed a more positive attitude toward Mrs. D. considered her to possess greater insight into her problems, more adequate social adjustment, and higher motivation for therapy. Warmer attitudes toward this patient were also accompanied by estimates of a more favorable prognosis with treatment and greater ease of empathizing with the patient.

In addition to the statistically significant results already reported, more than 75 per cent of the nonsignificant comparisons showed trends in the predicted direction. The figures for these comparisons are given in Table 2.

ADDITIONAL ANALYSES: The theoretical possibility that basic dimensions might underlie the observed relationships among questionnaire items led to an attempt to isolate such factors. Since a factor analysis employing the intercorrelation of all 27 items seemed impractical, only the nine items already found to yield significant comparisons were utilized. For each case, these nine items were intercorrelated (product-moment coefficients of correlation). A centroid factor analysis was performed for each patient separately, three factors were extracted in each analysis, and both factor analyses were then rotated to an oblique simple structure.

The similarity of patterns of the intercorrelation matrices (see Table 3) for each case suggests that certain items are consistently related to other items and that these relationships are rather stable. That is, patient differences as represented by the two cases in this investigation have little effect upon the degree to which various therapist estimates and judgments are correlated, and the observed asso-

545

TABLE 2

SUMMARY OF STATISTICAL COMPARISONS BETWEEN PATIENTS' MOTIVATION FOR THERAPY, THERAPISTS' ATTITUDE, AND OTHER QUESTIONNAIRE ITEMS
(N=82)

Therapists' Estimates	Male Case		Female Case	
	Motivation†	Therapist Attitude	Motivation†	Therapist Attitude
Diagnosis	NS*	.02	NS	NS
Ego strength	.001	.01	.05	NS
Anxiety	.05	NS	NS	NS
Insight	.02	.001	.01	.05
Emotional maturity	NS	NS	.01	NS
Social adjustment	.05	NS	.01	.05
Degree of disturbance	NS	NS	.01	NS
Similarity to patients in therapy	NS	NS	NS	NS
Kind of treatment	NS	NS	NS	NS
Motivation		NS		.001
Chances of acting out	.1	NS	NS	NS
Frequency of sessions	.05	NS	NS	NS

Extensiveness of change in character structure	NS	NS	.1
Length of treatment	NS	NS	NS
Permissiveness	NS	NS	NS
Encourage free association	NS	NS	NS
Recommendations to patient	NS	NS	NS
Change of usual therapy	.01	.05	NS
Prognosis without therapy	NS	.05	NS
Prognosis with therapy	.05	.02	.05
Willingness to accept patient in Rx.	.01	.001	.001
Ease of empathizing with patient	.01	.001	.001
Environmental stress	NS	NS	NS
Therapist's attitude	NS	.001	.001

* *NS*—not significant at .10 level (chi square, two-tailed tests).   † Patient's motivation as perceived by therapist.

547

TABLE 3

INTERCORRELATION AMONG SELECTED ITEMS

(N=75 to 82)

Item	Ego Strength	Insight	Social Adjust- ment	Moti- vation	Alter Rx.	Accept Patient	Prognosis	Empathy
Male Case								
Insight	.30							
Social adjustment	.61	.28						
Motivation	.32	.50	.27					
Change of usual therapy	−.30	−.31	−.06	−.34				
Prognosis with therapy	.46	.32	.32	.26	−.51			
Willingness to accept patient	.34	.30	.20	.40	−.30	.40		
Ease of empathizing with patient	.43	.14	.25	.22	−.02	.22	.28	
Therapist's attitude	.52	.23	.10	.22	−.29	.42	.55	.44
Female Case								
Insight	.49							
Social adjustment	.37	.35						
Motivation	.40	.65	.37					
Change of usual therapy	−.27	−.15	−.07	−.18				
Prognosis with therapy	.41	.37	.28	.55	−.52			
Willingness to accept patient	.19	.39	−.08	.46	−.21	.68		
Ease of empathizing with patient	.08	.35	.20	.25	−.01	.32	.40	
Therapist's attitude	.30	.40	.31	.59	−.07	.48	.54	.44

548

ciation between items can be assumed to be mainly a function of therapist variables.

The three factors extracted for each patient are difficult to interpret, and the findings for the two patients often failed to parallel each other. However, common to both factor analyses was the emergence of what might be termed a "good patient" factor. For Mr. J. this factor includes high loadings on items that give the following description: the therapist is willing to accept a well motivated, insightful patient for his usual treatment procedure. For Mrs. D. high loadings occur on such items as: the therapist perceives the patient as having insight, high motivation for therapy, and is easy to empathize with; the therapist has a warm attitude toward the patient and is eager to accept her for treatment.

DISCUSSION

Since this investigation is not based on observations of psychotherapists in their natural setting, questions may be raised about the correlation between their behavior responding to questionnaires and their behavior in actual psychotherapy when they have the opportunity for direct acquaintance with the patient. It was pointed out in Chapter Nine:

It is not contended that the behavior of the psychiatrists in an initial interview with a "real" patient bears a one-to-one relationship to his performance in the experiment. . . . What is asserted is that the evaluative processes, as they were studied under experimental conditions, are sufficiently similar to the "normal" behavior of the therapist to generate important hypotheses about his behavior in a first interview. Hypotheses thus derived are valuable if they raise further questions for research, and if they can be applied to practice and training in psychotherapy.

Asch (1952) comes to a similar conclusion in evaluating the

549

generalizability of his experimental findings based on descriptions rather than on observation of actual persons: "certain processes occurring in response to indirect data about persons not present are also at work in reaction to actual persons [p. 219]." Nevertheless, the possibility that concrete relations with persons introduce additional variables cannot be dismissed lightly.

Regarding our findings, it is seen that certain therapist estimates pertaining to perceptions of, and treatment plans for, the patient are related to the therapist's professed attitude toward the patient. Estimates of diagnosis, ego strength, inclination to modify therapy, prognosis without treatment, social adjustment, and motivation for therapy appear to vary with the therapist's attitude and the patient's degree of disturbance (it will be recalled that the female patient was less seriously disturbed than the male patient).

It should be pointed out that only 10 of the 24 multiple-choice items yielded results that were consistently statistically significant. At the same time, the fact that these results were obtained for two patients adds weight to the evidence. Furthermore, the fact that the vast majority of statistically nonsignificant comparisons were in the predicted direction, coupled with the respondents' frequently expressed claim that the written case histories did not allow them to use all the cues they ordinarily employ, suggests that many of the relationships are probably underestimates.

The direction of causation obviously remains indeterminate. It is not clear whether the therapist's attitude "causes" the character of his clinical estimates, whether the therapist feels more favorably disposed toward patients who are better therapeutic risks to start with, or whether both possibilities are more complex functions of other variables. It seems clear, however, that insight, or the capacity for insight, is a key variable entering into prognostic estimates, the therapist's eagerness in accepting the patient for treatment, and his (self-rated) ability to empathize with the patient. Therapists tend to profess a more positive attitude

550

toward a patient who meets these criteria. On the other hand, the data suggest that the patient's motivation for therapy influences the therapist's attitude in the predicted direction only when the degree of disturbance is not too great. In other words, a therapist "likes" a patient who has the capacity for insight and is eager to be helped provided the clinical evidence supplies no contraindications.

These findings show some interesting parallels to the ingenious experiments of Asch (1946) on the formation of impressions of personality. Among many other findings, Asch reports that "a central trait determines the content and the functional place of peripheral traits within the entire impression" but that central characteristics are "themselves affected by the surrounding characteristics [p. 276]." In his studies, the "warm-cold" dimension appeared to occupy such a central position. In this investigation, motivation for therapy similarly seems to determine a number of clinical estimates as well as the therapist's attitude. (For further evidence on this point, see the preceding chapter.) Our results also seem to corroborate Asch's conclusions that one can see another person only as a unit, that qualities enter into a particular relation and become organized, and that the system of the traits points to a necessary center. Altogether it seems that application of Asch's technique to the investigation of the formation of clinical judgments presents a fascinating research task.

Regardless of a patient's motivation for therapy, however, therapists profess a more positive attitude toward patients who are less severely disturbed. While this investigation has nothing to say about therapeutic outcomes, it dovetails with the findings of a number of such studies summarized by Luborsky (1959): "Those who stay in treatment improve; those who improve are better off to begin with than those who do not; and one can predict response to treatment by how well they are to begin with [p. 324]." We may add, on the basis of our findings, that therapists are more enthusiastic about treating patients whom they view

551

as having a better prognosis—perhaps, because they are perceived as having greater capacity for profiting from psychotherapeutic procedures that rely both on the patient's intellectual as well as emotional understanding. Our first hypothesis may be recast thus: A "warm" therapist attitude toward a patient is more likely to be present when the patient is well motivated for therapy, provided the severity of his emotional disturbance is not too great.

The one result that ran counter to the prediction showed a negative relationship between a favorable therapist attitude and his willingness to alter his usual method of therapy. In the context of other findings here reported, this disinclination to alter his usual method of therapy seems to reflect the therapist's conviction that the patient can profit from the kind of psychotherapy the therapist employs most often and has the greatest faith in and that there is no need to press into service other techniques and therapeutic adjuncts—the use of which may, at times, signify a subtle rejection of the patient as a person.

Estimates of the patient's insight into his problems showed the highest degree of association with the patient's motivation for therapy and the therapist's attitude. This finding supports the notion that estimates of insightfulness are highly descriptive of the good (potential) learner as far as psychotherapeutic achievement is concerned. It also substantiates the belief that psychotherapeutic success requires, among other things, the patient's ability to achieve insight and the therapist's ability to foster a warm, understanding, and accepting environment. Fiedler (1950) found these factors to be mentioned prominently in therapists' descriptions of the ideal therapeutic relationship, and he observed that agreement on these variables was higher among experienced therapists regardless of theoretical orientation than among experienced and inexperienced therapists of like orientation.

The demonstrated relationships between therapists' attitudes and their clinical evaluations and treatment plans in general support the second hypothesis. This may also be interpreted as discrediting the conception of an impersonal, mirror-like therapist, a view that has already become outmoded. By drawing attention to these associations, this study supports the increasing emphasis given to the effects of personality variables in the therapist upon his clinical operations. The extent to which these variables play a part in the therapist's intricate work remains to be explored much more exhaustively, but it is clear that they must come to occupy a more central place in selection, training, and therapeutic practice. From a methodological point of view, this study demonstrates the feasibility and potential value of quasi-clinical experimental designs, which permit the introduction of controls not otherwise possible.

SUMMARY

The hypothesized association between therapists' attitudes toward the patient and their perceptions of, and treatment plans for, the patient appear in general to be substantiated. The direction of causation, however, remains indeterminate and the degree of relationship between the therapist's "usual" performance and his performance in the present experimental situation is unknown. Nevertheless the evidence supports the assertion that personality factors of the therapist are an integral part of his clinical judgments and therapeutic procedures. A better understanding of these relationships might make an important contribution to more effective clinical practice as well as aid in the selection of candidates for training in psychotherapy.

References

Asch, S. E. 1946. "Forming Impressions of Personality," *J. Abnorm. Soc. Psychol.*, 41: 258-290.

————. 1952. *Social Psychology*. New York: Prentice-Hall.

Butler, J. M. 1952. "The Interaction of Client and Therapist," *J. Abnorm. Soc. Psychol.*, 47: 366-378.

Fiedler, F. E. 1950. "A Comparison of Therapeutic Relationships in Psychoanalytic, Nondirective and Adlerian Therapy," *J. Cons. Psychol.*, 14: 436-445.

Gitelson, M. 1952. "The Emotional Position of the Analyst in the Psychoanalytic Situation," *Int. J. Psychoanal.*, 33: 1-10.

Jackson, D. D. 1956. "Countertransference and Psychotherapy," in *Progress in Psychotherapy*, ed. F. Fromm-Reichmann and J. L. Moreno, pp. 234-248. New York: Grune & Stratton.

Luborsky, L. 1959. "Psychotherapy," in *Annual Review of Psychology*, Vol. X, ed. P. R. Farnsworth and Q. McNemar, pp. 317-344. Palo Alto, Calif.: Annual Reviews.

Mensh, I. N. 1956. "Research in Counseling and Psychotherapeutic Process," in *Progress in Clinical Psychology*, Vol. II, ed. D. Brower and L. E. Abt, pp. 340-360. New York: Grune & Stratton.

Parloff, M. B. 1956. "Some Factors Affecting the Quality of Therapeutic Relationships," *J. Abnorm. Soc. Psychol.*, 52: 5-10.

Winder, C. L. 1957. "Psychotherapy," in *Annual Review of Psychology*, Vol. VIII, ed. P. R. Farnsworth and Q. McNemar, pp. 309-330. Palo Alto, Calif.; Annual Reviews.

Wolberg, L. R. 1954. *The Technique of Psychotherapy*. New York: Grune & Stratton.

Part VII
Methodological
Developments

DEVELOPMENT OF A SYSTEM OF CONTENT-ANALYSIS:
The first chapter in this section sets forth the development
of a technique for describing and quantifying psychotherapeutic communications. Essentially, it is a system of content-
analysis designed to deal specifically with the form and
content of verbal utterances by psychotherapists in traditional dyadic psychotherapy. Its development was predicated on the assumption that in order to study phenomena
in nature it is essential to be able to order and classify them.

Systems for analyzing the content of written or oral
communications have been plentiful, but for the most part
they are not applicable to research in psychotherapy. Some
systems that antedated the present one were especially
designed for research on Rogers' nondirective or client-
centered therapy and did not appear to be relevant to other

557

forms of psychotherapy. Following my earlier research in which the Bales System of Interaction Process analysis was used (see Part II), I felt that a system of finer grain was needed. At the same time such a system should be sufficiently general to be useful in comparing the communications. The main purpose of the system is to facilitate comparisons between different psychotherapists, or comparisons involving the same therapist at different times or when working with different patients.

The system presented here has been used in a number of studies included in this volume; it has also been employed by other investigators.

DIMENSIONS OF PSYCHOTHERAPISTS' ACTIVITY: The second chapter in this part is an attempt to isolate salient aspects of psychotherapists' activity on the basis of self-descriptions and self-ratings. The strongest dimension emerging from factor analysis seems to relate to the therapist's "activity" level, that is, the extent to which he participates in a free and easy way in the interaction versus the degree of restraint (and distance) he imposes between himself and the client. This may well turn out to be one of the major defining characteristics of psychotherapists.

558

21

A SYSTEM FOR ANALYZING PSYCHOTHERAPEUTIC TECHNIQUES

In recent years there has been an increasing interest in the objective study of psychotherapeutic phenomena. This interest has been prompted by efforts to place psychotherapy on a firm empirical foundation, to resolve theoretical differences by investigating the actual therapeutic transaction, to simplify the language of therapy, and generally to facilitate the scientific study of interpersonal processes. To approach these problems it is indispensable to develop adequate research tools for dealing with the complexities of the interaction. The system of analysis outlined in this chapter represents an attempt to abstract certain salient features from the verbal behavior of the psychotherapist and thereby to promote the comparative study of psychotherapeutic techniques.*

What can the objective study of therapeutic techniques contribute? It is commonly taken for granted that the psychotherapist's personality, his theoretical orientation, and his therapeutic techniques are interrelated. From a knowledge of the therapist's personality, background, and training, it should be possible, therefore, to make predictions concerning certain relevant aspects of his therapeutic operations and, conversely, by studying his techniques it should be possible to make relatively specific inferences regarding his theoretical convictions and—perhaps to a lesser extent—concerning his personality. Apart from personality differences, it may be said that therapeutic technique is theory translated into action. Accordingly, fully trained therapists who subscribe to similar theoretical precepts should, within limits, employ similar techniques. On the other hand, divergences in theoretical position should also be mirrored in the therapist's technique. Assuming the existence of adequate research tools for analyzing therapeutic protocols, the demonstration of technique differences attributable to variations in theoretical viewpoint would provide powerful empirical evidence for the significance of a theoretical framework in doing therapeutic work. Failure to demonstrate differences or disclosure of differences other than those predicted from theory might give rise to such conclusions as:

---

*This research was supported by a research grant (M-965) from the National Institute of Mental Health, of the National Institutes of Health, U. S. Public Health Service, to the George Washington University School of Medicine, Department of Psychiatry. Grateful acknowledgment is made to Winfred Overholser, M.D., under whose general direction this work was carried out, and to Leon Yochelson, M.D., consultant to the project. I also wish to express my appreciation to Rebecca E. Rieger, A.M., who contributed materially to the formulations, and to Drs. Dorothy E. Green and Maurice Lorr for their advice on statistical problems. The responsibility for this article is, of course, mine.

1. The therapist's theoretical orientation exerts no demonstrable influence on his therapeutic operations.

2. The parameters of therapeutic operations lie on a different plane from what is stressed by the theories.

3. The technical operations of particular therapists are so idiosyncratic that more fruitful explanations of therapy might be sought in terms of nonverbal experiences, and so on.

While there is no lack of opinions on these matters, no definitive conclusions can be drawn simply because it has hitherto been impossible to subject the problems to rigorous research.

The lack of specific information on more empirical questions is equally conspicuous. For example, in what respects does an experienced therapist differ from an inexperienced therapist, even within the same "school?" How does therapist A behave with patient X at different stages of therapy? How does he behave with different patients? In terms of actual operations, how can psychoanalysis, psychoanalytically oriented therapy, supportive therapy, and so on be differentiated? These are important issues, and there can be little doubt but that the scientific status of psychotherapy will be enhanced as clear-cut answers are adduced.

Without losing sight of the complexities of the therapeutic enterprise, I would suggest that a pragmatic approach to the study of therapeutic phenomena can be of considerable value. The present focus is on the naturally occurring events in therapy and what can be learned from their systematic analysis. From this vantage point it is more important to investigate what the therapist *does* than what he talks about, which is to say that the practical value of a theory is largely determined by the operations to which it gives rise.

BACKGROUND

Almost 20 years ago Edward Glover surmised that

analysts, despite the presumed similarity of their training, might differ in their therapeutic practices, and that
many differences seemed to be obscured by what he called
"the psychoanalytic *mystique*." He designed a rather comprehensive questionnaire on technique, and solicited the
responses of 29 British analysts. From the replies of 24
respondents it became apparent that on only 6 out of 63
points raised was there unanimous agreement, and that
only one of the 6 points—the importance of analyzing the
transference—could be regarded as fundamental. Among
the areas of disagreement, the subject of interpretation
loomed large. There was a lack of agreement concerning
almost all aspects of interpretation, including mode, length,
timing, and depth. I shall not go into the details of this very
illuminating survey, but it is noteworthy that a pioneer
attempt was made, that it yielded valuable results despite
the smallness of the sample, and that it highlighted considerable divergences of opinion on both theoretical and
practical issues. If it is further remembered that Glover dealt
with *opinions* his respondents were willing to commit to
paper—probably after a good deal of soul-searching—
rather than the actual *therapeutic data*, it seems likely that
the degree of agreement was overstated rather than under-
stated.

In more recent years, Glover (1955b) has continued to
challenge the assumption that psychoanalysts "hold roughly
the same views, speak the same technical language . . . [and]
practice approximately the same technical procedures and
obtain much the same results, which incidentally are, by
common hearsay, held to be satisfactory [pp. 375-376]." He
states unequivocally that "without some reliable form of
standardization of technique there can be no science of
psychoanalysis, for if we cannot standardize the behavior of
the patient, we must at least be able to standardize the
behavior of the analyst [p. 383]," and that this is a problem

562

for research and not for discussion at a symposium.*

Glover's concern is shared by many American analysts. Marmor (1955), summarizing a symposium held by the American Psychoanalytic Association, states that:

one of the most important scientific tasks facing psycho-analysis today, is that of attempting to find the *common denominators* that underly [*sic*] the varying data and the therapeutic successes of these different schools of thought. Toward this end, tolerance toward dissident viewpoints, the elimination of semantic differences, the efforts at presentation of concepts in common everyday language, the breaking down of barriers toward free communication between differing groups, and the fostering of more interdisciplinary contacts and group research, are all steps which need to be strengthened and furthered [p. 505].

One of the stumbling blocks that has delayed progress is the question of how to evaluate the basic data of psycho-analysis and psychotherapy. With the advent of improved methods of sound recording and a greater willingness on the part of therapists to participate in research studies, there is a potentially large pool of data awaiting the ingenuity of the researcher. It is on the methodological side that psychologists during the past 10 to 15 years have made notable contributions. While these studies have rarely dealt specifically with *psychoanalytic* case materials, they provide a starting point for the investigation of the more intense forms of psychotherapy. (See Auld and Murray, 1955.)

Of primary interest in this connection are those investigations that have attempted to deal systematically with the

---

*There is now preliminary evidence—at least with regard to initial interviews—that an attempt to standardize the therapist's interventions leads to notable invariance or stability of certain interaction patterns (see Saslow, Matarazzo, Guze, 1955).

therapist's verbal communications. The general procedure has been to abstract certain relevant characteristics from the therapist's verbal behavior, to rate or to classify communications on the basis of operationally defined criteria, and to use the resulting frequencies or proportions as indices of the therapist's activity. Working within Rogers' "nondirective" framework, Porter (1943) set up a system consisting of some 20 categories—for example, defining the interview situation, bringing out and developing the problem situation, developing the client's insight and understanding, and so on. Despite his use of Rogerian terminology, Porter was careful to strive for a descriptive rather than an evaluative scheme. Another widely used system by a nondirectivist, Snyder (1945), subtly confounds description with evaluation. Both of these systems have been applied primarily to the data of client-centered therapy, for which they were originally constructed. They are in principle applicable to other forms of therapy, but since they stress aspects of technique more or less specific to the client-centered framework, they are not sufficiently analytical for other purposes.

Bales' 12-category system of interaction process analysis (1950), intended as a general-purpose framework for analyzing social interaction, has been used in a number of investigations having as their objective some problem pertaining to psychotherapeutic technique. This system has the advantage of not being encumbered by any theoretical predilections relative to psychotherapy, but it is relatively limited in its applicability to therapeutic data because of its overinclusiveness and generality. Built on the conception of social interaction as a problem-solving sequence, it does not go beyond characterizing a communication as a question, interpretation, restatement of the patient's content, and the like. Nevertheless, it has been useful in preliminary investigations. (See Chapters Six, Seven, and Eight.)

Collier's scale of depth of interpretation (1953) attempts an objective assessment of one important dimension of the therapist's activity. It fulfills the requirement of being theoretically neutral, hence applicable to the operations of therapists regardless of their theoretical preferences, and, more important, it objectifies a common denominator of diverse therapeutic operations. A variation of this scale has recently been described in Harway, Dittmann, Raush, Bordin, and Rigler (1955).

Like any scientific instrument, a system of content analysis must be *objective* and *reliable*—that is, the measurement units must be operationally defined, and the observations must be repeatable by independent observers with a high degree of accuracy. The most crucial requirement, however, is that a system of analysis be *valid*.* Validity is to some extent a matter of definition, and the schemes mentioned above are undoubtedly valid for the purposes for which they were constructed. Porter's system is valid—that is, relevant—to the Rogerian form of psychotherapy; Bales' system is relevant to problem-solving behavior in small groups; neither system may be valid for, say, intensive psychotherapy, and, indeed, no such claim has been advanced by their authors. It appears that there is at present no system of analysis that would permit the *comparative analysis of diverse therapeutic techniques*. Minimally, such a system should meet the following criteria:

1. It should take cognizance of the purpose and aims of psychotherapy as a unique form of social interaction and respect its complexities; it should show particular recognition of the therapist's role in the therapeutic process.
2. While being anchored to therapeutic operations, it should be sufficiently general to be applicable to the techniques of therapists whose theoretical positions may be divergent. In other words, it should stress the *common denominators* of different therapeutic approaches.
3. It should be primarily descriptive and nonvaluative,

---

*For a clear statement of the technical requirements for content analysis systems, see Berelson (1952).

on the assumption that the relative effectiveness of therapeutic techniques must be evaluated on the basis of external rather than internal criteria.

4. It should meet the requirements of objectivity, reliability, and system.

THE PROPOSED SYSTEM

In its present form the system proposed here comprises two sets of categories and three intensity scales. It is intended to be sufficiently general to cut across the various theoretical orientations, while at the same time being relevant to the purposes of psychotherapy. It views each communication by the therapist as a multidimensional datum, on which five simultaneous assessments are made. It takes advantage of some features of previously developed content systems and combines them into a single conceptual framework. Since the system was constructed with psychotherapy specifically in mind, it is inevitable that it reflects certain assumptions about the therapeutic process, personality change, and above all, the role of the therapist. It is hoped that the assumptions underlying the formulation of the concepts are relatively noncontroversial and generally acceptable so that the bias that may determine the results from this source is minimal.

For present purposes, psychotherapy may be viewed as a controlled interpersonal relationship, integrated for the purpose of effecting changes in the patient's feelings, attitudes, and behavior through the systematic application of psychological techniques. With regard to the therapist's role in the interpersonal process, the following implications of this definition may be stressed:

1. Psychotherapy is a planful interpersonal relationship between a trained professional person (the therapist) and a person seeking help for his difficulties in living (the patient). It is a personal relationship within an impersonal

566

framework. It is further implied that the relationship is integrated for the patient's benefit and that the totality of the therapist's activity throughout treatment is oriented toward this goal; thus, it precludes any participation or intervention in the patient's living that is not therapeutic in character.

2. It is hypothesized that the patient's difficulties in living are a function of emotional conflicts, of whose existence, significance, and consequences he is insufficiently aware, and that the application or institution of certain technical operations by a trained professional person (the therapist) in an interpersonal setting is peculiarly suited to bringing about a lasting amelioration of the patient's problems.

3. The uniqueness of psychotherapy derives from the application of psychological techniques, based upon scientific principles, in a controlled interpersonal setting. Irrespective of the ways in which the nature of the conflict is conceptualized, the following technical operations seem to be common to the major theoretical viewpoints:

(a) The therapist listens and attempts to "understand" the patient's verbal (and nonverbal) message. In contrast to the more usual forms of social interaction, he pays close attention to the connotative or symbolic content of the communications, which typically he explains in terms of certain theoretical conceptions.

(b) Sooner or later the therapist communicates to the patient some part of this "understanding." He may verbalize the feelings expressed by the patient or he may express a conjecture concerning the implicit meanings of the patient's message. In either event, he states a hypothesis or an inference, commonly called an "interpretation." The function of this activity is to increase the patient's self-awareness and to point out to him dynamic relationships that, it is hypothesized, have a bearing on the central emotional conflict or on one of its derivatives. Which aspects of the patient's com-

567

munication are singled out for interpretive activity depends on the therapist's theoretical leanings, his objectives, and the techniques considered most appropriate to achieve a desired therapeutic result.

(c) There are numerous technical operations that may be considered subsidiary to the interpretive function. Thus, the therapist may often consider it necessary to ask more or less specific questions to gain fuller information on a point, sometimes as a preamble to an interpretation. At other times, he may judge the patient's line of verbalization "unproductive" and deliberately change the focus by directing the patient's attention to an area that he thinks to be more promising therapeutically. Sometimes he may feel it necessary to alleviate a patient's anxiety by a word of reassurance or support; or he may wish to precipitate anxiety by being deliberately cold, aloof, or even sarcastic. Sometimes he has to explain something about the procedure, the goals, and the function of psychotherapy; on rare occasions, he may express an opinion or suggest a course of behavior or activity outside of therapy.

Ideally, there is always a rationale for the therapist's activity, so that, depending on the context, one approach is more desirable, therapeutically speaking, than another. In other words, some criterion of therapeutic effectiveness is implicit in what is considered the preferred technique. If it were true, as some maintain, that the relationship between patient and therapist is more "important" than the verbal exchange, it would be futile to speak of therapeutic techniques or to try to study them. If technique does make a difference, then presumably one technique is more effective than another. This is partly the *raison d'être* for the various schools of therapy that attempt to explain a set of similar phenomena in different terms and advocate different therapeutic approaches. From the point of view of empirical science, a first step would be to describe what techniques are actually practiced and to specify the conditions under which they are used. Such an exploratory survey might in itself suggest new hypotheses and leads, and pave the way for a comparative evaluation in addition to a comparative description. This reasoning is reflected in the scales and categories of the system proposed here, which attempt to provide specific answers on the following points:

What *kinds* of technique does the therapist employ? Does he primarily use questions, interpretive statements, authoritative opinions, and so on?

To what extent is his therapeutic behavior characterized by *inferential* operations? Are his hypotheses closely related to what the patient is expressing, or does he propound hypotheses that go far beyond the available data?

What is the *focus* of his therapeutic interventions? Does he try to stay within or close to the patient's frame of reference, or does he introduce and operate within a frame of reference of his own or that of his "school"?

Does he leave the *initiative* for structuring the content of the therapeutic hour with the patient, or does he assume the initiative for directing the patient's verbalization into a given channel? To what extent does he do either?

Are his communications predominantly emotionally "neutral," or does his attitude express *warmth* or *coldness*?

The scales and categories provide systematic information on each of the above questions for all verbal communication by the therapist.

The Scales and Categories

TYPE OF THERAPEUTIC ACTIVITY: These categories, presented in Table 1, appear to be the minimum number necessary to characterize most therapeutic communications without duplicating information obtained from other components. They are intended to represent meaningful abstractions from the therapist's intervention and are predicated upon commonly recognized differences in technique. They

569

TABLE 1

TYPE OF THERAPEUTIC ACTIVITY

(00) *Facilitating Communication (Minimal activity)*
(01) Silence.
(02) Passive acceptance, acknowledgment.
(10) *Exploratory Operations*
(11) Simple questioning : asking for further information, clarification, examples, elaborations; simple probes, case history questions; accenting by repeating one or more words.
Focal probes (with hypothesis), questioning to stimulate the patient's curiosity, encouraging self-exploration.
(20) *Clarification (Minimal interpretation)*
(21) Reflection of feeling, restatements for purposes of clarification (may include "?").
(22) Summaries (essentially noninterpretive).
(30) *Interpretive Operations*
(31) Interpretations, analysis of defenses, establishing connections, definitions of the patient's problem (interpretive).
(32) "Reality Model" : any operation by which the therapist's communication asserts the patient's rights, needs, and so on, and represents a reasonable model of reality (usually interpretive).
(33) Summaries (essentially interpretive).
(40) *Structuring*
(41) Structuring the therapeutic situation, describing the functions and tasks of therapy in general terms.
(42) Discussions about theory (relatively abstract).
(43) External arrangements, time, place, fees, and so on.
(50) *Direct Guidance*
(51) Direct suggestions for activity within the therapeutic framework.
(52) Direct suggestions for activity outside the therapeutic framework.
(53) "The therapist as an expert" : Giving information, stating an opinion, answering direct questions, speaking as an authority. Such communications may seem primarily objective, but they may also convey reassurance (warmth) or rejection (coldness).
(60) *Activity Not Clearly Relevant to the Task of Therapy*
(61) Greetings, small talk, endings, and so on.
(70) *Unclassifiable*

are based upon the general hypothesis that the techniques of therapists adhering to varying theoretical schools show specific differences. (See Chapters Six, Seven and Eight.)

The major categories and subcategories were developed empirically by analyzing a variety of therapeutic protocols; they are objective and essentially nonvaluative—that is, ratings are largely independent of the rater's theoretical outlook and his conceptions of what constitutes effective psychotherapy; and they are mutually exclusive.

DEPTH-DIRECTEDNESS: This scale, shown in Table 2, embodies the conception that any communication by the therapist, so long as it fulfills the requirement of being therapeutic (see the definition), carries with it an implication about, first, the patient's "problem" (as conceptualized by the various schools), and, second, the method of procedure best designed to bring about its alleviation or resolution.* This applies to the therapist's silences, probing questions, reflections of feeling, interpretations, summaries, or what not. Depending upon his theoretical orientation, he may deal with any of a number of levels implicit in the patient's communications, using the technique he deems most appropriate.

---

*This formulation may throw some light on the often-heard remark by therapists, "That's funny—*my* patients never bring up that kind of material!" (Marmor, 1955, p. 504), or on the Rogerians' disregard of defenses and transference. To some extent, at least, the patient's productions soon reflect the theoretical framework within which the therapist operates. Because of the reflexive nature of the therapeutic situation, in which the activities of both participants become almost inextricably interwoven, it is difficult to make observations that are not immediately influenced by the interaction itself, including the theoretical framework of the therapist through which his observations are filtered.

The Rogerian therapist is no different from other therapists in this respect, his claims of nondirectiveness notwithstanding, for his reflection-of-feeling technique is thoroughly interpretive in this sense. Certainly, the particular feeling that is singled out for "reflection" is a very definite inference in terms of the therapist's orientation. (See Kramish, 1954.)

TABLE 2

DEPTH-DIRECTEDNESS

0 *Noninferential*	1 *Mildly Inferential*	2 *Moderately Inferential*	3	4 *Highly Inferential*
Silence Passive acceptance Facilitating communication	Simple questioning: requests for further information, clarification, examples, elaboration Simple probes Case history questions Accenting (epitomizing) Nondirective leads Mild statements and opinions	Restatements of feeling (reflections) Focal probes (with hypothesis) Definitions of the therapeutic relationship Stimulating patient's curiosity about himself; encouraging self-exploration	Interpretations Analysis of defenses Establishing connections (pointing out inconsistencies) Hypothesis testing Definitions of the problem (interpretive)	Deep interpretations Direct confrontation (without preparation)

Degrees of interpretation

Intensification of therapeutic activity

The concept of depth-directedness refers to these levels. By this definition, a therapist's comment that operates upon the manifest meaning of the patient's communication is at the surface, whereas one that propounds a hypothesis, inference, conjecture, or interpretation is deep. Along this continuum, defined by the extremes, all therapeutic remarks find their place. The essential element in this conception is that inference is part and parcel of every therapeutic communication. Whatever differences occur are differences of degree, not of kind. Inferential depth is, perhaps, the most important single characteristic of psychotherapeutic communications.

The present scale differs from a similar one proposed by Harway and his co-workers (1955) in that it is not restricted to one class of therapeutic communications, usually labeled "interpretations," which these investigators define as "any behavior on the part of the therapist that is an expression of his view of the patient's emotions and motivations—either wholly or in part [p. 247]." A second difference refers to the relational definition of depth—"Depth of interpretation is a description of the relationship between the view expressed by the therapist and the patient's awareness [pp. 247-248]." While this definition seems useful, there is reason to believe that depth is more invariant and not solely dependent on the patient's current level of understanding.

There are five scale points, which are defined on an a priori basis rather than on the basis of empirical judgments. Raters are encouraged to use intermediate scores such as 1+ or 2−, which are statistically treated as half steps.

DYNAMIC FOCUS: The definition of psychotherapy as a planful and goal-directed enterprise implies some kind of theoretical orientation or framework that provides guidelines as to how the therapeutic relationship is to be structured, what goal or goals are to be pursued, and what technical procedures are to be utilized to achieve these objectives. The therapist's understanding of the therapeutic

573

process, in keeping with the particular theoretical formulations to which he subscribes, tells him what is "important" in the therapeutic situation and what is not, what he should focus on at a particular moment, and what is of no dynamic relevance, what is to be dealt with now rather than later, and so on. The way in which a therapist "sees" a situation is already an interpretation in terms of his particular framework—as well as a function of more personal factors.

To cite some examples, an orthodox Freudian may be expected to pay a great deal of attention to transference phenomena, manifestations of resistance, and the analysis of dreams and other fantasy productions, and to interpret the patient's productions in terms of infantile conflicts. Whether he accepts or rejects the libido theory, his emphasis will be on the *genetic* determinants.

A neo-Freudian, on the other hand, may be somewhat more concerned with *current* interpersonal conflicts. Instead of being primarily interested in genetic or historical antecedents, he may pay more attention to the ways in which past experience distorts the patient's contemporary interpersonal relations.

While both orientations stress the analysis of transference and resistance, their relative emphases might be expected to differ.*

A client-centered therapist of the school of Carl Rogers will focus on the patient's phenomenal self as it reveals itself in the therapeutic relationship. The dynamic concepts of transference and resistance are deemphasized and interpretations are shunned as "directive."

Examples could be multiplied, but the point is clear. Depending on his theoretical position, the therapist may be expected to engage in therapeutic activities congruent with his theoretical framework. An analysis of his focus alone may lead to an operational testing of his theoretical allegiance.

*Benjamin Wolstein (1954) attempts an analysis of the differences between orthodox Freudian and neo-Freudian formulations.

The concept dynamic focus, as shown in Table 3, refers to the frame of reference adopted at a particular juncture, by which the therapist structures the operational field and often elicits a particular content from the patient. Basically, the therapist can do one of two things: he can accept a patient's formulation as it is presented (Sector A), or he can introduce or superimpose a different frame of reference (Sector B). In the first instance, he may be silent, show

TABLE 3
DYNAMIC FOCUS

Sector A	Sector B
Therapist accepts the patient's formulation (minimal interference) without introducing a new frame of reference: Passive acceptance, facilitating communication, repeating word or phrase, reflections of manifest feeling	Therapist directs the patient's communication into a different channel and/or introduces a new frame of reference: B–1 Indications that additional information, clarification, examples, elaboration, and so on are needed to further the therapeutic operation B–2 Focus on *dynamic* events in the *past* B–3 Focus on *dynamic* events in the *present* B–4T Focus on the dynamics of the *therapist-patient relationship* (analysis of the transference) B–4 Focus on the *therapist-patient interaction* (therapist emerging as a person, authority, or expert)

interest, encourage the flow of communication, nod approval, reflect the feelings conveyed in the patient's communication, and the like. In the second instance, he may do a number of things: he may feel that further information is needed before a meaningful therapeutic intervention—perhaps in the form

575

of an interpretation—can occur (category B-1). He may focus on dynamic events in the patient's past that may have a dynamic bearing upon his current difficulties (B-2). He may focus on dynamic events in the present, such as interpersonal relations with contemporaries (B-3), and as a special case, with the therapist (transference) (B-4T). It also seems desirable to distinguish a class of communications in which the therapist responds to the patient by asserting his own role as an expert who states an authoritative opinion, expresses a value judgment, or something of the kind (B-4).

Dynamic focus, as defined here, is not a continuum but a set of categories that bear a meaningful relationship to the over-all heading. Two major sectors serve to differentiate whether the therapist is "going along" with the patient (A), or whether he introduces a different focus (B). Communications assigned to Sector A are not broken down further, but those assigned to Sector B are further analyzed with respect to the subcategories outlined in the preceding paragraph. Categories B-2, B-3, and B-4T are concerned with problems of function, in that they operate on the general hypothesis that the study of the patient's interpersonal performances, past or present, is effective therapeutically. In contradistinction, category B-1 is relatively static in its emphasis; the theoretical meaning of category B-4 is presently not clear. The rating on dynamic focus thus reflects the manner in which the therapist focuses the therapeutic spotlight.*

INITIATIVE: Consider the following statements addressed to a patient:

> Mmmh.
> Can you tell me more about that?
> Earlier in the hour you talked about your father. How did you get along with him?
> Now this is one of the ways this thing started. But the

---

*Eugene Pumpian-Mindlin's "frames of reference" seem to be closely related to this conception (see Marmor, 1955, pp. 498-499).

more insidious thing was that it kept up. When you see this clearly, you can do something about it.

In each statement the therapist gives a certain measure of direction to the patient and indicates the avenue along which he desires the patient to proceed. In the first remark the therapist is merely communicating: "I hear you; go ahead." In the last one, he outlines to the patient what is to be done in order to achieve a given result. Many fine shadings of directiveness can find their way into a therapist's remarks; in some cases the direction is clear, in others it is less apparent; but, typically, direction, guidance, or steering are never absent. Such guidance is even implied in deliberate silence in response to a patient's question, which says in effect: "If you ask direct questions, I am not going to answer them, at least until we find out the reasons. Communicate along different lines." This attribute of the therapist's communications may be called initiative, and defined as the extent to which he accepts responsibility for directing the patient's verbalization in a given channel.

By definition, all therapeutic activity is directed toward a goal. The goal, as well as the techniques for reaching the goal, may differ; but ideally all activities by the therapist guide the patient in a goal-directed channel. For present purposes then, the concept initiative has a specific meaning related to goal-directedness or therapeutic directiveness. In intensive psychotherapy with reconstructive goals, the therapist assumes the initiative by directing the patient toward self-exploration, self-understanding, abandonment of defensive systems, and so on. In other forms of therapy, the therapist may focus on a specific problem (sector), the phenomenal self, and so on. Less frequently will he take the initiative in the sense of telling the patient how to conduct his life. While he may assume the role of an authority or expert, he will usually not interfere with the patient's autonomy and will safeguard the patient's right to make his own decisions. Whether the patient welcomes this is another matter.

577

If initiative is an important component of the therapist's communications, it should be possible to make distinctions concerning the *degree* of initiative present in a particular statement or sequence of statements. The operational scale proposed in Table 4 is built upon the hypothesis that there is a continuum along which therapist communications may be arranged. Therapeutic statements may be regarded as ranging from a zero point (absence of initiative) through an area of mild and moderate initiative to an extreme of strong or authoritarian directiveness. The intensity of the therapist's initiative, rather than its quality, is the measurement attempted by this scale.*

THERAPEUTIC CLIMATE: This dimension hypothesizes an attitudinal-emotional continuum, which should be of considerable importance in the study of psychotherapeutic processes. There is a growing consensus that considers the existence of a warm, accepting relationship the *sine qua non* of effective psychotherapy. It is said that the therapist must be a warm, tolerant, accepting, and understanding person who is capable of integrating a relationship with the patient in which respect for the latter's personality is uppermost. The rationale for this assertion derives from the conception of the therapist as a more tolerant, reliable, and rational model of reality than was provided by the significant persons with whom the patient identified in his childhood. The presence of a climate of warmth, love, and understanding would thus constitute a precondition for the exploration and living through of painful experiences, which is often necessary for emotional growth.

The judgment of warmth or coldness transcends the symbolic structure of the communication and deals with its

---

*Notice that initiative is *not* defined as a function of the particular technique being used, nor is it asserted that interpretations are directive and reflections of feeling are nondirective. It should be apparent that the scale is not intended to perpetuate the time-worn controversy between so-called directive and nondirective therapy, which has been notably unproductive.

TABLE 4

INITIATIVE

0	1	2	3
Absence of initiative	*Mild* forms of initiative	*Moderate* initiative	*Strong* initiative

← — The therapist is "anonymous" — →

The therapist is more active, assumes the role of an expert

The therapist assumes the role of an authority

feeling tone. Admittedly, the measurements neglect to some extent the ways in which a therapeutic climate is fostered nonverbally; nevertheless, it is believed that, despite this restriction, useful inferences about the therapeutic climate can be made, by considering simultaneously the structure of the verbal communication and its emotional overtones.

The bipolar scale shown in Table 5 ranges from a neutral position to an extreme of acceptance, warmth, and the like in one direction, and to an extreme of rejection, hostility, coldness, and so on in the other.*

THE SYSTEM IN ACTION

Materials

Ratings are usually made from typescripts, which should be supplemented by sound recordings in order to preserve maximum realism of the original transaction. Typically, a single treatment hour is rated at a time.

Unit of Analysis

The single therapist communication occurring between two patient statements is treated as the common unit of analysis. This seems realistic since experience indicates that therapist communications are usually brief and concise. Moreover, even longer communications usually are devoted to the discussion of a *single* theme. In rare cases, it may be necessary to subdivide a therapist communication into two or three units.

---

*Some warmth, acceptance, and tolerance is probably a characteristic of all forms of successful psychotherapy, regardless of the therapist's theoretical position. See, in this connection, Fiedler (1953). However, there is some preliminary evidence (see Chapters Six, Seven, and Eight) of significant differences between experienced analysts and other analytically oriented therapists in this regard.

580

TABLE 5

THERAPEUTIC CLIMATE

-2 Coldness	-1 Withholding	0 Neutrality	+1 Giving	+2 Warmth
Rejection Sarcasm Cynicism Derision Hostility Criticism Brutality	Milder Degrees of -2	Objectivity Task-orientation		Milder Degrees +2: Acceptance Understanding Tolerance Empathy Respect

The Rating Process

In scoring a single treatment hour, the rater is guided by the history of the therapist-patient interaction as it has evolved up to that time. The background should be provided by studying the actual therapeutic proceedings rather than by reading a summary prepared by the therapist, which may be biased in unknown and unpredictable ways. Therapist communications should never be scored out of context.

Before embarking upon the ratings proper, the observer should listen to a sound recording of the treatment hour, perusing a typescript simultaneously. In case of doubt, he may refer to the sound recording later on. He will then begin the systematic scoring, taking one set of categories or dimensions at a time. This seems to have the advantage that it avoids constantly having to change one's frame of reference while considering a single scoring unit. It also tends to insure greater independence of the ratings on the several categories and scales.

The Rater's Role

The rater's vantage point is that of a "generalized therapist." He stands outside but midway between therapist and patient, and attempts to understand the patient's communications from the point of view of a therapist. Unlike the participating therapist, he need not be concerned with the effect of his activity upon the patient, which assures a greater measure of distance and—hopefully—objectivity. At any particular point, he must ask himself a number of questions that are systematically posed by the requirement of a score on the categories and scales. These determinations concern aspects of the communication itself as well as inferences relative to the therapist's intent expressed in the message. In order to score objectively, the rater must, as far as possible, divorce himself from his own theoretical predilections and attempt to empathize with the therapeutic goals of the therapist whose procedures he is observing. Nevertheless, he can never abandon the general conceptions of psychotherapy, which are basic to his understanding of the interactive process. He must be critical of the therapist's technical procedures, but not from the point of view of what he, the rater, would have done at a given juncture.

This is a difficult assignment, in view of the strong tendency to regard one's own procedures as the only true and effective ones. In some respects the rater's job is similar to that of a supervising therapist: he is to observe and to evaluate the treating therapist's techniques in the context of the ongoing interaction—that is, in terms of the therapist's personality and his modes of relating to people, rather than to assert how he, the supervisor, would have proceeded.

Objective criteria, definitions, and examples, compiled in a manual, are intended to maximize the objectivity of the observations, and the rater's familiarity with them should minimize his personal biases. However, in the final analysis it is the rater's self-knowledge, integrity, intellectual honesty, and technical competence that determine the usefulness of his observations. Even a precision tool is useless in unskilled hands; and this system is considerably less than a precision tool.

Rater Qualifications

It is apparent that a rater must not only have a familiarity with the characteristics of the system, which can be acquired relatively easily, but he must be thoroughly conversant with and sensitized to the phenomena of psychotherapy. Preferably, he should have experience as a therapist. Above all, he must have a solid grasp of the major technical operations used in therapy and their respective rationales. He should also have a working knowledge of the varying emphases of the major theoretical writers and schools.

Training of Raters

Following a study of the system and its components the rater must score a number of sample protocols and discuss points of difficulty with a more experienced person. Finally, it is necessary to conduct reliability studies to test intra- as well as inter-rater agreement.

STATISTICAL TREATMENT OF RESULTS

The system has been applied to a variety of interview materials, and systematic studies of rater agreement have been made. This preliminary evidence indicates that the system is highly reliable in the hands of trained raters and that it yields promising results. Chapter Thirteen illustrates an application to a complete case history (short-term, analytically oriented therapy) and presents data on rater agreement. For the present, the listing of a few indices that have been found useful may be apposite.

Summary and Analysis

The simplest method for summarizing the ratings consists of adding the frequencies made in each category and at each scale point. These totals may then be expressed as a proportion or as a percentage of the total number of interventions during an interview. In this way a profile of the therapist's activity for a given interview or series of interviews may be obtained. Comparisons between interviews may then be made by appropriate statistical techniques.

With regard to two continua (Depth-directedness and Initiative), mean ratings may be obtained for each interview. A series of interviews may then be compared by analysis of variance technique, t tests, and so on. For some purposes it may be more useful to deal only with the high-intensity (extreme) ratings, and to note their frequencies. This is advisable because the means tend to be heavily influenced by the low-level ratings, which are typically found to preponderate. With reference to Therapeutic Climate, it is almost indispensable to concentrate on nonzero scores, which are usually very few in number. A mean in this case is almost totally devoid of meaning.

If a comparison of interviews is desired on the categories (Type or Dynamic Focus), the chi-square technique appears to be the method of choice.

The foregoing suggestions pertain only to simple overall analyses, designed to answer such questions as: What is the therapist's typical profile? How does his activity vary between initial interviews, the middle phase of treatment, and the terminal stage? To what extent does his activity differ with different patients? In what respects does therapist A differ from therapist B? In other instances, the method of analysis of course depends on the hypothesis being tested.

Rater Agreement

An incisive analysis of rater agreement must deal with the ratings of independent judges on a unit-by-unit basis. In this way it becomes possible to determine whether raters agree on a given unit, and the possibility of compensating errors—frequently obscured in a comparison of totals—is excluded. Such estimates are conservative and will not indicate spuriously high agreement.

For the intensity scales that yield fairly large variance (Depth-directedness and Initiative), the product-moment coefficient of correlation appears adequate. The correlation between two independent raters, computed on a unit-by-unit basis, is a good index of their agreement. Concerning Therapeutic Climate, the preponderance of zero scores precludes this index. Although a zero score may be seen as a judgment, like a $+1$ or -2 score, the usual techniques are not applicable. One solution is to deal with totals of all plus and minus scores per interview.

With reference to the discrete categories (Type and Dynamic Focus), a simple but useful index is provided by determining the over-all per cent agreement, which is an index based upon the number of units on which two independent raters agree. If the agreement exceeds chance at a specified level, the result may be considered satisfactory. Obviously, this merely defines a lower bound. For a system to yield useful and usable results, the agreement must be considerably better than chance—just how much is a matter of judgment. A refinement is provided by analyzing the agreement for each category. This procedure indicates not only that two raters show a certain percentage of over-all agreement, but identifies the categories that are rated reliably and the ones that are not. By relating actually obtained agreement to agreement expected by chance one again obtains a lower bound as a basis for comparison.

LIMITATIONS

Certain limitations and cautions should be made explicit:

1. Since the system is restricted to the *therapist's* activity, it provides only a one-sided picture of the interaction. The information must, therefore, be supplemented by data on the patient's behavior. The interactive elements are taken into account in coding the therapist's verbalizations, but the resulting measures must always be considered in context. This illustrates the desirability of devising a parallel system for analyzing patient communications along similar lines, a task that seems quite feasible.

2. In its focus on the single communication the system is atomistic and disregards the idiosyncratic communication content. Therein lie both its strengths and weaknesses. On the positive side, it yields objective assessments of each intervention as it occurs, and is thus quite analytical. On the negative side, it does not throw light on the larger units of

therapeutic interaction, such as themes and phases of the therapeutic work. Additional descriptions of the therapeutic process in terms of its idiosyncratic content undoubtedly mitigate this shortcoming, and are indeed indispensable. In this respect, the information yielded by this analysis is the direct antithesis of the typical case history found in the psychoanalytic literature, which stresses the larger sweep of dynamic events, but usually disregards the single interaction units. The two kinds of approaches may complement and supplement each other.

3. The analysis is relatively time-consuming, requiring two to four hours for a typical therapeutic hour, and it requires highly qualified and trained raters.

4. Since the system is primarily descriptive and essentially nonvaluative, it makes no qualitative distinctions. Thus it provides no information as to whether an interpretation is "correct" or "incorrect," whether the therapist uses precise language, whether an intervention is properly timed, whether a remark is appropriate or anxiety-provoking, and so on. Such evaluations are contingent upon adequate external criteria.

5. The system is restricted to the analysis of verbal symbolic messages and their emotional overtones; it largely omits from consideration nonverbal forms of interaction. This is not to deny their importance, but points up the need for developing further special methodologies.

6. There is an elusive but significant limitation that derives from the assumptions in any quantitative analysis. It is assumed that each unit of analysis (therapist intervention) is equivalent to every other unit, that the units are additive, and that frequency of occurrence is an important heuristic indicator.

APPLICATIONS

The system should be useful in any research operation

587

requiring a quantitative measure of the therapist's verbal communications. A few specific uses are suggested in the following list:

1. The comparative analysis of therapeutic protocols: comparisons between different theoretical orientations; comparisons between therapists of varying experience levels, degrees and kinds of training backgrounds, professional affiliations, personality structures, and so on; comparisons between different forms of psychotherapy, such as psychoanalysis, psychoanalytically oriented therapy, nondirective therapy, supportive therapy, and so on.

2. Intratherapist analyses, such as comparisons of techniques used with patients of specific diagnostic categories—for example, different forms of neurotics, psychotics, and so on; longitudinal studies of single cases for the purpose of analyzing and comparing variations in technique as a function of the patient's problems, stage of therapy, therapeutic aims, and so on.

3. Validity studies in which techniques are related to therapeutic outcomes, evaluated by external criteria or by changes within the patient, judged independently.

4. The testing of specific hypotheses in so-called process studies. Examples would be reactions by the patient to, say, "deep" interpretations, focus on transference feelings toward the therapist, statements in which the therapist communicates "warmth," strongly assumes the initiative, and the like.

In conclusion, it should be emphasized that present formulations are tentative and subject to modifications as further relevant dimensions of the therapeutic process can be operationally defined.

References

Auld, F., Jr., and Murray, E. J. 1955. "Content-Analysis Studies of Psychotherapy," *Psychol. Bul.*, 52: 377–395.

Bales, R. F. 1950. *Interaction Process Analysis.* Cambridge, Mass.: Addison-Wesley.

Berelson, B. 1952. *Content Analysis in Communication Research.* Glencoe, Ill.; Free Press.

Collier, R. M. 1953. "A Scale for Rating Responses of the Psychotherapist," *J. Cons Psychol.*, 17: 321–326.

Fiedler, F. E. 1953. "Quantitative Studies of the Role of Therapists' Feelings Toward their Patients," in *Psychotherapy: Theory and Research,* ed. O. H. Mowrer, pp. 296–315. New York: Ronald Press.

Glover, E. 1955a. "Common Technical Practices: A Questionnaire Research," in *The Technique of Psychoanalysis,* pp. 261–350. New York: International Universities Press. Originally published in 1940 under the title *An Investigation of the Technique of Psychoanalysis.*

——— 1955b. "Therapeutic Criteria of Psychoanalysis," in *The Technique of Psychoanalysis,* pp. 374–386. New York: International Universities Press.

Harway, N. I., Dittmann, A. T., Raush, H. L., Bordin, E. S., Rigler, D. 1955. "The Measurement of Depth of Interpretation," *J. Cons. Psychol.*, 19: 247–253.

Kramish, A. A. 1954. "Problems in the Nondirective Therapist's Reflection of Feeling," *J. Soc. Psychol.*, 39: 201–209.

Marmor, J. 1955. "Symposium on Validation of Psychoanalytic Techniques," *J. Am. Psychoanal Assn.*, 3: 496–505.

Porter, E. H., Jr. 1943. "The Development and Evaluation of a Measure of Counseling Interview Procedures," *Educ. Psychol. Meas.*, 3: 105–126; 215–238.

Saslow, G., Matarazzo, J. D., and Guze, S. 1955. "The Stability of Interaction Chronograph Patterns in

589

Psychiatric Interviews," *J. Cons. Psychol.*, 19: 417–430.

Snyder, W. U. 1945. "An Investigation of the Nature of Nondirective Psychotherapy," *J. Gen. Psychol.*, 33: 193–223.

Wolstein, B. 1954. *Transference: Its Meaning and Function in Psychoanalytic Therapy.* New York: Grune & Stratton.

22

DIMENSIONS OF THERAPISTS' ACTIVITY (WITH M. S. WALLACH)

In recent years increasing attention has been given to the problem of devising operational definitions of psychotherapeutic techniques and other presumably relevant aspects of the therapist's activity. Such investigations are based upon the working hypothesis that therapists irrespective of their theoretical orientation and personality differences share certain conceptions and that some of the differences between therapeutic approaches that are stressed in theoretical expositions may be more apparent than real. On the other hand, there may be true (demonstrable) differences in the operations of therapists that may cut across theoretical orientations and personality differences. This approach focuses upon empirical data elicited from psychotherapists or observations made upon the psychotherapeutic process by external observers. Put more succinctly, we might say that

591

therapists of different theoretical persuasions may be more similar in their procedures than they realize or are willing to admit; however, they may also be more different, and both similarities and differences may be along heretofore unsuspected lines.*

The investigation discussed in this chapter represents a preliminary attempt to study therapists' preferences for and attitudes toward therapeutic practices that are fairly basic. We were not concerned with highly specific aspects of the therapist's operations, such as particular ways of handling therapeutic problems, methods of interpretation, and the like. Our concern was with more general attitudinal variations. In a number of respects this research is related to earlier studies by Glover (1955), Meehl (1960), Fey (1958), and to the comprehensive work of Sundland and Barker (1962), with whose findings, as will be seen, the present results showed marked congruence.

THE UTP SCALE

Relying on our own experience, the results of previous investigations by members of our group, and our general knowledge of the field, we constructed a 17-item scale dealing with what we considered to be major instances of the therapist's usual therapeutic practices (UTP). The respondent's task was simply one of stating on a six-point scale his agreement or disagreement with a given proposition.

METHOD

The UTP Scale was completed by two groups of respondents: Sample A consisted of 59 medical psycho-

*Grateful acknowledgment is made to Lyle V. Jones for helpful statistical advice and to the Computation Center of the University of North Carolina for assistance in the statistical analysis.

This research was supported by Research Grant MH-02171-05 from the National Institute of Mental Health, Public Health Service.

592

therapists at North Carolina Memorial Hospital, University of North Carolina, who were seen individually in connection with another project, which called for their participation as vicarious interviewers responding to a sound film of an initial psychiatric interview.

Sample B comprised 248 psychotherapists throughout the United States, who completed the scale as part of a questionnaire survey dealing with the *Weltanschauung* and values of psychotherapists.*

Pertinent biographical data for the two samples are presented in Table 1.

RESULTS

The responses of the 59 therapists of Sample A to the UTP Scale were intercorrelated and subjected to factor analysis. The principal axis solution was followed by varimax rotation to orthogonal simple structure, as programed by Johnson (1961) for the Univac 1105. The pattern of decrements in successive characteristic roots from the principal axes solution suggested that no fewer than four and no more than six factors should be retained for rotation. Rotated solutions were obtained based upon the largest three, four, five, six, seven, and eight principal axes. The six-factor solution was judged most suitable, since the smallest rotated factor still displayed sizable projections of two variables. To maintain consistency, six factors also were extracted and rotated for the data of Sample B. A comparison of the solutions from both samples appears in Table 2.

FACTOR I: For both samples, this factor emerged as the most distinct one. In both instances the highest loadings

---

*We are indebted to Peter N. Mayfield for making these data available. His questionnaire was mailed to 300 psychiatrists and 300 psychologists whose names were randomly selected from the directories of their respective professional organizations. A total of 248 therapists returned completed questionnaires. For details, see Mayfield (1962).

TABLE 1

BIOGRAPHICAL DESCRIPTION OF SAMPLES A AND B

| | Sample A*
Psychiatrists
($N=59$) | Sample B† | |
		Psychi- atrists ($N=91$)	Psychol- ogists ($N=157$)
Male	56	83	140
Female	3	8	17
Mean Age	35.9 years	41.5	40.1
Mean level of experience	5.3 years	8.5	8.2
Percent who had personal analysis	47	61	70
Primary theoretical orientation			
Orthodox Freudian		11	12
Psychoanalytic-general		57	61
Client-centered	0	6	23
Neo-Freudian and all others		17	61

Note.—Sample A was composed of therapists subscribing to the Freudian-Orthodox or Psychoanalytic-General orientations.
* 34 psychiatric residents, 21 psychiatrists, 4 analysts.
† In subsequent analyses, 6 cases omitted because of incomplete data.

TABLE 2

ROTATED ORTHOGONAL FACTOR MATRIX (VARIMAX SOLUTION) FOR TWO SAMPLES RESPONDING TO THE UTP SCALE

	Factor											
	I		II		III		IV		V		VI	
Item	A	B	A	B	A	B	A	B	A	B	A	B
1. Generally tend to be active.	-03	-21	-10	-06	-65	-30	29	12	02	-07	-08	01
2. Find it difficult to cope with patient's hostility.	-11	-06	-12	-13	01	-03	05	05	15	-11	51	39
3. Tend to be more effective with some patients.	04	05	00	03	09	-10	04	09	-05	-49	36	15
4. Rarely express own feelings in treatment	50	47	-38	-04	26	58	-24	-07	00	-06	10	-03
5. Rarely answer personal questions.	74	76	-13	-01	04	19	-06	-10	09	-09	-22	-08
6. Verbal interventions are usually sparing and concise.	02	17	-01	12	74	61	09	13	10	20	08	-05
7. If asked by my patient, would be willing to talk with a relative.	-17	-24	35	-18	-01	-12	-05	07	-16	-06	00	00
8. Prefer to conduct intensive rather than goal-limited therapy.	09	12	55	29	10	05	16	05	-11	02	03	-03
9. Almost never let silences build up during the therapy hour.	06	05	-43	-53	23	-16	34	10	02	04	-04	07
10. Keep all aspects of my private life out of therapy	76	70	08	-10	-03	28	-04	-03	-18	-17	-12	-19
11. Technique varies a good deal from patient to patient.	-06	-15	17	-32	-10	-06	-04	18	-50	-34	01	-07
12. Usually willing to grant extra interviews	-19	-22	-02	-08	-07	-08	57	22	24	-07	06	07
13. Consider psychotherapy much more an art than a science.	-15	-07	03	06	-05	-05	41	42	-19	-16	20	03
14. Almost never answer personal questions of opinion.	69	71	-06	-01	-08	04	-31	-17	23	17	11	02
15. A warm, giving attitude is the most important characteristic of a good therapist	-53	-16	-20	-18	-18	15	18	37	-28	06	-20	03
16. Therapist should be more like a "blank screen" than a person in therapy.	40	39	13	06	-11	18	-02	-22	34	12	26	21
17. Prefer patients not to develop intense feelings about me.	-15	09	-54	-34	07	12	13	01	-11	-02	28	07
Σa²/17	35	29	08	03	08	06	05	02	03	02	03	00

Note.—Decimal points omitted.

595

occurred on Items 5, 10, and 14, all of which are concerned with the extent to which the therapist allows himself to get personally involved in the treatment ("Rarely answer personal questions"; "Keep all aspects of my private life out of therapy"; "Almost never answer personal questions of opinion.") Clearly the theme here involves the *maintenance of personal distance.*

FACTOR II: The highest (negative) loadings occurred on Items 9 and 17 ("Almost never let silences build up during the therapy hour"; "Prefer patients not to develop intense feelings about me."). Another high (positive) loading was obtained on Item 8 ("Prefer to conduct intensive rather than goal-limited therapy."). This factor seems to be concerned with the therapist's *preference for intensive (psychoanalytic, uncovering) psychotherapy,* as well as his willingness to deal with transference feelings.

FACTOR III: High loadings, for both samples, occurred on Items 6, 4, and 1 (negative) ("Verbal interventions are usually sparing and concise"; "Rarely express own feelings in treatment"; "Generally tend to be active."). This factor appears to refer to a *preference for keeping verbal interventions to a minimum,* with the added implication that communications should be restricted to those that are clearly in the patient's interest, i.e., therapeutic.

FACTOR IV: This factor, which has its highest loadings on Items 12 and 13 ("Usually willing to grant extra interviews"; "Consider psychotherapy much more an art than a science."), is not entirely clear; however, it seems to refer to a view of psychotherapy as an *artistic and artful activity,* with an emphasis upon *flexibility* as opposed to a rigidly controlled procedure.

FACTORS V AND VI: These factors are referred to in the Discussion.

Differences between Experience Levels

In an effort to replicate pertinent findings reported by

Sundland and Barker (1962), we proceeded to investigate the relationship between the factors isolated in this study and the therapists' level of experience. Based on the highest loadings of the first four factors, we computed factor scores (using the z transformation) for each therapist and correlated these scores with the therapist's level of experience. No significant correlations were obtained for Sample A, and Pearson r's for Factors I, III, and IV for Sample B were in the vicinity of zero. For Factor II of Sample B (Preference for intensive therapy) an r of $-.15$ (significant at the .05 level) was obtained, signifying a tendency for the more experienced therapists to prefer intensive psychotherapy.

Differences between Theoretical Orientations

A comparable procedure was followed to investigate differences in factor scores for therapists subscribing to divergent theoretical orientations. Four subgroups of Sample B were sufficiently sizable for this analysis: Orthodox Freudian, Psychoanalytic-general, Sullivan, and Client-centered. Table 3 shows the means for each factor, together with the results of analyses of variance. Three of the obtained F's were statistically significant beyond the .05 level, with Factor I virtually reaching this level.

It will be noted that Orthodox Freudians were highest in maintaining personal distance, preference for intensive therapy, and keeping verbal interventions at a minimum, and lowest in considering therapy as an artistic activity. The client-centered group was distinct in considering psychotherapy as an art and in its lack of preference for intensive therapy. Other findings are apparent from the table.

DISCUSSION

While the six-factor solution was judged to be the most satisfactory for both samples, at best only four factors appeared worthy of serious consideration. Factor V appears

597

TABLE 3

MEANS AND F TESTS FOR THEORETICAL ORIENTATIONS AND FACTOR SCORES
($N=195$)*

Factor	Orthodox Freudian ($N=21$)	Psychoanalytic-general ($N=116$)	Sullivan ($N=28$)	Client-centered ($N=30$)	F
I Maintaining personal distance	13.59	12.35	11.71	11.74	2.63
II Preference for intensive therapy	6.85	6.04	6.37	5.03	3.47†
III Keeping verbal interventions at minimum	5.92	4.12	3.54	4.43	2.80†
IV Psychotherapy as art	7.87	7.78	7.87	8.30	6.52‡

* "Other" ($N = 26$) and subgroups containing few cases omitted. † $p < .05$. ‡ $p < .01$.

to relate to the therapist's view of technique as relatively invariant, and Factor VI may refer to an admission of countertransference potentials (particularly with reference to reactions evoked by the patient's hostility), but further study is needed for a better delineation of these dimensions. Indeed, on the basis of the present work, one is on safe grounds only regarding Factor I, which is the only factor that emerged with sufficient strength and clarity to enable one to be sure about its meaning. The remaining factors account for relatively small amounts of the total variance; nevertheless, the fact that it was possible to replicate them lends support to our belief that we are dealing with meaningful constructs. This conclusion is strengthened by two considerations: first, the replication employed a fairly large sample; and secondly, the utilization of machine procedures for computation and rotation obviated possible subjective biases that otherwise might intrude into the factoring process.

The findings of any factor analytic study are of course dependent upon the items representing a sample from the item universe. The present study points to dimensions of therapist activity that could have been posited on the basis of "armchair logic." The fact that the dimensions represented by the four factors were uncovered by actually asking therapists about their usual therapy practices lends stability to our initial conceptions. Worthy of particular note is the strength and clarity of the first factor, which emphasizes the importance of the therapist's personal distance (or, alternately, his direct personal involvement) in the interpersonal relationship with the patient. This factor shows marked congruence with Sundland and Barker's (1962) general factor, which was found to cut across a number of their scales. They considered it "the most significant single continuum upon which to compare therapists [p. 205]." This agreement is particularly noteworthy since our respective investigations proceeded quite independently. Note their description:

For convenience, one pole of the general factor will be labeled the "analytic" pole—using "analytic" in its broad sense as a mode of attending and responding, not as an abbreviation for "psychoanalytic." The other pole of the general factor will be labeled the "experiential" pole, congruent with its emphasis upon nonrationalized, nonverbal experiencing. In terms of the subjects with the higher loadings, the analytic pole stresses *conceptualizing, the training of the therapist, unconscious processes,* and *a restriction of therapist spontaneity.* The experiential pole deemphasizes conceptualizing, stresses the personality of the therapist, an *unplanned approach to therapy, deemphasizes unconscious* processes, and accepts therapist spontaneity [p. 205, authors' italics].

Somewhat in contrast to their conclusion, we tend to believe that "analytic" does refer to "psychoanalytic" in the sense of the therapist's studied and deliberate restriction of his free-and-easy participation in the therapeutic interaction. This restraint is viewed as a function of his training in psychoanalytic principles with its emphasis upon *analysis* of the transference situation, as opposed to a theoretical position that stresses the curative aspects of a good interpersonal relationship in and of itself.

In the present study, as in the report by Sundland and Barker (1962), therapists' levels of experience seem unrelated to reported therapy activity. Theoretical orientation, on the other hand, once again was related significantly to a number of the factors isolated. Usually the Psychoanalytic groups appear as most dissimilar from the Client-centered group.

At this point it is not possible to make more specific assertions about the kind of therapeutic relationship preferred by particular therapists or the degree to which such preferences might relate to other personality attributes or to the therapist's theoretical orientation. By the same token, the relationship of the personal distance variable to other

600

basic dimensions of therapist activity remains to be explored. The present findings, however, permit us to have somewhat clearer ideas about the kinds of items that might be used to strengthen the dimensions that were tentatively identified.

The results of this study emphasize the importance of the therapist's personal involvement versus his relative aloofness in the therapeutic relationship. They also call attention to variations in the therapist's willingness to accept and deal therapeutically with the patient's emerging transference feelings and attitudes. This may turn out to be an important dimension describing a basic orientation of psychotherapists: the extent to which they prefer to take an expectant attitude, let the transference develop, and analyze it; at the opposite extreme we may find therapists who are more interested in "manipulating" the transference (cf. Bibring, 1954). This dimension may also be closely related to the degree of indirection or restraint a therapist is willing to use in dealing with the patient's problem versus the extent to which he wishes to take an active part in directing the patient's efforts in solving his immediate life problems; indeed it may spell a basic temperamental difference between therapists regarding their preference for psychoanalysis or the various other forms of psychotherapy.

References

Bibring, E. 1954. "Psychoanalysis and the Dynamic Psycho-therapies," *J. Am. Psychoanal. Assn.*, 2: 745-770.

Fey, W. F. 1958. "Doctrine and Experience: Their Influence upon the Psychotherapist," *J. Cons. Psychol.*, 22: 403-409.

Glover, E. 1955. *The Technique of Psychoanalysis.* New York: International Universities Press.

Johnson, E. S. 1961. "Varimax Rotation, NCGFOI, Feb. 7." Programing Note 58, Computation Center, University of North Carolina, Chapel Hill.

Mayfield, P. N. 1962. "The *Weltanschauung* of Psychotherapists and Selected Correlates in a Quasi-Therapy Situation." Ph.D. Dissertation, University of North Carolina, Chapel Hill.

Meehl, P. E. 1960. "The Cognitive Activity of the Clinician," *Am. Psychol.*, 15: 19-27.

Sundland, D. M., and Barker, E. N. 1962. "The Orientations of Psychotherapists," *J. Cons. Psychol.*, 26: 201-212.

Part VIII
Psychoanalysis
and Its Discontents

The chapters in this section reflect my views and concerns about the status and future of psychoanalytic psychotherapy. It is a topic on which I hold strong convictions and, as is usually the case, my personal experiences inevitably color my outlook on science.

The chapters are primarily concerned with psychotherapeutic techniques rather than the broader theory (metapsychology) of psychoanalysis. This emphasis reflects my fundamental belief that as therapists and researchers we should concern ourselves with what therapists do, not what they say they do, and perhaps even less with the theoretical superstructure they invoke to explain their operations. For related reasons I greatly prefer to speak of psychoanalytic psychotherapy, and I have never felt very hospitable toward the distinction between "psychoanalysis" and "psychotherapy" or between "psychoanalyst" and "psychotherapist." These distinctions have always impressed me as a form of élitism, and while I understand the bases on which serious writers (e.g., Gill, 1954) have sought to differentiate these forms of therapy, I question very seriously whether this dichotomy can withstand critical scrutiny. The arrangements of the therapeutic situation, the therapist's stance, and the techniques he *thinks* he employs appear to me much less important than the actual character of the therapeutic influence he brings to bear on the patient. This influence, I have become increasingly convinced, cannot be defined in terms of the label pinned on a technique. An interpretation, for example, does not necessarily have the *effect* of producing "dynamic rearrangements" or giving the patient an understanding of some aspect of his motivations or behavior simply because the therapist's verbal communication is couched in the form of an interpretation. To classify communications on the basis of therapist's intent or by external criteria seems similarly artificial. Therapists of course recognize this, but a fair amount of research (including some of mine) has sought to measure differences in therapeutic techniques along these lines. By the same token, the "psychoanalyst," as much as the "psychotherapist," directs and manipulates the patient's behavior. It cannot be otherwise, yet this realization is dawning on many of us only gradually. In short, I believe that the distinction between "psychoanalysis" and "psychotherapy" is largely arbitrary and that there are large areas of overlap. It may turn out that the alleged differences (which have been maximized by orthodox writers) are quite inconsequential.

To avoid misunderstanding, let me emphasize my belief that there are significant differences between those forms of psychotherapy that are aimed at inducing changes in some central process (by which I mean the patient's unconscious strategies of dealing with other people, his self-system, etc.) and those designed to directly modify behavior, but even here the dividing line may be thinner than previously assumed. For example, it may be impossible to modify a symptom without changing the patient's view of the world and his self-confidence, and unless a change in inner processes somehow leads to changes in behavior one might be hard put to document its significance.

Freud was always ambivalent about the therapeutic effectiveness of the techniques he developed, particularly in his later years. I used to agree with analytic writers that we should not let ourselves be maneuvered into a position where we would have to defend the utility of psychoanalytic theory (I am speaking of those of its aspects relating to psychotherapy) on the basis of its therapeutic effectiveness. I now think this is an untenable position and that we must squarely face the question of whether psychoanalytic psychotherapy has something *unique* to contribute. I must concede that the evidence so far has been quite unimpressive. I am not a therapeutic nihilist—in fact, I continue to believe that psychotherapy can do a great deal for certain people in distress; however, I am skeptical whether psychoanalytic therapy (including orthodox analysis) offers anything "special" beyond its particular philosophy, which in the early decades of this century had considerable appeal to members of the intelligentsia, and to some extent still does in our metropolitan areas. Yet we cannot escape the conclusion that psychoanalytic psychotherapy has passed its zenith and is markedly on the decline.

Without in any way detracting from Freud's revolutionary contributions, I strongly agree with Engel (1968) that psychoanalysis has failed to "deliver the goods." For this failure I must squarely blame the orthodox psychoanalytic establishment that, almost from its inception, has vigorously dug its own grave. As soon as Freud began to think of his brain child in terms of a "movement" or "cause," he began to jettison what was perhaps his most unique contribution, that of open and honest inquiry into the causes and dynamics of man's neurotic turmoil and the search for effective ways of ameliorating it. Rejected by the medical

607

establishment of his day, Freud proceeded to set up his own, a trend that despite Freud's forebodings led to a merging of the two in this country. The history of psychoanalysis in America has increasingly been the history of a profession rather than that of a science. Excessively sensitive about establishing territorial rights for its practitioners, psychoanalysis in the United States has virtually become a "closed shop." To its detriment (and perhaps eventual downfall) it has systematically excluded from its ranks behavioral scientists, and indeed anyone who might question psychoanalytic doctrine, which has become progressively codified and stagnant. It is painfully obvious that any group that arrogates to itself the right to legislate what phenomena shall be investigated, what techniques shall be employed for such investigations, and—most destructively—who shall be considered qualified to undertake such inquiry is turning its back on the advancement of knowledge and retreating to a position that regards open communication with scientists in cognate areas as inimical and hostile to its own ends. While some belated corrections of this dismal situation have been attempted, it may already be too late. To be sure, what is viable and of lasting value in Freud's work will be absorbed by the mainstream of science. This occurs in any event, and it cannot be prevented by a professional guild. The latter, however, can have a powerful influence in delaying such amalgamation, and this is precisely what organized psychoanalysis in the United States has accomplished. In the process it has probably set back the scientific clock by 50 years or more, thereby ironically hastening its own demise.

Psychoanalytic psychotherapy, I am convinced, is in dire need of a thorough theoretical and technical overhaul. The developments that have occurred in the area during the past decades have been relatively minor. Much more trenchant changes are called for, and it is merely a question of time until they are made.

The rigidity and stagnation to which the psychoanalytic establishment has fallen victim are difficult to exaggerate.

608

I lived for a decade or more in a psychoanalytically dominated atmosphere, and thanks to some outstanding clinicians who were themselves analysts, I learned a great deal about the field (as well as myself). I continue to have abiding respect and even admiration for these individuals whose clinical and therapeutic acumen is unmatched by other therapists I have met before or since. Significantly, too, these persons—except when they wore the official hat of the establishment—were relatively openminded, searching, dedicated to their craft, and accepting of dissident views. But when a committee of senior faculty members denies another senior faculty member (an analytically trained psychotherapist but a nonanalyst) the right to treat a patient "on the couch," even when this is done under appropriate supervision, and when the patient's sitting or supine position ostensibly becomes the touchstone for the decision, one must begin to seriously question the rationality of the "system." (The foregoing incident, let me assure the skeptical reader, is not fiction; it occurred circa 1960.)

The emergence of new therapeutic approaches, particularly along the lines of behavior therapy, will be seen, I venture to predict, as a turning point in the development of psychotherapy as an applied science. Gaining momentum in the late Fifties, this trend has had the salutary effect of breaking with established doctrine by calling forceful attention to the need for dealing with empirical data rather than theoretical niceties. While the new trend was initially a reaction against psychoanalysis, it has long surpassed this tendentiousness. To be sure, behavior therapy was not long in developing an orthodoxy of its own, but it is quite clear that it has become quite impossible for any one group to exert the degree of control over divergent views and approaches that was once characteristic of psychoanalysis. The field is now much more open and much less fettered by shibboleths. Vigorous experimentation is sweeping the scene, and there is every reason to believe that a better synthesis will eventually emerge. Although the current techniques are hardly original and no one has learned to work miracles, it is true that therapy has become more sharply focused and the therapeutic results have become much more impressive. Withal, therapists are beginning to form a clearer awareness of what they *can* do, which is also beginning to highlight what they *cannot* do. As these lessons are learned, therapists undoubtedly will become more modest but they will establish a much sounder and more realistic basis for future developments. At the very least, the field is on the move again. For this we should be thankful!

References

Engel, G. L. 1968. "Some Obstacles to the Development of Research in Psychoanalysis," *J. Am. Psychoanal. Assn.*, 16: 195-204.

Gill, M. M. 1954. "Psychoanalysis and Explanatory Psychotherapy," *J. Am. Psychoanal. Assn.*, 2: 771-797.

23

PSYCHOANALYTIC THERAPY OF THE INDIVIDUAL

The observer of the psychoanalytic* scene who sets himself the task of discerning new developments in technique suffers disadvantages comparable to those of the interpreter of contemporary or near-contemporary history: he is too close to the events and too much under their sway to view them in proper perspective. Personal biases and idiosyncrasies are bound to influence his evaluations and judgments, which inevitably will bear the stamp of his time. Seemingly signifi-

*The terms "analyst" and "therapist" and their corollaries "psychoanalysis" and "psychotherapy" will be used more or less interchangeably, except where alleged differences are discussed. In general, the generic terms therapist and psychotherapy seem preferable because they are more neutral and less "loaded." Whatever the specific differences between psychoanalysis and psychotherapy may turn out to be, it seems reasonable to consider psychoanalysis a specialized form of psychotherapy.

cant advances may in the larger perspective of the history of science prove to be blind alleys; conversely, future advances may come from today's unnoticed or neglected developments. We still live under the shadow of Freud's revolutionary discoveries, in relation to which contemporary developments seem rather modest. This is not to denigrate their actual or potential importance, but merely to accentuate the great theoretical and technical innovations that flowed from such concepts as the dynamic unconscious, transference, resistance, and narcissism. The empirical cornerstones on which the psychoanalytic edifice firmly rests have neither been shaken nor replaced since Freud's time. History may show that Freud's most basic, trenchant, and lasting contributions consist of (1) the basic conception of the neurotic conflict and symptom formation; and (2) the contrivance of the psychoanalytic situation as a laboratory for the microscopic study and therapeutic modification of interpersonal and intrapsychic processes, subsuming most prominently the discovery, understanding, and "handling" of transference phenomena. But such judgments rightfully belong to future generations.

This chapter focuses on *technical* developments in the two-person treatment relationship in psychoanalytic psychotherapy. It attempts to discern changes in technique that have occurred over the last few decades, to cite examples of relevant empirical research, and to point up significant problems for future research. Theoretical contributions will be mentioned insofar as they seem to have found their way into therapeutic practice. The events leading to World War II and its aftermath had a stifling effect on the development of psychotherapy on the European continent, and the prevailing ideology in the Iron Curtain countries since the war has perpetuated this trend. By contrast, the English-speaking countries, notably America and to a lesser extent England, have played a leading role in this field. Therefore, the American scene will occupy the foreground of this presentation, and little will be said about developments elsewhere.

LACK OF PRIMARY DATA

In order to speak authoritatively of developments in the practice of psychoanalysis and psychotherapy one should be able to base his observations on *empirical* data. Furthermore, to discuss changes that have taken place over the years, it would be important to make comparisons between therapeutic techniques "then" and "now." Information permitting such comparisons unfortunately is not available. Freud's works on technique, as is well known, were not plentiful, and when he wrote on the subject he tended to speak in general terms. Besides, there is reason to believe that Freud's descriptions of technique are not an accurate guide to the manner in which psychoanalysis was practiced by him or anyone else. The descriptions tended to be "recommendations" rather than statements of what was actually done. It was assumed that any analyst, so long as he was properly trained, would follow "standard" technique in essential respects and that individual differences among therapists were negligible. In other words, therapists were regarded as interchangeable units, at least as far as their adherence to the basic tenets of psychoanalytic treatment was concerned. To be sure, Freud occasionally mentioned individual differences, but assigned them no great significance except in the context of countertransference reactions. He took it for granted that analyzed therapists were mature, reliable, and responsible individuals who in certain situations could act as mentors or serve as models to their patients (Freud, 1937). However, by and large, the personality of the therapist was seen as relatively inconsequential for the proper conduct of psychoanalytic therapy.

The view of therapists as "interchangeable units" was first challenged* by Glover (1940), who submitted a lengthy

---

*Anna Freud reported that "years ago, in Vienna," analysts discovered that they differed widely in their techniques. She states (1954): "So far as I know, no one has succeeded yet in investigating and finding the causes of these particular variations. They are determined, of

613

questionnaire to the membership of the British Psychoanalytic Association, eliciting information in their therapeutic techniques and practices. The form was sent to 29 practicing analysts, and the survey yielded responses from 24. While impressive, the results should have occasioned no surprise. Briefly, Glover found that British analysts, despite the marked homogeneity of their training, agreed on very few points, and indeed revealed marked divergence on many aspects of technique and practice. Glover had worded his questions in rather general terms and the responses reflected what the British analysts at the time *said* they did—not what they actually did. The *practical* significance of Glover's results is difficult to assess, because apparent discrepancies may have been of little practical import, but the opposite is more likely. In any event, the conclusion was justified that there are *true* differences in the techniques of therapists of comparable training and experience. There is no reason to assume that the situation is different today. The limited number of empirical studies bearing on this topic (e.g., Fey, 1958; see also Chapters Two and Seven) suggest that inexperienced therapists as a group are more "alike" in their techniques than experienced ones following the same theoretical orientation, but that there are palpable technique differences between therapists following divergent theoretical orientations. One series of studies (Fiedler, 1950a, 1950b, 1951) is often cited in support of the view that experienced therapists, irrespective of their theoretical orientation, establish therapeutic relationships whose "atmosphere" shows greater resemblance to each other than is true of novices. However, these findings have at best limited validity. By rigorous criteria, it must be asserted that the question is as yet unanswered.

---

course, not by the material, but by the trends of interest, intentions, shades of evaluation which are peculiar to every individual analyst. I do not suggest that they should be looked for among the phenomena of countertransference [p. 609]."

614

Primary data on psychotherapeutic techniques, such as transcripts or sound recordings, have been conspicuously scarce. Prior to 1940 such materials were virtually unavailable, and since that time the situation has not changed substantially, some notable exceptions notwithstanding. Examples of the latter are the sound films and sound recordings of psychoanalytic treatment produced by the late Franz Alexander and his co-workers at Mt. Sinai Hospital in Los Angeles (Levy, 1961) and by the late Paul Bergman at the National Institute of Mental Health in Bethesda. Comparable records of individual hours or segments of therapy have been somewhat more plentiful, but highly experienced therapists have, for the most part, been rather reticent to submit their therapeutic operations to public scrutiny. While the privacy of psychotherapy lends justification to the desire to maintain confidentiality, the fact remains that we are largely uninformed concerning the actual practices of the "average" psychotherapist. From case reports and theoretical discussions in the literature we know to some extent what therapists *say* they do, but there is reason to believe in the existence of discrepancies between writings on technique and actual practices. For these reasons, too, it is difficult to form a clear picture of changes that may have occurred over the years. (Judd Marmor, 1967, testifies from his personal experience over a quarter of a century that many changes have indeed occurred. Most of the changes mentioned by him will be discussed in this chapter.)

The alternative is to have recourse to the writings of those individuals who seem to have exerted the greatest influence on the field. This, largely, will be the procedure followed in this chapter. However, irrespective of the impact these contributions have had, it must be kept in mind that they are the products of the most articulate spokesmen who do not necessarily reflect the thinking and techniques of the rank and file of psychotherapists practicing today. Besides, therapists, while evolving their individual styles as their experience increases, undoubtedly are heavily influenced by their teachers, notably their training therapists, who belong to an earlier generation. For these reasons as well as the general conservatism of the field, it is probably fair to say that actual practices lag behind published writings.

FREUD'S CONTRIBUTIONS TO THE PROBLEMS OF TECHNIQUE

As already noted, Freud published little on the topic of technique, and while on several occasions he toyed with the idea of writing an *Allgemeine Technik der Psychoanalyse* (a general account of psychoanalytic technique), this plan was never realized. In his introduction to Freud's works on technique, Strachey (1958) reviews Freud's contributions, noting "some feeling of reluctance on his part" to write systematically on the subject. It is of historical interest to cite Strachey's speculations concerning the basis of Freud's reluctance. Reportedly, he disliked the idea of future patients knowing "too much" about the details of his technique, suspecting that they would scan his writings for "clues." Moreover, he was highly skeptical of the value neophyte therapists would derive from an exposition of technique. He considered that the psychological factors (including the personality of the analyst) were "too complex and variable" to lend themselves to hard and fast rules. Most important, perhaps, he remained convinced that once the "mechanism" of psychoanalytic therapy was properly grasped and understood by the student, everything else would fall into place. Underlying his discussions of technique there was the firm belief that mastery of psychotherapy could be acquired only from clinical experience, and, more fundamentally, from the therapist's personal analysis. This notion was advanced tentatively at first, but gained strong affirmation as time went on. In one of his last writings Freud (1937) urged every analyst to re-enter analysis, perhaps every five years. This recommendation, it should be noted, has been honored subsequently mainly in the breach.

616

In the same work Freud expressed his belief that the ways in which psychoanalytic technique achieves its aims have been sufficiently elucidated and that therefore it would be more appropriate to inquire into obstacles which therapy encounters. This statement seems overoptimistic, considering the many problems that continue to engage therapists in their published articles. Both Hartmann (1951) and Rapaport (1959) observed that expositions of technique have lagged behind theoretical developments, and Rapaport noted that a comprehensive theory of psychoanalytic *technique* still remains to be written.

Freud's works specifically dealing with technique constitute a series of six brief contributions published in rather rapid succession between 1911 and 1915 (Freud, 1911, 1912a, 1912b, 1913, 1914b, 1915). While they deal with important special topics, they can hardly be regarded as a systematic exposition. In addition, relevant comments are interspersed in the case histories and Introductory Lectures.* Significantly, Freud gave his fullest account of technique in *Studies on Hysteria* (Breuer and Freud, 1895), but this technique (which Strachey calls the "pressure technique") was of course soon to be superseded by what has since become the prototype of "orthodox" psychoanalysis.

PSYCHOANALYTIC THERAPY: DEFINITION AND PROBLEMS

One of Freud's (1914a) operational definitions of psychoanalytic therapy which is noteworthy for its simplicity and parsimony runs as follows:

The theory of *repression* is the corner-stone on which the whole structure of psychoanalysis rests. It is the most

---

*See Appendix, pp. 172-173, *The Standard Edition of the Complete Psychological Works of Sigmund Freud,* Vol. XII, for a complete list of Freud's writings dealing mainly with technique.

essential part of it; and yet it is nothing but a theoretical formulation of a phenomenon which may be observed as often as one pleases [Note the emphasis on empirical data!] if one undertakes an analysis of a neurotic without resorting to hypnosis. In such cases one comes across a *resistance* which opposes the work of analysis and in order to frustrate it pleads a failure of memory. The use of hypnosis was bound to hide this resistance; the history of psychoanalysis proper, therefore, only begins with the new technique that dispenses with hypnosis. The theoretical consideration of the fact that this resistance coincides with an amnesia leads inevitably to the view of *unconscious mental activity* which is peculiar to psychoanalysis and which, too, distinguishes it quite clearly from philosophical speculations about the unconscious. It may thus be said that the theory of psychoanalysis [here Freud clearly speaks of the theory of psychoanalytic *therapy*] is an attempt to account for two striking and unexpected facts of observation which emerge whenever an attempt is made to trace the symptoms of a neurotic back to their sources in his past life: *the facts of transference and resistance.* Any line of investigation [that is, therapy] which recognizes these two facts and takes them as the starting-point of its work has a right to call itself psychoanalysis, even though it arrives at results other than my own. But anyone who takes up other sides of the problem while avoiding these two hypotheses will hardly escape a charge of misappropriation of property by attempted impersonation, if he persists in calling himself a psychoanalyst [p. 16; italics mine—H.H.S.].

In this definition the essential ingredients of psychoanalytic therapy are explicitly stated as (1) transference and (2) resistance, which in turn are viewed as the result of (3) repression. The theory of repression, which has remained the prototype of all defense mechanisms, is rooted in the postulate of (4) the dynamic unconscious. The only ingredient not explicitly mentioned but clearly implied is (5) the analytic

618

situation which is prerequisite for the emergence of the foregoing phenomena.

One of the important ingredients in this definition is the absence of any attempt to differentiate "psychoanalysis" from "psychoanalytically oriented psychotherapy" (or similar terms)—distinctions that have been attempted by later writers. It seems clear that Freud espoused a broad and relatively unrestricted view of the psychoanalytic process, of which the development and resolution of the transference neurosis is *not necessarily* the touchstone. In this passage Freud undoubtedly had in mind the early dissidents whom he accused of "misappropriating" and distorting his ideas, but one cannot escape the impression that subsequent writers, in attempting to make finer distinctions, have grappled with pseudo-problems, or at least problems that were tangential to psychoanalytic therapy as Freud viewed is.

Freud's disinclination to spell out the technique of psychoanalysis was evidently based on similar considerations. In his well-known chess simile (1913) he explicitly stated that only the opening and closing moves are susceptible to specification whereas the grand strategy of "working through" with all its intricacies must be tailored to the problems and personalities of individual patients. Yet the basic tenets guiding this strategy are contained in the above paradigm. The complexity of therapy in the individual patient does not lie in departures from the basic principles; rather, the latter run like a red thread through every utterance and intervention of the therapist. Therefore, Freud believed that the mastery of technique flows directly from, and is firmly rooted in, the therapist's understanding of the theoretical premises of psychoanalysis.

A further corollary of this position is the relative de-emphasis of individual difference among therapists. From this point of view, it is inconsequential whether a therapist advances 10 interpretations that are aimed at the same transference manifestation during a single hour whereas another therapist, more sparing in his verbal interventions, attempts to achieve the same objective by making only two. Nor does the number of questions or the sheer number of words used by the therapist make a difference in and of itself so long as the immediate and long-range objectives of the therapeutic enterprise are clearly kept in mind. The immediate objective is always an answer to the question, where is the *current resistance*? How does it manifest itself? How does it interfere with the progress of therapy? The long-range objective is to be sought in the clarification and resolution of the transference.

The foregoing are well-known restatements of psychoanalytic axioms; yet they have often been misunderstood by researchers in the area who, since approximately 1940, have focused on increasingly smaller units of the therapeutic transaction, attempting to dissect it in the belief that if an interpretation is effective, its effect must be traceable to a single interaction between patient and therapist. The same error apparently has been committed by analysts who have spent many pages discussing the proper timing and the "mutative" effect of a single interpretation. Psychoanalysis, like any form of psychotherapy, is to be viewed as a *process* extending over a prolonged period of time, and its effect—as has often been pointed out—must be sought in the prolonged working through of basic pathogenic conflicts as they make their appearance in multiform guises.

Nevertheless, this question arises: Why is this process crowned by success in some instances and doomed to failure in others? Assuredly, there are reasons attributable to the patient's personality structure, the genesis of his neurosis, his constitution, and so forth. But there are also factors in the therapist's personality, life experience, attitudes, etc., and the manner in which they meet and interact with the patient via the therapeutic technique. It appears that, apart from his emphasis on countertransference phenomena, Freud did not explicitly formulate the *interactive* aspects of the patient-therapist relationship.

The therapist must understand the patient's transference maneuvers, his resistances, and the specific structure of his neurosis. But his communications must reach and make sense to the patient on a deep emotional level. Thus, crucial errors in technique do not arise to any significant degree from premature, partially incorrect, incomplete, or even false interpretations: rather they are to be seen as a failure to reach the patient at a level where therapy becomes *an experience that makes a difference.* Perhaps such failures may be subsumed under the heading of faulty empathy or faulty technique. Yet, ultimately, it is not the technique that is at fault; rather it is the therapist's failure to communicate in terms that are to the patient *emotionally significant and meaningful.* Herein lies the skill and the art of psychotherapy. Where technique is elevated to a position of preeminence, the groundwork for such failures is laid. It is very likely that this is precisely what occurred around 1920, when, according to Clara Thompson (1950), psychoanalysis in its search for the "infantile amnesia" reached a low ebb. The renaissance of psychotherapy was made possible by the realization that the technical devices Freud abstracted from his observations are only a means to an end.* Failure to heed this caution means courting a therapeutic impasse. Parenthetically, the latter-day popularity of existential analysis and its variants appears attributable—at least in part—to what is probably a basic misapprehension of the goals and procedures of psychoanalysis. On the other hand, it is easy to see how the reading of the typical psychoanalytic paper, with its astringent and impersonal quality, lends itself to misinterpretations of the essential goals aspired to by Freud in therapy.

A typical misapprehension concerns the nature of the transference, its technical handling, and resolution. One of

---

*I am also mindful of the developments ushered in by W. Reich's (1949) emphasis on the analysis of character defenses and the resulting emphasis on the ego's defensive functions.

the frequent criticisms of psychoanalysis by its contemporary opponents is the contention that the transference serves to resurrect problems of the past and to search for the childhood antecedents of the patient's current difficulties, usually at the expense of the therapist's interest in the patient's *current* problems in living. Evidently, this procedure was not infrequently followed by therapists a generation ago, but has been superseded by the newer emphasis on ego functions. As is well recognized, patients may dwell on the past as a resistance, just as they may become preoccupied with trivial events in their current lives. In short, resistance may take innumerable forms, and it is the therapist's task to recognize and deal with it in therapeutic ways. The latter constitutes an acid test of the therapist's skill.

An important question obviously concerns the relationship between a therapist's theoretical assumptions and his technique. To what extent does technique mirror underlying theoretical beliefs, and to what extent is it possible to make inferences about the therapist's theoretical assumptions by studying his behavior vis-à-vis a patient? Ideally, two therapists subscribing to identical theoretical tenets may be expected to employ identical therapeutic techniques, yet, as has been stated, such is not the case. Their communications will diverge on as many dimensions as one is willing to define: frequency of utterances, length, emotional quality, intonation, topics selected for comment—to name but a few. Such dimensions exemplify the kinds of variables content analysts (see, in this connection, the reviews by Auld and Murray, 1955, and by Marsden, 1965) have attempted to define and measure over the past 20 years in an effort to compare therapeutic techniques. It may be objected that such measurable differences are not the "real" ones, since two therapists might differ in their therapeutic styles and yet practice an identical form of therapy. This position is difficult to defend because the critic may ask about the criteria by which similarities or differences are to be decided. Surely, there must be a more solid basis than someone's opinion, but

622

even if one were to rely on expert opinion, a rater or judge will implicitly apply certain criteria, which are precisely the ones to be spelled out.

The issue is crucial because of the alleged theoretical differences between schools of psychotherapy, which their originators have done their utmost to accentuate. Typically, these systems are tied to conceptualizations about childhood development and the evolution of the adult personality. Many of these attempts, insofar as they are based on empirical clinical observations, are valuable contributions to the science of psychology, but this is not the present concern. To the extent that divergent theoretical positions include a theory of psychotherapy that gives rise to specific kinds of therapeutic interventions, the techniques must be operationally definable. Stated otherwise, the assertion that different systems lead to different therapeutic techniques is of little value unless the differences are in some way demonstrable. If a Rogerian, a Sullivanian, and a Freudian practice forms of psychotherapy that do *not* differ along the particular lines espoused by the originators of the system, then the uniqueness of the system may be a myth. To complicate matters, it may also be true that alleged differences in technique may lie along dimensions different from those postulated by the system, in which case the theoretical differences may be of negligible relevance as far as the practice of psychotherapy is concerned, and an entirely different theory of the nature of the psychotherapeutic influence may have to be written. Frank (1961) made a significant attempt to isolate common elements in diverse forms of psychological influence, including psychotherapy, religious conversion, "brainwashing," etc. Does the problem then have to be resolved by recourse to the kinds of *changes* effected by a given form of psychotherapy? Perhaps, but in that event criteria for the measurement of changes have to be evolved. The contention that orthodox analysis produces a restructuring of the psychic apparatus whereas other forms of therapy achieve modifications that are less far-reaching and profound

623

may be plausible, but the critics have a right to be shown that this is indeed the case. Again, it is necessary to point out that at present we lack criteria by which such personality modifications can be reliably and validly judged. Thus far, available methods are inadequate for such an undertaking.

If the nature of the psychological influence exerted by different forms of psychotherapy turns out to have only a loose articulation to the system espoused by the therapist, one may wonder about the nature of the significant dimensions. One important dimension that invites attention as a strong contender is the person of the therapist, including his attitudes toward the patient (for example, interest, dedication, and investment in the patient as a person) and his ability to make therapy a significant and meaningful experience for the patient. *How* he accomplishes this feat is the crucial problem that research in this area must answer. The therapist's depth of belief in the truth and usefulness of his theoretical system and his abiding willingness and faith in his ability to help the patient, as Frank suggested, probably play an important part. It may be also surmised that, depending on the patient's personality, cultural background, values, etc., different systems of psychotherapy have different degrees of intellectual and ultimately emotional appeal —over and beyond the person of the therapist who practices them. This possibility in no way denies that some conceptions of neurosis and emotional problems in living, apart from the person of the therapist, are more fruitful, heuristic, and capable of effecting deeper personality changes than others.

The preceding discussion puts in sharper focus the following question: To what extent is it necessary for a therapist to accept particular psychoanalytic tenets to practice psychoanalytic psychotherapy, including psychoanalysis? The answer, in terms of Freud's definition, is relatively simple, but troublesome questions remain.

For example, one might construct a continuum along which Freud's theoretical conceptions might be ordered on

624

the basis of their relevance to the practice of psychotherapy. Such a dimension might coincide with the degree to which phenomena are capable of observation. At one extreme, resistance, as evidenced, say, by blocking, evasiveness, and the like, is closest to observation; at the other, a concept like the death instinct, farthest. Freud's metapsychological concepts, which he termed "our mythology," appear to be the ones least relevant to psychotherapeutic operations. For example, it is hard to see that therapeutic practice is greatly affected by the therapist's acceptance or rejection of the concept of the death instinct, or whether he subscribes to the notion of an innate conflict-free sphere. However, it is of considerable consequence whether he accepts the concept of resistance and defense. At the extremes, the question is easily resolved; however, there is a large "gray" area where acceptance or rejection of a theoretical construct might make a practical difference. Therapy may take a different course if the therapist views the patient's "basic" problem as an "oedipal conflict" or as a "pregenital oral conflict." Here the question may be not so much acceptance or rejection of a theoretical construct but the relative emphasis the therapist assigns to it. Or, there may be differences of opinion about the layering of defenses and the proper sequence of analyzing them. In any event, the degree of articulation between theory and therapeutic practice represents an important problem. Freud, it has been noted, left the matter in rather general terms. He did not go beyond such general statements as: defenses are to be analyzed before content; negative transference must be interpreted expeditiously; etc. While therapist-supervisors make more specific recommendations to their students, generally applicable criteria have not been set forth, nor has empirical research succeeded in illuminating the problem.

There is another important reason necessitating the isolation of dimensions for the comparative study of therapeutic techniques. I am referring to the requirement of defining the *independent variable* (see Frank, 1959). While

625

the solution of this problem is of paramount importance for eventually comparing the effectiveness of different forms of psychotherapy, it is bound to have equally significant implications for the theory and practice of therapy. If the relative effectiveness of two medications is to be compared, it is scientifically inadequate to state that both are white, round, and weigh two grains. One may be a placebo and the other a potent drug, but one would not be able to tell from such a gross description. To define one form of treatment as "psychoanalysis" and another as "psychotherapy based on psychoanalytic principles"* is hardly more precise unless the "active ingredients" can be isolated. By this time it is apparent that the same form of therapy in the hands of two therapists, or the same form of therapy conducted by one therapist with two different patients, is *not* identical. Thus, it will be pointless to compare the relative effectiveness of different forms of psychotherapy, irrespective of real or apparent differences in outcome, as long as we cannot spell out the particular therapeutic interventions that are purported to be the operative ones.† The problem is of course vastly complicated by the fact that, concurrent with psychotherapy, the patient is undergoing a variety of life experiences that may have an inhibiting or facilitating effect on therapeutic progress. Among the practical consequences of isolating the nature of the psychological influences exerted by the therapist through his personality and technique, we may expect to see improved selection of particular patients for particular forms of psychotherapy with particular psychotherapists. Needless to say, this would be a major achievement.

To summarize principal problem areas that during the last few decades have received the attention of clinicians and researchers, we may list the following:

---

*The majority of research papers in the literature still rest content with such broad designations.

†This is one of the major shortcomings of comparisons between behavior therapy and psychoanalytic therapy (see pages 665-694).

1. There has been an increased emphasis on relating the childhood roots of the patient's neurosis to his contemporary functioning and adaptation, thereby rendering therapy a more vivid and potentially deeper-going process. Past events of the patient's life are of no intrinsic interest to therapy except insofar as feelings surrounding them are still alive in the present and continue to have an adverse effect upon the patient's current living. The influence of ego psychology here is particularly relevant.

2. Increasing attention is being paid to the personality of the therapist and the extent to which he succeeds in making therapy a significant experience for the patient. This interest is partly a function of a growing research interest, by sociologists and psychologists, in problems of two-person interactions in a variety of settings.

3. Intertwined with the foregoing has been the search for briefer, more economical, and more effective ways of treating patients by means of psychotherapy. Under this rubric should be mentioned attempts to regulate the length of therapy, frequency of visits, degree to which regression is fostered, and the like. More radical departures from the analytic model are exemplified by experimentation in the areas of verbal conditioning, behavior therapy, etc. (see pages 665-669).

4. While the scope of indications for psychotherapy has undergone considerable broadening from the base of the transference neuroses, efforts have been made to arrive at better criteria for selecting patients for particular forms of therapy. This effort has as yet been neither systematic nor exhaustive.

5. The same judgment applies to the definition and measurement of outcome criteria by which the effectiveness of therapy can be assessed. The assertion that the resolution of the transference neurosis by interpretation alone leads to more pervasive and more lasting personality changes than other forms of therapy in which "suggestion" is used more freely remains a credo of "orthodox" analysts, but has been

challenged by others, and as yet lacks clear-cut demonstration.

6. The philosophical assumptions and theoretical formulations underlying psychoanalytic therapy have been questioned from many quarters and for different reasons, leading to more or less radical departures from the "basic model" technique advocated by Freud. The emergence of numerous competing systems of psychotherapy (Harper, 1959, distinguished 36!) has probably contributed to the enrichment of the field as well as engendered confusion.

7. Advances of theory and research in sociology, anthropology (linguistics, kinesics), experimental psychology (learning theory, operant conditioning, etc.), information theory, communication theory, the use of psychoactive drugs in psychiatry, and in numerous other areas have been important but are hard to assess. The development of group therapy, family therapy, therapy with children, and other forms of psychotherapy, too, has had an impact on individual psychotherapy based on analytic principles. However, on the whole, these influences have led to comparatively few modifications or reformulations of basic psychoanalytic concepts and techniques.

In the following sections selected problems and trends will be elaborated in somewhat greater detail.

INFLUENCE OF EGO PSYCHOLOGY

While the theoretical contributions of ego psychology have been made explicit in numerous publications, the technical implications are considerably less clear and more difficult to delineate. Hartmann (1951), in one of the few essays specifically devoted to this topic, notes the lag between theoretical advances and practical applications, and frankly acknowledges that trenchant technical discoveries, comparable to abreaction and analysis of resistances, are not to

628

be found in the latest phase of analytic theory. Furthermore, he asserts that a great deal more is known on a theoretical level than can be utilized in practice.

Following Hartmann, ego psychology's major contribution to therapeutic practice has been in the area of handling resistances. The emphasis here rests on those aspects of the patient's psychic functioning that are concerned with his *adaptation to reality*. Clearly, the therapist never works with intrapsychic conflicts in isolation, but of necessity must deal with the patient's total personality in its intrapsychic as well as interpersonal struggles. To some extent this fact has always been recognized by analytic theory, but it was given increasing recognition by Freud (1926) in the *Problem of Anxiety* and by Anna Freud (1936) in *The Ego and the Mechanisms of Defence*. Both works have given direction to the theoretical developments that have since been subsumed under the heading of ego psychology.

How does the recognition that the ego serves a synthesizing and integrative function, that its structure comprises both conflicts and conflict-free components, and that stratification is one of its essential characteristics influence the therapist's technical maneuvers? These concepts, at least in rudimentary form, were spelled out in Freud's (1923) latest model of the psychic apparatus as formulated in *The Ego and the Id* and have since been elaborated rather than changed in any fundamental way. Hartmann points out that the evolution of analytic technique may be traced through gradually emerging changes in the original formula "making the unconscious conscious," already enunciated by Breuer and Freud (1895) in *Studies on Hysteria*. Subsequent developments occurred under the impact of the finding that a mere translation of the derivatives of the patient's unconscious conflict into consciousness was an inadequate therapeutic measure. Henceforth attention was directed upon the role and function of resistance, particularly of its unconscious aspects, which found its way into a broader conception of the structure and function of the ego. The practical yield

629

lies in an improved understanding of the varieties of defense, the manner in which impulse and defense are woven into character traits, the identification and management of the manifold forms of resistance, and a clearer conception of the patient as a *total* person. Thus, in analyzing a resistance, the working formula "defense—warded-off impulsive" provides only a crude blueprint for the therapist's interventions. Therapists could not escape the recognition that they are operating within a complex psychic field and that any interpretation sets in motion reverberations of the total psychic apparatus, which have potentially far-reaching dynamic, economic, and structural implications. We have as yet only very imprecise notions about the workings of this process, particularly with respect to *structural* changes. Indeed, structural changes seem far more difficult to achieve than was formerly believed, and it is as yet an open question whether psychoanalytic therapy is better equipped than other forms of therapy in effecting such modifications.

Field theoretical concepts are of course not unique to psychoanalysis, but rather represent special instances of developments in biology and psychology, among other sciences. However, instead of simplifying the understanding of the effects of therapeutic interventions (notably interpretations of resistance), such concepts add to the complexity. Nevertheless, by giving proper emphasis to the complexity of the psychic apparatus—in its intersystemic, intrasystemic, and adaptational functioning—ego psychology has performed a valuable service, most significantly by its implicit warning against the "empty organism" approach of behaviorism, which has been pitted against the alleged cumbersomeness of psychoanalytic theory and therapy, but fails to explain many relevant phenomena pertaining to emotional disturbances and their amelioration.

Psychoanalytic theory and practice—at least within the mainstream of its development—has remained rooted in Freud's instinct theory, of which the stages of psychosexual development are an integral part. Yet, in this area, too, reformulations have occurred, which probably will have a lasting effect on psychotherapeutic practice. Here Erikson's (1959) formulations of epigenesis, stressing as they do the psychosocial and adaptational aspects of personality development, deserve emphasis. It may be said that Erikson has broadened Freud's original formulations by placing the child's instinctual development more squarely with the broader context of his normal social and interpersonal relatedness. For example, the oral period is characterized not only by passive and active incorporation (together with associated fantasies) subserving a function of the id, but coincides with a particular way of relating to the world and significant people. This "way of life" is one of close physical contact, dependency, and receptivity. One of the important implications of Erikson's thinking is the evolution of the child's sense of *identity* as he successfully completes the developmental tasks set by each stage. The growth and consolidation of the ego are a concomitant of the achievement of competence and mastery. These in turn presuppose a sense of basic trust, instilled in infancy and early childhood, which may be viewed as the matrix for personality growth in normal development as well as in psychotherapy.

While the implications of these notions for psychoanalytic therapy are not nearly so clear as one might wish, they appear to be an integral part of the renewed emphasis on the *experiential* learning aspects of psychotherapy, particularly as opposed to intellectual (cognitive) insight. To illustrate further, while it was recognized that repressions in childhood had set the stage for fixations, it was more or less taken for granted that once the repressions were removed, the patient would soon "catch up" and close the gap between a disturbed childhood and present-day reality. Insufficiently taken into account, it appears, was the fact that by having suffered severe childhood traumata (resulting in massive repressions), the patient's ego development had sustained serious—and perhaps irreversible—damage. By analogy, a child who has dropped out of school because of an illness has

631

missed a significant portion of the curriculum. Merely to enable him to return to school after a year will not compensate deficits in learning and social maturation he has sustained. Similarly, the task of therapy in the "old" sense largely consisted of "returning" the patient to adult life. Freud initially believed that, when freed of his repressions, the patient would soon take advantage of the opportunities in social living and take his role among contemporaries. This process works smoothly where the patient's ego development is largely "intact." But, as every therapist knows, these cases are the exception rather than the rule. More typically, the patient, because of his neurosis, has been more or less seriously "retarded" in his personality growth, and ordinary life experience cannot be expected to fill the void. Psychotherapy, as part of its task, provides a new base of operations, or a new, if temporary, "home" from which the patient can venture forth, experiment in living, and return to enlist the therapist's assistance in helping him to understand errors in living he will unwittingly commit.*

Thus, the task of therapy is to clear away the impediments to emotional learning (repressions and other maladaptive defenses) and to create opportunities for new and more viable experiences. The advantages over the childhood situation lie in the patient's greater introspective powers, those aspects of his ego that form the therapeutic alliance with the therapist, and the therapist's comparatively greater objectivity (as compared with a parent). The disadvantages are to be sought in the fact that the maladaptive patterns the patient has learned in childhood are deeply entrenched and extraordinarily difficult to modify (Freud's repetition compulsion).

It may be said that the ego psychologists, by stressing man's problems in growth and adaptation, have partially

---

*This is another problem concerning which therapists who advocate desensitization and substitution of behavioral responses have remarkably little to say.

answered the accusation frequently leveled at Freud that he viewed *all* of man's behavior and psychological functioning as *nothing but* expressions of sexual and aggressive instinctual strivings. To be sure, one can find passages in his writings that tend to substantiate this conclusion, but the evolution of his thinking led from an emphasis on the dynamics of the unconscious to an increasing concern with the controlling functions of the ego. In keeping with this development, there has been a greater recognition that, in addition to mental functions that are embroiled in neurotic conflicts, there are parts of the personality that continue to serve important adaptive tasks, unless the person is completely incapacitated. How this shift in orientation has affected therapy practice is difficult to assess, all the more since psychoanalysis as yet lacks both an explicit learning theory and an explicit theory of psychotherapeutic change. Much remains to be learned about acquisition, maintenance, and—most important—modification of behavioral patterns (see Rapaport, 1959).

ANALYTIC THERAPY AS A LEARNING PROCESS

In this context it may prove helpful to compile an "operational inventory" of basic learning experiences occurring in psychoanalytic therapy.

1. The therapist *sets an example* of acceptance, respect, tolerance, nonpunitiveness, reliability, trustworthiness, punctuality, decency, nonretaliation, permissiveness, evenness of temper, predictability, truth, rationality, honesty, steady cooperation in constructive moves by the patient, nonavoidance of anxiety-provoking and "taboo" topics, reasonableness, etc. In this way he provides a certain gratification and stimulates in the patient the expression of wishes and impulses that become increasingly intense and primitive the less they are interfered with by outside pressure and the more they are guaranteed "safe" expression. The therapist

633

says, in effect: "It is all right for wishes and impulses to be experienced in awareness, but there is no assurance that they will be gratified." In fact, the patient will reject a good many himself once he becomes conscious of them. (This paradigm of the permissiveness of the analytic situation has of course been abundantly spelled out by Freud and others.)

2. The therapist *sets limits*: He strictly limits the time he devotes to the patient; he expects payment for services rendered; he expects punctuality, respect for his property, rights, privacy, and independence. He also abstains from participating in the patient's neurotic maneuvers (e.g. sado-masochistic strivings and a wide variety of other techniques of interpersonal control).

3. Through the foregoing and other devices the therapist teaches the *delay of gratification*—perhaps the most important lesson the patient has to learn. Tolerance of delay is taught by regulated frustration, such as nongratification of dependency wishes, terminating the hour by the clock rather than in accordance with the patient's desires, etc. The principle here is to awaken in awareness strong wishes typically dating back to early childhood, and by failing to gratify them, educate the patient to tolerate the unpleasure, tension, disappointment, discomfort, and unhappiness associated with them. In speaking about this process, Menninger (1958) observed that the patient's gain in psychotherapy is the product of his frustrations.

There is little doubt that in normal childhood development, ego strength is acquired in much the same manner: the child learns to accept frustration of his wishes (for dependency, sexual gratification, etc.) because he acquiesces in the privations imposed upon him by the parents as trustworthy representatives of reality. He suffers the pain of frustration and ultimately of separation from his love objects, because his love outweighs his self-seeking, narcissistic wishes, and he adapts to reality without developing excessive defensive controls resulting in neurotic symptoms.

The emotional learning occurring in psychoanalytic psychotherapy can thus be reduced to the following basic model:

1. The therapist provides a "good" climate, which the patient can come to recognize as a safe, protective environment. Thus, the therapist fills the role of a reasonable, accepting, and caring parent.

2. The patient—at least consciously—is willing to engage with the therapist in the collaborative venture of psychotherapy.

3. To the extent that the patient can emotionally come to experience the "good" aspects of Condition 1 (although they are controlled, restrained, and dosed), he begins to experience hitherto repressed wishes, impulses, fantasies, etc., toward the therapist. Also awakened are the negativistic and obstructionistic tendencies, commonly labeled resistance, by which the patient in accordance with his early life experience tries to engage the therapist in a neurotic struggle that, if successful (from the patient's point of view), would spell the failure of therapy. This phase comprises the spectrum of transference reactions.

4. The task of the therapist is to convince the patient of the irrationality, futility, and self-defeating aspects of his defensive maneuvers, thus encouraging their abandonment. As a substitute, he implicitly offers his own ego (attitudes, beliefs, values, etc.) as a new and better model for interpersonal collaboration.* This process, to a preponderant extent, is an emotional, not a cognitive one, and as Freud repeatedly observed, the balance of forces is determined entirely by the patient's emotional relationship to the therapist. It must also be pointed out that while psychoanalytic therapy in important respects is a process of socialization, this is only a part of it. It is more correct to say that in the

_____

*Clarification of *how* identification occurs appears to be another fruitful area for future research.

ordinary course of the child's socialization he comes to control (largely repress) his primitive instinctual strivings, which remain a central concern of analytic therapy. In the latter, various segments of unconscious processes are worked out in consciousness, interpreted in terms of their infantile roots, and integrated by the patient's adult, rational ego. The essence of analytic therapy is an intensive form of emotional learning in human collaboration and relatedness, carried on within an atmosphere of understanding and respect. The emotional relationship is mediated largely by the use of *language* and linguistic symbols, which raises the experiential aspects of the relationship to a more differentiated cognitive level.*

Psychotherapy (including psychoanalysis) appears to emerge more clearly as a learning process (Marmor, 1962, 1964), which is by no means restricted to the task of uncovering the patient's unformulated unconscious fantasies as they permeate his relationships to other people, life goals, and other facets of life. The making conscious of these derivatives (e.g., sadomasochistic, "homosexual," narcissistic trends) of course remains an undertaking central to analytically oriented therapy. It may be noted here, parenthetically, that the psychoanalytic emphasis on primitive, primordial fantasies, wishes, and fears separates this form of psychotherapy from the neo-Freudian dissidents, who by and large view the patient's problem to a much greater extent as a function of destructive interpersonal and cultural

---

*Stone (1961) characterizes the psychoanalytic situation as a state of "deprivation-in-intimacy," adding : "In my view, it represents to the unconscious, in its primary and most far-reaching impact, the superimposed series of basic separation experiences in the child's relation to his mother [p. 105]." "Underlying the entire dynamics and structure of the psychoanalytic situation, perhaps one of the inspirations of its genesis, is the driving force of the primordial transference, in its varying phase and conflict emphases, a phenomenon which is in itself derived from the successive states of separation from the mother [p. 106]."

636

influences. However, the "analyzing" of unconscious impulses proceeds concurrently with, or in the context of, a "good" human relationship, in which the patient has the unique opportunity to work, learn, and identify with a substitute parent-authority figure, whose function as a *model* has increasingly come to the fore. Thus, the therapist serves not only as a screen for the patient's transference projections, but in various ways (many of which have only been inadequately conceptualized so far) sets an example of strength, tolerance, patience, reliability—perhaps even wisdom!— that often provides a sharp contrast to the patient's early childhood experiences with significant adults. This all-important function Freud more or less took for granted— he saw it as *selbstverständlich*—yet it is anything but self-evident. Any form of psychotherapy mediates *a new experience in living,* and it is the extent to which the patient can derive *meaning* from this relationship that psychotherapy—at least in part—achieves its beneficial results.

The manner in which the therapeutic relationship becomes a meaningful experience for the patient remains essentially an unsolved problem. To be sure, the therapist, through self-knowledge, clinical experience, and formal training can do a great deal to prevent the therapeutic encounter from entering blind alleys or ending in an impasse. In addition, on the basis of his knowledge of the patient's life experience, presenting symptoms, and character structure, he can identify basic problems that in multifarious, idiosyncratic ways create the difficulties in living from which the patient is suffering. But he cannot *ensure* the emotional significance of the patient's experience in psychotherapy. At this point, technique ends and the imponderables of the human encounter assume the ascendancy. This also appears to be the juncture at which theoretical differences reveal the greatest divergence. More concretely, the two problems concern (1) the patient's suitability for psychotherapy, or, more precisely, the compatibility between a given patient and a given therapist; and (2) the essential nature of the therapeutic influence, which, after all, represents the personal view put forth by the therapist-proponent of a given theoretical system.

COMPATIBILITY BETWEEN PATIENT AND THERAPIST

There has been an increasing recognition that the chances for success in psychotherapy are markedly enhanced provided the prospective patient meets certain criteria, a number of which were already recognized by Freud, and others that have been isolated by systematic research undertaken during the last decades. Therapists, it is well known, have fairly specific—and presumably valid—notions about the kind of attributes a promising patient should possess, as well as those attributes that make a patient unsuitable for the more usual forms of analytic psychotherapy (cf. Goldstein, 1962, who critically discusses empirical research on the problems of therapist-patient expectancies). As a composite, patients considered good prognostic risks tend to be young, intelligent, physically attractive, well-educated members of the upper-middle class; to possess a high degree of ego strength, at least some anxiety that impels them to seek help; to have no seriously disabling neurotic symptoms, to have a relative absence of deep characterological distortions or strong secondary gains, to have a willingness to talk about their difficulties, an ability to communicate well, some achievements in the social-vocational area, a value system relatively congruent with that of the therapist, and a certain psychological-mindedness that makes them willing to take an objective look at themselves. As the work of Hollingshead and Redlich (1958) has shown, social class (which is of course linked to a number of the foregoing variables) plays an important role in the process of selecting patients for therapy. Understandably, a therapist tends to select patients who, in the therapist's judgment, are likely to benefit from the kind of therapy he has to offer. As clinical accounts by

Fromm-Reichmann, Searles, Will, and others demonstrate, these are necessarily the "easy" patients.

Furthermore, a cautionary note is essential to avoid the misinterpretation that promising candidates for psychotherapy are not really "sick." This inference would be quite unwarranted, and is in part a reflection upon the primitive status of currently available assessment techniques. By superficial standards a person may be described as "mentally healthy" if he meets gross behavioral criteria of performance, such as functioning in a particular social role, earning a living, absence of gross disturbances in interpersonal relations, or gross overt psychopathology. Yet, such conformity or seeming adaptation to the culture may be achieved at tremendous psychic cost, since the person may feel intensely unhappy, conflicted, inhibited, and ill at ease. There can be no doubt that psychoanalytic psychotherapy pays the closest attention to, and evinces the greatest respect for, the individual's intrapsychic organization and its function in the person's *fine* adjustment to himself and others. The latter is completely lost sight of in ordinary statistical tabulations of "improvement," as used in governmental statistics, outpatient clinic reports, and studies involving psychopharmacological agents.

Unfortunately, there are no adequate measures of self-respect, a sense of worthwhileness as a person, emotional well-being arising from an ability to be at peace with oneself and others, a sense of relatedness, identity, and true productivity—values that appear to become increasingly evanescent in the nuclear age. While existential analysts and therapists subscribing to related views have correctly called attention to the importance of these values, the impression has been conveyed that they are inconsistent with the goals of psychoanalytic psychotherapy. I do not think that this is so. As a corollary, symptom relief, while certainly important, should not be regarded as the ultimate goal of psychotherapy, no matter how often it may have to be compromised and modified for practical reasons. Rather, the integration and full unfolding of the human personality are worth striving for via psychotherapy, even though in the vast majority of cases, it may have to remain an unrealizable ideal. In this sense, Freud's conception of the psychoanalytic situation may be one of the few remaining bulwarks of the humanistic spirit in the twentieth century, for in no other human relationship is as much purposeful and dispassionate effort devoted to the "education" of a single human being.

THE THERAPIST-PATIENT RELATIONSHIP AND THE THERAPIST'S PERSONALITY: CHANGING CONCEPTS

The dynamics of the therapist-patient relationshp are the *sine qua non* of psychoanalytic psychotherapy, and all major contributions have taken as their point of departure Freud's conceptions of transference and countertransference. (See Orr, 1954; Thompson, 1950; Wolstein, 1954, 1959, for critical reviews.) It is clear that under the impact of operationalism in science certain modifications have occurred since the time of Freud. In general, there is an increasing tendency to deal with the dynamics of the therapeutic situation in process terms, to think of transference and countertransference as phenomena along continua instead of regarding them as either "positive" or "negative." Furthermore, greater emphasis is being placed on the here-and-now experience in the therapeutic relationship. Janet MacK. Rioch's (1943) formulation may serve as an example of this trend:

> The therapeutic aim in this process is not to uncover childhood memories which will then lend themselves to analytic interpretation. . . . Psychoanalytic cure is not the amassing of data, either from childhood, or from the study of the present situation. Nor does cure result from a repetition of the original injurious experience in the analytic relationship. What is curative in the process is that in

tending to reconstruct with the analyst that atmosphere which obtained in childhood, the patient actually achieves something new. He discovers that part of himself which had to be repressed at the time of the original experience. He can only do this in an interpersonal relationship with the analyst, which is suitable to such rediscovery. . . . Thus, the transference phenomenon is used so that the patient will completely re-experience the original frames of reference, and himself within those frames, in a truly different relationship with the analyst, to the end that he can discover the invalidity of his conclusions about himself and others [p. 151].

According to this viewpoint, the therapist is *more* than a sympathetic listener who interprets the patient's transference distortions, and his interpretations are not regarded as the only or the most effective factor in therapeutic success. Rather he must strive to create an emotional atmosphere in which the patient can reexperience significant aspects of his early life in which something went awry. By the same token, "countertransference" reactions are interferences with the therapist's positive emotional contribution—that is, instances in which the therapist's own personality through unresolved emotional problems impedes the full realization of the therapeutic goal.

When Freud (1910) introduced the term "countertransference," he revised his earlier view of the analyst as an impersonal mirror by recognizing that "blind spots" in the analyst's personality structure might interfere with his usefulness as a therapist. The emphasis of Freud's original formulation and that of subsequent elaborations has been on *interferences* with the analytic process occasioned by deficiencies, shortcomings, and characterological distortions within the analyst. This led to recommendations about dangers to be avoided, attitudes to be discouraged, and so on. The objective was to keep the analytic field clean and uncontaminated by minimizing unwarranted intrusions and involvements of the analyst in the patient's transference maneuvers. There is no doubt that this did much to augment the objectivity of observations in the analytic situation and to decrease the possibility of influencing the phenomena under scrutiny. Furthermore, it approximated a definition of the analytic situation as a laboratory situation for studying and modifying interpersonal processes (see, in this connection, Janis, 1958). The research potentialities of this method, it seems to me, have remained largely unexplored.

It is instructive to note that in the earlier formulations, countertransference was defined in relation to transferences of the patient, with little regard for the healthy or realistic aspects of the therapist's personality and attitudes. Even today, as Orr (1954) points out, there is widespread disagreement about the meaning of the term. For example, distinctions have been made between "positive" and "negative" countertransference; some writers insist that all feelings of the therapist should be included; others differentiate between whole and partial responses to the patient; still others restrict the term to the therapist's unconscious reactions. Berman (1949) suggests a distinction between countertransference in the classic sense and the therapist's reasonable and appropriate emotional responses, which he calls "attitudes." He also addressed himself to certain contradictions in Freud's writings, and reasons that "The answer could simply be that the analyst is always both the cool detached surgeon-like operator on the patient's psychic tissues, and the warm, human, friendly, helpful physician [p. 160]."

According to orthodox analytic principles, the therapist must not influence the transference situation by any means other than interpretations, which thus become the primary therapeutic agent. Furthermore, Freud and Fenichel imply that differences in the analytic atmosphere created by the analyst's personality do not exert an influence upon the transference situation and the therapeutic results. According to this view, *the* transference neurosis evolves more or less automatically, provided the therapist does nothing to interfere with its development.

In his last formulation Freud (1938) viewed the analyst as a new superego, who corrects errors in the patient's early upbringing. Strachey (1934), writing in the same vein, observes that

> The principal effective alteration consists in a profound qualitative modification of the patient's superego, from which the other alterations follow in the main automatically. . . . This modification of the patient's superego is brought about in a series of innumerable small steps by the agency of mutative interpretations, which are effected by the analyst in virtue of his position as object of the patient's id impulses and as auxiliary superego [p. 159].

The dosed introjection of good objects is regarded as one of the most important factors in the therapeutic process.

Bibring (1937) recognizes that the therapist makes a positive contribution through his own personality, but considers this to be essentially nonanalytical:

> [T]he therapeutic changes which take place in the superego are effected by purely analytical means, i.e., by demonstrating contradictions in structure and development and by making an elucidation of them possible. . . . In my opinion the analyst's attitude, and the analytical atmosphere which he creates, are fundamentally a reality-correction which adjusts the patient's anxieties about loss of love and punishment, the origin of which lies in childhood. Even if these anxieties later undergo analytical resolution, I still believe that the patient's relationship to the analyst from which a sense of security emanates is not only a precondition of the procedure but also effects an immediate (apart from an analytical) consolidation of his sense of security which he has not successfully acquired

or consolidated in childhood. Such an immediate consolidation—which, in itself, lies outside the field of analytic therapy—is, of course, only of permanent value if it goes along with the coordinated operation of analytic treatment [pp. 182-183].

Why is the atmosphere created by the therapist in which a "reality-correction" takes place to be divorced from the interpretive essence of analytic treatment? It may be that both are integral parts of analytic psychotherapy and that they operate conjointly as therapeutic factors. To tease out their relative contributions is a research task of the first magnitude, the solution of which may approach an answer to the question of what is effective in psychotherapy.

A major factor in the revival of interest in the therapist's personality was Alexander's conceptualization of the "corrective emotional experience," and it is fair to say that during the past decades this renewed interest in the person of the therapist has gained momentum. (See Chapter Twenty-four for a review of typical research studies.) In his attempt to isolate the therapeutic factors in psychoanalysis, Alexander (1950) stated:

No doubt, the most important therapeutic factor in psychoanalysis is the objective and yet helpful attitude of the therapist, something which does not exist in any other relationship. . . . To experience such a novel human relationship in itself has a tremendous therapeutic significance which cannot be overrated. . . . This attitude, combined with correct interpretation of material which is about to emerge from repression, together with the analysis of the ego's defenses, is primarily responsible for the therapeutic effectiveness of psychoanalysis [p. 487].

The essence of the "corrective emotional experience" involves an experiential contrast between the therapist's attitude and the original parental attitude, which were pre-

644

sumably pathogenic. In a more recent essay, Alexander (1958) forcefully restated this emphasis:

The theory of corrective emotional experience leads to still another technical conclusion. This concerns the most opaque (in my opinion) area of psychoanalysis, the question of the therapist's influence on the treatment process by the virtue of being what he is: an individual personality, distinct from all other therapists. The evaluation of this most elusive element in the therapeutic equation is at present quite beyond our ken. We know only that the blank screen model is an abstraction, which is too far removed from the actual events during treatment [p. 311].

Frank (1959a) explored the hypothesis that the patient's attitude of trust or faith may play a significant part in his response to all forms of psychotherapy. He hypothesizes that this favorable expectation is fostered by the therapist's own confidence in his ability to help, his ability to inspire confidence in the patient, to care deeply about him, to communicate the message that help will be forthcoming; and furthermore, that "the patient's favorable expectation, which is a major determinant of the therapist's influence over him, may have direct therapeutic effects which are not necessarily transient or superficial [p. 37]." Frank views these ingredients as a common factor in the effectiveness of all forms of psychotherapy. It is my impression that despite his cautions and disclaimers he is inclined to regard this common factor as the *major* factor.

The foregoing hypothesis, if substantiated, would be particularly damaging to the orthodox Freudian position, which draws a sharp line between the therapeutic objectives of psychoanalysis and those of other methods, including those of hypnosis, faith healing, brainwashing, etc., that Frank draws upon as analogues.

Macalpine (1950) postulates the following distinction

between the nature of psychological influence in psychoanalysis and suggestion in hypnosis or similar situations:

> Both hypnosis and psychoanalysis exploit infantile situations which they both create. But in hypnosis the transference is really and truly a mutual relationship existing between the hypnotist and the hypnotized. . . . One is tempted to say that countertransference is obligatory in and an essential part of hypnosis (and for that matter of all psychotherapies in which the patient is helped, encouraged, advised or criticized). . . . In psychoanalytic therapy alone the analysand is not transferred to. . . . The analyst . . . is never a co-actor. . . . The analytic transference relationship ought, strictly speaking, not to be referred to as a relationship between analysand and analyst, but more precisely as the analysand's relation to his analyst. . . . It is thereby not denied that analysis is a "team work"; in so far as it is, an "objective" relation exists between the analyst and the analysand. Because the analyst remains outside the regressive movement . . . suggestion can inherently play no part in the classical procedure of psychoanalytic technique.
>
> To make transference and its development the essential difference between psychoanalysis and all other psychotherapies, psychoanalytic technique may be defined as the only psychotherapeutic method in which a one-sided, infantile regression—analytic transference—is induced in a patient (analysand), analyzed, worked through, and finally resolved [pp. 535-536].

Frank concedes that his position and the analytic viewpoint need not be mutually exclusive, although I believe that psychoanalytic therapy encompasses considerably more than the "favorable expectancy" envisioned by Frank. For one thing, it requires hard work from the patient and makes similar demands on the therapist. On the other hand, I hypothesize that significant therapeutic progress cannot be made unless the patient is convinced that the therapist is a reliable partner in the enterprise, and that his attitude reflects personal integrity, dedication, honesty, and faith in the fruitfulness of the task. I consider these elements central to psychoanalytic therapy, but they have not yet been adequately conceptualized (see Chapters One and Two). In this sense, there *is* an "objective relationship" between patient and therapist. I fail to see how its hypothesized existence defiles the "purity" of analytic therapy. Yet analysts have strained to postulate the absence of an interpersonal relationship as a defining characteristic of psychoanalysis in the "orthodox" sense. That interpretations also play an important, though probably secondary, part is not denied, but their curative effect has perhaps been overestimated. At any rate, we have only clinical experience to go on. In saying this, I do not wish to denigrate its value, but neither can it command blind adherence in the absence of hard-core evidence.

QUEST FOR INCREASED EFFICIENCY OF THERAPY

The search for ways and means to make analytic therapy more efficient and shorter took its start with the work of Ferenczi and Rank (1925), of which the subsequent efforts by Alexander and French (1946), Alexander (1956), and Rado (1956, 1962) are logical successors. Ferenczi and Rank maintained that the revival of childhood memories in the transference situation was secondary to the re-experiencing of childhood patterns in relation to the therapist, which they considered sufficient for therapeutic change. It had been observed earlier that the "lifting of the infantile amnesia" in and of itself was no guarantee of therapeutic success; on the contrary, therapists noted that interpretation of the transference phenomena, even without recollection of specific childhood patterns, seemed to be the principal and essential condition for therapeutic change.

Alexander made numerous technical suggestions aimed

647

at intensifying the patient's emotional experience in therapy and achieving more rapid termination of treatment. Changing the frequency of interviews during appropriate phases of treatment was one technical device to make the patient more keenly aware of his dependency needs by frustrating them. Alexander also called attention to the problem inherent in any intensive long-term psychotherapy—the danger of excessive regression and the patient's tendency to use the treatment relationships as a means for obtaining significant gratifications instead of attempting to achieve mastery of his neurotic problems in the real world. He recognized—quite correctly, I think—a widespread tendency toward "overtreatment," which he vigorously proceeded to counteract by the above techniques. Alexander's theory of the "corective emotional experience," a significant departure from orthodoxy in therapy, has already been discussed in the context of the therapist's personality.

The limitations of "the basic model technique" were already recognized by Strachey (1934), and while he drew attention to the importance of the patient's identification with the therapist as an important therapeutic factor, he did not recommend changes in technique. In contrast, Rado took the next step and addressed himself to the problem of how the patient's emotional insight leads to changes in his behavior. He advocated an active re-educational procedure, by means of which the patient hopefully achieves a better adaptation to his life situation. In all of these approaches there is a sharper recognition that the exploration of the past is not a goal in itself in therapy; rather, it represents only a waystation toward mastery and coping with difficulties in the patient's current life.

Rado, much like Alexander, attempted to counteract at appropriate times the patient's regressive tendencies. Of course, analytic therapy considers regression essential to the resolution of traumatic childhood experiences, but there is the ever-present danger that by encouraging regressive trends in the patient, the therapist may unwittingly infantilize the patient and discourage his undertaking the important adaptational tasks that ultimately are the goals of therapy. Systematic research is needed to determine the exact point in therapy at which regression, instead of being helpful, becomes a noxious interference by reinforcing the patient's dependency wishes. To illustrate the absence of hard-core research on most problems of technique, we even lack as yet data on differences between a patient's associations while facing the therapist or reclining on the couch.

A bond uniting a number of modern approaches to analytic therapy, irrespective of divergences in other respects, is the emphasis on the patient-therapy relationships as an interpersonal system, which contrasts sharply with Freud's conception, restated by Macalpine (1950), in terms of the patient's relationship *to* the therapist. Rado's and Alexander's conceptions fit the former paradigm, which has been elevated to a central position in the writings of Sullivan and those of his followers. Fromm-Reichmann (1950), for example, defines the task of psychotherapy as "the clarification of the patient's difficulties with his fellow-men through observation and investigation of the vicissitudes of the mutual interrelationship between doctor and patient; the encouragement of recall of forgotten memories; the investigation and scrutiny of the anxiety connected with such recall, including the patient's resistance against this recall and his security operations with the psychiatrist who tries to effect it [p. ix]." The patient, according to this view, is suffering from disturbances in his interpersonal relationships, and the therapeutic factor is conceptualized as "discharge of affect plus insight gained by the patient [p. x]." In such statements it is left vague *how* insight changes the character of the patient's interpersonal relationships and leads to the kind of personality changes regarded as the goal of intensive psychotherapy. Nor is it clear how the interpretive process, upon which the neo-Freudians also rely, differs from the therapeutic interventions of a Freudian analyst.

Fromm-Reichmann observes in this connection: "There

are great differences of opinion, however, among various schools of psychoanalytic thinking in regard to the genetic frame of reference in which interpretation is done and about the patients' selection of content matter for repression and dissociation [p. 83]." She proceeds to note "an interesting transition" in the work of Fairbairn between Freud's psychosexual concepts versus the interpersonal interpretations of Sullivan. According to her, at the turn of the century, when Freud began his pioneering work, "sexual fantasies and experiences were the main entities and phenomena which had to be barred from awareness and to be resolved by interpretation. At the present time feelings of hostility, antagonism, and malevolence between any two individuals seem to be more subject to disapproval in our Western culture, therefore to more repression, than any other unacceptable brand of human experience and behavior [p. 3]." Examples of other "unacceptable thoughts and feelings" are said to include "the infantile overdependence of adults, interpersonal overpossessiveness or magic thinking, ideas of grandeur, etc." The impression is conveyed that these phenomena are taken at face value, rather than as complex resultants of more primitive processes originating in infancy or childhood.

Fromm-Reichmann exemplifies another major departure from Freud's conception of the transference situation. This deviation is rooted in a revised account of childhood development, which places much less emphasis on the oedipus constellation or at least questions its universality as a causal factor in neurosis. "In my experience," she states, "the wish for closeness and tenderness with the beloved parent and the envious resentment about the authoritative power of the hated one, both without recognizable sexual roots, constitute a more frequent finding in childhood histories of healthy, neurotic, and psychotic people than do their sexual oedipal entanglements with the parents of their childhood [p. 99]."

In the foregoing, a few examples have been given of

650

prominent attempts to render analytic therapy more effective. These efforts involve changes in the activities of the therapist, regulation of the transference situation, and certain reformulations of the kinds of pathogenic conflicts to be interpreted.* Controversy has surrounded all of these innovations, none of which have as yet been subjected to systematic investigation to assess their respective merits. It will be seen in the following sections that efforts to improve the effectiveness of analytic therapy are implicit in other contributions, although ostenisbly they may have been written for other purposes.

"WIDENING SCOPE" VERSUS RIGOROUS SELECTION OF PATIENTS

In a series of papers published under the general heading, "The Widening Scope of Indications for Psychoanalysis," Stone (1954) calls attention to Freud's basic conservatism in wishing to restrict the applicability of psychoanalysis essentially to the so-called transference neuroses, coupled with a persistent emphasis on a "basically reliable ego." Yet, a broadening of applications gradually occurred, encompassing the treatment of psychoses, character disorders, perversions, behavior disorders in childhood and adolescence, borderline states, psychosomatic conditions, and numerous others. Furthermore, with the rise of "the affluent society" in America, there is scarcely a human problem that has not

---

*In this connection, Alexander (1954) makes the interesting point: "The time has come when our technique must be adjusted to the therapeutic exigencies of each type of patient [p. 70]." In keeping with this assertion, Alexander questions the validity of the time-honored dictum that in psychoanalysis, therapy and investigation run parallel. The reason for this divergence is seen by Alexander in a potentially antitherapeutic result when the therapist pursues his interests in the genetic roots of the patient's illness at the expense of dealing with his oral dependency wishes, which can often act as a powerful and sometimes insurmountable resistance.

651

been brought to or treated by psychoanalysis, which thus has become the panacea for all human ills. This lack of discrimination may have been partly a function of the great social pressure for psychotherapeutic services, which has been mounting steadily, but therapists as a group must share some of the blame for undertaking tasks that often lay beyond their technical means. This problem was perhaps more severe some years ago than it is today, but it may account, at least in part, for the disenchantment with psychoanalytic therapy and its potentialities that currently seems to afflict the public, practitioners, and foundations supporting research.

In this context we again are brought face to face with the problem of defining more clearly the nature of the therapeutic influence as well as the conditions under which it is effective. Anna Freud (1954) comments: "If all the skill, knowledge and pioneering effort which was spent on widening the scope of application of psychoanalysis had been employed instead on intensifying and improving our technique in the original field (hysteric, phobic, and compulsive disorders), I cannot help but feel that, by now, we would find the treatment of the common neuroses child's play, instead of struggling with their technical problems as we have continued to do [p. 610]."

For example, there are as yet no clear-cut demonstrations that the development and resolution of a transference neurosis is the *only* (or indeed the best) method by which lasting ego modifications are achieved, and that the quality and extent of such changes are highly correlated with the therapeutic method. Gill (1954) attempts to draw a sharp line between "psychoanalysis" and "psychotherapy," reserving for the former the development of a regressive transference neurosis and the resolution of this neurosis by techniques of interpretation *alone*. In this connection, the relatively impersonal attitude of the therapist is seen as an attempt to hold constant an important variable—certainly a laudable objective on scientific grounds, and one whose potentialities still remain to be fully explored. Gill notes that in recent years there has been an increase in what he calls "intermediate techniques" which borrow heavily from the "basic model technique," but include departures dictated by various clinical and practical considerations. Nevertheless, Gill believes that psychoanalysis practiced in the strict sense achieves more lasting personality changes than any other technique. With the advent of many new techniques competing with intensive long-term analytic therapy, conclusive answers to this question would be particularly welcome.

THE CRITERION PROBLEM

In addition to specifications of the "active ingredients" in the treatment method, future progress appears to depend heavily on improved measures of outcome (see Chapter Sixteen). Clearly, there is no simple relationship between diagnostic indicators and therapeutic outcomes, yet, while much remains to be learned about the problem, in principle it should be amenable to conceptual analysis and empirical research. Traditionally, the "classical" neurotic conditions, like hysteria, have been regarded as ideally suited for psychotherapy and psychoanalysis, whereas severe character disorders and the psychoses have been considered more or less refractory. Such judgments are partly based upon clinical experience; but they also reflect subtle value judgments about the kinds of persons with whom psychotherapists prefer to work, as well as an appraisal in sociocultural terms of the patient's character structure and symptoms. Consequently, a patient meeting the psychotherapist's explicit as well as implicit criteria of a "good" or "promising" patient not only has a better chance of finding a competent therapist, but he may from the beginning elicit greater interest from the therapist, who in turn may become more willing to make an emotional investment in the treatment program and to devote greater energy to the treatment. It is as yet unknown to which extent the patient may fulfill the therapist's unverbalized prophecy.* However, it may turn out that a great deal more can be done for certain patients psychotherapeutically once it is possible to approach them and their difficulties in living more objectively.

Once the pertinent variables have been systematically studied, it may turn out that only a relatively restricted band of the population meets "good patient" criteria. The available evidence points to a convergent trend, which was aptly summarized by Luborsky (1959): "Those who stay in treatment improve; those who improve are better off to begin with than those who do not; and one can predict response to treatment by how well they are to begin with [p. 324]." It may be noted that the criteria of suitability that have been identified by research coincide remarkably well with those outlined earlier by Freud. What about the much larger group of people who by these standards are unsuitable for those forms of psychotherapy that place a premium on the patient's verbal skills and his ability to take some distance from his feeling?

From a practical point of view, the answer seems to lie not in making them more amenable to available methods of psychotherapy—sometimes this can be done, although it is a difficult and time-consuming effort—but in becoming more selective about making the limited facilities and the limited professional manpower available to those who can most readily benefit from them. Rather than being "undemocratic," this appears to be a counsel of reality. Research might make an important contribution by refining the selection of particular patients for particular therapists and for particular therapeutic methods. The challenge for the development of alternative techniques and treatment methods for those who cannot readily benefit from analyti-

---

*This problem has been studied by the present writer through experimental investigation designed to explore therapists' emotional reactions to patients presented via sound films and in other settings (see Strupp, 1960 as well as Chapters Twelve and Nineteen).

654

cally oriented psychotherapy of course continues and is beginning to be met. There is a strong possibility that a segment of the failure or near-failure cases can be curtailed through more judicious selection of candidates for therapy.

Before the advent of the "modern era" in psychotherapy research, that is, before sophisticated methodologists and researchers versed in matters of objective investigation and experimental design concerned themselves with these matters, a group of prominent psychoanalysts, including Glover, Fenichel, Strachey, Bergler, Nunberg, and Bibring (Symposium, 1937), addressed themselves to the issue at the 1936 International Congress of Psychoanalysis at Marienbad. While this group did not make any formal recommendation for judging outcomes, it dealt with the aims of psychoanalytic therapy and its modus operandi. Knight (1941) returned to the problem, listing three major groups of criteria:

1. *Disappearance of presenting symptoms*

2. *Real improvement in mental functioning*

    a. The acquisition of insight, intellectual and emotional, into the childhood sources of conflict, the part played by precipitating and other reality factors, and the methods of defense against anxiety that have produced the type of personality and the specific character of the morbid process;
    b. Development of tolerance, without anxiety, of the instinctual drives;
    c. Development of ability to accept one's self objectively, with a good appraisal of elements of strength and weakness;
    d. Attainment of relative freedom from enervating tensions and talent-crippling inhibitions;
    e. Release of the aggressive energies needed for self-preservation, achievement, competition and protection of one's rights.

655

3. *Improved reality adjustment*

a. More consistent and loyal interpersonal relationships with well-chosen objects;

b. Free functioning of abilities in productive work;

c. Improved sublimation in recreation and avocations;

d. Full hetrosexual functioning with potency and pleasure.

Knight also called attention to certain limitations that may detract from the full effectiveness of the therapeutic method. These will be recognized as the counterparts of the "good patient" variables previously mentioned. Limitations may be due to: (1) the patient's intelligence; (2) native ability and talents; (3) physical factors, such as muscle development, size, personal attractiveness, physical anomalies, sequelae of previous injury of illness, etc.; (4) permanent crippling of the ego in infancy and childhood; (5) life and reality factors that might impose frustrations, privations, etc., against which the patient must do battle, and that might produce relapses; (6) the patient's economic status, whether there is too little or too much money.

Clearly, Knight's criteria go far beyond a definition of disabling illness and in fact attempt a definition of positive mental health. It is also clear that the objectives of psychoanalytic therapy have always aspired to this ideal, and the outcome statistics reported by the various psychoanalytic treatment centers leave no doubt on this point (Fenichel, 1930).

Knight seems to take it for granted that the evaluations are to be made by the therapist. While the therapist's knowledge of the patient provides a unique vantage point for such appraisals, his objectivity is suspect on several counts, such as personal involvement as well as the segmental view he obtains of the patient's life.

In an effort to meet these criticisms, numerous efforts

have been made during the last two decades to develop more reliable and valid measures of therapeutic progress. In one group of studies, various apects of the patient's behavior—notably his verbalizations—have been quantified (see Auld and Murray, 1955, and Marsden, 1965, for summaries of this literature). Another large group of studies has followed the phenomenological approach, by asking the patient to evaluate his own status (e.g., see Chapter Nineteen). A third approach, has dealt with assessments by means of psychological tests. Zax and Klein (1960), following a review of several hundred investigations, conclude that the most serious failing of these approaches is that the criterion measures have not been systematically related to externally observable behavior in the life space of the patients. Their own proposed solution is to develop "criteria of sufficient breadth that they are meaningful and representative of a wide range of functioning and yet, at the same time, circumscribed enough to be measured with reliability [p. 445]." They concede that the development of such criteria is in its infancy, largely because there is no unifying set of principles (a theory of "normal" behavior) to guide observations. Finally, they express the hope that it might be possible to develop "a relatively limited number of norms reflecting basic interpersonal environments which can be useful [p. 446]." The basic problem here seems to be one of bridging the gap between the person's inner psychic experience and his adaptation to an interpersonal environment.

Clearly, there can be no single criterion of mental health or illness. As Jahoda (1958) in her review of current concepts points out, mental health is an individual and personal matter; it varies with the time, place, culture, and expectations of the social group; it is one of many human values; and it should differentiate between the person's enduring attributes and particular actions. One prominent value in American culture is that the individual should be able to stand on his own two feet without making undue demands or impositions on others.

657

From the research point of view, Jahoda discerns six major approaches to the subject: (1) attitudes of the individual toward himself; (2) degree to which a person realizes his potentialities through action (growth, development, self-actualization); (3) unification of function in the individual's personality (integration); (4) individual's degree of independence of social influences (autonomy); (5) how the individual sees the world around him (perception of reality); and (6) ability to take life as it comes and master it (environmental mastery).

In discussing directions for further research Jahoda indicates that we must seek better empirical indicators of positive mental health in all of the above areas; furthermore, it is necessary to specify the conditions under which mental health is acquired and maintained. The need for developing outcome criteria in psychotherapy largely overlaps these requirements and must follow a similar course. While the patient's behavior in therapy will scarcely suffice as an ultimate criterion, it will occupy an important place in the cluster of criteria that will undoubtedly emerge. While the therapy situation is a unique "test situation," intratherapeutic criteria must have a counterpart in the external world, that is, a validity beyond the therapeutic situation. It is noteworthy that in discussing various mental criteria, Jahoda assigns the therapeutic situation an important role for gathering empirical data. I agree that the therapeutic situation could be used to a much greater extent for the purpose of generating criteria of outcome because of the unequaled opportunities it offers for making systematic observations over a prolonged period of time. One of the major working hypotheses of psychoanalysis asserts that the patient's relationship to the therapist (the transference) is a faithful replica of the patient's patterns of intimate interpersonal relatedness. As a corollary, it is maintained that the patient's adaptation to his human environment outside the therapeutic situation "improves" (in the sense of becoming less conflictual and more satisfying) to the extent that he is able to relate (less conflictually) to the therapist. The skilled therapist is certainly sensitive to shifts in the patient's patterns of relatedness to the therapist and regards them as valuable indicators of therapeutic change and improvement. Research could do a great deal to systematize and objectify these intratherapy observations (Bellak and Smith, 1956; also see Chapter Fifteen) and, wherever possible, relate them to the patient's interpersonal performances outside therapy. In this and other respects, the necessity of "calibrating" the therapist-observer is of prime importance. As long as there is poor agreement on the observations made in the therapy situation, any inferences or predictions are on shaky ground.

AN EXAMPLE OF A COMPETING VIEW: DASEINSANALYSIS

Psychoanalytic therapy clearly has been influenced by a wide variety of developments in the biological and social sciences, and it would be a major undertaking to trace their effect. The theoretical and technical contributions of the various "schools" of psychotherapy have been described by numerous authors, e.g., Munroe (1955) and Ford and Urban (1963). The new "schools" range from basic acceptance of psychoanalytic teachings with various qualifications (e.g., the neo-Freudians) to more or less complete rejection of Freudian principles (e.g., operant conditioning, behavior therapy, etc.). Perhaps it may be said that the phenomenologists (exemplified in Europe by the *Daseinsanalysts* and in America by Rogers' client-centered therapy) occupy, broadly speaking, a middle ground. In singling out the *Daseinsanalytic* approach for brief discussion, I do not wish to imply either a personal preference or a judgment about its intrinsic importance for the future development of psychoanalytic therapy. The selection merely reflects a desire to present a view that, while recognizing the significance of Freud's contributions to psychotherapy, advances a sophisticated challenge to the naturalistic foundation of psychoanalytic therapy.

659

Daseinsanalysis, which has enjoyed a certain popularity in America for some years, is a European import purporting "to combine the assumptions of existential philosophy about the nature of man with the phenomenological method, to achieve a more effective understanding and psychotherapeutic treatment of patients" (Ford and Urban, 1963, p. 445).* To some extent, existential analysis represents a reaction to the naturalistic approach to psychotherapy implicit in psychoanalysis, which the proponents of existentialism consider inadequate to deal with the "essential concerns" of man as a mortal and finite being. This view is pitted against a normative (nomothetic) approach, which has been the underlying philosophical assumption of psychoanalysis as well as scientific psychology based on the British empiricist tradition. Essentially, existential analysis is a viewpoint, not a system. Indeed, the very notion of system is anathema to its proponents.

The question of primary importance in the present context relates to the operations of psychotherapy, and the extent to which existential therapy differs from analytic psychotherapy as commonly understood and practiced. In this area one gets little help from the writings of the existentialists although a number of case histories have been published. May (May, Angel and Ellenberger, 1958) has made a serious attempt to explain to American readers what the existentialists mean by "technique." "One might infer," Ford and Urban (1963) observe, "that they [the existentialists] have developed a new way of *thinking about* patients, but it does not lead them to *do anything different* in treatment [p. 469]."

Existential analysis, May (May *et al.*, 1958) explains,

is a way of understanding human existence, and its representatives believe that one of the chief (if not *the* chief)

---

*For reviews of the background and objectives of this movement, see May, Angel, and Ellenberger (1958), Ruitenbeek (1962), Ford and Urban (1963), Boss (1963), and Binswanger (1963).

blocks to the understanding of human beings in Western culture is precisely the overemphasis on technique, an overemphasis which goes along with the tendency to see the human being as an object to be calculated, managed, "analyzed." Our Western tendency has been to believe *that understanding follows technique*; if we get the right technique, then we can penetrate the riddle of the patient.... The existential approach holds the exact opposite; namely, that *technique follows understanding*. The central task and responsibility of the therapist is to seek to understand the patient as a being and as being-in-his world. All technical problems are subordinate to this understanding [pp. 76-77].

The role and function of the therapist are stated as follows: "The therapist is assumedly an expert; but, if he is not first of all a human being, his expertness will be irrelevant and quite possibly harmful [p. 82]." Without rejecting such concepts as transference, it "gets placed in the new context of *an event occurring in a real relationship between two people* [p. 83]." The term *encounter,* frequently used to describe this "real relationship," has a mystical quality setting it apart from the prosaic concept of the ordinary human relationship. In other respects, too, *Daseinsanalysts* charge psychoanalysis with a variety of flaws, of which the encouragement toward intellectualization and cognitive understanding, as opposed to "true insight," is one. *Daseins-analysis* stresses the now widely recognized truth that " ... the human being who is engaged in studying the natural phenomena is in a particular and significant relationship to the objects studied and he must make himself part of his equation. That is to say, the *subject*, man, can never be separated from the *object* which he observes [p. 26]." Existential analysis is intended to "heal" the subject-object split in Western thought.

In a real sense, the difference between existential analysis and psychoanalysis reduces itself to a schism between the

661

European approach to psychology as a *Geisteswissenschaft* and the American approach to psychology as an empirical science. Yet, the existentialists deny a lack of interest in the canons of science. They assert that their approach has its own method of investigation and that the frequently voiced countercharge of scientific inexactitude, mysticism, and a terminology that lacks precise meaning is a result of deficient understanding of the basic tenets of existentialism.

No doubt, the existentialists' emphasis on psychotherapy as a deeply personal and meaningful experience is well taken, and the possibility that a system such as psychoanalysis offers an invitation to substitute impersonal formulations about a patient for a human "encounter" cannot be dismissed lightly. Yet these shortcomings are not necessarily inherent in the system. By the same token, there is no guarantee that an unperceptive practitioner following the existentialist viewpoint can successfully avoid the danger of getting lost in the vagaries of a patient's idiosyncratic experience. Nor is it clear that the advancement of an empirical science is possible without efforts to organize the data of observation in terms of a coherent system.

To the person with aesthetic, artistic, literary, philosophical, and humanistic interests, the existentialist position has a powerful appeal, particularly when viewed in contrast to the "empty organism" approach prevalent in American psychology, that impresses the existentialists as "human engineering" and "manipulation." The tradition of American technology demands that the therapist *do* something, "fix" something, or "set things right." On the other hand, being with another human being, sharing his experience suggests a meditative, passive approach, whose intrinsic therapeutic value has face validity, but whose vaunted superiority is as yet undemonstrated. Psychoanalysis, on the other hand, while having very different philosophical underpinnings from American behaviorism, tends to view man as an "object" governed by psychic forces that can be objectively described and conceptualized. The battle between the competing positions is largely fought on philosophical grounds, and there are insuperable divergencies in *Weltanschauungen* rooted in the culture and history of Western man. For these reasons it is all the more amazing that existentialist thinking has gained a foothold in American psychotherapy (as well as in other areas of human pursuits).

Still, when all is said and done, psychotherapy is not intended to take the place of a new faith, a philosophy of life, nor is it a solace for the inescapable fact of man's mortality, his limited powers, and his susceptibility to existential suffering, loneliness, and anxiety. While firmly supported by humanistic values, analytic therapy *is* a technique and a technology for helping the patient to deal more effectively and adaptively and less conflictually with himself and others. What sets it apart from religion and philosophy is the attempt to discover and apply psychological principles to problems in human living. In short, it aspires to become a science. A patient, for example, who suffers in his interpersonal relationships because of destructive fantasies, often benefits from interpretation of his emerging fantasies. This requires painstaking work, and the result is an achievement in which both patient and therapist share. Is this an encounter? Is there anything mystical about their relationship? To be sure, the relationship must be simply meaningful in a human sense, but there need to be no pathos nor a glorification of the "I-Thou." One may well agree with Sullivan's pragmatic dictum that much of psychotherapy is plain hard work. Encounters there may be as well as occasional "peak experiences," but they appear to be the end result, the culmination of work in which resistances have been cleared away and the patient has become amenable to more direct, less defensive, and less complicated ways of relating to another human being. The therapist must possess empathy, but he also must have technical skill. The seeming paradox that the existential therapists do not do anything "different" in treatment may find its resolution in parsimonious formulations that hew as closely as possible to observable clinical data.

It must also be recognized that in all forms of psychotherapy the patient seems to acquire a conviction, a faith, or a system of beliefs that sustains him in the struggle against his neurotic trends and his relationships with other people and the environment at large. The essence of this faith is difficult to define and may take multiple forms. It may express itself as a sense of trust in the benevolence of a superior being (a personal God); a conviction of the strength of one's own powers, a belief that one can master adversity, cope with the vicissitudes of life and retain a sense of integrity and wholeness, a conviction of the truth of a set of scientific principles—all of which may express that *one is not alone in a hostile world*. The root for this faith may lie in the patient's identification with the therapist, which in turn is based upon the child's trust in his parents (seen by Freud as the prototype of the Judaeo-Christian belief in God as a Good Father). Trust, belief in the essential goodness and protective powers of another person, and love with its counterpart, humility (as opposed to narcissism), appear to be essential components of a person's ego strength. It is difficult to see how any form of psychotherapy can be successful that fails to mediate these qualities through the patient's relationship with the therapist. As noted, we are as yet unclear about *how* this process succeeds in producing therapeutic change—terms like identification and introjection do not really explain it—but observation shows that it happens. The task for research is to spell out the conditions, thus insuring a greater likelihood of their occurrence. This sets psychotherapy apart from religions and other forms of psychological influence. It is apparent, however, that the major world religions have a long priority in their recognition of the overriding importance of what for lack of a better term may be called *basic trust*.

"BEHAVIOR MODIFICATION": A CHALLENGE TO PSYCHOANALYTIC THERAPY?

Another challenge to analytic therapy has come from a diametrically opposed quarter, a group of scientists who avow a "hard-nosed" approach to psychotherapy. Their banner, "behavior modification," refers to techniques that are broadly related to the field of learning, "but learning with a particular intent, namely clinical treatment and change" (Watson, 1962, p. 19). Major variants include *operant conditioning* (a term used by B. F. Skinner and his followers), *behavior therapy* (whose most vocal spokesman is H. J. Eysenck), and psychotherapy based on *reciprocal inhibition* (a designation preferred by J. Wolpe). The emphasis of these approaches rests on behavior. To quote Ullmann and Krasner (1965):

> The working behavior therapist is likely to ask three questions: (a) what behavior is maladaptive, that is, what subject behaviors should be increased or decreased; (b) what environmental contingencies *currently* support the subject's behavior (either to maintain his undesirable behavior or to reduce the likelihood of his performing a more adaptive response); and (c) what environmental changes, usually reinforcing stimuli, may be manipulated to alter the subject's behavior [pp. 1-2].

Historically, behavior modification has its roots in the experimental work of I. Pavlov on the conditioned response, in learning theory as developed within American psychology, and in the behaviorism of John B. Watson. Clinical applications have been spearheaded by Eysenck, Mowrer, Dollard and Miller, Wolpe, and the followers of Skinner. A vast literature attests to the viability and popularity of the approach within American (and to some extent British and South African) psychology. For summaries, see Krasner and

Ullmann (1965), and Ullmann and Krasner (1965). The appeal to academic psychologists is supported by the behavior therapists' focus on experiment, empirical proof, and the use of concepts that make a minimum of theoretical assumptions. The proponents believe these tenets are continually ignored by therapists following psychoanalytic teachings, of which behavior therapists as a group are highly critical. The attack on the alleged inutility of intrapsychic variables is epitomized by Eysenck (1959): "Learning theory does not postulate . . . 'unconscious causes,' but regards neurotic symptoms as simple learned habits; there is no neurosis underlying the symptom, but merely the symptom itself. *Get rid of the symptom and you have eliminated neurosis* [p. 65]."

Behavior modification, therefore, is aimed at elimination or modification of the maladaptive response itself, which is considered the problem to which the therapist should address himself. Contrary to psychoanalytic therapy, which views any behavioral act as a complex (overdetermined) resultant of motivational forces, behavior therapy rejects all intrapsychic determinants hypothesized by analytic therapy. Neurotic symptoms thus are seen as analogous to habits that are more or less fortuitously learned without subserving important motivational functions for the individual.

If, as psychoanalytic psychology asserts, a symptom is merely a surface manifestation of an underlying intrapsychic conflict, which fulfills an important albeit abortive function in the individual's adaptation, the suppression or modification of the symptom without change in the underlying psychic structure should lead to the substitution of another neurotic symptom. Citing experimental results, behavior therapists assert that symptom substitution rarely occurs, and they consider it of little consequence. The psychoanalytic model of symptom formation is often regarded by behavior therapists as a "medical model" (supposedly because it postulates underlying causes), whereas the beha-

666

vior therapy model is extolled as a "psychological" one. Without getting involved in semantics, a rather convincing case can be made that the psychoanalytic theory of neurosis, insofar as it is based on purely psychological concepts, is as much a "psychological" theory as a theory based on conditioning principles.

In any event, behavior therapists have attacked psychoanalytic therapy on account of its inordinate length, expense, its narrow range of applicability, and—above all—its alleged ineffectiveness. Beginning with Eysenck's (1952) article questioning the effectiveness of psychoanalytic therapy, increasingly bolder claims have been advanced (Eysenck, 1961; Wolpe, 1958) for the superiority of behavior therapy, particularly in the treatment of phobias, but more recently also in modifying many other conditions. In view of the difficulty of providing adequate experimental controls, the fluidity of outcome criteria and their consequent noncomparability, the issue, despite the zeal of the behavior therapists, must be considered unsettled at the present time. The fact that a given technique "works" in particular instances does not necessarily prove the superiority of the underlying theoretical system: all systems of psychotherapy can point to successes (as well as failures), and as pointed out elsewhere in this chapter, the measurement of psychological change is as yet so tenuous that meaningful comparisons in terms of percentage improvements are untrustworthy and have little more than propagandistic value.

To the credit of the behavior therapists it must be said that their insistence on empirical indicators, their critical scrutiny of concepts that resist validation by scientific methods, and their eagerness to experiment with novel techniques are unmatched by any comparable effort on the side of analytically oriented investigators. The utter simplicity of the approach, too, has an enormous appeal.

Behavior therapists aver that analytically oriented therapists, too, employ reinforcement principles albeit in an

667

unsystematic way and that there are common elements in all forms of psychotherapy. Both of these assertions are probably true. For example, the analytically oriented therapist tends to "reward" patients through more active verbal participation and interpretations when they are working on their problems in nondefensive ways, whereas resistance is "punished" by the therapist's silence. A common element in all approaches is probably the therapist's interest, dedication, and conviction of the "truth" of his theories (Marmor, 1962, calls attention to the self-validating character of all therapeutic theories).

By the same token, analytic therapists use the same ploy ("My opponent does the same thing I do, only less effectively or in an inferior manner") by pointing out that the "indoctrination" of patients in behavior therapy achieves its success largely through a crass exploitation of the transference relationship, and they cite historical evidence to show that, for example, persuading patients to expose themselves to phobically avoided situations is an old technique.

One of the most impressive criticisms of behavior modification is its simplistic view of human behavior and neurosis. It has little to say about such complex problems as neurotic depressions, obsessive-compulsive disorders, character problems, and the wide range of difficulties in living that patients typically present to the therapist, in addition to specific neurotic symptoms (like phobias). The number of patients who complain of isolated neurotic symptoms, as any clinician can testify, is exceedingly small. On the other hand, behavior therapists have pioneered in treating patients whose intellectual and personality resources usually make them unsuitable candidates for analytic therapy, which clearly places a premium on the patient's ability to verbalize, to enter into a collaborative relationship with a therapist, and to immerse himself in the "as if" relationship of the transference.

The argument of objectivity, scientism, and the "proven principles" of learning theory, with which behavior therapists buttress the claims of superiority for their position, has recently been challenged from an unexpected source—by psychologists versed in learning theory (Breger and McGaugh, 1965). Characterizing the behavior therapists' position as "untenable [p. 340]," these authors adduce evidence to show that learning-theory principles are not nearly so well established as is maintained by the behavior therapist. They conclude that "there seems to be enough question about what goes on in verbal conditioning itself to indicate that it cannot be utilized as a more basic explanation for complex phenomena such as psychotherapy [p. 346]." Furthermore, "Wolpe's case histories are classic testaments to the fact that he cannot, and does not, apply the symptom approach when working with actual data [p. 350]." Breger and McGaugh argue that the phenomena of neurosis do not fit a stimulus-response theory and that intrapsychic variables are a more adequate way of conceptualizing neurotic disturbances.

> To sum it up [Breger and McGaugh state], it would seem that the behaviorists have reached a position where an inadequate conceptual framework forces them to adopt an inadequate and superficial view of the very data that they are concerned with. They are then forced to slip many of the key facts in the back door, so to speak, for example, when all sorts of fantasy, imaginary [sic], and thought processes are blithely called responses [p. 350].

The therapeutic effectiveness of a system, even if it could be convincingly demonstrated, which at present seems impossible, remains only one criterion by which to judge its value. Perhaps a more important one is its actual and potential explanatory value to account for the major phenomena within its domain. In this realm, I believe, psychoanalytic theory has no serious contender.

CONCLUDING COMMENTS

In critically assessing the current status of psychoanalytic psychotherapy one cannot fail to record a certain disappointment with the achievements and promise of this method of therapy. While continuing to occupy a position of high prestige in the United States, psychoanalysis has sustained a loss in scientific status. This conclusion emerges despite the fact that the last few decades have witnessed the emergence of research studies dealing with aspects of the *general* theory of psychoanalysis. Furthermore, there has been an unprecedented increase in the number of therapists whose training has been deeply influenced by Freudian principles, which in more or less diluted form make up the core of the "psychodynamic viewpoint." The steady rise in the number of therapists has been a result of the momentous growth of psychiatry, clinical psychology, and psychiatric social work. Graduates of these training programs, under the impact of the enormous social need for their services, have broadened their activities to include brief psychotherapy, group therapy, family therapy, and numerous other variants. In this connection, a fair amount of informal experimentation has occurred. Many therapists who have been trained in "orthodox" psychoanalysis, too, appear to treat sizable numbers of patients by forms of psychotherapy other than strict psychoanalysis. Withal, there has been a growing awareness of the necessity to tailor psychotherapy to the needs of an ever-expanding patient population, many of whose members do not meet the rigorous criteria originally postulated for psychoanalytic treatment.

Contrary to a trend of the 1940s, when psychoanalysis was considered the panacea for virtually all of modern man's ills and solution of difficulties in living, there is now a reluctance on the part of both patients and therapists to engage in long-term intensive treatment, which seemingly had a tendency to occupy longer and longer time spans. Analyses lasting 6, 8, or even 10 years were at one time not at all uncommon but now are becoming rarer. This is not to deny the need for intensive therapy in certain cases, but therapists also realize that psychotherapy eventually reaches

670

a point of diminishing returns, beyond which further therapy becomes inexpedient if not possitively harmful. However, in the absence of conclusive research, only broad clinical indicators are available to guide the therapist in determining this juncture.

Although there continue to be heard the strident voices of caustic critics who would dismiss the value of psychoanalytic therapy altogether, there seems little question that patients do improve and that they benefit from psychotherapy carried on over an extended period of time. Clinical experience amply documents the value of psychoanalysis and psychotherapy based on psychoanalytic principles with a good many patients. This assertion seems warranted despite the absence of ironclad criteria by which to measure the effectiveness of therapy. The problem is that other forms of psychotherapy can point to comparable successes, and the superiority of any method of therapy remains a moot question.* There are no reliable criteria for differentiating "structural changes in the ego" from "transference cures," nor can we as yet explain, except on a post hoc basis, why the outcomes of therapy are sometimes impressive and at other times disappointing.

Among additional factors accounting for the lessening enthusiasm for psychoanalytic therapy is the absence of incisive advances in the technology of psychotherapy during the last quarter of a century. This lack of progress beyond Freud's discoveries is particularly striking in comparison with rapid developments in such fields as psychopharmacology, genetics, and psychophysiology—to name but a few. Whether such comparisons are relevant or justified shall be left undecided; the fact remains that with the increasing recognition of the mental health problem by governmental

---

*I cannot take seriously Eysenck's contention that a large proportion of patients with serious neurotic problems in living "spontaneously improve" within one to two years of "onset." Such a statement is simply at variance with clinical observation.

bodies and the public at large, the clamor for efficient, inexpensive and "easy" solutions has received a great impetus. In contrast, it is alleged in various quarters that psychoanalytic psychotherapy has failed to answer the challenge, and —what amounts to a more serious charge—has blithely ignored its existence. The accusation has been made that instead of objectively examining its premises and systematically studying its operations in collaboration with cognate sciences, psychotherapy (and particularly organized psychoanalysis) has withdrawn to an ivory tower, from which it contemplates increasingly esoteric problems without paying attention to the societal problems that urgently demand solution.

These feelings of dissatisfaction are voiced not only by unsympathetic or uninformed critics, but also by prominent therapists and theoreticians whose extensive training and experience command respect. It will not do to call their strictures "unresolved transferences" or worse. Too, it must be recognized that the psychoanalytic *mystique* (Glover's term) has exerted an untoward influence on the free development of the field. The close alliance of organized psychoanalysis with psychiatry and medicine, the likelihood of whose occurrence Freud already viewed with foreboding (see Szasz, 1961; Eissler, 1965) and the guild character of organized psychoanalysis in America have been constricting influences that have impeded research and unfettered inquiry. As Shakow (1965) observed, "A scientific area belongs ultimately to its investigators, not to its practitioners. No field can maintain its vitality, in fact, its viability, without such a group. One of the most cogent criticisms that can be made of psychoanalysis at the present is that it has neglected this indispensable rule for growth [footnote 1, p. 355]." Because of its largely self-imposed isolation, psychoanalysis has deprived itself of the help and collaboration of well-trained investigators (notable exceptions notwithstanding) and engendered negative attitudes in governmental and private organizations that control the purse strings of research sup-

672

port. Some of these deficiencies are gradually being remedied (e.g., a somewhat larger number of candidates is
receiving analytic training for research purposes) and to
some extent thorough training in psychoanalytic therapy
and research is available to persons with background training in a variety of fields from organizations other than the
"official" training institutes.

It is quite possible that astounding advances are not to
be expected in a field like psychoanalytic therapy. With
respect to the problem of personality change, therapists, beginning with Freud, have been impressed with the generally
slow rate, and perhaps it bears underscoring that analytic
therapy is not aimed at rapid cures but strives for "gradual,
unconscious emotional rearrangements" (Hammett, 1965).
Precisely how such rearrangements come about is a problem about which much remains unclear, but they do occur
and may be broadly viewed as a function of an emotional
learning process.

However, even in the absence of radically new discoveries, systematic inquiries dealing with the selection of
patients, the effect of the therapist's attitude, and emotional
commitment, the handling of transference manifestations,
the problem of making therapy a maximally meaningful
affective experience, and so on, are by no means impossible.
Many of these problems, despite great technical and practical difficulties, *are* amenable to research, given the good will,
patience, and persistence of investigators working in collaboration with therapists. Advances, too, may come from laboratory investigations and from hitherto unsuspected sources.
However, I believe that the predictability of psychotherapeutic outcomes can be significantly enhanced by research
conducted *within the framework* of the psychotherapeutic
situation. While psychotherapy may be destined to remain a
clinical art,* it seems reasonable to hope that its technical

---

*The high level of skill achieved by some practitioners is truly impres-
sive, and better ways should be sought to communicate this expertise.

tools can be sharpened by investigative efforts. So far, it must be admitted, objective research in the area has had few practical applications for clinical practice. But it must also be kept in mind that psychotherapy is still a young science, with a long historical tradition but a short scientific history.

If, in conclusion, I may indulge in some speculation about promising areas of advance, I would say that the basic discoveries of Freud relating to the dynamic unconscious, the emergence of transference phenomena and their handling in the unique dyadic relationship of the analytic situation continue to hold our best hope for the future. Among the emergence of transference phenomena, and their hand-would name: (1) investigations aimed at studying characteristics of patients for whom this form of therapy (or empirically proven variants) is most suitable; (2) intensive study of variables in the personality of the therapist that, in conjunction with his technique, mediate the therapeutic influence.

With respect to (1), systematic study may serve to restrict psychoanalytic therapy to patients for whom it is clearly applicable and who are most likely to profit from it. Furthermore, systematic investigation along these lines may lead to the development of more specific therapeutic techniques for patients with particular personality structures and problems in living. Such specification is an urgent requirement.

With respect to (2), we may succeed in isolating better methods for ascertaining "patient-therapist compatibility," thus heightening the chances for an emotionally meaningful experience and re-education. Experimentation with variations in technique (coupled with a clearer formulation of technical principles) should be undertaken in the context of the personality of the therapist, from which technique is inseparable.

Advances in these areas, of course, are contingent upon the solution of a variety of technical problems, including the measurement of therapeutic change (Luborsky and Schimek,

674

1964), and specifications of the character of the therapeutic influence.

With honest and sustained effort, psychotherapy may show steady, if not stupendous, progress. Just as any educational process is gradual, so psychotherapeutic changes may remain slow and even tedious. As in the field of education, not all persons are equally educable. There seems little doubt that for a long time to come problems in living, created or aggravated by untoward interpersonal events in a person's emotional development, can be effectively resolved by more favorable human experiences as provided through psychotherapy. This is not to gainsay the possibility that personality changes can *also* be achieved in other ways, including techniques of psychotherapy that are based on divergent theoretical assumptions. But analytic psychotherapy, insofar as it remains rooted in empirical observations, aims at a theory of rational and planful personality change that does full justice to the complexities of the human personality. In this respect, it has a great advantage over the variety of simplistic schemes that are tending to preempt the contemporary scene. What the field can ill afford is an attitude of smugness, an air of finality, or unsupported claims of superiority over all contenders. It may turn out that pharmacological agents or other measures may be more "efficient" for certain purposes than psychotherapy. However, by working toward realistic goals, and by abandoning grandiose aspirations, analytic therapy seems to be assured of its value as a potent weapon in man's continued fight against neurotic suffering and misery. We may be sure that the future will not be utopia, but neither need there be cause for despair.*

---

*I am indebted to the following friends and colleagues for critical and constructive comments : Drs. Ron Fox, Ken Lessler, Lester Luborsky, and Judd Marmor.

References

Alexander, F. 1950. "Analysis of the Therapeutic Factors in Psychoanalytic Treatment," *Psychoanal. Quar.,* 19: 482-500.

—— 1954. "Some Quantitative Aspects of Psychoanalytic Technique," *J. Am., Psychoanal. Assn.,* 2: 685-701.

——1956. *Psychoanalysis and Psychotherapy.* New York: Norton.

—— 1958. "Unexplored Areas in Psychoanalytic Theory and Treatment," *Behav. Sci.,* 3: 293-316.

—— and French, T. M. 1946. *Psychoanalytic Therapy: Principles and Applications.* New York: Ronald Press.

Auld, F., Jr., and Murray, E. J. 1955. "Content-analysis Studies of Psychotherapy," *Psychol. Bul.,* 52: 377-395.

Bellak, L., and Smith, M. B. 1956. "An Experimental Exploration of the Psychoanalytic Process," *Psychoanal. Quar.,* 25: 385-414.

Berman, L. 1949. "Countertransferences and Attitudes of the Analyst in the Therapeutic Process," *Psychiat.,* 12: 159-166.

Bibring, E. 1937. "Symposium on the Theory of the Therapeutic Results of Psychoanalysis," *Int. J. Psychoanal.,* 18: 170-189.

Binswanger, L. 1963. *Being-in-the-World: Selected Papers of.* . . . New York: Basic Books.

Boss, M. 1963. *Psychoanalysis and Daseinanalysis.* New York: Basic Books.

Breger, L., and McGaugh, J. L. 1965. "Critique and Reformulation of 'Learning Theory' Approaches to Psychotherapy and Neurosis," *Psychol. Bul.,* 63: 338-358.

Breuer, J., and Freud, S. 1895. "Studies on Hysteria." *Complete Works,* Vol. II, pp. 1-305. London: Hogarth. (Also published as *Studies on Hysteria.* New York: Basic Books, 1957.)

676

Eissler, K. R. 1965. *Medical Orthodoxy and the Future of Psychoanalysis.* New York: International Universities Press.

Eysenck, H. J. 1952. "The Effects of Psychotherapy: An Evaluation," *J. Cons. Psychol.*, 16: 319-324.

—— 1959: "Learning Theory and Behavior Therapy," *J. Men. Sci.,* 105. 61-75.

—— 1961. "The Effects of Psychotherapy," in *Handbook of Abnormal Psychology,* ed. H. J. Eysenck, pp. 697-725. New York: Basic Books.

Fenichel, O. 1930. "Statistischer Bericht über die therapeutische Tätigkeit, 1920-1930," in *Zehn Jahre Berliner Psychoanalytisches Institut,* pp. 13-19. Vienna: Internationale Psychoanalytischer Verlag.

Ferenczi, S., and Rank, O. 1925. "The Development of Psychoanalysis," *J. Ner. Men. Dis.* Monograph No. 40.

Fey, W. F. 1958. "Doctrine and Experience: Their Influence upon the Psychotherapist," *J. Cons. Psychol.,* 22: 403-409.

Fiedler, F. 1950a. "The Concept of an Ideal Therapeutic Relationship," *J. Cons. Psychol.*, 14: 239-245.

—— 1950b. "A Comparison of Therapeutic Relationships in Psychoanalytic, Nondirective, and Adlerian Therapy," *J. Cons. Psychol.,* 14: 436-445.

—— 1951. "Factor Analyses of Psychoanalytic, Nondirective, and Adlerian Therapeutic Relationships," *J. Cons. Psychol.,* 15: 32-38.

Ford, D. H., and Urban, H. B. 1963. *Systems of Psychotherapy: A Comparative Study.* New York: John Wiley.

Frank, J. D., 1959a. "The Dynamics of the Psychotherapeutic Relationship: Determinants and Effects of the Therapist's Influence," *Psychiat.,* 22: 17-39.

—— 1959b. "Problems of Control in Psychotherapy as Exemplified by the Psychotherapy Research Project of the Phipps Psychiatric Clinic," in *Research in Psychotherapy,* ed. E. A. Rubinstein and M. B. Parloff, pp. 10-

26. Washington, D.C.: American Psychological Assn.

———— 1961. *Persuasion and Healing: A Comparative Study of Psychotherapy.* Baltimore: Johns Hopkins Press.

Freud, A. 1936. "The Ego and the Mechanisms of Defence." New York: International Universities Press, 1946.

———— 1954. "The Widening Scope of Indications for Psychoanalysis: Discussion," *J. Am. Psychoanal. Assn.,* 2: 607-620.

Freud, S. 1910. "The Future Prospects of Psycho-Analytic Therapy," *The Standard Edition of the Complete Psychological Works,* vol. XI, pp. 141-151. London: Hogarth. (Also in *Collected Papers,* vol. II, pp. 285-296. New York: Basic Books, 1959.)

———— 1911. "The Handling of Dream-Interpretation in Psycho-Analysis," *The Standard Edition of the Complete Psychological Works,* vol. XII, pp. 89-96. London: Hogarth. (Also in *Collected Papers,* vol. II, pp. 305-311. New York: Basic Books, 1959.)

———— 1912a. "The Dynamics of Transference," *The Standard Edition of the Complete Psychological Works,* vol. XII, pp. 97-108. London: Hogarth. (Also in *Collected Papers,* vol. II, pp. 312-322. New York: Basic Books, 1959.)

———— 1912b. "Recommendations to Physicians Practicing Psychoanalysis," *The Standard Edition of the Complete Psychological Works,* vol. XII, pp. 109-120. London: Hogarth. (Also in *Collected Papers,* vol. II, pp. 323-333. New York: Basic Books, 1959.)

———— 1913. "Further Recommendations on the Technique of Psychoanalysis I. On Beginning a Treatment," *The Standard Edition of the Complete Psychological Works,* vol. XII, pp. 121-144. London: Hogarth. (Also in *Collected Papers,* vol. II, pp. 342-365. New York: Basic Books, 1959.)

———— 1914a. "On the History of the Psychoanalytic

Movement," *The Standard Edition of the Complete Psychological Works,* vol. XIV, pp. 7-66. London: Hogarth. (Also in *Collected Papers,* vol. I, pp. 287-359. New York: Basic Books, 1959.)

——— 1914b. "Further Recommendations on the Technique of Psychoanalysis. II. Recollecting, Repeating and Working Through," *The Standard Edition of the Complete Psychological Works,* vol. XII, pp. 145-156. London: Hogarth. (Also in *Collected Papers,* vol. II, pp. 366-376. New York: Basic Books, 1959.)

——— 1915. "Observations on Transference Love," *The Standard Edition of the Complete Psychological Works,* vol. XII, pp. 158-171. London: Hogarth. (Also in *Collected Papers,* vol. II, pp. 377-391. New York: Basic Books, 1959.)

——— 1923. "The Ego and the Id," *The Standard Edition of the Complete Psychological Works,* vol. XIX, pp. 12-66. London: Hogarth.

——— 1926. "Inhibitions, Symptoms and Anxiety," *The Standard Edition of the Complete Psychological Works,* vol. XX, pp. 87-156. London: Hogarth.

——— 1937. "Analysis Terminable and Interminable," *The Standard Edition of the Complete Psychological Works,* vol. XXIII, pp. 216-253. London: Hogarth. (Also in *Collected Papers,* vol. V, pp. 316-357. New York: Basic Books, 1959.)

——— 1938. "An Outline of Psychoanalysis," *The Standard Edition of the Complete Psychological Works,* vol. XXIII, pp. 144-207. London: Hogarth.

Fromm-Reichmann, F. 1950. *Principles of Intensive Psychotherapy.* Chicago: University of Chicago Press.

Gill, M. M. 1954. "Psychoanalysis and Exploratory Psychotherapy." *J. Am. Psychoanal. Assn.,* 2: 771-797.

Glover, E. 1940. "Common Technical Practices: A Questionnaire Research." In *The Technique of Psychoanalysis,* pp. 261-350, New York: International Universities Press, 1955.

Goldstein, A. P. 1962. *Therapist-Patient Expectancies in Psychotherapy*. New York: Macmillan.

Hammett, V. O. 1965. "A Consideration of Psychoanalysis in Relation to Psychiatry Generally, circa 1965," *Am. J. Psychiat.*, 122: 42-54.

Harper, R. A. 1959. *Psychoanalysis and Psychotherapy: Thirty-six Systems*. Englewood Cliffs, N.J.: Prentice-Hall.

Hartmann, H. 1951. "Technical Implications of Ego Psychology," *Psychoanal. Quar.*, 20: 31-43.

Hollingshead, A. B., and Redlich, F. 1958. *Social Class and Mental Illness*. New York: John Wiley.

Jahoda, M. 1958. *Current Concepts of Positive Mental Health*. New York: Basic Books.

Janis, I. L. 1958. "The Psychoanalytic Interview as an Observational Method," in *Assessment of Human Motives*, ed. G. Lindzey, pp. 149-182. New York: Rinehart.

Knight, R. P. 1941. "Evaluation of the Results of Psychoanalytic Therapy," *Am. J. Psychiat.*, 98: 434-446.

Krasner, L., and Ullmann, L. P., eds. 1965. *Research in Behavior Modification: New Developments and Implications*. New York: Holt, Rinehart, & Winston.

Levy, N. A. 1961. "An Investigation into the Nature of Psychotherapeutic Process: A Preliminary Report," in *Psychoanalysis and Social Process*, ed. J. H. Masserman, pp. 125-140. New York: Grune & Stratton.

Luborsky, L. 1959. "Psychotherapy," in *Annual Review of Psychology*, vol. X, ed. P. R. Farnsworth and Q. McNemar, pp. 317-344. Palo Alto, Calif.: Annual Reviews.

————— and Schimek, J. 1964. "Psychoanalytic Theories of Therapeutic and Developmental Change: Implications for Assessment," in *Personality Change*, ed. P. Worchel and D. Byrne, pp. 73-99. New York: John Wiley.

Macalpine, I. 1950. "The Development of the Transference," *Psychoanal. Quar.*, 19: 501-539.

680

Marmor, J. 1962. "Psychoanalytic Therapy as an Educational Process," in *Psychoanalytic Education*, ed. J. H. Masserman, pp. 286-299. New York: Grune & Stratton.

―――― 1964. "Psychoanalytic Therapy and Theories of Learning," in *Science and Psychoanalysis,* vol. VIII, ed. J. H. Masserman, pp. 265-279. New York: Grune & Stratton.

Marsden, G. 1965. "Content-analysis Studies of Therapeutic Interview: 1954 to 1964," *Psychol. Bul.,* 63: 298-321.

May, R., Angel, E., and Ellenberger, H. F., eds. 1958. *Existence: A New Dimension in Psychiatry and Psychology,* pp. 37-91. New York: Basic Books.

Menninger, K. 1958. *Theory of Psychoanalytic Technique.* New York: Basic Books.

Munroe, R. L. 1955. *Schools of Psychoanalytic Thought.* New York: Dryden Press.

Orr, D. W. 1954. "Transference and Countertransference: A Historical Survey," *J. Am. Psychoanal. Assn.,* 2: 621-670.

Rado, S. 1956, 1962. *Psychoanalysis of Behavior: Collected Papers of...,* Vol. I (1922-1956), Vol. II (1956-1961). New York: Grune & Stratton.

Rapaport, D. 1959. "The Structure of Psychoanalytic Theory: A Systematizing Attempt," *Psychol. Is.,* 2, No. 2 (Monograph No. 6).

Reich, W. 1949. *Character-Analysis.* New York: Orgone Institute Press.

Rioch, J. MacK. 1943. "The Transference Phenomenon in Psychoanalytic Therapy," *Psychiat.,* 6: 147-156.

Ruitenbeek, H. M. 1962. *Psychoanalysis and Existential Philosophy.* New York: Dutton.

Shakow, D. 1965. "Seventeen Years Later: Clinical Psychology in the Light of the 1947 Committee on Training in Clinical Psychology Report," *Am. Psychol.,* 20: 353-362.

Stone, L. 1954. "The Widening Scope of Indications for Psychoanalysis," *J. Am. Psychoanal. Assn.*, 2: 567-594.

———— 1961. *The Psychoanalytic Situation: An Examination of Its Development and Essential Nature.* New York: International Universities Press.

Strachey, J. 1934. "The Nature of the Therapeutic Action of Psychoanalysis," *Int. J. Psychoanal.*, 15: 127-159.

———— 1958. "Papers on Technique: Editor's Introduction," in *The Standard Edition of the Complete Psychological Works of Sigmund Freud*, vol. XII, pp. 85-88. London: Hogarth.

———— 1937. Glover, E., Fenichel, O., Strachey, J., Bergler, E., Nunberg, N., and Bibring, E. "Symposium on the Theory of the Therapeutic Results of Psychoanalysis," *Int. J. Psychoanal.*, 18: 125-189.

Strupp, H. H. 1960. *Psychotherapists in Action.* New York: Grune & Stratton.

———— 1962. "Patient-Doctor Relationships: Psychotherapist in the Therapeutic Process," in *Experimental Foundations of Clinical Psychology*, ed. A. J. Bachrach, pp. 576-615. New York: Basic Books.

———— Wallach, M. S., and Wogan, M. 1964. "Psychotherapy Experience in Retrospect: A Questionnaire Survey of Former Patients and Their Therapists," *Psychol. Monog.*, 78 (Whole No. 588).

Szasz, T. S. 1961. *The Myth of Mental Illness: Foundations of a Theory of Personal Conduct.* New York: Paul B. Hoeber.

Thompson, C. 1950. *Psychoanalysis: Evolution and Development.* New York: Hermitage House.

Ullmann, L. P., and Krasner L., eds. 1965. *Case Studies in Behavior Modification.* New York: Holt, Rinehart, & Winston.

Watson, R. I. 1962. "The Experimental Tradition and Clinical Psychology," in *Experimental Foundations of Clinical Psychology*, ed. A. J. Bachrach, pp. 3-25. New York: Basic Books.

Wolpe, J. 1958. *Psychotherapy by Reciprocal Inhibition.* Stanford, Calif.: Stanford University Press.

Wolstein, B. 1954. *Transference: Its Meaning and Function in Psychoanalytic Therapy.* New York: Grune & Stratton.

——— 1959. *Countertransference.* New York: Grune & Stratton.

Zax, M., and Klein, A. 1960. "Measurement of Personality and Behavior Changes Following Psychotherapy," *Psychol. Bul.,* 57: 435-448.

24

FERMENT IN PSYCHOANALYSIS AND PSYCHOANALYTIC PSYCHOTHERAPY

The problem of success and failure in psychotherapy (under which I include psychoanalysis) entered a new phase in the 1960s. Some salient features of that stage may be briefly characterized as follows:

1. In the research literature—here it is important to mention that serious research in this area has increasingly become the province of American psychologists, with some help from colleagues in Great Britain and on the Continent —one finds a growing disenchantment with psychoanalysis and psychotherapy based on psychoanalytic principles. The arguments have essentially followed this pattern:

a. Psychoanalytic psychotherapy in general and ortho-dox psychoanalysis in particular are hopelessly inefficient methods for coping with the inexhaustible reservoir of human misery for which the services of psychotherapists are needed. The available professional manpower is grossly inadequate and it is demonstrably impossible to narrow the gap in any significant way by training a larger number of therapists.

b. This form of therapy and its variants has always been and remains restricted to a narrow band of the population who are young, intelligent, affluent, verbal, psychological-minded, and endowed with other superior qualifications. Conversely, the vast majority of people who need help neither meet these qualifications nor can they afford the services of a highly trained psychotherapist. Thus it follows inexorably that other methods—cheaper, more efficient, less demanding—must be developed. Indeed, a wide variety of such techniques has been made available and is already widely applied. Most prominently here are techniques derived from learning principles. The avowed aim is "behavior modification" (a term that has begun to supersede "psychotherapy"), which is now regarded as encompassing such "traditional" methods as psychoanalysis, client-centered therapy, and other forms of one-to-one therapy in an office setting. The enormous appeal of the former methods derives in part from these considerations: (i) They are applicable to a considerably larger segment of the population, including mental hospital patients, lower-class individuals, and many others; (ii) they are said to be more efficient and far less expensive; (iii) they often do not require a high level of therapeutic skill, so that subprofessionals and even laymen can function in the therapeutic role; (iv) they are claimed to be more effective than the so-called traditional methods.

2. The issue of therapeutic effectiveness has become the prime criterion of any approach and the touchstone of its popularity and value. This issue was forcefully brought to the fore by Eysenck (1952), who alleged that psychotherapists in general have failed to demonstrate the efficacy of their procedures. While his initial argument, buttressed by data open to other interpretations besides the ones he chose,

emphasized the absence of strong positive evidence, he and a growing host of followers have more recently asserted the superiority of behaviorally oriented methods. They have also presented a considerable body of empirical data to substantiate their points. This kind of research is frequently cited as demonstrating conclusively the superiority of the newer approaches to psychotherapy. Whatever the merits of these therapeutic techniques and the associated research, their impact on the field as a whole, notably through university training programs, has been extraordinary.

3. Whereas research-oriented psychologists (and a few psychiatrists) have labored to expand the therapeutic armamentarium along the lines sketched above, tested new approaches, conducted laboratory research to shed light on the psychological mechanisms at work, published a vast number of more or less well-controlled studies, and in general extolled empiricism as the ultimate standard for any therapeutic endeavor, psychoanalysts and other dynamically oriented therapists have essentially conducted "business as usual." I believe this judgment is substantially correct despite the emergence of a certain number of research studies dealing with the process and outcome of this form of therapy, developments along the lines of group psychology, community mental health, brief psychotherapy, etc., and a mild interest in empirical evidence. In the large metropolitan areas such as New York or Los Angeles there is a concentration of analytically oriented psychotherapists, typically organized in tightly knit professional groups, whose patients are recruited from the upper-middle class and seen in intensive psychotherapy for several years. As professionals, these therapists show little interest in research, the egregious needs of society at large, the extent to which their therapeutic interventions are effective, or ways in which they might be improved.

Lest the foregoing be misunderstood as a wholesale indictment of a professional group, many of whose members as a matter of fact I hold in high esteem, let me point out that I make these statements out of a sense of profound regret. By turning their collective back, as it were, upon serious and open inquiry, by discouraging free communication with other behavioral sciences, by taking for granted and treating as gospel truth a set of procedures that basically has undergone little change over the years, by being insufficiently self-critical and preponderantly unresponsive to social needs, analytically oriented psychotherapists have abdicated important responsibilities. Largely because of this failure—not because of demonstrated therapeutic ineffectiveness—Freud's significant contributions are being overshadowed and in the future may indeed be eclipsed by techniques that in terms of psychological sophistication, clinical penetration, and humaneness represent a retreat from a hard-won bastion (see the preceding chapter).

The clinician, typically, is convinced of the worthwhileness of his therapeutic endeavors and, like Freud, he is unimpressed by "statistics." A large majority of patients, too, feel benefited by their psychotherapeutic experience. To an important degree, the question revolves around one's definition of "improvement." As I pointed out in Chapter Sixteen, the kinds of improvement psychoanalysts are talking about are vastly different from the criteria Eysenck (1952, 1961) invoked, but in either case the criteria must be *specifiable*. If a behavior therapist is willing to consider the alleviation of a snake phobia in an otherwise well-functioning personality a "cure," this is his privilege, and he cannot be challenged (nor can he challenge) by other therapists who may prefer to work toward different objectives. But it is incumbent upon all therapists to be explicit about their goals. In this connection, Knight's (1941) criteria may be too vague to serve as guidelines, but they are specifiable in principle.* The scientific community and the public

---

*His major rubrics were: (1) disappearance of presenting symptoms; (2) real improvement in mental functioning; (3) improved reality adjustment.

have a right to know the rules by which the therapeutic game is played, and they are entitled to pass a value judgment on them. Analytic therapists, it seems to me, have devoted insufficient attention to this problem and in general shrugged off the researcher's insistence upon hard-core evidence as indicative of ignorance or ulterior motives. If it is true, as Szasz (1967) asserts, that the kind of learning in psychoanalysis is entirely different from that occurring in behavior therapy; if it is true that the former is principally concerned with increasing the patient's sphere of autonomy rather than alleviating his symptoms, there must exist *some* criteria by which such changes can be judged. These criteria must be communicable and they must, at least in some way, refer to aspects of the person's behavior. I contend that the issue is a legitimate one and it can be ignored only at the risk of ultimate disastrous effects. Some of these are already becoming apparent. The chaos pervading the entire area of psychotherapy and psychotherapy research to which several authors (Colby, 1964; Matarazzo, 1965) have called attention is at least partly attributable to the failure of specifying the precise nature of the operations designed to achieve a given objective in a particular person. Too often, unfortunately, therapists have acted as if the problem did not exist, or that it did not merit their attention. We cannot negate the simple fact that a patient comes to a psychotherapist because of a "problem" for which he is seeking a solution. No matter how the problem is conceptualized or attacked, the end result must be a form of change demontrable by the scientific rules of evidence.*

The therapist is entirely justified in specifying his goals and the criteria he is willing to accept. Other members of

---

*For this reason I have omitted from consideration a large number of "humanistic" or "existentialistic" approaches to psychotherapy that have achieved prominence in this country in recent years. Many of these appear to have a mystic or semireligious flavor, and their proponents seemingly show little interest in, or openly disparage, a scientific attitude toward personality and behavior change.

the community may consider these goals unimportant, incommensurate with the expended effort, impractical, or trivial. These are value judgments—as is true of all outcome criteria in the final analysis. But once the therapist has stated his goals and his techniques, he must abide by the rules and have the fruits of his work judged accordingly. Personally I am convinced that if concerted efforts were made along these lines, the showing of psychoanalytic therapy would be vastly more favorable than the existing literature suggests, but at the same time I am prepared to admit that personal opinion (even if augmented by clinical experience) will not decide the issue.

To elaborate on the *choice* of criteria, in this country we find today a strong emphasis on behavioral criteria, epitomized by the question: Does the patient *act* differently after psychotherapy? Following psychotherapy, he may interact differently with his spouse, his children, his boss, he may become more assertive with people in general, engage in activities he previously avoided, etc. To be sure, these are exceedingly important indices, not only because they are open to observation, measurement and verification. I agree that any form of psychotherapy worthy of the name must be capable of producing such changes (or inducing the patient to make them). But there is also a wide area of *internal* changes that are notoriously difficult to specify, observe, and measure. Investigators committed to a behavioristic orientation and society may not consider them important, but until therapists working toward internal changes become more articulate about their goals and subject them to systematic study, their assertions that the patient becomes more mature, self-reliant, independent, and more skillful in handling interpersonal situations will be ignored. To this end it will be necessary to place greater weight on the patient's own testimony, as our research group (together with some other researchers) has attempted to do, and a bridge must be built between subjective (necessarily fallible) and objective data. But in principle, internal changes are as real as behavioral ones, although one's personal preference may be for one rather than the other.

Consider an outstanding characteristic of neurosis, regardless of whether it is viewed as an "illness" or as a "problem in living." I am referring to intense suffering, misery, anxiety, hopelessness, and despair. Novelists, poets, and philosophers have at times articulated these feelings which defy quantification but are undeniably real to anyone who has experienced them or has the capacity to empathize.

Like any pain, neurotic suffering is a subjective feeling state that cannot be captured by behavioral measures no matter how sophisticated they may be. To assess it in any meaningful way we must rely on the patient's testimony. But how can one compare a person's pain with someone else's? Feelings fluctuate; they are elusive; people are suggestible; and their testimony may be highly unreliable. In the face of these obstacles, the behaviorist throws up his hands and turns to "behavioral indicators" that are observable by others and concerning which a consensus can be reached. But do we have a right to ignore salient aspects of a person's life simply because we have found no effective ways of measuring them? It appears that the chaotic state of outcome statistics from psychotherapy is at least partially due to the researcher's inability, unwillingness, or imperviousness to recognize this problem. It is symptomatic of our time that it is not often discussed.

To be sure, changes in feeling states often accompany changes in behavior but there is no one-to-one relationship nor can one serve as a substitute for the other. Every therapist and patient can cite abundant examples of behaviors that remain unchanged throughout therapy, but a given situation may be perceived and reacted to differently as a result of therapeutic work. What value are we to place on such changes? As I suggested, if a form of psychotherapy never or rarely produced changes in the patient's overt behavior there would be considerable ground for skepticism about its utility; however, it seems inordinately narrow to

690

restrict evaluations of psychotherapy to changes in overt behavior. Nevertheless, therapists do not have the right to label as "therapeutic" *any* procedure or activity they wish to dignify by this label. In fact, the term "psychotherapy" is used far too loosely today and often has little specific meaning. The burden of proof is upon the therapist not upon the critic. This does not mean that the therapist is obligated to play the game by *any* rules the critics might impose, particularly if they are based on ignorance of the therapist's concerns and objectives.

To illustrate my points two studies of psychotherapy follow, the first purporting to demonstrate the superiority of behavioral approaches over "traditional" methods. I contend that it achieves its objective only in a highly circumscribed sense and at the expense of defining psychotherapy in a very special way. The second investigation, conducted by my research group, focuses on internal changes experienced by patients who underwent psychotherapy of a more conventional sort. Neither study *proves* the effectiveness of psychotherapy as a technique for helping solve *real* problems in living, nor does it demonstrate that one approach is better than another. My purpose is to highlight the assertion that

1, the term psychotherapy as used today is a multifaceted conglomerate with fuzzy meanings;

2, as long as there is no reasonable consensus about methods, objectives, and outcomes, comparative studies will remain largely meaningless; and

3, the effectiveness of psychotherapy is largely a definitional problem involving value judgments about the kinds of outcomes a given investigator (or the public at large) deems worthwhile.

A COMPARATIVE OUTCOME STUDY

A study by Paul (1966) is often cited as strong evidence for the superiority of behavior therapy over "traditional"

691

approaches. Singling out anxiety as a research focus, Paul was interested in examining the relative efficiency of therapeutic procedures derived from "disease" and "learning" models in the treatment of anxiety in public speaking situations. Specifically, the study was designed to compare insight-oriented psychotherapy with modified systematic desensitization.

Measures included a sizable battery of self-report tests, autonomic indices of anxiety and physiological arousal, and a behavioral check list of performance anxiety.

The therapists were five experienced practitioners representing a mixture of the Freudian, neo-Freudian, and Rogerian orientation. They were paid for their services by the investigator.

Three methods of treatment were employed:

1. Insight-oriented psychotherapy, described as consisting of traditional interview procedures aimed at insight:

2. modified systematic desensitization based on the procedures advocated by Wolpe (1958), including prominently progressive relaxation and desensitization to anxiety-provoking stimuli; and

3. attention placebo, a procedure administered by the same therapists for the purpose of determining the extent of improvement from nonspecific treatment effects, such as expectation of relief, attention and interest on the part of the therapist, and "faith." Subjects ingested a placebo pill, represented to them as a "fast-acting tranquilizer," and underwent a task described as very stressful.

Two control groups were employed, a no-treatment classroom control, which followed the same procedures as the experimental groups except for the treatment itself; and a no-contact classroom control, which took the pre- and follow-up battery but otherwise did not participate in the investigation.

Subjects were undergraduate college students enrolled in a public speaking course. A letter accompanying the pretreatment battery, which was administered to 710 students, stated that the study was designed to determine "which people benefit most from various types of psychological procedures used to treat anxieties." About half of the original group expressed a desire for treatment. After screening, subjects identified as highly anxious were assigned to the various groups. Each treatment group comprised 15 subjects, the control groups 22 and 29 respectively. These individuals appeared to be "good bets" for psychotherapy in terms of motivation, degree of disturbance, intelligence, age, social class, etc.

Following a pretreatment test speech, which was preceded by the stress measures, the students were given an interview. They then entered therapy with their respective therapists. Each person had five hours of individual therapy over a period of six weeks. Upon termination, they gave a posttreatment test speech, accompanied by the same measures.

It is noteworthy that the five therapists administered all forms of therapy, a procedure that controlled for therapist differences. However, since they were not familiar with the desensitization treatment, they were given special training. It may be assumed that they felt more "at home" with the "traditional" procedures they ordinarily used in their therapeutic work.

The results based on extensive statistical analyses showed systematic desensitization to be consistently superior to the other methods. No differences were found between the effects of insight-oriented psychotherapy and the nonspecific effects of the attention-placebo treatment, although both groups showed greater anxiety reduction than the no-treatment control groups. Follow-up studies showed that the therapeutic gains were maintained and that no symptom substitution had occurred. On the basis of his results Paul concluded that "treatment based upon a learning model is most effective in alleviating anxiety of a social-evaluation nature, [p. 99]" and that "the bulk of the evidence in the

693

literature favors the superiority of direct treatment based upon principles of learning over traditional 'depth' approaches [p. 76]."

The study is a good example of a contemporary investigation of psychotherapy that reveals careful attention to problems of measurement and control. However, does it prove what it set out to prove?

1. *Are the patients "real" patients?* As already mentioned, this is in part a definitional problem. Paul was certainly at liberty to define the term as he did; however, it may be argued that his subjects actually had little in common with persons who typically apply for psychotherapy to an outpatient clinic or to a private practitioner. They were presumably well-functioning young adults who saw no need for psychotherapy prior to being approached by the investigator. True, the evidence showed that they experienced "public-speaking anxiety," but it is questionable whether this constituted a serious problem in their lives. Certainly, they did not see it as an incapacitating symptom for which they actively sought help.

There were other differences: whereas the bona fide neurotic patient must take the first step in enlisting professional help, the students in this study were *offered* psychotherapy. Little inconvenience or sacrifice in terms of money or time was involved, and they were spared the painful decision often faced by prospective patients whether or not to admit defeat and seek help. There is little evidence that these students were suffering in any sense of the word. Besides being *invited* to participate, the professional services were provided as a courtesy. In sum, it appears that the students were more comparable to subjects participating in a psychological experiment than they were to patients seeking help for neurotic problems.

2. *Does the study provide a fair test of the relative merits of different forms of psychotherapy?* In order to examine this question it is necessary to consider the goals of

694

the two forms of therapy being compared. Insight-oriented psychotherapy was defined solely in terms of "traditional interview procedures" used by these therapists in their daily work. "With this approach," states Paul, "the therapist attempts to reduce anxiety by helping the client to gain 'insight' into the bases and interrelationships of his problem [p. 18]." While the therapists asserted that "insight" was an important therapeutic goal in their work, there is no evidence that they focused specifically in the five hours allotted to them upon the reduction of the symptom defined as public-speaking anxiety, nor would one ordinarily expect them to do so. Evidently, they were given no instructions about the therapeutic goals the investigator had postulated nor was an effort made to insure uniformity of the therapeutic procedure. It is safe to infer that each therapist proceeded very differently, a problem that was not adequately solved by administering to them a check list intended to assess the frequency with which they used a series of techniques *in general*. It appears that "traditional insight-oriented therapy" was inadequately defined and that the therapists were a rather heterogeneous group, as shown also by the mixture of theoretical orientations they professed.

While some therapists subscribing to a dynamic orientation specialize in brief or goal-limited psychotherapy, no evidence was presented that the therapists in this study typically worked along those lines. As is well known, most dynamic therapists are not primarily concerned with the alleviation of an isolated symptom and they do not accept patients on that basis. Paul apparently induced them to work toward *his* goals rather than toward their own. Many therapists would have refused such an assignment.

The dynamic psychotherapies (and this is true also of client-centered therapy) are generally concerned with "real" patients, that is, individuals who are motivated to seek help for problems in interpersonal relations and affects they experience as troublesome. Contrary to the behavior therapist, who focuses on specific symptoms he views as "the problem," dynamic therapists regard symptoms as manifestations of a neurotic process that permeates the person's total functioning. Their therapeutic efforts, therefore, are aimed at helping the patient gain a different view of himself and achieve greater mastery, independence, and autonomy. To be sure, all therapists hope that as a result of their interventions the patient's symptoms will abate and that he will feel more comfortable with himself and others. Behavior therapists of course argue that the modification of specific behaviors will achieve the same end (besides doing it more efficiently), and that dynamic therapists have failed to adduce substantive evidence in favor of pervasive personality changes. But what constitutes acceptable evidence?

As I have suggested, this question concerns the criteria of change or improvement one is willing to accept. A specific symptom, as well as changes in a symptom, can be defined with far greater precision than changes in the person's self-concept, subjective comfort, competence in interpersonal relations, productivity, self-realization, and the like. Available measuring instruments, like tests and rating scales, are for the most part inadequate for this kind of assessment. Does it follow that the changes desired by dynamic therapists do not occur? I do not think so. What seems to follow is that our measuring instruments are insufficiently sensitive. Of course, it is possible that if we had fully adequate tools, the alleged personality changes might be shown to occur only infrequently or sporadically, which would be a more serious indictment, but even if this were true, a therapist and a patient might still want to take the risk, either because this form of psychotherapy appeals to them as an educational process, because other forms of therapy do not seem any more promising, or for other reasons. This does not mean that therapists subscribing to diverse orientations could not agree on certain rules or criteria, but as long as such common ground has not been established, one cannot conclude that a given technique or outcome is superior on scientific grounds.

696

The dynamically oriented therapist would contend that there are valid reasons for a person's reluctance to speak in public, which manifest themselves as an inhibition. If he goes against this inhibition or is forced to do so by the requirements of a college course, he may experience anxiety, which is also reflected in physiological and autonomic indices. He wants to master the course, he is concerned about the instructor's and fellow students' approval, but something within him says no. Subjectively, he feels "I can't," which could also mean "I don't want to." In short he is in conflict. Now contrast the approach of the behavior therapist with that of the dynamic therapist.

The behavior therapist is not interested in "underlying reasons"; he will assert that at some time in the past the anxiety response has become conditioned to a previously neutral stimulus. But this is not essential for the therapy. His approach basically is to countercondition the anxiety response. The therapist achieves this by asking the patient to imagine anxiety-provoking situations in a graduated series and by teaching him to make responses antagonistic to anxiety, notably relaxation, whereupon the anxiety response is gradually diminished. Having in this way achieved mastery over his anxiety, the therapeutic gain may radiate to other areas of the patient's living.

The dynamic therapist, on the other hand, views the anxiety response as a possible manifestation of more general personality dispositions, such as avoidance of challenging situations and dependence (Andrews, 1966). If this hypothesis is correct, he may find that there are numerous situations, besides public speaking, in which the patient experiences anxiety, shrinks from challenges, and fails to assert himself. He may gradually isolate a common theme linking these experiences, which he will bring to the patient's attention as the evidence accumulates. Throughout he will enlist the patient's cooperation in verbalizing his associations, fantasies, etc. As the therapeutic work proceeds, it may develop that the patient is fiercely competitive with his peers (to whom he may react as younger siblings) or he may fantasy that whenever he asserts himself (as in public speaking) he is in danger of expressing rage toward an authority figure who may retaliate, with dire consequences. He gains insight into his feelings and behaviors by experiencing the effect in relation to the therapist, who interprets the patient's current feelings in terms of his past experience and demonstrates to him how seemingly diverse situations are interrelated and the manner in which he misconstrues the present in terms of the past. Clearly, this work requires time and cannot be accomplished in five hours. It proceeds on the general hypothesis that as implicit processes are made explicit, and as the patient struggles with his difficulties, he will achieve greater control and mastery.

Is this tedious excursion necessary? Is it worth the trouble? The answer obviously depends upon the circumstances. If the patient is greatly disturbed by his phobic fears, if clinical assessments show that the public-speaking anxiety is an instance of a more pervasive disturbance, if the patient is interested in gaining an understanding of his feelings and motives instead of merely being relieved of his symptoms, and if other conditions are met, the answer may be in the affirmative. In the case of Paul's subjects, none of whom apparently saw the need for psychotherapy until they were solicited, and for whom the fear of public speaking seemed to be an isolated symptom of minimal severity, there clearly was no need.

"Insight therapy" is not designed for the purpose intended by Paul, and it seems absurd to restrict therapists following some semblance of the approach sketched above to five hours, to see how much "insight" the patient can acquire and to what extent the symptom might yield.

What Paul's study has shown is that, given the circumstances he contrived, desensitization appears to work quite well, and numerous other studies support his findings. He is entitled to conclude that under the stated conditions (and presumably similar ones), this form of psychotherapy—for

698

which he personally shows a preference—is helpful. What he has failed to do, as I have attempted to show, is to study dynamic psychotherapy as it is commonly practiced (he instead devised a form of brief psychotherapy arbitrarily defined as "insight therapy"); and to demonstrate the superiority of therapies based on a learning model to those based on dynamic conceptions. In my judgment Paul's generalizations are not justified, largely because the comparisons he performed are not the proper ones to make. If Paul's findings are restricted to the conditions of his experiment, they may be accepted as such. One should be extremely wary, however, of generalizing the conclusions, as Paul and others citing his work have done. There are as yet no adequate comparisons of the type intended by Paul. Consequently, there is no reliable evidence for the superiority of one therapeutic approach over another, and even less of the effectiveness of psychotherapy compared to no treatment.

AN EXAMPLE OF RETROSPECTIVE OUTCOME RESEARCH

The work of our research group (Strupp, Fox, and Lessler, 1969), was prominently concerned with former patients' retrospective accounts of their psychotherapy experience. Briefly, we obtained extensive questionnaire data from 2 samples of former patients (a sample of 44 patients seen by private practitioners for a mean of 166 interviews, and a second, larger sample of 122 clinic patients who for the most part were seen by psychiatric residents for a mean of 70 interviews). These were bona fide patients and the severity of their difficulties was evidenced by the fact that about one-third had previously been hospitalized for psychiatric reasons. All underwent either psychoanalysis or psychoanalytically oriented psychotherapy. The subjective data supplied by the patients were complemented by ratings from their therapists and data abstracted from clinic charts.

Unlike Paul's study, this was not an experimental investigation in which the form of psychotherapy was manipulated nor was it possible to exercise control over many other variables. The principal merit of this research, in our judgment, derived from the patients' own observations, comments, and evaluations, the comparisons with objective data we were able to perform, and the extent to which the patients' assertions about their therapy experience dovetailed with observations typically made by clinicians and also found in the clinical literature.

On the basis of several indices we concluded that two-thirds to three-quarters of the patients participating in our surveys considered their therapy experience as valuable; they reported that they had greatly benefited from it; and they attributed significant changes in personality and behavior to their psychotherapy. What was the nature of these changes?

Most noteworthy perhaps was the relatively minor emphasis they assigned to improvements of the common neurotic symptoms, such as anxiety, depression, and physical disturbances. This contrasted sharply with the more impressive changes (at least in terms of frequency of mention) in the areas of interpersonal relations and self-esteem. The conclusion emerged that the patients' view of therapeutic changes merged with that of all analytically oriented therapists; that is, therapeutic changes were seen not in terms of "symptom removal" but as changes occurring on a broader front and affecting the broad spectrum of their life experience. Since our respondents did not speak as clinicians but as laymen, we should put the matter more precisely by stating that these changes were most salient in the patients' awareness and were valued most highly. These findings argue against a conception of analytic psychotherapy as a technique for the "removal" of specific symptoms; instead they highlight more general character and personality changes. Patients frequently reported a new orientation toward life in general, a modified outlook on reality, and changes in their self-concept. Related findings pertained to

700

the patients' assertion that changes were apparent to close associates, and that they had occurred relatively rapidly once therapy got under way.

One of the trenchant accomplishments of psychotherapy with this population (as probably with most patients) was the transformation of seemingly mysterious and mystifying symptoms into phenomena that had explainable antecedents. Following therapy, the causes of the patient's difficulties were viewed in the context of his interpersonal relations. At the same time, this new understanding was accompanied by the development of techniques for more adaptive, less conflictual, and more satisfying ways of relating to others. An integral part of this learning experience undoubtedly was the achievement of a sense of mastery over experiences that hitherto had appeared as events to be passively endured. Conceptualizations of such therapeutic changes may of course be found in the writings of a host of therapists—from Freud to Erikson—but they have seldom been documented by reports of patients who had undergone psychotherapy. As Fromm-Reichmann (1950) stated:

In going over the literature on anxiety in children and adults, from M. Klein, Sharpe and Spitz, to Ferenczi and Rank, Freud, Rado, and Sullivan, Fromm, Horney and Silverberg, it seems that the feelings of powerlessness, of helplessness in the presence of inner dangers, which the individual cannot control, constitutes in the last analysis the common background of all further elaborations on the theory of anxiety.

It was precisely these feelings of helplessness and inability to cope that were ubiquitous both in the presenting complaints and in the areas of improvement listed by our patients. Gradually, in the course of therapy, feelings of self-confidence, self-assurance, and mastery replaced self-perceptions of helplessness, inadequacy, and overwhelming despair. Or, stated in different terms, the natural tendencies

701

toward synthesis, meaning, organization, competence, and growth supplanted the patient's previous sense of failure and helplessness.

No single variable emerged as highly predictive of therapeutic outcome and, in view of the complexity of the factors and their interacting effects, such a result was hardly to be expected. Patients, however, who met certain criteria appeared more assured of success than those who did not:

1. They were somewhat older, married patients, with children;
2. had a relatively recent onset of disturbance;
3. followed greater adherence to scheduled interviews;
4. felt greater internal pressure at the beginning of therapy;
5. showed relatively rapid improvement once therapy got under way;
6. showed less incapacitation, as judged by the clinic; and
7. exhibited greater motivation for psychotherapy, as judged by the clinic.

Finally, the therapist's attitudes toward the patient, the quality of their working relationship, and the patient's feeling of being respected by the therapist were shown to be important in determining the final outcome. In contrast, length of therapy, frequency of sessions, and the intensity of the emotional experience as perceived by the patient had no demonstrable bearing on outcome.

In the absence of comprehensive data on the patient-therapist interaction, specific information about the techniques employed, and gaps in our knowledge about the nature of therapy in general, we do not as yet know *how* personality and behavior changes are achieved. Our work, however, provided some important clues. The typical psychotherapy experience we examined was neither superficial nor very intensive (in the sense of attempting radical personality change). It helped the patient work through certain traumatic experiences; it succeeded in clarifying some patterns of neurotic interaction; and, above all, it provided a corrective emotional experience (Alexander and French, 1946).

The latter is perhaps the most important and central point of the therapeutic encounter we have studied; judging from their reports, patients experienced a hitherto unknown degree of acceptance, understanding, and respect; and within the framework of benevolent neutrality and warmth they were encouraged to examine some of the more troublesome aspects of their behavior and attitudes. Certainly, the therapeutic experience provided a sharp contrast to other human relationships the patients had previously known; it was an antidote to the criticism, exploitation, and dependency they had encouraged in themselves or of which they had been the victim; it permitted freedom to experience shameful, anxiety-provoking, and other painful feelings, and it supplied the patients with a professional helper who insisted that they look at themselves, examine some of the problems in their lives and work out—on an emotional as well as a cognitive level—a more viable solution. There is little question that this approach resulted in increased self-acceptance, self-respect, and competence. Therapists generally employed psychoanalytic principles (in a broad sense), rather than persuasion, suggestion, and the like. No matter how faltering and imperfect the procedure, the data demonstrated that they worked. Were the results due to suggestion? Did the patients become converts to a new faith? We cannot prove or disprove either possibility, but whatever their nature, the results in many instances were impressive and lasting. There is also reason to believe that they were achieved by rational means, that is, by procedures that at least in principle are teachable, communicable, and replicable. Could more have been achieved within the available time, by greater experts, by more incisive techniques? Perhaps. But something tangible was achieved, and it represented partly a measurable, partly a more elusive social and personal gain to the recipients.

The skeptic who insists on seeing the presenting symptom as the problem and denies the importance of intrapsychic conflicts and underlying causes will of course not be convinced by these demonstrations. He will counter that the patients' reports may merely reflect the therapist's success in persuading the patient or in instilling a new faith in the authority of the healer. True, we do not know what the patients' retrospective accounts would have been like had they been treated by therapists following a different theoretical orientation, but there can be little doubt that for these particular patients, treated by analytically oriented psychotherapy, a shift in outlook and orientation occurred, and that it took these particular forms.

It is probably true that most of our patients were reasonably mature, as shown by their ability to function in the community despite their neurotic handicaps. However, it is equally important to note that they often suffered from chronic and severe difficulties in living. The data showed that in an appreciable number of cases even such problems were helped markedly by psychotherapy of the kind studied by us. They also strengthened our conviction, which appears to be insufficiently appreciated by behavioristic psychology, that in effective psychotherapy the patient achieves subjective gains that defy quantification. Such gains include interpersonal competence, mastery, and concomitant increments in self-esteem.

Finally, it is important to draw attention to the uniqueness of the psychotherapeutic situation as a vehicle for personal growth and maturation. There are many elements that the psychotherapeutic relationship shares with other interpersonal experiences, characterized by openness, acceptance, and understanding. Such resemblance, however, does not signify identity. Qualities that set the psychotherapeutic situation apart from other human encounters include the therapist's objectivity, his sharply circumscribed involvement in the patient's life, his training that enables him to detect neurotic entanglements and self-defeating maneuvers, and his commitment to help the patient arrive at his own solutions by the process of examining and understanding factors within himself that contribute to his difficulties in living. At its best, individual psychotherapy creates conditions for such learning unequaled by anything human ingenuity has been able to devise, and it represents a powerful affirmation of the individual's worth, self-direction, and independence. While costly in terms of money, time, manpower, and dedication of the participants to the common task, it remains one of the few oases in a collectivistic society that fosters conformity and erodes individual values and autonomy in a host of ways. From a practical standpoint, it cannot begin to cope effectively with the enormity of human suffering caused by destructive interpersonal experience, and no amount of refinement in technique can significantly increase its effectiveness to a point where it could be considered a widely applicable weapon against neurotic problems. In essence, it remains an unrealizable ideal of self-discovery through learning and teaching in the context of a human relationship uninfluenced by ulterior motives of indoctrination or social control. What the patient, if he is fortunate, may expect is a glimpse or even a reasonable approximation.

On the basis of all our evidence we concluded that outpatient psychotherapy, as it is commonly practiced in this country, performs a highly useful function and that patients who meet certain criteria and have the good fortune of finding a competent therapist may expect to benefit substantially. At the same time we found little evidence to support the view that clinics operate at a high level of efficiency or that they offer a great deal to a sizable segment of the individuals who apply for help.

The two kinds of studies I have briefly reviewed obviously represent very different approaches to research in psychotherapy, but they share the view that the effectiveness of psychotherapy is a legitimate area for scientific inquiry, and that there must be a continuing search for methods more effectively and more efficiently meeting the enormous social needs for psychotherapeutic services. If "traditional" psychotherapy lived up to these requirements, obviously there would be no pressure to search for new techniques. Unfortunately, we are confronted with a growing hiatus between supply and demand (i.e., between the services offered and the patient's real or imagined needs), and it is this gap that will somehow be filled. As concerned citizens, scientists, and professionals it is our responsibility to ensure that the new approaches are sound, sophisticated, efficient, as well as humane.

In conclusion, because psychotherapy has traditionally been regarded as a variant of medical treatment, terms like "cure," "improvement," etc., have been employed as seemingly reasonable criteria. They are not. As I have tried to indicate, the issue is still foggy. It is safe to predict that clarification of the criterion problem, that is, the kinds of changes that may be expected from particular psychotherapeutic procedures, will be clarified to the extent that the medical analogizing will be abandoned. Paradoxically, psychologists who have pioneered psychotherapeutic techniques anchored to learning theory principles, have continued to measure the efficacy of their endeavors along similar "mental health" lines.

It would help greatly to view psychotherapy as a form of education, or as Freud called it, an "after-education." What the patient in psychotherapy acquires are new perceptions of himself and others; he learns new patterns of interpersonal behavior, but he also has to unlearn old maladaptive ones. There are vast individual differences in the capacity to profit from different kinds of learning situations, just as there are such differences in the educational realm. Psychoanalysis, as one form of psychotherapy, may be likened to a form of graduate education, and like graduate education it is suitable only for relatively few. As long as the patient's suitability for a given form of therapy is decided

706

on factual or clinical grounds, rather than in terms of his ability to pay for necessarily expensive services, there can be no quarrel. To be sure, some deserving students are excluded from advanced university training because they lack financial resources, but society is aware of the problem and attempts to remedy it through scholarships and the like. The same considerations should apply to prospective candidates for psychoanalysis or psychotherapy. Szasz (1965), who has done more than any other individual to advance Freud's revolutionary concept of the analytic situation as a unique learning situation, put it this way:

> The evidence suggests that, when the various forms of psychotherapy are clearly identified, each will appeal to and hence be useful for only certain kinds of *persons*. I am confident that this will be true, not only for psychoanalysis, but for other forms of psychotherapy as well. The scope of a particular psychotherapeutic method is limited, not so much by the nature of the client's "mental disease" as it is by his education, interests, and values. Different *people*, not different mental *diseases*, require differing psychiatric methods. Since psychotherapists cannot adjust their methods to the "needs" of their clients, the only rational solution lies in clearly identifying therapists. Clients will then be able to find therapists whose methods are compatible with their own interests and standards [p. 43].

Research can play an important role, it seems to me, in identifying which particular methods of psychotherapy are suitable for which particular people. Once a therapist works toward realistic goals with a given individual, we shall also be able to abandon futile attempts to determine the therapeutic method that is "most effective." For some persons, a form of "behavior modification" may be the best that can be hoped for; for others, the achievement of greater autonomy through self-discovery in psychoanalysis may be the goal. Within each category, there will be slow and fast "learners." In each instance, the method must be tailored to the individual, which is the reason general principles of psychotherapy can only provide the grossest guidelines. Different teachers (or therapists) also have their individual styles, and some can work more productively with some students (or patients) than with others. Each therapist-teacher, despite thorough training, is bound to make his share of mistakes, which suggests that patient effort, hard work, an inquiring attitude, and, above all, a sense of humility are the only sensible approach to psychotherapy.

References

Alexander, F., and French, T. M. 1946. *Psychoanalytic Therapy: Principles and Applications.* New York: Ronald Press.

Andrews, J. D. W. 1966. "Psychotherapy of Phobias," *Psychol. Bul.,* 66: 455-480.

Colby, K. M. 1964. "Psychotherapeutic Processes," *An. Rev. Psychol.,* 15: 347-370.

Eysenck, H. J. 1952. "The Effects of Psychotherapy: An Evaluation," *J. Cons. Psychol.,* 16: 319-324.

―――― 1961. "The Effects of Psychotherapy," In *Handbook of Abnormal Psychology,* ed. H. J. Eysenck, pp. 697-725. New York: Basic Books.

Fromm-Reichmann, F. 1950. *Principles of Intensive Psychotherapy.* Chicago: University of Chicago Press.

Knight, K. P. 1941. "Evaluation of the Results of Psychoanalytic Therapy," *Am. J. Psychiat.,* 98: 434-446.

Matarazzo, J. D. 1965. "Psychotherapeutic Processes," *An. Rev. Psychol.,* 16: 181-224.

Paul, G. L. 1966. *Insight vs. Desensitization in Psychotherapy.* Stanford, Calif.: Stanford University Press.

Strupp, H. H., Fox, R. E., and Lessler, K. 1969. *Patients View Their Psychotherapy.* Baltimore: Johns Hopkins Press.

Szasz, T. S. 1965. *The Ethics of Psychoanalysis.* New York: Basic Books.

—— 1967. "Behavior Therapy and Psychoanalysis," *Med. Op. Rev.*, June, 24-29.

Wolpe, J. 1958. *Psychotherapy by Reciprocal Inhibition.* Stanford, Calif.: Stanford University Press.

25

CURRENT TRENDS IN PSYCHOTHERAPY

During the past 10 to 15 years behavioral approaches to psychotherapy have had an enormous influence on the practice of psychotherapy. While this influence is only gradually making itself felt in psychiatry, it has already profoundly affected academic psychology and the training of clinical psychologists. Perhaps this is not surprising because behavioral approaches grew out of the psychological laboratory; they are based on the learning theories of Pavlov, Hull, Thorndike, and Skinner; and they represent psychology's unique contribution to psychotherapy. Indeed, the term behavior modification has begun to supersede psychotherapy in many quarters, and perhaps rightly so. It is difficult to overemphasize this influence. Judged by the sheer number of publications since 1960, the creation of new journals and societies, and the prodigious activity of researchers, there can be no doubt that behavioral approaches to psychotherapy are preempting the contemporary scene, at least in this country and in England. To be sure, we know that any new treatment in medicine and psychiatry commands initial attention often beyond its ultimate merit, but I believe we are dealing here with something different from a fad or a fashion. What is the tremendous appeal of the approaches whose major spokesmen are the followers of B. F. Skinner and Joseph Wolpe?

In large measure, I believe, the behaviorists derive their strength from a strong reaction to psychoanalytic doctrine with which both professionals and laymen have become deeply disenchanted. Here is a breed of men who are strongly action-oriented, who eschew the contemplative approach to man, who are willing to tackle problems in the area of mental health that others have long avoided because they were considered untreatable or unsuitable, who are developing a formidable technology that, moreover, is simple to teach and to apply, and who are strongly committed to the rapid achievement of therapeutic results. They are willing to proceed with a minimum of theoretical assumptions, and what is perhaps most important, they are eager to submit their work to public scrutiny and empirical test. They assert —and I believe they are right—that psychoanalysis has been in default on all counts: its practitioners have concentrated on the affluent middle and upper classes; they have been largely unconcerned with the crying needs for more manpower, more efficient services to all strata of society; their therapeutic results are often unimpressive or at least extremely difficult to assess; they have resisted innovation and refused to change practices in the light of society's needs; they have isolated themselves from the behavioral sciences in general; and they have been reluctant to engage in scientific investigation of their therapeutic work. To a society that is becoming increasingly interested in providing mental health services to all its members, the behavioral approaches obviously have a tremendous appeal. Personally,

711

as a researcher who continues to believe that there is much of lasting value in Freud's teachings, I think the behaviorists have gone overboard and their wholesale rejection of Freud's hard-won insights is quite inappropriate. However, their aims, methods, and—above all—their therapeutic results cannot be dismissed lightly. Beyond that, they have infused the field with energy and enthusiasm, and they have given it new viability.

In many respects the behaviorists are close to Freud's early work, which also focused on the alleviation of symptoms, and which was equally pragmatic in its aim to provide concrete solutions to what, at the time, he saw as concrete problems. The symptom may not be the disease, but as far as the patient is concerned, he comes to therapy with specific complaints for which he seeks relief, and his criterion of cure is equally simple: he wants to feel better and perform more effectively. The behavior therapist offers him this promise, and here lies one of its most important appeals. His methods may at times be crude, unsophisticated, and unduly simplistic, but the average patient—and here I am talking particularly about members of the lower classes—is neither interested in the methods by which results are achieved nor is he greatly concerned with such concepts as insight and self-understanding. To him, behavior therapy offers a straightforward approach.

The opposite end of the contemporary therapeutic spectrum is represented by the existentialist-humanistic position. Beginning in the late Fifties, this approach has claimed a growing number of adherents in this country. While the appeal of behaviorism to the pragmatic American *Zeitgeist* is easy to understand, the growing popularity of the humanist position is far more difficult to grasp. Yet here is a movement that forcefully opposes therapeutic technology, that is not interested in "symptoms" as a manifestation of disease or of faulty learning, that is concerned more fully and more completely than was ever true of Freud with the "inner man" and his strivings for meaning, self-realization

712

and self-actualization, and that views the therapist not as a behavioral engineer but as a guide to man's dilemma of being versus nothingness. The unrest of our time, the apparent emptiness of modern man's life, his compulsive search for material goods and values—all of these undoubtedly have lent the movement buoyancy and vitality.

From a somewhat different perspective, Thomas Szasz (1965) has discussed incisively the objectives of what he calls autonomous psychotherapy. He presents a convincing argument that Freud's conception of the psychoanalytic situation was one of the most significant breakthroughs in designing a human relationship that makes possible to the largest possible extent man's search for independence, autonomy, and individual freedom. To some extent Freud himself did not consistently foster and develop his creation, which represented a forceful antidote to the hypocrisy and duplicity of society in nineteenth-century Vienna; but his followers, by aligning psychoanalysis with medicine and psychiatry, have largely vitiated Freud's dream. Szasz admits, however, that this form of psychotherapy, which is much more akin to education than it is to any form of medical treatment, is applicable only to people who have already achieved a fair measure of independence, personally as well as economically. For reasons he makes abundantly explicit, this form of psychotherapy is unsuitable for the disadvantaged, the disenfranchised (primarily mental hospital patients), and others who in one way or another are oppressed by their families or society. In practice this means that autonomous psychotherapy excludes perhaps 97 per cent of the patients who seek help from outpatient clinics and similar treatment centers. Clearly, this form of psychotherapy is not for the masses, and, even more than psychoanalysis or psychoanalytically oriented psychotherapy, it is a therapy for the élite or the privileged few. I wonder very seriously whether humanistic or existentialist psychotherapy is not similarly limited in its applicability. I do not wish to be misunderstood as saying that the quest for meaning or self-actualiza-

713

tion is a luxury or, as has sometimes been alleged, that the patients who seek it are not really suffering, but we must realize that our society as it is currently constituted places relatively little value on the individual, his inner life, and his personal autonomy. I think this is unfortunate and regrettable; however, if my reading is correct, we are destined to move even further along the road of heteronomy and collectivism.

The term psychotherapy has become an umbrella term whose connotations are now so diffuse as to be almost meaningless. Is it art, science, religion, philosophy, behavioral engineering, thought control, brainwashing, mysticism? Psychotherapy is what psychotherapists do, not what they assert in their theoretical writings, their discussions, or their published case histories. It has frequently been pointed out that there is only a loose articulation between therapeutic techniques and their alleged theoretical underpinnings that often characterize their proponents as fiction writers of no mean proportions. I venture to predict, however, that the focus on empiricism, verification, and on science is here to stay and that we are destined to develop even more refined technologies for psychological influence and behavior change.

The psychotherapist, as Perry London, Szasz, and others have pointed out, represents a moral force and he cannot escape influencing the patient by his personal values and those of the society in which he lives. Like any parent or teacher, he indoctrinates the patient with what is good or bad, desirable or undesirable, adaptive or maladaptive, and he steers him—sometimes wittingly, sometimes unwittingly—in these directions. It cannot be otherwise and it is not necessarily reprehensible. However, we need to become increasingly clear about the role and function of the psychotherapist, and we must dispassionately appraise the nature of his influence.

Thus I take it for granted that, regardless of his assertions, the psychotherapist is a persuader and an influencer.

714

Indeed, this is what he is paid to do and it is what the patient expects him to do. The patient says, in effect, "I have inadequate control over my thoughts, feelings, attitudes, and behavior. Do something to enable me to exercise greater control over myself and others. I am willing to submit to your operations and I shall temporarily subordinate myself to your interventions whatever they may be." Here is one of the paradoxes that applies with equal force to child-rearing, education, and psychotherapy. How can freedom, self-determination, and autonomy grow out of dependence, submission, and control? The patient, like the child, has to learn discipline through love and acceptance. He must become socialized, curb his impulses and selfishness, and deploy his energies within the channel that society defines for him. As the poet Robert Frost aptly put it, freedom moves easy in harness.

It seems to me that in the future we shall see the emergence of psychotherap*ies*, the breakdown of barriers between schools (as Albert Bandura phrases it, "Let's retire the brand names!"), and we shall gradually isolate the common elements in all forms of psychotherapy. Psychoanalysis, behavior therapy, existential analysis, or what-have-you all employ to varying degrees common psychological principles, such as reward and punishment, learning by imitation of a model, suggestion, etc., and they provide the patient with an interpersonal relationship within which the patient can correct his attitudes, beliefs, and behavior patterns that have proven troublesome and problematic. In this context, too, he may forge a philosophy of life that can guide him in realizing his personal goals and ideals.

What are the implications of these observations for brief psychotherapy? Let me briefly list a few:

1. Psychoanalysis thus far has made few contributions to this problem, and while psychoanalytic principles are often being applied in brief therapy, the tangible results have remained relatively unimpressive. This is not to gain-

say the possibility that more could be done, but few people are bending their efforts to this goal.

2. Behavior therapy in its various forms has begun, vigorously and imaginatively, to tackle problems in this domain, and while there are many conditions that thus far elude its technology, this approach has made significant inroads on a variety of problems that propel patients to seek help. It is interesting to observe that many psychiatrists, sometimes even orthodox analysts, have found such techniques as desensitization useful in certain instances and incorporated them in their techniques.

3. Humanistic psychotherapy, despite its worthwhile emphasis on the "whole man," seems precluded by its very nature from developing techniques that are inexpensive, efficient, goal-limited, and widely applicable.

Society is nowadays more interested in small but significant changes for a great many patients than it is in extensive changes (even if they are possible) for a few selected members of the upper classes. In this trend, unfortunately, lies the danger of sacrificing scientific understanding of the psychotherapeutic process to technological developments. The fact that a given technique "works" does not prove the correctness of its theoretical assumptions nor do we necessarily learn in this way a great deal about the psychological forces at work. With regard to the last objective, I believe that the psychoanalytic situation, particularly in its transference aspects, provides an enduring investigative instrument, whose potentialities we have barely begun to explore. Finally, we must consider the moral implications of any form of psychotherapy. Any technology can be employed for good or evil. Atomic energy can be used destructively or constructively. Similarly, straitjackets and drugs can be used to subdue recalcitrant citizens who prove irksome to society. When we are dealing with a symptom like a phobia, the issue is reasonably uncontroversial; however, there are many situations in psychotherapy where the alternatives are

716

far less obvious. In the end, as therapists and researchers, we are dealing with human values about which we must be explicit.

References

Szasz, T. S. 1965. *The Ethics of Psychoanalysis.* New York: Basic Books.

26

THE FUTURE OF
PSYCHOANALYSIS

I have been and continue to be deeply committed to the insights into the nature of man that psychoanalysis has given us, and I have deep respect for the work of the dedicated practitioner whose foremost objective is to alleviate neurotic suffering. Indeed, it is precisely because of my abiding admiration for Freud's genius and the potentialities of psychoanalysis as a science that I must voice my deep concern for the embattled position of psychoanalysis today.

Once in the forefront of revolutionary change, psychoanalysis is with increasing monotony described as antiquated, passé, obsolete, and even defunct. The theory is seen as based on formulations and working assumptions that are in dire need of a massive overhaul; its therapeutic effectiveness has been seriously questioned; its applicability to the vast problems of contemporary society is being

718

doubted; and its status as a branch of the behavioral sciences appears to be approaching a nadir. Students are no longer "turned on" by what psychoanalysis has to offer; granting agencies have become profoundly critical of research proposals anchored to the psychoanalytic framework; universities have turned their attention to more exciting developments both within psychology and in the neighboring sciences; and the general public is deeply disillusioned. May I say that the *Zeitgeist* I am sketching here is not adequately represented by the climate in the metropolitan areas like New York, Boston, and a few other places; rather, in order to appreciate the extent of the disaffection it is essential to talk and listen to students at universities other than those of the Ivy League and to become attuned to psychotherapists other than psychiatric residents in training in psychoanalytically oriented medical schools. Without pursuing this theme further it is fair to say that psychoanalysis has failed. As George Engel (1968) bluntly put it, "We haven't delivered the goods." I am not saying that psychoanalysis is totally bankrupt and defunct, but I feel it is in mortal danger of being eclipsed by other approaches. The hard-won insights that brought a storm of hostility and vilification on Freud's head are being brushed aside as a historical curiosity, irrelevant to modern man. Where have we failed? What can be done to resuscitate a body of admirable clinical knowledge, a therapeutic tool of remarkable sophistication and profundity, a theory of mental functioning that has the potential of giving rise to outstanding research?

The basic problem and the common denominator of our difficulties, as I see it, lies in the failure of psychoanalysis to have cultivated a spirit of open inquiry, a chronic unwillingness to welcome new ideas and techniques no matter where they might come from, a pervasive disinclination to question time-honored ideas and practices, and to actively search for new departures (despite a few notable exceptions). Let me remind you that Freud saw the future of psychoanalysis as that of a science, and while, for reasons of self-preservation, he contributed a fair share to the evolution of professional guilds, he was adamant in his conviction that any theory is at best a temporary and transient formulation until something more adequate comes along; he would have been the first to show interest and curiosity in developments occurring in the biological and social sciences and to embrace knowledge from all quarters. A science, Shakow (1965) observed, does not belong to anyone—it belongs to all serious students regardless of their academic or professional credentials; a science is not owned by professional organizations; it cannot flourish if it becomes an exclusive club that denies opportunities for training to all but a selected few and that treats its theories, techniques, and insights as a secret lore, a kabbala, open only to the initiated. I realize that any self-respecting profession must develop qualifications for its practitioners, and I am also aware that in recent years there has been a liberal trend opposed to the one I have delineated. The basic issue, however, remains that for too long professional goals and research goals have been confounded and the science of psychoanalysis has been treated as the private property of professional guilds. Instead of welcoming scientists, researchers, critics—even hostile ones—psychoanalysis has fostered a spirit of "splendid isolation" that has proven calamitous.

It has frequently been pointed out that there are great temperamental differences between the clinician and the researcher, and perhaps therapeutic and investigative talents are diametrically opposed. While the clinical method has been the prime source of insights in psychoanalysis, it is by no means the only method for acquiring knowledge. For a long time psychoanalysts subscribed to the notion that doing therapy is doing research and that knowledge can be generated only within the clinical framework, preferably the "classical model," which must not be tampered with. Today we realize that the therapy-research equation is a convenient fiction. I am reasonably convinced by this time that the one-to-one therapy relationship, while remaining a

720

useful source of hypotheses, has grave limitations and very probably has already outlived its usefulness. I do not wish to be misunderstood as suggesting that we reject the clinical framework, but I believe that more or less uncontrolled observations made by a therapist in the course of psychotherapy as it is typically practiced are not very likely to lead to significant discoveries. With this general approach, I venture to speculate, we have gone about as far as we can go.

The second major issue that I see as consequent upon the open inquiry problem relates to the matter of therapeutic effectiveness. While I agree with Engel that we must not permit ourselves to be maneuvered into the position of having to defend psychoanalysis exclusively on the grounds of its therapeutic efficacy, it remains true that the outcome problem is always just around the corner, and society has become rightfully concerned about expectable returns from different forms of psychotherapy. I have long defended the view that psychotherapy in general and psychoanalysis in particular has a great deal to offer under appropriate conditions. Furthermore, I have contended that existing research methods do not permit us to assess the relative merits of different therapeutic approaches. It seems to me that psychoanalysis is in an excellent position to explore the scope of its applications, to spell out in convincing detail what psychotherapy can do and what it cannot do, the kinds of changes it can effect and the limitations it must face, the kinds of problems to which it is applicable, the kinds of patients for whom it is suitable, and the uniqueness of its approach in helping the patient achieve autonomy and independence as opposed to "modifying" his behavior. Not only is psychoanalysis well equipped to meet this challenge, but it has a responsibility to do so. In my judgment, it has shown few signs of taking this responsibility seriously. Since it has largely been out of touch with other sciences and, perhaps most important, with the spirit of the times, the needs of society for therapeutic services of all kinds and for a wide range of people, it has not done a good job of placing society's demands in proper perspective and delineating in a precise way what psychotherapy, on the basis of best available knowledge, can and cannot offer. It is partly for this reason that it has been unable to meet the challenge of vastly exaggerated claims for the wide array of psychotherapeutic approaches that have in recent years preempted the scene. How otherwise could the public readily believe that techniques like desensitization, operant conditioning, and "human relations" training of all kinds are panaceas and the last word? Objectives like "restructuring the personality" and "reducing excessive pressures of a primitive superego" have probably very little operational meaning to specialists, less to the informed critics, and none to the public at large.

In conclusion, I see the future of psychoanalysis as that of a science and all that this implies. To put it bluntly, psychoanalysis has lost its scientific respectability in 1970 and, in many quarters, has been degraded to an esoteric pursuit of a small cult that caters to affluent members of the upper-middle class, a cult that has nothing significant to say about important problems of modern man and his place in the world. My plea is that we should and can do better. In my judgment, the key is to be found in the abandonment of a smug attitude of narcissistic omnipotence and omniscience and an open recognition of the vast areas of ignorance that we all share in psychological and psychotherapeutic matters. To cite but one salient example, we can no longer be sure, as Freud was, about the specific therapeutic action of interpretations or, for that matter, any other therapeutic technique. If we do not conduct our own critical inquiries and push back the frontiers of science, it is a foregone conclusion that others, less well informed, will take up the cudgels. While what is valuable in a science will outlast fads and fashions, it is altogether possible that meanwhile the scientific clock will be set back a hundred years. In that kind of game, all will be losers.

References

Engel, G. L. 1968. "Some Obstacles to the Development of Research in Psychoanalysis," *J. Am. Psychoanal. Assn.*, 16: 195-204.

Shakow, D. 1965. "Seventeen Years Later: Clinical Psychology in the Light of the 1947 Committee on Training in Clinical Psychology Report," *Am. Psychol.*, 20: 353-362.

Part IX
Clinicians and Researchers—Toward Mutual Understanding and Collaboration

T he roles of the clinician and the researcher in psychotherapy have always been difficult to reconcile. The clinician has frequently been viewed as an artist, the researcher as a scientist, and their respective approaches have been regarded as antithetical and mutually exclusive. Part of the problem centers on one's definition of research; another aspect concerns temperamental differences.

Freud clearly aspired to the position of a scientist; he confessed that the role of the physician-healer was never congenial to him. Basically, anyone who systematically observes phenomena in nature, tries to order them, attempts to discern regularities and consistencies in them, and seeks to explain his observations in terms of general principles is engaged in research and follows the path of the scientist. Critics have disputed the scientific status of psychoanalysis,

727

but there can be no doubt that in his clinical work Freud was a scientist par excellence. His genius was manifested by (1) the perspicacity of his observations; (2) his ability to create a technique (the analytic situation) for making systematic observations over an extended period of time; and (3) his phenomenal skill and ingenuity in isolating important psychodynamic principles on the basis of what, after all, was a very small number of cases. The analytic situation, in particular, has always impressed me as a creative achievement of the first order. Where else in human affairs is there a comparable laboratory situation that makes possible the longitudinal study of interpersonal processes with a minimum of distortion? I believe that we have never taken full advantage of the immense research possibilities this superb method potentially provides.

Many of Freud's observations should have been stated as hypotheses rather than immutable truths, although in many cases they have been corroborated in clinical work. One of the troublesome problems with the clinical approach is the difficulty of isolating and manipulating single variables, so that the testing of hypotheses presents formidable obstacles. Freud, and to an even greater extent his followers, staunchly maintained that clinical phenomena can be studied only in a clinical context, and that the search for verification by other methods is doomed. However, while the clinical setting is a rich source of hypotheses, it is (in my judgment) not a very fertile ground for verifying them. Furthermore, if one approaches a patient (subject) with preconceived theoretical notions, it is very easy to produce a self-fulfilling prophecy, and alternatives become difficult to entertain. Many of Freud's followers seem to have fallen prey to this danger. That is, starting with Freud's assumptions, they found supportive evidence in their clinical work. Also, by subscribing to Freud's statement that research and therapy in psychoanalysis go hand in hand, they perpetuated the convenient fiction that every patient is a "research case." The presentation of a case history in and of itself is not research, although it may be the prelude to an investigative effort. It must be added that most clinicians, particularly if their background is in medicine, have not been trained as researchers.

For the sake of the advancement of psychotherapy as a scientific discipline it would be well to keep research and therapeutic functions apart. Freud himself came to see the psychoanalytic setting as predominantly an investigative instrument, and we have by now clear indications that if one's goal is to effect personality and behavior change there are more efficient and effective ways.

The second problem in this area concerns temperamental differences between clinicians and researchers. Rogers (1955) saw the two roles as diametrically opposed, and he felt that he could not function in both roles at the same time. While he built a convincing case, I believe he overstated the dichotomy, and undoubtedly there are great individual differences. My reply to Rogers comprises the second chapter paper in this section.

When research in psychotherapy began to be seriously pursued in the 1940s, it became clear that many researchers, primarily psychologists, showed a very rudimentary understanding of the clinical enterprise. In more recent years, this deficiency has been largely remedied, and many researchers now fully match the clinicians in sophistication and clinical understanding. Nevertheless, as I attempt to point out, the marriage between clinicians and researchers has always been an uneasy one. Traditionally, clinicians have suspected the motives of the researchers and they have not been particularly hospitable to his efforts, especially if the project required study of the ongoing process of psychotherapy. But even when I worked with analogues I encountered a fair amount of resistance and hostility. The researcher tended to be seen as an unwelcome intruder, a meddlesome detective who tried to expose the clinician or hold him up to ridicule, and the clinicians' mistrust often resulted in refu-

729

sals to cooperate in investigative ventures. Not infrequently it was couched in a (certainly legitimate) concern about the patient's welfare and the privacy of the therapeutic situation. Again, we have witnessed significant changes during the last two decades, and there are signs of far greater openness and increased willingness on the part of clinicians to cooperate in research. Also, the advent of sound and video recording and its use in training and supervision have brought about a significant change in therapists' attitudes. Finally, the researcher has vastly gained in prestige since the 1950s. Before that time, the clinician reigned supreme, and the researcher was at best a nuisance or a gadfly. Today, clinical activities have distinctly declined in prestige, and the researcher-scientist has assumed an impressive role of leadership.

There remains the problem that research in psychotherapy has had relatively little influence on clinical practice, a state of affairs continually deplored by researchers. The most significant influence perhaps has been an attitudinal change along the lines sketched in the preceding paragraph. As a consequence, clinicians have begun to question time-honored practices and to entertain alternative approaches to the resolution of problems presented by their patients. Therapists of all persuasions have started to experiment with techniques that heretofore were regarded as inferior or antithetical to their theoretical position. For example, even orthodox analysts have begun to see some virtues in such techniques as relaxation training and desensitization; hypnotherapy has again become respectable; and serious doubt has come to be cast on the potential value of radical personality reorganization, as advocated by psychoanalysis. Examples could be multiplied, but today there is a definite trend toward eclecticism, and it is fair to say that the activities of researchers have played a part in this development.

At the same time, researchers have yet to provide the clinician with conclusive answers on almost any problem in

730

the domain of psychotherapy. We know as yet little about how to select patients for particular techniques; the relative effectiveness of different techniques is unknown; we are unclear about the problem of outcome as well as the kinds of changes that may be expected under specific circumstances; and the personality of the therapist has remained shrouded in uncertainty. Nevertheless, progress is being made, and researchers in the 1970s are closer to the right track than they have ever been before. Esoteric pursuits have largely disappeared from the scene, and researchers are beginning to address themselves with serious effort to the hard-core questions that need to be answered if psychotherapy is going to have a viable future.

Greater collaboration between clinicians and researchers is still needed, as well as a better understanding and increased respect for their respective roles: researchers must be keenly attuned to the problems of the clinician, but the converse is also true.

The final chapter, written (in part) with Professor Allen E. Bergin, was the culmination of an intensive exploration spanning a period of three years. In the course of this work, whose primary objective was to determine whether collaboration on large-scale investigations in psychotherapy was feasible and to chart, as best we could, promising directions for future research, we carried out a comprehensive review of the research literature and subsequently interviewed some 30 authorities throughout the country. The chapter briefly summarizes this endeavor (omitting Dr. Bergin's own interpretations and conclusions). A full description of this work may be found in Bergin and Strupp (1972).

References

Bergin, A. E., and Strupp, H. H. 1972. *Changing Frontiers in the Science of Psychotherapy.* Chicago: Aldine-Atherton.

Rogers, C. R. 1955. "Persons or Science? A philosophical question," *Am. Psychol.* 10: 267-278.

27

THE FUTURE OF
RESEARCH IN PSYCHOTHERAPY

*As you know, we have never prided our-
selves on the completeness and finality of
our knowledge and capacity. We are just
as ready now as we were earlier to admit
the imperfections of our understanding, to
learn new things and to alter our methods
in any way that can improve them.*

Sigmund Freud

There is a growing consensus today that the future of
psychotherapy is that of a scientific discipline. In recent
years this point of view has been advanced by numerous
writers, who add that any other course would tend to rele-
gate psychotherapy to a doctrine, a faith, or a gospel (Kar-

diner, 1958; Kubie, 1956). While Freud often spoke of psychoanalysis as a "movement" and "cause," he never conceived of it as anything but a science. Moreover, he feared greatly that institutionalization would lead to stagnation and the emergence of a cult rather than to scientific development. This apprehension, it must be conceded, has not been altogether groundless, but fortunately there is a countertrend; and it is this countertrend with which many of the foremost thinkers in the area ally themselves. I am referring to the increasing emphasis on controlled research and experimentation, that is, the application of the scientific method to furthering our understanding of the psychotherapeutic process. During the past 30 years the quantity as well as the quality of research contributions has grown, and there is every reason to believe that the coming decades will see an intensification of this effort. Has research exerted a demonstrable influence on the theory and practice of psychotherapy? In my opinion, the influence has been slight, and I propose to examine some of the reasons for this seemingly pessimistic conclusion. I am also prompted by the belief that, somehow, we should be able to do better.*

First it will be necessary to clarify what "research contribution" is intended to mean in this context. The term "research" is broad indeed and connotes very different things to different people. To American psychologists and social scientists schooled in the tradition of empiricism, positivism, and operationism, the meaning is fairly clear: basically it means the formulation and testing of a hypothesis to aid in building a theory. The ground rules for this process are often intricate and complicated, but the insistence is always on empirical evidence for any assertion and an explicit statement of the means by which knowledge is derived. Such knowledge is public rather than private; it is demon-

*The writing of this paper was supported, in part, by Research Grant M-2171 of the National Institute of Mental Health, U.S. Public Health Service. I am deeply grateful to the National Institute of Mental Health for its continued and generous support.

strable, reproducible, and communicable. These stipulations are those of any science, and they must be adhered to insofar as psychotherapy aspires to the status of a scientific discipline.

To Freud and those working in the psychoanalytic tradition, "research" had a similar but not identical meaning. To be sure, he diligently searched for empirical evidence; he was concerned with making explicit the procedures by which knowledge was acquired; he recognized the need to replicate findings; and he strove for a distinction between clinical findings and the theoretical formulations he devised to explain them. Nevertheless, he was far less rigorous in his investigations than contemporary researchers, if—let it be noted—infinitely more productive. Certainly, one of Freud's greatest and probably most lasting achievements is that of having devised a novel and unique method of investigation (the psychoanalytic situation) and having incisively explored its essential ingredients. Psychoanalytic research was and largely continues to be done in the clinical setting; this setting led to the emergence of the cardinal principles upon which psychoanalysis as a therapeutic technique is built; this setting, too, by its very nature imposes serious restrictions on the rigor that is part and parcel of the scientific method. True, it has its built-in "controls": it defines the therapeutic situation as well as the role of the analyst (within rather broad limits); it seeks to maximize the patient's contribution to the situation while holding the analyst's constant; it imposes relatively strict rules upon the role behavior of the analyst; but it fails to insure that the analyst's observations (and the inferences he draws therefrom) are *reliable,* that is, more than purely subjective experience.*

---

*Not long ago a British follower of Melanie Klein reported that she was "shocked" to learn from a conversation with an American analyst that he and most practicing analysts in this country do very little research. As she saw it, *every* case at her institute is a "research" case. A similar comment was made to the writer by a British child analyst

Limiting the discussion to the American scene, it may be noted that knowledge about the psychotherapeutic process is enriched from two major sources: (1), analysts working in the tradition of Freud; and (2) research workers whose approach is more eclectic. The former group, largely on account of the restrictions imposed on psychoanalytic training, consists principally of analysts whose background training has been in medicine; the second group, primarily of psychologists whose training and experience have been in clinical psychology. With the rise of clinical psychology as a science and profession during the last decade, and as a result of increased contact of psychologists with psychoanalytic principles and techniques, research workers bring to bear upon their investigations a vastly greater understanding and appreciation of the subject matter, problems, and concerns of psychoanalysis than was true before 1940.† Psychoanalysts, on the other hand, have begun in some instances to seek the collaboration of psychologists whose training has stressed research design and methodology as well as clinical experience in psychotherapy. In short, there seems to be a tendency for psychoanalysts to know more about research (in a rigorous sense) and for research workers to know more about the dynamics of psychotherapy as an interpersonal process. Consequently, there is an expanding meeting ground, hence greater possibility for communication and collaboration.

---

trained by Anna Freud. There are indications that the younger generation of American analysts, perhaps as a result of more extensive training in the natural and social sciences, tends to use the term "research" in a stricter sense.

†A comprehensive survey prepared in 1943 (Sears) revealed a widespread preoccupation to "validate" psychoanalytic concepts and principles through methods then current in academic psychology. Significantly, Sears dispensed with reviewing "A few studies . . . of the psychoanalytic process itself, . . . since none of these was designed to test any theoretical point [Preface, p. x].

736

This statement is not intended to suggest that the millenium has arrived. The cleavage between the two kinds of research contributions—with a few notable exceptions—continues to be a rather sharp one. On the one hand, there is a plethora of papers that, while usually starting with clinical observations, pile inference upon inference and arrive at conclusions that typically are not capable of verification. On the other hand, there are numerous investigations whose attention to matters of methodology, sampling, quantitative assessment, and statistical control is reasonably adequate, but that fall short of illuminating the phenomena they purport to clarify. It is noteworthy that by and large the first kind of contribution tends to appear in "psychoanalytic" journals, the second kind in "psychological" ones. It is a hopeful sign that in papers of the first kind there is increasing emphasis on scientific rigor; with respect to researches of the second kind there is greater stress on meaningfulness and relevance. Very probably, the future will bring even greater rapprochement, and perhaps an eventual amalgamation of the two approaches. At present, however, it remains true that the former studies focus on the individual case, stressing longitudinal development, idiosyncratic richness, and depth; the latter place greater confidence in the cross-sectional approach, in which one or a few variables are systematically investigated in a sample of patients, therapists, etc. Here the individuality of the single case is subordinated to considerations of experimental design and statistical inference.

This problem is familiar to all who have witnessed the battle over psychometric versus projective tests, and it seems hardly necessary to belabor the issue. Although new statistical techniques (which are still not very widely employed) have opened new vistas for the study of the individual case, the problem remains with us. Let it be conceded without further discussion that both sides have a contribution to make, and that a scientific discipline of psychotherapy can and does profit both from exhaustive studies of individual

737

cases and from cross-sectional researches. The one may suggest hypotheses that can be more conclusively investigated by the other, and in general there is little danger that either approach will soon have to be abandoned for lack of problems.

At the same time, it is clear that the development of psychotherapy tends in the direction of greater specificity, explicitness, precision. This movement is inescapable if psychotherapy is to be taught, described, and explicated. Concepts must be defined more stringently, and the vagueness inherent in the subject matter must be diminished. The demands for operational definitions—or at least demonstrable empirical referents—can hardly be sidestepped. These desiderata are expounded with considerable vigor at scientific meetings, but, with the exception of a small minority of researchers, most practicing clinicians and psychotherapists are none too mindful of these injunctions, And, in a sense, rightly so; they cannot suspend their clinical work until such time as research sharpens their tools; they must go ahead, meet the vast clinical demands, and do the best under existing conditions.

The increasing split between the clinical function and the research function is undoubtedly due to many complex reasons, of which the technical difficulty of combining scientific rigor with therapeutic objectives is merely one. By contrast, it is interesting to note Freud's assertion that, in psychoanalysis, therapy and research always go hand in hand. Indeed, he considered this one of the distinctive features of the method. To him, each individual patient was the proving ground for his previous theories and the *fons et origo* of new clinical discoveries, which were then woven into subsequent formulations. He found it impossible to divorce research from the process of therapy, and conceived of himself more as a scientist than as a "healer." In fact, he came to the final conclusion that the possibilities of psychoanalysis as a research tool far overshadowed those of a treatment technique. To Freud, "research" meant *clinical* research, i.e., the painstaking study of individual patients. However, he applied the scientific method and, through the study of new cases, tested his hypotheses in an approximate way, without, however, achieving strict experimental control. In some instances, his observations led Freud astray, but it is a tribute to his genius that he succeeded in making valid generalizations on the basis of exceedingly small samples. At any rate, he found the roles of scientist and therapist quite congenial, and the thought of applying a therapeutic technique routinely was utterly alien to him. Nevertheless, as he envisaged the future of psychoanalysis, he foresaw a growing group of analysts who were primarily practitioners rather than researchers and who would rely on others to forge and refine the tools needed for clinical work.*

Furthermore, Freud held the view that research on psychoanalysis (as a therapeutic instrument) could be conducted *only* in the psychotherapeutic situation—at least he did not foresee other possibilities. Even today a strong belief is held in many quarters that in order to do research on the psychotherapeutic process, particularly long-term, analytically oriented psychotherapy, it is mandatory to leave the therapeutic situation undisturbed, even though various research techniques may be used as long as they do not interfere with the therapeutic situation proper. Another group of researchers seems to feel that relevant and meaningful research can be conducted experimentally or quasi-experimentally. The first group, harking back to Freud, asserts that the analytic situation represents a specific method of investigation, and that *psychoanalytic* research cannot be performed without this method; the latter group, without questioning the value of the method for therapeutic and other purposes, believes that other approaches, too,

*Rogers (1955), on the other hand, feels that he cannot simultaneously function in both roles : if, in the clinical situation he attempts to be a scientific observer, he feels his empathic ability suffers. He considers the two roles diametrically opposed and essentially irreconcilable.

739

may yield fruitful and provocative data, which eventually, may find their way back into the treatment situation.

So far, I have tried to indicate that essentially there are two kinds of research approaches to the psychotherapeutic process: the clinical, used preponderantly by practicing analysts and therapists; and the experimental, exemplified chiefly by clinical research psychologists. While changes are gradually taking place, it appears that clinical penetration and scientific rigor have varied inversely. Furthermore, the two approaches undoubtedly reflect the temperaments of the proponents. If the advances of psychoanalysis as a therapeutic technique are compared with the experimental research contributions, there can be little argument as to which has more profoundly enriched theory and practice of psychotherapy. Up to the present, research contributions have had exceedingly little influence on the practical procedures of psychotherapy. This, in view of the advocacy of more and more research, the expansion of facilities and the greater availability of federal and private financial support, is a deeply disquieting state of affairs requiring closer scrutiny. Why is this so? Why have research contributions had so little impact? Is it that they have nothing to teach the practicing therapist? Are therapists so impervious to scientific findings that they are unable to profit from them? Is our knowledge of the subject matter so rudimentary that at this stage research cannot possibly be expected to have left its mark on clinical practices? I raise these questions, not as a therapeutic nihilist but as a researcher who feels that important answers should come from research. But, I must confess that I am not fully convinced that they will. A closer look at the contemporary scene may not enable one to discern trends to forecast the future, but it may help to clarify the schism that divides practicing therapists and investigators doing research on the therapeutic process.

The therapist-clinician might speak as follows: Psychotherapy, first and foremost, is a clinical art, not a

740

science. My task is to aid and promote personality growth, or, more accurately, to help a troubled human being in his struggle with his emotional difficulties. I assume that the patient is fully capable of steering his own life course once the obstacles that stand in his way are removed. My task is to aid him in this process. I don't "handle" a case, I don't "manipulate" a person, I don't apply a "technique." My whole effort is concentrated upon *understanding* this person and his difficulties in living. If I am a psychoanalyst or an analytically oriented therapist, I follow certain technical rules (based on such concepts as transference, resistance, defense, etc.) that usually accelerate the therapeutic process. From this vantage point, I don't see how it would help me to know that persons having certain psychological character- istics are better candidates for intensive psychotherapy than persons having some other characteristics; that interpreta- tions of a certain kind tend to produce resistance in certain kinds of patients at a certain stage in therapy; that under certain conditions the therapist's personal problems tend to interfere with the therapeutic process; that certain patterns of personality characteristics in a therapist are more con- ducive to progress in therapy than certain others; that inter- pretive techniques are more effective in the hands of certain therapists with certain kinds of patients under certain cir- cumstances, etc. How do such findings help me to under- stand my patient, Joe Smith, whom I am seeing three times a week, who relates to me, a particular therapist, in a particular way, who tells me about his anxieties in highly specific situations and whose style of life, defensive patterns, life goals, fantasies, wishes are a unique constellation? True, there are important clinical papers that have influenced me deeply: they are the papers of a host of sensitive thera- pists—not the kinds of investigations that are based on a sample of patients often treated by student therapists, which report results at the .05 or .01 level of statistical confidence. I am in sympathy with the point of view that says that we must achieve greater clarity about our concepts and our operations, but I doubt whether an experimenter standing *outside* the therapeutic situation can deepen my understanding of patients qua living human beings.

The researcher-scientist might speak thus: I fully recognize that the major contributions to the theory and practice of psychotherapy are based on careful observations of perceptive clinicians. Freud and those who followed in his footsteps have revolutionized our thinking about psychic conflicts and developed a unique method for effecting fundamental and lasting personality change. Certainly, clinical observation and painstaking efforts by individual therapists have taught us most of what we know about the principles of psychotherapy and psychotherapeutic technique. It is possible that these insights will not be equaled or even approached in another century. However, we must not lose sight of the fact that Freud considered psychoanalysis a *science*, and he strove until his dying day to preserve the scientific attitude that formed the basis of his most notable discoveries. Unlike some of his followers, he did not consider his formulations as final pronouncements or immutable truths. To be sure, his methods were relatively uncontrolled, nor was he able to marshal the scientific rigor that is demanded of investigations today; but he applied the scientific method as clearly and unmistakably as an experimental psychologist who runs rats through a maze or a physiologist who measures the contractions of a muscle. The differences are quantitative rather than qualitative.

Furthermore, it must be recognized that our knowledge of psychotherapy is at a very rudimentary stage. As Kubie (1956, p. 102) points out, we stand at the threshold of a new era; discoverers like Freud have pointed the way, but it remains for others to systematize his insights, to document the wealth of his observations, to sift, discard, build, and revamp. Reluctant as the clinician may be to bring the searchlight of dispassionate and objective research to bear upon his clinical operations, no other course is open. It may be a long time before our knowledge is reorganized in revolutionary ways, and, compared to the sweeping discoveries of Freud, the patient and laborious investigations of the researcher may appear pedestrian, obsessive, and even picayune. Nevertheless, they are needed and may surely be counted upon to advance the frontiers of knowledge. Possibly none or very few of the current research investigations provide principles that *radically* change therapeutic technique or even have a marked influence on clinical practice. But neither have clinical insights during the last decades led to momentous changes in therapeutic technique. Progress in this area has been slow, but by no means negligible. Besides, the clinician's attitude of respect, empathy, and understanding has nothing to do with what research has to contribute; on the contrary, greater specificity coming from research will strengthen and illuminate the clinical framework of his practical operations and gradually enable him to be of better help to his patients.

These arguments, based as they often are on emotional commitments, have a familiar ring. They underline the nomotheticideographic controversy; they are mirrored in the fundamental differences between the *geisteswissenschaftliche* approach of German psychology and the naturalistic-positivistic approach of American psychology; they have recently been revived in existentialist thinking and *Daseinsanalyse* (May, Angel, and Ellenberger, 1958); and they are rooted in the subject-object schism of Western philosophy. These basic philosophic convictions determine one's view of psychology as a science, the methods by which knowledge is acquired about psychological processes, as well as one's conception of psychotherapy and of the role and function of the psychotherapist.

After having lived with Freud's discoveries for half a century, and viewed the individual patient as the battleground of impersonal forces shaping his destiny, we are still largely ignorant of the nature of the therapeutic action, and renewed attention is being focused on the psychotherapist as a *person*, who—some suspect—plays a larger part in the

743

therapeutic endeavor than has hitherto been acknowledged or made explicit.* Working with widely different methods of investigation, theoretical orientations, and therapeutic objectives, numerous investigators appear to converge on this point. Alexander (1958), after a lifetime of experience in psychoanalysis, refers to "the most opaque area of psychoanalysis, the question of the therapist's influence on the treatment process by the virtue of being what he is: an individual personality, distinct from all other therapists [p. 311]." Frank, speaking as a researcher concerned with

---

*In one of his last papers Freud (1952) makes this highly significant point:

Amongst the factors which influence the prospects of an analysis and add to its difficulties in the same manner as the resistances, we must reckon not only the structure of the *patient's* ego but the personal characteristics of the *analyst*. . . . The analyst. . . , because of the peculiar conditions of his work, is really impeded by his own defects in his task of discerning it in a manner conducive to cure. So there is some reason in the demand for a comparatively high degree of psychical normality and correct adjustment in the analyst as one of his qualifications for his work. And there is another point: he must be in a superior position in some sense if he is to serve as a model for his patient in certain analytic situations and, in others, to act as his teacher. Finally, we must not forget that the relationship between analyst and patient is based on a love of truth, that is, on the acknowledgment of reality, and that it precludes any kind of sham or deception [pp. 351-352].

As in earlier papers, the emphasis rests on those aspects of the therapist's personality that might create an impediment to therapy; however, Freud also recognizes that the therapist must be "in a superior position in some sense if he is to serve as model for his patient. . . ." Unfortunately, one is left to guess what is meant by "superior position," but I wonder whether Freud meant that the therapist had to be somewhat of a *Persönlichkeit*. If in the passage immediately following he expressed doubts that the candidate would acquire the "ideal qualifications" for his work *solely* in his personal analyis, he clearly had the removal of "blind spots" in mind; but perhaps he also questioned whether the candidate could ever become a *Persönlichkeit solely* through his personal analysis unless his analyst in turn embodied the "model qualities" Freud alluded to.

744

experimental controls, sees as a chief problem "to distinguish the effects of the therapist's personality or attitude, from the effects of his technique" (Frank, 1959). And further: "The most important, and unfortunately the least understood, situational variable in psychotherapy is the therapist himself. His personality pervades any technique he may use, and because of the patient's dependence on him for help, he may influence the patient through subtle cues of which he may not be aware." Elsewhere Frank considers the possibility that the patient's faith and trust in the therapist may be the single most important variable in therapeutic change (1958). Rogers (1957) speaks of the therapist's "genuineness in the relationship," his "unconditional positive regard," and "empathy." He views the therapeutic relationship "as a heightening of the constructive qualities which often exist in part in other relationships, and an extension through time of qualities which in other relationships tend at best to be momentary [p. 101]." In the same paper, Rogers comes to the conclusion that "the techniques of the various therapies are relatively unimportant [p. 102]" and, stressing the overriding importance of the therapist's attitudes:

Any of the techniques may communicate the fact that the therapist is expressing one attitude at a surface level, and another contradictory attitude which is denied to his own awareness. Thus one value of such a theoretical formulation as we have offered is that it may assist therapists to think more critically about those elements of their experience, attitudes, and behaviors which are essential to psychotherapy, and those which are nonessential or even deleterious to psychotherapy [p. 103].

The present writer, basing his conclusion on a study of psychotherapists in an experimental situation, regards the therapist's contribution to the treatment process as both personal and technical (see Chapter Nine):

745

His personal attributes (maturity, warmth, acceptance, etc.) enable him to create the kind of interpersonal relationship in which constructive personality change can take place; his knowledge of psychodynamic principles permits him in and through this relationship, to initiate the kinds of emotional unlearning and learning experiences that are considered necessary to the alleviation or resolution of neurotic conflicts. The latter would be impossible without the former; the former, by itself, would never be sufficient.

There appears to be, then, a growing disenchantment with psychotherapy as a "technique," American preoccupations with technology notwithstanding. The keynote of this development was perhaps sounded by Freud himself. His attention to the technical aspects of psychoanalytic therapy declined toward the middle and end of his career, and contrary to his theoretical revisions in other areas he had relatively little to add to his earlier papers on technique. While he considered the therapist's personal attributes important, he stressed their potentially noxious influences, leaving the positive aspects largely unformulated (Freud, 1952). True, at one time he conceived of psychoanalysis as a kind of "after-education" but later on expressed a distaste for the conception of the therapist as an "educator" or "mentor." (See, in this connection, Burchard, 1958.) He feared that the therapist might make similar mistakes as the patient's parents in "indoctrinating" him with a set of values and rules that would impede his free development and self-direction. In the 1920s and 1930s much emphasis was given to interpretations, their timing, correctness, and adequacy. Concomitantly, the person making the interpretations tended to be lost sight of, and under Freud's impetus the essence of psychoanalytic therapy was seen as the resolution of the transference neurosis through appropriate interpretations— a process, one surmised, that would reel off, regularly, automatically, and inexorably, if but the "correct" technical

746

procedures were followed. This is not the place to trace subsequent developments except to draw attention to a trend culminating in the "rediscovery" of the therapist as a person, whose attitudes, personality, and values presumably play an exceedingly important, if not crucial, part in the therapeutic process. Increasing effort must be expended to elucidate his personal influence, which may far transcend his technical contribution.*

Could it be that we have come full circle? Starting from the age-old view of the potentially beneficial effects of love, friendship, and acceptance of one's emotional well-being, we seem to have traversed an era in which a highly technical procedure (psychoanalysis) came to the ascendancy. Here the therapeutic task was conceived as an effort to bring about a reconciliation of impersonal forces—to help the ego come to terms with an irrational id and an unreasonable, overly severe superego. Moving along a spiral, the developments of ego psychology have stressed a conception in which the ego's autonomy and integrative functions again came to the fore. Contemporaneously, the psychotherapeutic situation is again seen as an encounter between two *persons*. The patient is regarded as an individual with problems in living, but also as a human being striving to realize his potentialities. The therapist is viewed, not as an analytic manipulator or technician, but as a human being who, aided by technical training *and* experience in living, attempts to *understand* the patient as a person. This understanding is to be accomplished through emotional participation in living with the other person over an extended period of time, to the end that the therapist's influence conduces to constructive personality growth. The focus is upon the experiential components of the situation, to which everything else becomes subordinate, including the technical operations by which the experience is facilitated. Consequently, the operations of psychotherapy are not simply to be explained by rules telling the novice when to interpret and what; rather they presuppose a deep

*For a more extended discussion of this point, see Chapter One.

understanding of the principles governing the whole gamut of human collaboration. Aware of this complexity, though speaking in a different context, Freud (1955, Vol. XII) said:

> Anyone who hopes to learn the noble game of chess from books will soon discover that only the openings and end-games admit of an exhaustive systematic presentation and that the infinite variety of moves which develop after the opening defy any such description. This gap in instruction can only be filled by a diligent study of games fought out by masters [p. 123].

This analogy illustrates a point, but like all analogies it has its limitations. It asserts that:

1. there are rules governing the conduct of psychotherapy;
2. that these rules are explicit and communicable, hence teachable;
3. that there is an over-all strategy in psychotherapy as there is in chess, i.e., there is a specific objective;
4. while knowledge of the basic rules is a prerequisite, it does not, in and of itself, enable one to play the game with any degree of skill; in other words, the general rules must be applied in highly specific and concrete situations, and once a measure of skill is acquired, the basic rules seem to recede to the background, so that the player is largely unaware that he is employing them;
5. that one learns the skill by watching and studying closely the operations of experts; in doing so, one learns to avoid pitfalls and refines his technique, which ultimately becomes interwoven with one's personality.

One of the important shortcomings of this analogy is that the rules of psychotherapy are established empirically, not, as in chess, a priori. Furthermore, they are modifiable

748

in the light of empirical findings, that is, their validity is to be established by reference to an external criterion. As the analogy suggests, the expert is more "successful" in playing the game than a novice, as evidenced by the fact that he wins more games. Is the expert psychotherapist more "successful" than the novice? This is a purely empirical question, which so far as I know has not been answered to anyone's satisfaction. One of the important reasons that it has not been done is the difficulty of *comparing* the performance of an expert with that of a novice, under rigidly specified conditions, and to note differences in outcome. Such a comparison presupposes the definition and measurement of dimensions that are hypothesized to make a difference (maturity, technical skill, for example). In all probability, the expert does differ in his therapeutic performance from the novice, but this must be demonstrated unequivocally, beyond a reasonable doubt. One approach might be to study the therapeutic behavior of a group of experts to see what they have in common. One might then search for the same common characteristics (therapeutic ingredients) in a group of beginners and determine whether differences exist. If so, they should lead to predictably different outcomes. If not, the results may be due to other factors yet to be defined. Freud attributes the results of psychoanalysis primarily to certain technical operations on the therapist's part; Rogers is inclined to search for them in the area of the therapist's "unconditional regard"; Frank hypothesizes a series of nonspecific factors, such as faith and trust. I suspect that technical skill and salient characteristics of the therapist's personality interact to make possible a new emotional experience, cognitive learning, and the gradual acquisition of new attitude patterns.

Preoccupations with psychotherapeutic technique have increasingly come under criticism in recent years. In this country, Rogers has been an eloquent spokesman for the view that *understanding* the patient is the therapist's first and foremost task. In Europe, the rise of existential psychotherapy has brought with it a further deemphasis of technique. In explicating this point of view to American readers, May (*et al.,* 1958) states: "Existential analysis is a way of understanding human existence, and its representatives believe that one of the chief (if not *the* chief) blocks to the understanding of human beings in Western culture is precisely the overemphasis on technique, an overemphasis which goes along with the tendency to see the human being as an object to be calculated, managed, 'analyzed' [p. 76]." And farther on: The central issue is "whether the human being is an object to be analyzed or a being to be understood [p. 81]." However, the emphasis on the here-and-now relationship neither obviates technical training nor should it discourage research on problems of technique. In May's (1958) words, this relationship

... is in no way an over-simplification or short cut; it is not a substitute for discipline or thoroughness of training. It rather puts these things in their context—namely, discipline and thoroughness of training directed to understanding human beings as human. The therapist is assumedly an expert; but, if he is not first of all a human being, his expertness will be irrelevant and quite possibly harmful. The distinctive character of the existential approach is that understanding *being human* is no longer just a "gift," an intuition, or something left to chance; it is the "proper study of man," in Alexander Pope's phrase, and becomes the center of a thorough and scientific concern in the broad sense. The existential analysts do the same thing with the structure of human existence that Freud did with the structure of the unconscious— namely, take it out of the realm of the hit-and-miss gift of special intuitive individuals, accept it as the area of exploration and understanding, and make it some extent teachable [pp. 82-83].

Thus, it is of little avail to investigate whether psychotherapy "works," or even whether one technique is more "effective" than another. Rather one must ask: Is this particular therapist, by virtue of being a particular person, capable of creating the kinds of conditions in which a given technique or techniques can attain their maximum usefulness? The question of the relative effectiveness of techniques still has to be answered, but the primary focus is on the *person* of the therapist by whom a particular technique is used. Can he understand the patient as a human being struggling with life's problems? Can he communicate this understanding, to the end that the patient feels deeply understood? For methodological reasons, research may emphasize one aspect or the other, but the totality of therapist and technique in interaction with a particular patient cannot be ignored.

There appears to be a serious danger in overemphasizing either relationship or technique at the expense of the other. To avoid these pitfalls it would appear that ways and means must be found to conduct investigations that do justice both to the demands of scientific rigor and the depth and breadth of the therapeutic undertaking. To this end, researchers must become better and more insightful clinicians, and clinicians must develop a greater awareness of the ideals which the scientist espouses. Among other things, such a rapprochement may result in a larger number of research contributions that are meaningful and relevant to the therapist. Similarly, it may inspire that tentativeness, caution, and respect for error in human observation that is still lacking in many clinicians.

The subject-object split that still pervades the science of psychology seems a particularly grave obstacle to the interpenetration of clinical practice and research in psychotherapy. Russell (1948), quoted by Szasz (1957), has eloquently dealt with this issue and defined psychology as a science dealing with essentially private experience. Among psychologists, Allport (1955) has taken issue with the prevailing behaviorist tendency to regard the human person as

751

"empty." In the area of psychotherapy, the investigations of Rogers and his students are perhaps the best illustration that fruitful research on the process of psychotherapy can be done, while retaining something of the uniqueness of the persons participating in the process (Rogers and Dymond, 1954). These are but beginnings, but they seem important beginnings in studying objectively the subjective experiences of patient and therapist in interaction.

Erwin Straus's dictum (May *et al.*, 1958) that "Whatever is related to my particular existence lessens and obscures knowledge [p. 145]" seems to strike at the core of an important dilemma in research on psychotherapy. In order to expand scientific knowledge of the therapeutic process, it is necessary to objectify essentially subjective experiences, but as one succeeds in doing so, one runs the danger of sacrificing the essence of what one is studying. Therefore, the obverse of the quotation likewise appears to be true. Knowledge lessens and obscures whatever is related to my particular existence. This, of course, is precisely what science attempts to do in all areas of investigation. Is psychotherapy an exception? If so, it can hardly become a science. If not, the search for invariance amidst change must go forward; common elements must be abstracted; and the unique aspects of the therapeutic encounter may have to go by the board. In one sense, I seem to have suggested that the future *may* bring the development of techniques for *simultaneously* achieving both objectives. This is a hope that may never materialize. We may find that we can't have our cake and eat it. In that event, the therapist and the researcher in psychotherapy may move further apart, unless the clinician abandons his commitments, which seems to be as doubtful as that the researcher will forsake the ideals of science.

Among other things, it will be fruitful to learn how a particular patient is perceived, experienced, and reacted to by a particular therapist and vice versa. But if "objective" knowledge in psychotherapy is possible we must also learn more about what patient and therapist are "really" like, as seen by *external* observers. There is reason to suspect that preconceptions on the therapist's part (e.g., notions about the treatability or nontreatability of certain "conditions") may blind him to the patient's potentialities and assets (see Chapter Nine). Of course, the therapist should develop maximal self-awareness of all factors that might adversely affect his therapeutic attitudes. But, important as the study of subjective elements and biasing factors may be, it must not overshadow the thorough scrutiny of interpersonal processes (e.g., transference manifestations) qua objective facts, which, as every analyst knows, usually emerge in the treatment process irrespective of the therapist's unique personality characteristics even though they may be colored by the latter. And—to continue on this side of the fence—it seems that the latter-day emphasis on "encounter," "here-and-now experience," "understanding," etc., does scant justice to the painstaking and prolonged process of "working through"— a highly *technical* operation—which is considered an integral part of all fundamental personality change achieved through intensive psychotherapy. Difficult as controlled research on these problems will be, I am sure the limits have not been tested. However, I am not fully convinced that it will be possible to reconcile successfully scientific rigor with the richness and subtle complexity of interpersonal dynamics.

CONCLUSION

The questions raised at the beginning of this chapter still loom large. It is disquieting to contemplate the large discrepancy between clinical and philosophical insights on the one hand, and research accomplishments, on the other. As researchers we seem to lack methods for making greater inroads on the phenomena with which psychotherapy deals —the broad spectrum of human experience. For instance, how do we assess and measure such qualities in the therapist as respect for the patient's struggle toward self-realization

753

and self-direction, capacity for empathy, warmth, acceptance of the human-ness of another person, depth of one's *Weltanschauung* and life experience, emotional maturity, ability to serve as a model of reality, and so forth*—all of which undoubtedly play an important role in determining the extent to which the therapist can participate in and collaborate with the patient's striving for realizing his human potentialities? By contrast, the quantitative and comparative analyses of technique, formidable as they are, appear like child's play.

The fact that techniques for measuring significant personality attributes are in their infancy does not mean that they are doomed to remain there. The fact that so far the contributions from researchers to psychotherapeutic theory and practice have been relatively slight need not remain an immutable truth and omen for the future. The task poses a challenge to our imagination as researchers. We must show greater penetration in forging our research tools and refuse to purchase precision in measurement at the expense of shallowness of concepts. If we agree to the proposition that psychotherapy's future is that of a scientific discipline, we have no choice but to undertake the laborious and painful drudgery of checking the empirical value of brilliant clinical insights glimpsed by intrepid pioneers and to sharpen our research instruments that they may become adequate to deal with the phenomena in our domain. It is just barely possible that a few crumbs of insight left over by the giants may be the reward of the patient researcher, not to mention the gratification of demolishing along the way some hypotheses that contemporaneously enjoy the status of a creed.

*We need to specify those qualities of character that give the therapist stature as a mature personality and model of reality. Compare the footnote on page 744 for a statement of Freud's position.

References

Alexander, F. 1958. "Unexplored Areas in Psychoanalytic Theory and Treatment," *Behav. Sci.,* 3: 293-316.

Allport, G. W. 1955. *Becoming: Basic Considerations for a Psychology of Personality.* New Haven: Yale University Press.

Burchard, E. M. L. 1958. "The Evolution of Psychoanalytic Tasks and Goals," *Psychiat.,* 21: 341-357.

Frank, J. D. 1958. "Some Effects of Expectancy and Influence in Psychotherapy," in *Progress in Psychotherapy, Vol III,* pp. 27-43, ed. J. H. Masserman and J. L. Moreno. New York: Grune & Stratton.

——— 1959. "Problems of Controls in Psychotherapy as Exemplified by the Psychotherapy Research Project of the Phipps Psychiatric Clinic," in *Research in Psychotherapy,* ed. E. A. Rubinstein and M. B. Parloff, pp. 10-26. Washington, D.C.: American Psychological Assn.

Freud, S. 1952. "Analysis Terminable and Interminable," in *Collected Papers, Vol V,* pp. 313-357. London: Hogarth.

——— 1955. "Further Recommendations in the Technique of Psychoanalysis," in Standard Edition of the *Complete Psychological Works.* London: Hogarth.

Kardiner, A. 1958. "New Horizons and Responsibilities of Psychoanalysis, *Am. J. Psychoanal.,* 18: 115-126.

Kubie, L. S. 1956. "Some Unsolved Problems of Psychoanalytic Psychotherapy," in *Progress in Psychotherapy 1956,* pp. 87-102, ed. F. Fromm-Reichmann and J. L. Moreno. New York: Grune & Stratton.

May, R., Angel, E., and Ellenberger, H. F., eds. 1958. *Existence: A New Dimension in Psychiatry and Psychology.* New York: Basic Books.

Rogers, C. R. 1955. "Persons or Science: A Philosophical Question," *Am. Psychol.,* 10: 267-278.

————— 1957. "The Necessary and Sufficient Conditions of Therapeutic Personality Change," *J. Cons. Psychol.*, 21: 95-103.

————— and Dymond, R. F., eds. 1954. *Psychotherapy and Personality Change.* Chicago: University of Chicago Press.

Russell, B. 1948. *Human Knowledge: Its Scope and Limits.* New York: Simon & Schuster.

Sears, R. R. 1943. *Survey of Objective Studies of Psychoanalytic Concepts.* New York: Social Science Research Council.

Szasz, T. S. 1957. *Pain and Pleasure: A Study of Bodily Feelings.* New York: Basic Books.

28

OBJECTIVITY VERSUS SUBJECTIVITY

If indeed the therapist's participation in the interpersonal venture of psychotherapy is reduced to a totally subjective experience, the antithesis of objectivity versus subjectivity becomes an acute one. Rogers' article, "Persons or Science" (*Am. Psychol.*, July 1955), is in many ways an admirable analysis, but I submit that an important factor in his dilemma arises from his particular conception of psychotherapy and the role of the therapist.

Speaking as a clinician, Rogers regards the therapeutic process, as experienced by the therapist, as a thoroughly subjective phenomenon. He uses such emotionally charged terms as "trance-like," "fullness of experiencing," and " 'out-of-this-world' quality" to characterize the situation. The same tenor is expressed by the client-centered therapist in "The Case of Mrs. Oak" (Rogers and Dymond, 1954):

"To me the thought of trying to guide or direct such an intricate human process is literally abhorrent, and I never felt any such impulse in regard to Mrs. Oak. To try to understand her, to go with her on the paths she was exploring, to let her feel the acceptance I experienced toward her, this seemed to be a fully satisfying task to me [p. 264]."

Every therapist with empathic capacities (and there should be none without them) has undoubtedly felt something of this ineffable experience Rogers has attempted to put into words, and will regard it as a *sine qua non* of the psychotherapeutic process. This question, however, arises: Is this the *essence* of psychotherapy as we know it today, or is it merely a precondition, however indispensable? Rogers, of course, recognizes that a new kind of emotional learning takes place within this matrix, but he asserts that "The most that one person can do to further it in another is to create certain conditions which make this kind of learning possible." It is undeniably true that learning in psychotherapy, as probably in most situations, is in the final analysis self-learning. The verbal exchange in psychotherapy, from beginning to end, is placed in the service of effecting such learning. We can agree with Rogers that the patient's verbal description of this process, once he has experienced it, is quite immaterial. The important thing is that he has felt it.

For the Rogerian therapist the creation of a benevolent emotional climate is quite enough. Now contrast this conception with one that does not deny the importance of this precondition, but which in addition assigns to the therapist an active, reconstructive, and re-educative task. Sullivan's description will serve as a good example. Commenting on the factors that bring about favorable change in a person, he (Sullivan, 1954) sees the patient as having "been *restrained from using the totality of his abilities.* The problem of the psychiatrist in treatment is to discover what the *handicaps* to the use of his abilities are. . . . I try to find out why he *can't* do the simplest thing, and in such investigation may come to solve the problem [p. 237]. . . . [The task is to] work toward uncovering those factors which are concerned in the person's recurrent mistakes, and which lead to his taking ineffective and inappropriate action. There is no necessity to do more [p. 239]."

The role of the therapist as more than a subjectively involved partner is made even more explicit in the following quotation (Sullivan, 1954):

From beginning to end, to the best of his ability, the psychiatrist tries to avoid being involved as a person— even as a dear and wonderful person—and keeps to the business of being an *expert*; that is, he remains one who, theoretically and in fact, deals with his patients only because he (the psychiatrist) has had the advantage of certain unique training and experience which make him able to help them. . . . He may feel that interviewing is hard work, as I recommend everyone should. It is, beyond perchance, very hard work [p. 36].

What Sullivan calls respect for the patient, what Braatøy (1954) (following Ferenczi) calls love, what Rogers calls acceptance these factors must be present before therapy can begin. But does it end there?

Rogers' dichotomy between the therapist as a participant and as an observer appears to be somewhat of an artifact. It is difficult to see how a therapist who is completely subjectively immersed in the experience can be of constructive help to the patient. Freud, too, stresses the technical factors in the analyst's work. He likens the therapist to a surgeon who calmly employs his skill for the sole purpose of effecting a successful termination of the operation.

This emphasis on skill, expertness, work, far from making psychotherapy "directive" or reducing it to a mere technology, points to the rational nature of the therapeutic task, and the possibility of scientific explanation. It brings to the fore the importance of *technique,* with the implication of manipulation in Rogers' nonvaluative sense. Without

759

skill, without technique, psychotherapy is unthinkable. It is the technique, and indirectly the scientific basis upon which it rests, that differentiates modern psychotherapy from spiritual guidance, the confessional, and similar procedures.

Technique implies the deliberate employment of skill, and introduces from a different vantage point objectivity and science into the relationship. As soon as the therapist observes what is happening in the therapeutic situation—and I am convinced that he should never stop doing so—he brings the process of therapy closer to objective description and scientific understanding. Implicit in the activity of the therapist is a constant shifting between the role of participant and the role of observer. Freud's singular ability to objectify the subjective elements of his therapeutic experience is probably the best case in point. Ideally, each psychotherapist should function in both roles.

We may deplore the slowness and crudity of our research efforts in this area, but there is no reason to conclude that the richness of the therapeutic experience is destroyed by our increasing success in bringing the scientific method to bear upon it. As our powers of observation are sharpened, rather the opposite should be the case.

References

Braatøy, T. 1954. *Fundamentals of Psychoanalytic Technique.* New York: Wiley.

Rogers, C. R., and Dymond, Rosalind, F., eds. 1954. *Psychotherapy and Personality Change.* Chicago: University of Chicago Press.

Sullivan, H. S. 1954. *The Psychiatric Interview.* New York: Norton.

29

WHO NEEDS
INTRAPSYCHIC FACTORS
IN CLINICAL PSYCHOLOGY?

Why shouldn't the emphasis on intrapsychic variables—certainly a hallmark of psychoanalytic theory*—be banned to the hinterland as a more or less esoteric pursuit and left in the hands of specialists who, like biblical scholars, wish to concern themselves with fine points of exegesis irrespective of the bearing on the practical world of affairs and pragmatic interests? The impetus for that question came from some observations I made (1966). To set the stage, I shall recapitulate them here:

1. When Freud's revolutionary ideas first attracted

---

*Throughout this chapter I shall link an interest in intrapsychic variables with psychoanalytic theory although this concern is not restricted to the latter, nor is psychoanalytic theory *exclusively* concerned with intrapsychic variables.

public attention, attacks on them centered on his emphasis on sexuality (particularly the child's psychosexual development) and on the dynamic unconscious, which posed a threat to man's vaunted rationality. Freud threatened the "establishment" of clinical psychiatry, and was thoroughly out of step with the academic psychology of his day.

2. Despite the profound influence Freud's ideas have had since then, we are now witnessing a growing ambivalence about the lasting value of psychoanalytic theory, particularly insofar as its underpinning of psychotherapy is concerned. (As Rapaport had occasion to point out, the *general* theory of psychoanalysis, as opposed to the *clinical* theory, is a waif properly understood only by few.) Freud had hoped that his brainchild would become a part of psychology—not just "abnormal" psychology—and he had serious misgivings about the prospect of its being swallowed up by organized medicine and psychiatry. The latter fear, as developments in America have shown, was only too well founded. The former hope, I am afraid, is not being realized. (I recall an obituary on David Rapaport, one of the few great systematizers of psychoanalytic theory. The writer spoke of the tragedy, that in spite of Rapaport's contribution, he was never fully accepted either by organized psychoanalysis or by American psychologists.)

3. During the last ten years, particularly, we see a steady and progressive disillusionment with psychoanalytic theory and psychoanalytic psychotherapy. Factors that play a part in this development are the length, expense, and relative inefficiency of psychoanalytic psychotherapy; the absence of clear-cut demonstrations of its effectiveness; the fuzziness of psychoanalytic concepts and the persistent difficulty of designing rigorous research with them; the search for cheaper, quicker, and more "direct" treatment to reach larger and more varied populations; the competition by other theorists and therapists who claim superiority for their particular approaches (e.g., behavior therapy); the lack of new developments within psychoanalysis; the impact of

762

psychoactive drugs; the progress of genetics, biochemistry and brain physiology, which offer themselves as a new *biological* basis for psychological variables.

From various quarters one hears the criticism that psychoanalytic theory has been oversold, that it has failed to provide promising leads to the solution of pressing problems in the field of mental health.

4. In conclusion, I expressed my concern over these emerging trends. The immenseness of the social need is a responsibility we cannot afford to shirk. What distresses me, however, is the widespread lack in interest in furthering our understanding of psychological factors as such. It is one thing to allay chronic anxiety by tranquilizers that block the conscious experience of anxiety; it is quite another matter to understand the intricate structure of a neurosis. I happen to believe that much remains to be learned about psychological factors in the etiology of neurotic problems and the manner in which one person, for better or worse, exerts a psychological influence upon another. I do not see that there are any short-cuts to such an understanding that ought to remain the psychologist's interest and concern. Toward this objective psychoanalytic theory has a great deal to offer, but it remains a question whether this potential will be realized. All too often a theory is rejected before it is properly understood.

For example, community psychology, crisis intervention, and behavior therapy (e.g., Wolpe, 1958; Krasner and Ullmann, 1965; Ullmann and Krasner, 1965), particularly in treating severely disturbed children, present a formidable challenge that cannot be brushed aside. These workers, like it or not, are here to stay, and the onus is on the proponents of psychoanalytic theory, not on its critics.

The emphasis in these endeavors is on *action,* e.g., changing a particularly disturbing or self-destructive pattern of behavior in a child, intervening in a situation of marital discord, dealing with a suicidal threat, consulting with

763

school principals or teachers about slow learners, helping with pressures that are in addition to the welter of neurotic difficulties that traditionally have propelled adult patients into individual psychotherapy. In the latter area, too, what can be done for this person that is of maximum benefit in the shortest possible time?

American culture always has been pragmatic, it is concerned with what "works," and we have seen in recent years a particularly strong emphasis on programs of social action designed to attack problems on a broad front, for example, the antipoverty programs, the attack on mental retardation, "Head Start," etc.

The emphasis on application was recently given forceful expression by President Johnson in a message addressed to the activities of the National Institutes of Health. He said:

> Only in recent years has death from tuberculosis ceased to be considered the will of God. Only since the early fifties and the development of the Salk vaccine has polio no longer struck terror in the heart of every mother, every parent in this country.
>
> A great deal of basic research has been done. I have been participating in the appropriations for years in this field. But I think the time has now come to zero in on the targets by trying to get our knowledge fully applied. There are hundreds of millions of dollars spent on laboratory research that may be made useful to human beings if large-scale trials on patients are initiated in programming areas. Now Presidents, in my judgment, need to show more interest in what the specific results of medical research are during their lifetime and during their administration. I am going to show an interest in the results [quoted in *Science,* 1966a].

The call for action and practical applications of scientific knowledge assumes that a great deal of basic knowledge is available, but left unused. While this may be true in some fields, it is hardly true in clinical psychology.* We are caught up in the prevailing social climate, which has the tendency to chase us out of the laboratory into the arena of social action. The large sums of money available to the applied worker are a powerful incentive. In the prevailing climate the slow, painstaking acquisition of bits of knowledge through research, which may or may not have immediate applications, ranks lower in the scale of social values than direct interventions in societal ills. It is in this context that the disenchantment with intrapsychic factors gains full meaning.

The question society asks clinical psychology, which hovers between basic and applied science without as yet having found its true identity, is this: What can your theories *do*? What is their *utility*? What *practical difference* do they make? Scientists in other fields whose research is much less likely to have an immediate social impact are caught up to a much lesser extent in this cross-fire.

Commenting in a different context on the slow progress of quantification of intrapsychic variables in psychoanalytic theory, Rapaport (1960) states:

---

*This point was clearly recognized by Dr. Alvin M. Weinberg, director of the Oak Ridge National Laboratory, at a recent conference devoted to biomedical research policies: " . . . there is a difference between the physical and biological sciences with respect to the degree to which their underlying scientific structure can be efficiently mobilized for achieving practical goals. The physical sciences and engineering, though they have started independently . . . have now been so intertwined and integrated, and the physical sciences themselves are so advanced, that given an applied goal in engineering, there is often nothing but money that stands in the way of achieving the goal, provided basic science has shown this goal to be achievable. I can't stress too strongly the importance of this latter proviso. The bulk of biomedical research is in the prefeasibility stage, and therefore, the underlying basic research must be done broadly. I think it is fair to say that most basic molecular biologists would work directly on a cure for cancer rather than on what they are now doing, if only they knew how to make real progress [quoted in *Science*, 1966b]."

We are blinded by the rapid development of new sciences in our time. The rapid growth of biochemistry and biophysics was possible because they had the solid foundations of several thousand years of physics and chemistry. Some psychologists are bent on linking psychology to those sciences *now,* hoping for an equally spectacular growth of psychology. Others are more patient. They do not deplore the present state of the theory, nor consider the experimenters to be fools. In their eyes these difficulties are phenomena of a *very early phase* in the development of a science. Clinical observation shows that conscious information does not eliminate symptoms rooted in unconscious forces and that conscious intent is usually no substitute for the lack of unconscious motivation. Likewise we may assume that consciously borrowed sophistication, however much it may help otherwise in developing psychology, cannot circumvent the long and time-consuming process all sciences have gone through. The process of development which brings about the interplay between the observables and the theories is always slow. Quantification and methodological sophistication are late products of any science and as such they should be long-range goals: mistaking them for proximal goals can render a science impotent [pp. 37-38].

Rapaport assumes that psychoanalytic theory is fruitful and worth developing, an assumption seriously questioned by many psychologists today. A major claim he advances rests on the comprehensiveness of the system, drives, and primary processes, as well as adaptation and reality relationships.

The main classes of variables in psychoanalytic theory, we may remind ourselves, include: motivations and structures, behaviors (including thought and affect as well as observable action), and external reality (Rapaport, 1960, p. 69). Rapaport says:

We may conclude that psychoanalytic theory requires the exploration of all possible functional relationships among its variables. One wonders whether or not
there is an intimate connection between the rigid decisions
of various schools of psychology on systematic variables
(e.g., those of S-R and Gestalt psychology—and we may
now add behavior therapy) and the limited range of observables acceptable to each of them. Any limitation on
the choice of variables seems to result in a limited range
of observables and observational methods, and it is the
dearth of methods which is probably the major obstacle to
bridging the gap between psychoanalysis and academic
psychology and between the various schools of psychology
[p. 72].

What commends psychoanalytic theory to the clinician
and the researcher is its comprehensiveness. In this respect
it is unequaled by any other existing theory and in fact has
no serious contender. It is sufficiently broad to encompass
"normal" as well as "abnormal" behavior; its explanatory
power extends to, say, depression, character disorders,
dreams, the psychopathology of everyday life, interests,
thought processes, grief reactions—to name but a few facets.
Contrast the breadth of this framework with that of
behavior therapy, which has been characterized as follows
(Breger and McGaugh, 1965):

. . . it would seem that the behaviorists have reached a
position where an inadequate conceptual framework
forces them to adopt an inadequate and superficial view
of the very data that they are concerned with. They are
then forced to slip many of the key facts in the back door,
so to speak, for example, when all sorts of fantasy, imaginary, and thought processes are blithely called responses.
This process is, of course, parallel to what has gone on
within S-R learning theory where all sorts of central and

767

mediational processes have been cumbersomely handled with S-R terminology (e.g., Deutsch, 1956). Thus, we have a situation where the behavior therapists argue strongly against a dynamic interpretation of neurosis at some points and at other points behave as if they had adopted such a point of view [p. 350].

A distinction must be made between the explanatory power of a theory and its pragmatic value, that is, what it permits one to do. The proponents of behavior therapy, for example, claim superiority in terms of therapeutic results, a claim that is far from being substantiated at the present time. As I have stated in Chapter Sixteen, the claim that behavior therapy is demonstrably superior to psychoanalytic therapy does not rest on acceptable scientific evidence. It is at best premature to reject psychoanalytic theory and its intrapsychic variables on the grounds of its therapeutic inefficiency. They seem to be saying, "Our technical operations are based on more scientific principles. Unless it can be shown that psychoanalytic theory results in socially effective technical interventions, there is no need to pay close attention to what it otherwise has to offer."

The search for techniques that permit the behavioral scientist to intervene effectively in social problems thus has become an urgent goal for psychologists and other behavioral scientists. The development of a theoretical base adequately accounting for these techniques, while important and desirable, has come to occupy a secondary place.

Since the major question here concerns intrapsychic variables, I shall examine further the following points:

1. Psychoanalytic theory is a comprehensive theory and as such it may greatly aid in *understanding* the psychological functioning of individuals, including personality development, intrapsychic adjustment, interpersonal relations, etc. However, its technical operations may be far less comprehensive, and indeed its therapeutic applications may be distinctly limited.

768

2. Other techniques, whatever their theoretical basis, may be more effective under certain conditions and with certain individuals. Such techniques, while having intrapsychic implications, may be applied without intensive interest in intrapsychic factors.

3. The value of a theory lies in its explanatory power, which is not necessarily synonymous with the efficiency of its technical interventions, although certainly correlated with it.

Understanding an individual's psychological functioning is worthwhile regardless of whether it permits one to "change" that person. There is no *a priori* reason to assume that the better one understands a person, the easier it is to exert a therapeutic influence on him. Freud, for example was known to be a poor *Menschenkenner* (the word has the connotation that "knowing" a person permits one to control and manipulate him) but he clearly understood a great deal about psychic development, neurotic problems, and the like.

Psychodiagnosis is rapidly becoming a lost art, not only because it is frequently regarded on a par with a laboratory technician's blood count reports. Its neglect probably has to do also with the predictive value of psychodiagnostic formulations and, true to the *Zeitgeist,* what they permit one to *do.* Often the diagnosis has no effect whatever on the planned therapy, its sole bearing being on the diagnostic code to be assigned to the patient. On the other hand, a comprehensive diagnostic study can have tremendous value. It may throw a great deal of light on the patient's intrapsychic functioning, although in many cases it may not be directly translatable into hard-and-fast predictions or recommendations for therapeutic action. I would argue that this in itself does not prove its futility, nor does it stamp diagnostic skills as useless.* Any clinician can learn a great deal

---

*This trend unfortunately is abetted by our training programs in which not infrequently courses in diagnosis are taught by inexperienced staff members or nonpracticing clinical psychologists.

from diagnostic work. But he needs a theoretical framework which helps him to order his data. To illustrate, a purely empirical instrument, like the MMPI, may be useful, but it acquires greater usefulness when the findings are viewed within a theoretical framework.

No claim has ever been advanced that psychoanalytic psychotherapy produces "quickie" cures. The transference relationship characterizes psychoanalytic therapy as a relatively long-term undertaking. But there has been a decided tendency for psychoanalyses to occupy longer and longer periods of time. In Freud's day, analyses lasting 9 to 12 months were quite common, but are nonexistent today. Efforts to shorten analytic therapy are not new (Ferenczi and Rank in 1925 and numerous therapists since that time, e.g., Franz Alexander, 1946, 1956, 1958). However, I know of no research that shows that five years of psychoanalysis with a given patient achieved more than three. The onus is on the analysts to conduct such research.

Assuming that psychoanalytic theory has advanced to some extent during the last 25 years—an assumption questioned by some—therapeutic techniques should have advanced concomitantly. Despite many new departures, there are no signs that such progress has occurred.

Several authors (e.g., Stone, 1954) have called attention to Freud's restriction of the applicability of psychoanalysis to the transference neuroses, coupled with a persistent emphasis on a "basically reliable ego." In his last years, he was more impressed with psychoanalysis as a theory than with its therapeutic potential. The broadening of applications that has gradually occurred, encompassing the treatment of psychoses, character disorders, perversions, behavior disorders in childhood and adolescence, psychosomatic conditions, etc., may not have been a wise one, if one is chiefly interested in the rapid achievement of therapeutic results. Anna Freud (1954) commented on this point:

If all the skill, knowledge and pioneering effort which was

770

spent on widening the scope of application of psychoanalysis had been employed instead on intensifying and improving our technique in the original field (hysteric, phobic, and compulsive disorders), I cannot help but feel that, by now, we would find the treatment of the common neuroses child's play, instead of struggling with their technical problems as we have continued to do [p. 610].

It is quite possible that psychoanalytic therapy has indeed limited applicability, which, if true, would not detract from its value. Accumulating research evidence has specified empirically Freud's concept of the "basically reliable ego." Youth, education, intelligence, likability, psychological-mindedness, relative absence of secondary gains, attractiveness, ability to verbalize feelings, motivation to seek help, moderate anxiety and distress, achievements in the social and vocational areas, etc., seem to define the limits of analytic therapy. Even if it should turn out that this form of therapy is restricted to a rather narrow band of the population, this is nothing to be ashamed of. A given form of therapy need not be suitable for everyone and not everyone may be a suitable patient for it. To realize this and to specify the range of applications, including limits set by the therapist's personality, would be a distinct research contribution. Perhaps we are heading toward a healthy development.

If this is so, then techniques like operant conditioning or behavior therapy may be equally and perhaps even more effective with certain classes of patients that are unsuitable for a form of therapy demanding the above qualifications. For example, therapy patterned after analysis may not be effective with autistic and self-destructive children, and some adults may fare better with a short course in desensitization than in psychoanalysis. However, a theory adequate to describe the operations and its antecedents is necessary and the question remains whether it is existing now or has a chance of being developed from the operations.

A major reason, in my opinion, for the disagreements between the various therapies derives from divergent outcome criteria. It is one thing to discharge a patient from a state mental hospital as "improved" after drug therapy; it is quite another matter to have contributed to his emotional maturation through prolonged therapy. The latter improvements are difficult to measure and document, but every therapist knows that they exist. They are unimportant only if one insists on applying narrow criteria of "cure" or "improvement." To be sure, in all therapies the patient must "feel better," but this can mean many things. If experts in the field have trouble in spelling this out, how much more difficult is it to communicate the differences to a legislator! All he may be able to see is that in one instance the patient costs the state seven dollars a day because he is hospitalized. But intrapsychic suffering has a price tag, too. The unhappiness of lonely people, their marital difficulties, their tensions and physical symptoms often can not be measured in dollars. So far, behavior therapy or operant conditioning has shown no signs of being able to deal with these problems any more effectively than other therapies.

Finally, I should like to say a word about the role of intrapsychic factors in community mental health and related fields, in which there has been so much interest in recent years. In order to help a school teacher deal with behavior problems in the classroom, to intervene in a marital crisis, etc., it seems essential that the behavioral scientist possess as broad and deep a knowledge about psychological functioning as possible. The layman can build a radio set from instructions that come with a do-it-yourself kit; but the designers must know basic principles of electronics. By the same token, in the final analysis *someone* must have the basic knowledge underlying the principles he is teaching to the layman, and this basic knowledge cannot and should not be based on a truncated understanding of the psychological man or on a simplistic engineering conception of behavior modification.

The same requirement holds for the advancement of

research in psychology. As Shakow (1965) has cogently observed, "A scientific area belongs ultimately to its investigators, not to its practitioners. No field can maintain its vitality, in fact, its viability, without such a group." While Shakow's admonition was directed at psychoanalysis, it applies with equal force to all forms of therapy which espouse a crude empiricism as the "royal road."

Clinical psychology is a young science at a very early stage of development. It must guard against overselling its wares in the market of applications despite the buyer's need for panaceas. It must beware of the *furor sanandi* and the sense of omnipotence present in all of us. It can ill afford to sacrifice the hard-won knowledge about the inner man, even though that knowledge does not provide a ready technology for changing the world.

References

Alexander, F. *et. al.* 1946. *Psychoanalytic Therapy: Principles and Applications.* New York: Ronald Press.

—— 1956. *Psychoanalysis and Psychotherapy.* New York: Norton.

—— 1958. "Unexplored Areas in Psychoanalytic Theory and Treatment," *Behav. Sci.,* 293-316.

Breger, L., and McGaugh, J. L. 1965. "Critique and Reformulation of Learning-theory Approaches to Psychotherapy and Neurosis," *Psychol. Bul.,* 63: 338-358.

Deutsch, J. A. 1956. "The Inadequacy of Hullian Derivations of Reasoning and Latent Learning," *Psychol. Rev.,* 63: 389-399.

Ferenczi, S., and Rank, O. 1925. *The Development of Psychoanalysis.* New York and Washington: *Ner. and Men. Dis. Monog. Ser.,* 40.

Freud, A. 1954. "The Widening Scope of Indications for Psychoanalysis: Discussion," *J. Am. Psychoanal. Assn.,* 2: 607-620.

Krasner, L., and Ullmann, L. P., eds. 1965. *Research in Behavior Modification: New Developments and Implications.* New York: Holt. Rinehart & Winston.

News and Comment: NIH. 1966a. "Demand Increases for Applications of Research," *Sci.,* 153: 149-152.

———— 1966b. "Biomedical Policy: LBJ's Query Leads to an Illuminating Conference," *Sci.,* 154: 618-619.

Rapaport, D. 1960. "The Structure of Psychoanalytic Theory: A Systematizing Attempt," *Psychol. Is.,* 2 (2).

Shakow, D. 1965. "Seventeen Years Later: Clinical Psychology in the Light of the 1947 Committee on Training in Clinical Psychology Report," footnote, p. 355, *Am. Psychol.,* 20: 353-362.

Stone, L. 1954. "The Widening Scope of Indication for Psychoanalysis," *J. Am. Psychoanal Assn.,* 2: 567-594.

Strupp, H. H. 1966. "Is the Demise of Psychoanalytic Psychology Imminent?" *Bul. Psychologists Interested in the Advancement of Psychotherapy,* 5: (2) 1.

Ullmann, L. P., and Krasner, L., eds. 1965. *Case Studies in Behavior Modification.* New York: Holt, Rinehart & Winston.

Wolpe, J. 1958. *Psychotherapy by Reciprocal Inhibition.* Stanford, Calif.: Stanford University Press.

30

PSYCHOTHERAPISTS AND (OR VERSUS?) RESEARCHERS

John Warkentin said to me, "As you know, most active therapists are, by nature, unwilling to take an interest in serious research, and make do with their clinical experience. If you could say something that would make the word 'research' more enticing and less threatening to therapists, that would be a major contribution to the field of psychotherapy." I think John correctly perceived a certain rift—perhaps even animosity—between psychotherapists and researchers, something of which I have been keenly aware ever since I entered the field some 20 years ago. This feeling existed then, it still exists, and I regret its existence. It reflects a deep-seated prejudice on both sides, and like all prejudices it is doing a great deal of harm. Above all, it presents a serious obstacle to the pursuit of the primary goal in which all of us are—or should be—interested: the advancement of knowledge and the development of better techniques for helping people cope with their emotional problems.

My work over the years has brought me in close contact with psychotherapists and researchers, and from personal experience I know something about the patient and therapist roles. Most of us are engaged in the work we are doing for deeply personal reasons, and our therapeutic techniques like our theoretical preferences are dictated more by our life style than by intellectual or scientific considerations. I am firmly convinced that we are analysts, client-centered therapists, existential therapists, or behavior therapists for reasons largely unrelated to the scientific or pragmatic merits of these approaches, and our attitudes toward research or clinical practice are colored by similar factors. The line should be drawn not between researchers and therapists, any more than it should be drawn between "basic" and "applied" scientists. There are therapists who are very fine scientists even though they never used an analysis of variance design or computed a chi square. Freud, to my mind, remains the most outstanding example of this kind of man. At the other extreme, the field today is full of individuals who correctly use all the available tools of science; their controls are impeccable, and their results are significant at the 1 per cent level; nevertheless, they are completely impervious to the concerns of the psychotherapist, the essence of the subject matter, and their publications are a sterile exercise. The therapist frequently subscribes to this stereotype of the researcher, whereas the researcher tends to view the therapist as a woolly thinker, a mercenary practitioner, or worse. While objective research in psychotherapy has undergone unprecedented growth since the forties, there are as yet very few contributions the psychotherapist would find helpful in his daily work with patients. On the other hand, it cannot be asserted that therapists have achieved significant breakthroughs in understanding or technique during the past quarter of a century.

776

Is psychotherapy a science? Can it become a science? The analyst Kenneth Mark Colby, for one, does not think so. He compares it to an art like wine-making, which however can be passed on from master to apprentice. The trouble with research, according to him (1962) is this: "A practitioner needs a 'causal relation' or variable he can manipulate *with this particular patient*. Research thus far has not given him a reliable guide in this direction because it has mainly been in the tradition of an extensive design. Extensive designs yield only weak group averages, not specific causal mechanisms (cf. Chassan, 1967)." And further:

> [The clinician] wants help with failures, with troubles, with lapses from the expected. . . . Guided by the artisan, a scientist must select a certain crucial problem in the art and judge whether the problem is ready and accessible to a systematic inquiry using currently available procedures. A scientist hopes to reduce the degree of (blind) empiricism in the art by finding that some acute problem in it can be solved through understanding an underlying explanatory principle [p. 75].

What acute problems can future psychotherapy research profitably elucidate? Says Colby:

> We are not trying to solve the problem of justified inductive generalization. Physics, chemistry, and medicine (e.g., heart transplants in single patients) progressed without representativeness of samples. They relied on repeatability of observations by independent observers and the development of a series of cases one by one. The population of observations we should be interested in at this time is a series of single-case populations. It is hopeless to generalize about "all" patients. No "all" exists about anything [personal communication].

One of the things this suggests to me is that there needs

777

to be closer collaboration between psychotherapists and researchers. The researcher, at least in principle, can help the practitioner in resolving "acute problems in the art." By the same token, no therapist should rest content with the current level of practice. Who would be foolhardy enough to assert that his techniques are beyond improvement, even if the conditions are rigorously specified? Many practitioners have turned their back on systematic inquiry—and this charge, I regret to say, must be leveled particularly at psychoanalysts—while quoting liberally from the work of Freud as if it were the Bible. Freud would have been the first one to reject such codification. Exemplifying the spirit of open inquiry, Anna Freud wrote:

> If all the skill, knowledge and pioneering effort which was spent on widening the scope of application of psychoanalysis had been employed instead on intensifying and improving our technique in the original field [hysteric, phobic, and compulsive disorders], I cannot help but feel that, by now, we would find the treatment of the common neuroses child's play, instead of struggling with their technical problems as we have continued to do [p. 610].

No one, of course, is opposed in principle to the advancement of knowledge, and we can readily agree that we have much to learn. There is one issue, however, that has done more than any other to alienate psychotherapists and researchers from each other. I am referring to the time-honored question of the effectiveness of psychotherapy. Essentially, it seems to me, one can approach this problem with three different preconceptions: on a deep emotional level, reinforced by personal experience and therapeutic work with patients, many therapists consider the question a pseudo issue; that is, they are firmly convinced that in an appreciable number of instances, sufficiently large to sustain their faith and self-respect, psychotherapeutic work benefits their patients. Such therapists need no "demonstrations" from scientists or anyone else. Secondly, there are cynics, not infrequently disillusioned by personal experience, who are dedicated to the proposition that psychotherapeutic changes are either illusory or due to placebo effects but in any case unimpressive. A variation on this theme is represented by those whose zeal causes them to reject violently one theoretical system while espousing the alleged virtues of another. Finally, there are those who make a serious effort to approach the problem as dispassionately as possible. To be sure, it is difficult to lay one's preconceptions aside, but one can try. If one takes this approach, it becomes possible to raise such questions as: Under what conditions does this particular technique work well? What kind of changes can one expect from a given form of therapy in the hands of a particular therapist with a particular patient? Are alternative approaches perhaps more promising under a given set of circumstances? This listing is purely illustrative but it suggests a spirit of open inquiry, which is all the scientist should be committed to. Theoretical boundaries as such are of no intrinsic interest to him, but he is vitally concerned with elucidating the conditions under which therapeutic learning occurs, what kind of learning occurs and when, and he takes it for granted that the last word has not been spoken on any issue. It is heartening to note that today there is a growing trend in this direction. Therapists and researchers are becoming more open-minded, despite many signs to the contrary; they are becoming more sophisticated about each other's endeavors and more tolerant of ambiguity; and they approach controversy in a somewhat less doctrinaire spirit. I am not suggesting that the millennium has arrived. Far from it. But the above developments do bode well for the future.

I have consistently maintained that we are not yet in a position to deal meaningfully with the question of therapeutic outcomes, at least not in the manner in which this problem has usually been approached. The psychotherapeutic interaction is far too complex to lend itself readily to comparisons which can be translated into percentage figures of success. The popularization of such "statistics" published under the aegis of "Science" in magazines has done a tremendous disservice and has misled the public. First the reader is told that one cannot compare apples and oranges, but as soon as this has been said, outcomes of different forms of therapy are being compared anyway, with the added assertion that some 70 per cent of all patients "recover" from neurotic disorders "spontaneously." The therapist is thus challenged to prove the effectiveness of his procedures against almost impossible odds whose validity he rightly questions.

It has been asserted by somewhat more friendly critics that, if psychotherapy were indeed a very potent method, it should not be difficult to demonstrate its effectiveness. That is, granted the methodological and practical difficulties in carrying out controlled research, if dramatic changes were a regular occurrence, they should be self-evident. To be sure, both patients and therapists in several studies have reported "improvements" in the 75 to 90 per cent range, but such assessments cannot be taken at face value, nor can the potency argument be blithely dismissed.

The fact is that, like it or not, we must live with the outcome problem, and the critics, despite some of their ill-founded allegations, have prevented the field from sinking into a state of complacency and stagnation. As researchers or therapists, it is our responsibility to face the issue, not to evade it.

A therapist of whatever theoretical persuasion is certainly at liberty to define his goals and the outcome criteria he is willing to accept. As one of my colleagues aptly put it, criteria are purely a matter of taste. One therapist may rest content if a snake phobic patient can hold a snake for 10 seconds following certain therapeutic interventions; another therapist may want to help his patient develop better interpersonal strategies; a third therapist may work toward the mastery of existential despair. Assuredly, one cannot compare these outcomes with each other, nor can one argue that one is trivial and another profound. Therapies must be tested on their own home ground but testable they must be. In other words, the criteria must permit specification and communication in the sense that impartial observers can reach agreement on the presence or absence of change. The field is abandoning the view that a little bit of (undefined) psychotherapy may be good for everyone; instead, the more pertinent questions are raised: What kind? For whom? Under what conditions? No form of psychotherapy is a panacea, nor need it be. But we should become increasingly explicit about its potential as well as its limitations.

The researcher's job does not end there because he is equally interested in the kinds of therapeutic interventions which lead to specific changes. He is concerned with the psychology as well as the technology of change. This is a task of gargantuan proportions, for which he needs all the help he can get—and then some.

Personally, I don't think it is possible to do meaningful research on any aspect of psychotherapy without extensive first-hand experience as a therapist or patient; on the other hand, one can practice the art of psychotherapy without being aware of the principles one is employing. Ideally, the researcher should approach the phenomenon of psychotherapy with a clinical attitude, and the therapist should have a critical and inquiring mind. In this way, there may also develop greater rapprochement between researcher and clinician.

At its best, psychotherapy is not faith healing, religious conversion, or brainwashing, nor does it traffic in the sale of friendship, as has been alleged. Admittedly, it may share some elements with all of these activities, but that is not its defining characteristic. What sets psychotherapy apart from other forms of "psychological healing"—and of course medicine—is the planful and systematic application of psychological principles, concerning whose character and

effects we are commited to become explicit. As psychotherapists and researchers, we want to learn more about what we
are doing; we want to be able to do it better; we strive to
be objective; and we are willing to work hard toward this
end. To me, these are the beginnings of science, if not its
essence.

References

Colby, K. M. 1962. "Discussion of Papers on Therapist's
Contribution," in *Research in Psychotherapy*, Vol. II,
ed. H. H. Strupp and L. Luborsky, pp. 95-101. Washing-
ton, D.C.: American Psychoanalytic Assn.
Freud, A. 1954. "The Widening Scope of Indications for
Psychoanalysis," *J. Am. Psychoanal. Assn.*, 2: 607-620.

31

NEW DIRECTIONS IN PSYCHOTHERAPY RESEARCH (WITH A. E. BERGIN)

Three national conferences on research in psychotherapy, held in Washington, D. C., 1957; Chapel Hill, 1961; and in Chicago, 1966, pointed up the need for investigators to pool their resources and to consider the design of research projects that might be executed on a collaborative basis. Precedents for such ventures were of course available in biomedical research, but had been conspicuously absent in psychotherapy. Informal suggestions at the first two conferences evidently were not followed by any action; the situation, however, was different at the Chicago conference. For one thing, a small group of investigators was more articulate about the problem; for another, the Clinical Research Branch of the National Institute of Mental Health—all three conferences had been supported by grants from the National Institute of Mental Health—was taking an active interest in the possibilities of collaborative research in this area.*

As a first step, John M. Shlien, the conference chairman, appointed an informal committee of conference participants to explore the feasibility of a collaborative study of psychotherapy. The following individuals were asked to explore the feasibility issue: Kenneth M. Colby, Jerome D. Frank, Howard F. Hunt, Joseph D. Matarazzo (Chairman), John M. Shlien, and A. Hussain Tuma.

Although the committee was informal and had no standing with any official group or organization, it consisted of researchers who believed that examination of the feasibility of coordinated or collaborative research was long overdue and that concerted action should be taken toward this end.

The committee met several times during the 18 months that followed the conference. At the initial meeting, it was concluded that an answer to the feasibility question required, as a first step, a critical review of the psychotherapy research literature. It seemed essential that a hard look at what the

*Reflecting this programmatic interest, A. Hussain Tuma attended the conference as an official observer, and subsequently both he and Donald Oken, then Chief, Clinical Research Branch of the National Institute of Mental Health, worked with us closely throughout this effort. The work described in this chapter has been supported by the National Institute of Mental Health through Contracts PH-43-67-1459 and PH-43-67-1386, awarded to Allen Bergin and Hans Strupp, respectively; and through Grants MH16244 and MH16250, awarded to Allen Bergin and Hans Strupp, respectively. We are most grateful for this support and for the devoted interest and help provided in all phases of our work by A. Hussain Tuma of the National Institute of Mental Health and by Joseph D. Matarazzo of the University of Oregon Medical School. We are also grateful to Jerome D. Frank and John M. Shlien, who served as advisors, and to the nearly three dozen consultants and colleagues who gave unreservedly of their talents in response to our requests. They have significantly stimulated our thought and enriched our lives. Requests for reprints should be sent to Allen E. Bergin, Department of Psychology, Teachers College, Columbia University, New York, New York 10027.

784

field had produced to date was necessary in order to determine whether studying other aspects of the feasibility issue would be fruitful.

The authors of the present report were asked by the committee to undertake this critical review of the literature and agreed to do so. We devoted the period from June through December 1967 to this undertaking, carried out under contracts from the National Institute of Mental Health. The results of our analysis were published as the February and March 1969 issues of the *International Journal of Psychiatry* (Bergin and Strupp, 1969; Strupp and Bergin, 1969a). A bibliography of research in psychotherapy was completed as a by-product (Strupp and Bergin, 1969b).

In our review, we reached the conclusion that the field might possibly be ready for one or more major collaborative studies, pending further feasibility testing and pilot work. Concomitantly, we outlined several studies that might prove fruitful.

We subsequently met with the originating committee in January 1968, by invitation of the Clinical Research Branch of the National Institute of Mental Health, and discussed future plans. Donald Kiesler, Nathaniel Raskin, and Charles Truax were also present. As a group, we discerned two possible next steps:

1. Independent investigators might on their own pursue one or another of the Strupp-Bergin recommendations for promising lines of inquiry; or

2. Further investigation of the feasibility issue in greater depth might be undertaken.

The latter would involve consideration of such problems as (*a*) kinds of variables to be studied, by whom, under what conditions, and in which settings; (*b*) research designs that might most profitably be explored; (*c*) consultants who might be approached for help on such matters as research design, statistical analysis, and professional and practical issues in collaboration; (d) whether independent investigators could be persuaded and motivated to participate in a coordinated or collaborative study; and (e) whether such an undertaking would be economically feasible. Clearly, such an inquiry might also lead to the equally important conclusion that collaborative research, while perhaps desirable, is either not feasible or premature.

At this point, stimulated by our own previous work and the undeniable importance of the problem as reflected by the interest of the originating committee and the National Institute of Mental Health, the present authors decided to embark on an examination of the questions outlined under 2. Accordingly, we submitted an application for a research grant to the National Institute of Mental Health, which received favorable consideration, and we began work on the project in the fall of 1968.

THE FEASIBILITY STUDY

In order to answer the questions posed by the present authors and the originating committee, we proposed to:

1. Explore in depth the relative merit and priority of several major psychotherapy research questions and relevant experimental designs in consultation with experts on substantive and methodological issues; and to scrutinize those designs that we had already identified as promising (in our review),* and determine the relative merits, power, feasibility, and potential contribution of the specific studies to the furtherance of knowledge in psychotherapy. This step involves the possible combination, amalgamation, modifica-

---

*These designs followed classical experimental models involving therapy, control, and other technique comparison groups along with rigorous selection procedures and preoutcome and postoutcome measures. They were heavily influenced by the tradition of outcome experimentation associated with H. J. Eysenck, C. R. Rogers, R. I. Watson, M. Scriven, D. J. Kiesler, etc.

786

tion, and specification of projects in an effort to arrive at optimal designs. This phase of the planning began from the vantage point of a considerable body of past research and the thinking of many insightful investigators who seriously concerned themselves with (a) general problems of strategy and of individual efforts versus collective or coordinated efforts; (b) problems of experimental design, choice of variables, and their measurement; and (c) strategies of collaborative research on psychotherapy or other areas of investigation of comparable complexity, and who have acquired considerable sophistication and a general realization of the limitations of research in a complex area where, administratively, treatment studies are extremely difficult to implement and variables are hard to define, measure, control, or manipulate.

2. Inventory resources available at various centers in the nation for undertaking major responsibility for collaborative work. It was not our intention at first, to begin organizing a large national network of collaborating centers nor to elicit specific commitments from them; rather, we planned to test, through visits and interviews with key personnel at differing levels in each center, the depth of interest and motivation for undertaking coordinated research and at the same time survey the clinical and research resources available. Through intensive work in conjunction with consultants and research centers, we hoped to arrive at progressive approximations representing a reasonable balance between such factors as precision of measurement, adequacy of controls, potential contribution to the advancement of basic knowledge, investment of manpower, facilities, and financial resources.

3. Keep a record of information and evaluations thus obtained, which would eventually form the basis of a detailed report on the feasibility of specified collaborative research projects. With this goal in mind, we gave special attention to the following considerations: (a) that several models or designs for collaboration might prove feasible

787

and they might or might not be like those implemented in other fields; (b) that the planning should aim for ends that could not be accomplished by individual investigators or agencies; (c) that master plans might include core variables and standardized measurements, but would not preclude measures preferred by or unique to any cooperating therapist or treatment center; (d) that it is important to be cognizant of the potential value of a variety of therapeutic techniques, influences, and innovations not yet studied extensively but that might be profitably included in future research, such as any of a variety of group techniques, nonprofessional and natural therapeutic influences, personality change under induced emotional arousal, etc.; and (e) that a central coordinating mechanism for collaboration would have to evolve from our efforts and our report if one or more projects were actually implemented.

4. Devote the first year primarily to the testing of feasibility, development of a research plan (or several alternate plans), including identification of potential participants, investigators, clinical settings, and patient populations. Should a collaborative study of major consequence appear unfeasible, then the planning phase would terminate and a final substantive report would be submitted. However, should the indications be positive, the planning would move into the second year. We would then devote more of our energies to actually working out specific details needed for mounting a study. This would involve obtaining specific commitments from potential collaborators and then deciding on a specific plan of study with appropriate design and specific measuring instruments, control variables, screening and selection procedures, procedures of selecting and training of raters, and the actual implementation of pilot work.

Consultants were selected in terms of their known expertise and their potential contribution to the objectives outlined in the foregoing. Prior to our visits, we sent each person a copy of our review, the grant proposal, and a set of 18 questions we had formulated as stimuli for discussion.* Between October 1968 and July 1969, we spent from half a day to a full day with the following consultants: Arnold A. Lazarus, Lester Luborsky, Arthur H. Auerbach, Lyle D. Schmidt, Stanley R. Strong, Paul E. Meehl, Bernard F. Riess, Howard F. Hunt, Arnold P. Goldstein, Thomas S. Szasz, Gerald C. Davison, Bernard Weitzman, J. B. Chassan, Kenneth Mark Colby, Albert Bandura, Robert S. Wallerstein, Harold Sampson, Louis Breger, Howard Levene, Ralph Greenson, Milton Wexler, Carl R. Rogers, Joseph D. Matarazzo, Charles B. Truax, Neal E. Miller, Henry Linford, Peter Knapp (with Martin A. Jacobs, Louis Vachon, and Douglas M. McNair), John M. Shlien, David Bakan, Jerome D. Frank, Peter J. Lang, and Marvin Smith.

Following each visit, we independently prepared critical résumés based on notes taken during the meeting. In addition to exchanging these documents, we prepared various working papers, met at regular intervals for the purpose of assessing the progress of our endeavor, read extensively (often following up on suggestions made by the consultants), and shared our impressions with selected colleagues. The extent of this material is evidenced by approximately 500 pages of manuscript, which remain to be organized and digested for publication.

Pending later elaboration and documentation of our findings, we are presenting our conclusions in this chapter with a minimum of context and only limited justification. It should be emphasized that these conclusions represent a synthesis of our own views and those held by prominent persons in the field. Needless to say, we are expressing our personal interpretations and judgments concerning the status of the field, which are not necessarily shared by our consultants.

---

*Copies of the stimulus questions used during these interviews may be obtained from either of the authors.

CONCLUSIONS REGARDING COLLABORATIVE STUDIES

Based on a large number of convergent considerations, we have reluctantly reached the conclusion that large-scale, multifactorial studies of the kind sketched by other investigators and ourselves are not feasible at the present time or in the immediate future. On balance, we believe that the expectable returns, in terms of research findings that might contribute to the accretion of knowledge as well as practical applications of such findings, do not justify the very considerable investment of manpower and financial support such studies would inevitably entail. In stating this, we are not saying that such studies are in principle futile or that all efforts at collaboration on large-scale ventures should be abandoned; however, we are asserting that the *likelihood* of success at the present time impresses us as low or at least incommensurate with the required expenditures in terms of effort, manpower, and funds. Major reasons supporting this judgment include the following:

1. Because of the complex interactions among patient, therapist, technique, and socio-environmental variables, it will prove extraordinarily difficult to isolate the effects of one or a limited number of variables, with the result that large-scale multifactorial studies are almost certain to lead to "weak" results. As a corollary, the necessary experimental controls that would be required to counteract these tendencies are virtually impossible to achieve at the present time, a problem that is aggravated if studies are carried out in different locations by therapists of diverse theoretical orientations whose techniques (even within a given "school") are bound to be heterogeneous and on patient samples whose homogeneity may be questionable.

2. Because the preceding weaknesses of large-scale studies will not be remediable in the near future, it is predictable that such studies will have minimal effect on

prevailing practices and are not likely to sway clinicians from their personal beliefs.

3. There are virtually no research centers that would be willing or able to observe meticulously the requirements called for by large-scale efforts.

4. With few exceptions, we found insufficient motivation and commitment on the part of leading researchers and clinicians to design and execute such studies.

5. The implementation of large-scale studies necessitates the creation of complex administrative machinery that would be costly to inaugurate and maintain. In view of the above factors, it seems unlikely that a central coordinating agency, even if it had broad executive powers, would be able to effectively implement the necessarily stringent design and bring to a successful conclusion the elaborate data collection and analysis.

6. Large-scale studies would at best serve as demonstrations that one set of techniques seems to be preferable to another set of techniques under broadly defined conditions, but they are not likely to shed much light on specific mechanisms of psychological change, specific techniques that might be necessary to produce such changes in patients of a certain "type," and the nature of therapeutic change. Stated otherwise, we believe that such studies will add only insignificant amounts to existing scientific knowledge.

7. In view of the current state of knowledge and technology in the area, it is considered more desirable to encourage research developments along lines other than large-scale collaborative studies, such as systematic research on basic mechanisms, naturalistic observations of psychological change, and intensive study of single cases.

It is important to note that we approached the issue of collaborative research with a positive bias (Strupp and Bergin, 1969a) and came away with a much less optimistic conclusion.

While collaboration on a large scale does not appear

propitious at this time, more efforts at coordination should be encouraged. For one thing, it is considered essential to improve communication, exchange of research ideas, plans, and research findings among productive investigators, and to stimulate collaboration on smaller scale projects. We have begun to explore several possibilities and shall devote further effort toward this objective. Under such arrangements, investigators might begin to apply common measures in their respective studies, pool research data, and design coordinated studies that would directly further their research programs. A few attempts in this direction have already occurred, but more are needed. For our own part, we expect to devote a portion of our own future effort to the furtherance of this kind of small-scale collaboration.

CONCLUSIONS REGARDING OTHER DIRECTIONS OF THERAPY RESEARCH

While our primary goal was to determine the feasibility of large collaborative efforts, a corollary objective was to explore theoretical issues, research strategies, therapeutic techniques, and relevant variables in order to determine whether selective research emphases might possibly accelerate advances in the field. Some of our salient conclusions follow. Again, because of space limitations, they are presented without documentation; however, we believe that each assertion can be adequately defended.

We have become convinced that further study of the therapeutic process and evaluations of outcomes resulting from traditional therapeutic practice offer little hope for significant scientific advance. While such studies may further expand our understanding of the therapeutic process and lead to refinements of traditional procedures, the potential yield resulting from pursuing other pathways appears incomparably greater. One exception would be to study the performance of unusual therapists. In this case, one might, through naturalistic study, succeed in extracting from their performance principles or strategies that make their therapeutic operations unusually effective. Even here, however, the inquiry may be expected to lead rapidly to the formulation of new techniques on the basis of the principles so extracted.

The foregoing conclusion is of course a relative judgment. No doubt, further inquiry into psychotherapy as it is ordinarily practiced will continue to bear fruit, particularly if such studies are systematic and increasingly responsive to the special problems in the area. However, at present there is no "normal science" in Kuhn's (1962) sense in psychotherapy; therefore, research in the area is not likely to lead to a questioning of a "paradigm," and even less to a "revolution." In general, no field of scientific inquiry can be advanced by synthetic efforts, and lines of advance are impossible to predict. Nevertheless, we venture the prognostication that in psychotherapy, advances will not come from dissection of the therapeutic process as it generally occurs, no matter how precise or sophisticated such studies become. Instead, new departures appear called for. As we see it, this means a movement away from the gross, complex, and relatively nonspecific traditional therapeutic operations. Stated positively, we must achieve greater specificity and, concomitantly, greater power in the sense of making therapeutic operations and strategies count therapeutically. Efforts in this direction would also make technique more adequately teachable and learnable.

While there is limited promise in the naturalistic study of the therapeutic process, there does seem to be a significant source of hypotheses and methods in the observation of spontaneous change processes occurring in the natural course of life events. It seems likely that a careful study of "the psychotherapy of everyday life' will yield valuable results. Accordingly, at the present stage of knowledge it may be valuable to study in greater depth "experiments of nature." Many examples in other sciences (e.g., the discovery of Vitamin C) underscore the merit of this approach. It has frequently been pointed out that the study of complex psychological processes requires approaches that are radically different from those employed in the physical and biological sciences, but the implications of this proposition still remain to be taken seriously. We have in mind studies that might deal with documentation of conditions under which personality changes occur "naturally," a "natural history of the neuroses," and similar investigations. Such work may also lead to new ideas regarding methods that will more effectively and more straightforwardly produce desired personality change.

During the last decade, the field of psychotherapy has undergone considerable proliferation. The classical model of psychotherapy, exemplified by the psychoanalytic situation, has receded to the background and largely lost its appeal to therapists and patients. Originally conceptualized as a form of medical treatment, the meaning of the term psychotherapy has become increasingly fuzzy and more than ever defies precise definition. Diverse human interactions, from individual psychotherapy to encounter groups, from aversive conditioning in the laboratory to token economies in mental hospitals, are subsumed under the heading of psychotherapy or under the new rubric, behavior modification. To characterize the field as chaotic is hardly an exaggeration.

Particularly noteworthy in this respect is the emergence of a wide diversity of new techniques and therapeutic modalities, most of which may be viewed as a response to modern man's insistent clamor for self-awareness, interpersonal intimacy, surcease from alienation, and the constraints of a "sick" society. New treatment methods in this area, it may be observed, do not arise from the efforts of researchers or as a result of experimentation in the laboratory; instead, they emerge in response to social needs that are met by the ingenuity or inventiveness of charismatic therapists whose individual temperament and philosophy of life are thoroughly intertwined with the therapeutic approach they espouse.

794

The "system" or "theory of psychotherapy" propounded by them is inevitably a belated attempt to conceptualize what they have found to be of pragmatic value. Obviously, this is not to deny that theories of psychotherapy contain important psychological principles, although often, because of divergent conceptualizations, they are impossible to compare. It follows that (1) new techniques in psychotherapy, unlike new drugs, are not developed in the laboratory, tested, and then applied, but typically are "invented" and applied long before they are tested; (2) psychotherapeutic techniques are very loosely articulated to theories of psychotherapy, which largely preclude the testing of any theoretical formulation per se; (3) the researcher in psychotherapy, in comparison to the innovative clinician, has been relatively uninfluential as far as developments in the field are concerned; (4) the field of psychotherapy is at an extremely rudimentary stage of development, and it seems safe to predict that neither research nor clinical ingenuity are about to produce a dazzling technology for psychotherapeutic change (measured against what therapists have been able to accomplish in the past). This is not to assert that the field can afford to rest content with its achievements or that progress is impossible; however, it seems only realistic to recognize the formidable difficulties confronting both clinicians and researchers in this murky field.

I conclude that the field as a whole is currently beset with innumerable fads, considerable conceptual unclarity, muddy theories, and grossly unwarranted claims for the effectiveness of simplistic techniques. All of these factors have conspired to impede progress and to retard dispassionate examination of basic scientific issues. There exists at present a dire need for separating the wheat from the chaff, for taking full advantage of earlier insights that, in terms of their sophistication, often surpass contemporary formulations, and for discarding obsolete theoretical notions that have questionable relevance to empirical data. Withal, a serious return to empirical data is imperative.

While the preceding conclusion has emphasized the arena of clinical practice, it is equally important to acknowledge the substantial growth of research in psychotherapy since the late 1950s, supported by a new wave of enthusiasm. The preponderance of this work has been inspired by behaviorally oriented researchers and, to a lesser extent by client-centered investigators, whereas psychoanalytically oriented workers have all but abdicated serious research interest. It seems premature to assess the lasting value or promise of these endeavors, a fair segment of which must certainly be characterized as crude; however, there can be no doubt that the work has had the inestimable merit of providing a renewed focus on empirical data that had been all but lost in sterile discussions about the relative merits of theoretical propositions. Furthermore, there is an increasing recognition that psychotherapy (in the sense in which I propose to use the term) consists of a set of specifiable technical operations to reach specifiable objectives. If this assumption is granted, it follows that we must work toward the specification of problems we seek to solve as psychotherapists, the goals we aim to achieve, and the procedures we employ to reach these objectives. Thus, if psychotherapy in an important sense is a technology, we must concede that a set of technical operations can be more or less effective in reaching a particular goal. While psychotherapy is likely to remain a practical art for a long time, the task of the researcher is to document, with increasing precision, the conditions under which a therapeutic strategy or a set of techniques forming part of that strategy is relatively effective or ineffective. Accordingly, he must succeed in defining "the problem" (that is, the patient state to be modified), the kinds of personality and behavior changes to be achieved, and the procedures to be employed in reaching them. In short, the therapist and the researcher must become increasingly explicit about the operations of psychotherapy and the nature of the therapist's influence. Existing knowledge, while undoubtedly embodying important psychological principles, is altogether too general, broad-gauged, and imprecise. It can be concluded then that future research in this area must firmly rest on empirical data; it must tend toward increasing explicitness and specificity; and it must seek to isolate psychological principles embedded in, and often obscured by, divergent theoretical formulations.

There has been insufficient clarity about the role of the researcher in psychotherapy and the kinds of contributions he may reasonably be expected to make. The fact is that to date research has exerted little influence on clinical practice, and the clinical work of therapists has generally not been informed, much less altered, by empirical research results. It is possible that the researcher's insistence on empirical evidence and intersubjective verification has subtly modified the attitudes, at least of the younger therapists, toward the subject matter, but that influence appears to be rather intangible. It may be concluded that the researcher has not provided the clinician with insights or useful information which he can employ in his daily work. However, there may be an important lesson from scores of studies that almost any set of procedures in the context of a benign human relationship, presented to, or viewed by, the patient as having therapeutic value will result in psychological or behavior change describable as therapeutic. At times, such changes produced by nonspecific techniques may be quite impressive and rival in significance those attributed to planned technical interventions. As a corollary, it may be noted that the theoretical formulations invoked by the therapist to explain the effects of his work may grossly lack parsimony and be deficient on other grounds.

Despite certain appearances to the contrary, research in psychotherapy, as it has evolved since approximately 1940, has failed to provide incisive answers to important issues, such as the problem of outcome, the relative effectiveness of different techniques, etc. While a form of cultural lag may in part be responsible, the prevailing investigative model may not be the proper one to use. For example, the

797

clinician has no way of using statistical trends based on mean differences between samples of broadly defined patient groups; he cannot be guided by findings that certain diffuse techniques *in general* tend to lead to certain patient responses under poorly defined conditions, etc.

As one of our consultants, Colby, has pointed out, not everything can be a problem for the scientist, at the same time, and for fruitful results to occur it is of crucial importance to ask questions that permit relatively unequivocal answers. In psychotherapy research, it appears, we have not yet reached great sophistication in asking the "right" questions.

The field urgently needs greater collaboration of a different sort. We need improved communications between clinicians and researchers, and between researchers of divergent theoretical orientations. I believe Scriven (1964) is correct in asserting that progress in psychology is hampered not by a lack of knowledge but rather by a surfeit of commonsense knowledge shared by all individuals (e.g., the effects of reward or punishment on behavior). Since the time of Freud, largely as a function of his contributions, which remain close to empirical observations, therapists have acquired a vast fund of knowledge, exemplified by man's ingenious tendencies to hide painful truths from himself, to disguise to himself and others primitive and self-defeating beliefs that profoundly influence the manner in which he construes himself and others, the profound but hitherto unrecognized effects of early traumatic experiences "stored" in memory, etc. The therapist, above all, is an expert in decoding the scrambled human communications the patient continually sends to himself and others. This fund of knowledge is impressive, but it is largely ignored by researchers and others who restrict their focus to observable behavior. Thus, it is a strange phenomenon that the importance of "cognitive factors" is currently being rediscovered. The point is that clinicians and therapists build as yet insufficiently on each other's work, and because of theoretical or

798

temperamental blinders they reject data that colleagues in other camps have to offer.

It is likewise important to record that the fund of clinical knowledge to which I have referred, poorly formulated as much of it is, has been acquired not through the study of mean differences between samples but through painstaking study of individual cases, by a process of "listening" that is closely akin to Polanyi's (1966) concept of indwelling. Man's capacity for discerning patterns, organization, and structure of beliefs, etc., in another person is infinitely greater than that of any man-made machine or rating instrument, and while the researcher can undoubtedly provide great help in systematizing and objectifying clinical observations, he hamstrings himself if he *substitutes* crude measuring devices for clinical insights instead of *articulating* his observations to the subtle functioning of the sensitive clinician. A wedding of clinical observation and research operations has yet to occur. From everything that has been said, it follows that significant increments in knowledge, at least within the therapeutic framework, are likely to come from the intensive study of individual cases in which disciplined observation is complemented by, and takes account of, the complex interaction of variables, a task that cannot be accomplished by statistical manipulations, although certain statistical techniques may be helpful in other respects.

It is conceivable that significant advances in the area will not come from within the traditional clinical framework, since it will prove extraordinarily difficult to disentangle the clinical complexities. It is also questionable whether "part processes" can be productively simulated in the laboratory or in quasi-therapeutic situations. Thus, it appears that new insights may come either from basic research in disparate areas, or, stated less esoterically, through a combination of clinical and experimental methods within the clinical context. In the latter kind of investigation, it may be possible to introduce, at selected points in time, specific experimental interventions whose effects, albeit in a relatively gross way, may then be assessed. This approach is reminiscent of the work of all clinical innovators, from Freud to Alexander to the behavior therapists, in which experimentation with relatively specific techniques occurs within the clinical situation. The current research on therapeutic learning through conditioning of autonomic responses (as pioneered by Miller, 1969) may be an important area for significant advances.

There is no question that greater specificity and a return to empirical data are absolutely essential, but it seems unlikely that the therapeutic process can effectively be broken down into "parts" capable of being studied in isolation (e.g., the research on "empathy"), and then of being "reassembled." The scientist, as Colby observed, must first isolate a problem he can do something about and he must then test its limits. The identification of important problems is solely a function of his ingenuity and intuition, and no prescriptions can be given.

As part of this effort, we need to achieve greater clarity concerning the principles of psychological change at work in all forms of psychotherapy and to articulate them to relatively specific therapeutic operations. Comparable to the researcher, the therapist must learn to recognize problems he can do something about and to employ better strategies to reach a particular goal. With varying degrees of emphasis, all forms of psychotherapy employ a limited number of psychological principles, but the theoretical formulations in which they are couched typically obfuscate these commonalities. The task of reformulating these principles in terms that do greater justice to the phenomena in need of explanation remains an important assignment for the future.

The foregoing set of conclusions embodies of course certain guidelines for the kinds of research directions we consider promising, investigations we ourselves might undertake or which we, as individual researchers, would find congenial. It would seem presumptuous, however, to make

800

categorical assertions about the potential promise of research proposed or currently being carried forward by other investigators. No one can forecast future developments in as poorly developed a scientific discipline as psychotherapy, and as indicated previously, significant increments in knowledge may come from quite unsuspected sources. For this reason, too, it appears unwise at the present state of knowledge to propose complex research programs or to recommend the creation of research centers or institutes that might undertake concerted research efforts to "solve" specific problems in the area. Since we cannot identify the nature of the problems currently capable of solution and for other reasons, it appears best to leave the initiative for creative work with individual investigators who may succeed in bringing new ingenuity to bear on the field. However, we feel that the time for discerning a new gestalt in the multifarious concepts and bits of evidence may not be too far off. Intuitively, we feel that future research will build on and produce a closer integration between experimental and clinical approaches.

The foregoing conclusions clearly imply certain negative recommendations, that is, classes of investigations we consider to be of limited promise at the present time or in the foreseeable future. This list prominently includes large-scale collaborative studies, naturalistic studies of psychotherapy as it is usually practiced, traditional outcome studies, comparative outcome studies pitting broad-gauged therapeutic techniques against each other, and studies attempting to evaluate the respective merits of divergent theoretical orientations. Our emphasis on studies dealing with the mechanisms of psychological change regardless of which particular "school" has laid proprietary claims to them suggests the desirability of "retiring brand names" (see Bandura's, 1969 description) that at present continue to cloud major issues in the field.

We also wish to note the great importance of wedding the study of change more closely to biological disciplines.

801

The recent successes in instrumentally conditioning visceral responses and the advances in behavioral genetics are only two of several strands of evidence that have convinced us that research in therapy will be more fruitful when coordinated more closely with that of specialists in biological areas. We witness today a renewed emphasis on a holistic view of man that is beginning to take seriously the interaction between psychological variables and biological variables Thus, increasing collaboration between psychologists and biologists should certainly be welcomed. We would like to see a center, for example, where the mechanisms of change were focused upon by various experts in the psychological, medical, and biological aspects of psychosomatic problems.

Among researchers as well as statisticians, there is a growing disaffection from traditional experimental designs and statistical procedures that are held inappropriate to the subject matter under study. This judgment applies with particular force to research in the area of therapeutic change, and our emphasis on the value of experimental case studies underscores this point. We strongly agree that most of the standard experimental designs and statistical procedures have exerted and are continuing to exert a constricting effect on fruitful inquiry, and they serve to perpetuate an unwarranted overemphasis on methodology. More accurately, the exaggerated importance accorded experimental and statistical dicta cannot be blamed on the techniques proper—after all, they are merely tools—but their veneration mirrors a prevailing philosophy among behavioral scientists that subordinates problems to methodology. The insidious effects of this trend are tellingly illustrated by the typical graduate student who is often more interested in the details of a factorial design than in the problem he sets out to study; worse, the selection of a problem is dictated by the experimental design. Needless to say, the student's approach faithfully reflects the convictions and teachings of his mentors. With respect to inquiry in the area of psychotherapy, the kinds of effects we need to demonstrate at this point in

802

time should be significant enough so that they are readily observable by inspection or descriptive statistics. If this cannot be done, no fixation upon statistical and mathematical niceties will generate fruitful insights, which obviously can come only from the researcher's understanding of the subject matter and the descriptive data under scrutiny.

This conclusion may be perceived as a rather broad and unwarranted repudiation of hard-won methods of rigor; but we are gratified to note the increasing concurrence in this viewpoint by knowledgeable statisticians (Bakan, 1969; Tukey, 1969).*

There is a renewed appreciation that internal, intrapsychic, or experiential processes, whether they be of a feeling or of a cognitive nature, have considerable power to influence bodily processes, behavior, and the general state of the organism. Since these processes are obviously private and unobservable directly, their study will require development of a sophisticated technology for studying private experience. Massive denials of the problem since the time of J. B. Watson have not obviated its importance, and more than ever, it is with us demanding recognition. The revival of interest in cognitive processes is exemplified by recent studies of conditioning that have shown that verbal reports of various kinds are absolutely critical for an understanding of the processes under study. While the behaviorists have traditionally eschewed efforts to conceptualize or *objectify* inner experiences, there is no question that this task can no longer be avoided. To be sure, this is a major technical problem to which scores of psychologists and therapists have made notable contributions (e.g., in the heyday of the dynamic theories) but which has not been blessed by impressive breakthroughs. It will be absolutely necessary to take full

---

*We do not by this argument deny the significance of the distinctive contributions by psychologists to research on behavior, especially in basic fields, but the unique sophistication of psychologists in experimental design has led to compromises with crucial clinical issues, which implies that a new style of *clinical* research must emerge.

account of intrapsychic processes as we seek to imbue the study of psychotherapeutic change with greater specificity, objectivity, and precision. This could be an exciting and productive area of future inquiry beckoning the imaginative researcher.

We are impressed with the impoverished character of the major theories in the area. Running the gamut from psychoanalysis to behaviorism, we fail to see fertile theories emerging. While the global theorizing that has dominated the field of personality has become largely defunct, more appropriate mini-theories centered on specific clusters of data have not emerged. We view the need for new theories as a vital one. Crucial concepts such as "repression," "defense," "cognitive mediation," "conditioned response," and "experiencing" all need major overhauling or replacement. We view this as a prime task for advancing the field.

We have been deeply impressed with the personal human aspect of the scientific enterprise that became particularly vivid as a result of visiting a number of people in rapid succession. Largely because of this human element, we came to realize the virtual impossibility of artificially stimulating particular lines of investigation short of massive (and probably futile) external inducements. It is clear that proposals for programmatic inquiry, besides being contingent on a certain maturity of the field of inquiry, must match to a significant extent the basic motivations and personal styles of researchers. Collaboration of any kind must emerge from these personal bases and cannot be superimposed upon them. This is a vital lesson, learned at great expense by the designers of some previous collaborative efforts in other areas. It appears that crucial ingredients for successful collaboration include a confluence of intellectual interests, mutual need, and social rapport among collaborators that can neither be dictated nor deliberately "arranged." Any attempt to mount collaborative efforts must consider these variables to be as central as the scientific ones, regardless of the difficulties they pose.

804

Numerous additional points could be made but perhaps these highlights will suffice to indicate the direction of our current thinking and provide interested colleagues with a general picture of our basic conclusions. This project has been a most illuminating experience for us, and we hope our digest adequately conveys to the reader the important shifts in direction we believe are now needed in this field.

References

Bakan, D. 1969. *On Method.* San Francisco: Jossey-Bass.

Bandura, A. 1969. *Principles of Behavior Modification.* New York: Holt, Rinehart & Winston.

Bergin, A. E., and Strupp, H. H. 1969. "The Last Word (?) on Psychotherapy Research; A Reply." *Int. J. Psychiat.,* 7: 160-168.

Kuhn, T. S. 1962. *The Structure of Scientific Revolutions.* Chicago: University of Chicago Press.

Miller, N. E. 1969. "Learning of Visceral and Glandular Responses," *Sci.,* 163: 434-445.

Polanyi, M. 1966. *The Tacit Dimension.* New York: Doubleday.

Scriven, M. 1964. "Views of Human Nature," in *Behaviorism and Phenomenology,* ed. T. W. Wann, Chicago: University of Chicago Press.

Strupp, H. H., and Bergin, A. E. 1969a. "Some Empirical and Conceptual Bases for Coordinated Research in Psychotherapy," *Int. J. Psychiat.,* 7:18-90.

——— 1969b. *A Bibliography of Research in Psychotherapy.* Washington, D. C.: National Institute of Mental Health.

Tukey, J. W. 1969. "Analyzing Data: Santification or Detective Work?" *Am. Psychol.,* 24: 83-91.

Index

808

Index of Names

811

Fromm, E., 93, 416n, 418, 701
Fromm-Reichmann, F., 13, 37, 43, 54, 101, 159, 172, 182, 185, 187, 188, 202, 317n, 327, 497, 516, 639, 649, 650, 679, 701, 708
Frost, R., 715

Geller, J. J., 28n
Gill, M. M., 28n, 521, 522, 606, 610, 652, 653, 679
Gitelson, M., 322, 327, 537, 554
Glasser, W., 92, 102
Glover, E., 22, 57, 83, 152, 156, 283, 501, 510, 561, 562, 563, 589, 592, 601, 613, 614, 655, 672, 679, 680
Goethe, J. W., 372
Goldin, P. C., 367, 373
Goldstein, A. P., 86, 102, 638, 680, 789
Green, D. E., 186n, 204n, 560n
Greenacre, P., 427, 475
Greenson, R. R., 789
Grinspoon, L., 514, 515, 516, 517, 518
Guze, S., 563n, 589

Haggard, E. A., 445, 476
Haley, J., 24, 26, 133, 134, 135, 136, 147
Ham, G. C., 329n
Hammett, V. O., 673, 680
Harper, R. A., 628, 680
Hartmann, H., 617, 628, 629, 680
Harway, N. I., 565, 573, 589
Heine, R. W., 498, 510
Heller, K., 86, 102
Hilgard, J., 126, 147
Hoffman, J. L., 210n

Hollingshead, A. B., 435, 436, 638, 680
Holt, R. R., 57, 80, 432, 476, 491, 492, 499, 510, 534, 536
Horney, K., 27, 483, 701
Hull, C. L., 85, 710
Hunt, H. F., 784, 789
Hyman, H. T., 488, 489n, 510

Jackson, D. D., 537, 554
Jacobs, M. A., 789
Jahoda, M., 504, 505, 507, 510, 657, 658, 680
Janis, I. L., 427, 476, 642, 680
Jenkins, J. W., 329n, 332, 336n, 342n, 373
Jessner, L., 28n
Johnson, E. S., 349, 373, 593, 601
Johnson, L. B., 764
Jones, E., 488, 510
Jones, L. V., 329n, 592n
Jones, W. S., 70, 71, 80
Jung, C. G., 147, 483

Kardiner, A., 733, 734, 755
Kelly, E. L., 523, 536
Kessel, L., 488, 489n, 510
Kiesler, D. J., 83, 102, 785, 786n
Kirtner, W. L., 495, 510
Klein, A., 504, 510, 657, 683
Klein, M., 701, 735n
Knapp, P. H., 789
Knight, R. P., 483, 488, 501, 502, 503, 510, 655, 656, 680, 687, 708
Kramish, A. A., 571n, 589
Krasner, L., 665, 666, 680, 682, 763, 774
Kubie, L. S., 57, 80, 283, 286, 415, 418, 734, 742, 755

813

814

816